ARCHITECTURE IN LOS ANGELES

A COMPLEAT GUIDE

ARCHITECTURE IN LOS ANGELES

A COMPLEAT GUIDE

DAVID GEBHARD
ROBERT WINTER

JULIUS SHULMAN,
Photographic Consultant

➜P

GIBBS M. SMITH, INC.
PEREGRINE SMITH BOOKS
SALT LAKE CITY
1985

First Edition

Published by Gibbs M. Smith, Inc. Peregrine Smith Books, P.O. Box 667, Layton, UT 84041

Designed by J. Scott Knudsen.

Manufactured in the United States of America.

Library of Congress Cataloging in Publication Data

Gebhard, David.
  Architecture in Los Angeles.

  Bibliography: p. 499
  Includes index.
  1. Los Angeles (Calif.)—Buildings—
Guide-books. 2. Architecture—California—
Los Angeles—Guide-books. I. Winter, Robert.
II. Title.
NA735.L55G39   1984   917.94'930453   84-5519
ISBN 0-87905-087-X

Contents

Preface

This is the third guide the authors have written on the architecture of Los Angeles and Southern California. With some reluctance—for we quite enjoyed the abbreviated telephone book quality of our 1977 *Guide to the Architecture of Los Angeles and Southern California*—we have decided to divide the material into two volumes. This first volume is devoted to Los Angeles and the other communities in Los Angeles County; the next volume will present the rest of Southern California. With the growth of Orange and San Diego counties, three volumes will eventually be necessary.

Our first *Guide* in 1965 arose from special circumstances. Although we recognized a general need for a survey of architecture in Southern California, we were especially interested at the time in providing a guide for Easterners and Midwesterners who would be coming to the joint meeting of the College Art Association and the Society of Architectural Historians taking place in Los Angeles in the winter of 1964. We knew that without some sort of help, these outlanders would find it difficult to cope with the vast distances of Los Angeles and would, therefore, miss outstanding examples of architecture.

Circumstances beyond our control put off publication until 1965, but this special intention of the *Guide* was to give it some quirks. We figured that the visitors would not be much interested in Victorian architecture since they had so much around them at home. Nor did we feel that they would have an interest in Los Angeles's great surge of traditional imagery of the years 1900 through 1941. Less understandably, we all but neglected the Craftsman movement. We consciously weighted our selections toward twentieth-century High Art Modern buildings, particularly those designed after 1920. The result was to underrate the nineteenth century and early twentieth century.

Something else has happened since 1964. We ourselves have become older, even mature. Our taste has broadened, perhaps even become a bit perverse. It is amusing to look back at our pride in our "catholic taste." We are still rather proud of some of the things we included that went against the high taste of the time. Zigzag and Streamline Moderne (Art Deco) and Hansel and Gretel, and the Period Revival styles of the 1920s, were given some prominence, though not as much as they should have had. We left a back door open when we noted that the book might become "a period piece," but we did not realize how right we were.

Since 1964, moreover, long friendship and the consequent appreciation of each other's attitudes has brought us to the point of almost invariable agreement on what should be included and why it is important. The elder of us was brought up and thoroughly conscious in the 1930s. He was told that the Streamline Moderne (then called "Modernistic") architecture was *petit-bourgeois*. When he went to college he learned to despise "eclectic" architecture and learned the terms "dishonest," "meaningless ornament," etc. He has, under the influence of his somewhat younger colleague, discovered that ornament, wherever it occurs, usually has great meaning and that "dishonesty" in art is sometimes just as well-intentioned and aesthetically successful as honesty.

A concern for the difference between the East and West still preoccupies us, both Midwesterners by birth and rearing. In choosing buildings to list, we have had to make our single most important criterion the necessity of emphasizing the areas where Southern California and Los Angeles are stronger — often stronger than other parts of the country, even Northern California.

There is no question that we have widened our list of buildings, both in our 1977 edition of the *Guide* and in the present new book. Nevertheless, it is by no means a complete listing of works by major architects. We have tried to limit the list to buildings that can be seen from the street, but this high motive has been difficult to enforce. So many of the buildings that were easily seen in 1964 and in 1977 are, thanks to plentiful water and fertilizer, today immersed in foliage. Some of these are so important in the history of architecture or in an important architect's aesthetic development that we had to list them in the hope that you might have a chance to see them someday. We do try to let you know about the problems of viewing particular monuments.

Very early in our studies we found it impossible to map everything in a totally logical fashion, not surprising in an area whose cities' boundaries often defy logic. Enclaves of outstanding buildings, such as in Pasadena, West Los Angeles, and Pacific Palisades, occur rarely in the greater Los Angeles area, and even in these places the idea of walking from one major building to another is usually ridiculous. In general we have tried to use freeways to separate regions, but every student of the area knows freeways, particularly when they are depressed below the land or raised above it, do not set limits except on maps. The problem remains that you may visit one building only to find later that there was another that you wanted to see just a few blocks away, but it was on another map. We suggest planning.

Another insoluble problem has been our inability to develop maps to please everyone. Difficulties occasionally arise from our very efforts to make it easy for you to go from one place to another. We have, for instance, usually left out minor streets where nothing that we have recommended exists. The maps vary in scale depending on the number of outstanding buildings in an area and their proximity to each other. Orientation is the same in all cases, with north being at the top of the map. In many areas you may want a more detailed map. We suggest buying at least the *Thomas Guide,* Los Angeles County edition, which is updated annually and available at major bookstores.

A final plea: the inclusion of buildings in this *Guide* does not mean that the owners have given permission to enter the grounds or the building. Privacy and security are especially sacred today. Some people love to show you through their houses, honored that you would think enough of their taste to notice them. But this attitude is becoming rare, especially among owners who have houses by well-known architects. Some people don't even want their homes photographed from the street. We counsel diplomacy in the form of a telephone call to the architect who may arrange a visit for you. Where that is impossible, a note to the occupant may have good results. A few rebuffs are par for the course. *But please respect the privacy of the occupants of these buildings.*

We hope that in publishing *Architecture in Los Angeles* we have not omitted anything that is really important. We know, however, that because we have not been able to cover every road and every street in Los Angeles, we may have left out some good things. We invite your comments and criticisms. Everyone will be the wiser for them when we publish the next edition.

Acknowledgement

Although in a book of this sort the authors must take full responsibility for its errors as well as its strong points, the final result must be a compilation of the work and knowledge of many people, most of whom will have to go unsung except as they may recognize themselves in this enterprise. We are grateful for the many leads that we have received in telephone calls, in comments after lectures, or in casual conversation. To the literally hundreds of people who have contributed to this volume we acknowledge our enormous debt.

All cannot be relegated to anonymity. Esther McCoy recognized the architectural richness of the Los Angeles area long before we arrived on the scene and has been a constant source of information as well as a close friend. Julius Shulman and Marvin Rand have been generous with their photographs and their knowledge. John Chase and John Beach, both enthusiasts for the city, have donated ideas and given inspiration to us. Ray Girvigian, the late Carleton M. Winslow, Jr. and Jay Frierman opened their files to us, as did Ileana Welch, the coordinator of the Cultural Heritage Program in the Cultural Affairs Department at City Hall.

John Miller and Richard Mouck have continued to prowl the area looking for things we missed in our earlier books and have turned up some wonders. The Los Angeles Conservancy, with Ruth Ann Lehrer, Paul Gleye, Bart Phelps, and Bruce Boehner in the lead, has called our attention to other important architecture that needs preservation or that is simply outstanding. Tom Owen, the encyclopedic mind at the Los Angeles Public Library, continues to mete out delicious morsels, as have other librarians around the city and county. Surely the Pasadena City Urban Conservation Program, formerly under the direction of Jane Ellison and now managed by Paul Gleye, is the best such organization in the state, if not the country. Its survey, formerly spearheaded by Leslie Heumann and now by Ann Scheid and Denver Miller, has archives that have enabled us to identify the architects and dates of buildings that would otherwise be poorly documented.

Besides the photographic collections of Marvin Rand and Julius Shulman, we have used those of the History Center of the Los Angeles Branch of the California Historical Society, the History Section of the Los Angeles County Museum of Natural History supervised by William Mason, The Huntington Library and Art Gallery, the Los Angeles Public Library, and the Special Collections of the UCLA Research Library. For the mechanical chores of typing, we are indebted to Grace Allen of the Word Processing Center at Occidental College and Judy Randolph of the History Department at the same institution, as well as Flor Vera and Yvonne Volkay.

For frequent contributions to our knowledge of Los Angeles architecture, we would also like to thank:

Gregory Ain, Los Angeles
Robert Alexander, Los Angeles
Timothy Andersen, Pasadena
Margaret Bach, Santa Monica
Mary and Reyner Banham, Santa Cruz
Mary Ann Beach, Los Cerritos
Harriette von Breton, Picayune, Mississippi
Lauren Weiss Bricker, Santa Barbara
David Bricker, Santa Barbara
Douglas Byles, Pasadena
Regula Campbell, Los Angeles

ACKNOWLEDGEMENT

David Cameron, Santa Monica
Richard Carrott, Riverside
Alson Clark, Pasadena
Richard Crissman, Pasadena
Frank O. Gehry, Santa Monica
Calvin Gogerty, Newport Beach
Barbara Goldstein, Los Angeles
Marlene Grossman, Los Angeles
Harwell H. Harris, Raleigh, North Carolina
Allen Hess, San Anselm
T.M. Hotchkiss, Monrovia
Thomas Hines, Los Angeles
Shelley Kappe, Pacific Palisades
Paul Laszlo, Los Angeles
James and Janeen Marrin, Pasadena
Cliff May, Los Angeles
Margaret Meriwether, Pasadena
John Merritt, San Francisco
Kennon Miedema, Pasadena
Denver Miller, Pasadena
Charles W. Moore, Los Angeles
Dion Neutra, Los Angeles
Dione Neutra, Los Angeles
Helen Park, Santa Monica
John Pastier, Los Angeles
Jean Bruce Poole, Pasadena
James Pulliam, Pasadena
John August Reed, Los Angeles
Ann Scheid, Pasadena
Kathryn Smith, Los Angeles
Msgr. Francis J. Weber, San Fernando
Betty Lou Young, Pacific Palisades
Marilyn Zubler, Los Angeles
The students of the Los Angeles Architecture class, Occidental College
The students of the Nineteenth and Twentieth Century Architecture classes, University of California, Santa Barbara

Old friends who have died since the publication of the last edition of *A Guide to Architecture in Los Angeles and Southern California* but to whom we continue to be deeply indebted are Carl Dentzel, A. Quincy Jones, Wallace Neff, Pauline Schindler, and Lawrence Test.

Photo Credits

Most of the photographs were taken by the authors. Exceptions are as follows:

Julius Shulman: pp. 20; 36(#6); 44; 48; 80; 104; 112; 113(#12); 120; 121(#35); 124; 125(#25); 141; 154(#19); 164; 171(#74); 174; 181(#35); 184; 186(#21); 188(#4); 194(#1); 207(#38); 268; 278; 322(right); 447(top); 452(bottom); 453; 455(bottom); 456(bottom)

Marvin Rand: pp. 19; 36(#7); 72(#12); 75(#12); 87; 170(#65); 364; 376(#11); 426; 429(bottom); 45l(bottom)

C. Winslow: p. 16

Miles Berné: p. 58

Jack Laxer: pp. 100; 488

Luckhaus Studio: pp. 128; 443(bottom)

Graphic Studio: p. 142(#21)

Maynard L. Parker: pp. 145(#6); 192; 448(bottom)

D. C. Lang: p. 145(#3)

Ralph Samuels: p. 185(#14)

W. P. Woodcock: pp. 143(#17); 198; 483

W. M. Clarke: pp. 277; 389; 438(top)

Robert C. Cleveland: p. 309(#5, 10)

Vanguard Photography: pp. 326; 333; 419(bottom)

Hiller Studios: p. 336

Padilla Studios: pp. 390(#27); 485

Frederick W. Martin: p. 416

Norbert Lopez: p. 450(top)

Tom Vinetz: p. 464(top)

Guide To This Guide

This is a *Guide* to the man-made structures, gardens, parks, and other features that make up the physical environment of Los Angeles County. The time span covered began with the Missions of Spanish California and will end with projects to be completed in 1984.

We suggest that a good way to begin exploring Los Angeles is to start wandering down the beach, and then proceed slowly inland. So we have started off with Malibu, and proceed all the way around Palos Verdes Peninsula to Long Beach, and then back up north. Eventually we will reach the San Fernando, San Gabriel, and Pomona valleys.

The only area of Los Angeles County we have not included is that portion of Westlake Village which we have chosen to place in the second volume. This area seems more related architecturally to Thousand Oaks and Ventura County than to Los Angeles.

The entries section comprises the bulk of the *Guide*. Each entry lists the building, design date, name of architect or designer (if available), address, and brief comments.

Federal, state, county, and city public buildings are generally open between the hours of 10 A.M. and 5 P.M. on weekdays. We have included a number of historic buildings open to the public. Information about these buildings is included either in the introduction to the section or in the individual entry. Museums are generally closed on Mondays.

Photographs within the entry section are generally located with their entries, but, in each case, have been identified clearly.

Following the entries section is a Photographic History of Los Angeles Architecture, showing buildings representative of each time period. That, in turn, is followed by a Glossary of Architectural Styles which provides a listing of the styles identified in the *Guide*, along with photographs and descriptive text to aid in style identification. A list of readings and the index complete the book.

Within the entries section, a black square ■ beside an entry indicates that the building is illustrated in the Photographic History section.

Introduction

The views and reactions which Los Angeles has evoked for well over a century have been delightfully rich and varied. Every American city has always had its boosters, and most have attracted at least a smattering of critics. Los Angeles's (and, of course, this is true of the whole of Southern California) regal distinction has always been the intensity of these reactions, ranging from vehement hatred to gushing enthusiasm. In a way, Angelinos have always enjoyed this, for, as Jack Smith sagely observed, almost everything people say about Los Angeles has some truth in it.

Los Angeles, like all of Southern California, sometimes seems to be as much a mirage as a reality. Walter Lindley and J. P. Widney were at pains to create this image when they wrote their extremely popular *California of the South,* first published in 1888. "The health-seeker who, after suffering in both mind and body, after vainly trying the cold climate of Minnesota and the warm climate of Florida, after visiting Mentone, Cannes, and Nice, after traveling to Cuba and Algiers, and noticing that he is losing ounce upon ounce of flesh, that his cheeks grow more sunken, his appetite more capricious, his breath more hurried, that his temperature is no longer normal. . . , turns with a gleam of hope toward the Occident."

Many followed that gleam and found that it was something more than hope.

The Southland (always capitalized) provided a place that, given water, fertilizer, toil, and imagination, could be transformed into almost anything that the human mind could conceive. A Midwestern farm, a Southern plantation or, best of all, a South American jungle — even something that had never before been seen. And the environment could be changed in a hurry so that the settler could enjoy the fruits of his or her labor in but a few months or a few years at the most. Foreigners and Americans had, of course, been busy transforming the continent since the seventeenth century, but in Southern California *instant* paradise was possible.

A place which lends itself so readily to transformation is by its very nature a fragile environment. Casual Southern California living hinges at best on a harmonious interplay of cool ocean breezes and warm desert air. A protracted period of Santa Ana winds, when air is drawn down and baked on the mountain slopes then suffused over the lower lands, can be disastrous, as can an overly wet rainy season. Rain usually appears in good amounts (often causing landslides) in the winter months, but when it does not (and it often does not) water must be hoarded in almost every area except Los Angeles, which in the early part of this century literally bought the Owens River Valley to the north and dried it up in order to get a constant water supply from the High Sierra.

Hotel Arcadia. 1887. Santa Monica. Boring and Haas. Razed.

The Big Orange, as Jack Smith has called L.A., also lives on Colorado River water, and more recently on Feather River water, both of which it pipes hundreds of miles. All this costs millions, but it works. Nevertheless, and because of the danger that all this might be cut off, Los Angeles with its teeming millions is the most tenuous civilization in Southern California, utterly at the mercy of human caprice or error—not to mention divine intervention. Nietzsche told us to live dangerously. In Los Angeles there is no other choice.

If the supreme existential predicament exists in this area, its residents are all but oblivious to it. They are intent upon an individualistic hedonism rarely experienced on such a wide scale since Sodom and Gomorrah. On the surface it would seem that people who, like the Athenians, live out of doors and who are constantly swarming at shopping centers, beaches, Disneyland, would have developed public virtues to their highest point. Not so. Southern Californians are among the most privacy-conscious people on earth. Outdoor living means backyard and private swimming pool areas, not the Agora. Historians have recently noted that the settlement of America was achieved not by Daniel Boones looking for *Lebensraum* but by groups of people moving together to establish communities. But once the communities were settled, the myth of the self-made man (and woman) has predominated over the concept of community.

Southern California is the most complete realization of the myth of the self-made, self-reliant, self-oriented individual that the world has ever seen. Its denizens live by one of the most ingenious and complex commercial, industrial, and transportation systems ever developed. Yet they accept this marvelous concatenation of forces as given, assuming that its main reason for being is to serve individual needs. The ideal of a democratic society in which public and private enterprises and activities are intended to enhance the pursuit of individual happiness is at the very heart of the Southern California experience.

This attitude has some negative ramifications, the most important naturally being a shirking of social responsibility. Signs of this lack of public concern are everywhere. The breaking up of communities by freeways and urban renewal and the destruction of the past in the name of progress are only the most glaring signs. When faced with this problem, Southern Californians are in the habit of saying that in a real emergency they will come together, but in the meantime—privacy. Sometimes they are right, but often they sense the emergency too late, and they reap the whirlwind.

Bryson-Bonebrake Block. 1888. Los Angeles. Joseph Cather Newsom. Razed.

On the other hand, positive physical symbols of individualistic hedonism occur—single-family dwellings and freeways. The latter, besides servicing real estate promotion in distant places, were built to get the individual into the landscape and as far away from the city as possible. Someone has said American history is mainly the story of the westward movement, and because Americans have always been moving, a proliferation of freeways is the natural reaction of people who, when stopped by the sea, want to keep going. There is poetry in this, but it is more likely that the reason for the freeways is to give the Southern Californian a means by which to roam into places where he or she can be free. It is true that the freeways have caused a sort of fungus growth that has helped to wipe out the landscape that the Southern Californian was seeking, but it is also true that the multiplication of freeways gives Southern California an identity unlike any other region of the globe. That is one reason, for instance, why it is absurd to compare Los Angeles to any other city on earth, save perhaps London. It simply cannot be measured by conventional standards set by cities which are centripetal. Los Angeles is a pioneer, and, unless you have some tolerance for the mobility provided by freeways, you will misunderstand Los Angeles and other Southland cities. Probably you will hate them.

Freeways, though appearing on the scene rather late, are closely related to the other much older architectural embodiment of the ideal of individual freedom — the single-family dwelling. It is significant that in America the terms "house" and "home" are used interchangeably, and that when viewing American architectural history, domestic architecture is usually emphasized much more strongly than government, ecclesiastical, or even commercial building. There has been in this country a sentiment for the single-family dwelling from the seventeenth century to the present when the apartment house, even in California, is encroaching on the American dream. Moreover, it has been the house standing on a good-sized lot, providing space for a garden and, in the twentieth century, a swimming pool that has drawn people to California. In fact, it is a part of the myth of the garden that the house should be only an element in the richness of nature, closing a vista as a temple or pagoda in an English landscape garden. Needless to say, the ideal has been honored in the breach. Rarely does any section (excepting Bel Air and portions of Palos Verdes, Pasadena, and San Marino)

resemble Frank Lloyd Wright's idea of "Broadacre City." But the semblance of an estate surrounds even the humblest bungalow. Even as the apartment house and condominium craze has lately struck the area, it is significant that these are usually called garden apartments, though the garden may simply be a swimming pool with a few potted plants (sometimes artificial) strung around to keep up pretenses.

Bradbury House, 1887. Los Angeles. Samuel and Joseph Cather Newsom. Razed.

The history of Los Angeles architecture is essentially an analysis of the process by which Americans adapted European ideas to the special needs of an unusual environment. The missions, all derived from Mexican design, had to be relatively simple in comparison to Mexican churches. The simplicity of life and the paucity of workmen who understood the fine points of Spanish Churrigueresque or Neo-Classical design mitigated against an elaborate civilization. Thus the special excitement of a relatively sophisticated facade such as that on the mission at Santa Barbara. The interiors were also chaste, with some painting, usually done by the Franciscan monks or their Indian converts, decorating the area near the altar and the trim along the lower parts of the walls. Remember that most of the present glittering altars have been added since 1900.

Early domestic architecture was equally simple, the chief material being adobe brick like that used in Mexico. No mansions the size of the Casa Grande at the Vallejo rancho near Petaluma were ever built in the Southland. In fact, it is somewhat disappointing to discover that a number of the adobes now extant were built after the American Conquest and often by gringos who made that adaptation of the Classical Revival to adobe architecture that we have come to call the Monterey style. And as in the case of the mission churches most of these adobes have been imaginatively restored, particularly in the 1920s, so that only rarely can the observer sense the plainness of existence before 1850.

First Congregational Church. 1888-89. Los Angeles. Ernest Coxhead. Razed.

After 1850, Southern California architecture reflected the current fashions in New York, Boston, Philadelphia, or later of St. Louis and Chicago, given the cultural lag in importing new ideas thousands of miles from their source. Thus there were, before the more intense use of land, urban renewal, and freeway construction wiped most of them out, many examples of Greek Revival, the Italianate vogue in its various phases, the Eastlake craze, the Richard-sonian Romanesque and the Shingle, Queen Anne, and Colonial Revival styles. As in Northern California, there was a curious mixture of the Queen Anne and Eastlake that would not often be found in the East. Nevertheless, except for palm trees and exotic flowers and shrubs, Los Angeles in 1895 would have greatly resembled, say Milwaukee.

But if the architecture was similar, the role of the architect was somewhat more expansive. The eastern architect, from Charles Bulfinch onward, had often been a speculator in futures as well as a designer of buildings. But the great land boom of the 1880s threw the Southern California architect directly into large speculative enterprises. Architectural firms such as the famous partnership of Samuel and Joseph Cather Newsom devoted a considerable amount of their professional energies to designing new towns, housing developments, hotels, and office buildings, and sometimes even invested their own monies in these speculative ventures. This was often done foolishly. The collapse of the boom in 1888 did most of these architects in. But we see here the beginning of the special Southern California invention of the large architectural firm that was in every way a business enterprise, promoting progress as much as any booster in the Chamber of Commerce. Moreover, we see in the late nineteenth century the full emergence of the architectural office involved as much with planning and financing as with the design of buildings.

It has been noted often that in California material and spiritual values tend to become confused. Just as the architect was becoming a businessman, the culture spawned the Mission style, a symbolic attack on the materialism which had made California. Again, the intellectual background of this "truly California style" was eastern.

There has always been ambivalence in American ideas about progress. Usually the aggressive spirit is credited with having made America great, but always there has been a parallel feeling that its end result may be catastrophe. There are many aspects of this mood in American literature, art, and even

Los Angeles Post Office and Federal Building, 1887-93. Will A. Ferret. Razed.

politics. The architectural manifestation of it was expressed, as Vincent Scully, Jr. has noted in his *The Shingle Style,* in several Colonial revivals toward the end of the nineteenth century. People coming west naturally brought these styles (Shingle, Tudor, and Georgian) with them, and there are still examples of all these styles in Los Angleles and Southern California. But their incongruity amidst palm trees was not missed by some emigrés. What was indigenous and Colonial in the Southland? The most obvious relics were the missions, reminders, like seventeenth and eighteenth century eastern architecture, of a better day before the industrial technological revolution swept over the Virgin Land.

The result was the beginning of the restoration of the missions, almost all of them moldering into ruins since the Mexican secularization of their lands in the 1820s. Amateur scholars such as Charles F. Lummis and his arch-rival George Wharton James propagandized for the missions both at home and nationally as did the architect Arthur B. Benton. In 1894 Lummis and other celebrants of the Spanish-Mexican culture founded the California Landmarks Club, one of the earliest state-wide preservation organizations to be established in the United States. The members not only talked about missions, but also involved themselves in the actual stabilization and restoration of mission buildings.

Even more interesting was the wholesale exploitation of mission elements, often with Moorish effects that the Franciscans had not thought of, into a new style—the Mission Revival or simply the Mission style (ca. 1891-1915). Benton was an active promoter of this style and, of course, designed its greatest monument, the Glenwood (now Mission) Inn at Riverside. But other architects such as Lester S. Moore and Sumner Hunt were just as successful in adapting it to houses, museums, railroad stations, school buildings, city halls, and churches, to the point that—much more than in Northern California—it became an emblem of a region.

Ironically, like Frederick Jackson Turner's winds of democracy, the Mission style blew east, becoming a favored style for amusement parks and recreational buildings and here and there a house (without palm trees). There is, indeed, a Mission Revival band instrument factory in Elkhart, Indiana! More importantly, the style looked two ways. On one hand it heralded the treasure trove of Iberia and anticipated the San Diego Fair of 1915 where Churrigueresque, Plateresque, and Moorish details were displayed, causing a craze for a Spanish Colonial Revival in the twenties. On the other hand the broad white stucco surfaces and deep recesses indicated the possibilities of a style which would reflect the Spanish-Mexican heritage and the climate of a country where the sun usually shines and, at the same time, an economy of ornament which might lead to a new style. Thus, while buildings in the Mission style are often awkward (even ugly), in the hands of a consummate artist such as Irving J. Gill the style could be beautiful. In fact, Gill's work often resembles the European International Style Modern, which was developing at the same time. But Gill was far in advance of his European contemporaries in his sensitivity to nature. Where foreign designs seem to have been intended to contrast with the natural surroundings, Gill took great interest in bringing nature to the house. His favorite device was the pergola, but it is also significant that he went so far as to put an almost imperceptible green tint into what otherwise seems to be white paint and used it on interior walls in order to complement the natural surroundings.

Sawtelle Veteran's Administrative Center, 1901, Los Angeles. Luther Peters and Silas Burns. Razed.

Unfortunately, Gill was almost a prophet without honor in his own country. His essays in abstraction and simplification were rarely imitated, and what has happened to most of his buildings forms a sorry chapter in the history of the destruction of the usable past.

The mention of Gill and his connection with the Mission style should be a reminder that both he and his style were part and parcel of the contemporaneous Arts and Crafts or Craftsman movement. The Craftsman movement is usually associated with the woodsy mountain cabin, and Gill with stucco and concrete. But read Gill's article, "The Home of the Future," in Gustav Stickley's magazine *The Craftsman* (1916) and you will find him very conscious of his fascination with fine craftsmanship albeit in a different material.

The epicenter of the Craftsman movement was not East Aurora, Eastwood, Oak Park, or even Berkeley, but Southern California. It is surprising that a style which used so much wood as a symbol of the love of work that the machine had wiped out should have gained such enormous popularity in an area where there are few forests and where the danger of dry-rot and infestation by termites would seem to make it the worst possible material. It has been suggested that the opening of the harbor at San Pedro was accompanied by a promotional campaign which was extremely successful with the lumber barons of the north. This would perhaps explain the popularity of the wood frame, but it does not explain the use of so much exposed wood on exteriors in the form of shakes or shingles and in interiors in the form of panelling and beamed ceilings. Rather, the use of so much wood has intellectual, even ideological, sources. It is not surprising in light of the vision which promoted Southern California as a haven from the cruelties of life and automatically promoted a style which would fit into picturesque surroundings. This explains the popularity of the style in the Arroyo Seco at Pasadena where it was particularly favored by the intellectual and artistic elite who are always conscious of the necessity to wage eternal war on crass materialism.

It was also in Southern California that the bungalow, the apotheosis of William Morris's notion of a proletarian art that he could never himself attain, found its true home. Here a young family on the make, a sick family on the mend, or an old family on meagre savings could build a woodsy place in the sun with palm trees and a rose garden. The California bungalow, whatever its size or quality of workmanship, was the closest thing to a democratic art that has ever been produced. Even when it became a high-art product, as in the work of Charles and Henry Greene of Pasadena, it was as much a tribute to the carpenters who lovingly put together the wood details as to the architects who designed them. The high-art Gamble House and the low-art bungalow both convey a message that you can do it yourself if you only have the moral conviction. In the bungalow court—another of Southern California's great inventions—which started around 1910 in Pasadena, the advantage of the bungalow was reduced to doll-house-like dwellings which still managed to convey the sense of the single-family dwelling set in a garden.

A very important concern was the relationship of house to garden. *The Craftsman* magazine became a devoted admirer of Southern California architecture and gardens. The *Ladies Home Journal* and the *Architectural Record* were no less enthusiastic. Old pictures of the Blacker House by the Greenes show its broad-sweeping eaves and horizontal lines blending into magnificently landscaped grounds—the house a kind of continuation of the garden. What is not now noticeable, since the gardens have been subdivided, is that the living room chandeliers, with water lilies designed in Tiffany glass, were intended to echo the aquatic plants that once graced the lily pond near the living room windows. Even more striking is the intent, dimly apparent in many bungalow books but very explicit in Eugene O. Murmann's *California Gardens* (1914), that the person of modest means should live in a house set in a landscaped garden.

House. ca. 1905. Santa Monica. Remodelled beyond recognition.

Popular and widespread as the Craftsman aesthetic became, it was, nevertheless, the Spanish Colonial Revival (or more broadly the Mediterranean Revival) of the 1920s which captured the imagination of the popular and professional journals, and architects and critics in the East as well as the West. Here was a style which reflected the storybook romance associated with Californians—one into which Americans, tired of the nastiness of war and modern life, could retreat. The highly successful Los Angeles firm of Morgan, Walls, and Clements was one of several firms which introduced the elaborate details of Spanish and Mexican Churrigueresque and Plateresque forms.

Though the Southland was eventually to become intensely involved with the myth of her Spanish heritage, classical Beaux Arts forms were popular from 1900 on for the staid conservatism of business establishments, and above all for financial institutions. Downtown L.A. still possesses an array of ten- to twelve-story office blocks built within the Neo-Classic tradition of McKim, Mead, and White, and Daniel Burnham (Burnham and Company). And most of the towns and cities of the region have one or more exercises in this mode. These Beaux Arts designs, which were produced from 1905 through 1925, are knowingly designed buildings, and they are little different from what we find elsewhere in the country. Almost all of these designs were produced by one or another of the large L.A. architectural firms—Morgan, Walls, and Clements, Albert C. Martin, John Austin, Parkinson and Parkinson, and Walker and Eisen. These firms employed designers like Stiles Clements who were trained in the Ecole des Beaux Arts mode and brought the prestige of their Parisian education to the Southland.

The well-organized Beaux Arts traditions underlay the work of most influential architectural offices and were openly enunciated in the more circumspect and controlled Italian designs of Myron Hunt, Sumner Spaulding, Gordon B. Kaufmann, and Reginald D. Johnson. But the most remarkable evidence of

Parisian influence was the "City Beautiful" movement that had touched California city planning as early as 1900 and that had, by the twenties, been embraced by all the major cities in the region and many small ones. Los Angeles, Long Beach, and Pasadena seized upon planning during the first decades of the century with the same enthusiasm with which they had accepted the Mission style and the Spanish Colonial Revival. Los Angeles itself was the first city in the United States to adopt (1909) a comprehensive zoning ordinance. In 1915 a city planning association was organized. In 1920 an official Planning Commission was established. Of even greater significance was the creation in 1923 of a Regional Planning Commission for the huge Los Angeles area. All this in a city which is known for its apparent disorganization!

Some of the outlying communities such as Palos Verdes went further than Los Angeles. They created architectural and landscape architectural reviewing agencies that extended the force of planning far beyond the conventional American practice in the twenties and thirties, which was almost always solely concerned with zoning (land use) and street planning. In a sense, as these review boards directed the transformation of the dry hills and flatlands into a jungle and the domain of the Spanish Colonial

Cottage, ca. 1907, Echo Park, Los Angeles. Razed.

Revival, they were reinforcing familiar symbols of a golden past; and the results of their efforts at Palos Verdes and in several other Los Angeles enclaves are most impressive.

Planning is traditionally the work of an elite and is often most visible to the layman on maps. The buildings of the twenties speak more loudly of the Age of Prosperity. From a high art point of view, the Spanish Colonial Revival was generally at its best when drawing upon the vernacular architecture of Andalusia and rural Mexico. In spite of the occasional flourish of a Churrigueresque doorway, the message of Spain and Mexico was simplicity, even when the house was very expensive and lavish in its spaces and gardens. The major architects of this style — Roland E. Coate, Reginald D. Johnson, John Byers, Wallace Neff, Gordon B. Kaufmann, Marston, Maybury, and Van Pelt — left a legacy of buildings which illustrate American architecture of the twenties.

Unquestionably the most talented of the Spanish Colonial Revivalists was the Montecito architect George Washington Smith. His houses and villas in and around Santa Barbara, up the coast, and in Bel Air and Pasadena still seem remarkable for their informality of plan, studied composition, and attention to landscape. Indeed, at risk of sounding one note, the concern of the architects of the twenties for the manipulation of outdoor spaces in the planting of flowers and trees and the building of terraces and garden walls has often been lost in our present romance of white stucco walls and red tile roofs. The nineteenth-century horticulturalists, men like Joseph Sexton and Francesco Franceschi, set the stage for the brilliant landscape architects who began to practice after 1900: Olmsted and Olmsted, Kate Sessions, Mildred Davis, Edward Huntsman-Trout, Katherine Bashford, Paul Thiene, Lloyd Wright, Florence Yoch, Lucile Council, A. E. Hanson, W. D. Cook, Lockwood de Forest, Ralph D. Cornell, and more recent figures like Garrett Eckbo and Emmet Wemple.

It is obvious to anyone who has looked at the popular home magazines and the professional architectural journals of the twenties that the Spanish or Mediterranean revivals were not the only styles that were beautifully designed. All of these architects were equally proficient in other historic modes—the Norman French Provincial, the English Tudor, the Colonial Revival, and later the Monterey Revival and even the Art Deco (Zigzag) Moderne.

The twenties dipped into three other historic images that are of great interest. The Egyptian Revival, touched off by the discovery of King Tut's tomb in 1922 and the themes of the ancient Nile presented through the silent Hollywood films and their exotic stage sets, are certainly delightful. The apartment houses designed and built by J. M. Close suggest in their decorative detail that the return to Karnak was a gag. But Bertram G. Goodhue's use of Egyptoid elements in the Los Angeles Public Library must be taken somewhat more seriously. The truth is that the spirit of the twenties recognized that architecture, like the other arts, is an art of effect. If the effect is good, try anything. Perhaps this explains the Pueblo Revival and the pre-Columbian Revival, both of which also occurred in the twenties. In these revivals the architect Robert Stacy-Judd is a name to reckon with, though it should be noted that an interest in pre-Columbian architecture had been reflected as early as 1912 in the Abbey

Hotel (Hener and Skilling; now destroyed) in downtown Los Angeles and the entrance and tunnel to the elevator of the Southwest Museum (Hunt and Burns) built in 1917. By the 1920s free and imaginative design in that idiom was being produced by architectural firms large and small. Probably the craziest of all these efforts was the Mayan Theatre (1926) by Morgan, Walls, and Clements in downtown Los Angeles. Fortunately it is still standing, the only changes having been to make the decoration even more lurid than it originally was.

Some have suggested that the popularity of pre-Columbian motifs may have something to do with the adoption of the Native American art of the Southwest by the Santa Fe Railroad, an interesting idea. It is also possible that the special interest of the *National Geographic* magazine in the Yucatan and Peru during this period may have touched off pre-Columbian notions. The *National Geographic* magazine was then and still is the comic book of the intellectuals, so this idea seems plausible. But another source is even more likely. Frank Lloyd Wright, well recognized in the early twentieth century, had been deeply influenced by pre-Columbian architecture as early as the second decade of the twentieth century and had given the first dramatic evidence of this influence in his A.D. German Warehouse in Richland Center, Wisconsin, in 1915.

When Wright came to Los Angeles (actually his first California dwelling was built in Montecito in 1909) he continued his exploration of Native American forms. The Barnsdall House (1917-1922) was a variation on the cruciform plan of his earlier Prairie style to which he applied Mayan and Zapotec massing and detail, adding such standards of Southern California as patios and pergolas. The pre-Columbian motif persisted in his impressive series of pre-cast concrete block houses, ranging from the Millard House ("La Miniatura," 1923) in Pasadena to the Ennis House (1924) which has the effect of a terraced Mayan temple on a hill.

Wright's oldest son Lloyd supervised a number of these buildings and even

Dodge House, 1916, Hollywood, Los Angeles. Irving J. Gill. Razed.

Von Sternberg House, 1936, Northridge, Los Angeles. Richard J. Neutra. Razed.

added design elements of his own. Lloyd Wright had come to California as a landscape architect with the firm of Olmsted and Olmsted, then developing plans for the Panama California Exposition at Balboa Park in San Diego. Wright settled in Southern California and became an associate of Paul G. Thiene. As he moved from landscape architecture to buildings in the twenties, it was not surprising that he continued to see architecture as an environment where human designs and natural features were in harmony. Neither was it surprising that he picked up on his father's interest in pre-Columbian forms. His Sowden House (1926) in Hollywood and other of his buildings outside the Los Angeles area demonstrate his recognition of Native American influences as well as his knowledge of Moderne and Expressionist sources.

As if to prove that from Frank Lloyd Wright all blessings flow, the exciting ideas of the Master also drew two other immigrants to Los Angeles in the twenties—the Austrians, R. M. Schind-

ler and Richard J. Neutra. Of the two, Schindler was closer to Wright in his romantic personalism in design and manipulation of spaces. Nevertheless, his knowledge of modern architecture in his native Vienna prompted him to develop forms which were not in Wright's vocabulary, at least in the twenties. His own house (1922) on Kings Road in West Hollywood was one of the most radical designs in America at the time. The orientation of his complex spaces to nature indicates how quickly he came to understand what was now a Southern California tradition. In a very different setting his Lovell Beach House (1922-26) at Newport Beach is unquestionably one of the true monuments of modern architecture. And Schindler continued to produce ingenious experiments in form and space until his death in 1953, all of them characterized by ideas not always fully carried out but certainly stimulating. In fact, his great charm is a quality of improvisation not quite completed.

Schindler, like Gill, was until recently admired but not tremendously influential. Richard J. Neutra, however, was without doubt the most influential Los Angeles Modernist architect from the 1930s until his death in 1970. His steel-frame Lovell House (1929) in the Hollywood Hills is, like Schindler's beach house for the same client, one of the very few buildings in America in the twenties which deserve to be called monuments in the history of the Modern movement in architecture. But he was not just another talented International Style Modern architect. His sensitivity to the natural environment, existing and potential, caused him to go further than anyone before him to bring house and garden together (literally, in the Perkins House in Pasadena, bringing the garden into the house). Neutra's example was not lost on his younger contemporaries in the thirties — Harwell H. Harris, Gregory Ain, and Raphael S. Soriano — who, with a little help from their clients, simply landscaped their brilliant designs out of sight.

The decade of the twenties represented a period of phenomenal growth in Southern California. In Los Angeles, for instance, the population increased from 576,000 in 1920 to 1,238,000 in 1930. In this same period as the city grew 114.7 percent, Los Angeles County advanced by 136.9 percent. One essential ingredient of this dispersal of population was the convenience of an inter-urban railroad network, the Pacific Electric "Big Red Cars," probably the finest public transportation system in the country until its planned obsolescence. But more and more Southern Californians came to rely on the automobile, a kind of extension of the single-family dwelling.

This turn to the automobile was accompanied by linear (or strip) commercial development, the classic example being Wilshire Boulevard, which as early as the twenties was beginning to take on its present look of being commercial from the central city to the Pacific Ocean.

Also significant, and closely related, was the invention of shopping centers, large and small, still evidenced rather quaintly in cut-out street corners (for parking) with Spanish Colonial or Art Deco (Zigzag) Moderne buildings lined in an L-shape around them. The orientation of stores to parking lots rather than the main street was to become a major break with commercial architecture of the past.

No less innovative was the development of eye-catchers to attract passing motorists — Programmatic buildings such as a real estate office in the shape of a sphinx, an orange juice stand sculpted as a large orange, and restaurants, premonitory of the sculpture of Claes Oldenburg, looking like brown derbies, hotdogs, owls, milk cans, toads, dogs, igloos, shoes, and doughnuts. Most of these regrettably have vanished, but they looked forward to less naturalistic but more dramatic pop-culture city scenery today.

It was inevitable that an era of growth would also make Southern California rich in the fashionable styles of the times. Certainly, next to New York City, Los Angeles exhibits, even today, more examples of the Art Deco (Zigzag) Moderne than any other part of the country. Bullock's Wilshire (1928), by Parkinson and Parkinson, is the best remaining example of Art Deco in the area, but there are literally hundreds of examples in Los Angeles, Pasadena, Long Beach, and even San Pedro. Sadly, the greatest of these, the shimmering black-and-gold-sheathed Richfield Building (1928-1929; Morgan, Walls, and Clements), is no longer with us.

Southern California was deeply affected by the Depression of the thirties. Ironically, it is for this reason that the area has so many outstanding examples of Streamline and Classical Moderne buildings. The Depression was generally catastrophic to the building industry. But one operation that was not curtailed was the building of moving picture theatres, the cheap movie ticket being one of the few luxuries still available to most Americans during the thirties. Even more important to architecture was public building, stimulated by the United States Public Works Administration (PWA), which helped to finance schools, libraries, and post offices in order to give people work. Its companion relief organization was, of

NBC Building, 1938-39, Hollywood, Los Angeles. John C. Austin Company. Razed.

course, the Works Progress Administration (WPA) whose Arts Project engaged in the revolutionary act of giving work to artists. The results of the activities of these federal agencies are everywhere, especially in the Classical Moderne (PWA Moderne) mode.

As historians have noted, not many millionaires jumped out of skyscrapers or off bridges as a result of the Great Crash. Generally, after a period of shock, the rich and the well-to-do went on building houses in the period revival styles of the twenties, giving employment to architects in the period styles. Wallace Neff, Paul R. Williams, Roland E. Coate, John Byers and Edla Muir, and H. Roy Kelley developed free-flowing interior spaces and indoor/outdoor relationships, then clothed them in forms which delicately suggested the past — the Spanish Monterey, the English Half-timber, the Colonial, and the Regency. By the end of the decade, Cliff May and others had fully developed the California Ranch house which was to dominate the single-family house after World War II.

A casual look through the pages of the national architectural journals, *Pencil Points, Architectural Record,* or *Architectural Forum,* readily attests to the recognition which the proponents of modern architecture received during the 1930s. In addition to the "Old Masters"— R. M. Schindler, Richard J. Neutra, and Lloyd Wright — there were the European expatriates — Kem Weber, J. R. Davidson, and Paul Laszlo. And by the mid-1930s there was an impressive younger generation of modernists including Harwell H. Harris, Gregory Ain, Raphael S. Soriano, Whitney R. Smith, Wayne Williams, A. Quincy Jones, Richard Lind, and John Lautner.

World War II was a great stimulus to business and often directed architecture into previously untouched areas. There was little work in mansions or public and commercial buildings, but for the first time since the First World War the federal government took an interest in public housing. By the end of 1942, Los Angeles had twelve public housing projects. In general these differed greatly from similar projects in other parts of the United States. The density of all of them was decidedly low, and they were styled in forms ranging from the California Ranch house to the International Style Modern. Unquestionably the most impressive of these projects was Neutra's Channel Heights Project (1941-42) above San Pedro, as always in Neutra's hands beautifully sited and landscaped. It is a matter of public shame that this project has been allowed to disintegrate, and finally disappear.

The war years also set the stage for an increased dispersal of population. In 1941 the Los Angeles Regional Planning Commission drew up the basic guidelines for development for the next quarter century. Los Angeles was not to be a classical city with one or two centers but a complex entity with a variety of commercial and industrial centers. The region was to continue to stress the single-family house. To realize this scheme, the private automobile was to be cultivated as the major means of transportation. All this meant a complete devotion to freeways. The Arroyo Seco Parkway (1934-1941, now Pasadena Freeway) had been the first freeway in the West. By 1941 the first sections of the Cahuenga (now Hollywood) Freeway were finished, connecting Los Angeles with the San Fernando Valley. The next two decades saw a freeway mania. By the seventies, when building tapered off due to the economy and a growing skepticism, almost everyone in Los Angeles was less than four miles from a freeway, the goal of the transportation experts.

In the period after World War II, Southern California experienced a building boom, mostly of tract housing, which demolished the orange groves of the San Fernando Valley and populated almost every square inch of it. The same development spread east almost to San Bernardino and south to the point that, at least along the coast, Southern California had indeed become a megalopolis. Only territories far beyond the reaches of Los Angeles, such as the Owens River Valley, the San Joaquin Valley, and the Mojave Desert, preserved communities that today still reflect some of the old charm of small-town America.

Nevertheless, within Los Angeles and other cities of California the chief building type, the ranch house, continued to exhibit the old values: the two-car garage near the street, the open family room and patio, the outdoor living space. Again, California pioneered a style of life for America.

In the same period, and especially after 1960, high art came to be high architecture. In an effort, often only cosmetic, at urban renewal, almost all the cities went to medium- or high-rise in their downtown areas. These buildings, without exception, were clothed in the machine image International Style Modern garb, many, following Mies, displaying dark and later reflective glass walls and creating in most instances a really unbearable monotony. Domestic architecture fared better. Whitney Smith and Wayne Williams, Harwell H. Harris, and A. Quincy Jones (Jones and Emmons) maneuvered the International Style Modern in a mellow, woodsy fashion. A domestic housing experiment, the Case Study House program (1945-1960) of John Entenza and his *California Arts and Architecture* magazine, was launched with fear and foreboding. No one really thought very many people would be interested in the high-art designs of

Lowes House, 1924, Eagle Rock, Los Angeles. R. M. Schindler. Razed.

Raphael S. Soriano, Gregory Ain, J. R. Davidson, Craig Ellwood, Pierre Koenig, and others. However, the first six houses that were opened received 368,554 visitors, though the architects rarely made any attempt to cultivate the popular taste. As Esther McCoy noted (*Perspecta 15,* 1975) the popularity of these avant-garde buildings spread to the beautifully designed furniture exhibited in them. A number of retail outlets for the products of such designers as Charles Eames and Marcel Breuer were opened, and they were a huge success. Later, the attendance at Eudorah Moore's "California Design" exhibitions was a clear sign that "modern design" had caught on with an influential minority of Southern Californians.

Naturally, there were counter-tendencies to the Miesian "less is more" machine esthetic. Throughout the postwar period, John Lautner's highly imaginative futuristic designs had a popular following, as did the Los Angeles buildings of Edward D. Stone and Associates, and others. Through the post-World War II years, and up to the present, there were the Ahmanson and Home Savings banks, which in their design and use of sculpture, mosaics, and murals proclaimed that the Classical tradition was not dead, and that "more was more." In the domestic architecture of the sixties and seventies, the movie set image of the thirties Hollywood Regency was replaced by the French Empire mode with its applique of mansard roofs, elongated windows, double front doors, and classical urns. Here, as John Chase has indicated, the Hollywood boudoir was turned inside out.

Architecturally and environmentally the early and mid-1970s were a confused period for Los Angeles and Southern California, probably much more so than for the rest of the country. Like a balloon, the ideologies of progress, growth, upward, and onward seemed to have burst, and no one seemed sure of the future any longer. Smog, the congestion of people (and their extension—the automobile), the continual destruction of productive farm land, and potential and real water shortages created doubts of such magnitude that even the usual

Hoot Owl Cafe, 1930, South Gate, Los Angeles. Razed.

boosterism of Southern California found it increasingly difficult to reassert the old beliefs. At first the negativism of these reactions produced a number of positive results. A surge of interest in planning occurred, ranging from the initiation of statewide coastal planning to elaborate requirements of environmental review for industrial and other types of projects. Architectural design itself became subject to public scrutiny. It appeared the days of planning and architectural laissez-faire were over.

The desire for continuity with the past reasserted itself in the seventies—albeit in a far different fashion than had been experienced in the decades from 1900 through the thirties. Though interest in historic preservation in Southern California had begun early, this involvement generally restricted itself to the missions and the adobes of the early 1800s. In the late 1960s Angelinos and others began to look at other inheritances from the past: from Victorian architecture of the late nineteenth century to the Streamline Moderne of the thirties. This involvement became evident in the demand to retain living relics, and in the increased usage of historic images derived from California's delightful, but at times mad, past.

The popular California Ranch house, which had slowly assumed Modern elements in the 1950s, began to revert to its Hispanic sources. Acres of tract houses, apartments, and later condominium row houses appeared—some on the remaining open land of the San Fernando Valley, others on leftover bits of land near the Orange County line. Retail establishments and shopping centers exhibited Hispanic themes of stucco, arches, and tile roofs. But all of this, at best, testified to lacking conviction. Still, there was an inkling of the past and, in this case, California's own past.

The Modern image was, however, in no way completely abandoned in the seventies. The established corporate architectural firms such as Albert C. Martin and Associates, Welton Becket and Associates, the Charles Luckman partnership, and William Pereira and Associates stood by the machine image of the Modern. As was the case in Albert C. Martin and Associates's Atlantic Richfield Towers (ARCO Plaza, 1968) they might have clothed the building in polished stone, but its image remained faithful to the Modern, the Corporate International Style.

Unquestionably, the most impressive of the larger commercial designs came from the offices of Daniel, Mann, Johnson, and Mendenhall and from Gruen Associates. Operating out of these offices, Cesar Pelli and Anthony J. Lumsden took up the fashionable theme of the mirrored glass box, employing it to create impressive pieces of minimal sculpture. One wonders, however, what these fragile pieces of glass sculpture had to do with Los Angeles's physical environment or its history. Cesar Pelli was perhaps conscious of this when he designed his small Pacific Savings Bank in San Bernardino (1972), with its masonry walls and drive-in facility composed of a regimented forest of palm trees. One of the ironies of the seventies in Los Angeles was that at the same

time there was an increased awareness of environment and history, the design and imagery of the city's larger buildings became more arbitrary (High Art objects, not architecture) and anti-regional.

Just as we can, for the convenience of history, present certain individuals and events as touchstones for changes in the past, so we can look to particular personages and events of the seventies which helped set the stage for Los Angeles of the eighties. Though Cesar Pelli left the Southland for Yale at the end of the seventies, he left an inheritance that encouraged a rather specific L.A. brand of High Tech imagery.

But High Tech of this period developed along two separate paths. One was a direct descendant of the glass-sheathed box; the other a delight in playing with building and mechanical technology to create High Art objects. The first approach can be seen in the swatch of low- and high-rise buildings constructed from the palisades of Santa Monica to Lake Avenue in Pasadena. These machine image buildings, such as the 1982-83 Wells Fargo Building (Albert Martin and Associates) in downtown Los Angeles, are, like their predecessors, purposely oblivious to their world, though it might be admitted they are often sophisticatedly detailed.

The second contingent of High Tech practitioners carries on the Victorian division of architectural practioners into the separate camps of art-architects and architects. Our present cadre of art-architects looks at technology not through the eyes of the contemporary computer, but through the historic and nostalgic eyes of the early Modernists of the 1920s—especially those of Le Corbusier. Most examples of these High Tech buildings are small-scaled condominiums, generally designed by young practitioners. The vigor of many of these buildings cannot be denied, though one is often left with the feeling that their irrationalism would disappear if they were, like Alice, miniaturized and placed in an art gallery.

Other "events" of the seventies had an impact on the L.A. scene. Though Charles W. Moore's first Los Angeles building dates from 1968-69, his real influence came through both the Southern California importation of his Sea Ranch image—for hundreds if not thousands of townhouse condominium units—and through the direct effect of his work and presence at UCLA. His involvement in history and his fascination with the long tradition of the stucco box in Southern California has inspired many architects practicing in the area.

A second figure of inspiration for the eighties has been Frank O. Gehry and his associates. Gehry's use and visual "misuse" of commonplace materials and structures from chain link to exposed wood studs has indeed created an unthought of chapter to Robert Venturi's "Complexity and Contradiction." Gehry carries the game a step further by playing off the practical everyday architect against the art-architect (the latter triumphing, of course). The lessons of Moore and Gehry have been energetically taken up by many other L.A. practitioners, including Eric Owen Moss. While no one would question the demanding presence and even humor of the buildings produced by these avant-gardists, there is a self-indulgent narcissistic quality that is often disturbing.

Popular American architecture in Southern California never abandoned traditional imagery. Most domestic tract housing from 1945 throught the 1970s retained some links with the past. And, as noted, the California Hispanic tradition reasserted itself in the late 1960s. As in the twenties and thirties, the Hispanic/Mediterranean tradition has increasingly shared the limelight with other heritages—the Medieval, whether English Tudor or French Norman, and the American Colonial. These images were and are employed for the complete gambit of building types, from single-family housing to apartments and restaurants. Interestingly, it is in the smaller shopping centers of the eighties that the concept of California as the New Spain predominates. And while many of these historic image buildings are expensive and display wonderful horticulture, few of them give evidence that their architects or landscape architects have any real understanding of the language they use.

Municipal Utilities Building, 1939, Long Beach. Razed.

There are, however, notable exceptions. The J. Paul Getty Museum (Langdon and Wilson; Stephen Garrett; Norman Neuerberg) at Malibu, characterized by the period-piece critics of the "old" Modernism as "camp," stands as perhaps the major California monument of the 1970s. And now, in the eighties, it is joined by the new (1982-83) gallery at the Huntington Library in San Marino (Warner and Grey). J. Paul Getty looked to Rome and the lava-covered Villa of the Papyri near Herculaneum for his inspiration, while the Huntingtons' architects had recourse to the buildings of one of America's great twentieth-century classicists, John Russell Pope. The fine line between illusion and reality embodied in these two buildings illustrates one of the often repeated themes of the architectural history of Los Angeles and Southern California, an essential ingredient also found in the work of Moore, Gehry, Moss, and others. Los Angeles is, for America, the new Rome (in the sense of illusion). And it will, like Rome itself, influence popular and High Art taste "for the good life" for years to come.

Historic Preservation in Los Angeles

C ontrary to popular belief, organized preservation efforts have had a long history in Los Angeles. The California Landmarks Club, founded in 1894 under the leadership of Charles F. Lummis, pioneered conservation of historic architecture, though, to be sure, these efforts were largely limited to a few missions. In the late twenties Christine Sterling and many local merchants set out to save and restore notable structures in the Old Plaza area including Olvera Street, a project in which the city, county, and state took an interest in the 1950s and administered jointly for awhile. Saddened by the destruction of Victorian Bunker Hill in the same period, a group of citizens joined to found the Cultural Heritage Foundation (1969) and moved the last two derelicts on the Hill to a newly designated Heritage Square on an unused piece of land next to the Arroyo Seco and the Pasadena Freeway in Highland Park. In 1978 the Los Angeles Conservancy appeared as a watchdog and galvanizer of preservation energy throughout the city. In fact, the seventies saw an active development of urban conservation programs, notably in Pasadena, South Pasadena, Santa Monica, Claremont, and more recently Long Beach, and other communities in Los Angeles County.

The Conservancy has not existed long enough to make any serious mistakes, nor regretably has it won some of its most publicized battles. The Cultural Heritage Foundation, whose Heritage Square has been dubbed "an architectural petting zoo" by the head of the National Trust for Historic Preservation, has been criticized for its limited scope and tendency to channel its monies into the moving of houses onto a rather undesirable piece of land, both charges lacking in appreciation of the fact that the Foundation has saved from the bulldozer or other vandals some very distinguished pieces of architecture that would otherwise have been destroyed.

Until recently the effect of the tripartite administration of the Plaza area has been a disaster for true preservation to the point that, although Olvera Street is a business success, the nearby Pico House, Garnier Block, Masonic Lodge, and Merced Theatre are unfinished and, except for the theatre, unused. Not all the blame can rest on managerial rivalry. Even ethnic jealousies have entered the fray, and now that the project is under the single administration of the city it is obvious that the problems, now mainly political, have not ended.

Similarly, the old Landmarks Club's concern for the missions has gone somewhat astray. At San Gabriel and San Fernando the efforts at preservation, particularly at the latter, have resulted in elaborate misinterpretations of history that would have led that sainted preservationist, William Morris, to renew his battle to limit preservation to shoring up old buildings.

All the while, the official city agency responsible for urban conservation has been the Los Angeles Cultural Heritage Board. Founded by ordinance in 1962 it is thus one of the oldest such agencies in the country and, among the large cities of the United States, one of the weakest. Ironically, when the ordinance was written, largely by Carl Dentzel (director of the Southwest Museum) and William J. Woollett (of the American Institute of Architects), it was one of the strongest. Under its provision that the Board can withhold permits for demolition or extensive remodelling for up to one year if progress were shown in efforts to preserve, many old and treasured buildings are today standing that otherwise would be demolished. But, until recently, the Board has felt limited by the ordinance to designating "cultural-historic monuments" and under the ordinance has been specifically barred from owning property or handling money. In 1980 an inventory of the architecture and other resources of the area was inspired by the Board but is administered by the Department of Engineering. It is doing fine work but is discovering that the process of surveying a huge, sprawling city is long and painstaking. While it is going on, much destruction of important buildings is taking place.

It is a tragedy that the county government's preservation legislation is non-existent. Furthermore, it must be stated candidly that, in spite of the hopeful signs that we have noted, architectural preservation in the Los Angeles area does not have the *elán* that it has in Charleston or even New York. After all, in spite of the victories of the L.A. Cultural Heritage Board and the Los Angeles Conservancy and similar commissions and preservation organizations in the County of Los Angeles, the retention of old or even middle-aged buildings depends on the will of the owner to save and, if necessary, re-cycle them. The owner's mind may be swayed by public opinion, but concentrated, well-directed public opinion is still very hard to come by in Los Angeles County.

In the period since World War II Los Angeles has been one of the few American cities to expand economically and to flourish even in a period of recession. It is very difficult for the staunchest preservationist to knock destruction in the name of progress. Recently, largely due to the strong and well-deserved publicity given to the restoration work being done by the developers Ratkovitch and Bowers, the idea is getting around that preservation can pay off financially. The success of this observation broadly interpreted, will, we believe, conserve more buildings than municipal ordinances can protect.

A revision of the old Cultural Heritage Ordinance is in the works and, if passed, promises to strengthen the official arm. Already an excellent

Historic District Ordinance has been established by the City Council. Historic Preservation Zones can now be set up under the supervision of the Cultural Heritage Board and the Planning Department. One, the Angelino Heights District, has its machinery in order and two others (South Carthay and the Plaza) have been recommended to the City Council. Again, this work is probably more important than designating individual landmarks, but, in a city where there are few concentrations of distinguished buildings but many isolated landmarks, the Cultural Heritage Board must keep in the business of individual designation.

The Los Angeles Freeway System

Ventura Freeway *1958-1971*
San Diego Freeway *1957-1964*
Corona Freeway *1958 (not completed)*
Glendale Freeway *1958 (not completed)*
Santa Monica Freeway *1961-1966*
Santa Paula Freeway *1963 (not completed)*
San Gabriel River Freeway *1963-1971*
Antelope Valley Freeway *1963-1973*
Garden Grove Freeway *1963 (not completed)*
Pomona Freeway *1965-1971*
San Fernando Valley Freeway *1968 (not completed)*
Orange Freeway *1969-1973*

As the list above indicates, there have been very few changes or additions to the Los Angeles freeway system in the last ten years. It now appears that the Century Freeway (to the Los Angeles Airport) will be built; and there are continual hints made that the Long Beach Freeway will be completed into Pasadena. Perhaps the most apparent change in the freeways over the past few years has been the addition of masonry noise-barrier walls along many sections, and the addition of concrete barriers in the central medians. One continues to hope that vines and other vegetation will eventually cover over these not very handsome walls.

Planning for what was to become the most famous freeway system in the world started in the early 1930s. By 1940 the Los Angeles Regional Planning Commission had adopted a "Parkway" scheme for the whole of the Los Angeles basin. In the following year the Pasadena Freeway (the Arroyo Seco Parkway) was completed, and the Cahuenga Pass section of the Hollywood Freeway was open to traffic. During the years of the Second World War two freeways were started— the San Bernardino and the Santa Ana. But it was the fifteen year period between 1950 and 1965 that most of the freeways of the system were begun.

In the chronological list below we have indicated the date when construction, (not planning) began, and the date they were basically completed. A number of the freeways have not yet been completed, and a number will most likely never be started.

Pasadena Freeway (Arroyo Seco Parkway) *1934-1941*
Hollywood Freeway *1940-1968*
San Bernardino Freeway *1943-1957*
Santa Ana Freeway *1944-1964*
Harbor Freeway *1952-1970*
Long Beach Freeway *1952-1965 (not completed)*
Golden State Freeway *1955-1976*
Foothill Freeway *1955-1976 (not completed)*
Artesia Freeway *1956-1975*

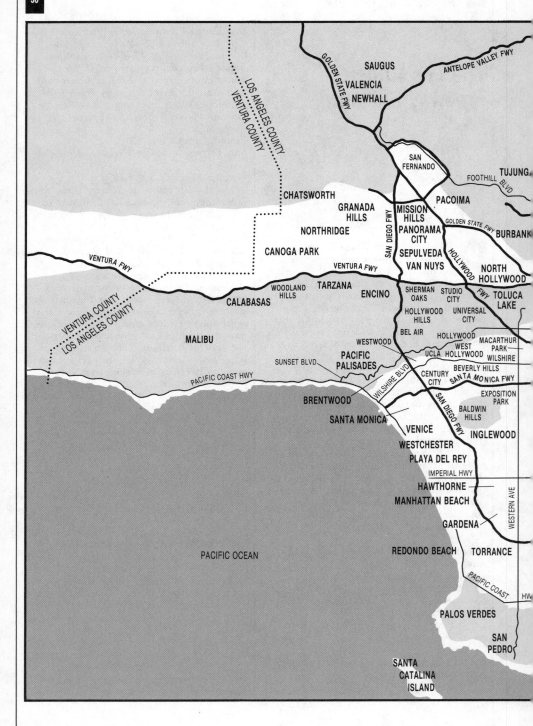

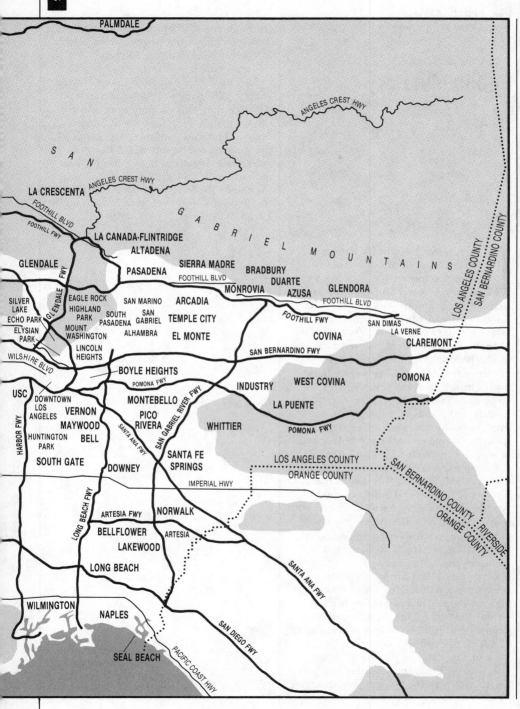

Public Murals

L os Angeles has always had its
share of public murals ranging
from the impressive high art work
of José Orozco and Howard Warshaw to the popular work of Hugo Ballin and Millard Sheets. During the
Depression years of the 1930s a number
of interior murals were painted as part
of the Federal Arts Project in post
offices, schools, and other public buildings. During the late 1940s and 1950s
large scale billboards and the exterior
murals and mosaics of the Home Savings Association branch office con-
stituted the major outlet for public art.
It was in the 1960s that Los Angeles
began to experience a growing rash of
external wall murals. The two centers
for this art were (and still are) East Los
Angeles and Venice. As with other
major American cities, these readily divide themselves into two categories:(1)
those which are really folk-painted by
amateur and self-trained artists (almost
always ethnic, and aimed generally at
conveying a political or social message);
and (2) those which aspire to high art.
In the 1950s the Fine Arts Squad
produced a number of epic pieces, some
of which are still around. In 1973 the
City of Los Angeles started its Inner
City Mural Program, and this has continued down to the present day. Starting
in 1983 both the city and the state
(through the California Department of
Transportation) has promoted an array
of murals related to the Olympic
Games—either as to subject or to help
spruce up the city's visual image for the
games. While most of these are well
painted, they still cannot compete with
the giant lighted billboards of Sunset
Strip. The rapid comings and goings of
the painted public murals of Los Angeles make it impossible to complete a
decent list. If you are interested in seeing them, the best solution is to drive
the freeways, and then visit Venice and
East Los Angeles.

Malibu

Malibu Beach did not begin its development until 1929 when the Pacific Coast Highway finally was forced through the Rindge Ranch. Earlier, in 1926, some Malibu land at Malibu la Costa was put up for lease, but the construction of houses at the edge of the beach did not really take place until after 1928. It was in the 1930s that the Malibu Colony became a fashionable place to have a beach house. The hilly coast land west of Malibu Colony remained basically rural and untrammeled until the 1960s. Increasingly in recent years that area between the Highway and the beach is being filled with numerous large-scaled houses. In the sixties and early seventies most of these houses were Modern in imagery, but in recent years historicism (usually grossly misunderstood) ranging from the Medieval to the Spanish Colonial Revival has prevailed. The land adjacent to the highway is slowly being condominiumized, again with disappointing versions of varied architectural images.

The Malibu Colony continues to acquire houses of distinguished design, but the Colony is a private, well-guarded world and is not open to the public. At 32348 Pacific Coast Highway you can look down towards the beach and see one of John Lautner's impressive concrete shell houses (1983-4). You'd better do it quickly because within a very few years the vegetation will block it out.

1. Pierson House, 1961-64
Craig Ellwood
32320 Pacific Coast Highway, Malibu

A carefully delineated volume, closed off from the road by thin walls and intervening courtyard. An urban design on three sides, and an open beach house on the west.

2. Berns House, 1951
Gordon Drake
31654 W. Broad Beach Road, Trancas Beach

A screened patio forms the center of this dwelling. The frame is articulated by vertical wood posts, primarily with an infill of glass. Rational, but warm.

3. House, ca. 1967
David Ming-Lowe
30860 Broad Beach Road, Paradise Cove

A two-story pavilion suggestive of the faraway Orient.

4. LeBrun House, 1963
Thornton M. Abell
6339 Bonsall, Zuma Beach

An entrance gallery, small courtyard, and office connect the living wing to the studio section of the house. Enclosed terraces and gardens effectively carry the enclosed space outward. Certainly one of Abell's most successful houses.

5. Lyndon House, 1950
Maynard Lyndon
28820 Cliffside, Paradise Cove

A 1950s ranch house close to the post and lintel Case Study House tradition.

6. Holiday House Motel, 1950
Richard J. Neutra; 1954, Dion Neutra
27400 Pacific Coast Highway

Two layouts of living/sleeping rooms, each with its own balcony, look out over the Pacific. The upper unit has two stories, the lower has one. Balconies are supported by L-shaped out-riggers, and the buildings are sheathed in board and batten. The original buildings plus the twelve units added in 1954 are effectively worked into the hillside bluff.

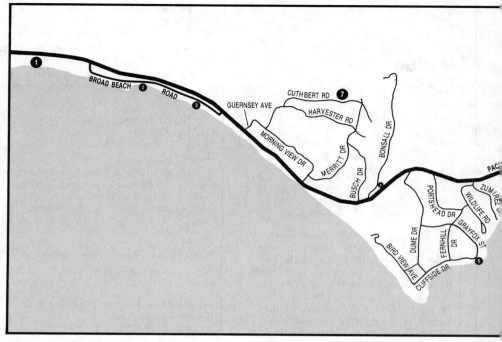

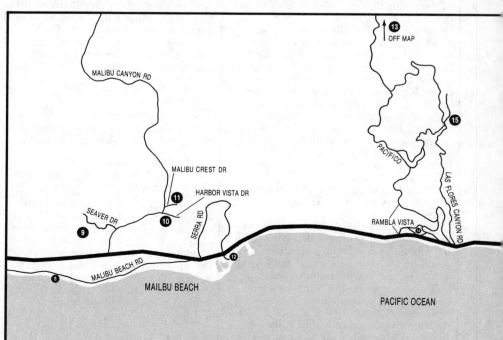

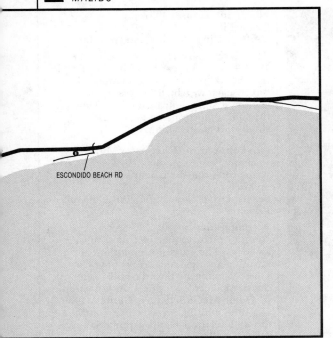

ESCONDIDO BEACH RD

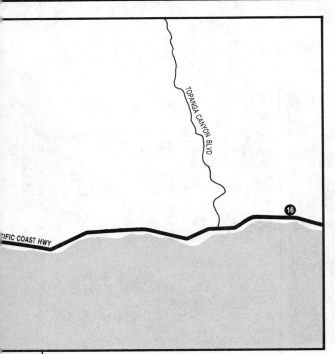

TOPANGA CANYON BLVD

16

PACIFIC COAST HWY

6. Holiday House Motel

7. Davis House, 1972
Frank O. Gehry and Associates
29715 W. Cuthbert Road, Trancas Beach

A trapezoidal building, covered by a low-pitched shed roof creates a neutral interior space which can be arranged at will. The exterior, including roof, is sheathed in corrugated metal. The shape as you see it from a distance creates some unusual problems of perspective.

7. Davis House

8. Hunt House, 1957
Craig Ellwood
24514 Malibu Beach Road, Malibu

The Case Study House image of the 1950s—Miesian, cardboardy, and fragile in a Southern California manner. Two boxes, each of which houses a garage, enclose a small entrance court. Down the hill, almost on the beach, is the single-volume dwelling.

9. Pepperdine University, 1971-73
William Pereira Associates
Armstrong and Sharfman, landscape architects
Seaver Drive, west of Malibu Canyon Road

A composition of cut-into stucco volumes picturesquely set on a hillside location. The carefully maintained lawns, plantings, and trees convey a sense of being in Beverly Hills. One of the most recent buildings on the campus in **Odell McConell Law Center** (1979; Neptune and Thomas) which continues the architectural forms originally established in 1971.

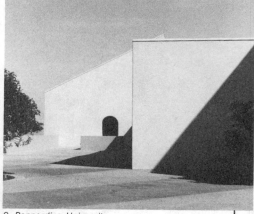

9. Pepperdine University

10. Rucker House, 1971
Douglas W. Rucker
Off Malibu Canyon Road at 23704 Harbor Vista Drive, Malibu

A hillside Schindleresque design which can be seen as far away as the Pacific Coast Highway.

11. Hodges Castle, 1977-79
Thomas Hodges
23800 Malibu Crest Drive

Dr. Hodges's towered and crenelated castle poses just as a castle should—on a high hill which overlooks and guards the inland approaches to Malibu.

12. Adamson House, 1928
Morgan, Walls, and Clements (Stiles Clements)
Pacific Coast Highway at Serra Road

The Adamson House is now included in Malibu Lagoon State Park, and can best be viewed from the beach itself. It is one of the few domestic commissions of Stiles Clements, who is best known for his many commercial and institutional designs either within Morgan, Walls, and Clements, or on his own after 1936. The house is a two-story Andalusian farmhouse which exhibits some splendid examples of metal work and also decorative glazed tile produced by the Malibu Tile Company.

13. Arch Oboler House, 1940, 1941, 1944, 1946
Frank Lloyd Wright
32436 Mulholland Drive

The grand and spectacular main house "Eagle Feather" was never built. From the road you can see the gate house (1940); below is the small wood and stone "retreat" built in 1941, and added to in 1944 and 1946. The vocabulary that Wright used here is directly related to the 1939 Sturgis House in West Los Angeles and the burned 1940 Pauson House in Paradise Valley north of Phoenix. This house was itself badly damaged in a November 1977 fire.

14. Reed House, 1960
John Reed
21536 W. Rambla Vista, Malibu

Projecting horizontal and vertical volumes in wood create a dramatic hillside composition.

12. Adamson House

16. J. Paul Getty Museum

15. Lyman House, ca. 1963
Frederick Lyman
3810 Las Flores Canyon Road, Las
Flores Beach

Two rows of heavy posts support a corrugated metal roof. Glass doors open between each pair of vertical posts. As a
design it seems simple, yet is highly
sophisticated.

16. J. Paul Getty Museum, 1972-73
Langdon and Wilson; Stephen Garrett;
Norman Neuerberg, consultant; Emmet
L. Wemple and Associates, landscape
architects
17985 Pacific Coast Highway

Here is Southern California as it should
be — the past as seen through the perceptive eyes of the 1970s, and a landscape
which puts the old world of the Mediterranean to shame. The Museum is
modelled after an ancient Roman villa,
the Villa of the Papyri, which was buried in the famous eruption of Mount
Vesuvius in A.D. 79 and excavated in the
eighteenth century by tunneling under
the hard lava crust. J. Paul Getty, who
commissioned the building, wrote:
"What could be more logical than to display it [classical art] in a classical building?" You approach the building through
a Roman gate along a Roman road and
enter the parking garage which is within
the podium. Ascending to the courtyard,
you obtain a view of the Pacific Ocean
(with no idea that the busy Coast Highway and beach lie below). Turning
around, you face the main Museum
building across the long reflecting pool.
Once in the building, a cross axis from
the central atrium leads to smaller
atriums and walled gardens (one of
which contains a restaurant). The classical Greek and Roman sculptures and
mosaics all appear at their best in their
environment, an environment created by
the building as well as the landscaping.
As one would expect the building and
the landscaping (as the architects and
the landscape architect planned) has
mellowed and improved each year. One
must call three or four days in advance
for reservations to visit the museum,
which is open 10 A.M. to 5 P.M. daily except holidays and Mondays.

Pacific Palisades, North

The area inland from the coast from Malibu to Santa Monica is rich in important High Art architecture, and fortunately much of it is visible from the streets. If Highland Park was the art center of Los Angeles at the turn of the century, Pacific Palisades took the title in the twenties, thirties, and forties. Moving picture figures soon discovered that it was only a short distance by Pierce-Arrow from Hollywood to the coast and settled in. Then writers, artists, and musicians, many of them fleeing Nazi Germany, found it a haven for their creativity. And under the leadership of John Entenza, the editor and publisher of *Arts and Architecture,* Pacific Palisades and nearby Santa Monica Canyon attracted the most advanced Modernist taste in architecture.

The community began its architectural life in the late 1860s when Los Angelenos came for the summer breezes off the ocean and pitched their tents just north of where Channel Road now cuts off from the Pacific Coast Highway. It remained a summer beach colony until 1921 when a group of Methodists, sensing a perfect place for Chautauqua and a resting place for retired ministers, established a colony on the highlands.

Castellammare, which lies to the north of Pacific Palisades, was developed in the twenties by Alphonzo Bell, Sr. who had already profited handsomely from the development of Bel Air. Some Mediterranean villas were built on the hills and cliffs overlooking the Pacific, but like the Methodists to the south, Bell never saw his posh Riviera realized.

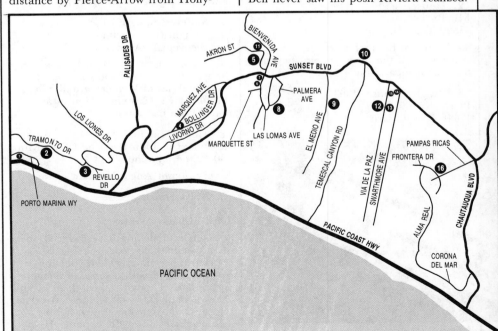

As you travel up the hill on Sunset Boulevard from the Pacific Coast Highway, take note of the **"Lake Shrine"** at 17190 Sunset Boulevard. Here in the middle of what looks like an African jungle is a spring-fed lake (with houseboat), a "Golden Lotus" archway, and domes of gold. This earthly paradise was built by the Self-Realization Fellowship in 1950 under the direction of Paramahanda Yogananda. The Fellowship and its instant paradise are pure Southern California.

1. Villa de Leon, 1927
Kenneth MacDonald
17948 Porto Marina Way

A memorable feature of the coast drive as you come down from Santa Barbara is this classical Mediterranean villa perched high on the edge of the cliff overlooking the entrance to the Getty Museum. Much of its splendid landscaping has now disappeared in continual landslides but the house is still sensational not only from the ocean side but also close up. Other Spanish and Italian villas of the twenties are situated nearby.

2. House, ca. 1935
Mr. Bird
17526 Tramonto Drive

The name of the architect is also a description of the house, quaint beyond dreams of sugarplums.

3. Beagles House, 1963
Pierre Koenig
17446 Revello Drive

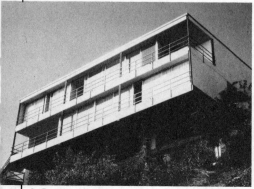

3. Beagles House

An intellectual statement of the "less is more" school. Incidentally, unless you follow a recent map you will probably get into trouble since part of Revello collapsed in a mudslide a few years ago.

4. Hill and Dale Nursery and Kindergarten, 1949, 1965
Lloyd Wright
16706 Marquez Avenue at Bollinger Drive

A handsome, horizontal redwood structure.

5. House, 1952
Jones and Emmons
16310 Akron Street

A single-level post and beam spec house for the never completely realized Southdown development. The plan is an open one, with the rooms oriented outward towards terraces and garden.

6. House, 1952
Jones and Emmons
North of northwest corner of Bienvenida Avenue and Marquette Street

Another variation on the small Southdown development spec housing.

7. Soffer House, 1973
Eric Wright (remodelling)
665 Bienveneda Avenue

Austere on the street front, all glass on the garden side, this house has all the good qualities of Wright's grandfather's (Frank Lloyd) "Usonian" Houses and none of the bad ones.

8. House, ca. 1935
Attributed to John Byers and Edla Muir
630 Palmera Avenue

A very quaint Anglo-Norman cottage.

9. Moss House, 1979
Eric Owen Moss
708 El Medio Avenue

A major remodelling has produced one of Moss's characteristic buildings. Architecture here is High Art, but fortunately tinged with a sense of delight and humor. Though radical in form and color, it really fits well within a street of typical California spec ranch houses. The original house (1949; James H.

9. Moss House

Caughey), was a sophisticated Modern version of the California Ranch house.

10. Presbyterian Conference Grounds, 1922-later
North end of Temescal Canyon Road

Once this belonged to the Methodists and was the site of the yearly Chautauqua performances which were so much a part of the cultural "uplift movement" for the common man at the turn of the century. By the time the small cottages were built to service the huge tent show, the Chautauqua movement was already declining. The Presbyterians took it over and used it as a retreat. Behind it are some beautiful nature trails which may be used by permission of the caretaker at the main gate.

11. ■Saint Matthew's Episcopal Church, 1982-83
Charles W. Moore (Moore, Ruble, Yudell); Campbell and Campbell (Regula Campbell), landscape architects 1030 Bienveneda Avenue

The present church is the third structure on the site. The original Carleton M. Winslow church of 1942 was moved to the site in the early 1950s and was then remodelled in 1953 by Jones and Emmons. This building burned in one of Southern California's hillside fires. The present church by Moore is close to being domestic in scale. It manages to declare its public nature by the barn-like contours and tall campanile, while at the same time it snuggles into its site and the excellent landscape scheme of Regula Campbell. Internally the sanctuary of the church has the quality of an informal meeting hall dominated by a pair of wood arches and an apse which suggest the traditional cruciform plan of a church. North of the church are remains (including windmill) of the French Norman Barnett Estate designed by John Byers and Edla Muir.

13. Palisades Elementary School

12. Community United Methodist Church, 1929
801 Via de la Paz

The church was organized in 1922, but the structure was not begun until 1929. Even then the congregation was small, hinting that Methodism would not triumph. The edifice began in the usual Spanish Colonial Revival mode with the belltower showing the influence of the Moderne. Much of the original character of the building has been covered up by modern (1972) facilities.

13. Palisades Elementary School, 1930
800 Via de la Paz

Spanish Colonial Revival again, this school with Moorish tower was slated for destruction after the 1971 earthquake. Even though it suffered no serious damage, the building's construction did not meet contemporary safety standards. A wise citizenry, proud of the architecture of the old building, engaged an architect who showed that gutting the building, reinforcing the walls, and constructing new interiors would not only satisfy the building inspectors but would cost less than building a new structure. As in the case of the Lapiths and the Centaurs, civilization occasionally wins.

14. Santa Monica Land and Water Company, 1924
Clinton Nourse
Southwest corner of Sunset Boulevard

A fine Spanish Colonial Revival business block. The very name suggests that promoters were early trying to lure buyers to their Riviera.

15. Department of Water and Power Building, 1935
Frederick L. Roehrig
Northeast corner of Sunset Boulevard and Via de la Paz

Did you ever think you would see an example of Regency Moderne? Now you have!

16. House, ca. 1929
629 Frontera Drive

This beautifully turned-out Monterey Revival house must be by John Byers. But the real reason we take you into this area is that we want you to experience the town planning of Olmsted and Olmsted, who also laid out Palos Verdes Estates. The houses are all expensive. Some like this one are good. Most date after 1929, which says something about the gravity of the Great Depression for the rich.

Pacific Palisades, South

behind the street wall and garage. It was sensitively modernized in 1982 by Gwathmey, Siegel, and Associates.

3. Canyon Elementary School, 1894
Northeast of intersection of Ocean Avenue and Channel Road

A nice Classical Revival one-room schoolhouse (now a children's library) said to be the second oldest school building in Los Angeles County.

4. Pumphrey House, 1939
Harwell H. Harris
615 Kingman Avenue

This horizontal, wood-battened house is quite Wrightian and very difficult to see behind fences and foliage.

S anta Monica Canyon initially contained small, quite modest summer beach houses and year-round cottages. In the later 1930s it began to acquire serious examples of Modern design by Harwell H. Harris, Richard J. Neutra, and others. After 1945 other prime examples of high art Modernism were built, especially in the area in and around Chautauqua Boulevard.

The Olmsted Brothers, whose father had laid out Central Park in New York City, platted a picturesque maze west of Chautauqua Boulevard where some of the most pleasant houses in the traditional imagery of the twenties and thirties remain. The old canyons attracted a varied congeries, from the Uplifters on Latimer Road to Will Rogers and Thomas Mann in the highlands.

1. Bradbury House, 1922
John Byers
102 Ocean Way

One of the first adobe houses that Byers designed, this was instrumental in establishing his reputation as a Spanish Colonial Revivalist.

2. ■Sten-Frenke House, 1934
Richard J. Neutra
126 Mabery Road, off Ocean Avenue

A classic Neutra with a Streamline Moderne curved-glass bay which overlooks the Pacific. The house, which is close to impossible to see, lies up the hill

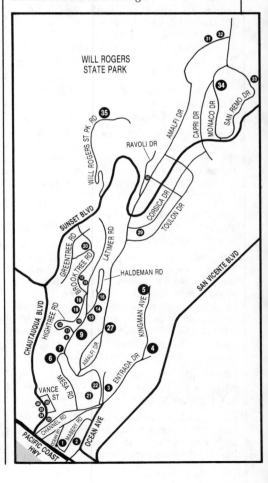

5. Gibbons House, "Delores del Rio," 1929
Douglas Honnold and Cedric Gibbons
757 Kingman Avenue

An early and impressive example of the Modern, somewhat formal and monumental (Art Deco) towards the street, but almost pure doctrinaire International Style Modern in the two-story facade which overlooks Santa Monica Canyon.

6. Entenza House, 1937
Harwell H. Harris
475 Mesa Road

Built for John Entenza, the editor and publisher of *Arts and Architecture,* as a declaration of his commitment to modernity. His curved-wall carport, spiral staircase, and metal railing make it more Streamline Moderne than classical International style. The Entenza House was Harris's only realized example of Streamline Moderne.

7. Abell House, 1937
Thornton M. Abell
469 Upper Mesa Road

A gem of the regionalized International Style Modern, this house depressed on the side of the hill is barely visible. The house consists of a series of stucco volumes stepped down a steep hillside. It is all quite nautical in feeling.

8. Haines House, 1943
Thornton M. Abell
477 Upper Mesa Road

An angled, single-floor, Modern image (stucco volumes) dwelling set far down the hillside. The garden side of this wood frame, concrete block, and fiberglass structure is almost entirely of glass to take advantage of the view. At the base of the hill is a combined studio and garage. This house, just two doors from Abell's own, is equally difficult to see.

9. Kaplan House, 1973
Michael Leventhal
514 Latimer Road

Parts of old wharfs and houses have been used to construct and decorate this highly expressionistic monument of the late Craftsman movement.

10. House, 1976
Paul Thoryk
532 Latimer Road

A tribute to the enormous popularity of the Moore and Turnbull ideas of the late 1960s, this house turns out in the end to be another example of the late Craftsman style.

11. House, ca. 1925
Southwest corner of Latimer and Hilltree roads

Additions have been made to this house which was once a tiny Hansel and Gretel delight.

12. Gertler House, 1970
Raymond Kappe
14623 Hilltree Road

A handsome wedding of the woodsy Craftsman aesthetic of Frank Lloyd Wright and Charles and Henry Greene to the bold angular forms of the International style. Kappe, whose own house is nearby, has a very personal style well suited to these ancient groves of eucalyptus and cypress.

12. Gertler House

13. Uplifters Club, 1923
William J. Dodd
Haldeman and Latimer roads

The watered-down Spanish Colonial Revival of the clubhouse is certainly not as interesting as the club itself. In the early teens the members of a splinter group of the Los Angeles Athletic Club devoted themselves to High Jinx, and in the early twenties under the leaderhip of Harry Marston Haldeman, a local executive of the Crane Plumbing Company, and L. Frank Baum, the author of the Wizard of Oz books, the club bought property on Latimer Road (named for one of its members) and set out a sort of retreat, not to be confused with the later settlement of high-minded Methodists on the highlands above. Architecturally this meant the building of cottages (often log cabins) and later more elaborate houses. While not really important individually, as a group they compose a fascinating complex, a significant reflection of the change in taste occurring in the late teens and early twenties. Although we have not thoroughly researched the architects of each of these houses, it would appear from a review of meagre records and general observation that the firm most responsible for the whimsical styles of these houses was that of Arthur S. Heineman, whose brother Alfred was the chief designer.

The log cabins, some of them authentic, some of them stagesets, are probably of chief interest. The first at 1 Latimer Road is the **Kley House** (1923), a log-faced lodge, now almost completely cut off from public view. It is probably by the Heinemans as are other log-faced cabins at 3 and 18 Latimer Road. Others are on Haldeman Road at 31, 32, and 34. At 36, 37, and 38 are authentically constructed log cabins in which 38, the **Marco Hellman Cabin,** is the most interesting.

14. Marco Hellman Cabin, 1923-24
Alfred Heineman
38 Haldeman Road

Tradition has it that this house, as well as those at 36 and 37 Haldeman Road, was part of a movie set transported to the canyon by Hellman, a very rich banker. Alfred Heineman who, under the firm name of his brother Arthur designed the Hellman banks in the Los Angeles area, was responsible for the rustic decor of the interior of Hellman's own cabin. It is probable that Heineman also was responsible for the interiors of the other cabins and also for the exterior as well as interior design of Heather Hill (1922-23) at 7 Latimer Road, whose shingled roof in imitation of thatch was a trademark of a number of Heineman houses in Pasadena.

15. Abel House, 1978
Charles W. Moore, Ron Frank, and Robert Yudell (Urban Innovations Group)
747 Latimer Road

This elongated house picturesquely rambles over its Rustic Canyon site, but, as in many of Moore's designs, a thin central core holds all of the wings and bays together. The entrance and a walled courtyard are in the fashion of the late seventeenth century New England colonial house. A large chimney and stairs dominate the design (both externally and internally).

16. Ruben House, 1936
Richard J. Neutra
50 Haldeman Road

Actually this is a rare case of a Neutra remodelling. The original shingled ranch-style house was built in 1923-24 by Ralph Hamlin, a bicycle manufacturer who had the dubious distinction of owning the first motorcycle west of the Rockies.

We have by no means listed all of the interesting architecture within Rustic Canyon; much of it is well hidden from public view. A case in point would be the extensive remodelling (1982) of an older California Ranch house by the architectural historian Charles Jencks and by the architect Buzz Yudell. This is a classic example of Post Modernism, but it cannot be seen from the road. The student of lifestyles in the twenties and the thirties will find many more houses of significance. After all, Aldous Huxley, Emil Ludwig, Johnnie Weismuller, and other worthies once lived in this area.

17. Emmons House, 1954
Jones and Emmons
661 Brooktree Road

A very neat post and beam International Style Modern product which has weathered the years extremely well.

18. Anderson House, 1950
Craig Ellwood
656 Hightree Road

A thin brick wall and aluminum garage door form the austere street facade of this house by one of Los Angeles's most distinguished followers of Mies van der Rohe.

19. Elton House, 1951
Craig Ellwood
635 Hightree Road

If the Anderson House is private, this Miesian house is very open and in a strikingly different style from its neighbor.

20. ▪Kappe House, 1968
Raymond Kappe
715 Brooktree Road

A virtual treehouse poised over a steep hillside. Glass has been used almost exclusively as the infill between the vertical and horizontal wood frame of the building. Within, wood bridges and staircases join the principle interior spaces. This house is another example of Kappe's inventive ability to meld the Craftsman aesthetic and the International Style Modern into a very personal style. Other examples of Kappe's work are nearby: **Pregerson House** (1966) at 680 Brooktree Road, and the **Gates-Dorman House** (1961) at 737 Brooktree Road.

21. Burns House, 1974
Charles W. Moore
230 Amalfi Drive

The Los Angeles version of the Spanish Colonial Revival of the 1920s. The pink stucco dwelling boasts an array of shed roofs and skylights, along with the basic necessities of Hispanic Los Angeles—a

21. Burns House

walled and tiled entrance court and a swimming pool. Within, an organ dominates the two-story living room.

22. Haines House, 1951
Thornton M. Abell
247 Amalfi Drive

A refined pavilion; sheathed in horizontal redwood and with a flat roof, brick chimney, and brick terraces.

23. West House, 1948
Rodney A. Walker
199 Chautauqua Boulevard

A romantically sited, single-floor, five-room house sheathed in striated plywood. This was one of the early Case Study House projects.

24. Eames House and Studio, 1947-49
Charles Eames
203 Chautauqua Boulevard

One of America's great twentieth century houses which is as impressive today as when it was built as part of John Entenza's Case Study House program. The two metal-framed boxes, set against a eucalyptus covered hillside, dramatically illustrate how personal and humane the image of the machine can be in the hands of a gifted designer. The interior furnishings chosen and arranged, with both Ray and Charles Eames collaborating, are an integral part of the design.

25. Entenza House, 1949
Charles Eames and Eero Saarinen
205 Chautauqua Boulevard

The steel frame and roof design is not as assertive in this Case Study House design as in the adjacent Eames House. A single rectangular form contains all of the spaces, including the two-car garage. As with the Eames House the open interior is most impressive with the furnishings of Saarinen chairs and built-in angular sofa.

26. Bailey House, 1946-48
Richard J. Neutra (with later additions by Neutra)
219 Chautauqua Boulevard

Esther McCoy has noted the similarity of this house to Neutra's Nesbitt House

of 1942, where he "made a virtue of redwood — even brick." The property is partly enclosed by a serpentine brick wall. A Case Study House.

27. Cernitz House, 1938
Milton J. Black
601 Amalfi Drive

If you look carefully behind the post-World War II remodelling you will see one of Black's Streamline Moderne delights.

28. Anderson House, 1922
390 Vance Street

Anderson, whose first name seems to have disappeared, was supposed to have been a merchant who brought treasures from all over the world to this tiny house. Most of his travels seem, however, to have been in Mexico. This house, with its magnificent tile, art glass windows, and mosaic of Mexican dancers in front of a mission arcade, is a real stunner.

28. Anderson House

29. Kenaston House, 1936-37
John Byers, Edla Muir; remodelled in
1963 by Edla Muir
914 Corsica Drive

The Spanish Colonial Revival made
modern.

30. House, 1950
Raphael S. Soriano
1080 Ravoli Drive

Almost invisible now, this is the first of
the pure steel-frame Case Study Houses
sponsored by *Arts and Architecture* magazine. It has been extensively remodelled.

31. Kingsley Houses, 1946
J. R. Davidson
1620 and 1630 Amalfi Drive

Absolutely simple builder's houses distinguished only by the name of their
architect.

32. House, ca. 1925
John Byers (with Edla Muir)
1650 Amalfi Drive

One of the loveliest of Byers's designs. A
long unfenestrated wall in front opens
only at a gate which allows you to see
into the central patio of this Spanish
Colonial Revival house.

33. Mann House, 1941
J. R. Davidson
1550 San Remo Drive

It is almost impossible to see this stucco
and glass two-story Modern image house
built for the great novelist Thomas
Mann. It is a pity since the Manns were
so deeply involved with the planning.
We list it because of the thrill of knowing it is there.

34. Barclay House, ca. 1927
John Byers (with Edla Muir)
1425 Monaco Drive

Monterey Revival.

35. Will Rogers Ranch, 1921-later
14243 Sunset Boulevard

This is one of those houses that is more
important in evoking the spirit of its
owner than for its architecture, though
the house does succeed very well in conveying the feeling of early California. It
was where Will could occupy himself
"messing around doing this and that and
not much of either. Get on old 'Soap-
suds' and ride off up a little canyon I
got here." When the Rogers moved to
the ranch permanently in 1928, they expanded their simple vacation cottage.
Again in 1933 when his wife and daughter were in Palestine, Will "raised the
roof" of the living room in order to
make room for him to do his rope tricks
comfortably. The house with its curios is
open 10-5 daily to the public. See also
the barn whose two bays are actually the
halves of an old barn Rogers found in
West Los Angeles.

33. Mann House

Santa Monica

Dubbed the "Zenith City of the Sunset Seas," Santa Monica was open ranchland until Senator John P. Jones of Nevada went into partnership with Colonel Robert S. Baker, the owner of the ranch, and laid out a town which he believed would become the port of Los Angeles, given railroad connections. A map of the town, with a characteristic grid pattern of streets, was filed with the recorder on July 10, 1875. A few days later lots went on sale. In nine months Santa Monica had 1000 residents and seemed destined, with the railroad and wharf built by Senator Jones, to become one of the great ports of America. Though it gained more residents during the land boom of the late 1880s, the idea of a major metropolis was doomed when San Pedro and Wilmington became the port of Los Angeles.

Santa Monica became, and still is, a beach city. Senator Jones and Mrs. Baker, the widow of the ranch owner, gave the land atop the palisades to the city. Palisades Park is one of the few places in California where a city has maintained the ocean view for the enjoyment of the people, and the people are there, every day of the week in the summer and on good weekends in the winter, playing cards, sunning themselves, jogging, and chatting in a babble of tongues.

Below the Palisades cliff, between the highway and the beach, lots were sold so that the beach became accessible in only a few places. Since the 1940s the State has bought back many of these properties; but a few houses remain, and are, of course, in great demand.

The town on the highland developed slowly. Third Street (now Santa Monica Mall) became the main commercial street with residential areas moving northwest, particularly in the twenties and thirties. Grand hotels were built. The Arcadia, long gone, was a Queen Anne pile near the pier at Colorado Street. Later hotels took to the highlands across from Palisades Park. Now the Miramar, some parts dating from the 1920s, is the only hotel reflecting any part of its former glory, though its gardens have been filled in with a new building. The whole frontage of Ocean Avenue has changed over the past decades: commercial buildings and highrise apartments taking the place of the old summer homes of wealthy Angelenos. From a distance the ocean frontage of Santa Monica is beginning to approach the wall-like look we associate with Miami Beach.

Most of Santa Monica's dwellings of the teens, twenties, and thirties were modest in size, but in and around San Vicente Boulevard the upper-middle-class quality of neighboring Pacific Palisades and Brentwood prevailed. Santa Monica was the home of the architect John Byers and has many houses designed by him, often in association with Edla Muir. Though Byers was self-trained as an architect, he early developed an interest and sensitivity to the Hispanic architecture tradition. His adobe, Spanish, English, French Norman, and American Colonial designs set an example which others followed to good effect making northern Santa Monica an architectural monument of traditional images of the twenties and thirties.

Within the past decade Santa Monica has been transformed bit by bit. The modest single-family houses have been and currently are being replaced by large houses, or even more often by condominium units. The newest of these condominiums spans a wide range of images, from High Tech to Spanish Colonial Revival and Tudor. And in the downtown areas high-rise office buildings are beginning to line Wilshire Boulevard and other major streets.

Santa Monica, North

1. La Mesa Drive
Enter opposite 19th Street off San Vicente Boulevard

No other street in Los Angeles County (not even Prospect Boulevard in Pasadena) is so beautifully landscaped. In this case Moreton Bay figs, seemingly planted by the pioneers, line the parkways on both sides of the street. The architecture is worthy of the trees. You will have your own favorites, but we begin with:

2. Crenshaw House, 1925-26
Gable and Wyant
1923 La Mesa Drive

The romantic ideal of the Spanish house.

3. Thompson House, 1924-25
John Byers
2021 La Mesa Drive

A blend of Spanish, Mexican, and California details.

4. Byers House, 1924
John Byers
2034 La Mesa Drive

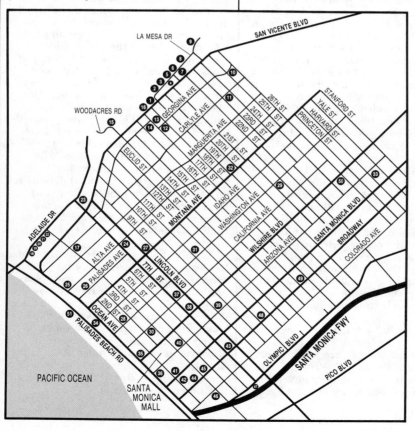

The architect chose the balconied Monterey style for his second home in Santa Monica. It was within walking distance of his office.

5. Zimmer House, 1924
John Byers
2101 La Mesa Drive

A single-floor adobe with a high central portal enclosed by end walls. Uncluttered stucco walls and the low-pitched tile roofs are the dominant theme.

6. Bundy House, 1925
John Byers
2153 La Mesa Drive

A good example of Byers's personal version of the Hispanic tradition.

7. Tinglof House, 1925-26
John Byers
2210 La Mesa Drive

Hispanic.

8. Nables House, 1949
Lloyd Wright
2323 La Mesa Drive

A low-lying yellow brick house, almost impossible to see.

9. Stothart-Phillips House, 1937-38
J. R. Davidson
2501 La Mesa Drive

You can catch only a glimpse of this elegant thirties International Style Modern house. The principle front of this house, with extensive glass doors and windows, overlooks the terrace and has a view to the west.

9. Stothart-Phillips House

5. Zimmer House

10. Byers Office

10. Byers Office, 1926
John Byers (with Edla Muir)
246 26th Street

This small and very romantic office building with magnificent wrought iron gate is simply beautiful.

11. Hromadka House, 1937
2320 Carlyle Avenue

Southern California's version of what the eighteenth century Colonial house should have looked like.

12. Fuller House, 1920-22
John Byers
304 18th Street at Georgina Avenue

A typical early Byers design with living and sleeping quarters separated by a pergolated patio. Certainly this is one of his best designs, only slightly less interesting than his similar house on Amalfi Drive in Pacific Palisades.

13. Laidlow House, 1924
John Byers
217 17th Street

Byers as a medievalist — in this case French Norman.

14. Carrillo House, 1925
John Byers
1602 Georgina Avenue at 16th Street

A monumental California adobe. The house next door at 1638 Georgina Avenue was designed by G. C. McAlister in 1937.

15. Ullman House, 1955
Thornton M. Abell
800 Woodacres Road (in Pacific Palisades; extension of 14th Street, Santa Monica)

This concrete block and vertical wood batten house in a rationalist version of the post-World War II International Style Modern is just visible through a magnificent grove of trees.

16. Armstrong-Cobb House, 1926
John Byers
1717 San Vicente Boulevard

A large-scale version of a Spanish farm house (*cortijo*). Especially successful is the varied layering of the tile roofs which conveys a sense that the dwelling has been added to over the years.

17. MacBennel House, 1921-22
John Byers
404 Georgina Avenue at 4th Street

One of Byers's first real adobes. At this stage in his career he was a manufacturer of adobe bricks, a builder, and an architectural designer.

18. Jones House, 1907
130 Adelaide Drive

A big, wholesome example of the turn-of-the-century Colonial Revival.

19. Weaver House, 1910-11
142 Adelaide Drive

A gorgeous example of Craftsman orientalism, worthy of Charles and Henry Greene.

20. Milbank House, 1910-11
236 Adelaide Drive

A two-story Craftsman masterpiece, with a strong surge of Oriental details, romantically situated in a lovely garden.

21. Gorham-Holliday House, 1923-24
John Byers
326 Adelaide Drive

Certainly one of Byers's most impressive Andalusian houses. A patio occupies the center of the U, and a projecting Monterey balcony overlooks the patio and garden.

22. Gorham House, 1910
Robert Farquhar
Southwest corner of Adelaide Drive and 4th Street

A low stucco house, reminiscent of the Pasadena Culbertson House by the Greenes. The entrance, otherwise classical, is capped by an Oriental porch roof.
    Across 4th Street (southeast corner) is the **Gillis House** (1906), a large T-shaped structure set out around a patio. It was designed by Myron Hunt and Elmer Grey during their woodsy, Arts and Crafts mode.

23. Worrel House, 1923-24
Robert Stacy-Judd
710 Adelaide Drive

A Pueblo Revival fantasy, more fantastic the longer you look at it.

24. Byers House, 1917
John Byers
547 7th Street near Alta Avenue

Board and batten and stucco walls hint more at the hills of Berkeley than the highlands of Santa Monica. This was the first house Byers designed for himself. The Craftsman bungalow (**Jones House,** ca. 1913) at the northeast corner of Alta Avenue and 7th Street is well worth a look, as is the 1925 **Boswell House** (John Byers) at 624 Alta Avenue.

25. Shorecliff Tower Apartments, 1963
Jones and Emmons
535 Ocean Avenue at Alta Avenue

A quiet and elegant version of the late International Style Modern of the early 1960s.

26. Witbeck House, 1917
Charles and Henry Greene (Henry Greene)
226 Palisades Avenue

A two-story, faintly Tudor dwelling, sheathed in shingles.

26. Witbeck House

27. Roosevelt School, 1935
Marsh, Smith, and Powell
801 Montana Avenue and Lincoln Boulevard

PWA Streamline Moderne with wonderful lettering over the major entrance.

28. Sovereign Hotel and Apartments,
1928-29
Meyer Radon
205 Washington Avenue

There was no reticence here on the part of the architect as to how many Spanish Colonial Revival forms and details should be used.

29. Gehry House, 1978
Frank O. Gehry and Associates
Southeast corner of Washington Avenue and 22nd Street

A helpless Dutch Colonial has been maneuvered into one of Gehry's perplexing compositions. A new wall separates the house from the street to the north, and to the rear a courtyard has been created. Fragments of the two-by-four-inch studs of the original house have been revealed, new windows have been added here and there, and of course there is a small swatch of chain link. Within, not withstanding the asphalt driveway floor of the kichen, the atmosphere is Craftsman.

30. Claremont Apartments, 1929-30
Max Meltzmann
330 California Avenue

Spanish Colonial Revival of the late twenties with a splash of colored tile in the forecourt.

31. Voss Apartments, 1937
947-953 11th Street near Washington Avenue

Exuberant Streamline Moderne. There was a surge of multiple housing units built in Santa Monica at the end of the 1930s. The two favored images were the Streamline Moderne and the classical-flavored Hollywood Regency.

32. ■Villa de Malaga Townhouse,
1982-83
926-930 20th Street near Montana Avenue

Two-story townhouses in the Andalusian mood, organized around a central courtyard. In this instance the Hispanic of the early 1980s has been carried out

29. Gehry House

31. Voss Apartments

with both knowledge and reticence. The long central court of the complex conveys the feeling of a Spanish village street.

33. Condominiums, 1980
Urban Forms (Steve Andre and Alan Tossman)
1319 Harvard Street

Contemporary high art surface pattern, accompanied by a sense of mechanical technology to suggest that it is all rational.

34. Gates to Palisades Park, ca. 1912
Across from entrance to Idaho Avenue

Craftsman orientalized gates with tile by Ernest Batchelder of Pasadena.

35. Lawrence Welk Plaza, 1973;
General Telephone Building; Wilshire West Apartments
Daniel, Mann, Johnson, and Mendenhall (Cesar Pelli; P. J. Jacobson and Dwight Williams)
Wilshire Professional Building, 1979-80
Gensler and Associates
100 Wilshire Boulevard at Ocean Avenue

Ocean Avenue facing on to Palisades Park is still a fascinating blend of new, middle-aged, and old architecture, though the old and middle-aged buildings of modest size are being continually replaced by modest high-rise buildings. The Lawrence Welk Plaza should have been a major focal point not only for Santa Monica, but also for L.A., for here Wilshire Boulevard reaches its western terminus with only the Pacific beyond. The DMJM buildings are at best dull; the newer eleven-story **Wilshire Professional Building** (1979-80; Gensler and Associates) with its stepped back floors and angle to the street is a better building; but while it is more satisfactory as a design it still does not really establish the importance of this intersection.

36. Shangri-la Apartments, 1939-40
William E. Foster
Southeast corner of Ocean and Arizona avenues

An eight-story Streamline Moderne block with a suggestion of a curved tower dominating the street corner of the building. Next door (at least at the moment) is a charming Eastlake-Queen Anne dwelling (1890).

37. Saint Monica's Roman Catholic Church, 1925
Albert C. Martin
Northwest corner of California Avenue and 7th Street

A stone-sheathed Romanesque church with an impressive barrel-vaulted interior. The exterior sculpture is by Joseph Conradi. As intended, the building presents the case for traditional imagery realized through the modern technology of reinforced concrete.

38. Miles Memorial Playhouse, 1929
John Byers
In Lincoln Park on Lincoln Boulevard between Wilshire Boulevard and California Avenue

A public auditorium theatre in the guise of an Andalusian building.

39. Drive-in Market, 1928
Paul R. Williams
Northeast corner of Wilshire Boulevard and 9th Street

Drive-in retail markets became a popular form in Southern California in the late 1920s; by the mid-1930s they were replaced by the larger scale supermarkets with their accompanying parking lots. In this complex Paul Williams utilized the Spanish Colonial Revival image.

40. Santa Monica Post Office, 1937
Neal A. Melick and Robert A. Murray
1248 5th Street at Arizona Avenue

A single-story PWA Moderne building with excellent ornament. The offset of the interior horizontal planking evokes the pioneering nineteenth century of the West. The Art Deco (Zigzag) Moderne decoration, especially that of the interior chandeliers, hints more at the Native American art of the Southwest than that of Paris.

41. Bay City Guaranty Building and Loan Association Building (now Crocker Bank), 1929-30
Walker and Eisen
1225 Santa Monica Mall

41. Bay City Guaranty Building and Loan Association Building (now Crocker Bank)

For a number of decades this was Santa Monica's only tall office building. The ground floor has been altered and signage has hidden the corner clock tower, but one can still make out its Art Deco (Zigzag) Moderne ornament.

42. Elmiro (now Cinema) Theatre, 1933-34
Norman W. Alpaugh
1443 Santa Monica Mall

A transitional design with a little of the Streamline Moderne embellished upon the earlier Art Deco Moderne. Though Moderne in detail, the flavor is really quite Beaux Arts.

43. Central Tower Building, 1929
Eugene Durfee
1424 7th Street

An eight-story classical Art Deco Moderne building that seems to have had problems getting off of the ground.

44. Keller Block, ca. 1890
Northwest corner of Broadway and 3rd Street

A rare pre-1900 which still retains its cast-iron street front.

45. Santa Monica Place, 1979-81
Frank O. Gehry and Associates
315 Broadway

45. Parking Garage, Santa Monica Place

The in-downtown enclosed shopping mall which has enjoyed great currency throughout America in the late seventies and on into the eighties. Though the multi-story mall space is tight, Gehry's design conveys a sense of being rational and delightful. Gehry's chain link fencing of the exterior surface of the parking garage creates a strange visual illusion, especially with its signage and palm trees on the south and west facades. Within the mall Frank O. Gehry and Associates (1981) have designed the interior of **Bubar's Jewelers.**

46. Store and Office Building, 1927
Eugene Durfee
1501-15 4th Street

Los Angeles's own improved version of Spanish and Mexican Churrigueresque.

47. ▪Santa Monica Bus (Transportation) Center, 1982-84
Kappe, Lotery, and Boccato
Between Olympic Boulevard, 5th and 7th streets, just north of the Santa Monica Freeway

The image of the futuristic machine, Buck Rogers brought up-to-date via science fiction films of the early 1980s.

48. Van Tilburg Office Building, 1979
Johannes van Tilburg and Partners
1101 Broadway

A formal composition of a white stucco box, with cut-in patterns accompanied by projecting volumes.

49. Packard Show Rooms, 1928
Edward James Baume
Southwest corner of Wilshire Boulevard and 17th Street

Spanish Colonial Revival with wrought iron grillwork reminiscent of old Spanish choir screens.

50. Home Savings and Loan Association Building, 1969
Millard Sheets
Southeast corner of Wilshire Boulevard and 26th Street

Another of Home Savings's attacks on the coldness and dullness of post-World War II Modern. The exterior mosaics are by Nancy Colbath, the stained glass window by Susan Hertel.

51. Flint Houses, 1928

John Byers
701 and 703 Pacific Beach Road (Highway 1)

Here Byers utilized the form of a Barcelona urban house, oriented around a high spaced interior court. There are a few other houses still standing on this strand of Pacific Beach Road. Among these is John Byers's **Netcher House** (1926) at 1020 Pacific Beach Road and Richard J. Neutra's **Lewin House** of 1938 at 512 Ocean Front.

52. Colorado Place, 1981-84
Welton Becket Associates

North side of Colorado Avenue between Cloverdale Boulevard and 26th Street.

A mixed use development consisting of offices, shops, and eventually a 392-room hotel. The first phase is now completed and consists of low-rise exposed concrete volumes that are insistently Modern in their horizontal striping of dark window bands and light-colored spandrels. A small public park is tucked into one corner, but at this moment the most noticeable elements are the parking garages with their important auto entrances.

51. Flint House

Santa Monica, South

The section of Santa Monica south of the Santa Monica Freeway has always been mixed in its usage — small beach cottages west of Ocean Avenue, then a mixture of residential and commercial buildings reaching up and beyond Lincoln Boulevard. This area, like Venice just to the south, is currently experiencing an intensity of multiple housing, ranging from high-rise towers to two- and three-story townhouses. Santa Monica's wall of high-rises has continued to work its way south overlooking the beach. Of these the **Sea Colony** at 2910 Nielson Way (1980; Landau Partnership) is unquestionably the best, though it could well be argued that none of these complexes (at least in their present size) should have been built.

1. Santa Monica Pier, 1909-21
City of Santa Monica Engineering Department
West end of Colorado Avenue

The pier was severely damaged in the heavy storms of the winter of 1982-83 and it is now being rebuilt. For decades the pier has been one of the joys of Santa Monica, rain or shine. On weekends the railings are lined with people fishing or just walking and looking. Restaurants, curio shops, and amusement palaces line the south side of the pier. But the hit architecturally (and otherwise as well) is the merry-go-round, with its 1900 Wurlitzer organ whooping it up over the weekends and during fine summer days.

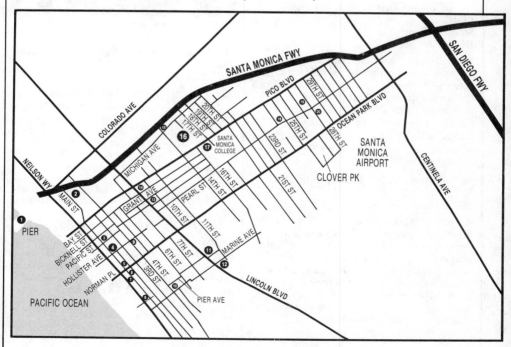

2. Santa Monica City Hall, 1938-39
Donald B. Parkinson and J. M. Estep
1685 Main Street

This PWA Moderne building with its
beautiful tile entrance was to have been
the central focus of a formal Beaux Arts
grouping of buildings which, as so often
happens, never took place.

2. Santa Monica City Hall

3. ■Condominium Townhouses,
1981-82
Stafford/Bender
116 Pacific Street

The ultimate in High Tech imagery.
Though not specifically derived from
classical European Modern of the 1920s,
the atmosphere of their constructivist design conveys that feeling. The design of
the building, and especially of the facades, is that of pure architectural pat-
terning, *a la* the high art image of the
machine.

4. ■Horatio West Court, 1919-21
Irving J. Gill
140 Hollister Avenue

As Esther McCoy has pointed out, this
four-unit complex is Gill's closest ap-
proximation to the later European International Style Modern of the 1920s. The
arched entryways and the small patio-
courts indicate Gill's attachment to the
early Mission Revival of California. The
buildings have recently been restored,
and though there have been some

changes, they do present an excellent
sense of Gill's puritanical and abstract
approach to design.

5. Merle Norman Building, 1935-36
Attributed to George Parr
2521-29 Main Street, at Norman Place

A large and delightful mixture of the
earlier Art Deco Moderne and the later
Streamline Moderne, the later winning
out. Its upper section conjures up a vision of a Streamline ocean liner.

5. Merle Norman Building

6. First Methodist Episcopal Church,
1875-76
2621 2nd Street

Santa Monica's first church building has
been, as was so often the case in the
nineteenth century, moved twice; once in
1893, and then in 1900. Architecturally
of interest, because the building could
just as well have been built in Iowa City
as on the far reaches of the Pacific
Coast.

7. Jones House (now **Heritage Square
Museum**), 1894
2620 Main Street

This simply detailed Queen Anne dwelling, and its neighbor, the **Trask House**
(1903; Hunt and Eggers), were moved to
this site in 1977. Both houses, originally
in the 1000 block of Ocean Boulevard
have been restored. The Trask House is
now the Chronicle Restaurant.

8. Parkhurst Building

8. Parkhurst Building, 1927
Norman F. Marsh and Company
Northwest corner of Main Street and
Pier Avenue

This Spanish Colonial Revival building
with its beautiful exposed brickwork
might have come out of a Hollywood
film on old Seville. It has been restored
to its former glory.

9. Two Bungalows, ca. 1910
Southeast corner of 4th Street and
Hollister Avenue

Almost identical Mission style bungalows. They were once pink and
trimmed in blue.

10. Vawter House, 1900
504 Pier Avenue

A shingled Queen Anne dwelling, which
with its extensive porches on two sides
suggests the ideal of the seaside resort
that Santa Monica was seeking to create
at the turn of the century.

11. Condominium Townhouses, 1981
Janotta-Breska Associates
1016 Pier Avenue

The High Tech image, perhaps in this
instance more romantic than other new
condominiums in Santa Monica and
Venice.

12. Condominium Townhouses, 1981
Janotta-Breska Associates
1015 Marine Street

A further continuation of the machine
image expressed in the condominiums at
1016 Pier Avenue.

13. Condominium Townhouses, 1979
A Design Group; David Cooper,
Michael W. Folonnis, George Blain, and
Richard Clemenson
831 Pacific Street

A not-to-be-missed High Tech image
which is resplendent with arbitrary high
art forms and surfaces. One comes away
with a feeling that it belongs in model
form within a museum rather than on a
city street.

14. Condominium Townhouses, 1981
A Design Group/Janotta-Breska
Associates
821 Bay Street

This stucco-sheathed unit is a little more
believable as High Tech, and as a place
to live, than its neighbor at #831.

15. Conference Room, 1982
Carde/Killefer
1638 19th Street

A tiny-gabled roof-building situated in a
garden, it has been treated in part as an
abstract exercise of exposed sticks (two-
by-four-inch studs, plus).

16. Woodlawn Cemetary Mausoleum, 1924 and later
Pico Boulevard between 7th and 14th streets

The 1924 section of this building (which faces towards the south) can be seen from Pico Boulevard and boasts a handsome Plateresque/Churrigueresque facade. Note as well the **BPO Elks Monument** (ca. 1910) to the west. It is an open, round, classical temple surrounded by cast iron elks.

17. Santa Monica College: Business Education and Vocational Building, 1981
Daniel, Mann, Johnson, and Mendenhall
Pico Boulevard at 17th Street

A blend of post-World War II International Style Modern with a suggestion of the Streamline Moderne of the thirties, and even a slight nod to recent High Tech. Do go to the rear (south side) of the building to see this elevation with its exposed metal stairs.

18. ■Sun-Tech Townhouses, 1981
Urban Forms; David Van Hoy and Steve Andre
2433 Pearl Street

An eighteen-unit condominium, the ultimate in current High Tech imagery. Though the machine is supposedly a rational creature, High Tech imagery such as this is related to Art with a capital A more than with pragmatic humane planning. Still, we must admit that it is impressive from the street and from within, especially in the two-story living spaces.

19. Putnam Place Townhouse, 1983
2332 28th Street

A perfect model of Post Modernism: classical columns, false walls, and other classical elements.

16. Woodlawn Cemetary Mausoleum

19. Putnam Place Townhouse

20. Condominium Townhouses, 1980
A Design Group (Michael Folonis and
David Cooper)
Street

Yet another well-designed example of
High Tech. The image in this case is
somewhat stronger in nostalgia for the
"Heroic" period of modern architecture
of the 1920s.

21. Condominium Townhouses, 1981
Tossman/Day
835 Grant Avenue

A three-story stucco unit, whose cut-out
forms, shed roofs, and window pattern
directly carry on Charles W. Moore's recent vocabulary.

**22. Santa Monica Freeway, Inter-
change with the San Diego Freeway,**
1961-66
Lammers, Reed, and Reece, Engineers

The Santa Monica Freeway begins at its
western end with a graceful swoop
through a curved tunnel, and it then
proceeds all the way to West Covina to
the east. The interchange with the San
Diego Freeway is certainly one of the
most spectacular interchanges in the
world—Norman Bel Geddes's *Magic
Motorways* of 1940 realized in fact. At the
freeway's west end murals are beginning
to appear upon the concrete retaining
walls. While these are folksy, they hardly
add a positive note to the machine
image of the freeway or of its park-like
landscaping.

23. Jacobs Studio 1984
John Chase and Claudia Carol
303 12th Street

An addition of L.A.'s recent spate of
small, two-story, rear-lot studios. This
one delightfully suggests a Craftsman
image which seems to live a strange life
of its own separate from the building.

Venice

In January 1906, the architect Norman F. Marsh wrote of California's new improved version of Venice: "Like the Aladdin's lamp of nursery days, wealth and labor have been the wand that has transformed an uninviting landscape in the southern part of California into scenes that delight the aesthetic." In a period of twelve months the architectural firm of Marsh and Russell had (according to Marsh's words) designed "a magic city (built for the generations) with its stately arcades, shimmering lagoons, floating pennants, and glistening minarets." Venice was the brainchild of Abbot Kinney, who came to California in 1880. His dream was to create an exotic city resembling the architecture and waterways of the famous northern Italian city. It would not be an ordinary beach community but one devoted to high culture and equipped with a 3,600 seat auditorium and even a "great university or institute." In 1904 Kinney had engaged Norman F. Marsh and his associates to lay out the site plan and to design the first of the community's buildings. The new city was officially opened by Kinney himself on June 30, 1905. But within a few years it was evident that the city would only succeed if it oriented itself to amusements and to the beach. In 1907 a casino was constructed, and other entertainment buildings followed reaching a high point in the 1912 "Race through the Clouds" roller coaster (designed by A. F. Rosenheim).

Nevertheless, while tourists came and went, few palaces were built along

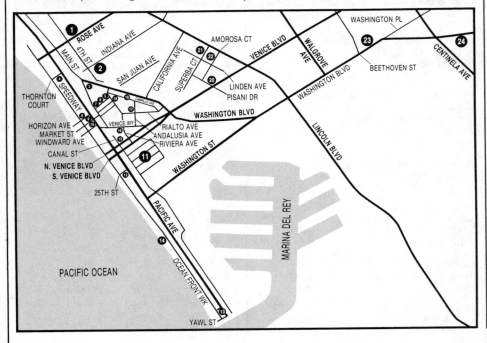

Venice's canals. A fair number of dwellings were built, but they were modest in scale and their image was in the lake or seaside manner of the Craftsman mode. Kinney himself died in 1920 and within a few years any thought of Venice as a cultural center was thrown to the winds. The canals began to be filled with silt and junk, many of them were filled in in 1930, and the gondoliers went home. Oil wells sprouted along a few of the canals and the center of Venice in and around Windward and Pacific avenues became increasingly shabby and run down. The final blow came in 1925 when Venice lost its independence and became a part of Los Angeles.

In the 1960s and early 1970s changes began to occur. To the south, Victor Gruen Associates laid out **Marina Del Rey** (1966-74), a new boat-oriented community checkered by low- and high-rise housing units (located southwest of Lincoln and Washington boulevards). **Marina City** (Daniel, Mann, Johnson, Mendenhall; Anthony Lumsden, and Richard L. Tipping) was built in 1971 and other additions followed, including **Mariner's Village Apartments** (1980, Kamnitzer and Marks). In the end neither the planning nor the buildings in Marina del Rey are really worth a visit, unless you want a lesson on what should not be done. It was in the sixties and early seventies that Venice became a Bohemian quarter and began to boast not only artists and their garrets, but also a wide array of public murals. From the late seventies on, Venice and the southern section of adjoining Santa Monica have emerged as the center for self-conscious, avant-garde, High Art Modern architecture — usually in the form of housing and artist's studios. A walk and drive through Venice today evokes the feeling of a visit to an art gallery.

1. Store Building, ca. 1937
Mid-block on the north side of Rose Avenue between 4th and 5th streets

A tiny building with an oversized oval window in the Streamline Moderne idiom.

2. Arnoldi Triplex, 1981
Frank O. Gehry and Associates
322 Indiana Avenue

Everything looks ordinary until one considers the box-like volume at the corner which seems to have been tipped on end.

3. Duplex, 1978-81
George Mayers
921-923 Washington Boulevard

A late 1970s Victorian Revival via details derived, at least in spirit, from an Eastlake pattern book.

4. Michich-Small House, 1981
Milica Dedijer-Michich
120 Thornton Court

Viewed from the walkway, its stuccoed angles and curved columns and balconies come from the Modern of the twenties and thirties. On the alley side, an angled greenhouse is almost a rationalist image via James Stirling.

5. Apartment Building, ca. 1905
Attributed to Marsh and Russell
235 San Juan Avenue

This is one of several of the early designs of Marsh and Russell which reflect the influence of the Midwest work of Louis H. Sullivan and of Frank Lloyd Wright.

6. Caplin House, 1979
Frederick Fisher and Thane Roberts
229 San Juan Avenue

A white stucco box with a partial barrel roof, *a la* Adolf Loos and Vienna in the early years of the century. The facades, on the other hand, are self-consciously composed of a pattern of rectangular openings and seem to have more to do with art than architecture.

7. Store Building, ca. 1937
1332-1380 Main Street between San Juan and Horizon avenues

A two-story complex of shops and offices clothed in the popular Streamline Moderne.

8. Spiller House, 1980
Frank O. Gehry and Associates
39 Horizon Avenue

A three-level townhouse with roof deck. Most of the building is clad in galvanized corrugated metal, while sticks (two-by-fours) and plywood occur in part of the inner court of the living room. Within, the stick-like quality of some exposed posts of the building creates a woodsy Craftsman atmosphere.

9. Gargosian Art Gallery and Apartments, 1980-81
Studio Works; Hodgetts and Mangurian; with Frank Lupe and Audrey Mitlock
51 Market Street

The grey stucco street elevation with its upper curved studio facade with glass brick suggests the Streamline Moderne of the 1930s. Within, a circular court interrupts the basic volume of the buildings.

10. Venice Center, 1904-1905
Windward Avenue between Pacific Avenue and Speedway

The best remaining group of the original buildings are those on the north side of Windward Avenue. At the northeast corner of Windward and Pacific avenues is the arcaded three-story **Hotel Saint Marks** (Marsh and Graham).

10. Venice Center

11. Venice Canals, 1904-05
Southeast of Pacific Avenue and Venice Boulevard
Strong and Dickerson Canal Subdivision

Venice's major system of canals and the Venice Lagoon have long since been filled in. To the north, Venice Canal is now San Juan Avenue, and to the south the Grand Canal is now Grand Boulevard. A few of the canals still exist south of Venice Boulevard, and four of the Venetian bridges still stand.

11. Venice Canal

12. Norton House, 1982-84
Frank O. Gehry and Associates
2509 Ocean Front at the end of 25th Street

This project is supposedly a remodel, but it is really a new house. Steps lead up from the beach in a grand fashion, seemingly all the way to the top of the building. Hovering over the single front section of the house is a viewing study, set as a box on a pole. As with so much of Gehry's work, what appears to be arbitrary and capricious turns out in plan to be highly rational.

13. Doumani House, 1982
Robert Graham
Southwest corner of Ocean Front Walk and Yawl Court

A white stucco U-shaped volume. Its step pattern windows, and the sculptured open metal grillwork at ground level tilt the design toward the Art Deco Moderne of the 1920s.

14. Stone Condominium, 1973
Kahn, Kappe, and Lottery
3815 Ocean Front Walk

Stucco volumes and walls serve as a foil for the west-facing glass and wood sections of the building. The placement of the wood members separating the glass areas creates an unusual horizontal scale.

15. Apartment Building, ca. 1910
Northeast corner of Venice Boulevard and Canal Street

A three-story delight, designed in a kind of parody of Oriental Craftsman architecture.

16. Ming-Lowe Office Building
David Ming-Lowe
308 Venice Way, near Riviera Way

High Art architecture realized by the commonplace (materials, structure, methods of assembly). You could easily drive by and not notice the building, but once your attention is fixed, Art is self-evident.

17. House, ca. 1907
Northwest corner of Andalusia and Rialto avenues

Although altered in later years, this dwelling still evidences the exotic, far-away qualities of Islamic India and the Near East.

18. House, ca. 1907
Cabrillo Avenue and Market Street

An arcaded two-story porch with dome suggests Islamic North Africa, or perhaps Moorish Spain.

19. University of Arts, 1904-05
Marsh and Russell
1304 Riviera Avenue

One of Abbot Kinney's original buildings, this one intended as part of his cultural institute. The design, like others at Venice, is both Sullivanesque and Wrightian.

20. Police and Fire Station of Venice, ca. 1930
Northeast corner of Venice Boulevard and Pisani Drive

A two-story PWA Moderne building in exposed concrete, with relief sculptures

13. Doumani House

14. Stone Condominium

over the entrance. Next door, to the west, is the former **Venice City Hall,** slightly garbed in the Mission Revival image.

21. Sedlak House, 1980
Morphosis (Thom Mayne and Michael Rotundi)
North side of Superba Court, between Linden Avenue and Lincoln Boulevard

One of an increasing number of two-story alley units built as a second dwell-ing on a city lot. This gabled roof unit plays all sorts of aesthetic games with common materials and structures; but all of this formal inventiveness is used with delight rather than high seriousness.

22. 2-4-6-8 House, 1979
Morphosis (Thom Mayne and Michael Rotundi)
North side of Amorosa Court, between Linden Avenue and Lincoln Boulevard

A four-part window as a playful theme, set in front of the pieces of asbestos shingle siding. Bright colors enhance the doll-house quality of the design.

23. Baldwin Motel, ca. 1934
12823 Washington Boulevard, Culver City

A small Streamline Moderne motel, with a drive-through gate.

24. Automobile Service Garage, ca. 1925
12129 Washington Boulevard, Los Angeles County

The onion dome atop the small tower, together with the row of ogee arches, establishes the Islamic image of this L-shaped corner garage unit.

20. Police and Fire Station, Venice

Airport
Westchester
Playa Del Rey

Since the 1950s the area directly around the Los Angeles International Airport has developed into an aerospace-related industrial zone, supplemented especially on the east and north by a good supply of hotels and office buildings. North of the airport is Westchester which is almost exclusively residential housing (with the exceptions of Loyola University and Northrup Institute of Technology). To the west is the beach-oriented community of Playa del Rey, which in the 1960s was substantially reduced in size by the removal of blocks of residences which once existed at the west end of the airport's runways. All that remains now is the picturesque pattern of the streets. The removal of these houses has meant the loss of a number of excellent Spanish Colonial Revival, French Norman, English Tudor, and Streamline Moderne houses of the twenties and thirties. Two major losses were R. M. Schindler's Zaczek Beach House (1936-38), and Thornton M. Abell's Shonerd House (1935). Within the past ten years there has been renewed building activity in what remains of Playa del Rey. The usual pattern of two- and three-story townhouses and of attached townhouses is occurring, as it is along much of the coast of Southern California.

South of the airport is El Segundo, the name of which was derived from the early (1911) oil fields in the area. The section of El Segundo to the west is composed of single family spec houses—most of which were built just after World War II—while industrial and

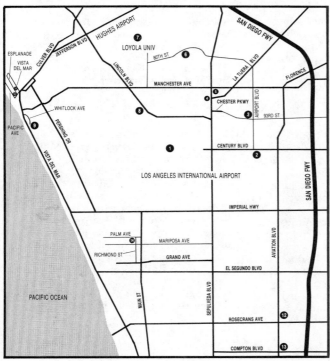

commercial activity characterize the eastern and northern portions of the community.

1. ■Los Angeles International Airport, 1925-present
Enter from the east on Century Boulevard

The site of the Airport was at first a general flying field, which was established in 1925. In 1928 it became the Municipal Airport for the City of Los Angeles. Through much of the 1930s the Municipal Airport was secondary in public use to other fields located in Burbank, Glendale, and Santa Monica. In 1940-41 Sumner Spaulding and John Austin were commissioned to design an extensive new passenger terminal and a number of secondary buildings. Because of the Second World War, this expansion of the public aspects of the airport was put aside. From 1959 through 1962, William Pereira and Associates provided a new master plan for the airport, and they designed a new group of terminals, the Administration Building, and the central theatrical flying saucer restaurant. Their scheme of a group of terminals built around a central space devoted to parking worked for a time, though the only things of interest in the terminals were the Islamic-like domes which hover above the escalators and staircases.

Pereira's scheme for the Airport worked well during the 1960s and early 1970s, but eventually the intensity of usage far out-stripped what had been planned. Added to this was the traffic congestion on Century Boulevard, the short surface street connecting the airport to the San Diego Freeway. Various proposals were made for the airport, including moving it out onto the eastern desert at Palmdale, but nothing came of these proposals. Finally the impetus of the 1984 Olympic Games prompted an extensive rebuilding of the airport, including a new two-layer road system, new and enlarged terminal buildings and an expanded parking system. This new expansion has been designed by William Pereira Associates, Daniel Dworsky and Associates, Bonito A. Sinclair and Associates, and John Williams

and Associates. When you fly in and out of the airport, look to the south and you will see a group of Spanish Colonial Revival buildings of the 1920s. The most important of these is **Hanger No. 1,** built in 1929, designed by Gable and Wyant (the hanger is located at 5701 W. Imperial Boulevard).

2. Worldwide Postal Center, 1967
Daniel, Mann, Johnson, and Mendenhall (DMJM) (Cesar Pelli and Anthony Lumsden)
5800 W. Century Boulevard

This building's character is created by the vertical and horizontal units of its two-story frame; left open in parts, and filled in in others. The exposed concrete frame, thin infills, and rounded corners suggest that the building is some type of fancy machine, housing not postal workers, but computers. The siting of the building and its design in no way suggest that it is in fact a public building.

3. Hertz Vehicle Maintenance Turnaround Facility, 1982
Daniel, Mann, Johnson, and Mendenhall
9000-9029 Airport Boulevard

A machine object, a two-story curved box with a curved canopy projecting in front of the building.

4. ■Millron's Department Store Building (now Broadway), 1949
Gruen and Krummeck
Northwest corner of Sepulveda Boulevard and Manchester Avenue

The three-block commercial strip on Sepulveda Boulevard (between Manchester Avenue and Lincoln Boulevard), which serves as the center of Westchester, was developed during the years 1948-52. Like the Miracle Mile section of Wilshire Boulevard the stores on Sepulveda Boulevard face towards the street in a traditional manner, while their parking and major entrances are at the rear. The two-story Millron's Department Store Building not only provides parking at the rear, but on its roof as well. Millron's itself and most of the adjoining stores employ the usual post-

World War II motifs — an angular or curved high pylon sign, curved surfaces, and bands of verticle supports.

5. Loyola Theatre, 1946
Clarence J. Smale
Southeast corner of Sepulveda Boulevard and Manchester Avenue

Post-World War II Streamline Moderne, partially transformed into Hollywood Regency. The marquee and its curved sign *are* the building.

6. Westchester High School (now Wright Jr. High School), 1952
Sumner Spaulding and John Rex
Southwest corner of Cowan Avenue and 80th Street

Miesian pavilions arranged around courtyards.

7. Loyola University, 1865-present
80th Street between McConnell Avenue and Fordham Road

Loyola University (at first named Saint Vincent's College) is one of the oldest academic institutions in California. The Westchester site of the University is open and suburban in character. There are several buildings worth visiting. These include:

Sacred Heart Chapel, 1953
Spanish Colonial Revival carried on successfully into the post-War years. The tower and the street facade work well, especially when seen from a distance.

Loyola University Theatre, 1963
Edward D. Stone

A characteristic Stone "Palladian Villa," used in this case for an auditorium, all tinselly and lighthearted.

Library, 1977
David C. Martin

A Modern image design with a central skylighted atrium.

University Gymnasium, Athletic and Recreational Complex, 1978-80
Kappe, Lotery, Boccato

The graceful, concave shape of the roof is a result of the cable-hung suspension system employed.

8. IBM Aerospace Headquarters, 1963
Eliot Noyes; A. Quincy Jones, and Frederick E. Emmons
9045 Lincoln Boulevard

An exposed concrete grid clothes a late-fifties International Style Modern box.

9. House, ca. 1938
5740 Whitlock Avenue

The perfect image for a site overlooking the ocean: a Streamline Moderne design equipped with nautical pipe railing, corner windows, glass brick, flat roofs, and white stucco walls.

7. Sacred Heart Chapel, Loyola University

9. House

10. Esplanade Del Rey Townhouse, 1982
Convoy Street between Esplanade and Culver Boulevard

Modern historicism: a block-long row of townhouses which seems to hearken back to the twenties work of J. J. P. Oud in Holland.

11. Duplex, 1977
Eric Owen Moss and James Stafford
6672-74 Vista del Mar

Except for its light yellow color and the exposed metal flues, this Streamline design could have been done in the early 1930s by Norman Bel Geddes.

11. Duplex

12. Scientific Data System Building (now Xerox), 1966-68
Craig Ellwood and Associates
555 S. Aviation Boulevard

Once you grant the Miesian design principles of Ellwood's work, his buildings remain impressive. The symbols of logic and order dominate this three-story post and lintel box. The plan is a perfect cruciform with semi-enclosed courtyards at the north and south. The hand of the designer is evident everywhere.

13. Federal Aviation Agency Building, 1973
Daniel, Mann, Johnson, and Mendenhall (Anthony Lumsden, Cesar Pelli, P. J. Jacobson, Dwight Wilson)
15000 S. Aviation Boulevard

An early 1970s image of the machine product, on the fragile and breakable side.

14. El Segundo Elementary School, 1936
Northwest corner of Mariposa Avenue and Richmond Street

PWA Moderne in exposed concrete.

12. Scientific Data System Building (now Xerox)

South Beach

The South Beach region comprises the communities of Manhattan Beach, Hermosa Beach, and Redondo Beach (also the district called Hollywood Riviera, which is a part of the City of Torrance).

Manhattan Beach was laid out in 1897 and slowly developed into a quiet bungalow colony. Hermosa Beach to the south was established in 1901, and by the twenties it was referred to as a "family resort." Both Manhattan Beach and Hermosa Beach received a continual influx of visitors from Los Angeles during the years 1900-1920 via the Pacific Electric Line. The entire beach strand of both communities is public, though you often have to gain access to the beach by what seem to be small, secret spur streets. The beach is mostly well hidden and does not form a strong element in the townscape.

Redondo Beach, the largest of the beach communities, was founded in 1881 with the hope that it would develop as a major port for Los Angeles. At this time a pier, hotel, and narrow gauge railroad (completed in 1888) to Los Angeles was built. In 1888 the Santa Fe Railroad constructed a line to the town. But the hoped-for commercial harbor never materialized. In 1938 work did begin on a pleasure marina (**King Harbor Marina**), which was completed after World War II. Redondo Beach, along with the neighboring section of the Hollywood Riviera, possesses an extensive beach

park which runs from Vista del Mar to Torrance Boulevard.

Several large-scale townhouse condominium projects have been built in the beach communities in the 1970s and early 1980s. In other sections of these communities density is being substantially increased. Examples of this can be seen on Blanche Road between 30th and 31st streets in Manhattan Beach where newer Spanish Colonial Revival townhouses (1981) now occupy their entire lots. On Myrtle Street in Hermosa Beach similar intensification of land use can be experienced, only here the occasional image is "Victorian."

1. Marsh House, 1974
John Blanton
469 28th Street, Manhattan Beach

Located close to the street is this three-story single dwelling, tied to its site by an extensive pergola. The slope of the shed roof is interrupted by a slot for a balcony.

2. Provost House, 1975
John Blanton
204 Manhattan Avenue, Manhattan Beach

A tall, thin, vertical shed roof volume with an assertive composition of windows, the whole topped by a projecting chimney. Other works in the area by the same architect are the **McNulty House** (1975) at 420 Manhattan Avenue, and the **Shelton Apartments** (1974) at 480 Rosecrans Avenue.

3. House, 1983
Morphosis (Mayne and Rotondi)
3410 Hermosa Avenue, Hermosa Beach

A borrowing of the Modern image of the thirties with a hint of High Tech, especially in the walls sheathed with galvanized sheet metal.

4. Pier Avenue School, 1939
Marsh, Smith, and Powell
Southwest corner of Pier Avenue and Pacific Coast Highway, Hermosa Beach

Classical PWA Moderne; its conventionalized ornament suggests Native American art of the Southwest.

3. House

5. Redondo Beach Civic Center, 1962
Victor Gruen and Associates
200 Pacific Coast Highway, Redondo Beach

A well-sited and handsomely-scaled community center, composed of low boxes connected by free-standing post and lintel passages. It is all early sixties International Style Modern, designed with delicacy. Regrettably, building activities of the seventies and early eighties have tended to obscure its civic prominence.

6. Redondo Beach High School, 1931 and later
Allison and Allison
Pacific Coast Highway between Diamond and Vincent streets, Redondo Beach

PWA Moderne, with the horizontal pattern of the board forms revealed in the concrete walls. Note the cast concrete sculpture on the Manual Arts Building extolling education and work.

6. Redondo Beach High School

7. Wardrobe Cleaners Building, ca. 1950
120 Catalina Avenue, Redondo Beach

An excellent example of a fifties commercial design with angled piers and plate glass windows, somewhat held in place by a strong horizontal cornice.

8. Eagles Building, 1949
Northwest corner of Catalina Avenue and Garnet Street, Redondo Beach

An almost pure late thirties Streamline Moderne building, constructed ten years later. Two groups of bands run horizontally across the two facades, connecting all the windows together. The entrances are emphasized by vertical projections which crawl up and over the parapets.

8. Eagles Building

9. United California Bank Building
(now **First Interstate Bank**), 1970
Roland E. Coate, Jr., Stanley Kamebins
1720 Elena, Redondo Beach

A cut-away passage leads one between two tightly-enclosed volumes. One of the volumes rises to form a natural pylon for the sign. Within, warm wood detailing contrasts with the coldness of concrete surfaces.

10. Riviera Methodist Church,
1957-58
Neutra and Alexander
575 Palos Verdes Boulevard, Hollywood Riviera, Torrance

A single, long, rectangular block houses the sanctuary and the Sunday School rooms. An openwork constructivist post and lintel composition of steel and wood emphasizes the entrance to sanctuary.

11. Reid House, 1928
Mark Daniels
124 Via Monte d'Oro

Daniels was one of California's gifted exponents of the Spanish Colonial Revival—in both architecture and landscape gardening. The Reid House clearly illustrates his understanding of Spain's rural Andalusian forms. The house and its siting also indicate how the original concept of the Hollywood Riviera was intended to be composed of large villas, set within ample grounds, something which did not occur.

12. Von Koerber House, 1931-32
R. M. Schindler
408 Via Monte d'Oro, Hollywood Riviera, Torrance

Though little known, the Von Koerber House is one of Schindler's most interesting designs. The interior is composed of a number of levels which open outward onto various decks, terraces, and courtyards. Narrow bands of clerestory windows provide light at the ceiling levels. Because of design restrictions Schindler was required to utilize the Spanish Colonial Revival image, and he responded with humor and satire to these requirements. Roof tiles not only cover the roof, but also sections of the walls, and are even used in an inverted manner around the fireplace.

12. Von Koerber House

Palos Verdes, North

n 1913 the New York banker Frank A. Vanderlip acquired 16,000 acres comprising almost all of the Palos Verdes Peninsula. He then engaged Olmsted and Olmsted, Howard Shaw, and Myron Hunt to lay out a "Millionaire's Colony." The entire 16,000 acre tract was planned to include a number of large estates, parks, clubs, an elaborate pattern of roads, and three model villages. The intervention of

World War I prevented the project from developing. After the war a pared-down version of the initial scheme was begun. Between 1922 and 1923 Olmsted and Olmsted, together with Charles H. Cheney, laid out a master plan for the 3,200 acres which occupied the northwestern portion of the peninsula. They provided for four commercial centers — Lunda Bay, Valmonte, Miraleste, and Malaga Cove. Of these only Malaga Cove was built (1922-25).

The Spanish (Mediterranean) architectural tradition was established as *the* allowable architectural style, and in 1922 an art jury was formed to review all designs. A number of major Spanish Colonial Revival designs were built, including F. L. Olmsted. Jr.'s house (Myron Hunt and H. C. Chambers, 1924-25) the Buchanan House (Kirkland Cutter, 1927) and the Cameron House (Kirkland Cutter, 1926). These and other houses are effectively hidden from view today.

In 1932 the landscape architect A. E. Hanson became the manager of the Palos Verdes Ranch, and it was he who suggested the name Palos Verdes Peninsula to describe the area. The commu-

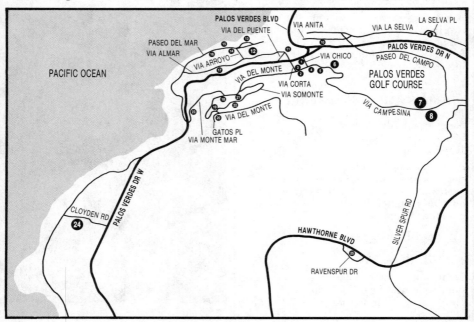

nity just kept its head above water during the Depression, and finally, with the economic recovery of the late 1930s, A. E. Hanson turned his attention to the northern part of the Ranch and began to develop Rolling Hills, whose theme was "own your own dude ranch." Again, as in Palos Verdes, architecture was to utilize two images—in this case the Colonial and the California board and batten ranch house. A Western-style gate led into handsome, shake-roofed ranch houses (designed by Lutah Maria Riggs) and to Williamsburg Colonial houses (designed by Paul R. Williams). In 1937 Rolling Hills was incorporated, and it has remained as a gate-guarded, upper-middle-class enclave to the present day.

The landscape and architectural beauty of Palos Verdes remains, especially in and around Malaga Cove. Palos Verde Drive (originally laid out by the Olmsteds) has recently been refurbished and replanted (1983). But one can immediately sense the qualitative difference between planning and design in the 1920s and that of the 1970s by comparing the linear shopping center which has developed just west of Crenshaw Boulevard on Silver Spur Road, with that of Malaga Cove Plaza. Even tile roofs, stucco walls, and some arches (and a Home Savings Bank with its public art) does not redeem the place.

1. Malaga Cove Plaza, 1922 and later
Olmsted and Olmsted; Charles H. Cheney; Webber, Staunton, and Spaulding
Palos Verdes Drive between Via Corta and Via Chico

Each of the four community centers planned for Palos Verdes was to be organized around a plaza and lined with two- and three-story arcaded buildings. The Malaga Cove Plaza was the only one built, and even it was not fully completed as planned. The buildings were all designed in 1924 by Webber, Staunton, and Spaulding, while Cheney and the Olmsteds provided the general plan. Both the plan and the architecture are highly successful, including the "Sally Port" over Via Chico. Note the fountain

(installed in 1930) which is a two-thirds-reduced reproduction of La Fontana del Nettuno of 1563 in Bologna.

1. Malaga Cove Plaza

2. Palos Verdes Public Library, 1926-30
Myron Hunt and H. C. Chambers; Olmsted and Olmsted, landscape architects
South of Via Campesina at Via Corta

One of Hunt's most successful designs, fitted with great care into the steep hillside. Stone walls form the base of the building and extend outward to form terrace walls for the garden. The library is on the second level. Below is an exhibition room and public meeting room.

2. Palos Verdes Public Library

3. Garden Apartments, 1937
Attributed to Pierpont Davis
2433 Via Campesina
A thirties Spanish Colonial Revival complex, including a picturesque minaret.

4. Apartment Buildings, 1939
2508, 2510, and 2512 Via Campesina

A reserved but well-organized International Style Modern group of buildings which step up the hillside away from the road.

5. Stein House, 1928
Kirkland Cutter
2733 Via Campesina

Spanish Colonial Revival, by one of Palos Verdes's major architects of the twenties.

6. Gard House, 1927
Kirkland Cutter
2780 Via Campesina

To be read as Spanish, but in truth many of its details came from the rural villas of Tuscany.

7. Palos Verdes Golf Course, 1922
and later
Olmsted and Olmsted; Charles H. Cheney
3301 Via Campesina

One can obtain a good idea of Olmsted's and Cheney's approach to designing in California by driving around the boundaries of the golf course. Today it all looks natural, but the contours of the land were appreciably modified, and almost all of the plant material is nonnative. The Spanish Colonial Revival **Club House,** designed by C. E. Howard, has been much altered (and not for the good) over the years.

8. Bowler House, 1963
Lloyd Wright
3456 Via Campesina

The low, hovering roof dramatically extends the interior outward onto balconies and terraces.

9. Sias House, 1927
E. Millard
3405 La Selva Place

An Andalusian farmhouse with a separate weaving studio.

10. Goodrich House, 1928
H. Roy Kelley
2416 Via Anita

This modest dwelling was the 1928 Model Home for the Palos Verdes Estates — Spanish Colonial Revival, of course.

11. Gartz House, 1930
Wallace Neff
Northeast corner of Via Almar and Via Del Puente

One of Neff's large villas; more Italian than Spanish.

12. Malaga Cove School, 1926
Allison and Allison; Olmsted and Olmsted, landscape architects
North of Via Almar at Via Arroyo

Mediterranean, with a tower which seems to be derived from late fifteenth or early sixteenth century Spanish examples.

13. Olmsted House, 1924-25
Myron Hunt and H. C. Chambers
Northwest corner of Paseo Del Mar and Via Arroyo (on the ocean side)

A rural Spanish farmhouse complex with a walled garden.

13. Olmsted House

**14. Palos Verdes Estates Project
House #2,** 1925
W. L. Risley
408 Paseo Del Mar

A modest Spanish Colonial Revival dwelling, indicating one of the housing types planned for Palos Verdes. Other housing types included connected townhouses, garden apartments, and extensive villas and gardens.

15. Haggerty House (now **Neighborhood Church**), 1928
Armand Monaco; Olmsted and Olmsted, landscape architects
415 Paseo Del Mar

An extensive seaside villa, once again more Italian than Spanish. The house is impressively detailed, especially in its ironwork. If Pliny the Younger could have seen this villa and its gardens, we feel he would have been very happy.

16. Moore House, 1965
Lloyd Wright
504 Paseo Del Mar

The extensively cantilevered roof ends in a sharp dramatic point and low horizontal terraces extend the dwelling outward on its site.

17. Stannard House, 1974
John Blanton
432 Via Monte Mar

A mid-seventies version of the Hispanic tradition, with white stucco walls and balconies.

18. Cheney House, 1924
Charles H. Cheney and C. E. Howard
657 Via Del Monte

Although not easy to see, this is an important Spanish Colonial Revival dwelling and garden. It was designed as his own home by one of California's foremost city planners, an advocate of community architectural control. While the house is Spanish, the garden tends toward the Italian.

19. La Venta Inn, 1923
Pierpont Davis; Olmsted and Olmsted, landscape architects
736 Via Del Monte

When built it was one of the landmarks of Palos Verdes. The image was that of a whitewashed Mediterranean church set on a steep hillside. Now the planting has grown so high and thick that only the very top of the tower is visible. A pergola encloses one side of the fountained courtyard.

20. Lombardi House, 1965
Lloyd Wright
804 Gatos Place, off Via Del Monte

In this house Lloyd Wright transforms some of the visual excitment of the L.A. commercial strip into domestic architecture.

21. Buchanan House, 1927
Kirkland Cutter
700 Via Somonte

Andalusian Spanish, with an outer and an inner court.

22. Schoolcraft House, 1926
Edgar Cline
749 Via Somonte

A rural Tuscan villa with extensive tilework, iron work, and windows and doors brought from Italy.

23. Beckstrand House, 1940
Richard J. Neutra
1400 Via Monte Mar

America's own domesticated version of the International Style Modern of the late thirties. Floor-to-ceiling glass visually connects the interior spaces with the surrounding terraces and gardens.

24. Palos Verdes High School, 1961
Neutra and Alexander
600 Cloyden Road

An effective modernist composition of low-pitched gable tile roofs. The buildings are arranged around courts and connected to one another by low, flat-roofed, open passageways.

25. Ravenspur Condominiums, 1966
Raymond Kappe
5632 Ravenspur Drive, off Hawthorne Boulevard

Constructivism of the 1960s, composed of vertical and horizontal wood members with an infill of wood surfaces and glass.

Palos Verdes, South

1. Miller House, 1948
Thornton M. Abell
3201 Palos Verdes Drive West

Post-World War II Modern, almost classical in its clarity and reserve.

2. Marineland of the Pacific, 1954 and later
Pereira and Luckman
Long Point, off Palos Verdes Drive, on the ocean side.

A period piece of the 1950s, of more interest for the pros and cons of its siting than for its architecture.

3. ▪Wayfarer's Chapel, 1949 and later
Lloyd Wright
Portuguese Bend at Abalone Cove, north of Palos Verdes Drive South

This chapel is Lloyd Wright's most widely-known and visited building. His concept, as with so much of his work, was to create a sense of place via architecture and landscape architecture. His "Natural Church" was a glass structure hidden in a grove of coastal redwoods. (These did not survive and they were replaced by other

trees.) Today one sees from the road only the thin, angular, stone and concrete tower rising from the forest. Once inside the building you will see how successful Lloyd Wright was in creating a sense of a mysterious, almost fairy-tale forest.

4. Ekdale House, 1948
John Rex
3500 Palos Verdes Drive South

A two-story, glass-walled interior looks out from a handsome redwood container.

4. Ekdale House

5. Pray House, 1969
Thornton Abell
4500 Palos Verdes Drive South

The 1950s *Arts and Architecture* post and lintel vocabulary successfully carried on a decade or so later.

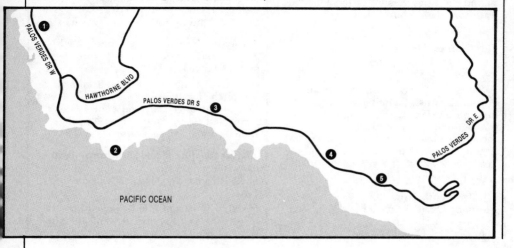

Santa Catalina Island

Santa Catalina Island, the largest of the Channel Islands, was first mentioned by the Spanish explorer Cabrillo in 1540. In the 1820s the Island was granted to Pio Pico, who later deeded it to Nicolas Covarrubias. Later in the nineteenth century it was purchased by James Lick, and it was he who introduced sheep and goats to the island. During the American Civil War a **barracks** was built on the island. But Catalina's architectural history really began when the shipping interests of William Banning established Avalon (1877) as a summer resort with a Hotel Metropole and a tent city. It was G. Shatto who laid the city out into small lots (in 1885). The hotel is long gone, but evidence of this early city remains in the tiny lots now occupied by cottages just behind the commercial strip along the waterfront.

The real development of Avalon came when William Wrigley, Jr. bought the island from the Banning interests in 1919. Wrigley, the owner of the Chicago Cubs, wanted a place for his team to do spring training. Also, like so many businessmen of the time, he hankered after the life of a landed aristocrat. The thousand acres of land provided plenty of substance for cattle and horses, as well as the buffalo imported later for a movie and domesticated. (They can still be seen on the island.)

Without attempting to project Catalina as an architectural mecca, we do suggest that there are a number of in-

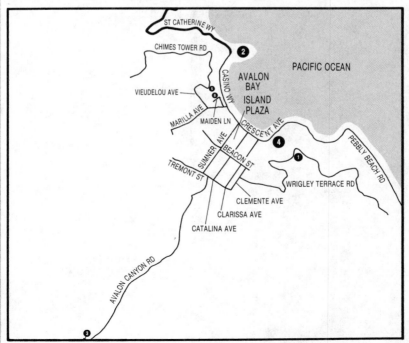

teresting walks which one can take around the town. There are many old cottages, including a row of Spanish Colonial Revival **workers cottages** on Fremont Street put up by Wrigley, who further hispanified the town in 1934-35 by employing commercial artist Otis Shepard to supervise facelifting the commercial center. It was at this time that controls of signage went into effect, and many of the old wooden fronts were stuccoed and often tiled.

1. Mount Ada, 1921
D. M. Renton; Albert Conrad, landscape architect
Wrigley Terrace Road (From Crescent Avenue take Claressa Avenue to Beacon Street; right one block then right on Clement Avenue. Wrigley Terrace Road begins half a block on the left.)

It would be pleasant to report that Mount Ada, the mansion that Wrigley had built by his Pasadena contractor, David Renton, was an architectural pearl. But like their Pasadena home (now headquarters of the Tournament of Roses) it is more of a curiosity than a work of architecture. It is mildly Anglo-Colonial Revival both inside and out. Its real plus is its wonderful orientations which look out towards magnificent views. One of these views, from Wrigley's study, offers an excellent view of the playing field on which the Cubs worked out. The house is now used by the University of Southern California as a conference center. The grounds, designed by Wrigley's head gardener at his Pasadena home, are well worth a visit, especially the cactus and succulant gardens.

2. Casino, 1928
Webber and Spaulding (Sumner Spaulding)
1 Casino Way (Casino Point, northeast side of Avalon Bay)
Wrigley employed the architect to design a grand Casino featuring moving pictures on the first floor and a ballroom on the second floor. Both of these rooms certainly do evoke the spirit of the 1920s, but it is the theatre organ with its bird calls and automobile horn stops that seems to thrill the tourists most.

2. Casino Box office

The exterior, which looms out of the sea as you approach the island by boat is a strange mixture of Spanish, Moorish, and Art Deco (Zigzag) Moderne styles, along with Art Deco murals on the porch as you enter. The ground floor (bay side) houses the headquarters and museum of the Catalina Island Museum Society (open Easter through October 1-4 and 7-9; weekends and holidays the rest of the year).

3. Wrigley Monument, 1924
Bennett, Parsons, and Frost

Top, west end of Avalon Canyon Road 1½ miles from Bay, train service from Island Plaza.

Wrigley's family employed this Chicago planning and landscape firm to design a suitable monument to Wrigley. Its grand staircase with insets of flamboyant Catalina tile ends in the austerly Goodhue-esque, Spanish with Art Deco enrichment mausoleum, which was apparently never used. (The Wrigleys are buried in Los Angeles.) The view from the monument is indeed handsome. The memorial is approached through a small but fascinating **botanical garden** (set out by Ralph Roth from 1933 onwards). On the way up Avalon Canyon Road you will pass **The Bird Cage,** an aviary now fallen into ruin.

4. Gano House, 1889
718 Crescent Avenue
Attributed to Dr. Gano

"Holly Hill," as the Gano House was called, is a large, picturesque Queen Anne cottage recently placed on the National Register of Historic Places. It is occasionally opened under the supervision of the Catalina Historical Society, usually for groups by appointment as a fund-raising project.

5. Wolfe House, 1928
R. M. Schindler
124 Chimes Tower Road

The design principles of the Modern expressed in exposed wood frame and stucco walls. An exterior ramp leads up to the pergola roof deck. This monument of modern American architecture in America in the 1920s is rarely open, but it can easily be seen from the path below and from the street.

6. Murdock House, 1929
Elmer Grey
103 Maiden Lane, on the corner of Crescent Avenue

In contrast to Schindler's nearby Wolfe House, designed about the same time, the image of the Murdock House is Spanish Colonial Revival, handled in Grey's usual fashion, so that it ends up being classical rather than picturesque.

5. Wolfe House

San Pedro

The open roadstead east of San Pedro was the harbor for the missions of San Gabriel and San Fernando in the late eighteenth and early nineteenth centuries. Beginning in the 1920s it continued as the principle shipping point for the growing town of Los Angeles and for the surrounding ranches. A revealing portrait of San Pedro in 1834 and its difficult open harbor is contained in Richard Henry Dana, Jr.'s *Two Years Before the Mast* (1840). In the late 1850s, Wilmington, which was established by Phineas Banning at the entrance to the Los Angeles River (yes, it actually used to have water in it), emerged as the most used harbor for Los Angeles. The community of San Pedro participated in a marginal way in the various harbor improvements which took place from 1877 on. The most extensive of these improvements began in 1892, and in 1909 both San Pedro and Wilmington were incorporated into Los Angeles.

In 1846 a "five-hundred vara square" had been established by the Mexican government as a governmental reserve. This square, which was located on the low cliff in San Pedro overlooking the harbor, was set aside by the U.S. govern-

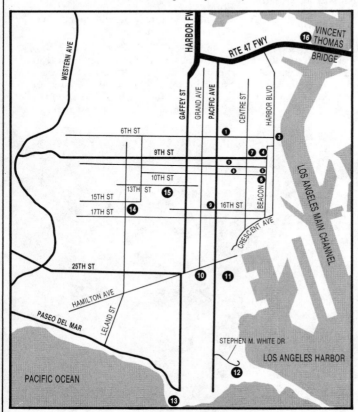

ment in 1888 as a military reservation. In 1914 Fort MacArthur was established, comprising not only the "five-hundred vara square," but extensive acreage in and around Point Fermin. Through the 1950s this installation remained as the principle defense for Los Angeles Harbor.

Just before and during the Second World War a number of Defense Housing projects were built for ship workers and others. These included Banning Homes (1942), Harbor Hills (1939-41), Rancho San Pedro (1942), and Richard J. Neutra's Channel Heights Housing Project (1941-43). Of these the **Channel Heights Housing Project** was justifiably the most famous, both for its excellent site planning and for the quality of its architecture. Regrettably there is so little left of this project that it is hardly worth a visit.

Though railroads, freeways, and the high **Vincent Thomas Bridge** connect San Pedro and Wilmington to Los Angeles and Long Beach, the feeling of both of these communities is that of small coastal towns, certainly not that of a large seaport.

1. Fox-Warner Brothers Theatre, 1931
B. Marcus Priteca
478 W. 6th Street

Modest in size, but still a highly effective example of a Moderne Art Deco (Zigzag) theatre.

2. YWCA Building, 1918
Julia Morgan
437 W. 9th Street

The Bay Tradition of San Francisco brought to San Pedro. A board and batten building which has been remodelled on several occasions.

3. Municipal Ferry Building (City Hall/Harbor Department Building), 1939-41
East end of 6th Street at Harbor Boulevard

A PWA Streamline Moderne Building, the Beaux Arts tradition made Moderne. The low, central tower with its clock face and ladder suggest the nautical origin of the Moderne of the 1930s.

3. Municipal Ferry Building

4. U.S. Customs House and Post Office, 1935
Northwest corner of Beacon and 9th streets

A classic PWA Moderne building. Within is a forty-foot-long mural by Fletcher Martin. The building has recently been recycled by Pullman and Matthews to house a Maritime Museum.

5. McCafferty Studio House, 1979
Coy Howard
1017 Beacon Street

A three-story structure with false gables at each end and a central gabled space which houses the stairway. The highly complex geometry of the street facade does not add much to the streetscape, nor has it much to do with the interior.

5. *McCafferty Studio House*

6. Seaman's Center Building, 1954 and 1962
Carleton M. Winslow, Jr., Warren Waltz; Andrew Joncich and William Lusby
Southwest corner of Beacon and 11th streets

The Modern at the end of the fifties. Here we have one example which has held up well.

7. House, ca. 1898
918-20 Centre Street

A Queen Anne/Colonial Revival dwelling with an expansive highly detailed corner bay-tower.

7. *House*

8. ■House, ca. 1885
324 W. 10th Street

An early Queen Anne Revival with some earlier Eastlake details. The house has a two-story spindled porch and a corner bay-tower whose third floor is open.

9. Commercial Building, ca. 1938
Northwest corner of Pacific Avenue and 16th Street

A Streamline Moderne building with a strong commitment to the horizontal. If you continue on down Pacific Avenue you will discover a good number of fragmented remains of the thirties Moderne.

10. Old Saint Peter's Episcopal Church, 1884
South end of Grand Avenue at 25th Street

A simple, unpretentious Carpenter's Gothic in wood.

11. Fort MacArthur, 1914 and later
East side of Pacific Avenue between 24th and 27th streets

Though the fort is not open to the public (it is presently being used by the U.S. Air Force) one can see many of the Mission Revival buildings from Pacific Avenue. These were all constructed between 1916 and 1918. Just barely visible are some of the double NCO Spanish Colonial Revival houses which were built in 1933-34. At the east end of the parade grounds is the site of the **Casa San Pedro** (the Hide House) which was the first Anglo adobe constructed in Southern California (1823). The former

13. Point Fermin Lighthouse, 1874
Point Fermin, south end of Gaffey Street

Out of what appears to be a modest Eastlake dwelling emerges a tapered, four-sided lighthouse tower.

14. San Pedro High School, 1935-37
Gordon B. Kaufmann
Leland Street between 15th and 17th streets

The most impressive aspect of this PWA Moderne building is the curved front auditorium. Its narrow marquee, three louvered openings above, and the relief sculpture are all expressive of Beaux Arts design principles of the 1930s.

15. Dodson House, ca. 1887
859 W. 13th Street

This two-story Eastlake dwelling was first located at the corner of 7th and Beacon streets. Much of its former lush ornament is now gone.

11. Fort MacArthur

Trona Corporation Building at the south end of the Fort (built in 1917-18) contains a spectacular timbered interior.

12. Cabrillo Maritime Museum, 1981
Frank O. Gehry and Associates
3730 Stephen M. White Drive

A pipe framework, open in part and covered in other areas by chain link fencing, provides an introduction to a series of separate enclosed pavilions. Each pavilion is sheathed in corrugated metal and stucco. The central courtyard, exhibit spaces, and the auditorium work well.

16. Vincent Thomas Bridge, 1961-63
North of the Catalina Terminal; enter from the northeast corner of Gaffey and Oliver streets.

The Thomas Bridge, which connects San Pedro to Terminal Island, and thence to Long Beach, is California's third largest suspension bridge. The bridge is Southern California's one-upmanship to San Francisco's Golden Gate Bridge and the Bay Bridge. There is something delightfully stage-set about the Thomas Bridge, for while it does indeed lead somewhere, one is not quite sure why it is really there.

Wilmington

Wilmington, first named New San Pedro, was founded in 1858 by Phineas Banning. It was he who started the process of developing the harbor by constructing a pier and providing warehouses. In

1869 Wilmington was connected to Los Angeles by rail. Though the community was incorporated in 1872, its independence was lost when it was absorbed into Los Angeles in 1909. **Banning Park and the Banning House** still form, as they did in the last century, the most important place in the community.

1. Los Angeles Department of Social Service Building, ca. 1925
Southeast corner of Anaheim Street and Broad Avenue

A two-story Spanish Colonial Revival building.

2. Saint Peter and Saint Paul Roman Catholic Church, 1930
Henry C. Newton and Robert Dennis Murray
515 W. Opp Street

Italian Romanesque, the concrete walls with board pattern of the forms exposed.

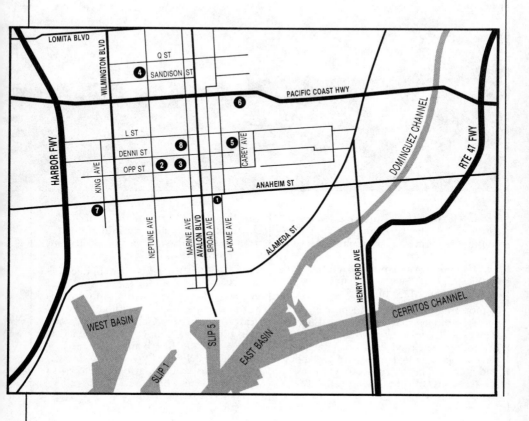

3. Wilmington Branch Public Library, ca. 1926
Marston, Van Pelt, and Maybury
309 W. Opp Street

A T-shaped, single-floor Spanish Colonial Revival building. The children's library room leads out onto a pergola and garden.

4. Saint John's Episcopal Church, 1883
1537 Neptune Avenue

A Queen Anne Revival church building, small in size.

5. Drum Barracks, 1859
1053-55 Cary Avenue

A two-story try at Greek Revival which really ends up more Federal than Greek. The officers' quarters is all that is left of an extensive group of wooden buildings constructed here in the late 1850s and early 1860s.

6. Banning House, 1864
Banning Park at Lakme Avenue and Pacific Coast Highway

A luxurious version (at least for California) of the Greek Revival, resplendent with two-story balconied porch and elegant entrances on both floors. Glass doors with transoms open out onto the entrance porch and the balcony porch above. The Banning House illustrates how late the Greek Revival as a style continued into the 1860s, not only in California, but also in many areas of the East and Midwest. A central cupola crowns the eighteen-room house. The present park only hints at what the grounds around the house were like in the 1870s. A long avenue of eucalyptus led to the house, and gardens of flowers and shrubs abounded.

7. Lucy Banning House, ca. 1900
Southwest corner of Anaheim Street and King Avenue

Mission Revival of a sort, with Japanese overtones.

8. Memorial Chapel, Calvary Presbyterian Church, 1870
1160 N. Marine Avenue

A rarity in Southern California—an Italianate church building. The original curved roof of the tower is now missing, and originally there were two entrances, one to each side of the projecting tower.

6. Banning House

Torrance

The City of Torrance was established in 1911. It was named for its founder, Jared Sidney Torrance, who sought to build an ideal small industrial city. He selected Olmsted and Olmsted to design his new city. They in turn engaged Lloyd Wright to supervise the landscaping and they prevailed upon their client to have Irving J. Gill design the first public, commercial, and residential buildings. They organized the city around a two-and-a-half block park—El Prado. Symbolically the southwest end of the park was terminated by the high school, while to the northeast the orientation was towards a distant view of Mount San Antonio. A commercial center was placed around the Pacific Electric Station. Beyond this to the north and east the land was laid out for factories and other types of industrial use. The residential areas of the city were placed around the Prado and the high school.

In the mid-1930s a small-scaled civic center was built facing Cravens Street, from El Prado to Post avenues. The thirties civic center has now been abandoned for a new one located at the northwest corner of Torrance Boulevard

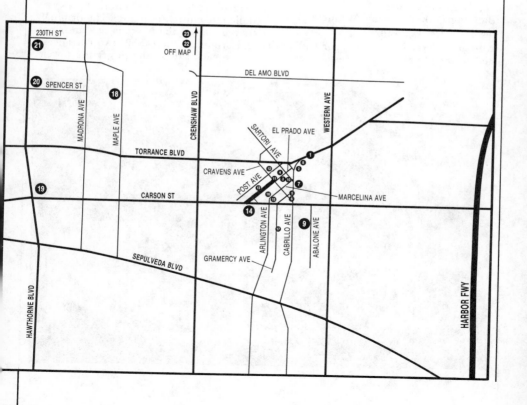

and Maple Avenue. In the twenties a residential area—the Hollywood Riviera—was developed on the western hills which overlooked the Pacific. In the post-World War II years there has been a slow infill of the area between the Olmsted center of Torrance and the Hollywood Riviera section. This infill is highly mixed, ranging from office complexes and other commercial uses to single- and multi-family housing.

1. Pacific Electric Railroad Bridge, 1912
Irving J. Gill
Torrance Boulevard between Western and Cabrillo avenues

In effect this reinforced concrete, six-arched bridge serves as a ceremonial entrance into Torrance from the east. This bridge was one of Gill's first projects at Torrance.

2. Pacific Electric Railroad Station, 1912
Irving J. Gill
610 S. Main Street on the west corner of Torrance Boulevard and Cabrillo Avenue

2. Pacific Electric Railroad Station

1. Pacific Electric Railroad Bridge

The design of the station originally incorporated a red tile roof and dome, so that it read more effectively as Mission Revival than is currently the case. The two miniature segmented domes on top of the side spur walls illustrate Gill's abstracted used of Mission Revival elements. As with other buildings at Torrance, the structure is that of hollow tile and brick, sheathed in stucco.

3. Roi Tan Hotel, 1912
Irving J. Gill
1211 El Prado Avenue

This three-story commercial structure is one of a group of buildings which Gill realized in downtown Torrance. The proportions of the building and of its openings are a hallmark of Gill's approach to design. Architecturally the building sways between the bland and the aesthetically abstract. Though this building was referred to as being of reinforced concrete it, like his other commercial buildings in Torrance, is of steel, brick, and hollow tile covered with stucco.

4. Murray Hotel, 1912
Irving J. Gill
1210 El Prado Avenue

Similar to the Roi Tan Hotel across the street. The eyebrow of red mission tile at the top has been removed.

5. Colonial Hotel and United Cigar Building, 1912
Irving J. Gill
1601-05 Cabrillo Avenue on the south corner of Cabrillo and Gramercy avenues

A triangular-shaped building with retail uses on much of the ground level and two floors of hotel rooms above. The narrow brick cornice at the top of the building has been removed.

6. Brighton Hotel, 1912
Irving J. Gill
1639 Cabrillo Avenue, on the north corner of Cabrillo and Cravens avenues

A second triangular building almost identical to the Colonial Hotel, with the usual retail stores on the ground level and hotel rooms and small apartments above.

7. Retail Commercial Building, ca. 1928
1420 Cabrillo Avenue

A Spanish Colonial Revival design with a highly dramatic entrance.

8. Fuller Shoe Manufacturing Company Building (Casa Del Amo), 1912
Irving J. Gill
1860 Torrance Boulevard

The single (false) shed roof and the scale of the symmetrical facade convey more of a domestic than a manufacturing quality. Fittingly, the building has been converted into apartments.

9. Salem Manufacturing Company Building, 1913
Irving J. Gill
1805 Abalone Avenue

A single-story box which, though of wood, appears to be of reinforced concrete. Another nearby Gill industrial building is the **Rubbercraft Corporation of California Building** (1913) at 1800 W. 220th Street. This two-story stucco structure has a pair of false stepped gable ends.

10. Retail Commercial Building, ca. 1916
2266 Sartori Avenue

The Mission Revival image is evident here. Buildings such as this had a much wider popular appeal than most of Irving J. Gill's more puritanical buildings.

11. Torrance City Hall and Municipal Auditorium (now Home Savings Branch Bank), 1936-37
Walker and Eisen
North corner of Cravens and El Prado avenues

A modest, single-story, PWA-Classicized Moderne building.

12. Torrance Public Library, 1936
Walker and Eisen
North corner of Cravens and Post avenues

PWA Moderne, one of the group of buildings which composed the original thirties civic center of Torrance.

13. House, ca. 1916
1504 Post Avenue

A two-story bungalow improved by references to the Midwest Prairie style.

14. Torrance High School, ca. 1920; 1929, and later
Southwest end of El Prado Avenue at Carson Street

The main building, which was axially oriented to El Prado, utilized a Classical and somewhat Beaux Arts image. The Assembly Hall with its relief sculpture over its entrance is an excellent example of the PWA Moderne.

15. Villa Sonora, ca. 1922
East corner of Marcelina and Arlington avenues

A Spanish Colonial Revival bungalow court, with single-story units towards the street and a two-story section at the rear of the property.

16. United Methodist Church, ca. 1916
Northeast corner of Marcelina and Arlington avenues

Mildly Midwest Prairie in style, the whole terminated by a wonderful octagonal dome.

17. Worker's Single-Family Housing, 1912
Irving J. Gill

Gramercy Avenue contains several of the concrete (actually hollow tile) bungalows designed by Gill. These are located at 1815, 1819, 1903, 1904, 1907, 1916, 1919, and 1920 Gramercy Avenue. These L-shaped single floor dwellings have their entrances to the side within the L. A low-pitched roof projects between the two corner parapets. Gill had planned streets of these and double connected bungalows for Torrance, but they were not popular with the workers and their families, who much preferred the more romantic and traditional California bungalow.

18. South Bay Industrial Park, 1974
Matlin and Dvoretzky; Emmet Wemple and Associates, landscape architects.
300 Maple Avenue

The romantic, picturesque (seemingly natural), landscaped industrial park is what is important here. The non-assertive, two-story buildings serve as a backdrop to Wemple's landscape.

19. Ohrbach's Del Amo Fashion Square, 1971
Gruen and Associates (Cesar Pelli)
Northeast corner of Carson Street and Hawthorne Boulevard

A fragile-looking blue container looks out onto acres of parked cars.

19. Ohrbach's Del Amo Fashion Square

20. Bill Hopkins Lincoln-Mercury Agency Building, 1966
Daniel L. Dworsky and Associates
20460 Hawthorne Boulevard (at Spencer Street)

A well-conceived sixties Modern design of modular brick walls and steel.

21. Tomanjan Professional Building, 1979-80
Neil Stanton Palmer
Northeast corner of Hawthorne Boulevard and 230th Street

A pyramid in brick and stone.

22. "The Courthouse," 1978-79
Northwest corner of Crenshaw Boulevard and 185th Street (just southwest of the San Diego Freeway)

The owner of this building, Dudley Gray, purchased fragments from the 1885 Pottawattamie Courthouse in Council Bluffs, Iowa, and then incorporated them into his own version of a classical courthouse. As a design it works best when it is seen at a distance, from the San Diego Freeway.

23. Castle Park Recreation Center, 1978
2410 Compton Boulevard

In the late seventies a wonderful group of castle image recreation centers were built in the Los Angeles area. Within, the castle houses video games of all sorts. Externally, the grounds are a miniature golf course. The castles are large in scale so that they can be seen from the freeways—and this one situated close to the San Diego Freeway works very well. Within the landscaped grounds are a delightful array of miniature buildings.

22. "The Courthouse"

Long Beach, Downtown and West

The city was founded in 1880 by Englishman W. E. Willmore, and it was first named the "American Colony." "The project," it was noted in the local press at the time, "includes an ample townsite, college grounds, and all the latest improvements." This plan was especially generous in providing a varity of open public spaces. The entire beach front was to be public, and a number of parks were provided throughout the townsite. Shortly after the first sale of land commenced the city was named Willmore City. Though widely advertised, it was not successful. In 1887 it was taken over by the Long Beach Land and Water Company and touted as an ideal seaside resort. A wharf was built and a large wooden hotel was constructed on the cliff overlooking the beach. In 1902 the Pacific Electric connected the city with Los Angeles. Four years later, work began on the harbor which eventually would transform Long Beach into a major West Coast port. The culmination of all of these efforts was reached in November 1925 when at long last navigation was open to deep draft ships.

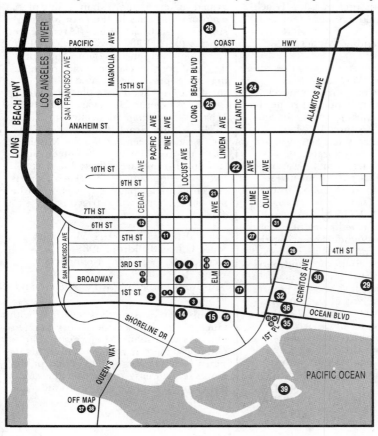

In the teens and twenties, efforts were made to impose a "City Beautiful" plan on the city. The major axis, Long Beach Boulevard, was to be lined, close to Ocean Beach Boulevard, with classical public buildings. The major result of this scheme was the construction of a Civic Auditorium (1930-32) at the south end of Long Beach Boulevard. In the early thirties a more modest scheme for a Civic Center was built around Lincoln Park.

In 1928, The Pacific Southwest Exposition was held in Long Beach. The site for the Exposition, at the south end of 7th Street, became an Islamic stageset (it was referred to as "Tunisian"). Regrettably, all of the Exposition buildings were temporary (designed by Hugh R. Davies), so that nothing was handed on, including the site itself.

In 1933, a severe earthquake destroyed or damaged many of the downtown masonry buildings in Long Beach. Many of these buildings were replaced or remodelled into Art Deco Moderne or later into Streamline Moderne buildings.

Like many other American cities after the Second World War, Long Beach plunged headlong into urban redevelopment. In this case it happened somewhat later than other cities, in the 1960s and 1970s. In 1981 it was noted, "Major redevelopment surgery has removed six blocks of the city's deteriorated downtown business district to make way for a $100-million mall as part of an investment of more than $1.25 billion in the heart of the city." (*Los Angeles Times,* February 22, 1981, VIII, 1) And as is the continually repeated story of urban redevelopment throughout America, the results are at best mixed. The landscaping of Long Beach Boulevard and parts of Ocean Boulevard is unquestionably a plus. The new plan for the area ignores what little was realized of the earlier Beaux Arts plan, The "surgery" within and outside of the six block area destroyed a number of commendable buildings including the 1930-32 Long Beach Municipal Auditorium with its great colorful mosaic by Henry R. Nord (the mural has been reinstalled on the south side of the new parking structure),

and the group of civic buildings situated facing Lincoln Park—the 1933-34 Long Beach City Hall, the 1932 Long Beach Municipal Utilities Building, and the 1936-37 Long Beach Veteran's Memorial Building. All of these were very good examples of the PWA Moderne.

The usual pedestrian mall ("**The Promenade**") has been built on the east end of Pine Avenue between Ocean Boulevard and 3rd Street. Its only asset is that it does have a symbolic termination at its north end. Here an arched section of the parking structure contains Nord's old Auditorium mosaic, and although the piece was never meant to be seen at eye level and close up, it is still impressive. As with most pedestrian malls "The Promenade" is not overrun by people.

The high-rise buildings which have been constructed either in or adjacent to the redevelopment area are undistinguished. There is more than a hint of overdone theatrics in the twin fourteen-story, semi-cylindrical glass **Arco Center Towers** (at 200-300 Oceangate, 1979-82 Luckman Partnership, Inc.). And nothing very positive can be said for the setting or design of the faciated, glass-sheathed **Crocker Plaza** office building (at 180 W. Ocean Boulevard, 1980-82, Maxwell Starkman Associates) or the 1974-78 **Long Beach Convention Center** (a sad replacement for the Municipal Auditorium). The 1974-75 **Queen Surf Condominiums** are regrettable. Extensive redevelopment of the beach front is currently taking place but it is doubtful that these efforts will retrieve past glories.

1. California Veteran's Memorial State Office Building, 1981-82
Kenneth S. Wing, Sr., Kenneth S. Wing, Jr.
Northwest corner of Cedar Avenue and Broadway

A four-story constructivist exercise, with much of the exposed metalwork painted blue. As with many Modernist public buildings, there is nothing about this design which suggests the civic and public, nor is it even easy to discover the entrance or to find one's way around.

1. California Veteran's Memorial State Office Building

4. Parking Structure, Long Beach Plaza

2. Long Beach City Hall and Public Library, 1973-76
Allied Architects; Hugh Gibbs and Donald Gibbs; Frank Holmelka and Associates; Killingsworth, Brady, and Associates; Kenneth S. Wing, Sr. and Kenneth S. Wing, Jr.
333 W. Ocean Boulevard

The fourteen-story City Hall office tower reads as a glass box held in place by projecting concrete piers. The Library (if you can find it) is a concrete pillbox hidden in the ground (*a la* the Oakland Museum). As with the nearby **California Veteran's Building** there is little of a proud civic sense about the site design or the architecture.

3. Downtown Plaza Building, 1981-82
Gruen Associates
Northeast corner of Ocean Boulevard and Promenade N.

A faciated and stepped glass-sheathed building, more suburban than urban.

4. Parking Structure, 1981-82
Gruen Associates
North end of The Promenade at West 3rd Street

As already mentioned, the arched wall of the parking structure which contains the 1930s Federal Arts Project mosaic by Henry Nord and others saves not only the parking structure but the mall as well. The adjacent enclosed **Long Beach Plaza** shopping mall was in part to have many of its ground floor shops open to the adjacent streets, but as has happened elsewhere, this has not really worked.

5. Buffum's Autoport, ca. 1937
North side of 1st Street between Pine and Pacific avenues

A classic example—including its name—of the Streamline Moderne of the thirties. Horizontal bands terminate in a vertical plane, from which project three small, curved balconies. The only change is the open concrete grillwork on the street level.

6. Commercial Building (now 115 Pine Building), ca. 1915
115 Pine Avenue, Northwest corner of Pine Avenue and 1st Street

A rather severe six-story Beaux Arts design, with the exception of a fanciful corner clock tower.

7. Security Trust and Savings Building (now Security Pacific National Bank), 1925
102 Pine Avenue, northeast corner of Pine Avenue and 1st Street

A fourteen-story Beaux Arts skyscraper. Large two-story windows occur between the fluted pilasters on the ground floor, and elaborate multicolored relief panels are located above the office tower entrances.

7. Security Trust and Savings Building (now Security Pacific National Bank)

8. Retail Store and Office Building, ca. 1932
Northeast corner of Pine Avenue and Broadway

The ground floor of retail shops has been remodelled, but the second floor displays a wonderfully inventive and colorful array of Art Deco Moderne motifs in terra-cotta. Note also the second floor of the adjoining building to the north—another Art Deco Moderne facade in terra-cotta.

9. Farmers and Merchants Bank Building, 1922
Northeast corner of Pine Avenue and 3rd Street

A ten-story white terra-cotta-sheathed skyscraper, whose image seems both Beaux Arts and Spanish Renaissance.

10. First Congregational Church, 1914
H. M. Patterson
Southwest corner of Cedar Avenue and 3rd Street

By the mid-teens the northern Italian Romanesque had been found to be highly appropriate for the image of California as the new, improved Mediterranean world.

11. YWCA Building, 1925
Julia Morgan
Southeast corner of Pacific Avenue and 6th Street

A four-story brick Italian Renaissance building. Visit quickly, for it may not be around very long. It has been slated to be replaced by a new structure.

12. Second Church of Christ, Scientist, 1916-25
Elmer Grey
Southwest corner of Cedar Avenue and 7th Street

Pure Beaux Arts, except in this instance there is a hint of the Byzantine rather than the Italian. Most impressive are the four large Corinthian columns which set off the high entrance porch.

13. Chemical and Physical Testing Laboratories, City of Long Beach, ca. 1915
1475 San Francisco Avenue

A single-story Mission Revival building.

13. Chemical and Physical Testing Laboratories, City of Long Beach

14. Jergins Trust Building, ca. 1928
100 E. Ocean Boulevard; southeast corner of Ocean Boulevard and Pine Avenue

A seven-story plus tower building sheathed in light-colored terra-cotta. Its rich, ornamented detailing points to Spain and the Churrigueresque.

15. West Coast Fox Theatre, 1925
Meyer and Holler
333 E. Ocean Boulevard

Spanish Renaissance. Within the facades upper arch is "Bulova, Goddess of Time," which dominates the scene.

15. West Coast Fox Theatre

16. Hotel, ca. 1932
334 E. Ocean Boulevard

An Art Deco (Zigzag) Moderne concrete structure set back from the street in a heavily planted garden.

17. Lafayette Hotel Building, 1930-31
W. H. Austin
Southeast corner of Broadway and Linden Avenues

A four-story vertical Art Deco (Zigzag) Moderne building. Surveying the scene, perhaps with some reservations, are two large-scaled heads of Native Americans looking down from the parapet.

18. Federal Building, 1931-32
Gordon B. Kaufmann
Northeast corner of Long Beach Boulevard and 3rd Street

PWA Moderne, accomplished within Kaufmann's restrained and sophisticated taste.

19. Great Western Savings Association Building, 1968
Daniel Dworsky and Associates
350 Long Beach Boulevard

A cut-into box with an exposed concrete frame and an infill of brick. The setback of the building has provided space for planting, brick walks, and walls.

20. Retail Store Building, 1932
315 Elm Avenue

A single-story Art Deco (Zigzag) Moderne store building with pattern of metal grillwork above the store windows.

21. Scottish Rite Cathedral, 1926
Park O. Wright and Francis H. Gentry
Southwest corner of Elm Avenue and 9th Street

A classical Italian Romanesque design, covered with grey mottled terra-cotta which suggests stone.

22. Saint Mary's Hospital, 1937
North end of Linden Avenue at 10th Street

A succession of three-story volumes terminated by a low tower with a hipped roof. It all adds up to a successful Art Deco (Zigzag) Moderne composition (with Beaux Arts overtones).

23. Long Beach Masonic Temple Building, 1927
829 Locust Avenue

A severe Beaux Arts block.

24. Long Beach Polytechnic High School, 1932-36 and later
Hugh R. Davies
Northeast corner of Atlantic Avenue and 15th Street

The 1934-36 Industrial Arts Building and the Commercial Arts Building by Davies lean more towards the International Style Modern of the thirties than the then-popular Streamline Moderne. Note the style of lettering for the buildings. Also, go inside the Industrial Arts Building to see the Federal Arts Project mural by Ivan Bartlet and Jean Swiggett.

25. Gasoline Service Station, ca. 1925
Southeast corner of Long Beach Boulevard and 15th Street

An early, prefabricated metal service station with a single, hipped roof which covers both the pumps and the office.

26. Pacific Auto Works, 1928
Schilling and Schilling
1910 Long Beach Boulevard

Art Deco (Zigzag) Moderne with both an art and programmatic intent. The central cartouche suggests a radiator of an automobile and the double seashell motif to each side creates the needed headlights.

26. Pacific Auto Works

27. Robert Louis Stevenson School, ca. 1936
West side of Lime Avenue between 5th and 6th streets

PWA Moderne. The ornament suggests both the Art Deco (Zigzag) Moderne and the pre-Columbian.

28. Hot Cha Restaurant, 1936
957 4th Street

A metal coffee pot for a giant sits on top of the clerestory of a small octagonal building.

28. Hot Cha Restaurant

29. Apartment Building, ca. 1928
1436 3rd Street

A two-story Spanish Colonial Revival apartment complex with an open garden-court.

30. Ebell Club Building, 1924
Attributed to Hugh R. Davies
Southeast corner of Cerritos Avenue and 3rd Street

A great rectangular box of a building with an exuberant Spanish Churrigueresque entrance.

31. Saint Anthony's Roman Catholic Church, 1952
Barker and Ott
Southeast corner of Olive Avenue and 7th Street

This simple, gable-roofed church was remodelled in 1952. Added to the older building were two fanciful (Gothic?) towers which now enclose the gable end mosaic depicting Pope Pius XII watching the Virgin's assumption. Below, a three-part entrance is set in a Gothic screen.

31. Saint Anthony's Roman Catholic Church

32. Apartment Building, ca. 1929
917 1st Street

A two-story Streamline Moderne building with all of the needed elements — curved corners, horizontal banded windows, steel railings, and glass bricks.

33. Villa Riviera Apartment Building, 1928
Richard D. King
800 E. Ocean Boulevard

One of the seashore landmarks of Long Beach. The image with its dormered, high-pitched, hipped roof and octagonal tower is French Chateauesque.

34. Pacific Coast Club, 1925-26
Curlett and Beelman
Southwest corner of East Ocean Boulevard and 1st Place.

A romantic French Medieval castle resplendent with towers and all. At the moment it is in need of sympathetic restoration.

35. Tichenor House, 1904
Charles and Henry Greene
852 E. Ocean Boulevard

A much-remodelled, two-story, Greene and Greene bungalow. The east facade faces onto 1st Place and contains a remarkable pattern of brick, wood, and glass.

36. House, ca. 1937
936 E. Ocean Boulevard

A Streamline Moderne dwelling, quite nautical in feeling.

37. The Queen Mary, 1931-34
At the edge of the harbor off of Queens Highway North

The interiors of this famous transatlantic ocean liner reveal the English approach to the Art Deco (Zigzag) Moderne, which was emerging into the Streamline Moderne.

38. Howard Hughes's Flying Boat (The "Spruce Goose") and Hanger, 1982
Temcor
Southeast of Queens Highway North

This immense aluminum dome houses this great post-World War II flying boat. The airplane's design has many points in common with the highly imaginative projects for flying boats designed in 1929 by Norman Bel Geddes.

39. Oil Drilling Islands, 1967-68
Herb Goldman; Linesch and Reynolds, landscape architects
Long Beach Harbor

A grouping of high, thin, sculptured walls seek to hide the utilitarian equipment of the man-made oil islands from public view on shore. As beautification the results are peculiar, though it all is a pure Southern California solution.

34. Pacific Coast Club

Long Beach, East; Naples, and Seal Beach

Raymond House is a concrete and hollow tile construction. Its proportions and general detailing are similar to the destroyed Dodge House in West Hollywood.

1. Raymond House, 1918
Irving J. Gill
2724 E. Ocean Boulevard

This is one of the few Gill houses in the Los Angeles area which still remains intact. As with many of his houses, the

1. Raymond House

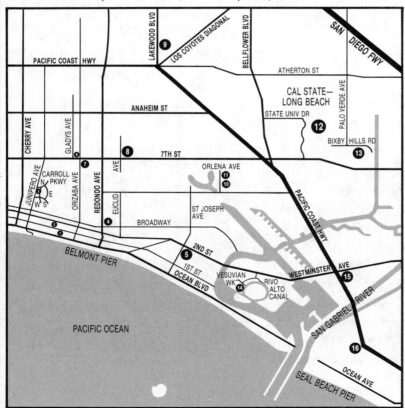

2. Bungalow, ca. 1915
2601 1st Street

A single-floor bungalow becomes respectable with a front porch displaying classical columns.

3. House, ca. 1910
363 Carroll Parkway West

A Mission Revival dwelling.

4. Bungalow, ca. 1909
4341 Broadway

An ordinary California bungalow assumes some importance with the concrete columns of its front porch cast in the form of rustic tree trunks.

5. Belmont Theatre Building, 1929
Reginald F. Inwood
Southeast corner of Saint Joseph Avenue and 2nd Street

Pre-Columbian architecture "improved" through the Art Deco (Zigzag) Moderne. The building is still exotic, though it has suffered the loss of the upper part of its corner tower, the addition of a new entrance, and of a marquee (in 1948). Recently it has been made "Old West."

6. Office/Dwelling, ca. 1925
708 Gladys Avenue

A narrow, Medieval Hansel and Gretel dwelling, more French than English.

7. Retail Store and Apartments, ca. 1927
Southeast corner of Orizaba Avenue and 7th Street

An imaginative crenelated tower stands guard over this complex of remodelled structures. Note the staircase and the entrance into the tower, and also the pink stucco. Style? Perhaps we should think of it as Spanish Medieval.

8. Jefferson Jr. High School Building, 1936
Northeast corner of Euclid Avenue and 7th Street

PWA Moderne in exposed concrete. The spiral motif ornamentation of the piers and spandrels is impressive.

7. Retail Store and Apartments

9. Duffield Lincoln-Mercury Agency Building, 1963
Killingsworth, Brady, and Associates
1940 Lakewood Boulevard

A steel grid frame, which is mostly infilled with glass, faces onto the street. The late 1950s Case Study House form enlarged into a elegant auto showroom.

10. House, ca. 1936
376 Orlena Avenue

One of a number of white stucco Streamline Moderne bungalows to be found in and around Long Beach.

11. Kimpson-Nixon House, 1939
Raphael S. Soriano
380 Orlena Avenue

Soriano as an advocate of the purist International Style Modern of the 1930s. Boxy volumes are articulated by horizontal bands of windows on both floors.

12. California State University at Long Beach, 1949 and later
State University Drive off Bellflower Boulevard on 7th Street

The architecture of the University, like that of most of the other state universities and colleges, can at best be described as bland "State College Modern." Though architect Edward Killingsworth has for many years been the master-planning architect for the University, the complex still has not developed much above the ordinary. The best element of the campus and its saving grace is its landscape architecture. The 1966 **Sculpture Walk** (Killingsworth, Brady, and Associates; Edward Lovell, landscape architect) is a good case in point. Fortunately the landscape is winning out.

13. La Casa De Rancho Los Alamitos, 1806
6400 E. Bixby Hills Road

This single-floor adobe ranch house is, according to tradition, the oldest domestic building still standing in Southern California. The ranch house and adjoining grounds are open to the public, Wednesday-Sunday, 1-5 P.M.

Naples

This waterside community was developed between 1903 and 1905 by Arthur Parson. Like Venice, south of Santa Monica, it was planned around a series of canals. (Needless to say no one had really looked around the bay of Naples.) The center of the place is an island within Alamitos Bay (itself a fake bay), and it is much more reminiscent of Venice, Italy, than is Santa Monica's Venice.

14. Frank House, 1957
Killingsworth, Brady, and Smith
5576 Vesuvian Walk, Naples

Arts and Architecture magazine's Case Study House No. 25. The two-story interior is arranged around a lath-covered interior court. The verticality of space, of wall surfaces, and of details indicates the course which much of California's Modern was to follow in the later 1960s.

15. The Market Place, 1976-77
Richard Nagy Martin
North corner of Pacific Coast Highway and Westminster Avenue

Several major shopping centers have been constructed in and around the intersection of Pacific Coast Highway and Westminster Avenue. Of these The Market Place is by far the most pleasant. The high points of the place are the connected lakes, the traditional large-scale Mexican fountain of Guadalajara Canterra stone, and El Torito Restaurant, a wonderful version of California's Mission Revival.

16. Bay City Center, 1979-80
Irwin and Associates
Pacific Coast Highway, between 5th and Marina streets, Seal Beach (off of map)

The centerpiece of this commercial development is the central thirty-five-foot-high cupola and dome of copper, which, it is said, was modelled after the dome of the 1920s Islamic Bay City Bath House.

11. Kimpson-Nixon House

Long Beach, North

1. Cambridge Investment Inc. Building, 1966
Killingsworth, Brady, and Associates
324 E. Bixby Road

An open post and lintel frame building, quite classical in concept.

2. Bixby House, ca. 1895
Ernest Coxhead
11 La Linda Place

We still have no idea how many residences Coxhead designed in Southern California, either during his stay in Los Angeles or after he moved to the Bay Region. This house was designed when he was in San Francisco, and as one would expect, it is similar in certain aspects to his work in the north. In the Bixby House he has blended the Shingle Colonial Revival tradition with the English Arts and Crafts.

3. Reeves House, 1904
Charles and Henry Greene
4260 Country Club Drive

A characteristic Greene and Greene two-story bungalow which was originally built at 306 Cedar Avenue. In 1917 it was moved to 1004 Pine Avenue, and in 1927 it was moved to its present site.

4. ■Adobe Los Cerritos, 1844
4600 Virginia Road

This large house was built by Don Juan Temple as the center for his extensive ranch located around the Los Angeles River. The dwelling is a U-shaped building enclosing a patio which was walled at its open end. The center section of the building is surrounded by a two-story wood porch and gallery. Originally the roof was flat, covered with "brea," but after 1866 a hipped shingle roof was added. The Adobe Los Cerritos is one of the finest existing Monterey style adobes to be found in Southern California. The romantic gardens around the house were restored by Ralph Cornell.

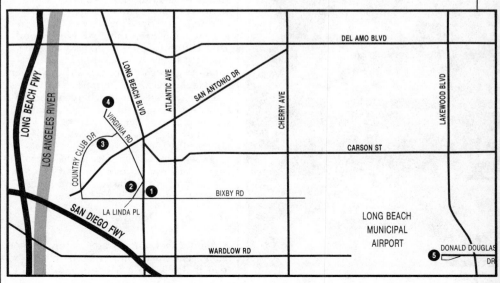

5. Long Beach Airport Terminal, 1940-41
Kenneth S. Wing, W. Horace Austin
West end of Douglas Drive off Lakewood Boulevard

The late thirties Streamline Moderne moving towards the bland Modern of the post-World War II years. The site planning, with its dominant axial road leading to a park in front of the two-story terminal building, is characteristic of the PWA Moderne. Regrettably the Federal Arts Project murals and mosaics by Grace Clements are no longer visible.

Inglewood, Hawthorne

5. Long Beach Airport Terminal

Inglewood was one of the many boom towns which were established in the late 1880s on the flat plain south of Los Angeles. It was platted in 1887. A large hotel was built and plans were made for the establishment of the Freeman College of Applied Arts. Then came the bust of 1889-90. The hotel was left standing, but the college never got underway. The town grew very slowly until the late 1930s, when several large tracts of modest spec housing were built, and such streets as Manchester Avenue, Crenshaw Boulevard, and La Cienega Boulevard began to develop as typical, auto-oriented, retail commercial strips. The city's chief fame for years has been the 1937 **Hollywood Turf Club** designed by Stiles Clements. The city today is well supplied with small neighborhood parks and the larger **Centinela Park** (off Florence and Centinela avenues). Much of the city lies right in the center of the east jet pattern for the Los Angeles Airport, but it has somehow managed to survive remarkably well.

Hawthorne, which lies to the south of Inglewood, was founded in 1906. Its system of grid streets basically continues those of Inglewood.

1. Randy's Donuts, 1954
805 W. Manchester Avenue

A giant doughnut sits atop a tiny, canted-glass, early fifties Modern fast-food building. In a Modern fashion, the

vertical steel supports for the doughnut plunge right through the building below. A classic example of fifties programmatic architecture where the sign (the three-dimensional doughnut) is the design and the building below is merely a base.

2. Centinela Ranch House (Ygnacio Marchado Adobe), after 1844
7636 Midfield Avenue

The Rancho Aguaje de Centinela was granted in 1844, and it is likely that shortly after this date the adobe ranch-house was built. As is generally the case with adobes, the house was added to from time to time, especially in the early 1860s. It is a single-floor adobe with a wood shingle roof, fireplaces, and deep window reveals.

3. Three Speculative Houses, 1940
Edward Lind (office of R. M. Schindler) 423, 429, and 433 Ellis Avenue

Three single-floor spec houses which mirror a number of Schindleresque design motifs. Their garages at a lower level face towards the street, and the houses open up to enclosed gardens at the sides and rear.

4. Stanford M. Anderson Water Treatment Plant, 1977
Kappe, Lotery, and Boccato
Southwest corner of Eucalyptus and Beach avenues

A two-story Miesian, steel-and-glass box looks out onto a gay world of brightly painted pipes, tanks, and other machine elements. A colorful diagram on the front wall-sign explains it all.

5. Inglewood Civic Center, 1973
Charles Luckman Associates; Robert Herrick Carter, landscape architect
Northwest corner of Manchester Avenue and Hawthorne Boulevard

Within this twenty-nine-acre civic center has been placed a nondescript eight-story City Hall situated on a two-story base. Within its own separate garden is the two-story library building. Other buildings located within the Civic Center are a police facility, a fire station, and a public health complex. The landscape is slowly hiding most of the buildings.

6. Los Angeles Railroad, Inglewood Station, 1928
Southeast corner of Prairie and Florence avenues (within Inglewood Park Cemetary)

A small Spanish Colonial Revival passenger station which poses as an Andalusian church.

7. Hollywood Turf Club, 1937
Stiles O. Clements, with later additions by Fred Barlow, Jr.; Edward Huntsman-Trout, landscape architect
Northwest corner of Century Boulevard and Prairie Avenue

A Streamline Moderne clubhouse and grandstand, easily visible from Century Boulevard. The master plan, which was laid out by Clements and Huntsman-Trout, can best be seen from the window of your jet as you approach the Los Angeles International Airport. Note that they provided spaces for twenty-two thousand cars (in 1937).

8. ▪Academy Theatre, 1939
S. Charles Lee
3100 Manchester Boulevard

Notwithstanding recent remodellings, this theatre marks a high point of the Streamline Moderne in the United States. Stucco-sheathed cylinders play into one another, and culminate in a thin, 125-foot-high tower. The spiral fins of this tower and of the parking sign were originally lighted by blue neon.

9. Brownfield Medical Building, 1938
Gregory Ain
Northwest corner of Manchester Boulevard and Third Avenue

A small, tastefully-proportioned "rationalist" design by one of L.A.'s pioneer modernists.

10. Avalon Gardens Public Housing, 1941-42
Roland E. Coate, Carleton M. Winslow, and Samuel E. Lunden; Katherine Bashford and Frederick Barlow, Jr., landscape architects
701 E. 88th Street

Sixty-three stucco California Ranch house units which contain 164 living units. A hint of the Moderne is suggested by horizontal bands and the thin fascia of the overhanging wood roofs.

11. Milk Bottle (Knudson's Dairy), ca. 1935
1914 W. Slauson Avenue

A good-sized milk bottle sits on top of a dairy building so that we are all aware of what it is about.

12. Pepperdine College, 1937
Thomas Cooper; Katherine Bashford and Frederick Barlow, Jr., landscape architects
West of 79th Street and South Vermont Avenue

The college campus contains several excellent examples of the Streamline Moderne, and there are several buildings which come close to being thirties International Style Modern. The older President's House at 7851 Budlong Avenue and the Pepperdine Center

Building on the west side of South Vermont Avenue at West 78th Street are Spanish Colonial Revival.

13. Mount Carmel High School Building, 1934
7011 S. Hoover Avenue

An excellent exercise in the more abstracted version of the Spanish Colonial Revival of the 1930s.

14. The Teapot, ca. 1931
607 W. Manchester Avenue

A little programmatic restaurant in the form of a metal teapot.

15. One-Hundred Fifty-Third Street School Building, 1957
Ain, Johnson, and Day
1605 W. 153rd Street between Harvard Boulevard and Denker Avenue

A fifties one-story finger-plan school accomplished with Ain's characteristic reticence.

16. Northrop Electronics Division Headquarters, 1982
Daniel L. Dworsky and Associates
2301 W. 120th Street

International Style Modern, made fashionable through contemporary High Tech imagery. Many of the glass-walled areas of the building open onto well-landscaped terraces.

Gardena

G ardena, which was located at the junction of the Pacific Electric Railroad lines from San Pedro and Redondo Beach, was founded in 1906. The town center of Gardena (located at Gardena Avenue between Western and Normandie avenues) still conveys a 1920s Spanish Colonial Revival image. Newer buildings of the past three decades have somewhat modified the original unity of the place.

At 2501 W. Rosecrans Avenue is the 1952 Gardena Office of **Great Western Savings and Loan Association,** designed by the San Francisco office of Skidmore, Owings, and Merrill. The building utilizes the then-fashionable Edward Stone Pavilion mode, except that in this case massive concrete was used. The building has been remodelled, but you can still see the architects' original intent. At 3312 El Segundo Boulevard are the **Goldwater Apartment Buildings** designed by Carl Maston in 1964, with the landscape designed by Emmet L. Wemple and Associates. Each of the fourteen two-story units has its own private court and in addition there are larger, more public courts. The imagery is early 1960s *Arts and Architecture* Modern, with an open courtyard created between the stucco-sheathed boxes and the constructivist pergolas.

Just east of the San Diego Freeway interchange with Redondo Beach Boulevard is **El Camino College** (at 16067 S. Crenshaw Boulevard). The Administration Building and the Library were designed in 1951 by Smith, Powell, and Morgridge. These buildings indicate how well the architects of the immediate post-World War II years could apply both the 1930s lesson of the International Style Modern and the popular Moderne to produce a functional and convincing image.

Great Western Savings and Loan Building

Baldwin Hills

This section of Los Angeles (County and City) contains the Palms District (laid out in 1886), and Culver City (platted in 1913). Palms, which was established alongside the Santa Monica Railroad, was planned as a grain shipping center, and until the early 1900s agriculture was the primary use made of the land.

Culver City, founded by the real estate promoter Harry Hazel Culver, has long been famed for the major film studios which began to be located there from the late teens into the twenties. Land use in the area now varies considerably. Light industry occurs here and there, extensive commercial strips abound (Venice, Washington, Culver, and Jefferson boulevards). For the vernacular commercial strip fancier, a long, leisurely drive along Pico Boulevard or Washington Boulevard from Santa Moncia to downtown Los Angeles is a must. If your interest is in middle class suburbia and its planning, then visit a development such as **Monte Mar Vista,** a 130-acre development south of Rancho Park (north off the Santa Monica Freeway, east of Overland Avenue, west of Robertson Boulevard). This development was laid out in 1924 by Cook, Hill, and Cornell. In Palms, in and around Overland Avenue between National Boulevard and Venice Boulevard, is **Westside Village,** a spec development of small single-family houses which was built between 1939 and 1941. The small, clap-

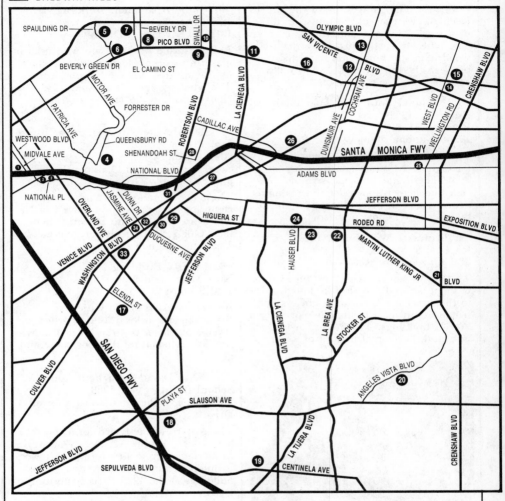

board houses with their shuttered windows evoke the then-popular Anglo Colonial Revival image.

1. ■Petal House, 1982
Eric Owen Moss
2828 Midvale Avenue

This complex of buildings (it is in part a remodelling) displays the architect's inventive ability to carry pedestrian architecture over into the world of high art. The commonest of materials coupled with the most common of architectural forms produces a very uncommon composition. Though the design, includ-

ing its strong colors, is highly assertive, it fits with ease into a neighborhood of typical, modest, post-World War II spec houses. And, as is true of other designs by Moss, the forms and details of this house convey a sense of charm and delight. See the house close up from the street, and also observe how it works from the Santa Monica Freeeway.

2. Garden Apartment Building, 1955
Carl L. Maston
10567 National Boulevard

The building consists of a series of volumes which step down the hillside to the street. The garages are at the street level. Above, each of the units has its own small, enclosed courtyard garden. The building is sheathed in vertical redwood. Glass in horizontal bands occurs between the top of the redwood walls and the thin fascia flat roofs.

3. National Boulevard Apartment Building, 1954
Raymond Kappe
10565 National Boulevard

This building provides a good neighbor for Carl L. Maston's apartments next door. The design concept is similar, except that here Kappe's detailing is more delicate, and in places there is a hint of his later wood constructivism.

4. Strauss-Lewis House, 1940
Raphael S. Soriano
3131 Queensbury Road

This single-story dwelling arranged in a U-shape around a patio (the fourth side to the street is walled in) is far less doctrinaire than most of his other pre-World War II buildings. The house is sheathed in a thin, horizontal pattern of wood.

4. Strauss-Lewis House

5. Karaski House, 1960
Lloyd Wright
436 Spalding Drive, Beverly Hills

Lloyd Wright at his best; a wonderful essay in stucco, concrete open grillwork, and stone. The grillwork encloses courts and parts of the balconies. The two-story rear of the house has the visual appearance of the bridge of a ship.

6. Colby Apartment Building, 1950
Raphael S. Soriano
1312 Beverly Green Drive

Pure post and beam design with infill of glass and stucco. Corrugated fiberglass panels are used for the balcony fronts. The whole design is light and airy, characteristic of Soriano's work after 1945.

7. Beverly-Landau Apartment Building, 1949
Alvin Lustig
Southwest corner of Olympic Boulevard and El Camino Drive

These two rectangular volumes, set at right angles to each other, have facades which are divided into repeated modules. One strongly feels here the hand of a careful designer.

8. Liberty Building, 1966
Kurt Meyer and Associates
1180 S. Beverly Drive

An L.A. version of the sixties New Brutalism. Its awkwardly-proportioned, seven-story form is a reminder of how rapidly architectural fashions come and go.

9. B'Nai David Synagogue and School Building, ca. 1929
South side of Pico Boulevard at Swall Drive

The pattern of the board forms has been left exposed in this Art Deco (Zigzag) Moderne concrete structure. The tower is mildly reminiscent of several of the buildings at the 1925 Paris Exposition of Decorative Arts.

10. Ellwood Office Building, 1965-66
Craig Ellwood Associates
1107-11 S. Robertson Boulevard

A close-to-magical transformation of two fifty-year-old buildings into one of Ellwood's thin, refined versions of the post and beam Miesian grids.

11. Supermarket Building, ca. 1940
Attributed to Stiles Clements
Northeast corner of Pico and La Cienega boulevards

The Streamline Moderne street facade of this building culminates in two thin, vertical fin-signs which turn out to be relief sculpture of a Hugh Ferriss skyscraper from his 1929 *Metropolis of Tomorrow*.

11. Supermarket Building

12. Dunsmuir Apartment Building, 1937
Gregory Ain
1281 S. Dunsmuir Avenue

A mid-1930s classic of Modernism, often illustrated during those years in magazines and books on housing. It was this building, presented through the revealing photographs of Julius Shulman, which established Gregory Ain's national reputation. The building is composed of four two-story units which are stepped back up the low hillside with a narrow entrance walkway on one side and a small terrace and garden for each unit on the other side. Each of the second-floor bedrooms per unit opens onto an upper pergola-covered deck.

12. Dunsmuir Apartment Building

13. Mackey Apartment Building, 1939
R. M. Schindler
1137-41 S. Cochran Avenue

Each of the building's elevations is composed of projecting and cut-into volumes, articulated by a carefully-designed pattern of windows and doors. Within, some of the spaces are two stories in height.

14. Sears, Roebuck, and Company Store Building, 1939
John Reddon and John G. Raben
Southeast corner of Pico and Westwood boulevards

This building beautifully presents the ideal of the pre-World War II suburban department store. The building itself serves as a quiet Streamline Moderne backdrop to the automobile, parked either in the large parking lot to the west, or on top of the roof of the store. The automotive and garden shop buildings are separate structures within the parking lot. Originally, small mechanical elevators brought the merchandise up to the roof parking deck.

15. The Radio Building, ca. 1941
North side of Pico Boulevard, 4500 Block

Pure Streamline Moderne. Also note the 1930s Art Deco (Zigzag) Moderne building across Pico Boulevard.

16. Washeteria, ca. 1955
5800 Pico Boulevard

A low structure dominated by a giant clothespin.

17. Robert Lee Frost Auditorium, Culver City High School, 1965
Fleweling and Moody
4401 Elenda Street

A concrete shell in the form of an open folded fan. At its open end is a low cylinder which houses the secondary spaces of the complex.

18. Fox Hills Shopping Mall, 1973-76
Gruen Associates (Cesar Pelli)
Southeast corner of Sepulveda and Slauson boulevards below Freeway

A form seemingly designed to make an impression from the Freeway interchange. The landscaping and buildings do not work as well close up.

19. Ladera Center, 1983
Urban Innovations
Corner of La Cienega Boulevard, Centinela Avenue, and La Tijera Boulevard

A small, older shopping center brought up-to-date by a new stage-set facade which looks to the classical tradition (in a strange way). A successful revamping.

20. California Military Academy (now **Foundation for the Blind**), 1934-35; 1936
Richard J. Neutra
5300 Angeles Vista Boulevard

A single-floor, L-plan building constructed of a metal frame and sheathing. Each of the classrooms opens to its own out-of-doors space through sliding glass walls. Skylights balance the light in the classrooms and the interior corridors. (Note that Neutra's buildings lie to the rear of the site.)

21. Broadway/Crenshaw Shopping Center, 1949
Albert B. Gardner
Northwest corner of Crenshaw and Martin Luther King, Jr. boulevards

Two forms are combined in this shopping center: the Wilshire Boulevard type, which presents a traditional front to the major street and has its principle entrance in the back facing the parking lot; and the self-contained shopping center which is oriented exclusively to its own parking lot. An open L-plan accommodates the four-story Broadway Department Store at the center with the other stores spread out to the sides. A service station/auto center occupies one end of the parking lot. A tunnel runs under the parking lot to provide for delivery to all of the stores. The imagery of the stores is fifties Modern, which is matched across Martin Luther King, Jr. Boulevard by the equally well-planned **May Company Department Store Building** (1948; Albert C. Martin).

22. Baldwin Hills Shopping Center, 1954
Robert E. Alexander

Southwest corner of La Brea Avenue and Rodeo Road

A small, neighborhood shopping center directed primarily to the residences of nearby Baldwin Hills Village. Changes in shop fronts and signage have tended to destroy its unity of design.

23. Baldwin Hills Village, 1940-41
Reginald D. Johnson, Wilson and Merrill, Robert E. Alexander; Clarence S. Stein, consultant and site planner; Fred Barlow and Fred Edmunson, landscape architects
5300 Rodeo Road

At the time it was built, and in the years which have followed, Baldwin Hills Village has continually been mentioned as a successful example of multiple medium-density housing. The project was and still is an excellent solution to group housing. Two-story units are arranged around open, well-landscaped spaces which lead into the central tri-part village green. In addition, each of the units has its own small, walled courtyard, which helps to separate the buildings even further from the more public open spaces. Parking and garage courts were laid out on the edge of the site and near the center are the clubhouse and the offices. The buildings, with their stucco and wood walls and low-pitched, hipped roofs, are neutral in design, and it is the trees, shrubs, grass, and flowers which dominate. Recently the project has been turned into a condominium, with individual ownership of each unit.

23. Baldwin Hills Village

24. University Elementary School,
1948; 1950
Robert E. Alexander
Northwest corner of Rodeo Road and
Hauser Boulevard

Post and beam Modern of the fifties. A
good example of the indoor/outdoor
classroom building.

25. Two Retail Commercial Buildings,
ca. 1934
West Adams Boulevard, 4500 block,
north of Wellington Road

Two Moderne commercial buildings,
more Art Deco (Zigzag) Moderne than
Streamline Moderne. Each has a corner
tower and splended cast-concrete Zigzag
Moderne ornament.

**26. Kings Tropical Inn Restaurant
Building,** 1925
5879 Washington Boulevard

A domed Islamic building which one
supposes was to signify the exotic and
faraway lands of the tropics.

27. Helms Bakery Building

26. Kings Tropical Inn Restaurant

27. Helms Bakery Building, 1930
E. L. Bruner
8800 Venice Boulevard

The vocabulary of the PWA Moderne
(in this case pre-PWA) realized in an
extensive two-story building. Now missing is the regimented row of precisely
trimmed shrubs in front of the building
and the central rooftop sign advertising
Helms Olympic Bread.

28. La Casa de Rocha, 1865
2400 Shenandoah Street

This story-and-a-half adobe ranch house
is surrounded on three sides by a covered corridor. The upper walls of the
building are sheathed in shiplap siding.

29. Thomas Ince Studio Building
(now **Grayson Potchuck Products**), 1915
9336 W. Washington Boulevard

The offices of a motion picture company
as its own stage set—in this case a
Colonial Revival southern plantation
house. This was the first major studio
building to be constructed in Culver
City.

30. Culver Theatre, ca. 1950
Southeast corner of West Washington
Boulevard and Duquesne Avenue

A post-World War II theatre where the
facade ends up being all sign. Its design
is both Moderne and Baroque (*a la*
Hollywood).

31. Los Angeles Pacific Railroad Company, Ivy Park Substation (later **Pacific Electric Culver Substation**), 1907
Northwest corner of Venice and Culver boulevards

The Mission Revival image for a small, single-story railroad passenger station.

32. Garden Apartment Buildings, ca. 1925
3819-25 Dunn Drive

A Medieval fairy-tale world of Hansel and Gretel cottages in a witch-infested jungle with pools of water. It is delightfully unbelievable that it is situated here, only a block from the center of Culver City.

33. MGM Studios (Goldwyn Studios) Building, 1938-39
Claude Beelman
East corner of Washington Boulevard and Overland Avenue

The Beaux Arts in the guise of the monumental PWA Moderne. Rounded corners and decorative panels of concrete make it as official as any governmental building. The studios were established at this location in 1923, and there are both pre- and post-1938 buildings on the site. The 1923 building is an impressive classical columned structure just northeast of the corner of Washington Boulevard and Overland Avenue.

34. Saint Augustine Roman Catholic Church, ca. 1931
Northeast corner of Washington Boulevard and Jasmine Avenue

A Gothic church in revealed concrete, with the usual horizontal board patterns as a surface.

Brentwood

Originally part of the Rancho San Vicente y Santa Monica, modern Brentwood began when the Western Pacific Development Company acquired the land in the early 1900s and named it Brentwood Park. In 1906 the company platted the lots and streets in a manner consciously modelled on the plan of Golden Gate Park in San Francisco. The area bounded on the east by 26th Street, on the west by Cliffwood Avenue, on the south by San Vicente Boulevard, and on the north by the Santa Monica Mountains was intended from the first to be the home of the upper crust of society. It was determinedly residential, with thirty-four traffic circles interrupting the flow of rapid transit. All but seven of the circles (all on or near Bristol) have been eliminated by progress.
Bristol) have been eliminated by progress.

Our listing includes the area east to the San Diego Freeway. Originally this was part of the Bel Air District developed in the same period by Alphonzo Bell, Sr. Bell, an early alumnus of Occidental College, for some reason decided to separate his historically coeducational college into men's and women's divisions. The women were to remain in Eagle Rock and the men moved to Bel Air, not far from where UCLA was soon to settle. The old grads and students were generally disgusted with Bell's idea and nothing came of it except the name "Tigertail Road" in honor of the Oxy Tigers. His real estate, on both sides of the present freeway, sold well. Like Brentwood Park, it was bought by the upper-middle to upper-upper classes. By and large, the former class hired the better architects.

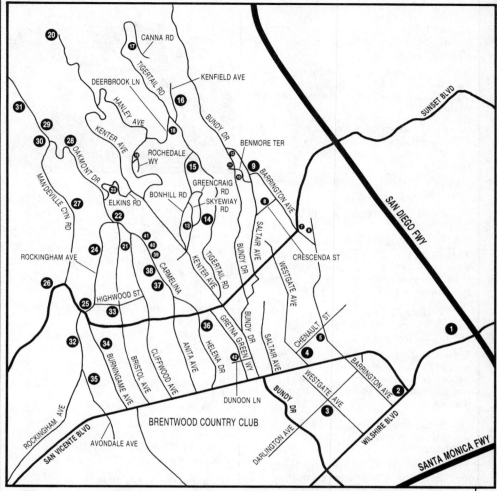

The new art complex for the **J. Paul Getty Museum** is to be situated on the hills just northwest of the junction of Sunset Boulevard and the San Diego Freeway. From a short list composed of Richard Meir, James Stirling, and Fumihiko Maki, the Museum has selected Meir to design the building. One can only hope that this conservative choice will lead to a major Southland building, both in its approach to function, and to the aesthetics of a wonderful site.

1. Sawtelle Veterans Hospital

Technically, this is not in Brentwood, but it is so near that it makes a good starting point. It was founded in the 1880s—one of the first veterans hospitals opened after the Civil War. The old buildings, called *Domiciliaries,* which have been destroyed over the last ten years, were excellent examples of Shingle style resort architecture. Little remains of the old hospital. The picturesque wooden **Chapel** (1900) is easily seen from Wilshire. Its architect, J. Lee Burton, mixed the Colonial Revival with Gothicism. The same architect designed a tiny Street-car Station (ca. 1900) at the corner of Dewey and Pershing, north of the chapel. The station, all arches and posts, is not really Eastlake, but the feeling is.

2. World Savings Center Building, 1982
Maxwell Starkman and Associates
Northwest corner of Wilshire and San
Vicente boulevards

A tall, late example of Corporate International Style Modern of no great distinction, but it is so big that you will wonder about it.

3. Four Apartment Units, 1966
J. R. Davidson
955 Westgate Avenue at Darlington
Avenue

Naturally-stained, diagonal flush boards mark this assemblage.

4. Abell Office Building, 1954
T. M. Abell
654 S. Saltair Avenue

This building, though visible, makes its statement from the interior court rather than the street facade. Offices and drafting rooms open into a garden.

5. Shairer House, 1949
Ain, Johnson, and Day
11750 Chenault Street

Very Neutraesque, though, as we have noted, the members of the Los Angeles School constantly exchanged ideas, making the subject of influences often beside the point.

6. Shopping Center, ca. 1935
Barrington Avenue and Sunset
Boulevard

Mainly Spanish Colonial Revival and dominated by a huge service station with tower. Many a Pierce-Arrow tanked up here on the way to the Hollywood studios.

7. Eastern Star Home, 1931-33
William Mooser and Company
11725 Sunset Boulevard

You can see a little of the Santa Barbara Courthouse here but it lacks the finesse of its northern relative. The huge concrete corbels are grained and painted to resemble wood.

7. Eastern Star Home

8. Goss House, 1950
Milton H. Caughey
11731 Crescenda Street

Understated vertical board and batten with the ends of the roof beams projecting.

9. House, ca. 1928
Northeast corner of Saltair and Barrington avenues

Obviously a work of one of the better architects, this Spanish Revival house dominates its neighborhood.

10. Evans House, 1936
Lloyd Wright
12036 Benmore Terrace

Big but less ornamented than most of Wright's work, this house can be seen from 554 N. Bundy Drive below and from its entrance on Benmore.

11. Samuel House, 1934
Lloyd Wright
579 N. Bundy Drive

The Bundy facade is saved from austerity by lush foliage. Strangely the eaves at the side which are carried into a sort of trellis do not hold vines.

12. Leslie House, 1950
T. M. Abell
525 N. Saltair Avenue

As usual, the garage is the street facade, and the International Style Modern house is set below street level.

13. ▪Sturges House, 1939
Frank Lloyd Wright
449 Skyewiay Road

Cantilevered from the hill, this house seems windowless from the street side although all the major rooms open through glass doors to the balcony deck. It is, of course, one of Wright's monuments.

14. House, 1973-74
Lomax-Mills Associates
548 Greencraig Road

The stucco volume has been dramatically cut into by deep, rectangular openings.

15. Herman House, 1948
Carl Louis Maston
650 Bonhill Road

A good International Style Modern house.

16. Bernheim House, 1961
Raymond Kappe
1000 Kenfield Avenue

A fine essay in fragile wood and glass.

17. Gould House, 1969
Raymond Kappe
12256 Canna Road

Again, glass and wood prevail in this house with stylistic affinities to Schindler's Wolfe House on Santa Catalina Island.

18. Shoor House, 1952
William S. Beckett
12336 Deerbrook Lane

Trim International Style Modern.

19. Mutual Housing Association Community, 1947-50
Whitney Smith, A. Quincy Jones, and Edgardo Contini; James Charlton, Wayne R. Williams and Associates, and Garrett Eckbo, landscape architects.
Hanley Avenue at Rochedale Way

The community comprises a number of houses, some now remodelled. We picked out 717, 727, 738, and 743 Hanley Avenue and 12404, 12408, 12414, and 12428 Rochedale Way as exemplary and visible. There are others on Broom Way and Bramble Way. The community remains a remarkable social, planning, and architectural development by three of Los Angeles's most important architectural figures. The informal siting and the woodsy detail suggest the Bay tradition plus Frank Lloyd Wright.

20. ▪Rodes House, 1978-79
Moore, Ruble, and Yudell
1406 N. Kenter Avenue, north end of pavement.

Moore says that this stucco box was based on ideas the architects had in their minds of "modernized eighteenth century houses in the south of France," i.e., Moore's version of the Hollywood Regency. It has a two-story convex facade that acts as a stage set for the owner's amateur theatrical productions.

21. Epstein House, 1949
Craig Ellwood
401 N. Cliffwood Avenue

A redwood facade by an architect who was soon to turn to glass, steel, and brick.

22. House, ca. 1972
Northwest corner of Rockingham and Bristol avenues

A house with huge wooden shafts pointing skyward. It must be very dramatic inside.

23. Rich House, 1968
T. M. Abell
689 Elkins Road

Unfenestrated stucco walls, broken only by a simple door. Pure architecture.

24. Avery House, 1934-37
Lloyd Wright
365 N. Rockingham Avenue

A pyramid!

25. ▪Temple House, 1935-36
John Byers (with Edla Muir); Benjamin Morton Purdy, landscape architect
231 N. Rockingham Avenue

This mixture of English and Norman farmhouse is a real delight. There is a fair view of it from the entrance gate and a view of an amusing fragment from Sunset Boulevard below.

26. Cliff May Office, 1952-53
Cliff May
Northeast corner of Sunset Boulevard
and Riviera Ranch Road

Tucked around the corner from Sunset
Boulevard, this wood panel house is very
uncharacteristic of May's work. Truth is,
like the firm of Buff, Straub, and Hensman, May likes to set his houses in
dense foliage or just around a hill.
There are many houses so situated in
the Brentwood and Bel Air districts. Actually the houses on Riviera Ranch and
Old Oak are all, with one exception, by
May. Through the foliage you can see
adobe and vertical board and batten
houses by this master of the ranch house
idiom. The **May House "Mandalay"** is
at 220 Old Ranch Road, but it is behind a gate and so deep in foliage that
you cannot possibly see the main house.
You can, though, see the gatehouse.

27. Rex House #1, 1949
Edla Muir; Edward Huntsman-Trout,
landscape architect
1888 Mandeville Canyon Road

The feeling is Craftsman through the
Bay tradition. The motor court is especially handsome.

Rex House #2, 1955
John Rex
1900 Mandeville Canyon Road

Orientalism seen through the eye of an
International Style Modern architect.

28. ■Rosen House, 1962
Craig Ellwood Associates
910 Oakmont Drive

This was new when our first architecture
guide was written. We put a picture of it
on the cover. Now the foliage has grown
up, mostly obscuring the building. You
can still catch a glimpse from the road
before you reach the gate.

29. Sperry House, 1953
Wurster, Bernardi, and Emmons
2090 Mandeville Canyon Road

A rational, post and beam house, rather
L.A. in spirit though by a Bay Area
firm.

29. Sperry House

30. Siple House, 1949-59
Allen Siple
2669 Mandeville Canyon Road

This dressed-stone house, obviously a
labor of love, was constructed by the architect and his wife — aided by
neighbors.

31. Seidel House, 1960
Pierre Koenig
2727 Mandeville Canyon Road

Two small Miesian pavilions, delicately
articulated, compose this Case Study
House.

32. Johnson House, 1919
Harry Johnson assisted by John Byers;
Edward Huntsman-Trout, landscape
architect
201 S. Rockingham Road

Byers, Harry Johnson's cousin, employed
Mexican laborers to make the adobe
bricks for the walls of this Spanish
Colonial Revival house. It was landscaped with native plants which have all
but obscured the view.

33. Siskin House, 1966
T. M. Abell
12822 Highwood Street

Set far back from one of the original
Brentwood circles, this International
Style house contrasts with its wooded
environment.

34. Newfield House, 1961
T. M. Abell
250 S. Burlingame Avenue

Buff-colored, Roman-laid brick. We thought that the art of the mason was fast disappearing, but here it is in wonderful shape.

35. Nesbitt House, 1942
Richard J. Neutra
414 Avondale Avenue

The Nesbitt House marks an early excursion by Neutra into warm, non-machine materials: wood and brick. Unfortunately for the architecture buff, few of its features can be seen from the street.

35. Nesbitt House

Carmelina Avenue.
There is a series of fascinating houses on Carmelina Avenue just below its intersection with Anita, and continuing south to San Vicente Boulevard. The best have been selected for listing here.

36. Boland House, ca. 1925
John Byers (with Edla Muir)
12322-23 Helena Drive

One of Byers's picturesque Spanish Colonial adventures!

37. ■Hamilton House, 1931-33
John Byers (with Edla Muir)
193 N. Carmelina Avenue

Monterey Revival.

38. Stedman House, 1935-36
John Byers (with Edla Muir)
363 N. Carmelina Avenue

A path leads from a typical Byers gate through carefully clipped boxwood hedges to the Colonial Revival front door.

39. Zimmerman House, 1950
Craig Ellwood
400 N. Carmelina Avenue

An interruption in the Byers boutique. A stark brick wall faces the street—the beginning of an L-shaped house which immediately breaks into glass and steel.

40. Kerr House, 1930
John Byers (with Edla Muir)
428 N. Carmelina Avenue

A very different version of the Monterey Revival when compared with the Hamilton House.

40. Kerr House

41. Murray House, ca. 1935
John Byers (with Edla Muir)
436 N. Carmelina Avenue

Colonial Revival.

42. Drucker Apartments, 1940
J. R. Davidson
Northwest corner of Gretna Green Way and Dunoon Lane

A curious blending of Schindler and Gill, though the greatest influence was the International Style Modern.

Bel Air

This hilly area above UCLA was developed by Alphonzo Bell in the teens and obviously sold well in the twenties. It is the last word in respectability, having its own security patrol years before other highbrow enclaves felt the need. It is a gorgeously landscaped area. The entrance to Bel Air is through imposing gates at Bel Air, Stone Canyon, or Bellagio roads. Much of the planning during the twenties was by architect Mark Daniels (Elmer Grey Associate), who also designed the **Administration Building** (ca. 1928) on Stone Canyon Road just north of the intersection with Bellagio. It is a handsome building of white walls and red tile roofs whose plan focuses on two patios.

The large and small estates exude wealth not by the imposing facades (most of which you cannot see) but by beautifully trimmed plantings literally inundating the sumptuous dwellings. Foliage hides residences by George Washington Smith (his only one in West Los Angeles), Gordon B. Kaufmann, Wallace Neff, Roy Selden Price, Palmer Sabin, Douglas Honnold, George Vernon Russell, Paul R. Williams, and Paul Laszlo. The following list only hints at what is hidden away.

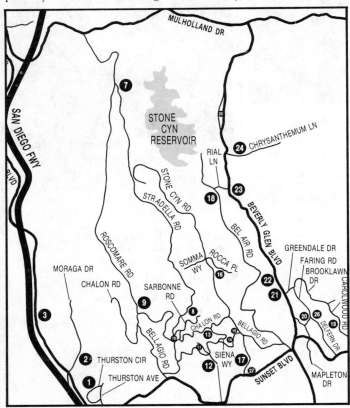

Stone Canyon Administration Building

1. Nordlinger House, 1948
A. Quincy Jones
11492 Thurston Circle

Very much under the influence of Frank
Lloyd Wright.

2. Winans Apartments (now Bel Air Gardens), 1948
A. Quincy Jones
850 Moraga Drive

The jutting roofs are very dramatic.

3. Leo Baeck Temple, 1962
Victor Gruen Associates
1300 N. Sepulveda Boulevard

A series of apparently thick walls of
varying shapes and a great hood of a
roof enclose the space of the sanctuary.
It all reads well, especially from the San
Diego Freeway.

4. Mirman School, 1972-3
Brent, Goldman, Robbins, and Brown
16180 Mulholland Drive (west of San
Diego Freeway, just beyond Mulholland
Place)

A good-looking group of stucco buildings obviously influenced by Charles
Moore—a good influence.

5. Steven S. Wise Temple, Chapel and School Facilities, 1975
Sidney Eisenstadt
North corner of Mulholland Drive and
Casiano Road (east of San Diego
Freeway)

Very impressive Expressionism with
great, leaning roofs.

6. Singleton House, 1959
Richard J. Neutra
15000 Mulholland Drive (east of Woodcliff Road)

Completely private, almost impossible to
see that it's there.

7. Rabinowitz House, 1960
J. R. Davidson
2262 Stradella Road

What a pleasure to actually be able to
see an International Style Modern house
by this architect.

8. Chappellett House, ca. 1925
H. Roy Kelley
848 Stradella Road

A beautiful Monterey Revival dwelling
in a style of which Kelley was a master.

8. Chappellett House

9. Beck House, 1955
T. M. Abell
952 Roscomare Road

With flush, horizontal wood boards, this
house still looks brand new.

10. Brown House, 1955
Richard J. Neutra; Dion Neutra
10801 Chalon Road

A steep hillside house of stucco and redwood, just barely visible from the road.

11. Anderson House, 1951
Honnold and Rex
621 Perugia Way

International Style Modern with Las
Vegas stone base.

9. Beck House

12. Healy House, 1949-52
Lloyd Wright
565 Perugia Way

The Usonian House updated as a California Ranch house with a little Orientalism added.

13. Norcross House, 1927
Roland E. Coate
673 Siena Way

Monterey Revival dwelling.

14. Japanese Garden, 1961
Nagao Sakurai, designer, assisted by Dudley Fridgett; Kazuo Nakamura, construction
Bellagio Road, west of intersection with Stone Canyon Road

The original garden was designed and laid out by A. E. Hanson for Harry Calandar in 1923. At that time it was picturesque Spanish, not Japanese. It was transformed into a Japanese garden in 1961. This beautiful hillside was given to UCLA in 1965. It may be visited 10-1 Tuesday and 12-3 Wednesday, by calling the UCLA Visitors Center.

15. Miller House, 1932
Wallace Neff
10615 Bellagio Road

An enlarged, two-story English cottage with some inklings of Charles F. A. Voysey's turn-of-the-century work in England.

16. Nilsson House, 1977
Eugene Kupper
10549 Rocca Place (can be seen only from end of Somma Way)

An elongated, two-story, skylighted spine serves as the core of this dwelling. Although the spaces and their relation to one another are complex, the general atmosphere of the house is Classical and Mediterranean. The garden, walls, and terraces beautifully integrate the house to its hillside site.

17. Curtis-Noyes House, 1950
Raphael S. Soriano
111 Stone Canyon Road

One of Soriano's largest commissions. About all that can be seen are the grid motif garages.

18. Case Study House #16, 1951
Craig Ellwood
1811 Bel Air Road

A steel-frame Miesian exercise based upon eight-foot modules. The infills are of Palos Verdes stone, wood siding, and glass.

19. Gordon B. Kaufmann House, ca. 1929
Gordon B. Kaufmann; Florence Yoch, landscape architect
245 Carolwood Drive

Mediterranean (Italian) style with Spanish Colonial aspects, this is much warmer than most of Kaufmann's houses. The house is close to the street and beautifully landscaped. Just below at 230 Carolwood Drive is the **Lohman House** (1925), also by Kaufmann, in a version of the Tudor style. Again, the landscaping is by Yoch.

20. Colbert House, 1935
Lloyd Wright
615 N. Faring Road

Here Lloyd Wright brings together the Moderne and the Colonial Revival.

21. Broughton House, 1950
Craig Ellwood
909 N. Beverly Glen Boulevard

Modular design, midway between traditional post-and-beam and the insistent Miesian steel beam.

22. Bernatti House, 1947
Rodney Walker
1025 N. Beverly Glen Boulevard

A simple, frame structure. You can see the garage best.

23. Lohrie House, 1940
Rodney Walker
1648 Beverly Glen Boulevard

The traditional California Ranch house emerging as a Moderne product with corner windows, sliding glass doors, and extending and overlapping horizontal planes.

24. Johnson House, 1949
Harwell H. Harris
10280 Chrysanthemum Lane

Here Harris simplifies and opens up the woodsy style of Charles and Henry Greene to terraces and gardens.

25. Sommer House, 1941
Rodney Walker
2252 Beverly Glen Place

Related to the 1930s San Francisco Bay tradition designs of William W. Wurster, Gardner Dailey, and others.

26. Singleton House, 1973
Wallace Neff
384 Delfern Drive, corner of Faring Road

A French Norman house.

27. House, ca. 1926
Northeast corner of Sunset Boulevard and Stone Canyon Road

A splended Moorish/Spanish house with an abundance of colorful tilework and an impressive, cusped arch loggia looking to the south. The garden, with its terraces, fountains, and water course is Moorish as well. From time to time in its existence, this house has been highly visible from Sunset Boulevard, on other occasions little could be seen. At the moment, it is as visible as it has ever been.

25. Sommer House

27. House

Westwood, West

Westwood was planned and developed by the Janss Investment Company during the early 1920s. By the end of the decade the area was composed of single-family residences with streets laid out in part to conform to the irregular pattern of the hilly terrain. In the center was the new UCLA campus, and to the south around Wilshire and Westwood boulevards was Westwood Village. Many upper-middle class, single-family houses utilized one or another of the historic images—Spanish Colonial Revival, Mediterranean, Monterey Revival, English and Norman Medieval, the Colonial, and Regency. Since the late 1940s a smattering of Modern (of one variety or another) housing has been built. Highly respectable multiple housing developed around the Village, along Wilshire Boulevard, and to the east of the UCLA campus (around Landfair Avenue and Strathmore Drive). The quality of these historic-styled houses and apartments is remarkably high and the buildings, coupled with the quality of the landscaping, make this section one of the most pleasant in L.A.

Before the advent of high-rises around **Westwood Village,** it was one of

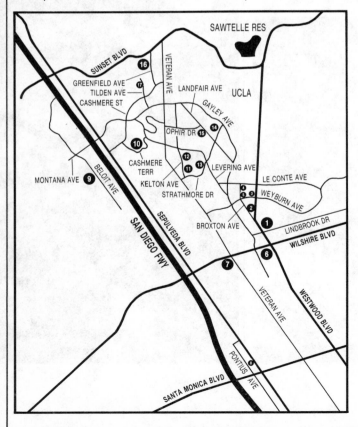

Southern California's most successful regional suburban shopping centers. It was laid out in 1928 by the planner Harland Bartholomew and an art jury was initiated to guide its architectural development. The style selected was loosely Spanish, and it all worked well through the 1940s. Later remodellings, modernizations, and replacements have somewhat destroyed its character. Probably the greatest losses have been the several Spanish Colonial Revival service stations with their high towers with illuminated signs. Currently there is the hint of a nostalgic urge to return Westwood to its original Spanish styling. Perhaps this urge can restore some of the visual unity which used to characterize the area.

1. Ralph's Grocery Store Building
(now a restaurant), 1929
Russell Collins
1150 Westwood Boulevard

Colonnades, extending along the two streets, culminate in a low, corner round tower, into which has been placed an impressive, pedimented entrance. The entablature of the tower has a band of corbelled arches, and a small lantern tops the conical roof of the tower. The walls were built in imitation of stone, but they have now been stuccoed over. In style the building is Spanish, both Romanesque and Renaissance.

2. "The Dome" Offices of the Janss Investment Company (now Glendale Federal Savings Association Building), 1929
Allison and Allison
Northwest corner of Westwood Boulevard and Broxton Avenue

This domed, octagonal building still remains as the dominant structure within the Village itself. Though on the dry side, the dome with its Islamic zigzag pattern of brightly colored glazed tile retrieves it all. The new lantern on top of the dome does not help the composition.

3. Holmby Hall, 1929
Gordon B. Kaufmann; John and Donald Parkinson
West side of Westwood Boulevard be-

tween Weyburn and LeConte avenues

A Spanish Colonial Revival streetscape of six stores. The corner building at Weyburn Avenue once had a pinnacled tower with four clock faces.

4. Bruin Theatre, 1937
S. Charles Lee
925 Broxton Avenue

A thirties Moderne theatre whose semi-circular facade above the marquee was used as the lighted sign to advertise the theatre.

5. Fox Westwood Village Theatre, 1931
P. O. Lewis
961 Broxton Avenue

Like "The Dome," the Fox Theatre and its tower turn the axis of Broxton Avenue toward the northeast. The theatre is essentially Spanish Colonial Revival with a touch of Moderne. The shaft of the tower rises to support projecting single columns and entablatures. On top a Fox sign is surrounded by Art Deco (Zigzag) Moderne patterns in metal.

5. Fox Westwood Village Theatre

6. Wilshire West Plaza, 1971
Charles Luckman Associates
10880 Wilshire Boulevard

Perhaps adequate as an urban high-rise complex, it is devastating in what it and the other high-rises around have done to destroy the scale of Westwood Village.

7. U.S. Federal Office Building, 1970
Charles Luckman Associates
11000 Wilshire Boulevard

An immense file cabinet which one can't miss. As depressing a comment on architecture as upon the bureaucracy of our society.

8. Siskin Companies Office Building, 1972
Thornton M. Abell
1617 S. Pontius Avenue

A modest, very-well-handled, late version of the *Arts and Architecture* aesthetic.

9. Plywood Model Experimental House, 1936
Richard J. Neutra
427 S. Beloit Avenue

This plywood panel house was designed so that it could easily be transported— and so far it has been moved twice. In the late thirties plywood was just coming into its own. The material conveyed modernity and the image of the machine. Nuetra's use of it here fulfills these ideals.

10. Buki House, 1941
J. R. Davidson
11149 Cashmere Terrace

Davidson, operating within the stripped-down Regency mode which was popular in the Los Angeles region before the Second World War.

11. Kelton Apartments, 1942
Richard J. Neutra
646-648 Kelton Avenue

Five apartments are grouped into two buildings. Each apartment is provided with its own outdoor terrace. The fenestration of the building is less insistently International Style Modern than one experiences in Neutra's earlier (1938) nearby Landfair Apartments.

12. Elkay Apartments, 1948
Richard J. Neutra
638-642 Kelton Avenue

A post-World War II extension of his earlier Kelton Apartments next door. The Elkay units are more woodsy and less committed to the image of the machine than the 1942 Kelton unit.

13. Strathmore Apartments, 1937
Richard J. Neutra
11005 W. Strathmore Drive

In these apartments Neutra updated the Bungalow Court providing it with a new image (the Modern), more light and air, and more extensive greenery. These four buildings contain eight apartments which, in part, face out onto the central garden and towards UCLA.

13. Strathmore Apartments

14. Sheets (L'Horizon) Apartments, 1949
John Lautner
10901-10919 W. Strathmore Drive

An eight-unit apartment which suggests the futuristic Modern of the twenty-first century. Visually this building is as fresh today as when it was built. Functionally it is a beautiful solution for multiple housing, with each apartment completely separated from the others, and each with its own terraces, decks, and outdoor garden space—all indicative of Lautner's understanding of readable images and of the environment of L.A.

15. Landfair Apartments, 1937
Richard J. Neutra
Southwest corner of Landfair Avenue and Ophir Drive

The Landfair Apartments are one of Neutra's most European International Style Modern designs of the decade of the thirties. This impressive exercise with its roof terrace is composed of patterned surfaces of stucco, metal, and glass bands.

16. ▪Tischler House, 1949
R. M. Schindler
175 Greenfield Avenue

Schindler set a 3-D de Stijl composition as a frontispiece for a stucco, gable-roofed volume. The roof of the house was originally made of corrugated fiberglass, which was to have been shaded by parallel rows of eucalyptus planted along each side of the house.

17. Galli Curci House, 1938
Wallace Neff; Florence Yoch and Lucile Council, landscape architects
201 Tilden Avenue

Neff took the theme of the informal rambling Andalusian farmhouse and produced a stunning composition of white stucco volumes terminated by a tile roof. The result, accompanied by one of his tall, picturesque chimneys, illustrates the vigor of the Hispanic tradition in the late 1930s.

17. Galli Curci House

Westwood, South and East

1. Kaufmann House, 1937
Richard J. Neutra
234 S. Hilgard Avenue

A beautiful example of Neutra's version of the International Style Modern. In this case the building works not only as a symbol of the machine but also as an excellent "machine for living." The house takes advantage of its site with the principal public spaces opening towards the garden, away from the street. The bedrooms on the second floor have glass doors leading onto a roof deck. Glass brick, stainless steel, and interior mirrors add a Moderne note.

2. Saint Alban's Episcopal Church, 1940 and later
Northeast corner of South Hilgard and Westholme avenues

This late 1930s chapel illustrates how stong and vigorous traditional imagery was in this decade—in this case Romanesque (both Italian and French) in brick, rough mortar, and stone trim. The post-1945 parts of the building do not convey any of the strength of the original.

3. Doheny Memorial Dormitory for Girls (now YWCA), 1931
Stanton, Reed, and Hibbard
794 Hilgard Avenue

If only the smaller buildings on the UCLA campus could have followed the Monterey tradition expressed in this building. The building is well sited on its hillside lot, and the landscaping works

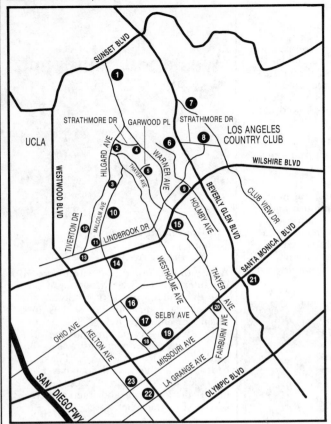

with the irregular form of the building to create its own world away from the very busy street.

4. Van Cleff House, 1942
Richard J. Neutra
651 Warner Avenue

All of the hallmarks of Neutra's Modern image are present in this single-story dwelling, though the roof form and the wood detailing help it to fit in with its neighbors.

5. Greenberg House, 1949
Richard J. Neutra
10525 Garwood Place

During the late 1940s Neutra designed several houses with low-pitched shed roofs, with walls of stucco and redwood. The Greenberg House exhibits these elements on its hillside site.

6. Dean McHenry House, 1940
Harwell H. Harris
624 Holmby Avenue

A two-story stucco dwelling hidden within a walled enclosure which provides privacy from the street and creates small enclosed garden spaces within. As with many of Harris's dwellings where the garden and the house are really one, we are asked visually to read the dwelling as a series of separate fragments (as with a traditional Japanese house).

7. Mudd House, 1969
Roland E. Coate, Jr.
420 Club View Drive

A formal (almost public in scale) wood-sheathed group of pavilions set within a concrete wall and base—a base which has Le Corbusian overtones. The interior spaces and the way in which they extend themselves to the out-of-doors is decidedly axial and Beaux Arts.

8. Maslon House, 1970
Thornton M. Abell
10345 Strathmore Drive

A U-shaped stucco volume faces toward the street. To the rear and sides the interior opens out through glass walls and doors to various terraces and gardens. The atmosphere, though Modern in image, is in fact quite classical.

9. Westwood-Ambassador Apartments, 1940
Milton J. Black
10427 Wilshire Boulevard

A textbook image of the Streamline Moderne before the Second World War, this two- and three-story U-shaped stucco apartment building has horizontal groupings of windows going around the corners, along with curved bays and terrace walls. This architect designed many of Los Angeles's Streamline Moderne apartment buildings of the 1930s.

10. House, ca. 1929
862 Malcolm Avenue

The avenues (not, it should be noted, streets) of Westwood curve in and out of the low hills both east and west of the UCLA campus. They are filled with excellent, well-designed, historic imagery houses of the 1920s and 1930s, all beautifully taken care of, including their grounds. In the twenties the preference was for Spanish/Mediterranean, English Tudor, and French Norman; in the thirties it was the Monterey and then the Anglo-Colonial Revival. All of these are present within the eastern section of the Westwood district. These houses illustrate how well the architects of that time could work with traditional images (in this case English Tudor) and at the same time produce a functional house for an upper-middle-class family.

11. Garden Apartment Building, ca. 1936
1001-09 Malcolm Avenue

Streamline Moderne with the prerequisite round corners accompanied, of course, by glass brick.

12. Monterey Garden Apartment Building, ca. 1930
James N. Conway
10840 Hilgard Avenue

A two-story garden apartment in the Monterey Style, built around a central court. Another **garden apartment building** is located at 10830 Hilgard Avenue. This one is mildly Spanish Colonial Revival (also ca. 1930). South of Wilshire Boulevard at the northeast corner of Westwood Boulevard and Wilkins Avenue is a combined **garden apartment and retail shop** building, designed in the Colonial Revival style (ca. 1931; J. E. Dolena).

13. El Greco Apartment Building, 1929
Pierpont and Walter S. Davis
1028 Tiverton Drive

A brick walkway leads from the street through an arched opening into a central courtyard furnished with plants, potted plants, and a central pool. A projecting, wooden, second-story balcony overlooks the courtyard of this Andalusian composition.

14. Branch Office Building, Perpetual Savings Association, 1962
Edward D. Stone and Associates
Southeast corner of Wilshire Boulevard and Malcolm Avenue

A small, circular, glass pavilion whose domed roof is supported by mushroom-like columns. Here one can see Stone at his elegant best. The nearby high-rises somewhat smother Stone's small structure. It worked best when this section of Wilshire Boulevard contained only one- and two-story buildings.

15. Ten Five Sixty Wilshire Boulevard, 1980-82
Maxwell Starkman and Associates
10560 Wilshire Boulevard

Wilshire Boulevard between the Los Angeles Country Club to the east and the San Diego Freeway to the west has, since the early 1960s, developed as a high-rise, double-wall corridor of expensive condominium apartment buildings and office towers. It looks great from the air, but its effect on the nearby single-family houses and on Westwood Village itself is devastating. None of the tall apartment buildings or the office towers are outstanding in design, but several of them are so visually aggressive that it is difficult to ignore them. A case in point is this 108-unit, twenty-two-story apartment building. This eight-cornered tower with its crowd of curved balconies does succeed in conveying a sense of transient luxury.

16. Church of Saint Paul the Apostle, 1930-31
Newton and Murray
Southeast corner of Ohio and Selby avenues

A classically reserved design, which the architects say they based on late eighteenth century Spanish architecture. As with so many of Los Angeles's churches of the late 1920s and early 1930s, it is constructed of reinforced concrete with the exposed surfaces (inside and out) revealing the wood pattern of the forms.

17. Ralph Waldo Emerson Junior High School Building, 1937
Richard J. Neutra
1650 Selby Avenue

This is a project which one should walk around and through to obtain an idea of what was going on in the thirties in school design in California and how Neutra responded to the California tradition of the open-air school. Though Neutra's image is out-and-out International Style Modern, the plan of the building and of the site is really quite traditional (especially for California). Behind the two-story section of the complex are classrooms which open out to their own individual out-of-doors gardens through sliding glass doors.

18. Moore/Rogger/Hofflander Condominium Building, 1969-75
Charles W. Moore and Richard Chylinski
1725 Selby Avenue

A version of a Spanish Colonial Revival auto court. A ground-level fountain provides the entry theme of this remarkable building. From the street one sees a cascading roof to the north interrupted by stepped dormers. To the south one can see a curved grouping of windows (forming a pattern like partial spokes of a wheel) that ends in another roof dormer. It is close to impossible to know what is going on inside, which is part of the romance of this design. In fact, it is difficult to know that there are three units in this building. Each of the units faces out to the west, away from the street, and each has walled terraces and balconies.

18. *Moore/Rogger/Hofflander Condominium Building*

19. Church of Jesus Christ of Latter-day Saints (Mormon) Temple, 1955
Edward O. Anderson
10741 Santa Monica Boulevard

Described by one high art observer as "Cocktail Lounge Modern," but on a scale which would put any Sunset Boulevard lounge to shame. The design, in fact, could best be described as modernized Classical. A gold-leaf statue of the angel Moroni graces the summit of the building. As is traditional in the best of L.A.'s public and semi-public buildings, the hilltop site of the Mormon Temple is beautifully landscaped with a precisely manicured lawn and low shrubs. The building and its site form a completely unified composition. As is frequently the case, the Temple is best seen from the San Diego Freeway.

19. Church of Jesus Christ of Latter-day Saints (Mormon) Temple

20. Psychoanalytic Building, 1968-69
Charles W. Moore and William Turnbull
1800 Fairburn Avenue

Driving along Little Santa Monica Boulevard one can easily miss this gem, for its stucco volumes set behind the trees appear right at home in Los Angeles. A complex stage-set gateway composed of a single plane of stucco wall leads into an interior courtyard. Double walls make one wonder what is building and what is the screen.

20. Psychoanalytic Building

21. The Barn, 1965
A. Quincy Jones
10300 Santa Monica Boulevard

Quincy Jones's two-and-a-half story "Barn" served as a place of work, of entertaining, and of living. It is a remodelled structure, though you would not know it once you were inside and able to experience the wonderful central space of the building. As with the best of Quincy Jones's work, it is not openly assertive. But its sense of proportions and detailing make it wear very well.

22. Westwood Hills Congregational Church, 1928
Northwest corner of Westwood Boulevard and LaGrange Avenue

A small Spanish Colonial Revival church coupled with some suggestions in detailing of the Art Deco (Zigzag) Moderne.

23. Kelton-Missouri Townhouses, 1980
Mutlow-Dimster Partnership
10925 Missouri Avenue

The basic forms of this building look back to the Dutch and German International Style Modern housing of the 1920s. But there are other features, such as the stepped window patterns and the greenhouse elements, which are pure late 1970s and early 1980s.

UCLA

The University of California at Los Angeles was established as a State Normal School in 1881 (on a five-acre site in downtown L.A., where the public library is now situated). In 1919 it became a two-year

southern campus of UC, and in 1924 it became a four-year school and was named UCLA. The institution's second location—a site at Vermont and Heliotrope avenues—was felt to be far too small for the projected major institution. In 1925 the site in Westwood was selected, and the cities of Los Angeles, Beverly Hills, Santa Monica, and Venice voted bonds to purchase the land. The new campus then became an element within the Janss Corporation development of Westwood. It was to be surrounded by single-family residences (with some multiple housing) on the east, north, and west sides and was to adjoin the commercial district of Westwood Village to the south.

The Los Angeles architect George W. Kelham was engaged to prepare a master plan for the campus. In 1925 Kelham presented his plan, a classic cross-axial Beaux Arts scheme. The main axis ran east/west from Hilgard to Westwood

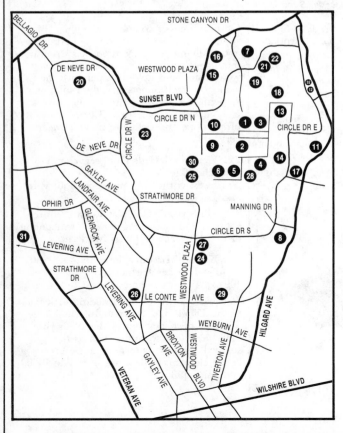

Boulevard. The hilly, irregular site provided the drama of terraces and steps leading down the west side of the hill to Westwood Boulevard. To the east a small *arroyo* created a contrasting English Romantic garden element, and over this Kelham placed a bridge. A circle on Westwood Boulevard created the major north/south axis. The architect's plan called for forty buildings, and he and the Regents "chose red brick Romanesque architecture of Milan and Genoa because Westwood's rolling hills and gentle climate were reminiscent of northern Italy." The selection of Northern Italian Romanesque for the Westwood campus was not, as the quote would seem to imply, based upon a careful look into appropriate styles. Italian Romanesque in brick was a fashionable style for educational buildings in California during the teens and twenties. Also, it was the style which had been used in the teens by Allison and Allison for the Vermont Avenue campus of the University ("executed in a style of architecture inspired from the Lombard Romanesque of northern Italy"). By 1931 ten buildings (plus the bridge) had been completed at the Westwood campus.

During the Depression years of the 1930s, only a few buildings were built. Kelham remained as supervising architect until 1935 when he was replaced by Allison and Allison (David C. Allison). After World War II David C. Allison and landscape architect Ralph D. Cornell prepared a revision of the Kelham plan. Retaining the essential ingredients of his plan, they still argued for low-rise buildings. They did, though, suggest the filling-in of the *arroyo* (in 1947, which in part now includes Dickson court and plaza) so as to obtain additional building sites. Their most far-reaching recommendation was to locate the Health Science (Medical School) on the Westwood campus, rather than to separate it as UC Berkeley had done by putting it in San Francisco. This decision, plus the ideal of having a 25,000-plus student campus, eventually led to immense buildings and the commitment to moderate high-rise.

In 1948 the firm of Wurdeman and Becket was appointed as supervising architects (the title was changed to *consulting architects*). After the death of Wilton Wurdeman, Welton Becket and Associates continued as consulting architects through 1968.

It was during the immediate post-World War II years that the decision was made to abandon the commitment to the historicism of the Northern Italian Romanesque and to embrace the "Modern." At first the Modern was approached gingerly through the style of Eliel Saarinen as you can see in such buildings as the first Dickson Art Building (now the School of Architecture and Urban Planning, 1952, Paul Robinson Hunter). Later, variations of the fifties Corporate International Style Modern were utilized. Today it is very difficult to discover anything positive to say about the UCLA campus. The pile-up of buildings comprising the Court of Sciences and the Medical Center is as depressing a grouping as you can experience. To the west on the hillside above the athletic field is a group of four high-rise dormitories (1959-64, by Welton Becket and Associates) which mars this side of the campus and adjacent residential district north of Sunset Boulevard.

The one saving grace of the campus is the landscaping, which is really outstanding. In 1937 the landscape architect Ralph D. Cornell was appointed. He and his firm continued to develop the wonderful imported vegetation of the place until his death in 1972. Cornell's firm, Cornell, Bridgers, Troller, and Hazlett, has continued to work on campus landscaping since 1972, with Jere H. Hazlett as the official landscape architect. While all the landscaping efforts have not been able to hide the tragedies of unfortunate planning and buildings, they have been able to create, throughout the campus, pockets of space which are pleasant, highly visible, and in many instances, simply beautiful.

Since the mid-1970s there have been a few refreshing buildings, such as Frank O. Gehry and Associates' Student Placement and Career Planning Center (1976-77), and Daniel L. Dworsky and

Associates' UCLA Parking Structure (1979-80). Currently Royce Hall is undergoing what we hope will be a sympathetic renovation (1983; John Carl Warnecke and Associates). There is also a proposal to re-excavate the bridge under the axial roadway adjacent to Dickson Court and to build a partial underground building under the bridge. But there are also disappointments, such as the UCLA Faculty Housing (1982-83; Samuel Wacht), and the John Wooden Center (1982; Parkin Architects). We would have thought that UCLA by now, with its distinguished School of Architecture and Urban Planning, would be constantly encouraging designs of real merit, but such does not seem to be the case.

1. Royce Hall, 1928-29
Allison and Allison

One of the key buildings in the Lombard Romanesque style, freely transcribed from San Ambrosio in Milan. Here one can see Allison and Allison's concept of UCLA as a Lombardian hill-top town. The court between Royce Hall and the Library Building to the south, along with the terraces and stairs leading down to Westwood Boulevard (now closed off) illustrate how they combined the picturesqueness of an Italian city with Beaux Arts axial planning.

1. Royce Hall

2. The Library (now the College Library), 1928
George W. Kelham

Italian Romanesque, as with Royce Hall. The library contains one of the best interiors within the style.

3. Haines Hall, 1928
George W. Kelham

Undistinguished, functional Romanesque.

4. Physics-Biology Building, 1928-29
Allison and Allison

Pared-down Romanesque.

5. Moore Hall of Education, 1930
George W. Kelham

More pared-down Romanesque.

6. Kerck Hall, 1930
Allison and Allison

A lone Gothic building, designed in this style supposedly because of the donor's insistence.

7. University Residence (Chancellor's House), 1930
Reginald D. Johnson

A northern Italian villa, exhibiting Johnson's usual sophistication and reserve.

8. Mira Hershey Residence Hall, 1930
Douglas McLelland

Spanish Colonial Revival rather than the usual brick Italian Romanesque. This complex, with its courtyards, low scale, and planting, is one of the most successful buildings on the campus.

9. Men's Gymnasium, 1932
George W. Kelham

This building and the Women's Gymnasium to the south form the lower terrace grouping for Kelham's main axis.

10. Women's Gymnasium, 1932
Allison and Allison

Lukewarm, brick Italian Romanesque.

11. Administration Building, 1937
Allison and Allison

More mild Italian Romanesque.

12. University Guesthouse, 1952
Burnett C. Turner

A two-story, wood-sheathed dwelling, combining the image of the Modern and the California Ranch house. This building is scheduled to be removed for additional housing.

13. Dickson Art Building (now **School of Architecture and Urban Planning Building**), 1952.
Paul Robinson Hunter. The new library within the building was designed by Thomas Vreeland.

This building attempts to play the game of being twentieth-century Modern and classical at the same time. It works reasonably well to the south, but the rest tends to be bland, especially the original interiors.

14. Schoenberg Hall, 1955
Welton Becket and Associates

Schoenberg Hall is a much more successful example of modernized classicism (Moderne Regency).

15. University Elementary School, 1957-58
Neutra and Alexander

16. University Nursery-Kindergarten School, 1957-59
Neutra and Alexander

Set in a wooded site near Sunset Boulevard, these single-story buildings illustrate Neutra and Alexander's excellent approach to siting and to the indoor/outdoor planning of educational buildings.

17. Faculty Center, 1959
Hutchinson and Hutchinson

A woodsy California Ranch house. The interiors are pleasant, as are the gardens around the building, but it has none of the vigor of a Cliff May design.

18. Bunche Hall, 1964
Maynard Lyndon

The one and only distinguished high-rise on campus, even though the size of the structure and walk-through scale is poorly related to the adjacent older buildings. The reason for the tower's success has to do with the proportioning of the skin and its components, the relationship of the enclosed box to its base, and the manner in which it projects out of the heavy planting which surrounds the structure.

18. Bunche Hall

19. University Research Library, 1964 and 1967
Jones and Emmons

A modest, non-assertive building which is very pleasant to work in.

20. Sunset Canyon Recreation Facility, 1964
Smith and Williams

This building climbs up its steep hillside site to create an impression of an elaborate child's treehouse.

21. Dickson Art Center, 1965
William Pereira and Associates

The only elements of character in this Modern design are the raised terraces and the steps leading up to them.

22. Murphy Sculpture Court, 1969
Cornell, Bridgers, and Troller, landscape architect

Perhaps the landscaping will eventually block out the adjacent buildings so that this space will really have the sense of a court within which are placed freestanding sculptures. Major pieces are by Henry Moore, Jacques Lipschitz, Louis H. Sullivan, and many other important sculptors.

23. Track and Field Stadium, 1969
Daniel Dworsky Associates

This structure might have worked on a site three or four times this size, but what was needed here was an underground non-building.

24. Untitled Mural, 1970
Howard Warshaw

The one and only reason to visit the **Reed Neurological Research Center** is to see the Warshaw mural. In comparison to so much of the well-publicized public mural art of the late sixties and seventies, Warshaw's mural illustrates the real understanding needed to accommodate high art to architecture. And in this instance the art easily triumphs over the building.

25. James E. West Alumni Development Center, 1974-76
Caudill Rowlett

Formal, undistingished Modernism which is being hidden by trees and shrubs.

26. UCLA Extension Building, 1976
H. Jones

A highly intellectual, rather than spatial, design of hooked-together boxes.

27. Jerry Lewis Neuromuscular Research Center, 1976-79
Daniel Dworsky Associates

A two-story concrete and steel structure with a shed roof greenhouse and a terraced patio roof.

28. Student Placement and Career Planning Center, 1976-77
Frank O. Gehry and Associates

This small-scaled, long, low box is loosely post-International Style Modern. Gehry's delight in exposing the equipment and structure hearkens back on the one hand to the Smithsons and the English New Brutalists of the mid-1950s. The suggestion of a building as a machine also ties the design into Los Angeles's own version of the High Tech image of the late seventies and early eighties. All of this has been accomplished with a characteristic Gehry high art image. At the same time, the build-

ing is well snuggled into its landscaped site, and the interior spaces have a comfortable, easy-going scale.

28. Student Placement and Career Planning Center

29. UCLA Hospital Parking Structure, 1979-80
Daniel Dworsky and Associates

Certain parts of this reinforced concrete parking structure are of the pure Brutalist tingle—quite handsome, especially the top roof deck's layer effect. Other sections of the structure are, as John Dreyfuss of the *Los Angeles Times* noted, "tediously fortresslike."

30. John Wooden Center, 1983
Parkin Architects

A sports center which looks on the exterior like a Southern California supermarket or department store.

31. Le Conte-Levering Faculty Housing, 1982-83
Samuel Wacht Associates
Located off-campus at 827 Levering Avenue

Considering the many examples of distingished multiple housing around the UCLA campus, ranging from Spanish Colonial Revival bungalow garden courts to the later work of Neutra and Lautner, it strikes us as unfortunate that these new units could not have carried on that tradition. Instead, they have the appearance of inexpensive spec housing.

32. UCLA Guest House, 1982-83
Field and Silverman

A row of shed-roofed stucco boxes, not much different from similar attached spec units which one finds all over the Southland.

Beverly Hills, Upper

Beverly Hills, entirely surrounded by the city and county of Los Angeles, lies on the land known in the early nineteenth century as the Rancho Rodeo de las Aguas, the "gathering of waters" from present-day Benedict, Coldwater, and other canyons near the site of what is now the Beverly Hills Hotel. In the 1850s and 1860s, the Yankees, with Benjamin Wilson, Henry Hancock, William Workman, James Whitworth, and Edson A. Benedict in the lead, took over land development and speculation. Several attempts to found a city were made. A German colony was planned in the 1860s, the only remnant of which is Los Angeles Avenue, now Wilshire Boulevard. Until the 1880s the area's chief contribution to civilization was lima beans.

In the 1887 land boom the town of Morocco was platted, but with the economic collapse the next year the real estate promoters' dream fizzled. The founding finally occurred in 1907 when the Rodeo Land and Water Company, under the leadership of Burton E. Green, conceived of a city for the swells, very much the way Beverly Hills has developed. The landscape architect,

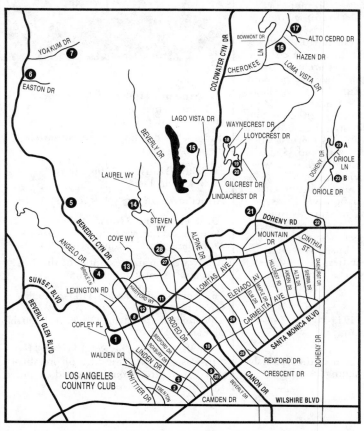

Wilbur Cook, planned the present business area with a grid running at forty-five degree angles north from Wilshire Boulevard. He laid out the gently curving streets between Santa Monica Boulevard and the hills to the north. In the hills north of Sunset Boulevard the landscape architects were the Olmsted Brothers, and they set out streets that undulated picturesquely off into the hills with equally undulating streets crossing them. The result of this plan is that driving, especially at the six-way intersection of Cañon Drive, Beverly Drive, and Lomitas Avenue, can be very interesting. In 1912 the extremely fashionable **Beverly Hills Hotel** was built on Sunset Boulevard just above this intersection, and fine houses, most of them on surprisingly small lots, were soon appearing all around. It is usually assumed that these houses were built by the motion-picture crowd, since so many stars live in them now. Actually, the first owners were usually lawyers, doctors, oil men, or wealthy retired people from the frigid zones.

It is remarkable how few of these houses, most of them in the varied styles of the 1920s, have strong architectural or landscape distinction. They are pleasant and highly visible, but not outstanding. It is only when you get into the radically-winding streets in the hills that you will discover distinguished buildings and gardens—some the Modernist work of Neutra, Schindler, Ain, and Harris, and an array of talented architects who employed period revival images.

The commercial section in the city below Santa Monica Boulevard was originally the strong mixture of Spanish Colonial Revival and Art Deco Moderne that you would expect. Some dazzlers still remain. But the business section has, since the mid-sixties, literally been transformed by high-rise. Some of it, particularly the most recent, has real artistic merit.

1. Helms House, 1933
Gordon B. Kaufmann
135 Copley Place

A highly correct version of the Spanish Colonial Revival dwelling.

2. Spadena House, 1921
Henry Oliver
Southeast corner of Carmelita Avenue and Walden Drive

Originally designed in Culver City as a movie set and office for Irvin V. Willst Productions, this masterpiece of the Hansel and Gretel mode was moved to a respectable neighborhood and set in an unconventional garden that matches it beautifully. Apparently, it has always been occupied by people who understand and respect its complete madness.

2. Spadena House

3. Menzies House, 1926
William Cameron
604 N. Linden Drive

Tudor with flamboyant stucco enrichment in the gable.

4. Gate House ("Doll's House")
1808 Angelo Drive

A medieval cottage too sweet for words.

5. Heidemann House, 1972
Pulliam, Matthews, and Associates
1236 Benedict Canyon Drive

An award-winning example of the cut-into box. Almost monumental.

6. Vorkapich Garden House, 1938
Gregory Ain
2100 Benedict Canyon Drive, just north of Easton Drive

A small, modular plywood house. Here Ain was exploring the idea of prefabricated structure, though it sould be noted that the statement of the house as

5. Heidemann House

prefabricated architecture is more symbolic than real.

7. Hale House, 1949
Craig Ellwood Associates
9618 Yoakum Drive

A single-story Miesian box on stilts.

8. Brown House, 1949
Craig Ellwood Associates
902 N. Roxbury Drive

Another box on stilts, this time with balancing, one-story wings. We must say that this house on Roxbury Drive, which Gore Vidal once described as "not so much a drive as a state of mind," is quite a sensation. It is now, shrouded in trees, as respectable as its Spanish and Tudor neighbors.

9. ■O'Neill House, 1978-83
Guest House and Pavilion; Don Ramos
House (Project); Santa Monica Architectural Group (Tom Oswald)
507 North Rodeo Drive

Presently the part that can be seen is in an alley behind 507 N. Rodeo Drive. Eighty years too late, but here is Los Angeles's first real Art Nouveau building—Gaudiesque in the extreme. We pant for the construction of the main house in the near future.

10. Forrest House, 1930-31
Roland E. Coate
612 N. Beverly Drive

The columned porch suggests both the nineteenth century one-story Monterey house and the later California Ranch house. As befitting its location in Beverly Hills, the Forrest House signals respectability.

11. Beverly Hills Hotel, 1911-12
Elmer Grey
9600 Sunset Boulevard

Old photographs reveal a rather complicated version of the Mission style. Aesthetically, a great deal has been lost in remodellings and additions, but the building and its lovely garden setting still evoke genteel hospitality.
Nearby, at the end of Elden Way (off Crescent Drive) is the entrance to the Robinson County Botanical Garden that surrounds the fascinating Beaux Arts ■**Robinson House** (1911; Nathaniel Dryden).

12. Anthony House, 1909
Charles and Henry Greene
910 Bedford Drive at Benedict Canyon Drive

It is significant that Earl C. Anthony, who monopolized the Packard agencies in California, would employ Bernard Maybeck to do his showrooms in San Francisco and Oakland and get the Greenes to design the interiors of his showroom (demolished) in Los Angeles and his first house, which once stood at the corner of Wilshire and Berendo. When relationships changed (Charles Greene sold his Packard and bought a Hudson), Anthony got Maybeck to design a castle for him near Griffith Park and a large addition to his showroom (also demolished). The Greene and Greene 1909 house is presently being conscientiously restored by the owners, and it is worthy of comparison with its contemporaries, the Gamble and Blacker-Hill houses in Pasadena. The Kerrys, who moved the house to its present site, got Henry Greene to design walls and garden appointments in 1925. A real surprise in an area mainly developed in the revivals of the twenties.

13. Familian House, 1971
John Lautner
1011 Cove Way

A huge house of stone cairns and wood, just as startling (in a different way) as the Greenes' Anthony House, not far away.

14. Quen House, 1959
Ladd and Kelsey
1211 Laurel Way

Except for the fact that it is all white, this house would pass for the Craftsman style.

15. English House, 1950
Harwell H. Harris
1261 Lago Vista Drive

A large house whose architect was inspired by Frank Lloyd Wright—in this case almost as if the Hollyhock House had been divested of ornament. The effect is stunning.

16. Rourke House, 1949
Richard J. Neutra
9228 Hazen Drive (off Coldwater Canyon Drive onto Cherokee Lane, then Bowmont Drive, then Hazen Drive)

Post and beam, stucco with wood trim. Neutra's famous spider-legs (bents) arch the entrance corridor.

17. Rodakiewicz House, 1937
R. M. Schindler
9121 Alto Cedro Drive, beyond Rourke House, right on Alto Cedro Drive—view obtained above on Alto Cedro Drive if you go beyond house, now obscured by tennis court.

17. Rodakiewicz House

Here, with plenty of money to spend, Schindler unleashed all the powers of his romantic vision of de Stijl. This is a classic. It was once set in a tropical rain forest, but the present tennis court pretty much wiped that out.

18. Grossman House, 1949
Greta Magnusson Grossman
1659 Waynecrest Drive

A simple, Modern, brown box sheathed in vertical board and batten.

19. Schulitz House, 1977
Helmut Schulitz (Urban Innovations Group)
9356 Lloydcrest Drive, near southwest corner of Gilcrest Drive.

Another spin-off from Charles Eames's Case Study house in Santa Monica Canyon. The aesthetic of scarcity can go no further.

20. Miller House, 1948
Ain, Johnson, and Day
1634 Gilcrest Drive

Very expressionistic for Ain, the roof angles jut every which way. A really handsome house, easy to see.

21. Doheny House ("Greystone"), 1925-28
Gordon B. Kaufmann; Paul Thiene, landscape architect
Greystone Park, 905 Loma Vista Drive

Tudor and Jacobean on the grandest possible scale. The house is no longer open except on rare occasions, but the glorious gardens are open every day, 10 A.M. to 5 P.M.

21. Doheny House ("Greystone")

Farther up Loma Vista Drive is the housing development, much of it on formerly Doheny land, called **Trousdale Estates**. It is essentially spec housing for the rich. Although there seems to be a strong predilection for the Neo-Classical, all styles exist here. Everything is so out-of-scale as to form a kind of unity.

22. Commercial Building, ca. 1935
9169 Sunset Boulevard

Rather elegant Streamline Moderne.

23a. Clarke House, 1950
Whitney R. Smith and Wayne R. Williams
1557 Oriole Lane

Not much can be seen of this house except the garage with exposed rafters and a little plywood sheathing.

23b. Sale House, 1949
Whitney R. Smith and Wayne R. Williams
1455 Oriole Drive

The last house was planted out of sight. This one is fenced, but you can see some of Smith's ideas from above. Simplicity in wood, beautifully crafted.

24. Hawthorne School, 1929
Ralph C. Flewelling
624 N. Rexford Drive

This exposed concrete building, with the impression of the board forms retained, is Spanish Colonial Revival. The tower, capped with a dome of glazed colored tiles, and the two story entrance portico off the courtyard are the focal points.

24. Hawthorne School

25. Howland House, 1933-34
Lloyd Wright
502 Crescent Drive

This house is a radical remodelling of a simple stucco box. The exterior is as restrained as the interior is flamboyant.

26. All Saints Episcopal Church, 1925
Roland E. Coate
Northeast corner of Santa Monica Boulevard and Camden Drive

The extensive areas of plain, uninterrupted walls and the restrained historical detail of this church show how close some aspects of the Spanish Colonial Revival were to the "new" architecture then developing in Europe and America.

26. All Saints Episcopal Church

27. Pendleton House, 1942
John Woolf
1032 Beverly Drive

A mansard-roofed Regency Moderne house with urns in niches at each side of the colonnaded entrance, this is a fine example of what John Chase calls "exterior decoration."

28. House, 1983-84
Kamran Khauakani
1081 Laurel Way

Paired Ionic columns grace this large testimony to the fact that Beverly Hills will always remain the same.

Beverly Hills, Lower

1. Wells Fargo Bank, 1973
Sidney Eisenstadt
9600 Little Santa Monica Boulevard

The architect's unusual way with glass creates the illusion that each floor of this multi-story building is cantilevered over the one below. Note also the entrance court with fountain supporting Jack Zajac's *Swan IV* (1971-73).

2. Barclay Bank and Shops Building, 1973
Kahn, Kappe, and Lotery
Northeast corner of Brighton Way and Bedford Drive

It is fascinating to find Kappe's ideas, which are usually seen in domestic building, applied to downtown architecture. The result is a pleasant relief from the usually bland Modernism of the late International style.

3. Manufacturers Bank Building, 1973
Daniel, Mann, Johnson, and Mendenhall
Northwest corner of Wilshire Boulevard and Roxbury Drive

A very large building encased in a curtain of black glass undulates around the corner. It has won much applause from people whose taste was jaded by the dry International Style Moderne tradition.

3. *Manufacturers Bank Building*

4. ■Perpetual Savings Bank Building, 1962
Edward D. Stone
Southwest corner of Wilshire Boulevard and McCarty Drive

A steel-caged high-rise encased in a shell of vaguely Oriental arches, the opposite of the idea expressed down the street at the Swiss Connection. The result, with window-boxes trailing real vine, might best be described as "Venetian Modern."

5. Nieman-Marcus Store Building, 1981
John Carl Warnecke Associates
9700 Wilshire Boulevard

Both the travertine monolith exterior and the spatially elegant interior completely express the essence of the Beverly Hills grand manner — and by a Frisco firm at that.

6. I. Magnin and Company Store Building, 1939
Myron Hunt and H. C. Chambers
Southwest corner of Wilshire Boulevard and Bedford Drive

Classical Moderne and very refined.

7. Security Pacific Place, 1969
Craig Ellwood Associates
Northeast corner of Wilshire Boulevard and Bedford Drive

Black Miesian austerity softened somewhat by a plaza and sculpture. The small

matching **State Savings Bank** (1972-73) is also by Ellwood.

8. Saks Fifth Avenue Store Building, ca. 1936-37
John and Donald B. Parkinson; Paul R. Williams
9600 Wilshire Boulevard

Elegant Hollywood Regency with enough curved surface to suggest that the thirties Streamline Moderne could be elegant.

6. *I. Magnin and Company Store Building*

9. Frank Perls Gallery Building (now Shaxted), ca. 1948
Alvin Lustig
350 N. Camden Drive

The International Style Modern given Beverly Hills classiness by a talented designer of the post-war years.

10. Anderton Court Building, 1953-54
Frank Lloyd Wright
328 Rodeo Drive

Said not to have been carried out precisely according to Wright's plans. It is as if the Guggenheim ramp had been zigzagged and shops put along it. This building by the Master has received little publicity, probably because it is one of his zaniest productions. Across the street (number 339) is a fancy **gallery** (1972-73) in black marble by Marvin Beck and Societe d'Etudes Santini Bouchard.

Another gallery notable for its opulence if not its good taste is the **Rodeo Collection** (1980-81, Le Sopha Group/Environmetrics, Inc.) at 421 N. Rodeo Drive.

11. Beverly-Wilshire Hotel, 1926
Walker and Eisen
Southwest corner of Rodeo Drive and
Wilshire Boulevard

The Italian Renaissance strained through
Beaux Arts ideas by a very productive
Los Angeles firm.

12. Beverly Theatre, 1925
L. A. Smith
206 N. Beverly Drive

The exterior, once imitating a mosque,
has been all but ruined. The interior,
with its Chinese moon-gate proscenium
arch, is pretty well preserved.

13. The Swiss Connection Restaurant,
1973
9444 Wilshire Boulevard

This had to happen! A Miesian glass box
encloses the facade of something that is
supposed to appear Swiss.

14. Commercial Building, ca. 1928
9441 Wishire Boulevard

Art Deco (Zigzag) Moderne.

15. Pacific Theatre, 1931
B. Marcus Priteca
9404 Wilshire Boulevard

Late twenties Art Deco with a Mexican
flourish.

16. ■Beverly Hills Post Office Building,
1933
Ralph C. Flewelling
Southeast corner of Cañon Drive and
Santa Monica Boulevard

16. Beverly Hills Post Office Building

A beautiful rendition of the Italian
Renaissance in terra-cotta and brick.

17. Beverly Hills City Hall, 1932
William J. Gage
East side of Crescent Drive between Santa
Monica and Little Santa Monica
boulevards.

Spanish Renaissance magnificence built
significantly at the beginning of the
Depression when the people in this vicinity felt little pain. The scheme of the
building—that of a low, classical base
(symbolizing government) surmounted by
a tower (signifying business)—was frequently employed for public buildings in
the United States from the teens on
through the 1930s.

In 1981 a competition was announced
by the city council for an expansion of
the Civic Center. Six architectural firms
were selected to present architectural
plans: Frank O. Gehry and Associates,
Arthur Erickson Architects, Gwathmey
Siegel and Associates, Moshe Safdie and
Associates, and Charles Moore/Urban Innovations Group. The winning design,
continuing the Spanish image of the City
Hall, was that of the Charles
Moore/Urban Innovations Group, who associated themselves with the firm of Albert C. Martin and Associates for the
production of the final design. The landscape design will be by Campbell and
Campbell. The project and its landscaping
should be completed in 1986.

**18. ■Music Corporation of America
Building** (now **Litton Industries**), 1940
Paul R. Williams
Burton Way between Crescent and Rex-
ford drives

A rambling California version of the work
of Robert Adam (American Federal Revival) by the distinguished black architect
of the twenties and thirties. Note especially the formal gates and garden to the
west.

19. Burton-Hill Townhouses, 1974
Widon-Wein and Associates
9323 Burton Way

Twenty-four units, extremely sophisticated
and understated seventies Modern in
wood and brick.

18. Music Corporation of America Building (now Litton Industries)

20. Payne Furnace Company Building, 1937
Milton J. Black
336 N. Foothill Road

A fine two-story factory in the Streamline Moderne mode. This architect produced a number of essays in West Los Angeles, Santa Monica, and Pacific Palisades.

21. Apartment Building, 1936
S. Charles Lee
344 S. Oakhurst Drive

Streamline Moderne by one of the masters of the mode.

22. VW Showroom Building, ca 1937
Northwest corner of Maple Drive and Olympic Boulevard

Here it is again. Los Angeles would seem to have more monuments to the Streamline Moderne than any other city in the United States.

23. Cañon Court, 1930
J. Raymond
9379 Olympic Boulevard, at northeast corner of Cañon Drive

This lovely Spanish Colonial garden court apartment seems out of place on this now noisy street.

24. Work House, 1982-83
Frank O. Gehry and Associates
440 S. Roxbury Drive

A two-story, very open house, full of surprises, including the fact that it has not as yet acquired any chain link fence.

25. Swimming Pool Building, Beverly Hills High School, ca. 1937
Stiles O. Clements
Between Heath Avenue and Moreno Drive above Olympic Boulevard

This elliptical-facaded building with its barrel-vaulted, sky-lighted interior contrasts with the knife-sharp Yamasaki towers behind it. The single-story entrance pavilion with rounded corners and rows of deep horizontal bands makes the building Streamline Moderne.

25. Swimming Pool Building, Beverly Hills High School

26. Le Colonnade, 1982
Luckman Partnership
9350-9358 Little Santa Monica Boulevard

A retail center that looks like its name.

Century City

Within what, to an Easterner, would seem easy walking distance of the Beverly Hills business district is Century City, built on what used to be the Twentieth-Century-Fox movie lot. This is a totally new complex of high- and medium-rise buildings, some by distinguished name-brand American architects. There is, however, none of the intimacy and human scale that characterize the buildings of Beverly Hills. In fact, the governing idea seems to have been to inspire awe with wide avenues and over-scaled architecture. If you accept the effort to impress, then the attempt, even at this stage, has been suc-

cessful. But there are problems. Except around the Century Plaza Hotel and a few theatres doing business, the place is pretty spooky on weekdays and downright frightening on Sundays. There is no on-street parking. In fact, there are few cross-walks. Pedestrians are forced to go under streets. One has the strange feeling that this city was planned not for people but for architectural photography. We have included only the buildings that we think are of architectural importance.

1. Century City Medical Plaza, 1969
Daniel, Mann, Johnson, and Mendenhall (Lumsden and Pelli; P. I. Jacobson)
Northeast corner of Olympic Boulevard and Century Park East

Both major architects have since gone off into attacks on the International Style Modern. This complex, a seventeen-story office tower and a ten-story hospital, stands at the turning point of their reaction.

2. Century Plaza Hotel, 1966
Minoru Yamasaki; Robert Herrick Carter, landscape architect
2025 Avenue of the Stars

A huge, high-rise ellipse enlivened by delicate detail.

3. ABC Entertainment Center, 1972
Henry George Greene
2040 Avenue of the Stars

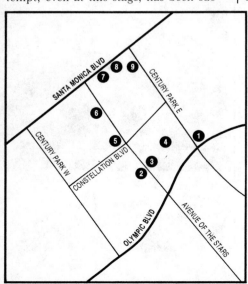

4. Century Plaza Towers

Big and dull—mildly Brutal below, crisper above.

4. Century Plaza Towers, 1969-1975
Minoru Yamasaki; Robert Herrick Carter, landscape architect
East of ABC Entertainment Center

These two soaring towers, indentical in height and triangular floor plan, are the focal point of Century City. They are truly stunning when viewed nearby and play strange optical tricks from the distant Santa Monica Freeway.

5. First Los Angeles Bank Building, 1975
Maxwell Starkman and Associates
Northwest corner of Avenue of the Stars and Constellation Boulevard

An extraordinarily fine building of brown brick and black glass tilted to give the effect of the skylight in an artist's studio.

6. 1900 Avenue of the Stars Building, 1969
Albert C. Martin and Associates

A twenty-seven-story building of aluminum and tinted glass.

7. ABI Tower, 1971
Skidmore, Owings, and Merrill (E. Charles Bassett)
10100 Santa Monica Boulevard

A twenty-six-story building of light aluminum and black glass.

8. San Diego Savings and Loan Association Building, 1972
Daniel, Mann, Johnson, and Mendenhall (Lumsden; P. J. Jacobson)
Southwest corner of Santa Monica Boulevard and Century Park East

A squarish, twenty-story building set at a diagonal to the corner. The mitred corners which do line up with the street indicate that the designer was perhaps trying to make some sort of statement. Or was he simply being playful? The building nevertheless seems askew and unrelated to anything else.

9. Northrop Complex, 1982-83
Welton Becket and Associates
1800 Century Park East

A nineteen-story Corporate International Style tower. An equally dull twenty-three-story tower is underway.

Carthay Circle

South Carthay

Carthay Circle was planned in 1921 by the landscape architects Cook and Hill. The area is bounded by Fairfax Avenue to the east, Olympic Boulevard to the south and Wilshire Boulevard to the north. It is bisected by San Vicente Boulevard. The founder of the 136-acre, mainly Spanish Colonial Revival community, was the developer J. Harvey McCarthy. It was originally planned around its own shopping center. Originally the main buildings and many of the lesser ones were designed by Alfred W. Eichler and H. W. Bishop. The chief feature of Carthay Circle was the theatre, now long gone. No major monuments remain—only a pleasanter-than-usual community.

This area just southeast of Beverly Hills and bounded by Olympic, Crescent Heights, Pico, and La Cienega boulevards was developed in the 1930s by a builder named Ponti. It is really all of one piece, mainly Spanish Colonial Revival, but also exhibits the other period revivals as well as the Moderne. It is mostly single-family dwellings, all in the same scale except for the fringes on Olympic and Crescent Heights where small apartment houses in the same thirties styles appear. There are very few intrusions from the succeeding decades, and where they do appear they are not liked. The sense of an organic community of period architecture caused the Los Angeles Cultural Heritage Board to recommend to the Planning Commission and the City Council that South Carthay be recognized as a cultural-historic district, or in officialese, a Historic Preservation Overlay Zone remarkable only for its consistent good design.

West Hollywood

Through a strange quirk of fate, most of the area known as West Hollywood is in the County but not in the City of Los Angeles and therefore not subject to higher city taxes. This has given it special attraction for interior designers who work and live here. Their Grand Palais is the **Pacific Design Center** at the corner of San Vicente Boulevard and Melrose Avenue—"The Blue Whale"—that houses the most prestigious wholesalers. But small shops, the mainstay of an earlier day, still abound. And not far from them are acres of bungalows, many being literally transformed by their designers-owners into miniature villas in a congeries of taste that stretches the imagination to the point that John Chase has written a book about them— *Exterior Decoration* (Hennessey and Ingalls, 1982).

The questionable part of Sunset Boulevard that is called "The Strip" is also in the unincorporated area. Also, some wonderful garden apartments of the twenties and thirties. And some very famous people lived here, some in very famous houses. Kings Road at one time was the home of Theodore Dreiser and Aldous Huxley, whose houses were undistinguished, and also the home of R. M. Schindler and Walter Dodge, whose houses were monuments of twentieth-century architecture. Indeed, one of the reasons that Irving J. Gill's great Dodge House (1916) was lost to cultural vandalism was that it was in unincorporated

West Hollywood and thus not covered by the Los Angeles City Cultural Heritage Ordinance.

Lloyd Wright's own studio-house is on Doheny Drive just below the Strip. But the hills above Sunset Boulevard are in Los Angeles proper and are full of excellent Period Revival houses as well as outstanding avant-garde work by Carl S. Maston, Raphael Soriano, Richard J. Neutra, John Lautner, Gregory Ain, Pierre Koenig, and R. M. Schindler. This is a wonderful part of the world.

We have taken the liberty of extending West Hollywood into these hills to the north and have pushed its southern boundary to Olympic Boulevard. At the same time we have observed the conventional western and eastern boundaries at Doheny Drive and Fairfax Avenue.

1. Sunrise Plaza Apartment Building, 1982
John Siebel Associates
1201 Larrabee Street

High Tech with all of its clichés.

2. ▪Sunset Plaza, 1934-36
Charles Selkirk; Honnold and Russell
8578-8623 Sunset Boulevard

Clustered near the intersection with Sunset Plaza Drive, most of these shops were designed by Charles Selkirk. Some are now being restored and rebuilt in their original Neo-Classical, Regency, and Colonial Revival styles. Advance respectability on the Sunset Strip! The crown jewel of them all is the shimmering white Ionic temple (1936) at 8619 Sunset Boulevard.

3. Lomax House, 1970-71
Lomax/Mills Associates
1995 Sunset Plaza Drive

An elegant cut-into stucco box, a reminder in the Modernist tradition that architecture can be minimal sculpture on a grand scale.

4. Wayne House, 1950
Alvin Lustig
1365 Londonderry Place

You can catch only a glimpse of this International Style Modern house.

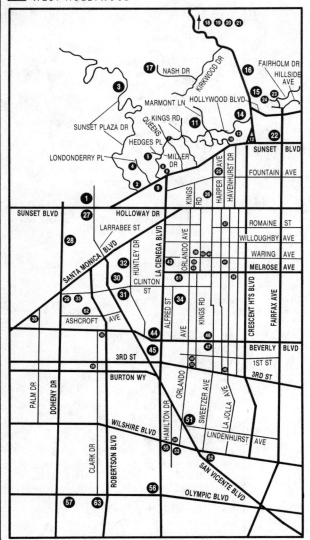

5. Wolff House, 1963
John Lautner
8530 Hedges Place

This steep hillside house is a characteristically dramatic statement of its architect. It is made of dressed boulders, concrete, and jutting glass. Its most salient feature from the street is the great extended lip of a carport.

6. Reis House, 1950
R. M. Schindler
1404 Miller Drive

In this single-floor dwelling Schindler hovered a thin roof plane over a set of quite fragile stucco planes. As in all of his work, and especially in his post-1945 designs, there are many ideas going on in this small dwelling. But here the roof planes hold everything together.

7. Polito House, 1939
Raphael S. Soriano
1650 Queens Road

A two-story, Modernist box character-ized by the abstract composition of stucco walls, horizontal banks of win-dows, and cantilevered balconies.

8. Carney's Restaurant
8361 Sunset Boulevard

A Union Pacific dining car brought to the site in the 1970s.

9. ■Sunset Tower Apartment Build-ing, 1929-31
Leland A. Bryant
18358 Sunset Boulevard, at Kings Road

The lower part of the tower is a first-class monument of the Zigzag Moderne while the upper portion anticipates the thirties Streamline Moderne. The build-ing has long been as much an emblem of Hollywood as the Hollywood Sign. Drive to the rear and note the stylized automobile radiator grills incorporated into the decoration of the garage.

10. Chateau Marmont, 1928
Arnold Weitzman
8225 Marmont Lane near Sunset Boulevard

Perhaps more important historically than architecturally, this Norman pile was a favorite of the screen stars. . .still is. It is being proudly restored by its owner.

11. Maston House, 1948
Carl Louis Maston
1657 Marmont Lane

Rather surprising to find this partisan of the "less-is-more" esthetic practicing here in what would seem to be a late Crafts-man technique — lots of wood.

12. Store and Office Building, ca. 1925
Morgan, Walls, and Clements
Northwest corner of Laurel Canyon and Sunset boulevards

Somewhat defaced but still recognizable as these architects' brand of the Chur-rigueresque, realized in cast concrete.

13. Mace House, 1958
Lloyd Wright
8292 Hollywood Boulevard

The facade right on the street is very private looking.

14. Storer House, 1923
Frank Lloyd Wright
8161 Hollywood Boulevard

Wright's romantic creation of decorated concrete block, wonderfully fitted into the hillside. The interior space of this house is dominated by a central, two-story living room which opens onto ter-races, both front and rear. The house was retouched in the 1970s by Lloyd Wright.

14. Storer House

15. House, ca. 1925
1808 Laurel Canyon Boulevard (actually a spur which veers off about 100 yards above Hollywood Boulevard)

A beautiful tribute to the Spanish Colonial Revival.

16. House, ca. 1910
2044 Laurel Canyon Boulevard (spur)

A horizontal, one-story house raised above the street level by the garage below. It is an example of the West Coast adaptation of the Midwestern Prairie School aesthetic.

17. Jones House and Studio, 1938
A. Quincy Jones
8661 Nash Drive (Laurel Canyon Boule-vard then left on Kirkwood Drive, right on Ridpath Drive to Nash Drive)

The influence in these buildings with broad eaves is Wright filtered through the San Francisco Bay tradition of the 1930s.

A little further up Laurel Canyon Boulevard, again jutting off to the left (west) is Lookout Mountain Avenue, which you will recognize by a suitable log cabin at the entrance. Lookout Mountain Avenue leads to some important houses.

18. Janson House, 1949
R. M. Schindler
8704 Skyline Drive (Lookout Mountain Avenue to Wonderland Avenue to Greenvalley to Skyline Drive)

A house on a scanty budget. It looks as if it were made of sticks. It is amazing to return to this house after many years and discover that, where in the 1950s it could easily be photographed, now it is almost invisible midst foliage and new neighbors. A number of changes also have been made to the house in the last ten years. If you look closely at this dwelling and then at the recent designs of Frank O. Gehry, you will see the connection.

18. Janson House

19. Case Study House #21, 1958
Pierre Koenig
9038 Wonderland Park Avenue (Lookout Mountain Avenue to Wonderland Avenue to Wonderland Park Avenue. House on left, just above Burroughs).
Koenig carried the elegance of the metal post and beam aesthetic to the point that it almost seems related to the popular Hollywood Regency of the thirties.

Another example of his refined approach can be seen in his **Case Study House #22** (1959), located at 1635 Woods Drive. In **#22** the idea of the glass pavilion is fully realized.

This elegant, precisely-detailed Modernist house of vertical wood panels is still very smart.

19. Case Study House #21

20. De Bretteville-Simon Houses, 1976
Peter de Bretteville
8067-71 Willow Glen Road off Laurel Canyon Road

The image of the twentieth-century dwelling as a machine. A spin-off from Charles Eames own house in Santa Monica Canyon.

21. Ain House, 1941
Gregory Ain
7964 Willow Glen Road

A narrow, room-in-a-line plan with all the major spaces opening toward a terrace and the view, the whole covered with a low-pitched, hipped roof.

22. Sunset Car Wash, 1972
Robert Barnett
7955 Sunset Boulevard

A monumental, almost Egyptian, object in concrete.

23. Kun Houses, 1938 and 1950
Richard J. Neutra; Gregory Ain, collaborator
7947 Fareholm Drive

Two adjoining machine image, International Style Modern houses on a precipitous hillside. The 1938 stucco-and-steel-windows dwelling was advertised as an "all-electric house." From the street you see only the top level. The rear elevation reveals that it is actually three levels.

24. Tucker House, 1950
R. M. Schindler
8010 Fareholm Drive

A two-story stucco frame design whose planes project and recede in a complex pattern.

25. Garden Apartments
Mainly on north-south streets between Sunset Boulevard and Fountain Avenue

Usually, as the name suggests, these are two- or three-story apartments in some way arranged around a garden, often elaborately landscaped with palms and other tall trees. A swimming pool is not usually a part of the ensemble though it may exist on some other part of the property or have been added to the sacred precinct more recently. They are at their best in the Spanish Colonial Revival mode, and are generally charming if not great architecture. A recent visitor from Canada was heard to say, "Why don't all the people in Los Angeles live this way?" For a discussion of these garden apartments see Stefanos Polyzoides, Roger Sherwood, James Tice, and Julius Shulman's *Courtyard Housing in Los Angeles* (Berkeley, 1982).

Here is a group that is within easy walking distance of each other:

a. Patio del Moro, 1925
Arthur B. Zwebell
8225 Fountain Avenue

Although not the first designer-builder to hit upon the garden court, Zwebell was certainly a very active pioneer. This Spanish design has a gorgeous entrance and an interesting garden.

b. The Ronda, 1927
Arthur B. Zwebell
1400 Havenhurst Drive

From the street all you can see is the three-story facade with a garage entrance to the side and a small garden entrance to the north. Within this complex are two courtyard gardens.

c. The Andalusia, 1927
Arthur B. Zwebell
1475 Havenhurst Drive

Two garage buildings to each side form a forecourt beyond which a large arch leads into the inner court. Cantilevered balconies, a round tower, and a loggia complete the composition.

25c. The Andalusia

d. Villa Sevilla, 1931
Elwood Houseman
1338 N. Harper Avenue

An Andalusian village scene set on the hillside. A narrow interior garden court contains the entrances and stairways.

e. Villa d'Este, 1928
Pierpont and Walter S. Davis
1355 Laurel Avenue

Vaguely modelled on the not-so-famous Villa d'Este on Lake Maggiore, this apartment house with garages as a forecourt on the street is surely the most beautiful of those we have listed. Beyond the entrance and pool lies the main courtyard. Each of the two-story units has a private patio.

25e. Villa d'Este

Actually, to have settled on the garden apartment house may seem perverse. Look around at the other delightful apartments in this area. The **Chateau Marmont** is only the most conspicuous.

26. Coral Gables Bungalow Court, ca. 1932
1233-39 Sweetzer Avenue

A two-story Spanish Colonial Revival complex.

27. Modern Creators Store Building
for W. Lingenbrink, 1937
R. M. Schindler
8750 Holloway Drive

Schindler supervised additions in 1947. Since then many remodellings have been made so that one can grasp Schindler's ideas only through illustrations in books. Oh, there is still a skyline.

28. Wright House, 1928
Lloyd Wright
858 N. Doheny Drive

The house is of stuccoed frame with elaborate pre-cast concrete block decoration within and without, suggested by the Joshua tree. It is easily missed under its pine tree, which acts as an insulating device. No more romantic scene could be imagined than when Mr. Wright lighted a fire on the hearth of the "great hall" and opened the canvas drapery which separates the room from the small patio over which the huge tree sprawls.

28. Wright House

29. Office and Showroom Building, 1982
Tom Roberts
Southeast corner of Melrose Avenue and Santa Monica Boulevard

A miniature brick takeoff on the "Blue Whale" (Pacific Design Center) down the street.

30. ■Pacific Design Center, 1975
Victor Gruen Associates (Cesar Pelli)
Northeast corner of Melrose Avenue and San Vicente Boulevard

Controversial, to say the least. Some critics have damned "The Blue Whale," usually because it obviously contradicts the scale of the area, which is mainly small shops and houses. Others have praised it for its break with high-rise. The Center is vast and, on its San Vicente side, reminds you of London's Crystal Palace in its roof line. With the exception of the top floor, its interiors are just big spaces, possibly because the architect expected them to be filled with color and people by the designer tenants. A grand exception is the **Sunan Showroom** (#206) designed by Michael Graves in 1981.

31. Thunder Thighs, ca. 1978
8642 Melrose Avenue

A restaurant intended (?) to look like a San Francisco whorehouse.

32. Maisson Huntley Apartment Building, 1982
625 Huntley Drive

A blocky expression of Post Modern.

33. William S. Beckett Offfice Building (now Hannold, Riebsamen, and Rex), 1950
William Beckett
9026 Melrose Avenue

International Style Modern elegance now almost hidden in foliage.

34. Center for Early Education Building, 1968
Kurt Meyer and Associates
536 N. Alfred Street

Very spartan in red brick but with Athenian blue doors.

35. Herman Miller Showroom Building, 1949
Charles Eames
8806 Beverly Boulevard

Its glass facade still looks crisp and bright though the Millers have moved to the Pacific Design Center.

36. Rapid Transit District Bus Maintenance Facility, 1982
Ralph Parsons Company (Engineering)
Santa Monica Boulevard at Palm Drive

About as Brutalist as we go in Southern California.

37. Duplexes, 1922
R. M Schindler
Northeast corner of Harper Avenue and Romaine Street; northwest corner of La Jolla Avenue and Romaine Street

These two identical, low-budget structures were built as spec investments. Their style is close to Art Deco Moderne.

38. Service Station, ca. 1935
8176 Melrose Avenue

Streamline Moderne.

39. Schindler Studio House, 1921-22
R. M. Schindler
833 N. Kings Road

Actually a double house, with guest quarters and a common kitchen, built for the Schindlers and R. M.'s engineer colleague, Clyde Chase. In this studio house, Schindler experimented with tilt-slab concrete walls, the vertical space between each slab being filled with glass. In a sense, the house follows historic precedent. The interiors, though now mostly painted, were once in the woodsy Craftsman style. The plan, which opens all rooms to courtyards, suggests both the Hispanic and Japanese traditions. It is a classic in modern architecture — and we use the word sparingly. God preserve it. It is on county land, not protected by a cultural heritage ordinance, but fortunately it is owned and administered by the non-profit Friends of the Schindler House. The studio house is open to the public and often presents architectural and design exhibitions. The house is open 11-4 on Saturdays, 1-4 on Sundays.

39. Schindler Studio House

40. Apartment Building, ca. 1925
Carl Kay
Northwest corner of Sweetzer and Waring avenues

An Islamic Revival complex beautiful to behold.

41. Duplex, 1936
William P. Kesling
754-56 Harper Avenue

Splendid Streamline Moderne, coming close to International Style Modern.

40. Apartment Building

42. Gemini Studios Building, 1976
Frank O. Gehry and Associates
8365 W. Melrose Avenue

A remodelling and addition to an older single-story commercial structure, this is so understated that you do not notice the subtle relationship of the new facade and addition to the huge sign on its roof. High Art successfully commenting on the common and everyday building behind.

43. Gerwin-Ostrow Office Building, 1960
Craig Ellwood Associates
Southeast corner of La Cienega Boulevard and Waring Avenue

Less glass than usual, the building still shows the influence of Mies.

44. Tail-O-the-Pup, 1946
Northwest corner of Beverly and La Cienega boulevards

A programmatic hot dog stand in the shape of a hot dog in a bun.

44. Tail-O-the-Pup

45. Beverly Center, 1982
Welton Becket Associates
8500 Beverly Boulevard

Just behind the Tail-O-the-Pup, so to speak, this monstrous shopping center with its department stores and shops is a sort of unintended joke on the Pompidou Center in Paris.

46. Janus Gallery, ca. 1928
Northwest corner of Beverly Boulevard and Sweetzer Avenue
Art Deco (Zigzag) Moderne.

47. Carson-Roberts Building, 1958-60
Craig Ellwood
8322 Beverly Boulevard

This building stands on stilts, providing a garage below. The front is made up of glass panels extended beyond the real walls. These give extra privacy from the busy street.

48. Crescent Professional Building, 1959
Richard J. Neutra
8105 W. 3rd Street

White, marblized, and unfenestrated to the street, the architecture is asserted by a stainless steel canopy extended over the side walls.

49. Apartment Building, ca. 1940
Southwest corner of 1st Street and South Kings Road

A late version of the Streamline Moderne.

50. House, 1936
Milton J. Black
127 S. Kings Road

As we have noted, this area is practically the home of the Streamline Moderne.

51. Marshall House, 1948
Konrad Wachsmann and Walter Gropius
6643 Lindenhurst Avenue (rear)

You cannot easily see it from the street, but we had to put it in because the prefabricated "panel houses" by these famous architects are rarities.

52. Century Bank Building, 1972
Daniel, Mann, Johnson, and Mendenhall (A. Lumsden)
6420 Wilshire Boulevard

A well-designed medium-rise with much
attention toward a break with 1960s
Modern, but it does inspire us to feel
like whipping whoever it was that in-
vented black glass.

53. Fox Wilshire Theatre, 1929
S. Charles Lee
8440 Wilshire Boulevard

A wonderful creation in Art Deco (Zigzag) Moderne.

54. Shopping Center (now **Porsche-
Audi**), ca. 1928
Northeast corner of Wilshire Boulevard
and Hamilton Drive

A specimen of Spanish Colonial Revival
architecture. Corner L-shaped shopping
centers of this vintage are rapidly fading
from the scene. It is good to find one in
this area.

**55. Great Western Savings Center
Building,** 1972
William Pereira Associates
Southeast corner of Wilshire and La
Cienega boulevards

This huge, black glass building with an
oval floor plan certainly makes a break
with International Style Modern
sermonizing.

**56. Beverly Hills Water Department
Building,** 1927

56. Beverly Hills Water Department Building

Salisbury, Bradshaw, and Taylor
Northwest corner of Olympic and La
Cienega boulevards

You will at first think that this huge,
poured-concrete structure with
Romanesque detail and reasonably accurate facsimile of "La Giralda" is a cathedral. And so it is in Los Angeles
County, where water is sacred.

57. Lyons Van and Storage Building,
1942
Ulysses Floyd Ribble
9016 Wilshire Boulevard

Late Streamline Moderne.

58. Temple Emmanuel and School,
1954 and 1965
Sidney Eisenstadt
300 N. Clark Drive

The temple is not as dramatic as much
of Eisenstadt's work, but it contains a
mural by Joseph Young who recently
designed the Triforium in downtown Los
Angeles. The school, comprised of very
low arches with brick and glass above,
reminds us in some ways of the Frank
Lloyd Wright civic building at San
Raphael.

59. Orlando/Waring Condominiums,
1974
Kenneth Dillon
8380 Waring Avenue at Orlando Avenue

A large complex in the cut-into box
idiom. Not great architecture, but the
planting around it is magnificent.

60. Senior Citizens Housing Project,
1978-80
Bobrow, Thomas and Associates; Charles
W. Moore/Urban Innovation Group
Northwest and northeast corners of
Kings Road at Waring Avenue

These 106 one- to three-story units in
stucco and tile spell Spanish Colonial.
Several exisiting Spanish Colonial Revival houses of the 1920s have been incorporated in the project and help to tie
the present to the past. The new buildings have been scaled and sited so as to
continue the low residential character of
Kings Road before the advent of apartment houses in the 1960s.

61. Woolf Studio Building, 1946-47
John Woolf
8450 Melrose Place

A one-story building, its out-size Pull-man door surround has been greatly admired by the interior designers in West Hollywood.

62. House Remodelling, 1961
Lawrence Limolti
8937 Ashcroft Avenue

A tiny, originally Spanish Colonial Revival bungalow entirely rejuvenated with mansard roof, complete with bust in the tower and topiary work in the front yard.

63. Owl Drug Store Building, ca. 1930
Southwest corner of Wilshire and Robertson boulevards

A version of the Art Deco (Zigzag) Moderne. Between fluted engaged columns on the upper floor are small, highly-decorated columns and spandrels with rich relief ornamentation.

63. Owl Drug Store Building

Central Hollywood

Since everything about this place is supposed to be fabulous, it is worth noting that the name may have been chosen by the developers, Mr. and Mrs. Horace Wilcox of Topeka, because Father Junípero Serra may have once said the Mass of the Holy Wood of the Cross near the site. Unfortunately, a much more prosaic explanation of the derivation is probable. But it is significant that the Wilcoxes were determined when they platted the town in the late 1880s that it would be a center of culture and morality, however contradictory these terms may be. They offered a free lot to any church that would build there. Their high tone was evidently contagious, for when movies were first developed in New York, they were banned in Hollywood, as were liquor and other forms of vice.

Needless to say this happy condition did not last very far into the twentieth century. Whatever its present resemblance to Sodom and Gomorrah, Hollywood is conspicuously a city of churches, the **First Presbyterian** being the largest of that denomination in the world. But the movies came seeking the sun like everything else that came to California. The result may still be noted on the map in the form of large areas devoted to movie studios which, incidentally, may be converted eventually to new uses, as in Universal City to the north and Century City to the west. Also, the city acquired some of the most

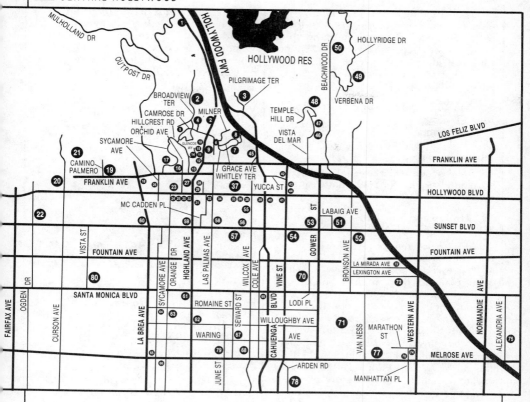

spectacular moving picture palaces that were built anywhere in the world in the twenties and thirties. **Grauman's (now Mann's) Chinese** is the most famous, but the **Hollywood Pantages** is the most magnificent.

The effect of movie madness on domestic architecture is less conspicuous. The taste of the stars and moguls, whatever their quest for opulence, was generally channeled into the Spanish. Tudor, and the Colonial revivals. Nevertheless, the imaginative atmosphere did encourage a taste for the exotic in some citizens—the Egyptian, Islamic, Hansel and Gretel, Medieval and Mayan tradi-

tions finding much favor. On the other hand, the same atmosphere seems to have encouraged other residents to employ some of the early Modernists— Gregory Ain, Richard J. Neutra, R. M. Schindler, Harwell H. Harris, Raphael S. Soriano, Pierre Koenig, and the Wrights, father and son. As a matter of fact, the Hollywood Hills, though full of commonplace architecture, is an area that no student of twentieth-century traditional or avant-garde architecture can ignore.

If you are such a student, be sure to have your car and your patience in prime condition. We have done our best to make the maps accurate, but they can forecast only a few of the steep, tortuous roads and barely suggest the many opportunities to get lost. Persevere! "Civilization" is always nearby.

We begin at the north in Cahuenga Pass:

1. Maston Architectural Office Building, 1967
Carl Maston
2811 Cahuenga Boulevard (west side of Hollywood Freeway)

An ideal Modern design—an austere, horizontal brick wall is all that meets the eye.

2. Hollywood Bowl, 1924 to present
2301 N. Highland Avenue

The first performance in the originally-natural amphitheatre was in 1922. In 1924 it was decided to improve the carrying power of the sound by building a shell, and Lloyd Wright was chosen as the designer. The result was a wood shell that was successful both visually and acoustically. In 1928 Wright was again employed to design a second shell which was elliptical in shape. In 1931 the Allied Architects of Los Angeles replaced that shell with a more pretentious one in concrete that never worked in spite of almost continuous remodelling. The latest shell (1982) is by Frank O. Gehry and Associates. Now the complaint is about the quality of the amplification system. The best thing at the Bowl is the **gate** on Highland Avenue. Three Federal Arts Project **sculptures** representing music, drama, and dance were sculpted by George Stanley (ca. 1935). Very inspirational, especially at night, when lighted (although the original colored lights were a nice touch).

3. House, ca. 1928
2403 Pilgrimage Terrace

At first this seems to be a Queen Anne house, but closer inspection suggests a later date, perhaps even later than our guess.

4. The High Tower, ca. 1920
North end of High Tower Road

Even if you do not decide to go up on the elevator, you will certainly want to admire this bit of whimsy, a small-scale version of the extravagances at Bologna. The two flanking Moderne **houses** are by Carl Kay (ca. 1937).

4. The High Tower

5. Otto Bollman House, 1922
Lloyd Wright
2200 Broadview Terrace (reached by elevator from High Tower Drive below or by footpath nearby)

Architectural Expressionism at its height. This stuccoed frame house had pyramidal roofs covered by a pattern of horizontal and vertical boards. The boards have been removed, but you can get the idea from the unaltered garden house visible from the public walkway.

5. Otto Bollman House

6. House, ca. 1928
Southwest corner of Milner Road and Las Palmas Avenue

A charming Hansel and Gretel in a storybook area. This area near the corner of Highland and Hollywood boulevards is one of the few in Los Angeles where you can actually park your car and walk to dozens of things. Of course, the natives will think you are mad!

7. Pike House, 1952
George Vernon Russell
6675 Whitley Terrace

A characteristic, rather delicate version of post-World War II Moderne, now painted brown. You can see this better than most of Russell's domestic work.

8. Lingenbrink House, 1930
Jock Peters
2000 Grace Avenue

Like other L.A. designers, Jock Peters used both Moderne and International Style Modern images. They are here in this house. In fact, Lingenbrink published several small books on both images in Los Angeles. Later in the 1930s he was a major patron of R. M. Schindler.

9. The Roman Gardens, 1926
Pierpont and Walter S. Davis
2000 N. Highland Avenue

The tower that you see does not look Roman (it could be from Moorish Spain or North Africa), but this is one of the more elaborate of Los Angeles's garden court apartment houses.

10. American Legion Headquarters Building, 1929
Eugene Weston, Jr.
2035 Highland Avenue

Goodhue's Los Angeles Public Library certainly was on the architect's mind when he designed this modern Classical spectacle, its glittering tile ornamentation still very fresh.

11. Shrader House, ca. 1915
Mead and Requa
1927 Highland Avenue

Spanish Colonial Revival via Gill by an important San Diego firm. It is amazing that it still exists.

10. American Legion Headquarters Building

12. Duplex for De Keysor, 1935
R. M. Schindler
1911 Highland Avenue

The walls and sloped roofs of this hillside house are covered with roll roofing material in a manner similar to the original condition of the Packard House (1924) in Pasadena.

13. First United Methodist Church, 1929
Thomas B. Barber
Northwest corner of Highland and Franklin avenues

English Gothic in revealed reinforced concrete.

13. First United Methodist Church

14. Koosis House, 1940
Raphael S. Soriano
1941 Glencoe Way

A delightful building because it does not seem to take the International Style Modern too seriously.

15. Freeman House, 1924
Frank Lloyd Wright
1962 Glencoe Way

Another of Wright's concrete "knit-block" houses which seems to begin Mayan and end Islamic. To have seen the Freeman House above the Methodist Church is to have reached Mecca! Much of the built-in and freestanding furniture was designed by R. M. Schindler in 1927. The house has been recently presented to the University of Southern California.

15. Freeman House

16. Lane House (now **Magic Castle,**)
ca. 1925
Dennis and Farwell
7001 Franklin Avenue at Orchid Avenue

This "French Chateau" has been transformed into a private club for magicians. Lucky are you if you get a chance to experience invisible Irma at her magic piano.

17. ■Bernheimer Bungalow (now **Yamashiro Restaurant,**) 1913
Franklin M. Small
1999 N. Sycamore Avenue

A stunning Japanese mountain palace and garden (with a real 600-year-old pagoda), built by two importers of orien-

tal art, Adolphe L. and Eugene Bernheimer.

18. Crippled Children's Society Regional Office Building, 1969
Ladd and Kelsey
Southeast corner of Franklin and La Brea avenues

A sleek brick edifice in the late International Style version of Modern.

19. Fuller House, 1924
Arthur S. Heineman (Alfred Heineman, designer)
Northeast corner of Franklin Avenue and Camino Palmero

A strange mixture of Colonial Revival and Italianate forms.

20. Erlik House, 1952
R. M. Schindler
1757 N. Curson Avenue

One of Schindler's last houses — an essay on how to use the typical Los Angeles stucco box. The interior of this single-floor house contains mirrored halls and much built-in furniture.

21. Wattles Gardens, 1908
Myron Hunt and Elmer Grey
1850 N. Curson Avenue

These Roman Italian Baroque gardens terraced toward the Hollywood Hills were once the talk of the town. They were highly architectural, with classical columns and balustrades everywhere. Now a couple of rows of ruined columns and some planting are the only reminders of past glory.

22. Henry Bollman House, 1922
Lloyd Wright
1530 N. Ogden Drive

An early use of textured "knit-block" construction combined with a wood stud frame covered with stucco. Lloyd Wright maintained that this was the first actual use of the concrete block "knit-block" system, which his father was to use in such later Los Angeles designs as the Storer House (1923), the Freeman House (1924), and the Ennis House (1924).

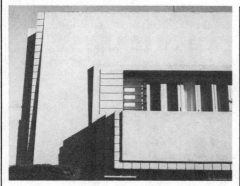

22. Henry Bollman House

23. Grauman's Chinese Theatre (now Mann's), 1927
Meyer and Holler
6925 Hollywood Boulevard

This giant tourist attraction surely must be familiar to everyone. Fortunately, nobody has tried to "modernize" it. The same cannot be said for **Grauman's Egyptian** down the street.

23. Grauman's (Mann's) Chinese Theatre

24. Hollywood Masonic Temple, 1922
Austin, Field, and Frey
Intersection of Hollywood Boulevard and Orchid Avenue

A magnificent Classical pile pushed up against the wildly Churrigueresque Paramount Theatre.

25. El Capitan Theatre Building (now Paramount), 1926
Morgan, Walls, and Clements; G. Albert Lansburgh, theatre designer
6834 Hollywood Boulevard

At first a combination theatre and furniture store, the store (six stories) has pulled out leaving the theatre to make ends meet. The South Sea interior by Lansburgh has been removed.

26. El Cadiz Apartment Building, 1936
Milton J. Black
1731 Sycamore Avenue

A large Spanish Colonial Revival garden apartment with nice tile trim and art glass. Notice that the garage is in the basement. A much smaller Hispanic charmer is **El Cabrillo** (1928; Arthur and Nina Zwebell) at 1832 Grace Avenue, at the corner of Franklin.

27. U.S. Post Office, Osbourne Station, ca. 1928
1767 Highland Avenue

Zigzag Moderne in extremely colorful tile.

28. Don the Beachcomber Restaurant, ca. 1937
1727 N. McCadden Place

Although far from eye-catching today, this restaurant was one of the first to openly employ the South Sea Island motif so popular today.

29. Los Angeles First National Bank Building (now Security Pacific), 1927
Meyer and Holler
6777 Hollywood Boulevard

A strange but effective Gothic and Spanish Colonial goulash.

30. Bank of America Building, 1914
Ellet Parcher

Classical facade added in 1920s. Remodelling 1935; Morgan, Walls, and Clements
6870 Hollywood Boulevard

This originally was a four-story building. It was cut down to its present one-story size by MWC, who added the tile roof.

31. Max Factor Building, 1931
(Remodelling) S. Charles Lee
1666-68 Highland Avenue

Lee was a fashionable theatre designer, e.g. the Los Angeles Theatre in downtown Los Angeles. He chose Regency Moderne to clothe this old warehouse giving it cosmetic richness with the use of pink and white marble. Take a look inside.

31. Max Factor Building

32. Rexall Drug Company Building (now Lee Drug), 1935
B. D. Bixby
6800-04 Hollywood Boulevard at southwest corner of Highland Avenue

Not as zappy Streamline Moderne as the nearby **Owl Drug Store** at the corner of Cahuenga and Hollywood boulevards, but it has its moments, such as the neon Coca Cola signs under frosted glass in the pavement of the entrance. At risk of didacticism, it should be pointed out that this intersection of Highland and Hollywood is one of the few areas in the Los Angeles area where there is a real sense of place. This is the result of the immediate architecture all around it, but also the more distant **Methodist Church** to the north at a curve in Franklin and Highland. As we move east along Hollywood Boulevard a generally grundgy look has covered some good to outstanding architecture.

33. Egyptian Theatre, 1922
Meyer and Holler
6712 Hollywood Boulevard

Here is an example of the grundgy look, though it is a result of remodelling rather than signage and filth. As noted

earlier, the wonderful Egyptian facade is completely gone and most of the interior madness has perished. Strangely, if you go down McCadden, at the west side of the theatre you will find some very fresh looking restoration of the original decoration.

34. Shane Building (now Hollywood Center), 1930
S. Norton, F. Wallis
6652-54 Hollywood Boulevard on the southwest corner of Cherokee Avenue

A marvelous Art Deco marquee on Cherokee Avenue calls attention to an equally distinguished lobby, almost completely intact.

35. Kress and Company Building (now Frederick's), 1935
Edward F. Sibbert
6606-12 Hollywood Boulevard

It is very tempting to leave out this lavender and purple horror, but behind the recent color scheme is a good Streamline Moderne building by a good New York architect. Note the set backs; try to ignore the window displays.

36. J. J. Newberry Company Building, 1928
Newberry Company
6600-04 Hollywood Boulevard

The most colorful Art Deco on Hollywood Boulevard but it is almost upstaged by **Frederick's** next door.

37. Baine Building (now U.T.B.), 1926
Gogerty and Weyl
6601-09 Hollywood Boulevard

Very lovely Spanish Colonial Revival above the "modernized" first floor.

38. Janes House, 1903
Dennis and Farwell
6541 Hollywood Boulevard

By a miracle, apparently soon to be lifted, this late Queen Anne house remains on this otherwise commercial boulevard. Farwell was a product of the New York office of McKim, Mead, and White.

39. Warner Theatre Building (now **Pacific Hollywood**), 1926-27
G. Albert Lansburgh
6423-45 Hollywood Boulevard

Somehow the architect combined Renaissance, Rococo, Moorish, and Art Deco ornamentation to produce a very effective piece of architecture.

40. Owl Drug Company Building (now **Julian Medical**), 1934
Morgan, Walls, and Clements
6380-84 Hollywood Boulevard, on the southwest corner of Cahuenga Boulevard

Surely this must be one of the crowning achievements of the Streamline Moderne, to be rated in the same class as Robert Derrah's Coca Cola Bottling Plant.

The old **Hollywood Public Library** at 1623 Ivar Avenue burned in 1982. It will be replaced by a new **Francis Howard Goldwyn Regional Branch Library,** designed by Frank O. Gehry and Associates. The design of the new building takes into account L.A.'s long tradition of walled gardens and stucco-sheathed volumes that read as both historic and contemporary.

41. Corner of Hollywood Boulevard and Vine Street

a. Taft Building, 1923
Walker and Eisen
6290 Hollywood Boulevard

b. B. H. Dyas Company Building (now **Broadway**), 1927
6300 Hollywood Boulevard

c. Hollywood Equitable Building, 1929
Aleck Curlett

6253 Hollywood Boulevard
These buildings are not great or even outstanding architecture. But for their time they were notable for their height—150 feet, the limit in the 1920s. They, therefore, represented a visible center of Hollywood. The Dyas (Broadway) Building has recently closed. Ironically, two lower buildings on the northwest corner were more notable—the **Laemmle Building** (1933) by Richard J. Neutra and **Sardi's Restaurant Building** (1932-34) by R. M. Schindler. Because of extravagant remodelling, neither has a sign of its architect's style.

42. Yucca-Vine Tower Building, ca. 1928
Gogerty and Weyl
Northwest corner of Yucca and Vine streets

French curvilinear ornament mixed with Art Deco (Zigzag) Moderne.

42. Yucca-Vine Tower Building

43. Capitol Records Tower Building, 1954
Welton Becket
1750 Vine Street

Symbolic architecture. What could be more appropriate for the headquarters of a recording company than it should look like a stack of records! Across the street at 1735 Vine Street is the old **Hollywood Playhouse** (now being refurbished as **The Hollywood Palace**), a Churrigueresque dream designed (1926) by Gogerty and Weyl.

44. Pantages Theatre Building, 1929
B. Marcus Priteca
6233 Hollywood Boulevard

On the exterior this theatre building does not have the sensational quality of Mann's Chinese down the street, but go inside. It is one of the most dramatic Baroque statements ever made.

45. Bungalow Court, ca. 1937
1935 Cahuenga Boulevard

Streamline Moderne.

46. ■Krotona Court (now Goldwater Patio Villa), 1914
Mead and Requa
2130 Vista del Mar Avenue

Originally built for the Theosophical Society, this complex is properly exotic, though its exoticism is played off against the purity of Irving J. Gill. The aura of the mystical East is suggested in the Islamic domes and the horseshoe and cusped arches.

47. Hansel and Gretel Cottages, ca. 1925
2234 and 2244 Vista del Mar Avenue

These two cottages look to the medieval rural English cottage. The **double cottage** with its central drive-through and folk paintings on its exterior walls, located at 6114-6116 Scenic Avenue, hints at the French rural cottage. Across the street, at 6111 Scenic Avenue, is a delightful **French Norman cottage** with a small tower attached to the hillside garage.

48. House, ca. 1920
6147 Temple Hill Drive

Islamic, with dome and all. A smaller **Islamic cottage** is situated nearby at 6106 Temple Hill Drive.

48. House

49. Mosk House, 1933
Richard J. Neutra
2742 Hollyridge Drive

The image of the Mosk House is intended to be machine repeatable. The living room serves as a focal point for the lower wings at each side. This house was meant to be the first of a colony of Neutra houses to be built on this site.

50. Hollywoodland Gates, 1923
Beachwood Drive at Westshire Drive

These sandstone, somewhat Gothic fairy-tale picturesque gates were built to tell you that you are entering a very prestigious part of Hollywood called Hollywoodland, on the lowest slopes of Mount Lee. The subdivision was advertised by the famous **Hollywood Sign** still standing high on Mount Lee. Originally, this sign of free-standing letters spelled out "Hollywoodland" but the "land" fell apart. The sign that is left has been restored and restored, a reminder that beneath the facade of materialism, Los Angeles hides a strain of sentiment. Both the gate and the sign are cultural-historic monuments of the city. The suburban area above the gates is fascinating for the student of period revivals.

51. Courtyard Apartments, 1952
Craig Ellwood
1570 Labaig Avenue

A Miesian complex in a strange area for "less is more" architecture to appear.

52. Warner Brothers West Coast Studios, 1922
Southeast corner of Sunset Boulevard and Bronson Avenue

A long, low building which salutes the street with a magnificent set of Doric columns.

53. Columbia Broadcasting System Building, 1937-38
William Lescaze and E.T. Heitschmidt
6121 Sunset Boulevard

A classic of the early (for America) International Style Modern now badly remodelled. You can still get the idea though if you erase the walls behind the pilotis.

54. Sunset-Vine Tower, 1964
Honnold, Reibsamen, and Rex
Corner of Sunset and Vine streets

Thin, late International Style Modern emphasizing the vertical.

55. U.S. Post Office, Hollywood Branch, 1937
Claude Beelman; Allison and Allison
1615 Wilcox Avenue

A small but impressive expression of the Classical PWA Moderne.

56. Retail Commercial Building, ca. 1928
6607 Sunset Boulevard

Lively Churrigueresque ornament around the entrance. We wonder how long such romantic buildings will last.

57. Hollywood Chamber of Commerce Building, 1925
Morgan, Walls, and Clements
Just west of Hudson Street on Sunset Boulevard

These architects always seem to treat their cast stone Churrigueresque ornament in a light-hearted manner. The building was more charming, however, with the large pepper trees which used to stand in front.

58. Crossroads of the World, 1936
Robert V. Derrah
6671 Sunset Boulevard

The theme is set by a Streamline Moderne ship sailing into Sunset Boulevard with a tall, open tower (supporting a lighted globe) on its prow. Go to the stern and you will find shops in the Spanish Colonial, Tudor, and French Provincial modes. It is perhaps significant that Derrah is one of the few architects to have two of his buildings

58. Crossroads of the World

declared cultural-historic landmarks by the Los Angeles Cultural Heritage Board. The other is the equally remarkable Coca Cola Bottling Plant near downtown Los Angeles.

59. Hollywood High School Science Building, 1934-35
Marsh, Smith, and Powell
Northwest corner of Sunset Boulevard and Highland Avenue

Monumental Streamline Moderne given juice by high-minded slogans at appropriate places and a characteristic Federal Arts Project bas-relief by Bartolo Mako over the door.

59. Hollywood High School Science Building

60. Tiny Naylor's Drive-in Restaurant, 1950
Douglas Honnold
7101 Sunset Boulevard, at the northwest corner of La Brea Avenue

A jutting angle of a roof marks one of the most famous (and probably the last) of the drive-in restaurants where you are waited upon in your car. This institution will probably be demolished before you get a chance to see it.

61. Toberman Storage Warehouse (now Bekins), 1925
Morgan, Walls, and Clements
1025 North Highland Avenue

This is an illustration of how a skyscraper could be clothed in the Spanish Colonial Revival mode and at the same time appear as an excellent example of the 1920s "American Vertical style." The building has lost some of its zest in remodelling.

62. Community Laundry Building (now **American Linen Supply**), 1927
W. J. Saunders
Northeast corner of Highland and Willoughby avenues

The piers of this Spanish Colonial Revival building are covered with shields. When the sun rakes over them about mid-day, the effect is that of the Casa de las Conchas in Salamanca. We never exaggerate.

63. Aaron Brothers Building, ca. 1928
East side of Orange Drive between Romaine Street and Willoughby Avenue

Spanish Colonial Revival with some good ornament. But its salient feature is its present unearthly color.

64. Producers Film Center, ca. 1928
Southeast corner of Romaine Street and Sycamore Avenue

A little gem of the Art Deco (Zigzag) Moderne.

64. Producers Film Center

65. Danziger Studio, 1965
Frank Gehry and Associates
7001 Melrose at Sycamore Avenue

Minimal architecture at its best; a common stucco box whose composition has raised it to High Art.

66. Telesound Studio, ca. 1945
6926 Melrose Avenue

65. Danziger Studio

The architect of this late Streamline Moderne building curved the corners into the entrance leaving a single column in the middle. This one, with its glass brick, is certainly not minimal!

67. EVCO Film Library Building, 1968
Leroy B. Miller
838 Seward Street

Minimal Modern architecture in brick.

68. Apartment Building, 1926
J. M. Close
747 N. Wilcox Avenue

It is amusing to speculate upon what on earth was in this builder-architect's mind when he conceived of buildings such as this, only one of several essays in the Egyptian Revival which he erected around Hollywood and elsewhere. As one would expect, that which is Egyptian is only the pylon front. The rest is pure L.A. stucco box.

69. Film Exchange, Inc. Building, ca. 1928
Southeast corner of Santa Monica Boulevard and Cole Avenue

A tiny relic of the Regency Moderne. There is a key on top of the tower which may someday release something.

70. Hollywood Studio Club Building, 1925-26
Julia Morgan
1215 Lodi Place

A mildly Italian Renaissance design; the second-floor loggia and the painted, decorated walls are carried out with real delicacy.

71a. Hollywood Cemetery, 1900
5950 Santa Monica Boulevard

With its mausoleums and ornate sculpture, not to mention the quantity of famous people buried here, this cemetery seems to be an annex of the Paramount Studio at the other end of the block. Probably the most distinguished architecture is the Classical **mausoleum of William Andrews Clark** designed (1922) by Robert Farquhar, though Egypt and other exotic sources are present in other monuments and mausoleums.

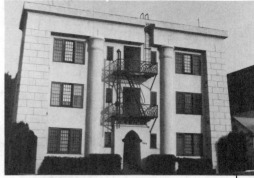
72. Karnack Apartment Building

71a. Hollywood Cemetery

71b. Paramount Studio Lot
5500 Melrose Avenue

Off limits to the public, but the main attraction is the old gates (ca. 1928) at the end of Bronson Avenue at Marathon Street. Here a Spanish Renaissance gate is posed between two white stucco, tile-roofed, Hispanic buildings. The script sign "Paramount Pictures" is as much a delightful period piece as the cast iron gates.

72. Karnak Apartment Building, 1925
J. M. Close
5617 La Mirada Avenue

Since there is another Egyptian Revival apartment house just a block from here, we suggest that urban renewalists investigate the possibility of building a pyramid in honor of J. M. Close. They could and have done worse.

73. Ahmed Apartment Building, 1925
J. M. Close
5616 Lexington Avenue

Almost a duplicate of the **Karnak**, this apartment house has been refitted with the original murals which were recently restored with considerable verve.

74. Jardinette Apartment Building, 1927
Richard J. Neutra
5128 W. Marathon Street, at southeast corner of Manhattan Place

This project began as a joint Schindler-Neutra venture, with Neutra finally doing it as an independent commission. Neutra provided bands of coloring between the windows, no longer apparent, that gave the illusion that this concrete building was composed of strongly contrasting horizontal bands of glass and projecting balconies.

74. Jardinette Apartment Building

75. House, 1939
Edward Lind
822 Alexandria Avenue

Lind was in Schindler's office in the mid-thirties. Here you can see how creatively he applied the lessons of the master to a small, one-story stucco dwelling.

75. House

76. Service Station, ca. 1928
5125 Melrose Avenue
Art Deco (Zigzag) Moderne.

77. Hollywood-Wilshire Health Center, 1968
Honnold, Reibsamen, and Rex
5505 Melrose Avenue

Some may write this low, concrete building off as sixties Brutalist. We think it has class.

78. Morgan House, 1917
Irving J. Gill
626 North Arden Road

One of Gill's prototype, single-family houses. As with most of his buildings, its walls are of hollow tile covered with stucco.

79. House, ca. 1925
717 June Street

A tiny mosque.

80. Four Apartment Buildings, ca. 1928
1128-1144 S. Vista Street, just above Santa Monica Boulevard

A whole row of Andalusian treasures.

Hollywood Hills

Although the roads were laid out in the twenties, the summit of this section of the Santa Monica Mountains did not begin to be developed until the thirties. Schindler's **Fitzpatrick House** (1936), which is so prominent when you finally twist to the top of Laurel Canyon Boulevard, was built as a real estate come-on to attract buyers to the area. The development of the summit before and after World War II is a dramatic illustration of how a landscape, even a rugged one, can be transformed by energy and water. Indeed, the vegetation is now far more significant than most of the housing.

Only a baker's dozen important and visible houses are up here, but they are so hard to find that we have tried to make this area as clear as possible. Otherwise, we set this section apart from Hollywood simply because when you are up this high, you might as well stay up. Incidentally, there are other things on and just off Mulholland Drive, a road that sticks with determination to the top of the hills almost as far as the ocean, many miles to the west. The nearest buildings are in the Bel Air section.

1. Johnson House, 1963
Lloyd Wright
7017 Senalda Drive

Nothing more nor less than ancient Mayan made Moderne. If the lavender hue isn't original, it should be.

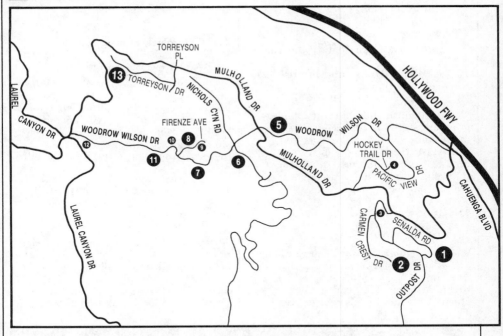

2. Wolff House, 1960
Ladd and Kelsey
2400 Carmen Crest Drive

A sheer stucco wall and metal doors seal this purist house from the curious.

3. Druckman House, 1941
R. M. Schindler
2764 Outpost Drive

A two-story house covered with one of Schindler's unique gable roofs. Now it's almost impossible to see, but we thought you would be happy to know that it's there.

4. Carling House, 1950
John Lautner
Pacific View and Hockey Trail drives

One of Lautner's most dramatic gestures, raised above your view.

5. Garred House, 1949
Milton H. Caughey
7445 Woodrow Wilson Drive

International Style Modern simplicity almost completely screened from the street.

6. General Panel House, 1950
Konrad Wachsmann and Walter Gropius
2861 Nichols Canyon Road

Of the four such houses by these famous architects in the Los Angeles area, this is the most easily seen. This single-story design exudes logic and dullness.

7. Bell House, 1940
John Lautner
7714 Woodrow Wilson Drive

Set far from Woodrow Wilson Drive on a very private road, the house can nevertheless be seen from certain points to the east. Like Lautner's own house in the Silver Lake district, the pre-World War II Bell House shares stylistic similarities with the works of Harris, Ain, and Wurster.

8. Branch House, 1942
Richard J. Neutra
7716 Firenze Avenue

About all you see from the street is the carport and some white clapboards. This house has been altered extensively.

9. House, 1937-39
Barcume and King
7777 Firenze Avenue

A mixture of Monterey and Moderne.

10. ▪Shulman House and Studio, 1950
Raphael S. Soriano
7875 Woodrow Wilson Drive

The distinguished architectural photographer's studio is connected to the main house by a small pergola and courtyard. He has landscaped the grounds so magnificently (including a Redwood grove!) that you cannot see the house from the street.

11. Granstedt House, 1938
Harwell H. Harris
7922 Woodrow Wilson Drive

We are pleased that this beautiful house can easily be seen from the street. A drive-through garage runs parallel to the street. Also, here you can see how Harris worked with his roof to create clerestory and other high sources of lighting.

12. Fitzpatrick House, 1936
R. M. Schindler
8078 Woodrow Wilson Drive

The de Stijl composition of overlaid volumes of horizontal stucco surfaces can best be seen from below on Laurel Canyon before it joins Mulholland and Woodrow Wilson. The front has been altered, but the southwest facade and the sunken garden to the west are still intact.

13. Malin House ("Chemosphere"), 1960
John Lautner
776 Torreyson Drive

At first it seems to be a flying saucer, but then you see that it is on a pedestal firmly riveted to the hill. The house is at the end of a private drive, but there are many places to view it on Torreyson Drive and Woodrow Wilson Drive.

12. Fitzpatrick House

East Hollywood, Los Feliz

1. MPA Office Building, 1928
S. Charles Lee
Southwest corner of Hollywood Boulevard
and Western Avenue

Art Deco (Zigzag) Moderne—but the
great effect is in the high relief sculpture
on the balcony fronts.

2. Hollywood Christian Church, 1922
Robert H. Orr
1717 North Gramercy Place

A great Ionic pile.

Kleihauer Memorial Chapel, 1967
Carleton M. Winslow, Jr. and Warren
Waltz

Austerely exotic, this building has no relationship to the older building.

3. Garfield Court Apartments, 1927
A. J. Waid
1833 Garfield Place

A really grand Spanish Colonial court
with beautiful trees. Even the fire escapes
are beautifully designed and crafted.

4. Security Pacific Bank Building,
1972-73
Craig Ellwood Associates
1811 N. Western Avenue

"Less is more" at a 45-degree angle to
the street.

5. Bungalow Court, ca. 1915
1742-1752 N. Western Avenue

An Oriental complex complete with entrance gate.

6. Taggart House, 1922-24
Lloyd Wright
5423 Live Oak Drive

One of Lloyd Wright's simplest and most picturesque stucco and wood buildings, carefully related to the hill to which it clings. Incidentally, **Ferndell Park** just below the house is one of the loveliest in Los Angeles.

7. Samuels-Navarro House

5. Bungalow Court

7. Samuels-Navarro House, 1926-28
Lloyd Wright
5609 Valley Oak Drive

Here Lloyd Wright translates the textured, pre-cast concrete Mayanesque block into pressed metal. The result hints at pre-Columbian Revival and Art Deco (Zig-zag) Moderne composition. The main (top) floor is cross-axial, with one arm terminating in an open court with swimming pool.

8. Ernest House, 1937
Gregory Ain
5670 Holly Oak Drive

Using large areas of glass in this house, Ain emphasizes the relationship between indoors and out. Some details of the house indicate his admiration for Schindler's designs of the late twenties and early thirties.

9. Edwards House, 1936
Gregory Ain
5642 Holly Oak Drive

This single-story house is comprised of a series of walled enclosures that give each space complete privacy.

10. Vinmont House, 1926
Roland E. Coate
5136 Los Feliz Boulevard

A characteristic Mediterranean/Spanish Colonial Revival two-story house by an architect who specialized in this mode but who also did equally well in the Tudor and Colonial Revival styles.

11. ∎Sowden House, 1926
Lloyd Wright
5121 Franklin Avenue

Built around an inner court which originally contained an elaborate fountain and Mayan-inspired stele, the building is entered through a door at the lower level, almost hidden under a huge, cave-like window framed in decorative concrete blocks.

6. Taggart House

12. Apartment Building, ca. 1938
Carl Kay
1941-43 Mariposa Avenue

A two-story Streamline Moderne
composition.

13. House, ca. 1925
David J. Witmer
2020 Edgemont Street

An unusual example of a reinforced concrete house with the wide board marks of
the forms strongly showing. Its image and
detailing are Tudor.

13. House

14. Moore House, 1964
Craig Ellwood and Associates
4791 Bonvue Avenue

Here Ellwood applies his personal Miesian
aesthetic to a structure that exhibits even
more wood than the Kubly House which
he was building in Pasadena at the same
time.

15. Skolnik House, 1952
R. M. Schindler
2567 Glendower Avenue

In several of his late works Schindler
concentrated on simple, stucco-covered
volumes, roofs extending over clerestory
windows, and thin linear wood members.
All are present in the Skolnik House.
Later additions were made by Gregory
Ain (1960).

16. ▪Ennis House, 1924
Frank Lloyd Wright
2607 Glendower Avenue

Variously called a mausoleum, a Mayan
temple, and a palace, this is without a
doubt the most monumental of Wright's
experiments with "knit-block" construction.
It is being carefully restored by the owner.

16. Ennis House

17. House, ca. 1924
Northwest corner of Los Feliz Boulevard
and New Hampshire Avenue

A striking revealed concrete house best
viewed from New Hampshire Avenue.

**18. Los Feliz Manor Apartment Build-
ing,** 1929
Jack Grundfor
4643 Los Feliz Boulevard

Art Deco (Zigzag) Moderne—white with
original green trim.

19. Greek Theatre 1929-30
Department of Parks
Vermont Canyon Road

A flat Doric facade masks an open theatre
seating four thousand people. It isn't
much as architecture, but you will
certainly notice it on the way up
Vermont Canyon.

**20. Griffith Park Observatory and
Planetarium,** 1935
John C. Austin and F. M. Ashley.
Obelisk and bas-reliefs (Galileo, Coper-
nicus, etc.), 1934, Archibald Garner.
Interior Murals, 1935, Hugo Ballin.
Western Canyon Road

PWA Classical Moderne in exposed reinforced concrete. A fine achievement of the
Depression years. High on the hill, it is a

very romantic object, completing many vistas in Los Angeles like a folly in a huge eighteenth century English garden. Its siting and entrance are pure axial Beaux Arts.

20. *Griffith Park Observatory and Planetarium*

21. Thirteenth Church of Christ, Scientist, 1930
Allison and Allison
1750 N. Edgemont Street

A very sophisticated Italian Renaissance ensemble.

22. Barnsdall Park

Entrance on Hollywood Boulevard about 100 yards west of intersection with Vermont Avenue.
■Barnsdall ("Hollyhock") House, 1917-1920
Frank Lloyd Wright

22. *"Hollyhock" House, Barnsdall Park*

Studio-Residence A, 1920
R. M. Schindler, under Wright's supervision

Garden Wall and Landscaping, 1924
R. M. Schindler

Wading Pool and Pergola, 1925
R. M. Schindler and Richard J. Neutra

Junior Arts Center, 1967
Paul Hunter, Walter Benedict, Herbert Kahn, Edward Tarrell

Municipal Art Gallery, 1971
Wehmueller and Stephens

Aline Barnsdall, like another oil millionaire, Gaylord Wilshire, toyed with Marxist ideas. She envisioned a veritable "peoples park" when she gave her estate to the city. In the latter day the fringes of her estate on Vermont and Sunset have been inundated with commerical buildings and a hospital that do nothing for the spirit of the place, to say the least.

But go up the drive and you are almost out of this skulchpile. The first important building that you see is Studio-Residence A, now called the **Arts and Crafts Center.** This was to be the first of several such artists' residences in the manner of the MacDowell Colony in New Hampshire. Even though designed by Schindler, the building is very beholden to the Prairie style of Frank Lloyd Wright, for whom Schindler acted as supervisor of the main house construction while the Master was in Japan. Studio-Residence B was razed in the 1950s.

The main house, with its pre-Columbian air and stylized hollyhock ornamentation, is in good condition, thanks to a recent restoration (by Wright's son, Lloyd). Some mistakes have been made. Nevertheless, to those who watched the house literally crumble in the fifties and sixties, the new look is generally praiseworthy. We look forward to the original elephantine furniture being reproduced and installed. Only the dining room furniture (chairs with hollyhock backs!) and a few other pieces are original. The moat in front of the fireplace was uncovered in the recent restoration but faced with common-colored tile. Wall-to-wall carpet was put over fine hardwood floors. But the building is shored up, alive, and well. It is open Tuesdays and Thursdays by appointment—call 485-4580. Needless to say, even with time's changes, the interior, particularly in the entrance, living room, and dining areas, displays Frank Lloyd Wright's magical spatial concepts. All is drama. Wright constructed a temporary gallery between the main house and the pre-Columbian Revival kennels in 1956. This was supposed simply to house a major showing of his drawings but was used as the municipal art gallery until the late sixties, when a new gallery was designed and constructed by another firm and the old gallery torn down. No loss, except that Wright had several interesting designs for a new museum. Perhaps it is for the better that he did not get the commission, since it is well known that when he designed a museum he made more problems for the museum directors than he solved. Suffice it to say that the present building, while not great architecture, has exhibition spaces that, though smaller, are much better adapted to the viewing of art than those in most other museums around town.

The Junior High Art Center is a much-needed facility in a light Wrightian ner. The garden structures were designed by Schindler and Neutra. The original landscaping was by Lloyd Wright.

23. House, 1924
Alfred Heineman
2234 Commonwealth Avenue

Important because with its roof swooping into the eaves and Hansel and Gretel ornament, it demonstrates a tendency of the Arts and Crafts movement toward sentimentality.

24. Schrage-Hallauer House, 1951
Raphael S. Soriano
2648 Commonwealth Avenue

Almost invisible, but it is here. A two-story, International Style Modern design in stucco, glass, and steel.

25. ■Lovell House, 1929
Richard J. Neutra
4616 Dundee Drive

Without question, this house and Schindler's house for the same clients in New-

port Beach are *the* greatest monuments of the early International Style Modern in Southern California. The Lovell House, with its open, free-flowing plan, its modern machine-age materials, and structural form, firmly established Neutra's world reputation. Today, more than fifty years after its construction and in spite of slight alterations, the Lovell House looks new—the highest compliment.

26. Apartment House, 1935
Northeast corner of Los Feliz Boulevard and Nella Vista Avenue

Regency Moderne.

27. Johnstone House, 1935
W. P. Kesling
3311 Lowry Road

Streamline Moderne, of course. We emphasize this style because it took an act of moderate courage to flout the conventions of the time.

28. Ulm House, 1937
3606 Amesbury Road

We are sounding one note. Just the same, this Streamline Moderne two-story house, with its dramatic curved staircase encased in glass brick, simply stands out.

28. Ulm House

29. Cole House, 1948
Ain, Johnson, and Day
3642 Lowry Road

A regional version of International Style Modern in stucco and wood.

30. House, ca. 1928
End of Lowry Road at Shannon Road

Ye olde English cottage.

31. Griffith Park Girl's Camp, 1949
Smith, Jones, and Contini
North end of Griffith Park Boulevard

A wood post-and-beam structure which is more of an open shelter than a building.

32. Farrell House, 1926
Lloyd Wright
3209 Lowry Road

An ordinary Spanish Colonial Revival bungalow of the twenties becomes pre-Columbian with a facing of textured concrete blocks.

33. Carr House, 1925
Lloyd Wright
Southeast corner of Lowry Road and Rowena Avenue

Originally this still-unusual house had a tent room at the side (overlooking Rowena) and a bent pattern of fine canvas awnings which provided privacy and kept the west sun off the side of the house. Portions of the exterior stucco walls were stencilled to suggest an ornamented concrete block pattern.

33. Carr House

34. Anthony House, 1927
Bernard Maybeck; Mark Daniels, landscape architect
3412 Waverly Drive

Now a Roman Catholic retreat, this is almost impossible to see unless you want to retreat, which might be a good idea. We include it because it is the only well-authenticated building by Maybeck in the Los Angeles area. It is one of the architect's most romantic houses, which is saying a lot. The general effect is Medieval, but of course Maybeck thought nothing of bringing in elements of other styles in order to get desired effects. It is fascinating to compare Maybeck's spatial explosions with Frank Lloyd Wright's equally dramatic but more integrated volumes. In 1968 impressive formal gardens and walled terraces were laid out by Lutah M. Riggs. They represent the most extensive formal gardens realized in Southern California in the post-World War II years.

34. Anthony House

35. McAlmon House, 1935-36
R. M. Schindler
2721 Waverly Drive

The house is a piece of architectural sculpture embracing the complete range of Schindler's de Stijl aesthetic. Actually you get two for the price of one. The house, with garage at street level, is an old bungalow which Schindler moved down the hill and clothed in modern dress.

36. Schapiro House, 1949
J. R. Davidson
Northwest corner of Waverly Drive and Maxwell Street

Almost all of Davidson's houses are hard to see, but here enough of the jutting roof is visible to make your trip worthwhile.

37. Bungalow Court, ca. 1925
2906-12 Griffith Park Boulevard

35. McAlmon House

Each of these eight units is a miniature Norman cottage. A matching tower stands at the rear to give visual focus. Certainly this is one of the outstanding bungalow courts in the Los Angeles area!

38. John Marshall High School, 1930-31
George M. Lindsey
Northeast corner of Tracy and Saint George streets

Collegiate Gothic. After the 1971 earthquake the School Board said that it had

38. John Marshall High School

to come down. But the neighborhood, after a fine battle, convinced the board that the shell could be stabilized and the interior remodelled.

39. Franklin Avenue ("Shakespeare") Bridge, 1926
J. C. Wright for City Engineer's Office
Built over Monon Street between Saint George Street and Myra Avenue

A great, open spandrel arch is laced by long Gothic arches. At both ends of the bridge are pairs of Gothic aedicules which cry out for sculptured saints.

40. Apartment Building for Dr. F. Haight, ca. 1937
Wesley Eager
4116 Franklin Avenue

The lines of this Streamline Moderne complex are muted in comparison to those of the spectacular bridge next to it.

41. Schlesinger House, 1952
R. M. Schindler
1901 Myra Avenue
From the street this dwelling is a deceptively plain design for Schindler, yet the interiors and his method of providing natural lighting for them are as successful and complex as any of his other houses.

42. Apartment House, 1939
J. Knauer
4230-4234 Franklin Avenue

Part of the fine effect of this Streamline
Moderne building is the result of its being
sited on the crest of a hill.

43. Elliot House, 1930
R. M. Schindler
4237 Newdale Drive

Schindler set the house far back on the
site in order to allow a view of the valley.
On the street level is a garage and entrance, both covered by a pergola. The
house is also partially covered by a pergola. The living space on the second level
opens to terraces, both front and rear.

43. Elliot House

44. Gogol House, 1938-39
Raphael S. Soriano
2190 Talmadge Street

Only a single floor is visible on the
Talmadge Street side of the house. A deck
and patio face toward the view. The style:
purist International Style Modern.

45. Walt Disney House, 1932
F. Scott Crowhurst
4053 Woring Way

As one would expect, this house is an
enlarged Hansel and Gretel cottage. A
large, squat, round tower with a high-
pitched conical roof houses the entrance.

Silver Lake

For so small a district, the Silver
Lake area has a high concentration of first-rate architecture,
making it one of the most important places to visit in the city. The most
interesting work is by the best Los Angeles Modernists: Schindler, Neutra,
Ain, Soriano, Harris, Lautner. These
works stand side by side with houses
designed in the Period Revivals of the
twenties and thirties. It is essentially this
latter work which gives Silver Lake its
special character. In fact, looking from
Schindler's ingenious **Walker House**
down over the flood of tile roofs to the
lake below reminds one, well, of Los
Angeles's version of Urbino. Obviously
the view (of hills, Los Angeles, and the
reservoir) was the attraction, and the architects have played up to it. Along the
eastern section of Sunset Boulevard running through the area is a sprinkling of
Spanish Colonial Revival and Moderne
commercial relics. There are also a few
delightful exotics scattered hither and
yon. For example, at 933 Parkman Avenue is a two-story **garden apartment**
(ca. 1920) which declares its allegiance
to Islam through its minarets, dome,
and arches. Here are our choices of the
most representative architectural finds in
Silver Lake:

1. Holy Virgin Mary Russian Ortho-
dox Cathedral, 1928
658 Micheltorena Street

A lovely Russian village church, the cathedral is even more attractive inside. It

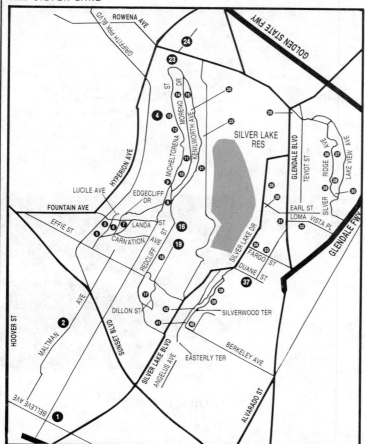

reflects the taste of the emigrès from the Revolution—Russian intellectuals of the Count Tolstoy school. Great simplicity with patches of opulence.

2. McIntosh House, 1939
Richard J. Neutra
1317 Maltman Avenue

One of the earliest of Neutra's wood-sheathed houses. The narrow plan with the garage, sleeping, and service areas in front and living area to the rear takes full advantage of the narrow lot and view over the city.

3. Landa Apartment Building, 1966
A. E. Morris
Southeast corner of Griffith Park Boulevard and Landa Street

A stepped design of connected stucco boxes certainly inspired by the earlier work of R. M. Schindler. This architect is even more Expressionistic than Schindler.

.3. Landa Apartment Building

4. ■Bubeshko Apartment Building, 1938 and 1941
R. M. Schindler
Southeast corner of Griffith Park Boulevard and Lyric Avenue

A dramatic setback of each level allows the building to hug the hillside and at the same time to continue internal spaces of each apartment outward to roof terraces and patios.

5. Falk Apartments, 1939
R. M. Schindler
Northeast corner of Lucile and Carnation avenues

Working with an extremely difficult hillside site, Schindler twists and turns the building so that each living unit has its own garden and roof terrace.

6. Manola Court (Sachs) Apartment Building, 1926-40
R. M. Schindler
1811-13 Edgecliff Drive

These apartments, designed for the artist/designer Herman Sachs, are examples of the studied abstraction which Schindler was beginning to develop. They are designed as steps leading from the lower street up the steep hillside to the next.

7. Westby House, 1938
R. M. Schindler
1805 Maltman Avenue

Schindler's late de Stijl aesthetic at work in a two-story house.

8. Daniels House, 1939
Gregory Ain
1856 Micheltorena Street

The stucco box as a fragile container, masterfully detailed and imaginatively planned. The architect angled the house on a steep hillside in order to allow for a private patio and garden.

9. Lautner House, 1939
John Lautner
2007 Micheltorena Street

Since World War II, Lautner has become one of the leading Expressionist architects in the country. Here we see him working in a subdued, controlled manner with redwood and concrete.

10. "Silvertop" House and Garden, 1957
John Lautner
2138 Micheltorena Street

Here's what we have just been talking about! This structure gets a high grade for exotic form. The total design includes the cantilevered driveway and swimming pool, the house, and of course, the landscaping. Actually it can be seen better from a rear entrance near 2134 Redcliff Street and best (with binoculars) from across the lake on East Silver Lake Boulevard.

10. Silvertop House

11. Olive House, 1933
R. M. Schindler
2236 Micheltorena Street

A house full of Schindler's wonderful contradictions. The house seems flat-roof International Style from the street, but it is all shed and gable roofs on the garden and view side. As a result, the interior is a syncopation of ceiling heights and changing axes. The living room, with its built-in furniture, is one of Schindler's most handsome.

12. Alexander House, 1941
Harwell H. Harris
2265 Micheltorena Street

Harris had learned a great deal from Frank Lloyd Wright about composition. Here he simplified Wright's Usonian concept. The low, hipped roof and simple walls seem to have as much to do with Wright as with the traditional California Ranch house.

13. Tierman House, 1938-39
Gregory Ain; Visscher Boyd,
collaborator.
2323 Micheltorena Street

A very ingenious house on two levels,
pivoting around a central core lighted by
a skylight. Essentially, the Tierman
House is a stucco box with an attached
garage, one-story on the street, two-story
on the garden side.

14. Orans House, 1941
Gregory Ain
2404 Micheltorena Street

The living room is covered by a gently
sloping shed roof that floats above bands
of glass.

14. Orans House

15. Van Patten House, 1934-35
R. M. Schindler
2320 Moreno Drive

This dramatic hillside house has been
fenced in and the garages with their
overlapping shed roofs have been converted to living space, but basically
Schindler's ideas have been maintained.

16. Wilson House, 1938
R. M. Schindler
2090 Redcliff Street

Here, in another of his hillside houses,
Schindler cantilevered three floors of
projecting and receding boxes out to the
rear and then connected them with
projecting balconies at the side.

17. Hopmans House, 1951
Harwell H. Harris
1727 N. Dillon Street

A subtle touch revealed in a wood
pavilion, the house has been modified a
bit since it was built.

18. Lipetz House, 1935
Raphael S. Soriano
1843 Dillon Street

The living room is in the form of a
Streamline Moderne ship's bridge. Bands
of horizontal steel windows and metal
railings extend the nautical theme, now
somewhat altered.

18. Lipetz House

19. House, ca. 1930
1824 San Jacinto Street (beyond the turn
of Dillon Street)

A doll house of a mosque with flashing
tiles on its lovely tower.

20. Droste House, 1940
R. M. Schindler
2025 Kenilworth Avenue

As this house was being finished,
Schindler asked the owners to sit where
their dining table would be on the second floor, so he could adjust the lintel of
the picture window so that they wouldn't
miss anything in the view.

21. Walker House, 1936
R. M. Schindler
2100 Kenilworth Avenue

The closed-in street facade reveals
nothing of the glass and projecting-
balconied, three-level drama to the rear
inside.

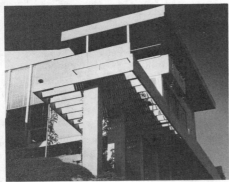

21. Walker House

22. Hansen House, 1951
Harwell H. Harris
2305 W. Silver Lake Boulevard

This stucco and wood beauty is rather surprising amidst the relatively conventional suburbia on this street.

23. Kenngott-Brossmer Design Studio Building, 1968
Carl Maston
2840 Rowena Avenue

A grey brick street facade almost hides a beautifully articulated court with much use of wood.

24. Avenel Housing, 1948
Ain, Johnson, and Day; Katharine Bashford and Fred Barlow, Jr., landscape architects
2839 Avenel Street

This is now painted pink, but the raking angle of the roof marks it as early Los Angeles International style mixed with L.A.'s tradition of the common stucco box and enclosed gardens.

25. Conrad's Drive-In, (now Astro's), 1958
Louis Armet and Eldon Davis
Southeast corner of Glendale Boulevard and Fletcher Drive

A striking example of People's Moderne of the 1950s with its angled roof. Other examples of Armet and Davis's designs are: **Romeo's, Times Square** (1955; now **Johnie's**), at the corner of Fairfax Avenue and Wilshire Boulevard; **Pann's** (1956), at the corner of La Cienega Boulevard, Centinela Avenue, and La Tijera Boulevard in Inglewood; and **Norm's** (1957), at the corner of Overhill Drive and Slauson Avenue.

26. Hawk House, 1939
Harwell H. Harris
2421 Silver Ridge Avenue

Although very close to the road, this house is easy to miss. It is in dense foliage, but you can still see enough of this horizontal board house with its low, hovering roof to recognize the work of a consummate artist. The serene Oriental interior has always been beautifully maintained.

27. Howe House, 1925
R. M. Schindler
2422 Silver Ridge Avenue

The exterior is horizontal board and batten and concrete, very boxy. The interior is a tour de force in interlocking spaces. Incidentally Eads Howe was known as the "King of the Hoboes." The floor of the house below street level was, according to legend, a sort of dormitory for tramps who would come up from the railroad below. We cannot vouch for this, but it should be true.

27. Howe House

28. Duplexes, 1958-62
A. E. Morris
2378-90 Silver Ridge Avenue

Morris is sort of a Schindler undisciplined by Loos, who was a great disciplinarian. These two-story buildings shoot out blocky stucco volumes with apparent abandon. Number 2390 is Morris's own Studio Building, (1957). The studio has a Wrightian flavor, realized in steel, glass, and brick. Equally theatrical is Morris's **Murakakami House** (1962) at 2378 Silver Lake.

28. Duplexes

29. Sabsay House, 1940
J. R. Davidson
2351 Silver Ridge Avenue

Rather quiet and bulky-looking from the street, this is one of the few works by Davidson that you can actually see.

30. Duplexes, 1964
A. E. Morris
2330-50 Silver Ridge Avenue

Another group of Morris's stucco box duplexes, similar to those nearby.

31. Bungalow Court, ca. 1926
Glendale Boulevard at Loma Vista Place

A lovely grouping of Hansel and Gretel Medieval bungalows.

32. House, ca. 1965
2384 Loma Vista Place

One of the most conscious imitations of Antonio Gaudi in America. It is most strange to see the Barcelona architect's special style coupled with louvered windows.

33. Eltinge House, 1921
Pierpont and Walter Davis; Charles G. Adams, landscape architect
2327 Fargo Street (reached from Apex Street)

A Spanish Colonial garage plus garden walls are about all you can see of this extensive Mediterranean villa and its terraced Italian gardens. The Eltinge House was one of L.A.'s first major essays in the Mediterranean style.

34. Presley House, 1946
Gordon Drake
2114 Fargo Street

Drake was one of California's gifted young architects in the immediate post-World War II years. His early death cut short a promising career. Unfortunately there are few of his houses in existence, and none of them remains unaltered. This is one of the the least changed.

35. Neutra House, 1964
Richard J. Neutra and Dion Neutra (principal)
2300 E. Silver Lake Boulevard

The original pure International Style Modern (Research) house, built in 1933, was partially burned in 1963. The present structure, though far from having the experimental quality of the first, is late, romantic, Neutra. It steps in three stages away from Silver Lake, and each layer has its own tiny roof-top lake.

36. Colony of Neutra Houses
Richard J. Neutra, Dion Neutra
Intersection of Earl Street with Silver Lake Boulevard and Argent Place

It is rare that you have the chance to survey the work of a major Modernist in such a concentrated form, particularly in Los Angeles.

a. Yew House, 1957
2226 E. Silver Lake Boulevard

b. Kambara House, 1960
2232 E. Silver Lake Boulevard

c. Inadomi House, 1960
2238 E. Silver Lake Boulevard

d. Sokol House, 1948
2242 E. Silver Lake Boulevard

e. Treweek House, 1948
2250 E. Silver Lake Boulevard

f. Reunion House, 1949
(Remodelled by Dion Neutra 1966 and later)
2240 Earl Street

g. Flavin House, 1958
2218 Argent Place

h. Ohara House, 1961
2210 Argent Place

i. Akai House, 1961
2200 Argent Place

37. Silverview Condominiums, 1983
EDC, Inc. Architects (Walter Abronson and Ko Kiyohara)
2330 Duane Street

A suitable neighbor for the Neutras, but the architects should have had Neutra's sensitivity to landscape architecture in order to tone down the white walls. Maybe the landscaping will come in time.

38. Koblick House, 1937
Richard J. Neutra
1816-18 Silverwood Terrace

A three-story, beautifully-sited house with windows ranked around the third-floor living room, which has a sensational view of the lake and mountains.

39. Walther House, 1937
Harwell H. Harris
1742 Silverwood Terrace

It is very interesting to see the two very different design philosophies of Neutra—the dwelling as an art-object machine—and Harris—the dwelling as a romantic shelter—on the same street.

40. Feldman House, 1953
Gregory Ain
1607 Angelus Avenue

The facade is mainly bands of windows. The setback of the second story makes the house almost classically composed.

41. Silverwood Duplex, 1965
A. E. Morris
1611 Silverwood Terrace

Nice, white, with Schindleresque interlocking volumes and details.

41. Silverwood Duplex

42. Three Houses, 1935-38
William Kesling
1530-36 Easterly Terrace
2808 W. Effie Street

Balance somewhere between High Art Modern and Streamline Moderne. Kesling designed other Streamline Moderne houses in this area, but they have been altered.

42. Three Houses

Echo Park, Elysian Park

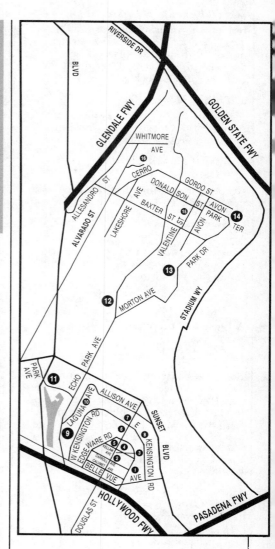

This area is cut off by freeway now from the Silver Lake area to which it is atmospherically related. The northern part has some funky things as well as high art. The district around Echo Park is much older. In fact, the 1300 block of **Carroll Avenue** in Angelino Heights has the highest concentration of Victorian houses still remaining in Los Angeles—not many in comparision to San Francisco but very choice—including two by Joseph Cather Newsom.

Don't miss the **lake** in Echo Park (1894), reminiscent, if you please, of the Public Garden in Boston with its peddle boats for rent and the most magnificent lotus plants you will find anywhere.

1. Betsford House, ca. 1890
801 E. Edgeware Road

The mansard tower, with original iron balustrade, deserves mention.

2. Carroll Avenue

This was once an esteemed residential district with a nice view of the city, previously reached by streetcar. It has been coming back in the last decade, due mainly to attempts by its proud residents to improve the surroundings. Two Victorian houses have even been moved in to take the place of ones demolished long ago. We begin at the east end of the block.

a. Philips House, 1887
1300 Carroll Avenue

Almost pure Queen Anne with just a little Eastlake decoration here and there.

b. Russell House, 1887-88
1316 Carroll Avenue

Again, Queen Anne, but this time with pronounced Stick style features.

c. Heim House, 1887-88
1320 Carroll Avenue

This time Queen Anne combines with Italianate brackets in the cornice and a wonderful round tower.

d. Scheerer House, 1887-88
1324 Carroll Avenue

A Queen Anne cottage.

e. House, ca. 1887
1321 Carroll Avenue

Both this house and the next, number 1325, were once on Court Street — 1145 and 1123 respectively. They were moved to Carroll Avenue in 1981. Both are late Eastlake working into the Queen Anne.

f. House, ca. 1887
1325 Carroll Avenue
Eastlake/Queen Anne.

g. ■Sessions House, 1888
Joseph Cather Newson
1330 Carroll Avenue

A fine Newsom creation recognized as such by the architect, who illustrated and described it in his *Picturesque and Artistic Homes and Buildings of California,* No. 3 (1890). The predominant Queen Anne theme of Carroll Avenue is here sustained and embellished by Moorish (Chinese?) detail, including "Moongate" openings on the second-floor porch.

h. Innes House, 1887-88
1329 Carroll Avenue

Built for a shoe store magnate, this house illustrates the peculiar California wedding of Queen Anne and Eastlake.

i. Haskin House, ca. 1888
1344 Carroll Avenue

Some authorities have dated this house in the nineties but it is such a pure example of Queen Anne (much spool-work and no Eastlake ornament) expansiveness that we suspect it was done about the same time as the other houses (if not earlier). It is immaculately maintained and constantly being used as a subject for painters and a backdrop for TV commercials.

j. Sanders House, 1887
1345 Carroll Avenue

Good Queen Anne with wrought-iron railing still crowning the roof.

2. Sanders House

k. Pinney House, 1887
1355 Carroll Avenue

Similar in style and scale to the **Sanders House** next door, this house is still in the Pinney Family. It seems to be in its original colors.

l. Cohn House, ca. 1887
1443 Carroll Avenue

A two-story Queen Anne house with an unusual corner bay tower.

m. Cottage, 1889
Joseph Cather Newsom
1407 Carroll Avenue

This story-and-a-half cottage falls basically into the Queen Anne style, though some portions, such as the angled bay and the roof, have an Eastlake quality. This was one of several spec houses built from Newsom's published "El Capitan" plan.

Other houses on Carroll Avenue are worthy of preservation and restoration. In fact, the whole of Angelino Heights is a delight to anyone who can, in the mind's eye, see these houses and their gardens restored to their original condition.

2m. Cottage

3. House, ca. 1890
1334 Kelham Avenue

A very late Queen Anne/Colonial Revival cottage.

4. Houses, 1890
1347, 1343, and 1341 Kelham Avenue

Obviously designed by the same Queen Anne inspired architect (builder?). Number 1341 has the most ornament.

5. House, ca. 1905
1405 Kelham Avenue

A large Mission Revival dwelling. This suggests that the Angelino Heights area is important for other styles besides the Victorian ones.

6. House, ca. 1887
917 Douglas Street

A rare, almost pure, example of the Eastlake style.

7. House, ca. 1896
1101 Douglas Street

A merging of the Queen Anne and Colonial revivals.

8. Weller House, 1887
824 Kensington Road

Certainly this Queen Anne gem is worthy of its neighbors on Carroll Avenue. The spindly porches and open belvedere tower add to its fairy tale quality.

8. Weller House

9. Saint Athanasius Episcopal Church, ca. 1890
Northeast corner of Echo Park and Laguna avenues

This mixture of Shingle style with diminutive Gothicism suggests the work of Ernest Coxhead, but it lacks the strong mannerist quality that usually marks his work.

10. Lacey Duplex, 1922
R. M. Schindler
830-832 Laguna Avenue

A remodelling of an older house, Schindler's design suggests both the Spanish Colonial Revival and the early Moderne.

11. Angelus Temple, 1925
A. F. Leicht
Northeast corner of Glendale Boulevard and Park Avenue

The architect of this concrete, classical-styled temple must have been inspired by the Mormon Tabernacle in Salt Lake City. Strange, since the egg shape is hardly symbolic of the Four Square Gospel once preached by the Temple's Amy Semple McPherson.

12. Apartment Building, ca. 1928
1650 Echo Park Avenue

A four-story Art Deco (Zigzag) Moderne structure further enlivened by a vivid floral motif.

13. Southhall House, 1938
R. M. Schindler
1855 Park Drive

As so often happens in avant-garde houses of this period, the garage is right on the street with the house secluded behind it. The plan of the house is a large rectangle from which three bayed spaces project. The whole is sheathed in plywood.

14. Atwater Bungalows, 1931
Robert Stacy-Judd
1431 and 1433 Avon Park Terrace
Northwest corner of Park Drive and Avon Park Terrace (best seen following northerly route along Park Drive as indicated).

This architect, who was best known for his advocacy of the pre-Columbian Revival, here shows himself equally the master of the Pueblo Revival in a most romantic rendering.

15. Ross House, 1938
Raphael S. Soriano
2123 Valentine Street

Again, a garage stands almost in front of one of Soriano's handsome early International Style Modern designs. The two-story glass and stucco house is one of Soriano's best works.

16. Meier House, 1942
Harwell H. Harris
2240 Lakeshore Avenue

You can't see it, but Harris is so rare that we thought we should include it.

13. Southhall House

Wilshire

As the map and dates of the following buildings suggest, Wilshire Boulevard, named for an oil millionaire who was also a Marxist, has had several spurts of growth. In the twenties it had already started its march west to Santa Monica and the Pacific, the complete apotheosis of the linear city. It was commercial about as far as Western. Beyond that, a great region of bungalows proliferated. Still further, starting near Crenshaw Boulevard, the rich took up their abodes north and south of Wilshire with a little commercial building here and there. The buildings on Wilshire Boulevard itself gradually began rising in height and ostentation until the beginning of the **"Miracle Mile"** at Hauser Avenue where ten-story or so office buildings and luxury shops were built at the end of the twenties and on into the thirties, and where a great deal of building has occurred since World War II.

In fact, it is great fun to drive the length from Number 1 Wilshire (in downtown Los Angeles) to the sea in an open car. In its own way it is as overwhelming as a similar drive along the length of Park Avenue in New York. Strangely, if you go off Wilshire on the streets above and below it, you will still find residential areas sometimes only a block away.

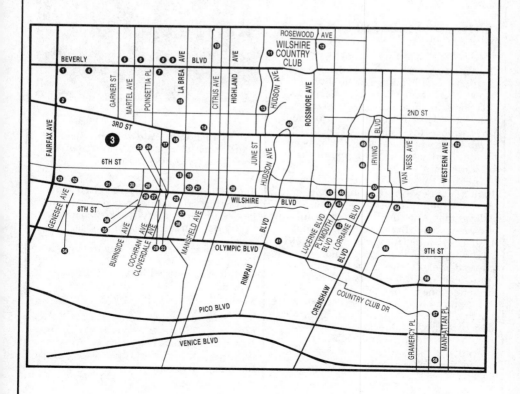

1. CBS Television City, 1952
Pereira and Luckman; major addition
1976, Gin Wong Associates
Southeast corner of Beverly Boulevard
and Fairfax Avenue

A fifties low modern cube, big and
bland but not without distinction. The
addition is in exactly the style of the
original.

1. CBS Television City

2. Farmer's Market, 1934-37 and later
Northeast corner of Fairfax Avenue and
3rd Street

Built by Roger Dahljolm to show off
Southern California's great ability to
grow magnificent fruits and vegetables,
this complex of buildings is more an institution than it is architecture. Its only
pretension is the somewhat Colonial Revival tower which replaces a wonderful
windmill advertising the name of the
building on a blade.

Behind Farmer's Market on Gilmore
Lane (cuts between 3rd Street and
Beverly Boulevard) is the ■Gilmore
Adobe that Antonio Jose Rocha built on
the Rancho La Brea in 1828-30. This
L-shaped adobe (the present south and
west wings) originally had a flat, tar-
covered roof. In the 1920s it was
remodelled by John Byers and Edla
present name). They added the north
wing and built a low second story over a
portion of the original adobe. They also
added pitched gable roofs covered with
tile. As we see the adobe today, it
reflects the 1920s ideal more than what
it actually looked like in 1830.

3. Park La Brea Housing (Metropoli-
tan Life Housing Development),
1941-42; Towers, 1948
Leonard Schultze and Son and E. T.
Heitschmidt; Tommy Tomson, landscape
architect; 1948 landscaping by Thomas
Church.
A 10½ acre development bounded by
3rd Street, Cochran Avenue, 6th Street,
and Fairfax Avenue

The first thing that strikes your eye from
a distance is that Carcassonne has been
transported to L.A.—the 1948 towers
merge to appear to be a medieval wall.
From a shorter range the more interesting features are the earlier, two-story
housing units which are in a sort of
stripped Regency Moderne mode.

3. Park La Brea

4. ■Pan-Pacific Auditorium, 1935-38
Wurdeman and Becket (Wurdeman)
7600 Beverly Boulevard

A major L.A. expression of the Streamline Moderne, probably the city's most
photographed and painted monument.
Notice the very pretty park that has recently been created just beyond it.

5. A. J. Heinsbergen Decorating
Company, 1925
Claude Beelman with A. B. Heinsbergen; details by Willard White
7415-7421 Beverly Boulevard

The general impression of this brick
building is English Medieval with a little
Baroque added here and there. Very picturesque and old world in a strange area
for that to happen.

6. Spanish Kitchen, ca. 1925
Northeast corner of Beverly Boulevard
and Martel Avenue

Not great Spanish Colonial, but the
windows appear to have the original
twenties paintings of caballeros and
señoritas. As of this writing the building
has no tenant, social change making it a
derelict, but the twenties chairs are still
piled on the twenties tables, only need-
ing to be dusted off before a good meal.

7. Commercial Building, 1930
J. R. Horns
Southeast corner of Poinsettia Place and
Beverly Boulevard

Art Deco (Zigzag) Moderne.

8. Commercial Building, 1929
L. Mulgreen
7223 Beverly Boulevard

Art Deco (Zigzag) Moderne.

9. Service Station, ca. 1925
Roland E. Coate
7201 Beverly Boulevard

Mission Revival with a dome!

9. Service Station

10. Beckman House, 1938
Gregory Ain
357 N. Citrus Avenue

An immaculately kept-up Los Angeles
conception of the International Style
Modern. In plan the house is narrow,
and the principle rooms open to small
terraces and enclosed courts.

**11. Meade House ("La Casa de las
Campanas"),** ca. 1927
Lester Scherer
350 June Street

Needless to say, you are among the
swells. This immense Spanish Colonial
Revival house on this gently winding
street has real distinction.

12. Apartment Building, ca. 1928
Southeast corner of Rossmore and Rose-
wood avenues

This huge, somewhat Spanish pile and
the **Ravenwood,** an Art Deco (Zigzag)
Moderne structure with Assyrian incli-
nations (at 570 Rossmore Avenue), and
a few rather nondescript lesser monsters
nearby are among the few large Los Angeles apartment complexes which would
compare in size to those of the apartment house craze in New York during
the same period.

13. Smith House, 1929-30
J. C. Smale
Northwest corner of 2nd Street and
Hudson Avenue

One of the few concrete Art Deco (Zigzag) Moderne houses in the Los Angeles
area and probably the greatest. It is
very elegant in an extremely elegant
neighborhood. Paris would be proud of
it.

14. Apartment Building, ca. 1928
Northwest corner of 3rd Street and
Mansfield Avenue

This two-story Art Deco (Zigzag)
Moderne building is a typical Los Angeles flat.

15. Retail Shop, ca. 1930
153 La Brea Avenue

La Brea was once a rich feast for the
connoisseur of the Moderne in its various ramifications and permutations.
Today almost all the shops in this mode
have been demolished or refaced. This
one seems pretty well tuckered out.

16. Apartment Building, 1930
J. C. Smale
364 S. Cloverdale Avenue

Another Art Deco (Zigzag) Moderne
flat.

17. Apartment Building, 1938
Milton J. Black and R. Borman
462 S. Cochran Avenue

A two-story Streamline Moderne structure. Black, who designed well in the Spanish Colonial Revival style in the twenties, has here kept up with the times.

17. Apartment Building

18. Automobile Showroom, ca. 1927
Morgan, Walls, and Clements
611 La Brea Avenue

Probably intended to be Moorish, this tiny building must have been very swanky in its day.

19. Courtyard Retail and Office Building, ca. 1926
Roy Selden Price
624 La Brea Avenue

A U-shaped Spanish building with Moorish arches.

20. Wilson Building, 1929
Meyer and Holler
Northeast corner of Wilshire Boulevard and La Brea Avenue

You know this firm for their Grauman's Chinese and Egyptian theatres in Hollywood. For them this Art Deco (Zigzag) Moderne tower is really straight.

21. Security First National Bank of Los Angeles (now **Security Pacific Bank Building**), 1929
Morgan, Walls, and Clements
5209 Wilshire Boulevard

A single-story, glazed, black-and-gold, terra-cotta-sheathed building similar to this firm's famous Richfield Building which was destroyed in 1968.

21. Security Pacific Bank Building

22. The Dark Room, 1938
Marcus P. Miller
5370 Wilshire Boulevard

Programmatic black vitrolite with silver trim. Streamline Moderne, the conventional nautical porthole in this case is placed in the middle of a plate glass window and thus becomes the lens of a camera. The new tenant has mainained the Streamline image but not, of course, the sign.

23. Dominguez-Wilshire Building, 1930
Morgan, Walls, and Clements
5410 Wilshire Boulevard

An eight-story Art Deco (Zigzag) Moderne tower placed on a two-story base. The detail is sharp and brittle.

24. Chandler's Shoe Store, ca. 1938
Marcus P. Miller
Northwest corner of Wilshire Boulevard and Cloverdale Avenue

One of the busiest buildings ever done in the Streamline Moderne idiom, this building is actually a remodelling of a Spanish Colonial Revival structure of the twenties.

25. Roman's Food Mart, ca. 1935
5413 Wilshire Boulevard

Streamline Moderne with a matching small tower at one end.

26. El Rey Theatre, ca. 1928
W. Cliff Balch
5519 Wilshire Boulevard

A small, angular Art Deco Moderne gem with marvelous box office and original signage, a king's head etched in neon.

26. El Rey Theatre

27. Commercial Building, 1927
Frank M. Tyler
5464 Wilshire Boulevard

Art Deco (Zigzag) Moderne framed by two small, and quite mad, towers.

28. Cochran Avenue Court, ca. 1928
Charles Gault
Just south of Wilshire Boulevard on Cochran Avenue

Small Spanish Colonial court covered with dense foliage.

29. Desmonds Department Store Building, 1928-29
Gilbert Stanley Underwood
5514 Wilshire Boulevard

Art Deco (Zigzag) Moderne with flamboyant ornament; an eight-story tower placed on a two-story base with enormous rounded corners.

30. Ralph's Supermarket Building, 1927-28
Morgan, Walls, and Clements
5623 Wilshire Boulevard

Once this was typical of the firm's work—a simulated cut-stone facade with Spanish Gothic arches and Churrigueresque ornament. It has been almost completely ruined by "modernization," but its proud tower still stands above the mess.

29. Desmonds Department Store Building

31. Prudential Building, 1948
Wurdeman and Becket; Ruth Shellhorn, landscape architect
5757 Wilshire Boulevard

A large office and commercial building in the International Style Modern, affected more by Gropius than by Mies. It thus shows its age stylistically, but well.

32a. Los Angeles County Museum of Art, 1964
Pereira and Associates
Wilshire Boulevard at Genesee Avenue in Hancock Park

Although salient, the architecture is not much. But it is, with the Getty and Pasadena (Norton Simon) museums, one of the greatest museums in Southern California. Set in the La Brea Tar Pits (see next entry), the buildings were once surrounded by a shallow moat with fountains popping up in it. This attempt at urbanity failed, however, and in 1975 the moat was filled in and replaced by an unimaginative **sculpture garden** designed by Bridger, Troller, and Hazlett. This will soon be replaced by a new **Atlantic Richfield Gallery** that will completely screen off the old building from Wilshire Boulevard. The architects are Hardy, Holtzman, and Pfeiffer (1981-84). The galleries of the existing museum have been remodelled (1982-83) by Frank O. Gehry and Associates. It seems too good to be true, but a new **Price Museum of Oriental Art** designed by Bruce Goff before his death is projected for the site as well.

32b. A Discovery of La Brea Museum, 1976
Thornton and Fagan Associates
Hancock Park

The park gets its name from the family which bought the Rancho La Brea (essentially our Wilshire District) in 1860, and, after having tapped it for almost all of its crude oil (*brea*), gave the tar pits to the city and sold off the rest to other rich people. In drilling for oil, Major Henry Hancock began digging up large bones but thought little of it until in 1906 Professor J. C. Merriman of the University of California recognized that these pits had trapped large numbers of prehistoric animals. Many of their skeletons can now be seen at the County Museum of Natural History in Exposition Park. The new museum, a sort of mound, celebrates this major scientific discovery, but we are sorry to say that in spite of the planners' good intentions, it makes further inroads on valuable open space.

33. May Company Department Store Building, 1940
Albert C. Martin and S. A. Marx
Northeast corner of Fairfax Avenue and Wilshire Boulevard

Streamline Moderne. The corner gold tower (really a sort of elegant perfume bottle) with its sign is *the* architecture of the building, especially when lighted at night. This also marks an entrance, but the main entrance is characteristically at the parking lot connected to the building. The multi-level parking structure was designed by Albert C. Martin and Associates in 1953.

34. Buck House, 1934
R. M. Schindler
Southwest corner of 8th Street and Genesee Avenue

All privacy on the exterior with just a touch of Streamline Moderne. The interior spaces open through great panels of glass into the south garden area. One of Schindler's finest houses.

34. Buck House

35. The Monterey Apartments, 1925
C. K. Smithley
754 Burnside Avenue

Extremely austere and absolutely impregnable Spanish Colonial garden apartments.

36. Apartment Building, ca. 1928
741½ Burnside Avenue

French Norman and very happy.

37. Firestone Garage, 1937
R. E. Ward, engineer
800 S. La Brea Avenue

Difficult to describe! A huge streamlined shell cantilevered over the corner.

38. Cedu Foundation Building, ca. 1928
842 La Brea Avenue

A very lovely Spanish Colonial Revival assemblage that has survived the change on La Brea.

39. AVCO Savings Building (now Imperial Savings), 1973
Burke, Kober, Nicolais, and Archuleta
4929 Wilshire Boulevard

This ten-story building is one great cube of bronze-hued glass. At least it's bronze and not black.

40. ■Reynolds House, 1958
John Woolf
200 Rimpau Street (cul-de-sac north of 3rd Street)

A tall, arched door, looking very much like a paper clip, cuts through a high mansard roof—one of Woolf's most imitated designs.

41. Memorial Library, 1930
Austin and Ashley
4625 W. Olympic Boulevard

Submerged in vines is this Tudor and Gothic branch library obviously intended to go with the old Collegiate Gothic Los Angeles High School, now replaced by repressed Brutalism. The fine art glass window with heraldic emblems on it was fashioned by the Judson Studios.

42. House, ca. 1935
814 Plymouth Boulevard

Streamline, then squared off.

43. Wilshire United Methodist Church, 1924
Allison and Allison
4350 Wilshire Boulevard

Quite Romanesque on the exterior, this exposed reinforced concrete church turns Gothic inside. To top that, it has another of those free interpretations of "La Giralda" that are so popular, whether in Florida or in Southern California.

44. Ebell Club, 1924
Hunt and Burns
4400 Wilshire Boulevard

The club building, auditorium, and garden are very sedate examples of the Spanish Colonial Revival.

45. Verbeck Mansion, ca. 1897
637 Lucerne Boulevard

A huge, 2½-story Queen Anne Revival house with Colonial Revival touches. It was moved here in the 1920s.

46. Gless House, 1924
Arthur Heineman (Alfred Heineman, designer)
Southwest corner of Plymouth Boulevard and 6th Street

45. Verbeck Mansion

Although rather late for the Craftsman style, this house has all the trappings. The faintly Tudor exterior shows traces of Frank Lloyd Wright and the magnificent interiors of teak reflect the ideas of Charles Greene. The art glass, designed by Alfred and carried out by the Judson Studios in Garvanza, is especially fine. Incidentally, it was moved to this area in the thirties, though it looks as if it had always been on this corner. It is one of the Heinemans' most important structures outside Pasadena.

47. Lytton Building (now Great Western Savings), 1968
William Pereira and Associates
4333 Wilshire Boulevard

Cleaned up Brutalism, there is a cocked-hat attitude to the roof.

48. Donovan House ("Sunshine Hill"), ca. 1910
419 S. Lorraine Boulevard
Theodore Eisen

A Classical giant portico disguises a house that is strongly Adamesque inside.

49. Van Nuys House, 1898
Frederick L. Roehrig
357 S. Lorraine Boulevard

A magnificent example of the emergence of the Colonial Revival Shingle style from the earlier Queen Anne style.

50. House, ca. 1915
Southwest corner of Irving Boulevard and 6th Street

55. Weber House

A Tudor effort betraying the peculiar attitude of the early twentieth century toward that style. This entire area is very strongly Tudor.

51. Wilshire Professional Building, 1929
Arthur E. Harvey
3875 Wilshire Boulevard

Unfortunately, the first floor of the nine-story-plus-penthouse Art Deco (Zigzag) Moderne building has been spoiled.

52. Commercial Building, ca. 1928
356 S. Western Avenue

Art Deco Moderne with a tall tower and urn.

53. Apartment House, ca. 1935
3919 W. 8th Street

This three-story-plus-penthouse Streamline Moderne structure with large parking area in basement is premonitory of present systems.

54. INA-PEG Building, 1960
Charles Luckman and Associates
Southeast corner of Wilshire Boulevard and Norton Avenue

This building, except for a little unnecessary detail, would pass for an Skidmore, Owings, and Merrill interpretation of Mies.

55. Weber House, 1921
Lloyd Wright
3923 W. 9th Street, at 4th Avenue

Lloyd Wright's first realized building in Los Angeles. It is a two-story modified Prairie style building, including art glass in geometrical patterns resembling those developed by his father.

56. House, ca. 1915
965 Gramercy Place

This has to be the supreme act of misunderstood Orientalism in America. Gable after gable protrudes, shaming the Greene brothers into insignificance.

57. House, ca. 1910
G. Lawrence Stimson
3340 Country Club Drive

Mission style mixed with Beaux Arts details.

58. Apartment Building, 1936
Earl D. Stonerod
1554-60 S. Saint Andrews Place

A symmetrical Streamline Moderne building.

MacArthur Park, West

This section of the city, west of downtown, developed early as a desirable place for middle class dwellings. At first it was the modestly hilly area just west of the present Harbor Freeway which became a

fashionable neighborhood. The grouping of houses on **South Bonnie Brae Street** and on **Alvarado Terrace** provides a glimpse of what this section of Los Angeles was like in the 1890s and early 1900s. The single-family residential nature of the area continued throughout the First World War, but the twenties introduced a strong pattern of auto-oriented strip commercialism along such streets as Venice, Pico, Washington, and Olympic boulevards, and along Western Avenue and other north/south streets. Multiple housing also became more frequent — at first bungalow courts, and two- and three-story apartment buildings. Later, in the twenties, a number of six- to eight-story apartment buildings were built. Generally the mixed use of the region — retail, commercial, and single and multiple housing — has continued right on down to the present day. Since the 1950s high-rise buildings of the downtown area have slowly spread into the area.

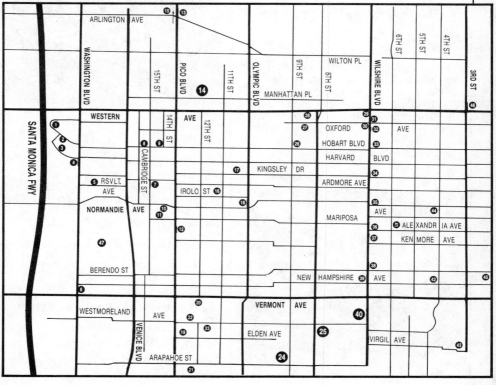

Two major public spaces occur in the midst of this area. **MacArthur Park** (at first named Westlake Park) with its small, picturesque lake provides thirty-two acres. **Lafayette Park** to the west has eleven acres. MacArthur Park was laid out in the 1880s and Lafayette Park was donated to the city in 1899. Wilshire Boulevard, which formerly went around MacArthur Park, was sliced through the middle of it in 1934, an advantage for the auto and the Boulevard, but hardly for the Park.

The glory of the MacArthur Park area has been and is Wilshire Boulevard, the "Champs Elysees of Los Angeles" as it was characterized in the 1920s. Beginning in the twenties, major churches, retail stores, and office buildings were built along it. Since the early 1950s new and even higher office towers have been added, so that Wilshire Boulevard as the prototype linear city is as vigorous today as it was in the twenties.

1. United Church of Christ, Scientist, 1945
South end of Oxford Avenue just north of the Santa Monica Freeway

A small but impressive Spanish Colonial Revival church building, whose tower is visible from the Santa Monica Freeway. The Hispanic borrowings in the design are varied. The tower is from the Mission Revival, the entrance of cast stone suggests the Churrigueresque, and the central rose window relates to the late Gothic in Spain. All of this mixture

1. United Church of Christ, Scientist

of sources has been carried out well. Originally the building was located where the Freeway now stands and it was moved to its present site in 1963.

2. House, ca. 1905
2068 Hobart Boulevard

Mission Revival with a wonderful entrance porch supported by stout, "primitive," cylindrical columns.

3. House, 1908
2091 Harvard Boulevard

A commodious box becomes picturesque and Mission by the addition of parapeted end wall gables, quatrefoil windows, and above all by the delightful, second-floor arcade with its cusped, Moorish arches.

3. House

4. Scott House, ca. 1906
Frank M. Tyler
1910 S. Harvard Boulevard

When built it was described as "an Italian design with the qualities of Moorish architecture incorporated." This all adds up to Southern California Mission Revival with a Moorish touch.

5. Apartment Building, ca. 1925
1817-19½ Roosevelt Avenue

Spanish Colonial Revival with a peculiar entrance.

6. Boulevard Theatre (now Intercity Repertory) 1925
Albert C. Martin
1615 W. Washington Boulevard

Spanish Colonial Revival with a penthouse on top.

7. Pacific Telephone Company Building, ca. 1926
Northeast corner of Ardmore Avenue and 15th Street

A Churrigueresque dress for a utilitarian building.

7. Pacific Telephone Company Building

8. Wheeler House, 1905
Charles and Henry Greene
2175 Cambridge Street

A modest, two-story Craftsman bungalow. The broad, cantilevered roof dramatically projects its rafter ends. The low attic gable is entirely vented, and stick-like posts and rails articulate the entrance porch.

9. Bungalow, ca. 1910
Henry L. Wilson
Southwest corner of Hobart Boulevard and 14th Street

A classic California bungalow which was published in Wilson's *Bungalow* magazine. Note the front door which goes right through the middle of the chimney.

10. Saint Sophia's Greek Orthodox Cathedral, 1948
Gus Kalionzes, Charles A. Klingerman, and Albert R. Walker
1324 S. Normandie Avenue

Anyone who has seen an eastern Mediterranean Greek Byzantine church will come away from this building wondering where all of these inventive ideas came from. Even though the elements are often in the wrong traditional place, the design still does manage to read as Byzantine.

11. Saint Thomas the Apostle Roman Catholic Church, 1905
Maginnis, Walsh, and Sullivan
1321 S. Mariposa Avenue

This church illustrates the inventiveness of these Boston architects who employed the Mission Revival image. The building conveys a strong primitive quality, and its towers and upper roofed arcade never occurred in this manner in original Mission architecture of the late seventeenth/early eighteenth centuries.

12. Retail Store/Apartment Building, ca. 1925
2713 W. Pico Boulevard

A three-story store and apartment block has been taken out of the ordinary by being clothed in a rectangular pattern of glazed and unglazed tile.

13. Arlington Avenue Christian Church, 1926
Harold Cross and A. F. Wicker
Northwest corner of Pico Boulevard and Arlington Avenue

A concrete church which employs detailing derived from the Spanish Renaissance. The gable roof has been highly simplified, with the tile pulled out to the edges of the walls. The tower is undecorated until the belfry, where cast concrete ornament provides decorative relief.

14. Wilshire Ward Chapel, Church of Jesus Christ of Latter-day Saints (Mormon), 1928
Harold W. Burton
1209 S. Manhattan Place

A Goodhuesque abstraction of Medieval architecture—a little Gothic mixed with the Byzantine and the Romanesque. The domed octagonal tower is impressive. The structure is of reinforced concrete with the form board pattern exposed.

15. Forum Theatre Building (now a church), 1921-24
Edward J. Borgmeyer
Southwest corner of Pico Boulevard and Norton Avenue (6th Street)

14. *Wilshire Ward Chapel, Church of Jesus Christ of Latter-day Saints*

The most refined example of a Beaux Arts theatre still standing in Los Angeles. Two pedimented porticos enclose a six-columned entrance porch. The fluted Corinthian columns, the cornices, entablatures, and the engaged piers are all richly decorated.

15. *Forum Theatre Building*

16. Bungalow Court, ca. 1920
1038-44 S. Ardmore Avenue

A single-story, narrow-courtyarded bungalow court in the guise of the Islamic. A sloped and painted archway leads from the street into the narrow entrance court. To the side pairs of small towers adorn each of the two wings.

17. Apartment Building, ca. 1922
1020 South Kingsley Drive

A typical L.A. stucco box apartment with an Egyptian Revival street facade.

18. VIP Palace Restaurant Building, ca. 1973
Southeast corner of Olympic Boulevard and Irolo Street

A return to the romanticism of the Orient. Not, of course, the real Orient, but one that must exist somewhere in a story book.

19. House, ca. 1912
1223 S. Elden Avenue

A 1½-story, shingle-and-stone, Colonial Revival dwelling.

20. American National Red Cross Chapter Building, 1939
Spaulding and Rex
1200 S. Vermont Avenue

A late-thirties, flat-roofed, California Modern house somewhat enlarged to serve as a small, one-story office building set in its own garden. The atmosphere is woodsy and suburban.

21. Double House, ca. 1900
Attributed to Joseph Cather Newsom
1214 S. Arapahoe Street

A central driveway entrance goes right through the 1½-story double bungalow. The main gable and the front dormers, which are now enclosed, were originally open sleeping porches.

22. House, ca. 1910
1229 S. Westmoreland Avenue

A large number of upper-middle-class suburban houses built in L.A. between 1900 and 1917 are clothed in respectable English Tudor, as is this one.

23. Apartment Building, 1936
1146-52 S. Westmoreland Avenue

Streamline Moderne with the usual strong nod to the nautical with portholes and steel railings.

24. House, ca. 1900
Attributed to Joseph Cather Newsom
957 S. Arapahoe Street

Knowing Newsom's inventive use of terms to indicate style, he would most likely have labeled this stucco, wood-detailed, and high-pitched-roof dwelling as "Rhinish."

25. First Unitarian Church, 1930
Allison and Allison
2936 W. 8th Street

One suspects that the architects had cast a quick glance at northern Italian churches of the early sixteenth century when they designed this exposed concrete church. They also included a small, pointed dome on the tower which seems somewhat Islamic. The sanctuary and the cloisters enclose a charming courtyard.

26. Apartment Building, 1936
Milton J. Black
Northwest corner of Hobart Boulevard and 9th Street

A Streamline Moderne apartment building of four units, designed by one of L.A.'s masters of the style. A horizontal bay with a row of fins dominates the street facade.

27. Val D'Amour Apartment Building, 1928
G. W. Powers
854 S. Oxford Avenue

Art Deco (Zigzag) Moderne. At the street entrance kneeling male figures somehow manage to hold up the five concrete stories above. Cast concrete figures stand guard along the parapet and alternate with Moderne relief ornament.

27. Val D'Amour Apartment Building

28. Parking Garage Building, ca. 1926
824 Western Avenue

The plan is that of an L-shaped structure with an open (on three sides) drive-in entrance facing onto Western Avenue. This automobile entrance is surrounded by a rich array of cast concrete Churrigueresque ornament. It all adds up to a remarkable composition in reinforced concrete. Note the stepped pattern of the walls which reflects the garage's ramp. Do not miss the building (ca. 1939) directly to the south. It is a sophisticated exercise in the Art Deco (Zigzag) Moderne.

29. Warner Brothers Western Theatre; Pellissier Building (now Wiltern Theatre), 1930-31
Morgan, Walls, and Clements, G. A. Lansburgh, and Anthony B. Heinsbergen
Southeast corner of Wilshire Boulevard and Western Avenue

A fully intact Art Deco (Zigzag) Moderne theatre and office tower building. The narrowness of the vertical recessed band windows and spandrels removes any reference to scale, so that from a distance you would think you were looking at a large skyscraper (in reality it is only twelve stories high). The Moderne theatre auditorium is currently being restored, as is the exterior.

29. Warner Brothers Western Theatre; Pellissier Building (now Wiltern Theatre)

30. Beneficial Plaza, 1967
Skidmore, Owings, and Merrill
3700 Wilshire Boulevard

An eleven-story ice cube tray set on end (it must have been cut out of graph paper), situated in a late sixties non-pedestrian plaza.

31. McKinley Building, 1923
Morgan, Walls, and Clements
Northwest corner of Wilshire Boulevard and Oxford Avenue

Morgan, Walls, and Clements developed their own version of the Spanish Churrigueresque, of which this is one example. The upper portion of the corner tower is encrusted with cast concrete ornament. Although the building has been modified over the years the original courtyard still lies within the building.

32. Ahmanson Center Building, 1970
Edward D. Stone Associates
3701 Wilshire Bouelvard

Ten floors plus a penthouse, this building is rather neutral Modern in spite of the curves.

33. Wilshire Boulevard Temple, 1922-29
Abraham A. Adelman, S. Tilton Norton, and David C. Allison
Northeast corner of Wilshire and Hobart boulevards

The mystery and the opulance of the Near East is suggested in this luxurious, Byzantine-inspired edifice. Black marble, inlaid gold, brilliant multi-colored mosaics, and rare woods were used throughout the interior. Hugo Ballin's murals add the final touch of richness to the interior.

34. Saint Basil's Roman Catholic Church, 1974
Albert C. Martin and Associates;
Emmet L. Wemple and Associates, landscape architects
Northwest corner of Wilshire Boulevard and Kingsley Drive

A forest of vertical concrete volumes creates an illusion through fuzzy, dark glass of a medieval northern Italian town, perhaps with Sir Basil Spence's Coventry Cathedral in mind. Herb Goldman did the interior sculpture of the Stations of the Cross and also other sculpture in the side altars.

34. Saint Basil's Roman Catholic Church

35. Wilshire Boulevard Christian Church, 1922-23
Robert H. Orr
Northeast corner of Wilshire Boulevard and Normandie Avenue

Northern Italian Romanesque, which was so popular in Southern California in the teens and twenties, was used for this church. The campanile and other features of the church are Italian, while the great rose window is French. The building is of reinforced concrete with the pattern of the form boards revealed.

36. Office Building, 1936
Walker and Eisen
Northwest corner of Wilshire Boulevard and Alexandria Avenue

Behind all sorts of odds and ends on the street level you will find an excellent version of a four-story Art Deco (Zigzag) Moderne office building. Wide, fluted piers encase a row of double, narrow piers. Above, double spirals provide the needed ornament.

37. Brown Derby Cafe, 1926
3377 Wilshire Boulevard

This structure, in the form of a gentleman's derby hat (hinting at "class"), has long been one of the visual symbols of Los Angeles. This programmatic building now sits partially demolished while "Save the Derby" cries come from across the country. We hope that it is still there (or somewhere) at the time of your visit.

37. Brown Derby Cafe

38. Tishman Building, 1956
Victor Gruen and Associates
3325 Wilshire Boulevard

A characteristic mid-1950s Corporate International Style Modern building—dull and dry. Now it is a real period piece of its time. Perhaps we will eventually come to respond to it in a positive fashion.

38. Tishman Building

39. ■One Park Plaza, 1971-72
Daniel, Mann, Johnson, and Mendenhall (Anthony J. Lumsden)
3250 Wilshire Boulevard

A twenty-two-story skyscraper clad in a thin, fragile glass skin set with a light metal frame. The form of the building, with the secondary towers projecting from each of the corners, suggests the shape of a Richardsonian Romanesque tower.

40. ■Bullocks-Wilshire Department Store Building, 1928
John and Donald Parkinson; Feil and Paradice; Jock Peters
3050 Wilshire Boulevard

Bullocks-Wilshire is a remarkable building, a treasure trove of late 1920s Moderne design. The store's management engaged some of the most notable L.A. artists of the time to design the interior of the building. The principal figure envolved with the interior was the architect-designer Jock Peters. His hand can be seen most forcibly in the sportsware shop as well as in the center foyer at ground level. Art abounds. If you go through the parking lot entrance, you will pass through Art Deco (Zigzag) Moderne gates (expressing the theme "Times Fly"). On the ceiling of the porte cochere is a mural by Herman Sachs. A relief sculpture *The Spirit of Sports* by Gjura Stojano adorns the walls of the sports shop. Other decoration are by Mayer Krieg, David Colins, George De Winter, and John Weaver. This store was one of the first on Wilshire Boulevard to provide a dual frontage, one (traditional) on Wilshire Boulevard (for advertising purposes), and the other facing on the extensive, well-landscaped parking lot to the rear (this is, of course, the real entrance in the store). The building is sheathed in light tan terracotta and trimmed with brown copper. The building as we see it today (five floors plus the tower), was to have been the first phase of a ten-story structure. What is remarkable about the building

40. Bullocks-Wilshire Department Store

today is that so much of its original Art Deco interior design remains, and is so beautifully maintained.

41. Chapman Park Market, 1928-29
Morgan, Walls, and Clements
Northwest corner of West 6th Street and Alexandria Avenue

A Spanish Colonial Revival shopping center which occupies the entire block between Alexandria and Kenmore avenues. The central court was an auto-park with the surrounding retail stores facing both onto the parking lot and onto the adjoining streets. Across Alexandria Avenue at the northwest corner of West 6th Street is the **Chapman Building** (Morgan, Walls, and Clements, 1928), a two-story Spanish Colonial Revival retail store and office building.

41. Chapman Park Market

42. Temple Sinai East (now **Korean Royal Church**), 1926
S. Tilton North
407 S. New Hampshire Avenue

A mixture from the Eastern Mediterranean area—Byzantine, Islamic, plus other odds and ends. A central dome dominates both the interior and the exterior, and hand-cut bricks of varied color create a rich tactile surface.

43. Virgil Apartment Building, 1950
Carl L. Maston
315 S. Virgil Avenue

A two-story building whose image is light post-World War II Modern. Each of the living units faces out onto an enclosed small patio.

44. Ninth Church of Christ, Scientist, 1924-27
Robert H. Orr
433 S. Normandie Avenue

This Classical English brick building lightly suggests the turn-of-the-century work of Sir Edwin Lutyens. In contrast, drive over to South Alvarado Street and see Elmer Grey's handling of the Romanesque in a highly traditional but vigorous manner in his 1912 **First Church of Christ, Scientist.**

45. Automotive Garage Building, ca. 1926
248 S. Berendo Street

A single-story Spanish Colonial Revival automobile garage, luxurious enough in its cast concrete ornate facade to accommodate Franklins, Packards, and Pierce Arrows.

46. Selig Retail Store Building (now **Crocker-Citizens National Bank Branch Offices**), 1931
Arthur E. Harvey
Northwest corner of Western Avenue and West 3rd Street

Though modest in size, this is one of L.A.'s most vigorous examples of the use of glazed terra-cotta tile of the late 1920s/early 1930s. The gold ornament is dramatically set off against the rich black tile background. The rich ornament is pure Art Deco (Zigzag) Moderne. The sheathing of this building will give you some indication of what the famous Richfield Building in downtown L.A. looked like.

47. Chapel of the Pines, Rosedale Cemetery, ca. 1900
West Venice Boulevard between Normandie Avenue and Catalina Street

Within the Rosedale Cemetery are a number of monuments and buildings well worth a visit. One of the most interesting of these is the Chapel of the Pines. The chapel itself is a round, low, domed building. It is approached through a classical Greek Doric temple front, the proportions of which are quite "correct."

MacArthur Park, North

46. *Selig Retail Store Building (now Crocker-Citizens National Bank Branch Offices*

1. Bungalows, ca. 1910-25
Arthur and Alfred Heineman

The Heinemans designed a number of bungalows in the northern part of the MacArthur Park district, including a group on South Ardmore Avenue. Those that are authenticated are situated at 110, 179, 201, and 228. They also designed two "Oriental" bungalows at 720 and 741 S. Irolo Street. The bungalow at 228 S. Ardmore Avenue is also Oriental, while the one at number 201 is Colonial Revival with a sandstone base and columns.

2. Studio Court, ca. 1925
4350 Beverly Boulevard

The French Norman mode was particularly popular in Los Angeles in the 1920s for small cottage-like commercial complexes and bungalow courts. With the continual intensification of land use in the west Los Angeles region, most of these have unfortunately disappeared. Here is a good remaining example — a fairy tale-scaled group of buildings.

3. Mount Vernon Office, Pacific Savings Building (now California Federal Savings) 1960
Rick Farver Associates
270 N. Vermont Avenue

This light-hearted version of George Washington's Mount Vernon was originally built at 400 N. Vermont Avenue where one could readily see it from the Hollywood Freeway. It has now been

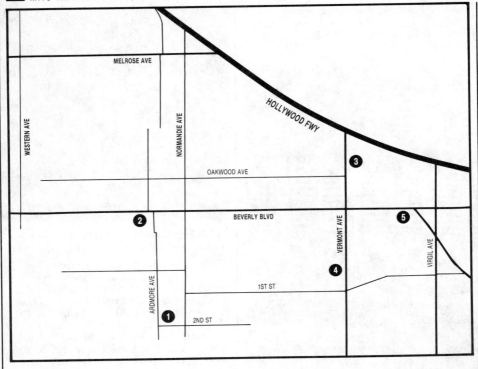

moved down the street where you will have to search it out.

3. Mount Vernon Office. Pacific Savings Building (now California Federal Savings)

4. KFL (KEHE) Radio Station Building, 1936
Morgan, Walls, and Clements
133-41 N. Vermont Avenue

Though altered, this radio station building is still one of Los Angeles's forceful examples of the thirties Streamline Moderne. The central pylon tower, designed for the display of the stations call letters, was originally surmounted by an open metal vertical tower 475 feet high.

5. American Storage Company Building (now Yellow Pages Building), 1928-29
Arthur E. Harvey
3639 Beverly Boulevard

A fourteen-story (supposedly ten plus) Los Angeles landmark. The thin verticality of the tower creates the illusion of great soaring height. In contrast to the Art Deco (Zigzag) Moderne tower, the base of the building exhibits a rich vocabulary of the Spanish Colonial Revival.

5. American Storage Company Building (now Yellow Pages Building)

MacArthur Park, East

1. Ponce de Leon Apartment Building, ca. 1905
1136 S. Alvarado Street

Compared to other American cities the Classical Beaux Arts image was not continually used in Los Angeles during the years 1895 through the early teens. Here a dignified, columned entrance provides the appropriate formal entry into this three-story building.

2. Cottage, ca. 1895
1805 12th Place

A small Queen Anne cottage.

3. Dora Apartments, 1906
1600 W. Pico Boulevard

Between 1900 and 1915 a good number of three-story Mission Revival apartment buildings, were built in the area west and south of the downtown. In the Dora Apartment Building a corner bay emerges above the tile roof as a low, octagonal tower. Gabled parapets, arched openings, and stucco walls help to create the needed Mission image. Apartment buildings with retail stores on the ground level such as this one, were common.

4. Pico Union Villa Building, 1980
John Mutlow
1200 S. Union Avenue

A three-story multiple-housing building for the elderly. It is in the form of a

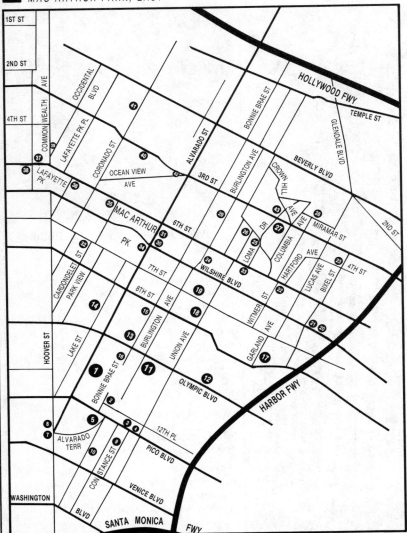

square with an interior courtyard. A diagonal passage pierces through the two opposite corners of the complex.

Freestanding pylons in the courtyard and at the entrance are, one assumes, to visually contradict the square and its diagonals. The idea of the interior courtyard comes from the traditional courts found within the Mediterranean tradition—though in this case its design suggests a prison exercise yard. The saving grace of the building (as art, not as a dwelling place) is the excellent use of colors on the walls.

5. Alvarado Terrace Houses,
Southwest of Pico Boulevard and Bonnie Brae Street

Alvarado Terrace, laid out as a gentle, curved, upper-middle-class residential street, was planned in the early 1900s by Pomery Powers, who was at the time president of the Los Angeles City Council. The development was at first called Windmill Links—named after the landmark of a nearby windmill and tank. The seven remaining houses on the north side of the street provide us with a good glimpse of L.A.'s suburban streets from about 1900 through the mid-teens. These houses indicate the wide smorgasbord of images employed by architects and clients.

a. Barmore House, ca. 1902
1317 Alvarado Terrace

English and Germanic Medieval styles establish the character of this suburban dwelling.

b. Cohan House, ca. 1902
Hudson and Munsell
1325 Alvarado Terrace

Late Queen Anne in concept, but simplified and made more classical with references to the Shingle Colonial Revival.

c. Gilbert House, ca. 1902
1333 Alvarado Terrace

A late Queen Anne Shingle dwelling with the usual hint of the Colonial Revival. The building with the round corner bay tower, is sheathed in Santa Barbara sandstone below and shingles above. There is an abundance of ornament, both inside and out.

d. Powers House, 1902
A. L. Haley
1345 Alvarado Terrace

This is the house which the developer of Alvarado Terrace laid out for himself—an exuberant Mission Revival piece (one of the best examples still standing in Los Angeles). The house was designed by A. L. Haley whose extensive practice was primarily in the realm of spec apartments and other commercial buildings. The front porch of the Powers House exhibits an arcade supported by short, thick, fat, "primitive" columns, and the roof presents a picturesque assembly of open and closed

towers, scalloped parapets, and quatrefoil windows.

5d. Powers House

e. Raphael House, ca 1902
Hunt and Egger
1353 Alvarado Terrace

A good-sized, two-story English Tudor dwelling. Note the beautiful entrance with its windows of bevelled glass.

f. Evanardy-Kinney House, 1902
Hunt and Egger
1401 Alvarado Terrace

Late Queen Anne modified by Colonial Revival details. The house is sheathed in sandstone and stucco below, and shingles above.

g. House, ca. 1905
1406 Alvarado Terrace

A good example of Los Angeles turn-of-the-century attachment to Anglo fashions, here in a Colonial Revival dwelling.

h. Milner Apartment Building, ca. 1925
1415 Alvarado Terrace

A multiple-housing unit intrudes in this single-family enclave. This apartment building utilizes an elaborate English Gothic image.

6. First Church of Christ, Scientist, 1912
Elmer Grey
1366 S. Alvarado Street

Northern Italian Romanesque as a source, but *strongly abstracted.* A high, semicircular temple porch with Corinthian columns looks out toward the street intersection. Another more delicately detailed porch faces east, and the tower has been reduced to a single rectangular volume, with a grouping of three vertical windows on each of its surfaces.

7. House, ca. 1897
1519 S. Hoover Street

A late Queen Anne dwelling.

8. House, ca. 1900
1515 S. Hoover Street

Another late Queen Anne dwelling, this time modified with classical American Colonial Revival detailing.

9. House, ca. 1900
1346 W. Constance Street

This imaginative composition, using seemingly all of the current images of the period, could well be labeled as the Bavarian Hunting Lodge style.

10. Bungalow Court, 1925
Edwin W. Willit
1428 S. Bonnie Brae Avenue

A miniaturized pylon gateway with relief sculpture establishes the Egyptian theme for this single-story, double-row bungalow court (the Hollywood film set brought into the world of "real" architecture).

11. House, ca. 1898
1030 Burlington Avenue

An unbelievable array of Islamic details in wood cover this simple wood building.

12. Loyola University Law School Building, 1981-84
Frank O. Gehry and Associates
1441 W. Olympic Boulevard

One of Los Angeles's really important buildings of the early 1980s. Here we can see Gehry and his associates at their best, in both planning and design. The main building is broken in the middle by a greenhouse-like gabled roof temple, which is approached from below by a long, narrow staircase. The smaller, single-story buildings in the court in front of the large building are rendered as small, abstracted classical temples.

12. Loyola University Law School Building

13. Houses
South Bonnie Brae Avenue

Bonnie Brae Avenue was one of a series of fashionable suburban streets situated west of downtown Los Angeles. Most of the single-family upper-middle-class dwellings which lined these north/south streets were built between 1890 and 1910. As one would expect, much has been lost. Still enough remains so that we can gain a sense of suburban Los Angeles at the turn of the century.

a. House, ca. 1897
1026 S. Bonnie Brae Avenue

"Palladian" (perhaps). Really a Queen Anne design with American Colonial Revival frosting.

b. House, ca. 1896
1032 Bonnie Brae Avenue

An additional example of the late Queen Anne open plan, with many American Colonial Revival references.

c. House, ca. 1898
1035 S. Bonnie Brae Avenue

Shingled late Queen Anne/Colonial Revival.

d. House, ca. 1895
1036-38 S. Bonnie Brae Avenue

One of the remaining architectural gems of the Avenue, this dwelling is French Chateauesque accomplished in wood, with small corner turrets and a low balcony between.

e. House, ca. 1897
1047 S. Bonnie Brae Avenue

A two-story, simplified, late Queen Anne house.

13e. House

f. House, ca. 1905
1053 S. Bonnie Brae Avenue

A boxy Colonial Revival dwelling with some imaginative touches, including a small Gothic window set in a frame with tiny columns, and a Romanesque window placed below. Fluted pilasters terminate the corners of the building.

14. Marlinex Apartment Building, ca. 1930
938 S. Lake Street

A seven-story Art Deco (Zigzag) Moderne apartment building. Perhaps its most impressive detail is the "Modernistic" lettering.

15. 800 Block of south Bonnie Brae Avenue

Another of Bonnie Brae's turn-of-the-century streetscapes.

a. Wright-Mooers House, 1894
818 S. Bonnie Brae Avenue

This house is one which is often illustrated in discussions of West Coast Victorian architecture. The open plan and the overall general design of the building are Queen Anne. The arched street entrance (in wood) with its two pairs of small columns is Richardsonian Romanesque, while the tower with its elongated domed roof and ogee dormers appears Islamic. And there are other suggestions as well, of the French Chateauesque, and of the American Colonial Revival. Note especially the stairhall landing window on the north side of the house.

b. House, ca. 1897
824 S. Bonnie Brae Avenue

A Colonial Revival design accompanied by a wide veranda which is wrapped around the corner bay tower. The tower is capped by an Islamic domed roof.

c. Flint House, 1888
Joseph Cather Newsom
842 S. Bonnie Brae Avenue

The Flint House illustrates one of the many variations of the Queen Anne side-hall plan worked out by the Newsoms. A square bay projects off of the southwest corner of the house, and above on the second floor was an open, spindled porch (now enclosed). A hallmark of their de-

15c. Flint House

signs is the dramatic stair landing bay which projects from the north side of the house. This house was one of many illustrated in Joseph Cather Newsom's *Artistic Buildings and Homes of Los Angeles* (1888).

16. House, ca. 1902
Attributed to Joseph Cather Newsom
1011 Beacon Street

Newsom employed a combination of images in all of his work in Los Angeles and elsewhere. He would probably have labeled this dwelling as an example of the "Bavarian Hunting Lodge Style." This meant a combination of a Queen Anne floor plan with medieval vernacular detailing from central Europe.

17. Dennis House, 1910
Dennis and Farwell
767 S. Garland Avenue

The architectural firm of Oliver P. Dennis and Lyman Farwell was one of Los Angeles's most productive offices from around 1896 through the mid-teens. A good number of their designs tend towards the Beaux Arts Classical and to the American Colonial Revival. (Farwell had worked in the New York office of McKim, Mead, and White.) Here in Dennis's own house we can see a Colonial Revival dwelling with a few leftovers from the earlier Queen Anne.

18. House, ca. 1905
740 S. Union Avenue

Colonial Revival of the stately type with a temple front, large-scale Corinthian columns and all.

19. Young's Market Building (now **Andrews Hardware and Metal Company),** 1924
Charles F. Plummer
1010 W. 7th Street

A Maybeckish romantic version of the Beaux Arts tradition. A row of classical columns supports the upper arcade. Between them is a "life-size frieze of genuine della Robbia style." The interior is decorated in a "Pompeiian" fashion with marble and antique mosaics.

20. Office Tower for the Signal Oil Company, 1958
Pereira and Luckman; remodelled in 1973-74 by Craig Ellwood and Associates
1010 Wilshire Boulevard

Ellwood re-sheathed a rather dull fifties Modern tower of 17 floors into his own version of the Miesian aesthetic.

21. Woodbury College Building, 1937
S. Charles Lee
1027 Wilshire Boulevard

A monumental Streamline Moderne building. The grand entrance and the basic symmetrical facade suggest the dignity of an institution.

22. Foy House, 1873
633 S. Witmer Street

One of the few remaining Italianate houses still to be found in Los Angeles. The house was built on a site near Wilshire Boulevard and was moved to this location. The design is a typical Italianate L-shape plan with a service wing and a central hall. Paired brackets support the extended roof over the gables and the eaves. The front porch has lost its upper railing and is now partially enclosed.

23. Scholts Advertising Company Building, 1937
Richard J. Neutra
1201 W. 4th Street

On the street side the one-story facade is divided into three extended horizontal bands of stucco with the windows carried up to the soffit of the flat roof and finally the thin facia line of the roof itself. The principle offices face north away from the street and out onto a landscaped court.

24. Office Building, ca. 1939
Southwest corner of 6th Street and Burlington

A small, but handsome single story Streamline Moderne office building displaying all of the hallmarks of the style — curved walls, glass brick, etc.

25. Loma Court, ca. 1925
380-88 Loma Drive

One of Los Angeles's many Mediterranean-styled bungalow courts.

26. Osiris Apartment Building, 1926
J. M. Close
430 S. Union Avenue

J. M. Close, who acted as both architect and builder, designed a number of Egyptian Revival apartment buildings in west Los Angeles. As in the Osiris Apartment Building that which is Egyptian (and it works well) is the pylon street facade. The rest of the building is a typical Los Angeles stucco box.

26. Osiris Apartment Building

27. Mary Andrews Clark Memorial Home (YWCA), 1912-13
Arthur B. Benton
306 Loma Drive

The master of the Mission Revival here turned his hand to the French Chateauesque. The building seems most satisfactory from a distance, where the towers and high roofs emerge out of the surrounding trees. Within, the more public spaces exhibit exotic woods and some splended leaded and colored art glass.

28. Lewis House, 1889
Joseph Cather Newsom
1425 Miramar Street

The Newsom brothers, Samuel and Joseph Cather Newsom, best known for their often-illustrated Carson House in Eureka, California, produced some of the wonderful inventive if not slightly "mad" Victorian houses in Los Angeles during the Great Boom of the 1880s. Regrettably, most of these houses have disappeared one by one over the years. The Lewis House is a delightful but subdued example of one of their Queen Anne designs. The effectiveness of their design would be more apparent if the second-floor porch above the entrance were not enclosed.

28. Lewis House

29. Bungalow Court, ca. 1937
428-32 S. Burlington Avenue

A Streamline Moderne bungalow court. Other nearby courts are to be found at 445 S. Burlington Avenue (Mission Revival, ca. 1914) and at 470-78 S. Burlington Avenue (a bit of Dutch Cottage imagery, ca. 1922).

30. World Savings Association Building, 1982
Eric Owen Moss
Northeast corner of Wilshire Boulevard and Alvarado Street

A subdued design composed of a single box, and then cut-into boxes within. Color has been used to both establish forms and to suggest more formal qualities. The building is situated at an important corner, but the design seems to address each of the streets independently.

31. Westlake Theatre, 1926
Richard M. Bates, Jr.
638 S. Alvardo Street

The interior was originally Adamesque, but both the interior and the exterior have continually been updated over the years. The interior is still worth a visit.

32. Hite Building, 1923-24
Morgan, Walls, and Clements
Southwest corner of Cardondelet Street and West 7th Street

The firm of Morgan, Walls, and Clements designed well over a dozen small retail/commercial buildings in the Mac-Arthur Park area. They utilized a Spanish image, but maneuvered it into something which always read as a pure twenties design. Ornament inspired by Spain and Mexico — the Plateresque, the Churrigueresque, and of the Renaissance — was placed as accent marks on simple stucco volumes. In the Hite Building the street elevation of the single-story section boasts a composition of a six-columned arcade balanced on each side by entrances with cast-concrete ornamented panels above. Two other Morgan, Walls, and Clements buildings nearby are the **Thorpe Building** (1924) at the northwest corner of Parkview and West 7th streets and the **Studio and Shop Building** for Mrs. Olive J. Cobb at 2861 W. 7th Street (1924).

33. Carl's Supermarket Building, 1933
Morgan, Walls, and Clements
1530-36 W. 6th Street

An early supermarket building. Its image is transitional between the Art Deco Moderne and the then emerging Streamline Moderne. Note the composition of the pylons to each side which sprout three layers of plant-like spirals at their tops.

34. Prometheus, 1935
Nina Saemundsson

MacArthur Park (near the southwest corner of Wilshire Boulevard and Alvarado Street).

An eight foot high cast-concrete figure placed on a wonderful high base with sunrays and other Moderne patterns. This is a Federal Arts Project sculpture which well sums up the aesthetic qualities of public art of the 1930s.

34. Prometheus

35. The Elks Building, (now Park Plaza Hotel,) 1923-24
Curlett and Beelman
607 S. Park View Street

A monumental Goodhue-esque composition with its prime reference being to the early Romanesque. The glory of the building externally lies in the groupings of large-scale sculptured figures at the upper ends of each of the wings of the building and the eight, larger-than-life-size figures near the parapet of the high central section of the building. The interiors were decorated by Anthony Heinsbergen.

36. Granada Building, 1927
Franklin Harper
627 S. Lafayette Park Place

A full block of retail stores, offices, and studio/apartments designed as a single Spanish village. Inner paseos, balconies, and courts create a series of pleasing, small-scaled spaces.

37. First Congregational Church, 1930-32
Allison and Allison
Northwest corner of Commonwealth Avenue and West 6th Street

37. First Congregational Church

A concrete structure with revealed horizontal form boards patterns on its wall surfaces. One assumes that the design was derived from English late Gothic, especially the central tower.

38. CNA Building, 1972
Langdon and Wilson; Emmet L. Wemple and Associates, landscape architect
Southwest corner of Commonwealth Avenue and West 6th Street

A mirrored glass cube — it works well as long as there is something around worthwhile to reflect.

39. Church of the Precious Blood, ca. 1932
Henry C. Newton and Robert D. Murray
North corner of Hoover Street and Occidental Boulevard

Italian Romanesque in reinforced concrete, beautifully sited in relation to the joining of the two major streets.

40. Charles Croze Studio, 1948
Harwell H. Harris
2340 W. 3rd Street

If only the MacArthur Park area could have developed after World War II with buildings and landscaping of this quality, it would have maintained the Arcadian image of Los Angeles. Here, within a grove of blue gum Eucalyptus trees, Harris has placed his beautiful L-shaped building with its dramatic cantilevered balcony and its forecourt of low planting and brick paving.

41. Hill House, ca. 1911
Walker and Vawter
201 S. Coronado Street

This Craftsman bungalow was frequently illustrated as the typical Los Angeles bungalow. The principle rooms of this bungalow open though glass doors to a terrace surrounded by a clinker brick wall. Long, heavy shingles cover the walls, and the Japanese exposed roof beams lend an oriental feeling.

42. Medical Offices, ca. 1935
Alfred Heinemann
West corner of Ocean View Avenue and West 3rd Street, just west of Alvarado Street

The form of a bungalow court used for a series of medical offices arranged around landscaped courts. The image is basically Streamline Moderne but there are occasional episodes of the Classical, the Spanish Colonial, and even of the Egyptian revivals.

43. Bungalow Court, ca. 1925
West corner of Loma Drive and Crown Hill Avenue

Hillsides were often used to advantage throughout Los Angeles for stepped patterns of bungalow courts. This example displays a Spanish Colonial Revival image.

44. House, ca. 1900
Southwest corner of Bonnie Brae Avenue and West Olympic Bouelvard

A Chateauesque Revival dwelling with the characteristic dominant round tower surmounted by a conical roof.

Downtown

Yes, Virginia, there is a downtown Los Angeles, although you continue, to this day, to wonder why. The present day central city lies southeast of the fabled multilevel interchange of the Hollywood, Santa Ana, Pasadena, and Harbor freeways. The northern section of this area occupying what remains of Bunker Hill is devoted to public buildings and spaces—both symbolic and bureaucratic. The remainder of Bunker Hill and south into the flatlands is given over to commerce (with some high-density housing).

Downtown L.A. is the product of three major building booms. The first was in the years 1900 through 1917, the second from the early 1920s through 1931, and the last which started in the late 1960s and is still very much with us. The first two booms utilized the imagery of the Classical Beaux Arts, and it is amazing how many ten- to twelve-story office buildings were built, especially on South Broadway and on South Spring Street. The second expansion moved towards the west from South Broadway to South Flower Street and was clothed in variations of the Art Deco (Zigzag) Moderne and the PWA Moderne. In the late thirties a few Streamline Moderne buildings were constructed and a number of street level frontages were remodelled. Little building activity occurred from 1945 through the early 1960s so there are few examples of post-World War II Corporate Modern buildings. The high-rise buildings constructed since the late 1960s are much more varied in form, and are more traditionally sheathed than was the case of those designed in the fifties and early sixties.

Since the early 1920s, downtown L.A. has been a constant disappointment for those who feel that a city should have a primary high-density urban core. Even today downtown finds itself battling with other urban cores and strips. During the 1930s the view that downtown should only be one among many urban centers was officially codified in the regional plan for the L.A. Basin. It was in the late 1930s, too, that the freeway system was planned, and as soon as World War II was over, work commenced on completing the Hollywood Freeway. A short time later, the Santa Ana and Harbor freeways were built. In the 1950s, these freeways (plus the pre-World War II Pasadena Freeway, 1934-41) were connected by the famous multilevel interchange known as "The Stack."

So far downtown L.A. has followed the classic approach to urban renewal, namely to bulldoze away the past and start anew. Many of the buildings which were situated on Bunker Hill could have been revamped and reused, but they are all gone now. With the exception of several restored nineteenth-century buildings near the Plaza (and of course the Bradbury Building), little or no evidence of Victorianism remains in downtown Los Angeles. The number of major buildings lost in the past ten to twelve years is, if nothing else, impressive. Included are the great black and gold 1928 Richfield Building (Morgan, Walls, and Clements) and the 1935 Sunkist Building (Walker and Eisen) with its roof gardens and abundance of sculpture and paintings. We have also lost through remodelling the wonderful Moderne Clifton's Cafeteria, and more recently Saint Paul's Cathedral, the Hotel Cordova, the Abby Building, the Bath Building, the Municipal Water and Power Building, and others. And the Los Angeles Public Library and its park are under continual assault.

Through urban renewal, the great houses of Bunker Hill were bulldozed off, and they are bit by bit being replaced with the big city illusion of high-rise towers. On the whole these towers are competent exercises, but they in no way address the specifics of Bunker Hill as a hill, or of the specific climatic and geographic environment of Los Angeles. As one finds over all of America (with the fewest of exceptions) the streets adjacent to these high-rises are not a pleasant experience for the pedestrians, notwithstanding a few very handsome ground-level plazas.

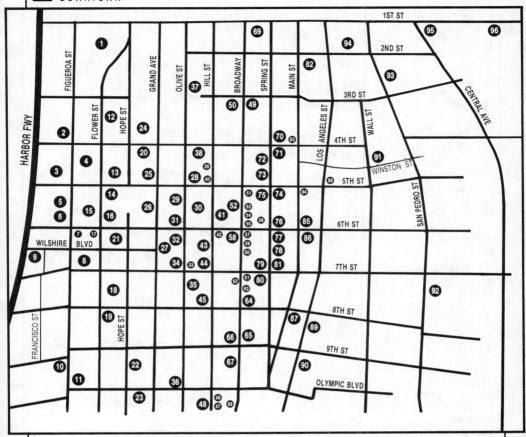

In 1980 five developer/architect teams were invited to submit their proposals for the last remaining large parcel of Bunker Hill, an eleven-acre site. The B. H. A. Associates with Arthur Erickson were finally chosen though even a casual look at the proposal of the Maguire Partners (which included a star-studded cast composed of Cesar Pelli, Lawrence Halprin, Charles W. Moore, Robert Kennard, Hardy, Holzman, and Pfeiffer, Richard Legoretta, Frank O. Gehry, Paul Krueger, Barton Myers, Harvey S. Perloff, and Edgardo Contini) would indicate that their proposal was far superior. Part of the accepted B. H. A. Associates scheme will be the Los Angeles Museum of Contemporary Art, designed by the Japanese architect Arata Isozaki.

An extensive redevelopment has been proposed around the central Los Angeles Public Library. The Library itself is to be expanded and revamped. North of the Library, between the Wells Fargo and the Southern California Edison buildings will be a circular tower (Henry Cobb of I. M. Pei). On the west side of this building will be an elaborate monumental stairway (Lawrence Halprin). At the northeast corner of Fifth and Grand is to be a 65-story high-rise by Johnson and Burgee. South of the Library, is to be a third tower (33 floors, Harwood K. Smith). There may be fragments of all of this which will really work and may even be handsome. Ultimately though, the approach taken illustrates that the prime consideration is still land as a speculative commodity.

1. Bunker Hill Towers, 1968
Robert E. Alexander
Northeast corner of Figueroa and West
1st streets

Three high-rise towers which are supposed to introduce mixed use (residential living) into downtown. In style and concept they are marginally respectable, but neither here nor there.

2. Sheraton Grande Hotel, 1978-83
Archsystems
Southwest corner of Figueroa and West
4th streets

A fifteen-story structure which plays off curvalinear and diagonal shapes. Like the Bonaventure Hotel, it is best when experienced from the freeway. The most acceptable thing about it is the use of palms.

3. Union Bank Building, 1968
Albert C. Martin and Associates
Figueroa Street between West 4th and
West 5th streets

A typical example of the late 1960s Corporate International Style Modern, here a vertical box set on a low podium.

4. ■Los Angeles Bonaventure Hotel, 1974-76
John Portman and Associates
Northeast corner of Figueroa and West
5th streets

The science fiction world of Buck Rogers and the twenty-first century have not left us. Five bronze-clad glass towers rise from their podium base—just like one of the 1940s drawings by Frank R. Paul for *Amazing Stories*. As a contribution to downtown L.A. they work best when seen from one of the freeways. Portman was quoted as saying of L.A. and his hotel, "Put cars in their place, put people on their feet, and put the city in order (1973)." Obviously his view of putting people on their feet meant inside of his building, not on the adjoining streets. As with many other recent downtown L.A. projects the streetscape of the Bonaventure is grim—the public sidewalk alongside the adjoining streets is not for pedestrians. And this is reinforced by four pedestrian bridges which connect the upper level of the Bonaventure Hotel with adjoining buildings. As seems typical of the design of skyways across America, all of these are dull—both for their users and as objects within the streetscape. The atrium space within Portman's hotel is visually exciting, but maddening when you try to find your way around.

5. Manulife Plaza, 1981-82
Albert C. Martin and Associates
515 S. Figueroa Street

Another vertical reflective box, in this case blue-green glass with a step-back facade. A suggestion of luxury is added to this twenty-story skyscraper by the use of green granite both externally and in the lobby. Below the shaft of the building are four levels of parking. The usual stageset plaza is provided, adorned by a sculpture of a family of bears fishing for salmon, the work of Christopher Keene.

6. Jonathon Club, 1924
Schultze and Weaver
545 S. Figueroa Street

A restrained, low-rise building realized in a dignified version of early sixteenth century Italian Renaissance architecture.

7. Linder Plaza, 1973-74
Honnold, Reibsamen, and Rex
888 W. 6th Street (at Figueroa Street)

A fifteen-story triangular skyscraper whose fragile skin is sheathed in silver and grey steel and glass. The fine and expensive machine-image detailing of the building is impressive.

8. Fine Arts Building (Havenstrite Studio and Office), 1925
Walker and Eisen
811 W. 7th Street

The street facade of this twelve-story building displays a highly original use of Romanesque (probably Venetian Romanesque). Twisted columns, sculptured corbelling, heavy arched windows, and elongated doomuns were all employed. The tripart division of the facade has taken into account how the building is viewed—subtle close up at the street level, large and bold at the top so that it will make an impact from a distance. The tour-de-force of the building (and a must to see) is the two-story arcaded Main Lobby with its rich surfaces and ornament produced by the tile maker Ernest Batchelder.

9. Office Building, 1978-80
Skidmore, Owings, and Merrill
(Chicago Office)
911 Wilshire Boulevard

One more horizontal grid skyscraper — twenty-three-stories high. This is a familiar type unfortunately found in urban environments across the U.S.

10. Hotel Figueroa, 1925
Stanton, Reed, and Hibbard
939 S. Figueroa Street

A learned Beaux Arts interpretation of northern Italian Renaissance townhouses.

11. Friday Morning Club (now **Variety Art Center,**) 1923-24
Allison and Allison
938-940 S. Figueroa Street

A Beaux Arts formula, in this instance there seems to be a suggestion of Byzantine or Romanesque.

12. Security Pacific Plaza, 1973-74
Albert C. Martin and Associates
Southeast corner of South Flower and West 3rd streets

The return of the Beaux Arts (the design principle, not the usual Classical vocabulary): the tower is fifty-five-stories high and its facades are accentuated by thirty-six vertical piers sheathed in light grey granite from Ponteverde, Spain. The gardens and their fountains are quite formal. A large arched sculpture in steel (painted red) by Alexander Calder is placed near the entrance to the tower. Across South Figueroa Street to the west is the full-block **World Trade Center** (1974-76; Conrad Associates) which, notwithstanding its twin eight-story towers, poses as an urban non-space.

13. Wells Fargo Building, 1979
Albert C. Martin and Associates
Northeast corner of South Flower and West 5th streets

When one considers that this forty-eight-story skyscraper replaced the handsome Sunkist Building (1935; Walker and Eisen), the demands for a building whose design would be far above the normal was to be expected. The emphasized horizontality of its stepped back rectangular volumes is well carried out, but hardly distinguished. The plaza with its palm trees heads in the right direction, but it does not end up saving the composition. Equally mixed is the sense of meaningful public sculpture, by Michael Hiezer, Bruce Nauman, Robert Rauschenberg, Frank Stella, and Mark di Suvero.

14. Los Angeles Public Library, 1922-26
Bertram G. Goodhue and Carleton M. Winslow
Southeast corner of South Flower and West 5th streets

This building and the Nebraska State Capitol at Lincoln, are Goodhue's two most significant works, and also two of his most influential designs. In both of these designs, Goodhue sought to bring the past and present together in a single readable image. From the past he borrowed far and wide — from Egypt, Rome, Byzantium, and from various Islamic civilizations. The present is expressed in his use of the skyscraper (implying modern business), his utilitarian planning, and his use of twentieth-century materials, here concrete.

Operating within a Beaux Arts tradition, he introduced a wide array of art; exterior sculpture by Lee Lawrie, the twelve murals in the second floor of the rotunda by Dean Cornwall, the thirteen murals in the History Room by Albert Herter. In the Children's Room, the fresco *Stampeding Buffalo* is by Charles M. Kassler, and the scenes by Julian Garnsey and A. W. Parsons convey episodes from Sir Walter Scott's novels. Planting, which looked like one of Goodhue's romantic Persian sketches, was originally integral to the building and this was especially notable in the axial walk, pools, fountains, and trees which led up to the west entrance of the building.

New Yorkers, with love and care, have recently restored their famed Beaux Arts Public Library (1898-1911; Carrére and Hastings) and through careful planning made it and its subsidary buildings highly useable. But Los Angeles has even gone so far as to suggest that this public park and its building should be torn down and sold, or at best sold and leased back to the city. And one would find it difficult to imagine that New Yorkers would allow Bryant Park to the west of their library to be torn up to provide parking for the library employees — and yet this is just what happened to Goodhue's west garden.

15. Atlantic Richfield Plaza, 1972
Albert C. Martin and Associates
West side of South Flower Street between West 5th and West 6th streets.

These two, thin, fifty-two-story towers (one of which houses the Atlantic Richfield Oil Company offices, the other the Bank of America) replace one of L.A.'s major monuments, the 1928-29 Art Deco (Zigzag) Moderne, black and gold, terra-cotta Richfield Building (Morgan, Walls, and Clements). The dark, polished-stone-sheathed twin towers of the new buildings are formal, dignified, and reticent. The plaza between the towers contains a fountain sculpture, *Double Ascension* (1973) by Herbert Bayer. Below the plaza are two levels of an underground mall, which in color and design is more self-consciously fashionable than the towers (Bielski and Associates, design consultants for the mall).

16. The California Club, 1929-30
Robert D. Farquhar
238 S. Flower Street

The classical tradition via the Beaux Arts in an eight-story structure. The architect carried out his instructions ". . . to use the best materials without elaboration and to provide an atmosphere of the finest type of American Club life." The exterior is of warm brown Roman brick with a thin tufa trim. trim.

17. Security Pacific Building, 1973
William L. Pereira Associates
Southwest corner of South Flower and West 6th streets

The picturesque aspects of Louis Kahn's Richards Medical Towers of the University of Pennsylvania are applied to a seventeen-story office tower, all a bit thin and of a decorative nature.

18. The Broadway Plaza, 1972-73
Charles Luckman and Associates
Southeast corner of South Flower and West 7th streets

This square block project contains the Hyatt Regency Hotel with its round revolving restaurant on top, a thirty-two-story office tower, the downtown Broadway Department Store, and the open-atrium Broadway Plaza Galleria. The two-story Galleria is pleasant, but the ground floor level of the building creates a grim experience — for both pedestrians and passengers in cars.

19. Southern Counties Gas Company Building, 1939-40
Robert V. Derrah
820 S. Flower Street

Forget the ground floor of the building. It has been hopelessly remodelled. But the five floors above indicate how well Derrah (who designed the Coca Cola Building and the Crossroads of the World) could work with the Streamline Moderne. The slightly recessed center is of glass, and the two concrete side sections curve into the center.

20. O'Melveny and Myers Office Building, 1982
Welton Becket Associates (Robert Taylor); the SWA Group, landscape architects
South side of 4th Street between South Hope Street and South Grand Avenue

A twenty-six-story tower of six sides sheathed horizontally in alternating bands of tinted reflective glass and polished brown granite. The tower is set at an angle on its site, and at ground level there is an ample plaza with a double row of sixty-eight Italian cypress trees. The lobby of the tower is composed of a fifty-foot-high greenhouse. The building's most distinguished feature from afar is its thirty-degree slope roof, suggesting that it is either a minimal piece of sculpture or that solar collectors are in use.

21. United California Bank Building, 1973
Charles Luckman and Associates
Northwest corner of South Hope Street and Wilshire Boulevard

A non-descript vertical shaft, sixty-two-stories high.

22. Apartment Building, ca. 1907
Attributed to A. L. Haley
928 S. Hope Street

There are still a remarkable number of these turn-of-the-century Colonial Revival apartment buildings still around in Los Angeles. This one has a classical-columned, two-story portico, behind which hides a simple, wood-sheathed box.

23. Standard Oil Company Office Building, 1928
George W. Kelham
605 W. Olympic Boulevard between South Hope Street and South Grand Avenue

The San Francisco architect George W. Kelham utilized a rusticated, late fifteenth century northern Italian "Palazzo" scheme for this urbane eight-story building. The Los Angeles building is similar to the 1921 office building which he designed for Standard Oil in San Francisco.

24. Crocker Center, 1982-83
Skidmore, Owings, and Merrill
Southwest corner of South Grand Avenue and West 3rd Street

Two 760-foot-high prismatic towers of polished brown granite and tinted glass. In the space between the two towers is a glass atrium "Garden Court" with an exotic garden designed by Lawrence Halprin. Within are pieces of sculpture by Jean Dubuffet, Robert Graham, Juan Miro, and Louise Nevelson.

25. Southern California Edison Building (now One Bunker Hill), 1930-31
Allison and Allison
Northwest corner of South Grand Avenue and West 5th Street

The slope of the two streets made it logical to place the main entrance of this twelve-story Art Deco (Zigzag) Moderne/Classical office building at the corner. Over the entrance are three relief panels by Merrell Gage: *Hydro Electric Energy, Light,* and *Power.* Once in the formal entrance, go on to the elevators, and there you will find a mural *Apotheosis of Power* by Hugo Ballin. The tower portion of the building is basically classical and massive, but the deep-cut vertical window/spandrel units create a strong vertical pattern.

25. *Southern California Edison Building (now One Bunker Hill)*

26. Mayflower Hotel Building, 1927
Charles F. Whittlesey
533-535 S. Grand Avenue

Externally it presents a restrained classical Beaux Arts facade. But internally its allegiance is to the Spanish Colonial Revival. Another example of the wide range of images used within the Beaux Arts tradition can be seen just down the street at 603 S. Grand Avenue (now **California Pacific National Bank Building**) where a 1925 thirteen-story office block imprints a Romanesque image on a classical frame.

27. One Wilshire Building, 1964
Skidmore, Owings, and Merrill (San Francisco)
East side of South Grand Avenue and Wilshire Boulevard

A big, bulky box with a stamped-out facade. Recent renovations have helped a bit.

28. Philharmonic Auditorium and Office Building and Temple Baptist Church, 1906
Charles F. Whittlesey; remodelled in 1938 by Stiles O. Clements
427 W. 5th Street

In 1938 the nine-story auditorium was stripped of its lush ornament, and an effort was made to attire it in Moderne clothes (not too successfully). Originally the building exhibited some of the most enthusiastic Sullivanesque ornament to be found in Southern California. If you can arrange to get into the auditorium you will be able to obtain an idea of how Whittlesey worked out variations on Sullivanesque ornamental themes. It should also be noted that the auditorium was one of Los Angeles's earliest re-inforced concrete buildings.

29. Biltmore Hotel, 1922-23 and 1928
Schultze and Weaver
Southwest corner of South Olive and West 5th streets

Designed by the New York firm which produced in the teens and twenties many of America's major hotels. Its composition and much of its detailing are faithful Beaux Arts. But if you look closely you will find that much of the brickwork and terra-cotta detailing are sixteenth century Italian. Internally, a variety of moods are created, including the Spanish Churrigueresque. Many of the ceilings were painted by Giovanni Smeraldi. In the mid-seventies the hotel was renovated and handsomely restored (Gene Summers and Phyllis Lambert).

30. Pershing Square (formerly La Plaza Abaja, Public Square and Central Park)
Between South Olive, South Hill, West 5th, and West 6th streets

This 5.02-acre park was part of the original public land of the Pueblo of Los Angeles. It was set aside as a public park in 1866. Up until the early 1950s it was known for its vegetation, among which were a wide variety of palm trees. All of this went out when Stiles Clements (1950-51) dug it all up and provided an underground parking garage, *a la* Union Square in San Francisco.

31. Pacific Mutual Building, 1912, 1922, 1926, 1937, and 1974
523 W. 6th at South Olive street

The original Pacific Mutual Building was a close-to-unbelievable, six-story, glazed, white terra-cotta Corinthian temple (1908; designed by John Parkinson and Edwin Bergstrom). In 1922, a new twelve-story building was contructed next door (designed by Dodd and Richards). In 1926 a three-story parking garage was added, and in 1937 Parkinson and Parkinson remodelled their Corinthian temple into a lukewarm Moderne building. Dodd and Richards's 1922 twelve-story building is a typical example, well done, of a Beaux Arts office tower. The H-plan building has an arcaded base which embraces three stories, then a seven-story shaft, and finally two floors hidden behind a colonnade and surmounted by a heavily-bracketed overhanging roof. The vaulted ceiling and engaged piers which line the walls of the ground floor elevator lobby are most impressive. The building was restored in 1974 by Wendell Mounce and Associates using Bond and Steward as design consultants.

32. Oviatt Building, 1927-28
Walker and Eisen
617 S. Olive Street

Though the building's design is essentially Italian Romanesque, it is the Art Deco (Zigzag) Moderne details of the building which attracted attention when it was built — it was described as "Ultra Modern." Extensive use was made of Lalique glass in the external store front, marquee, interior lobby, and sales room. According to publications of the time the shop front, marquee, and all of the other interior decorative work were designed and produced in France and were then shipped to Los Angeles accompanied by five French engineers and architects who had ". . . come over especially to supervise the installation of the fixtures." It was also noted at the time that "Mr. Oviatt has built a bungalow on the roof for his use." The two-story bungalow was no bungalow at all, but a sophisticated Art Deco apartment with "Modern" French furniture and decorative arts.

33. Los Angeles Athletic Club, 1911-12
John Parkinson and Edwin Bergstrom
Northeast corner of South Olive and West 7th streets

This steel-frame twelve-story building is certainly a knowing display of Beaux Arts principles of design. The exterior of the building is pressed brick with terra-cotta trim and a projecting iron cornice.

34. Clifton's Silver Spoon Cafeteria (originally Brock and Company Jewelry Store), 1922
Dodd and Richards
515 W. 7th Street

A small, four-story building with a theatrical parapet—almost Sullivanesque in feeling. The three upper floors of the building are treated as a picture within a frame.

34. Clifton's Silver Spoon Cafeteria

35. Los Angeles Pacific Telephone Company Building, 1911
Morgan and Walls
716 S. Olive Street

This is one instance where a recent renovation has enhanced an earlier design. The ca. 1930 remodelling of this building by Morgan, Walls, and Clements produced a good, but textbook, example of the Art Deco (Zigzag) Moderne. Timothy Walker and Associates in 1979, brightened it all up so

that its facade is more forcefully Art Deco today than it was in 1930.

36. Los Angeles Branch, Federal Reserve Bank of San Francisco, 1930
John and Donald Parkinson
Northwest corner of South Olive Street and West Olympic Boulevard

One's image of a Federal Reserve Bank building is that it should look like a vault—a cold, impersonal fortress. And that is just what the Parkinsons provided. The severe exterior is Moderne Beaux Arts. Over the entrance is a relief sculpture composed of a spread-wing eagle placed between two kneeling figures (by Edgar Walter). To the rear of the building is a vault-like door opening to a ramp which winds down to the basement level, so that armored cars can safely enter the building.

37. Angelus Plaza, 1981
Daniel Dworsky and Associates
Southwest corner of South Hill and West 2nd streets

A group of three sixteen-story, concrete, medium-rise apartment units for the elderly, with an accompanying parking structure to the east.

38. Subway Terminal Building, 1924-26
Schultze and Weaver
417 S. Hill Street

According to the architects, this large twelve-story building was based upon a sixteenth-century Italian prototype. From the street the four-bay division of the building makes it appear as four individual buildings. Rusticated masonry is used on the lower two floors, and the upper portion of the building is treated as a two-story Palazzo. Far below the ground level, five subway tracks enter the building. Trains entered the building from such faraway destinations as Santa Monica and San Fernando in the valley. The subway tunnel, which was a mile in length, brought trains in from the west. It was in operation from 1925 through 1955. The columned entrance lobby of the building has recently been restored. (by Bernard Judge).

39. The National Bank of Commerce, 1929-30
Walker and Eisen
439 S. Hill Street

Art Deco (Zigzag) Moderne as the language for a Beaux Arts design. The building's forte is the entrance and the three high relief panels above. Please take note of the message of the right-hand panel "Wealth means power, it means leisure, it means liberty."

39. The National Bank of Commerce

40. Title Guarantee Building (Guarantee Trust), 1929-31
John and Donald Parkinson
Northwest corner of South Hill and West 5th streets

A twelve-story Art Deco (Zigzag) Moderne skyscraper sheathed in light buff terra-cotta with a granite base. A suggestion of the Gothic is conveyed in the upper reaches of the building with its tower and flying buttresses. The building's verticality was accentuated at night by dramatic exterior lighting. In the lobby is a mural *The Treaty of Cahuenga* by Hugo Ballin.

41. International Jewelry Center, 1979-81
Skidmore, Owings, and Merrill (Los Angeles)
Northeast corner of South Hill and West 6th streets

A horizontal, ribbon-window, sixteen-story building with a faceted Siena granite and reflective glass facade. The building occupies approximately half of the east side of Pershing Square, and though its facade is broken up above its lower street level it is somewhat over-bearing for the scale of the park. If one looks to the west side of the Square at the Biltmore Hotel and the Pacific Mutual Building (on South Olive Street) one can sense how much more satisfactory is their contribution to the public space of the Park.

42. William Fox Building, ca. 1929
S. Tilden Norton
608 S. Hill Street

A mild Art Deco (Zigzag) Moderne office tower with an excellent black and gold vestibule and lobby.

43. Bankers Building (now International Center), 1930
Claude Beelman
629 S. Hill Street

The late twenties Moderne leaning towards the verticality of the Gothic. Unfortunately, the Moderne marquee has been removed, but the entrance/elevator lobby retains its Moderne elegance.

44. Warner Brothers Downtown Building and Pantages Theatre (now Jewelry Center Building), 1920
B. Marcus Priteca
Northwest corner of South Hill and West 7th streets

A Beaux Arts composition of the late teens—much more French than the typical designs of American architects of the 1920s. Heavy piers accent the corners and divide the two street facades into three vertical window bays. The corner of the building is rounded, forming an impressive bay surmounted by a Baroque Revival dome.

45. Garfield Building, 1928-30
Claude Beelman
408 W. 8th Street (northwest corner of South Hill Street)

The exterior is bland, but the Art Deco (Zigzag) Moderne entrance/elevator lobby is a gem with its dark marble walls and detailing in German silver and gold leaf.

46. Mayan Theatre, 1926-27
Morgan, Walls, and Clements
1040 S. Hill Street

Seven "Mayan" warrior-priests look down on you as you enter the theatre, and within you are a participant in a twenties Hollywood film recreating a pre-Columbian world as it should have been. The cast concrete sculptured facade of the building (by Francisco Comeja) has been brightly painted (originally it was left a light grey concrete color).

46. Mayan Theatre

47. Belasco Theatre (now Metropolitan Community Church), 1926
Morgan, Walls, and Clements
1060 S. Hill Street

Morgan, Walls, and Clements going forward at full steam with the Spanish Churrigueresque realized in concrete. The ground level of the street facade has been remodelled, so concentrate your gaze above.

48. White Log Coffee Shop (now Tony's Burger), 1932
Kenneth Bemis
1061 S. Hill Street

Here the best of the past and present are combined — the time-honored American theme of the rustic, non-urban world of the log cabin coupled with its white, steel frame and concrete logs, which signify the hygenic present as well as the Colonial past. By the end of the 1930s Kenneth Bemis had created sixty-two imitation log cabins on the Pacific Coast. The building is now painted brown, and the original roof sign (of steel) in imitation of logs has been replaced by an excellent sign typical of the late fifties.

48. White Log Coffee Shop (now Tony's Burger)

49. Bradbury Building, 1893
George H. Wyman
304 S. Broadway

You would hardly believe that this pedestrian exterior (mildly Romanesque) hides one of the most beautiful interior spaces to be found in L.A. The iron and glass-skylighted court contains open balconies, staircase, and elevators. The lacy quality of the metal work in the inner court plays off against its glazed brick walls.

50. Million Dollar Theatre, 1918
Albert C. Martin; William L. Woollett
307 S. Broadway

50. Million Dollar Theatre

A lush, Churrigueresque exterior is complemented by an equally sumptuous and rather mysterious Baroque interior designed by William L. Woollett. Symbolism abounds in Woollett's sculptured and painted decoration. What is needed is a Nancy Drew to ferret it all out. The lobby has been altered, but the Baroque auditorium remains as built.

51. Roxie Theatre, 1932
John M. Cooper
518 S. Broadway

Here the Art Deco (Zigzag) Moderne oozes over into the Streamline Moderne. This was the last major theatre to be built in the downtown theatre district.

52. Reed Jewelers, ca. 1929
533 S. Broadway

Art Deco (Zigzag) Moderne with an impressive bas-relief on the front. Don't miss **Hartfells** next door, which is equally committed to the Moderne.

53. Pantages Theatre (now Arcade), 1911
Morgan and Walls
534 S. Broadway

An early Beaux Arts theatre building.

54. Broadway Arcade Building, 1922-23
MacDonald and Couchot
542 S. Broadway

The lower three floors of this twelve-story building are wholeheartedly "Spanish Renaissance" while the upper nine floors are Beaux Arts. An open, skylighted shopping arcade runs through the building from Broadway to Spring Street.

55. Lunes Broadway Theatre (now Cameo Theatre), 1910
Alfred F. Rosenheim
528 S. Broadway

A nickelodeon with its interior fully intact, including the silk canopy over the auditorium ceiling.

56. The Dutch Chocolate Shop (now Finney's Cafeteria), 1914
Plummer and Feil (remodelling)
217 W. 6th Street (northwest of South Broadway)

Inside you will discover a world of Ernest Batchelder tile representing the designs and colors he used during his Craftsman years.

57. Story Building and Garage, 1916 and 1934
Morgan, Walls, and Clements
Southwest corner of South Broadway at West 6th Street

The often-repeated Beaux Arts formula of stacking one horizontal volume on top of another—here successfully realized in white terra-cotta. The upper zone uses arcaded openings, attic story, and heavy projecting cornice to effectively terminate the composition. On West 6th Street is a garage whose entrance was designed in 1934 by Stiles Clements. This entrance with its gates represents a high point of the Moderne in L.A.

58. Los Angeles Theatre, 1931
S. Charles Lee
615 S. Broadway

A Baroque motion picture palace. Twin Corinthian columns frame the central notched arch. Above, a varied skyscraper is provided with pinnacles and other sculptured forms. The interior grand staircases and rich decoration is as French Second Empire as the street facade. Probably the finest theatre building in Los Angeles.

54. Broadway Arcade Building

59. Schauber's Cafeteria, 1927
Charles F. Plummer
620 S. Broadway

A Spanish Colonial Revival eating establishment.

60. Orpheum Theatre and Office Building (now Palace Theatre), 1911
G. Albert Landsburgh
630 S. Broadway

A French Second Empire theatre, reserved on the outside and exuberant on the inside (with sculpture by Domingo Mora). Note the use of multicolored terra-cotta decoration throughout the building. The San Francisco architect G. Albert Landsburgh was the principal designer of theatres on the West Coast during the decades 1900 through 1930.

61. Tower Theatre, 1925-26
S. Charles Lee
Southeast corner of South Broadway and West 7th Street

A Spanish composition with Romanesque and Moorish details. The small but highly effective tower which rises from the corner of the building is quite Goodhue-esque. This was one of the earliest theatre designs by S. Charles Lee who was to emerge in the 1930s and 1940s as L.A.'s principal designer of motion picture theatres. As with most of the older theatres the present marquee was added after the end of World War II.

61. Tower Theatre

62. State Theatre, 1921
Weeks and Day
703 S. Broadway

One can assume that the Beaux Arts educated Charles P. Weeks of San Francisco was thinking of the Mediterranean when he designed this building.

63. Globe Theatre, 1921
Morgan and Walls
744 S. Broadway

A classical Beaux Arts design. As was usually the case, the interior reflects the influence of nineteenth-century Paris.

64. Charles E. Chapman Building, ca. 1923
756 S. Broadway

A twelve-story Beaux Arts office block, large Ionic columns gracing the ground-floor level.

65. Ninth and Broadway Building, 1929
Claude Beelman
850 S. Broadway

A thirteen-story Art Deco (Zigzag) Moderne office block, with an emphasis on the vertical. The lobby is especially worth a visit.

66. The Eastern Columbia Building (now 849 Building), 1929
Claude Beelman
849 S. Broadway

Now that the Richfield Building is gone, the Eastern Columbia Building assumes the mantle of being L.A.'s major Art Deco (Zigzag) Moderne building of the 1920s. In this stepped back design, vertical piers and shafts extend close to the top of the tower which houses four faces of a clock (neon-lighted). The exterior terra-cotta sheathing is in gold and blue-green. The building originally housed two retail stores: Columbia and Eastern Outfitting. An L-shaped arcade, with entrances on South Broadway and on West 8th Street, separated the two stores. Above the entrances are pierced grills forming a sunburst pattern, and these are stippled in gold.

67. Texaco/United Artists Building, 1927
Walker and Eisen; C. Howard Crane
929 S. Broadway

It is surprising that in Los Angeles the twenties rage for Spanish (and Mediterranean architecture in general) was not employed frequently for commercial building. As this building indicates, it is a shame that the style was not used more often. Terra-cotta and cast stone readily lend themselves to the style, and its richness can be fully expressed. In this building the style is Spanish Gothic. The lobby is modelled after the nave of a Spanish church, richly decorated with vaulting and murals.

68. Women's Athletic Club, 1924
Allison and Allison
1031 S. Broadway

Described when built as an example of Italian Renaissance architecture. The most interesting aspects of the design are the courtyarded roof garden, with its plantings, loggia, and stairs.

69. Times-Mirror Building, 1931-35
Gordon B. Kaufmann
Southwest corner of South Spring and West 1st streets

American newspapers have a fondness for assuming official governmental garb and, whenever possible, locating themselves so as to imply that they and the government are one. The L.A. *Times* building fulfills this image very well. The original building is monumental PWA Moderne, and its siting, just across the street from the buildings of the Civic Center, makes it seem as if it belongs. There are some wonderful spaces inside the Kaufmann building, if you can arrange to get inside. Above all see the Rotunda with Hugo Ballin's mural *Newspaper*. In 1948 Rowland H. Crawford designed a ten-story addition at the northwest corner of South Spring Street and West 3rd Street. It too is PWA Moderne, but in this case the classical monumentality has been mellowed quite a bit. Nevertheless the sculpture at the central parapet still helps the building to read with authority. To the west of the older building, William L. Pereira

and Associates added in 1970-73 a six-story addition consisting of two horizontal boxes hovering over various vertical boxes below. The marriage of the old and new is not a happy one, but then it seldom is in the hands of a "Modern" architect.

70. Hellman Building (now Banco Popular Center), 1903
Alfred F. Rosenheim
Northeast corner of South Spring and West 4th streets

A typically respectable turn-of-the-century Beaux Arts office building, similar to others erected across the country. Recently restored.

71. Brady Block (later Hibernian Building), 1904
John Parkinson
Southeast corner of South Spring and West 4th streets

This building has often been cited as L.A.'s first skyscraper. It is a twelve-story Beaux Arts office block which has an elaborately decorated attic with a colonnade in the Corinthian order.

72. Stowell Hotel Building (now Hotel El Dorado), 1913
Frederick Noonan
416 S. Spring Street

A sort of Neo-Gothic treatment of the facade, including extensive cantilevered canopies. The walls, sheathed in glazed green brick, contrast with the light tan cast stone ornament.

72. Stowell Hotel Building (now Hotel El Dorado)

73. Title Insurance and Trust Company Building (now **Los Angeles Design Center**), 1928
Walker and Eisen
433 S. Spring Street

Lightly Art Deco (Zigzag) Moderne. There are mosaic panels above the entrance and murals by Hugo Ballin. The lobby was decorated by Herman Sachs. Note the elevator doors.

74. Security Trust and Savings Bank Building, 1907
John Parkinson and Edwin Bergstrom

Security National Bank Building, 1916
John Parkinson
Southeast corner of South Spring and West 5th streets

The office building is textbook Beaux Arts with a pronounced cornice. The two-story bank is quite elegant, with its four pairs of Ionic columns behind which are windows which light the main banking room. In 1982 the bank building was converted into a theatre.

75. Alexandria Hotel, 1906
John Parkinson
Southwest corner of South Spring and West 5th streets

What counts in this building is the interior palm court with its stained glass ceiling. The palm court was refurbished in 1967-70 when the lobby was drastically remodelled in order to look Victorian rather than retain its original Baroque magnificence.

76. Merchants National Bank Building (now **Lloyd's Bank,**) 1915
William Curlett and Son
Northeast corner of South Spring and West 6th streets

Another L.A. squarish, but well-designed, Beaux Arts office block.

77. Pacific Coast Stock Exchange, 1929-30
Samuel E. Lunden; John and Donald Parkinson, consulting architects.
618 S. Spring Street

Monumental PWA Moderne (in somber grey granite) as an appropriately solid fortress. Four large-scaled fluted pilasters articulate the street elevation. Under the flat entablature are three panels symbolizing modern industry (by Salvatore Cartaino Scarpitta). Within is sculpture from the Wilson studio and murals by Julian Ellsworth Garnsey. Next door at 626 S. Spring Street is a handsome six-story Beaux Arts building with the space between the engaged piers now filled with glass.

77. Pacific Coast Stock Exchange

78. Banks-Huntly Building, 1929-31
John and Donald Parkinson
632 S. Spring Street

A vertical Art Deco (Zigzag) Moderne twelve-story building with its upper facade treated as a tower with vertical panels of chevrons.

79. Union Oil Building (now **Security Pacific National Bank**), ca. 1911
John Parkinson and Edwin Bergstrom
Northwest corner of South Spring and West 7th streets

An eleven-story Beaux Arts office block in white terra-cotta.

80. I. N. Van Nuys Building, 1910-11
Morgan and Walls
Southwest corner of South Spring and West 7th streets

Another eleven-story white terra-cotta exercise in the Beaux Arts tradition, with engaged Ionic columns at the street level. Next door at number 719 is a four-story Beaux Arts Annex (designed by Morgan, Walls, and Clements, 1929-30) with an office space in the center and garage doors to each side. The north garage entrance still retains its original classical metal gates.

81. Hellman Commercial Trust and Savings Bank Building (now **Bank of America**), 1924
Schultze and Weaver
Northeast corner of South Spring and West 7th streets

Four two-story Ionic columns bring dignity to the ground floor of this Beaux Arts office block.

82. Saint Vibiana's Cathedral, 1871-76
Ezra F. Kysor; W. J. Mathews
114 E. 2nd Street

This cruciform-plan church was supposedly modelled after the church of San Miguel del Mar in Barcelona. In 1922 John C. Austin added the present "more correct" entrance facade in stone. The rear elevation and the interior are, in spite of heavy remodelling, basically mid-nineteenth century Italianate.

83. Van Nuys Hotel (now **Barclay Hotel Building**), 1896
Morgan and Walls
103 W. 4th Street

A six-story Beaux Arts composition of repeated bays separated by four story high pilasters.

84. Charnock Block (now **Pershing Hotel**), 1888
Southeast corner of South Main and West 5th streets

84. Charnock Block (now Pershing Hotel)

A rare late-nineteenth century commercial building. As usual, forget the remodelled first floor and look at the second floor of this brick building. Five classical decorated oriel bays and a corner bay tower punctuate the facade.

85. Kerkhoff Building (now **Santa Fe Building,**) 1907 and 1911
Morgan and Walls
Northeast corner of South Main and East 6th streets

A ten-story Beaux Arts office block.

86. Pacific Electric Building, 1903-05
Thornton Fitzhugh
610 S. Main Street

The often encountered turn-of-the-century combination of Richardsonian Romanesque and the Beaux Arts. In this case huge pilasters with exaggerated Ionic capitals separate the major bays, while small arched bays occur within. A pergola garden with wonderful views was placed on top of this ten-story building.

87. California Theatre, 1918
Alfred B. Rosenthal
810 S. Main Street

The sculptured French Third Empire facade looks down (with disgust) at the modernized marquee and lobby.

87. California Theatre

88. Fire Station No. 29, 1910
Hudson and Munsell
225 E. 5th Street

Small, mild classicism in concrete.

89. Gray Company Building (now **824 Building**), 1928
Morgan, Walls, and Clements
824 S. Los Angeles Street

Stiles Clements convincingly demonstrated in this five-story building how well the Spanish Colonial Revival vocabulary could be used for a commercial structure. Here he used thin vertical piers which terminated in an entablature of cast concrete ornament.

90. Gerry Building, 1947
Maurice Fleischman
910 S. Los Angeles Street

A 1930s Streamline Moderne design built in the years immediately after the Second World War. The center of the facade, which is almost entirely of glass, curves inward on each side.

91. Wolfer Printing Company Building, 1929
Edward Cray Taylor and Ellis Wing Taylor
416 Wall Street

A Tudor Revival commercial building.

92. Commercial Block, ca. 1889
740-748 S. San Pedro Street

A two-story brick Queen Anne commercial building with a cast iron street front.

93. Japanese American Cultural and Community Center
San Pedro Street between Azusa and East 3rd streets

The area of Little Tokyo has been experiencing intensified building activity in the late seventies and now into the eighties. Note should be made of the theme tower of wood (1978; David Hyun) and now more recently Isamu Noguchi's stone sculpture *To Issei* (1983) placed in the Plaza of the Center. close by is the **Japan American Theatre** (244 S. San Pedro; 1982, by Kajima Associates, George Shinno), a gracefully curved, facaded building which looks out onto the Plaza.

94. Weller Court, 1982
Kajima Associates, George Shinno
123 Weller Street

The ground-level section of this building with its flat and curved volumes together with the plaza and its fountain and planting join together to provide a pleasant Modernist pedestrian space (but more planting and less hard surfaces would have helped).

95. "Temporary Contemporary Museum," Los Angeles Museum of Contemporary Art, 1982-83
Frank O. Gehry and Associates
134-152 Central Avenue

An extensive warehouse complex (partially of wood and partially of concrete) which has been remodelled to serve as exhibition space for the to-be-built Museum on Bunker Hill. The interior spaces work well for the exhibition of contemporary art.

96. 1st Street Viaduct Bridge, 1928
H. P. Cortelyon, engineer
East 1st Street, east of Santa Fe Avenue

Concrete homage to the classical tradition of Rome.

96. *1st Street Viaduct Bridge*

97. 4th Street Viaduct Bridge, 1930
Louis L. Hunt, architect, Merrill Butler, engineer

Mildly Medieval forms in concrete.

Downtown, Civic Center

As early as 1900 there were discussions of creating a "City Beautiful" Civic Center for the City and County of Los Angeles. In 1905 a Municipal Arts Commission was appointed and the group in turn engaged the pioneer city planner Charles Mulford Robinson to prepare a plan — which it formally published in 1909. In 1918 a commission was appointed to select a site. They recommended setting aside the location which is now occupied by the various buildings of the present Civic Center. The planning and landscape firm of Cook and Hall was commissioned to plan the details of the site. In 1923 the firm submitted a scheme which called for a Beaux Arts axial plan, with the major buildings grouped around Broadway and Main Street. The existing pattern of streets was essentially left intact, but provision was made for subways and extensive auto parking. The projected railroad passenger station was made integral to the plan. The following year (1924) the Allied Architects of Los Angeles proposed it's own scheme — a much more grandiose cross-axis Beaux Arts plan. Out of these two schemes finally emerged the "adopted plan" of 1927, which was as dull and unimaginative as one could ask, and which seemed to combine the worst portions of both plans.

Other architects also tried their hand at suggested schemes. William L. Woollett projected (in 1925) a romantic, highly imaginative, classical composition, and Lloyd Wright submitted (in 1925) his own "futuristic" cross-axial plan, composed of skyscrapers, airports, layers of streets, and integrated rapid transit and freeways. In 1939, Sumner Spaulding proposed a return to the basic concept of the 1924 Allied Architects plan, but, like the plans of 1920s, Spaulding's plan was never realized. After World

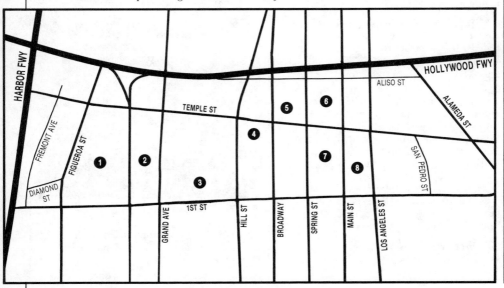

War II, the planning and construction of the Civic Center became closely involved with urban renewal and the razing of Bunker Hill (the hill as well as the buildings). What we have today is the ghost of Spaulding's 1939 scheme. An east/west axis runs from the Water and Power Building at the west end to the City Hall on the east. Lining the axis are the buildings of the Music Center, then to the north, the Hall of Administration, the Hall of Records, and the Criminal Court Building; to the south, the Courthouse, Law Library and State Building. The more recent (1975) Los Angeles Mall loosely seeks to gather together the civic buildings which lie east of the City Hall.

The criticism which Allied Architects leveled at the Cook and Hall plan—that retention of north/south streets would destroy the unity of the Civic Center—has proved to be absolutely correct. Today, there is simply no feeling of coherence or unity. Parts do work, like the plaza of the Music Center or the space between the Hall of Administration and the Courthouse, but they only function as fragments. As to the individual buildings themselves, none is great. But the following are worth a real look:

1. Los Angeles Department of Water and Power Building, 1963-64
Albert C. Martin and Associates
Northwest corner of South Hope and West 1st streets

Best seen at night from the Harbor Freeway to the north. The solidity of the

1. Los Angeles Department of Water and Power Building

building melts, and all that is left are thin vertical and horizontal lines of support, the floors and the sun screen. Unfortunately the forest of fountains around it is not allowed water.

2. Los Angeles Music Center, 1964-69
Welton Becket and Associates
North of West 1st Street between South Hope and South Grand streets

The building faces on an east/west plaza with a central pool dominated by a 1969 Jacques Lipschitz sculpture. To the south is the largest of the three buildings, the **Dorothy Chandler Pavilion;** to the north, enclosed by a free-standing colonnade, is the circular **Mark Taper Forum** and the **Ahmanson Center** (Theatre). Under all of this is the essential parking garage. The whole composition is light, fragile, but elegant. However, it should be noted that like most Modern designs it is not growing better with age. Functionally and aesthetically (given the premise of design in the 1960s) it all appears to be working very well.

2. Los Angeles Music Center

3. Los Angeles County Courthouse, 1958
J. E. Stanton; Paul R. Williams; Adrian Wilson; Austin Field and Frey
Northwest corner of Hill and First streets

Fifties Modern attempting to be classical and public. The higher portion of the building to the north has a clock face and the east facade, which is windowless and divided into squares, boasts some relief sculpture.

4. Hall of Records Building, 1961-62
Richard J. Neutra, Robert Alexander; Honnold and Rex; Herman Charles Light and James Friend
320 W. Temple Street

A rare, realized Neutra high-rise. Functionally it seems to fulfill its task, but as an object itself or of even more importance as an element within the Civic Center it does not contribute much.

5. Hall of Justice Building, 1925
Allied Architects of Los Angeles
Northeast corner of South Broadway and West Temple Street

This fourteen-story building in the Italian style indicates what the Allied Architects had in mind for the buildings of the Civic Center—pure Beaux Arts classicism of the early 1920s. The building is sheathed in grey granite with highly polished granite columns.

6. ■Federal Building and Post Office
(now U.S. Federal Courthouse), 1938-40
Louis A. Simon; Gilbert Stanley Underwood
Northeast corner of South Spring and West Temple streets

PWA Moderne of the late thirties, beautifully and convincingly carried out. When the *Architectural Record* in 1940 asked a number of Los Angeles citizens to cite their favorite buildings, the then-new Federal Building was one of them. Though seventeen stories high (on South Spring Street) the building manages to remain snugly within the classical tradition—albeit in an abstracted manner. Within, luxury and formalism are evident, ranging from rose marble and Siena travertine to James L. Hauser's larger-than-size sculpture *The Young Lincoln*, to Archibald Garner's eight-foot-high sculpture in stone, *Law*.

7. Los Angeles City Hall, 1926-28
John C. Austin, John and Donald Parkinson, and Albert C. Martin; Austin Whittlesey, interiors.
Southeast corner of South Spring and West Temple streets

7. Los Angeles City Hall

The approach which the architects took was a Goodhue-esque, combining the traditional classical temple as a base with the symbol of a skyscraper, commenting on the prowess of American business. In their presentation of the design the consortium of architects noted that "the first story of the City Hall would be of monumental character," and that the skyscraper tower ". . . was necessary to cut the skyline." The tower, with its sloping walls, turned out to be monumental as well, and the top of the tower seems to be a twenties interpretation of what the ancient Mausoleum at Halicarnasus should have looked like (although it should be noted that when the building was built it was referred to as "Italian Classic"). Following in the footsteps of Goodhue, Hartley Burr Alexander of the University of Nebraska furnished the inscriptions for the building. ("The city came into being to preserve life, it exists for the good life.")

In the interior public spaces, especially in the central rotunda, the mood is Byzantine, with the floor, wall, and ceiling decoration by Austin Whittlesey, who worked closely with Herman Sachs and Anthony Heinsbergen. It was fitting that when the building was dedicated in April of 1928, the three-day affair was under the direction of Sid Grauman.

Until the 1950s the twenty-eight-story tower was the only structure allowed to exceed the 150-foot height limitation. Now its tower is only one among many.

8. Los Angeles Mall, 1973-74
Stanton and Stockwell; Cornell S. Bridgers, Troller and Hazlett, landscape architects
East side of South Spring Street between West First and Aliso streets

This civic addition consists of a six-level mall, a four-level underground garage, and three buildings: **City Hall East, City Hall South,** and a small **Children's Museum.** The skyway which connects the mall to the original City Hall is as dull as the other buildings. The two objects which make a noble, but vain, attempt to lift all of this out of the mundane is Millard Sheets wonderful mural at the Spring Street entrance to City Hall East (Stanton and Stockwell, 1973-74) and Joseph Young's *Triforium* (1975), a sixty-foot fountain of light and music. The landscaping is well carried out, but now ten years after it was finished, it is all beginning to look a bit tired. Even the fountains run only intermittently.

Downtown, Plaza and Northeast

The section around the **Old Plaza** and east towards the present course of the Los Angeles River was the center of Los Angeles from 1781 through the mid-nineteenth century. The first public plaza, which lay to the northeast near Sunset Boulevard, was gradually filled in by early settlers. The present Plaza, which was essentially the church/government plaza, has continued to remain open and public, though some of the buildings to the north have extended into the public space (especially after it was "improved" in the 1840s). In 1862, the Plaza was replanned and replanted, this time with topiary work.

By the 1870s the business center of Los Angeles had moved south, and the Plaza area remained a low-density backwash. In the early 1900s, the area was somewhat rejuvenated by a renewed interest in things Hispanic, and during the 1920s **Olvera Street** and several of its adjoining buildings were restored. The plaza area has just missed extinction on two occasions: in the early 1920s it was proposed that the area be incorporated into the projected civic center, and in 1949-50 the plaza narrowly missed being devoured by the construction of the Santa Ana Freeway. Since the 1950s, and especially since it was made a state park, the Plaza area has increasingly become a tourist spot amid restored historic buildings.

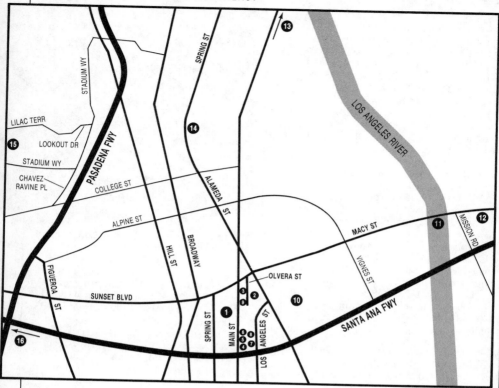

Chinatown originally developed from the 1870s where the Union Passenger Terminal now stands. New Chinatown lies in and around North Broadway and Alpine Street and was built after 1933 when clearing was begun for the Terminal.

1. ■La Iglesia de Nuestra Señora la Reina de Los Angeles (The Church of our Lady the Queen of the Angels), 1818-22; 1861-62; 1875; 1912; 1923 535 N. Main Street

The simple, gable-roofed adobe church was rebuilt and received a new facade in 1861. A bell tower was added in 1875. In 1912 the church was once more restored and enlarged, making it more "Mission" Spanish than it had been before. In 1923 a tile roof replaced the late-nineteenth century shingle roof. As originally built, the facade of the church had a single arched entrance placed

within a molded rectangle. Above was a single window which lighted the choir and nave. Above a horizontal molding which followed the parapet molding of the sides of the building was a single *espadana* (belfry wall). To the south of the facade was a *campanario* (single wall bell

1. Our Lady the Queen of the Angels

tower) which had a single opening (not a double opening as we now see it). And as was true of many of the early Spanish and Mexican buildings of California, the church was at first flat-roofed. Thus, what we see today (internally and externally) is a modest village church which essentially dates from 1861 on.

2. Avila Adobe, ca. 1818
10 Olvera Street

This is the oldest dwelling still standing in Los Angeles. As with most late eighteenth/early nineteenth century adobes it is uncertain as to what was originally built. By the 1830s the dwelling consisted of a traditional double row of rooms, one set facing a corridor (porch) looking out on the street; and to the rear was a second corridor facing toward the court. The house is now covered with a tile roof, but it is unlikely this was part of the original building. The adobe was damaged in an earthquake in 1971, and it has now been rebuilt with concrete reinforcing.

3. La Casa Pelanconi, 1855
33-35 Olvera Street

This two-story house was the first brick dwelling in Los Angeles. A winery occupied the ground floor, the living quarters were above. Note the wood balcony and the main fireplace on the ground level. Although not strong in character, the house is basically very late Greek Revival in style.

4. ▪Masonic Temple, 1858
416 N. Main Street

A cast iron balcony poses over the triple-arched street opening below. The Italianate style shows up in the widely projecting cornice.

5. Merced Theatre, 1870
Attributed to Ezra F. Kysor
420-22 N. Main Street

A three-story masonry building, Italianate in style. The second and third floors boast arched openings inset between simple pilasters. A cast iron balcony projects off the third floor. The ground level was planned as a retail store, the second floor as a 400-seat theatre, and the third floor as an apartment.

5., 6. Pico House and Merced Theatre

6. Pico House, 1869-70
Ezra F. Kysor
430 N. Main Street

This Italianate hotel was the first three-story masonry building constructed in Los Angeles. The openings are all arched and set between vertical pilasters and projecting horizontal cornices. The street elevations of the building were stuccoed over, and then painted to imitate light blue granite. The building has been completely rebuilt and has awaited some use for a number of years.

7. Garnier Block, 1890
415 N. Los Angeles Street

What we now see of this restored building is only half of the original block. The south half went in 1950 when the Santa Ana Freeway was built. The building is a two-story brick and stone structure, mildly styled in the Romanesque.

8. Old Plaza Firehouse, 1884
Southwest corner of Old Plaza and
North Los Angeles Street

A two-story brick building with an Eastlake balcony over the high entrance.

9. Sepulveda House, 1887
624 N. Main Street

This two-story red brick building was
constructed as a hotel and a restaurant.
The upper bay window balconies suggest
the Eastlake style.

10. ▪Union Passenger Terminal,
1934-39
John and Donald B. Parkinson; J. H.
Christie, H. L. Gilman, R. J. Wirth;
Herman Sachs, color consultant; Tommy
Tomson, landscape architect
East side of North Alamdea Street be-
tween Aliso and Macy streets

The last of the large metropolitan passenger depots to be built in the U.S.
The terminal provided for sixteen tracks
and for extensive parking (120 cars underground and 400 in front of the building). Landscaped grounds and courtyards convey an indoor-outdoor sense of
space seldom encountered in large-scale
public buildings. The design successfully
merged the Streamline Moderne and the
Spanish. The 135-foot-high observation
and clock tower, the principal interior
spaces, and the patios manage to convey
both modernity and tradition.

11. Macy Street Viaduct, 1926
Macy Street between Keller Street and
Mission Road

The most northern of the series of via-
duct/bridges which were built to cross
over railroad tracks and the Los Angeles
River. The reinforced concrete Macy
Street Viaduct is Spanish Renaissance
with Ionic and Doric columns.

12. Macy Street Residence, ca. 1890
1030 Macy Street

A brick Queen Anne dwelling.

**13. ▪Fuller Paint Company Warehouse
Building,** 1924-25
Morgan, Walls, and Clements
290 San Fernando Road

One of Morgan, Walls, and Clements
creative exercises in the Spanish
Colonial Revival for a five-story reinforced concrete warehouse building. The
facade is a classical tripartite division:
the base is decorated with low relief cast
in stone (with a wonderful three-unit
entry), above is a row of piers for three
floors, and then there is an attic with
perforated openings.

14. Capital Mills, 1884
1231 N. Spring Street

The Capital Mill is the oldest existing
flour mill in the city. The utilitarian
building is of brick and sections of it are
as high as four stories. The 1884 building incorporated parts of an even earlier
brick building constructed ca. 1855.

**15. U.S. Naval and Marine Corps Ar-
mory,** 1939-40
Stiles Clements
North side of Stadium Way, southeast of
Lilac Terrace

Late PWA Moderne terra-cotta-sheathed
design with engaged fluted piers and
panels of relief sculpture. The Armory is
a little-known late-thirties L.A. monument which is well worth a visit. Do not
miss the wonderful eagles.

**16. Bank Americard Building (Bank
of America Computer Center),** 1979
Skidmore, Owings, and Merrill
Beaudry Avenue between West Temple
and Mignonette streets

An eleven-story box, highly visible from
the freeway interchange. It seems purposely to be a non-building which con-
tributes nothing to one's experience, neither from the freeway nor close up.

Downtown, South

only major external mar is the closing in of all of the ground-level arches. Within, the main lobby is a luxurious Baroque space which no Mission Father would recognize.

1. Los Angeles Herald-Examiner Building

1. ▪Los Angeles Herald-Examiner Building, 1912
Julia Morgan
1111 S. Broadway

Phoebe Hearst and her son William Randolph provided Julia Morgan with numerous commissions throughout California. Supposedly the Los Angeles Herald-Examiner Building is based in part upon A. Page Brown's California Building at the 1893 World Columbian Exposition in Chicago. There is a vague resemblance—primarily because both employed the Mission Revival image. The Examiner Building is one of Julia Morgan's distinguished buildings, and its colorful domes, tile roofs, white walls, and arched openings are as pleasing today as when built. The

2. Morgenstern Warehouse, 1978
Moss and Stafford
1140-46 S. Main Street

This is an instance where even strong, exuberant architecture is having a difficult time maintaining itself against use—in this case the need for signage. The low stucco boxes with their cylinder end adjacent to the street are now on the tawdry side. Still it is a delightful, if somewhat self-indulgent, design.

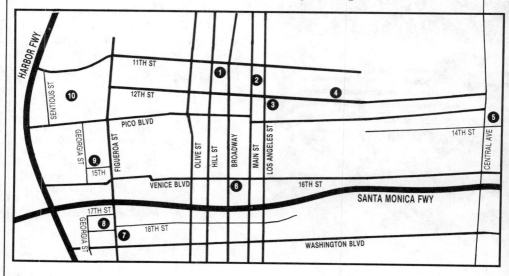

3. Saint Joseph's Roman Catholic Church, 1901
Attributed to Brothers Adrian and Leonard, OFM
218 E. 12th Street

A late Victorian Gothic brick church with extensive interior woodwork, stencilled designs, and stained glass windows. The structure was partially destroyed by a fire on September 4, 1983. Regrettably, it will not be rebuilt.

4. Cohn-Goldwater Building, 1909
525 E. 12th Street

This was the first Modern "Class A" steel-reinforced concrete building in the city.

5. ▪Coca-Cola Bottling Company Plant, 1936-37
Robert V. Derrah
1334 S. Central Avenue

The Streamline Moderne posing as ocean-liner. It is equipped with a ship's bridge, metal railings of a nautical feeling, port-hole windows, ship doors, and suggestions of metal rivets. "What, therefore, could more aptly express the bottling method of the Coca-Cola Company than a ship motif. . ." The interiors were originally as nautical as the exterior of this stucco and concrete flagship. The suggestion of a ship is still present internally, but not the way it used to be. The 1936-37 two-story ship is, in fact, a remodelling and addition to several older structures which were on the site.

6. Illing of California, 1946-47
Paul Laszlo
1600 S. Broadway

Most of Laszlo's work was domestic. Here you can see how the master of the Moderne created a classic statement.

7. Patriotic Hall, 1926
Allied Architects
1816 S. Figueroa Street

The impressive Beaux Arts facade works equally well from the street or from the Harbor or Santa Monica freeways. The west street elevation of the ten-story concrete building is "Italian Renaissance." The sides and back are just there.

8. Forthmann House, ca. 1887
Burgess J. Reeve
629 W. 18th Street

This elegant Victorian house boasts Eastlake details with Italianate brackets, plus a mansard-roofed tower.

9. Fifteenth Street Residence, ca. 1895
633 W. 15th Street

A late Queen Anne dwelling "in the Caribbean Style."

10. Los Angeles Convention Center, 1972
Charles Luckman Associates
1201 S. Figueroa Street

A classic and highly successful example of an L.A. building geared to the auto and the freeway. The center is located close to the interchange of the Harbor and Santa Monica freeways and is well-connected to the freeways. The slightly formal building sits on a podium with its parking structure situated across Sentous Street to the west.

5. Coca-Cola Bottling Company Plant

Boyle Heights

By the late 1880s Boyle Heights, which lies just east of the Los Angeles River, was connected with downtown Los Angeles by two street railroads which crossed the river on the East First Street and on the East Alison Street bridges. Boyle Heights itself is centered around Hollenbeck Park (acquired in 1892) and its lake, while Brooklyn Heights to the north has a similar center in and around the oval form of Prospect Park. By the time of the First World War, the area had declined as a home for artisans and the middle class. In the 1950s four freeways cut huge swaths through the area—the worst and the most unbelievably thoughtless was the placing of the Golden State Freeway adjacent to the once-quiet atmosphere of Hollenbeck Park. The past twenty years present a mixed picture of decay, restoration, well-kept yards and gardens, high, protective, chain link fences, and formidable watch dogs. The fame of East Los Angeles in the late 1960s and through much of the 1970s rested on the ever-changing **street murals.** A number of these can be seen on Whittier Boulevard from Soto Street east to Atlantic Boule-

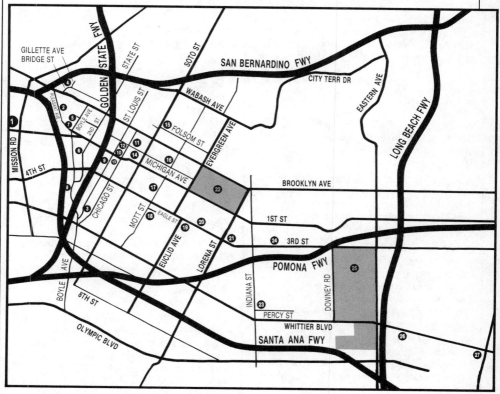

vard. Others are situated on First Street between Lorena and Indiana streets, on Brooklyn Avenue at Gifford Avenue, and on Brooklyn Avenue at Gage Avenue. Some of these murals are by professional artists, others are by self-taught painters and children.

1. Public Housing Projects, 1941-42

Several of these housing projects were started as low-cost developments of the later Great Depression years, and then with the approach of the Second World War they became War Housing Projects.

a. Aliso Village, 1941-53
George G. Adams, Walter S. Davis, Ralph C. Flewelling; Eugene Weston, Jr., Lewis E. Weston, Lloyd Wright; Katherine Bashford and Fred Barlow, Jr., landscape architects
Northwest corner of First and Mission streets

This housing project consists of thirty-three two-story, masonry/stucco/wood-framed, flat-roofed boxes. It was planned to house 2,975 persons on the 34.3-acre site. As is true of many public projects in Los Angeles, the site plan and the landscape design ended up being far more imaginative than the architecture.

b. Rosehill Courts Public Housing, 1942
W. F. Ruck and Claude Beelman
Northeast on Huntington Drive to Esmeralda Rose Hill Drive and Amethyst Street

A small World War II housing project of 100 living units contained in fifteen two-story frame and stucco-sheathed buildings. Existing eucalyptus trees were retained, which helps.

c. William Mead Homes, 1941-42
T. A. Elisen; A. R. Walker, Norman R. Marsh, David D. Smith, Herbert J. Powell, and Armand Monaco
1300 N. Cardinal Street (North Main Street to Elmyra Street, east on Elmyra Street to Cardinal Street)

These 449 living units were provided on a site of 15.2 acres. Corner windows, horizontal balconies, and other details slightly suggest the late 1930s Moderne.

d. Pico Gardens Public Housing, 1941-42
John C. Austin, Sumner Spaulding, Earl Heitschmidt, and Henry C. Newton
500 S. Pecan Street (South on Pecan Street off East First Street)

This project contains 250 living units in thirty-seven two-story buildings.

2. Mount Pleasant Bakery Building, ca. 1885
1418 Pleasant Avenue

This small, false-fronted wooden building is supposedly the oldest bakery building still standing in Los Angeles. It is essentially Queen Anne in style with some older elements of the Italianate.

3. House, ca. 1900
706 S. Chicago Street

What appears to be a late Queen Anne two-story dwelling moves on to suggest either the Richardsonian Romanesque or, more likely, the Mission Revival. Note the two rows of cobblestone arches.

4. House, ca. 1905
603 Gillette Street

A boxy, hipped-roof, turn-of-the-century Colonial Revival dwelling is yanked from the normal by the injection of a pointed Gothic window in the center of the street facade. And this feature is "balanced" on one side by an oversized round window. The design is a perfect one-ups-manship of the current fashion of Post Modernism.

5. Cottage, ca. 1885
914 E. Michigan Avenue

A rare (for Los Angeles) surviving example of a Second Empire mansard-roofed cottage. This story-and-a-half cottage exhibits a traditional street elevation which includes a small porch placed between two bay windows.

6. Cottage, ca. 1889
327 S. State Street

A story-and-a-half Queen Anne cottage with original chimney still present (which in Los Angeles is rare because of continual earthquakes). Sunburst patterns occur in the gable ends and jigsaw work is present on the entrance porch.

7. House (now a neighborhood center), ca. 1895
358 S. Boyle Street

A two-story Queen Anne/Colonial Revival dwelling with both first- and second-floor porches sporting an abundance of turned woodwork.

7. House

8. Hollenbeck Home for the Aged, 1896; 1908; 1923
Morgan and Walls; Morgan, Walls, and Clements
573 S. Boyle Avenue

Pure Mission Revival though, as often happens in that style, many design elements, proportions, and details came directly from the Richardsonian Romanesque style of the 1880s. One can see this in the entrance arcade, in the corbelling below the extended eaves, and in the engaged columns employed around openings.

9. Cottage, ca. 1885
2018 E. Second Street

Compared to cities of the East and Midwest, there were few Eastlake houses and cottages built in and around Los Angeles. And of these, very few remain. This small cottage displays a wide array of wood surfaces and sawed work which we associate with this style. The exterior surfaces include forty-five-degree shiplap, tongue-and-grove horizontal boards, and a small bit of fish scale shingles.

10. Grace Methodist Episcopal Church, (now **Free Methodist Church**), 1906
200 N. Saint Louis Avenue

A shingled Craftsman Gothic church building with leaded glass windows. The high points of this picturesque composition are the two miniature towers over the side entrance.

10. Grace Methodist Church (now Free Methodist Church)

11. First Hebrew Christian Church, 1905
Northeast corner of North Chicago Street and East Michigan Avenue

Here you will find a New Yorker's idea of architecture in Los Angeles: a stucco Austrian Secessionist/Islamic facade (with a corner dome) placed in front of a plain clapboard box. The culmination of the design is a large roof sign in the form of an open Near Eastern scroll.

11. First Hebrew Christian Church

12. Church Building (now **Iglesia Bautista Unida**), ca. 1900
East side of North Chicago Street south of Michigan Avenue

A wood Craftsman Romanesque church building. The design displays an assortment of different window shapes, including pointed Gothic windows. One is not certain whether we are to respond to the entrance porch as Richardsonian Romanesque or Mission.

13. House, ca. 1887
2123 E. 2nd Street

Shingled arches are supported by turned wood columns on the entrance porch of this Queen Anne cottage. Across the street at number 2126 is another, larger, **cottage** (ca. 1890) which represents more of the typical Los Angeles builder's spec cottage (Queen Anne in style).

14. Los Angeles Jewish Community Center, 1937
Raphael S. Soriano
2317 E. Michigan Avenue

Pre-World War II International Style Modern. A stucco-sheathed rectangular box with a strong emphasis placed on horizontality via bands of windows, the usual thin roof facia, and then the horizontal bands of the stucco itself.

15. Apartment Building, ca. 1925
East side of North Soto Street, north of East Folsom Street

A commonman's do-it-yourself version of Austrian Secessionism just emerging into the 1920s Art Deco Moderne.

16. Cottage, ca. 1890
2533 E. Michigan Avenue

A many-gabled Queen Anne cottage. It could be right out of any number of late nineteenth century architectural pattern books.

17. House, ca. 1895
South side of East Second Street west of Mott Street

A two-story Queen Anne/Colonial Revival dwelling. A round corner bay-tower is covered with a conical domed roof.

16. Cottage

18. House, ca. 1895
Southeast corner of South Mott and East Eagle streets

Another Queen Anne dwelling with the traditional corner-bay tower.

19. House, ca. 1890
South side of Euclid Avenue

A two-story Queen Anne dwelling with emphatic projecting boxed windows.

20. Cottage, ca. 1889
3059 E. Fourth Street

Clapboard, fish-scale shingles, flush tongue-and-grove boarding, and board and batten form the surfaces of this Queen Anne cottage. The cottage is now partially hidden from the street by a later, single-floor commercial building.

21. Cottage, ca. 1887
3407 E. Fourth Street

A picturesque tower roof projects above the bay and porch of this Eastlake/Queen Anne cottage.

22. Evergreen Cemetery, 1877
Southwest corner of Brooklyn Avenue and Lorena Street

Evergreen Cemetery is one of the oldest cemeteries in the City of Los Angeles, and it contains some interesting nineteenth century tombs and sculpture. Architecturally, the important object within the cemetery is **Ivy Chapel,** designed by Arthur B. Benton in 1903. The chapel is a medieval stone structure with a handsome front composed of four pointed windows along with a long narrow porch.

23. Bungalow, ca. 1910
3672 E. Percy Street

The porch of this modest bungalow establishes it as something almost regal. Four flat arches with stuccoed brackets are supported by thick, primitive columns. Above the eave a curved pediment marks the principle entrance.

24. Our Lady of Lourdes Roman Catholic Church, 1930
L. R. Scherer
3773 E. 3rd Street

An imaginative and forceful mixture of the Art Deco (Zigzag) Moderne and the Spanish Colonial Revival of the 1920s (plus hints of the Mission Revival and the Gothic). All of this imagery has been realized in a reinforced concrete church building.

24. Our Lady of Lourdes Roman Catholic Church

25. ■New Calvary Cemetery and Mausoleum, 1927
Ross Montgomery
4201 E. Whittier Boulevard

Ross Montgomery's **Mausoleum of the Golden West** is a concrete building which is in the same league as the Los Angeles Public Library and the Los Angeles City Hall. It is a major but little-known monument. The architect has beautifully succeeded in creating a picturesque and memorable building, by combing the past and choosing references (it would seem) to Babylonia, to the Hindu architecture of India, to the Mausoleum at Halicarnassus, to Italian and Spanish architecture, and finally to the then-developing Art Deco Moderne of the late twenties. Within the Mausoleum are paintings of California scenes and a great deal of art glass fabricated by the Judson Studios. Also within the cemetery is **Grace Chapel** (ca. 1900). The **entrance gates** off Whittier Boulevard were designed in 1923 by A. C. Martin.

26. Boulevard Theatre, ca. 1937
Balch and Stanberry
4549 E. Whittier Boulevard

A Moderne motion picture theatre, more angular than streamline. The nine letters of "Boulevard" project separately off the horizontally lighted tower.

27. Golden Gate Theatre, ca. 1928
Southwest corner of East Whittier and Atlantic boulevards

The design of this theatre is similar to the Fox Arlington Theatre in Santa Barbara. Both combine a courtyard entrance with what amounts to a small shopping center. Both are Spanish Colonial Revival, but the Golden Gate Theatre is Churrigueresque in its sources. The building turns the corner via an eight-sided tower surmounted by a lantern. The entrance to the theatre is one of the finest examples of the Churrigueresque to be found in Southern California.

28. Wyvern Wood Public Housing, 1938-39
David J. Wetmore and Loyal F. Watson
Between East 8th Street and East Olympic Boulevard, south off South Soto Street and South Grande Vista Avenue

The first low-cost public housing project to be built in Los Angeles (built with private, not public, funds). The seventy-acre site was designed with curved streets and open courts. The site included retail stores which face Olympic Boulevard and Soto Street and a school and playground which adjoin Grande Vista Avenue. The loosely Colonial Monterey style buildings are two-story stucco buildings, some with projecting balconies.

28. Wyvern Wood Public Housing

29. ■Samson Tyre and Rubber Company Building, 1929
Morgan, Walls, and Clements
5675 Telegraph Road (take the Santa Ana Freeway to the South Washington Boulevard exit, then northeast on Telegraph Road)

An architectural wonder of Los Angeles. An industrial office and manufacturing plant as a walled Babylonian (or is it Assyrian?) city, right out of a twenties Hollywood movie set. Babylonian priest-kings and other creatures adorn the walls, and add prestige to the production of automobile tires. The name Samson is associated with the Near East, as is Babylon. So now one does not have to travel to the Tigris and Euphrates rivers to see Babylon for here it is, improved upon in Los Angeles. Over the years various proposals have been made for the recycling of the building (since it no longer produces tires), and we hope that whatever is done will not compromise this landmark as we see it from the Santa Ana Freeway.

30. Lever Brothers Office and Soap Company Building, 1951
Welton Becket and Associates
6300 Sheila Street (take the Santa Ana Freeway to East Washington Boulevard exit, then to Sheila Street)

A period piece of the 1950s Modern, very well done. The most assertive element of the design is the glass penthouse placed on top of the principle building.

Exposition Park, West

Before and after the turn of the century, the northeast part of this section of Los Angeles was a prestigious residential area. This was especially true of the district around Chester Place and Saint James Park. The great residential street of the 1900s was West Adams Boulevard extending from South Figueroa Street to South Arlington Avenue. Though individual enclaves of upper-middle-class exclusiveness were maintained into the 1920s, this part of L.A. began to decay. It has in part become commercialized or has been turned into various types of multiple housing. The extensive flat plain south of Exposition Boulevard developed in the usual strip commercial fashion along major thoroughfares (South Western and South Vermont avenues, South Figueroa Street), with an infill primarily made of modest artisan bungalows and some small-scale multiple housing.

Though Exposition Park and adjacent USC to the north provided open space, those two enterprises really had very little to do with residential neighbors nearby. The 1960s redevelopment has torn down a number of blocks of houses and stores west of USC and replaced them with new commercial buildings (oriented around the auto), and now multiple housing. The streets north of USC used to have many examples of late nineteenth and early twentieth century residential architecture (ranging from the Queen Anne through the Mis-

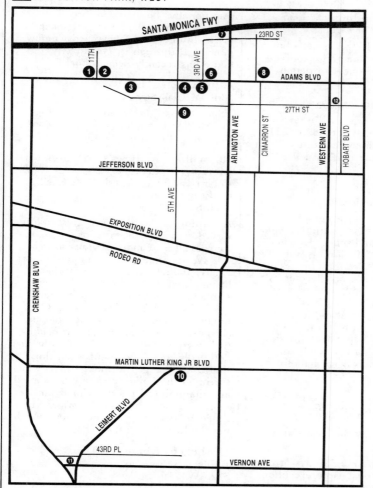

sion Revival and adaptations of English Medieval), but now there are few examples left.

A number of the late nineteenth century Victorian houses around USC have been renovated and a handful of others have been moved—even as far away as Pasadena. Probably the greatest continuous loss has occurred and is occurring along West Adams Boulevard. One of L.A.'s great formal Italian gardens with a hillside water staircase used to surround the **Murphy House** (ca. 1906; Hudson and Munsell) at 2079 W. Adams (landscaped in 1931 by A. E. Hanson), but only a few of the larger trees now remain. And more recently, the Colonial Revival **Childs House** at 3100 W. Adams Boulevard has been demolished.

1. McCarty Memorial Christian Church, 1931
Northwest corner of West Adams Boulevard and 1st Avenue

An excellent example of one of L.A.'s reinforced concrete churches of the late 1920s. The style in this instance is Gothic, partially English and partially French.

2. Apartment Building, ca. 1955
4025 W. Adams Boulevard

A post-World War II L.A. stucco box which emerges as something exotic because of its Japan-esque roof details.

3. House, ca. 1908
3820 W. Adams Boulevard

By 1910 there were over half a dozen Beaux Arts villas on West Adams. This one, somewhat eighteenth-century French, is one of the few still left.

4. House, 1905-06
Charles F. Whittlesey
3424 W. Adams Boulevard

This massive stone house comes close in spirit to Secessionist work from Vienna, though its arches and other elements help it to read as "Mission" as well. Two balls balance on projecting pinnacles at each side of the west front dormer. A heavy, arcaded balcony projects over the entrance porch. Whittlesey was one of L.A.'s gifted architects at the turn of the century. He, along with Irving J. Gill, was fascinated with the possibilities of reinforced concrete. Regrettably, most of Whittlesey's work has been demolished or defaced.

5. Walker House (now **Seventh-Day Adventist Building**), 1905-06
Charles F. Whittlesey
South side of Adams Boulevard at 3rd Avenue

Whittlesey's designs were always original and the Walker House is no exception. Half-timbering suggests the Medieval, but basically the stucco volumes and tile roofs are Mission Revival. Generous terraces face toward the street and the rear (south), overlooking the hillside and garden.

6. ■Fitzgerald House, 1903
Joseph Cather Newsom
3115 W. Adams Boulevard

Whatever Newsom touched, he transformed. This design is as inventively outrageous as any of his earlier Queen Anne or Eastlake designs. If you wonder what style it is, the architect labeled it "Italian Gothic." While it is Medieval in spirit, none of the details is handled traditionally. The tour de force is the elaborate entrance and large clinker brick chimney with an arched window punctured through it. Fortunately, the house has recently been restored.

7. House, ca. 1902
2301 W. 24th Street

"South Seas Edwardian"—a little bit of the Medieval coupled with the Colonial Revival and even a little Queen Anne.

8. William Andrews Clark Memorial Library (UCLA), 1924-26
Robert Farquhar; Ralph D. Cornell, landscape architect
2520 S. Cimarron Street

According to the literature, this building was "designed in the style of the Italian Renaissance." A more obvious source was Wren's addition to Hampton Court Palace, though for some reason Farquhar omitted the oranges from Wren's symbolic decoration and substituted yellow brick for Wren's lovely pink. One might also add that the design has the classical calmness which one associates with Farquhar's work. The villa was undoubtedly more successful when the walled and hedged formal gardens which surround the building were well planted and maintained. The interior is far more successful than the exterior. Arrangements to visit can be made by calling the library (731-8529).

9. Lukens House, 1940
Raphael S. Soriano
3425 W. 27th Street

The single-floor dwelling is arranged around an enclosed patio in a design much less insistently International Style Modern than most of Soriano's pre-World War II plans.

10. Touriel Medical Building, 1950
Raphael S. Soriano
2608-10 W. Martin Luther King, Jr. Boulevard

A steel-frame, post-and-beam building with a small entrance courtyard which carries the *Arts and Architecture* Case Study House aesthetic into the commercial realm (it all seems interchangeable).

11. Leimert Theatre (now **Jehovah's Witness Hall**), 1931-32
Morgan, Walls, and Clements
3300 43rd Place

This reinforced concrete theatre building is a direct result of the Paris Exposition of 1925, except for the open-work oil derrick tower and signing. The interior ceiling of the oval-shaped auditorium still retains its Moderne patterns. Also, note the murals in the lobby. The theatre, which faces onto **Leimert Park**, was a major element in this L.A. suburban development.

12. Fire Engine House No. 18, 1904
John Parkinson
2616 South Hobart Boulevard

A small, delightful, twin-towered Mission Revival building.

Exposition Park, East

1. ■Stimson House, 1891
Carroll H. Brown
2421 S. Figueroa Street

The Richardsonian Romanesque in stone never enjoyed as great a popularity in California for residences as it did in the Midwest and East. The Stimson House was one of the largest and most elaborate examples built in Los Angeles. In plan, with its great living hall, it is really Queen Anne. Externally the four-story octagonal tower with crenelated battlements is picturesque.

2. ■Saint Vincent de Paul Roman Catholic Church, 1923-25
Albert C. Martin
Northwest corner of South Figueroa Street and West Adams Boulevard

Certainly one of the principal landmarks of L.A. and of the Spanish Colonial Revival in California. The Spanish Churrigueresque of Mexico was used as a design source for this church. A richly decorated screen made of Indiana limestone dominates the entrance, and brightly colored tile covers the forty-five-foot-diameter dome. The interior ceiling decoration is by John B. Smeraldi.

3. Automobile Club of Southern California, 1922-23
Hunt and Burns; Roland E. Coate; Aurele Vermeulen, landscape architect
2601 S. Figueroa Street

The corner of this building, with its octagonal tower surmounted by a domed

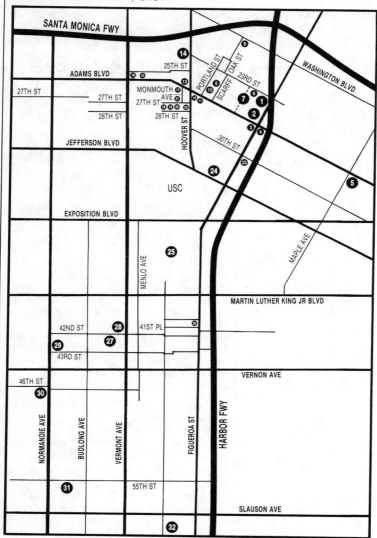

cupola, and the Baroque entrance screen are forceful elements of the Spanish Colonial Revival. Equally impressive is the interior, especially the public entrance and lobby space.

4. Saint John's Episcopal Church, 1922-23
Pierpont and Walter S. Davis
514 W. Adams Boulevard

The design for this church was the result of a competition juried by Ernest Coxhead of San Francisco, William Templeton Johnson of San Diego, and the Rev. George A. Davidson of Los Angeles. The historic source for the design was northern Italian Romanesque. The interior ceiling was modelled after the Church of San Miniato in Florence. The bas-reliefs around the rose window were designed by S. Cartaino Scarpitta. The surfaces of this reinforced concrete church reveal the horizontal board pattern of the forms.

4. *Saint John's Episcopal Church*

5. House, ca. 1900
426-28 E. Adams Boulevard

Medieval imagery of a sort, with a remarkable composition of connected dormers.

6. Severance House, 1904
Joseph Cather Newsom
650 W. 23rd Street

Joseph Cather Newsom designed a number of Mission Revival buildings during his second period of active practice in Los Angeles. Of these, the story-and-a-half Severence House was one of the most frequently illustrated. While for a Newsom design it looks reasonably calm from the street, it is anything but sedate behind and, above all, inside.

7. Chester Place
Between West 23rd Street and West Adams Boulevard west of South Figueroa Street

Chester Place was a private enclave of twenty acres which originally contained thirteen large dwellings. It was laid out as a residential park in 1895. The various houses within the park were built just before and after 1900. Of the houses that still remain, the two most interesting are the **Doheny House** at number 8, and the **Wilson House** across the street at number 7. The Wilson House was built about 1897, and in style is somewhat Mission/Islamic. Its cast orna-

ment was certainly inspired by the work of Louis H. Sullivan. The Doheny (originally Posey) House was built in 1898-1900 and was designed by Theodore A. Eisen and Sumner P. Hunt. Externally, the house is rather neutral (could it be called Chateauesque?). Internally, its most famous space is the Pompeiian Room, designed by Alfred F. Rosenheim and built in 1906. Much of the interior was remodelled in the French rococo style in 1933-34.

7. *Wilson House*

8. Apartment House, ca. 1905
2342 Scarff Street

An authorative Beaux Arts frontispiece set in front of a conventional apartment house.

9. Odd Fellows Temple Building, 1924
Morgan, Walls, and Clements
1828-34 Oak Street

A reinforced concrete building with cast concrete ornament, in this instance more Spanish Renaissance than Churrigueresque.

10. House, ca. 1875-79
2624 Portland Street

One of the once-many modest Italianate dwellings which formerly lined many Los Angeles streets from the late 1860s through the early 1880s.

11. Casa de Rosas (Froebel Institute), 1894
Sumner P. Hunt
950 W. Adams Boulevard

Charles F. Lummis labeled this as Mission and so it must be. It is stuccoed and has an arcade—supported, it should be noted, by short Tuscan columns. And above all it has a patio. It is an odd design, but historically it is important as one of the very early instances of the self-conscious cultivation of the myth of the Mission in a new building.

12. Second Church of Christ, Scientist, 1905-10
Alfred F. Rosenheim
948 W. Adams Boulevard

This Beaux Arts classical design was inspired by the Mother Church in Boston. The concrete dome is sheathed in copper. An authoritative bank of six Corinthian columns faces Adams Boulevard.

13. House, 1892
1140 W. Adams Boulevard

A two-story Queen Anne dwelling.

14. Rindge House, 1900
Frederick L. Roehrig
2263 S. Hoover Boulevard

An imposing Chateauesque dwelling with fat corner towers between which is a Richardsonian Romanesque porch.

15. Kerckhoff House, 1900
1325 W. Adams Boulevard

A shingled Queen Anne/Colonial Revival dwelling.

16. Cottage, ca. 1889
1308 W. 25th Street

This small wood cottage was moved in 1981 and handsomely restored. In style it exhibits both Eastlake and Queen Anne features.

17. Adlai E. Stevenson House, 1895
2639 S. Monmouth Avenue

A late, simplified Queen Anne dwelling, characteristic of many built in the Exposition Park area.

18. Kiefer House, 1895
Sumner P. Hunt and Theodore A. Eisen
1204 W. 27th Street

Queen Anne in concept, but with a turn-of-the-century nod to the Colonial Revival.

19. House, 1904-5
John C. Austin
1194 W. 27th Street

A Craftsman dwelling given Tudor roots and respectability.

20. House, ca. 1890
1160 W. 27th Street

A Queen Anne dwelling. Of special interest are the long, horizontal windows in the gable ends.

21. House, 1890
Bradbeer and Ferris
1163 W. 27th Street

A Queen Anne with a touch of the Colonial Revival. Its commanding feature is the third-floor tower set on the thin posts of the second-floor porch.

22. House, 1891
Bradbeer and Ferris
2703 S. Hoover Street

Queen Anne with an extensive, curved, wraparound veranda, plus the needed palm trees.

22. House

23. Bungalow Court, ca. 1920
627 W. 30th Street

A late Craftsman bungalow court. A group of clapboard bungalows faces onto a long, narrow, open court.

24. Shrine Civic Auditorium (Al Malaikah Temple), 1920-26
John C. Austin, A. M. Edelman, G. Albert Lansburgh
665 W. Jefferson Boulevard

Islamic imagery from somewhere (the Hollywood stage sets?) was employed externally and internally. The pair of domed cupolas and balcony loggia are the strongest features of the design. The auditorium seats 6,400 and a large ballroom pavilion adjoins at the north.

24. *Shrine Civic Auditorium*

25. Exposition Park
Between Menlo Avenue, South Figueroa Street, Exposition and Martin Luther King Jr. boulevards

This site was established in 1872 as a privately operated fairgrounds and racetrack. The Southern District Agricultural Society, which owned the park, went bankrupt in 1880. In 1898 the land was purchased jointly by the state, county, and city. The ▪**Museum/Exhibition Building** was started in 1910 and completed in 1913. In 1911 the landscape architect Wilber D. Cook, Jr. laid out the grounds of the park. The **California Museum of Science and Industry Building** (designed by Hudson and Munsell, with numerous later additions) was thought of as being an example of "Spanish Renaissance" architecture. The **Memorial Coliseum** was designed in 1921-23 by John and Donald B. Parkinson, and this was the central sports facility for the 1932 Olympic Games in Los Angeles. The high point of the park is the seven acres of sunken **rose gardens** which run parallel to Exposition Boulevard and the Beaux Arts Classical public space of the Museum of Science and Industry Building. One of the latest addi-

tions to the buildings within Exposition Park is the ▪**California Aerospace Museum** (1982-84) designed by Frank O. Gehry and Associates. This complex design, resplendent with references to technology, flight, and high art, contains spaces which enhance and dramatize the objects on exhibition. Two other new buildings are currently under construction and will be completed in 1984-85. These are the Museum of **Afro-American History** (designed by Jack Haywood and Vincent J. Proby, 1983-84) and the **Multi-cultural Center** (designed by Barton Myers, 1983-84). For the 1984 Olympic Games, the sculptor Robert Graham designed a gate composed of two bronze piers supporting two headless male/female figures.

25. *Memorial Coliseum*

26. Van De Kamp Building, ca. 1930
Northwest corner of South Figueroa Street and 41st Place

A windmill tower, sadly lacking its blades, brings attention to this corner. The suggestion of shingles, with their V-shaped forms, hints at the Art Deco (Zigzag) Moderne.

27. Apartment Buildings, ca. 1915
1016-18, 1020-22, and 1040-42 W. 42nd Street

A group of typical L.A. Craftsman apartment houses.

28. Manual Arts High School, 1934-35
John and Donald B. Parkinson
Northwest corner of South Vermont Avenue and West 42nd Street

A two-story, exposed concrete, PWA Moderne building, in this case Streamline. Don't miss the relief sculpture over the entrance to the auditorium, and of course the dramatically rounded corners of this concrete building.

29. Saint Cecilia's Roman Catholic Church

28. Manual Arts High School

29. Saint Cecilia's Roman Catholic Church, 1927
Northeast corner of South Normandie Avenue and West 43rd Street

A cruciform concrete church of the Romanesque order. A low, highly effective tower dominates the crossing. Sections of the concrete walls were originally tinted in reds, yellows, and tans.

30. Pilgrim Congregational Church, ca. 1905
West side of South Normandie Avenue at West 46th Street

A shingled Craftsman church, with some Gothic detailing.

31. Two Bungalows, ca. 1910
1102 and 1156 W. 55th Street

Two characteristic L.A. Craftsman bungalows. Nearby on West 54th Street east of South Normandie Avenue are other spec Craftsman bungalows.

32. Mount Carmel High School Building, 1934
7011 S. Hoover Street

Here, in a mid-1930s building, one can sense how the Spanish Colonial Revival tradition was being continually and creatively modified.

University of Southern California

USC was established in 1879 on an eighteen-acre site located adjacent to Exposition Park. In 1910 the architectural firm of Train and Williams prepared a general plan for the campus, followed in 1920 by a strong axial plan prepared by John Parkinson. The Parkinson plan projected the major axis—University Avenue—as being lined with three- and four-story northern Italian Romanesque buildings. The avenue itself was to be bridged at various points by Venice-like foot bridges. During the twenties a number of these buildings were constructed along University Avenue.

At the end of the 1930s, the strict adherence to the vocabulary of the northern Italian Romanesque was modified and modernized in the **Hancock Foundation Building** and in the **Harris Hall/Fisher Gallery Building.** After World War II, Marsh, Smith, and Powell prepared (in 1949-50) a revised master plan, but this was never really carried out. In 1961 William L. Pereira and Associates were engaged to provide still another master plan with additional changes in 1966. One ingredient of this last plan was the gradual closing off of

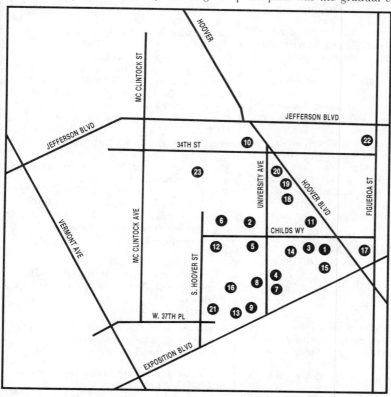

all the streets which cut through the campus, replacing them with pedestrian walkways. Another element was to intensify the density of the campus by introducing high-rise buildings.

From the early 1950s to the present, the tendency has been to infill the campus's older green spaces with new buildings, and also to slowly expand the campus into the residential area to the north. The newer high-rise buildings — some of which are up to fourteen stories high — do not, needless to say, fit in very well with the older buildings, and now there is not much open green space left (though some of the more recent landscaping has been handsomely carried out). USC's architectural image since 1945 has been self-consciously Modern, and, as is true in the case of most of America's academic architecture after World War II, the structures built during these years are, as a group, hardly distinguished. During this time the University has engaged an impressive array of national and regional name-brand architects and architectural firms including I. M. Pei, Albert Martin and Associates, Stanton and Stockwell, Robert E. Alexander, and others. But the overall results have, on the whole, been disappointing.

We wish that the situation was now improving in the 1980s, but such is not the case. The fourteen-story **Webb Tower** and the adjacent eleven-story **Flour Tower** are as mindless as the earlier high-rise designs. It is possible, as has been the case at the UCLA campus, that a distinguished landscape architectural program might rescue it all, but this will be a formidable task to carry out.

1. Widney Hall, 1880
Attributed to E. F. Kysor and Octavius Morgan

This two-story wood structure reads as an early example of the Colonial Revival, though it was in fact mildly Italianate when it was originally built. It was moved to its present site in 1958 and transformed into a Colonial dwelling by Lawrence Test, with the addition of green shutters and a widow's walk on the roof.

1. Widney Hall

2. George Finley Bovard Administration Building, 1920-21
John and Donald Parkinson

The first of this architect's brick northern Italian Romanesque designs to be built on the campus. It is interesting to note that the reactions to the building's architectural images varied. In the twenties it was described as a fine example of the Spanish Renaissance, while others labeled it Lombardian. The building's large square tower, with eight heroic sculptured figures (by Casper Gruenfeld) at each corner, was meant to dominate the new center of the campus. If one compares USC's version of the northern Italian Romanesque with that of UCLA's, it is apparent that Parkinson and others produced a group of buildings which were far more inventive, playful, and lively. Even the most distinguished of the northern Italian Romanesque designs at UCLA, Royce Hall, cannot be compared in quality of design and detailing to the Wilson Student Union Building, the Doheny Library or the Mudd Hall of Philosophy at USC.

3. Elizabeth Von Kleinsmid Hall (now **Student Administrative Services Building**), 1925
William Lee Woollett

A low brick complex which meanders over its site, similar in feeling to an English medieval collegiate building.

4. Law School Building (now **School of Social Work**), 1926

John and Donald Parkinson

Northern Italian Romanesque, with some excellent cast stone detailing around the windows and the main entrance.

5. Gwynn Wilson Student Union Building, 1927-28
John and Donald Parkinson

This version of the northern Italian Romanesque exhibits a first floor treated as an enclosed loggia and two upper floors which are rich in cast stone ornament. The southeast and the southwest corners of the building are particularly successful in their imaginative use of cast stone ornament and low- and high-relief sculpture.

6. Physical Education Building, 1928
John and Donald Parkinson

The centerpiece of this northern Italian Romanesque design is the west entrance with its single large arch and extensive use of cast stone detailing.

7. Bridge Hall, 1928
John and Donald Parkinson

A four-story interpretation of the nave of a northern Italian Romanesque church.

8. Science Hall, 1928
John and Donald Parkinson

A deep entrance passageway from the east leads through a pair of wrought iron gates to a ceramic tile panel depicting four figures captivated by the world of science (by Jean Goodman, 1937).

9. Colonel Seeley Wintersmith Mudd Memorial Hall of Philosophy, 1926
Ralph C. Flewelling

The high campanile of this complex was the dominant vertical element of the campus until it was supplanted in 1966 by the Carillon Tower of the Von Kleinsmid Center. Though the Parkinson buildings are very good examples of the northern Italian Romanesque, they do not come up to the quality of the "Lombardy Romanesque" entailed in this design. Its high point is the cloisters at the east side of the building.

10. Methodist Episcopal University Church, 1931
C. Raimond Johnson

Another important, but often neglected, monument of the campus. One enters this northern Italian Romanesque church through a partial cloister situated on the southeast side of the building. The building's picturesque skyline is enlivened by a pair of buttress towers surmounted by twisted, cast stone roofs.

10. Methodist Episcopal University Church

11. Edward L. Doheny, Jr. Memorial Library, 1932
Cram and Ferguson; Samuel Lunden

The Doheny Library is certainly the most luxuriant of the northern Italian Romanesque buildings on the USC campus. Cram modelled its design closely on the buildings which he and Bertram G. Goodhue had designed in 1910 for Rice University in Houston. The centerpiece of the building is the two-story-plus, square entrance hall with stained glass windows. Other interior spaces are impressive, especially the reading rooms. The Library Building to the east and Bovard Hall to the west create the central open space of the campus with its fountain and planting of sycamores.

12. Owens Hall, ca. 1930

This former fraternity house, now used for administrative offices, is a fine example of a twenties version of a rural northern Italian villa. The low walls of this two-story building are terminated by a wide, overhanging, hipped roof in tile.

13. Harris Hall of Architecture and Fine Arts (including the Fisher Art Gallery), 1939
Ralph C. Flewelling

The architect sought to modernize both the vocabulary of the Italian Roman-esque and that of the Beaux Arts, and he succeeded admirably. The brick and cast stone walls, and the scale of the building closely match his earlier Mudd Hall of Philosophy to the east. And the rambling character of the building is ad-mirably played against the more formal classical elements such as the two splen-did entrances on the south side of the building.

13. Harris Hall of Architecture and Fine Arts

14. Alan Hancock Foundation Building, 1940
C. Raimond Johnson; Samuel E. Lunden

Though its scale is compatible with the older twenties northern Italian Romanesque buildings around it, the four-story Hancock Building is in reality a version of the classical PWA Moderne. An abstracted portico is presented at the center of the west facade. The sculpture used around the building consists, as was so much the practice in the 1930s, of figures which float out in front of the wall surface. Do not miss the delightful group of animals and other forms (dominated by an elephant) cast into the

exposed concrete wall of the auditorium on the north side of the building.

15. Faculty Center, 1960
Jones and Emmons

A modest, non-assertive design by one of L.A.'s important early modernists.

16. Ahmanson Center for Biological Research, 1964
William L. Pereira and Associates

The dominant note of these connected, box-like five- and six-story buildings is a surface pattern of cast concrete hooded windows—the same on the north as well as on the south.

17. Information Center, 1964
Ladd and Kelsey

A delicate pavilion set on a low podium which employs the Miesian post and beam system.

18. Von Kleinsmid Center of International and Public Affairs, 1966
Edward D. Stone Associates

The block of the campus which contains the Von Kleinsmid Center to the north, the Social Science Building in the center, and the Phillips Hall of Education (all by Edward D. Stone Associates) is the finest of the post-World War II group of buildings on the USC campus. The U-shaped Von Kleinsmid Center is composed of three low, rectangular volumes placed on a podium and surmounted by a projecting roof. A four-sided, concave-surfaced Carillon Tower is situated to one side of the courtyard. The brickwork and the general exterior detailing enhance the polished feeling of the design.

19. Social Science Building, 1968
Edward D. Stone Associates

The square Social Science Building has been carefully sited and designed to be related to the Von Kleinsmid Center to the south and the tower of the Phillips Hall of Education to the north. The fa-cade of the Social Science Building is ar-caded, and the building looks out to the west upon a sunken courtyard with a central fountain.

20. Waite Phillips Hall of Education, 1968
Edward D. Stone Associates

The architect has articulated the four facades of his tower into thin, vertical, brick piers with narrow, intervining spandrels and windows. The building rises from a freestanding arcaded brick wall.

20. Waite Phillips Hall of Education

21. Ray and Nadine Watt Hall of Architecture and Fine Arts, 1973
Killingsworth, Brady, and Associates; Sam T. Hurst

A heavy, exposed concrete, savings and loan pavilion which does battle with the 1939 Harris Hall to the west. (Note that Harris Hall easily wins.) The interior public areas of Watt Hall convey a funereal-like atmosphere—a rather strange atmosphere within which to educate future architects and artists.

22. Charlotte S. and Dane R. Davidson Conference Center, 1975
Edward D. Stone, Inc.

A characteristic Stone pavilion, with the east and west facades centering on a recessed, three-arch loggia. The building stands on a podium, its brick walls held in place by a thinly detailed projection roof. There is a handsome sunken garden to the south of the building.

23. Schoenberg Center, 1978
Adrian Wilson and Associates

The Center is unquestionably an im- pressive piece of complex angular sculpture of exposed concrete walls and metal and glass windows and roofs. The whole composition is set above a really fine garden of ferns and trees.

23. Shoenberg Center

Vernon, Huntington Park, Bell, Maywood, South Gate

The southern section of the Los Angeles plain, west of the Los Angeles River, was the scene of extensive speculation during the great land boom of the 1880s. Some residential and commercial growth took place in the late 1880s and early 1890s, but basically the area was devoted to agriculture. The development of the communities of Vernon, Huntington Park, Maywood, Bell, and South Gate came after 1900. Huntington Park was incorporated in 1903, Vernon in 1905, and South Gate as late as 1923. In the teens and later, this section of Los Angeles County emerged as the industrial region of the basin, though it should be noted that the industrialization was accompanied by quite a bit of spec single-family housing. There are a few examples of turn-of-the-century housing to be found in Huntington Park, but almost all of the dwellings to be found today date from after 1920. These communities do contain several of L.A.'s major architectural monuments — the murals of **Farmer Johns**, **Watts Towers**, and several wonderful 1930s Streamline Moderne office and industrial buildings.

1. Pueblo del Rio Public Housing, 1941-42
Paul R. Williams, Adrian Wilson, Gordon B. Kaufmann, Wurdeman and Becket, Richard J. Neutra; Ralph Cornell, landscape architect
1801 E. 53rd Street, Vernon

Fifty-seven two-story units were placed on this 17.5-acre site. The brick and stucco buildings, with their long horizontal bands of windows and thin projecting facia of the roofs, show Neutra's strong influence. As part of the project, individual garden plots and fruit trees were provided. Another contemporaneous public housing project in south Los Angeles which Neutra was involved with is the **Hacienda Village** of 1942, located at 1515 E. 105th Street.

2. Farmer John's (Cloughtan Packing Company), 1953 and later
3049 E. Vernon Avenue, Vernon

Farmer John's expresses a high point in the use of painted illusionism to create its own world, despite what goes on within or in regard to the buildings. Here you will find little pigs romping along with nineteenth-century Tom Sawyer farm boys. The painted scenes continue along the fences, along the street walls of the buildings, and here and there the pigs become three-dimensional and climb onto or over the roofs. If you drive along Vernon Boulevard at thirty-five miles per hour, the small boulevard trees become a part of the scene. The fences and walls were painted in this public-scaled *trompe l'oeil* by Leslie A. Grimes, and since his death (he fell from a scaffold while painting), they have been repainted by Arco Sign Company.

2. Farmer John's

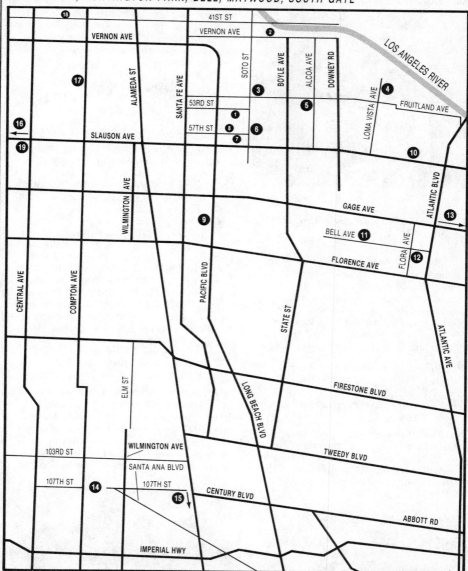

3. Owens-Illinois Pacific Building,
1937
H. H. Brunnier
Northeast corner of East Fruitland Avenue
and South Soto Street, Vernon

As you would expect from this company,
this is an ode to the glory of glass brick.

Best of all is the Streamline Moderne corner bay. As with well-designed glass brick
walls, the ones on this building work well
both in the day and at night.

3. *Owens-Illinois Pacific Building*

4. Central Manufacturing Terminal Building, 1923-28
Frank D. Chase, Inc.
4802-04 S. Loma Vista Avenue, Vernon

The high Spanish Baroque octagonal tower with its brightly colored, glazed dome is visible over much of Vernon, Huntington Park, and Maywood. Roof pergolas occur to each side of the tower and a handsome entrance is set in a rather plain, six-story concrete building.

5. Aluminum Company of America Building, 1938
Gordon B. Kaufmann
Southwest corner of Fruitland and Alcoa avenues, Vernon

Aluminum used as one of the new materials for Modern architecture. In style it is Streamline Moderne, except for the angular bay on the north side which is reminiscent of the turn-of-the-century

work in Glasgow of Charles Rennie Mackintosh. Be sure to see the lobby with its Moderne lights, and also the two cast aluminum spandrels which depict the virtue of hard work.

6. ■Lane-Wells Company Building (now Winnie and Sutch Company), 1938-39
William E. Myer
5610 S. Soto Street, Huntington Park

This and the adjoining buildings to the north (now W. W. Henry Company) represent one of L.A.'s really impressive Streamline Moderne buildings. "Rounded corners and three large continuous glass areas give the building a strong horizontal feeling, but the tall pylons provide interesting contrasts at the entrances," wrote the architect shortly after this reinforced concrete building was completed. Essentially, the buildings were placed in a park-like setting ". . . so that when one enters the plant nothing reminds him of manufacturing, for beautiful flowers and shrubs, well-kept grounds and distinctive buildings have removed the stigma of the old-fashioned factory."

7. Apartment Building, ca. 1925
2802 E. 57th Street, Huntington Park

A near-perfect solution (especially with the budget in mind) to bring history and fashion into an L.A. stucco box. Place a stucco-relief mission bell within a panel and then give a slight indication at the entrance of columns and an entablature. By magic it all becomes Mission Revival.

5. *Aluminum Company of America*

7. *Apartment Building*

8. Cottage, ca. 1889
2735 E. 57th Street, Huntington Park

A spec Queen Anne cottage. Further west on 57th Street at the southwest corner of Malabar Street, the bungalow court devotee will discover one which is attired in a Missionesque design.

9. Warner Brothers Theatre, 1930
B. Marcus Priteca
6714 S. Pacific Boulevard, Huntington Park

An Art Deco (Zigzag) Moderne motion picture theatre. The auditorium is still intact and has a multilayered ceiling and hidden lights.

10. Maywood City Hall, 1938
Wilson, Merrill, and Alexander
4319 E. Slauson Avenue, Maywood

A two-story PWA Streamline Moderne public building. If you look closely as you drive along Slauson Boulevard from Maywood west to Baldwin Hills, you will find the remains of a good number of late 1930s Streamline Moderne buildings.

11. Bell Avenue School (Corona School), 1935
Richard J. Neutra
3835 Bell Avenue, Bell

Neutra continued the early California tradition of the open air school in this building. Each of the classrooms opens through sliding glass walls to its own enclosed out-of-doors court. An open exterior corridor runs along the other side, and high clerestory windows balance the interior light of the classrooms. This stucco and wood frame building is an excellent example of pre-World War II High Art Modern.

12. Bell High School, 1935
Robert F. Train
Southeast corner of Bell and Flora avenues

This building, and especially its central section, is a characteristic example of the PWA Moderne in reinforced concrete.

13. Vicente Lugo Adobe (El Viejo Lugo Adobe), 1844
6360 E. Gage Avenue, Bell Gardens

An extensive, two-story Monterey adobe surrounded by a two-story wood-railed porch, and covered by a low-pitched, hipped roof, extended at a lower pitch over the porches. The Lugo Adobe indicates how universal the two-story Monterey adobe was in California. This adobe recently burned (1984). It will either be restored on the site or moved and restored.

14. Watts Towers, 1921-45
Simon Rodia
1765 E. 107th Street, Watts

L.A.'s most notable contribution to the architecture of folk fantasy, accomplished on a grand scale which fits the image of Los Angeles and Southern California. Broken tile, china, soda pop bottles, plaster, concrete, steel, and iron form the colorful lacework of these towers. Rodia said that he wished to do something big and memorable, and here it is: L.A.'s rival to Paris and its Eiffel Tower, and Barcelona and its Sagrada Familia Cathedral.

15. Dominguez Ranch House, 1826
18127 S. Alamenda Street, Compton

The front of this house, as we see it today, is pure Mission Revival, ca. 1910. The long, open corridor with its simple, square wood posts and Greek Revival double-hung windows is characteristic of Spanish-Anglo adobes from the mid-1830s on.

16. Green Dog and Cat Hospital, ca. 1936
1514 W. Slauson Avenue, Los Angeles

A sharp, angular, thirties Moderne build-

10. Maywood City Hall

ing which merges into a spectacular central tower-sign.

17. Bethlehem Baptist Church, 1944
R. M. Schindler
4900 S. Compton Avenue, Los Angeles

This is Schindler's only built church, and it is a must to see, though it is not in the best condition. The street front on busy Compton Avenue is composed of a series of wide overlapping stucco bands, closing off the main building effectively from the street and its noises. The principal natural light for the auditorium is introduced by skylights placed at the base of the cruciform tower.

17. Bethlehem Baptist Church

18. Thomas Jefferson High School, 1936
Stiles O. Clements
319 E. 41st Street, Los Angeles

Here is monumental PWA Streamline Moderne at its best. Horizontality asserts itself everywhere via moldings, bands of windows, and horizontal fins. The tour de force is the concave wall of the entrance with its band of dramatic lettering.

19. Root Beer Barrel Resturant, ca. 1932
1000 E. Slauson Avenue

A drive-in resturant in the form of the container of its product.

Highland Park

This community, still discernible in spite of merging with Los Angeles, was once one of the famous "suburbs in search of a city." Situated on the road to Pasadena (Figueroa Street in this area was once Pasadena Avenue), it was perhaps the first of the suburbs. By the turn of the century it had many fine homes and even exhibited a high cultural tone— Charles Fletcher Lummis, William Lees Judson, Clyde Browne, Mary Austin, and other luminaries lived there. It was the home of Occidental College until 1914. It must also be noted that near what is now Sycamore Grove Park was one of the most notorious red-light districts in Los Angeles County.

No more! The Sycamore Grove area, once the site of many dalliances, is now quite respectable. Occidental College flourishes today in nearby Eagle Rock. Most of the artists are gone (many younger ones are on Mount Washington nearby), as are most of the Victorian houses (one of them moved across the Arroyo Seco to Heritage Square). A sad note: the pre-Columbian Revival buildings that once comprised Luther Burbank Junior High School have been levelled.

But do not despair. Much fascinating material remains.

1. Hathaway Home for Children, ca. 1905
Train and Williams
840 Avenue 66

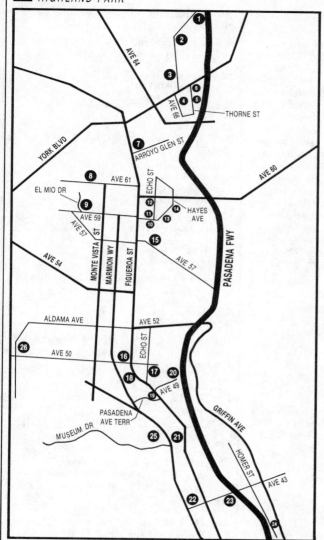

A huge, boulder-based, Craftsman piece, now painted but having some good interiors including a stair-hall with a large panel of stained glass designed by Judson Studios. Train and Williams's work was featured in the one and only issue of the *Arroyo Craftsman* (October, 1909).

2. Munger House, 1889
432 Avenue 66

Queen Anne, Eastlake, and Italianate styles have been merged here. The house has been altered but it still shows what the architect intended.

3. Bungalow, ca. 1905
201 Avenue 66

This is a true California bungalow, with strong Swiss Chalet influence and even a little Orientalism in its slightly upswept eaves. The vertical board and batten siding suggests the early date.

4. Judson Studios, 1901
200 Avenue 66

Originally, before the roof burned off, this was a three-story building in Islamic Revival style. It was the home of the Los Angeles College of Fine Arts founded by William Lees Judson, a prominent regional painter who came to the area in 1893. When the College became a part of the University of Southern California, the building was converted into a Guild Hall for the Arroyo Guild of Fellow Craftsmen, a group of workers inspired by Judson and George Wharton James, an editor of *The Craftsman,* to emulate William Morris and Gustav Stickley. Note the logo of the Guild, an arm and hammer and the motto "We Can" over the entrance. Still later it became the Judson Studios, the "Tiffany of the West," fabricating fine art glass — as it still does.

5. Judson House, ca. 1895
William Lees Judson
216 Thorne Street

Judson's interpretation of the Shingle style is a real curiosity.

6. Fargo House, 1908
Harry Grey
206 Thorne Street

The elevation is remarkably similar to a number of designs by the Greenes. The house is most picturesque viewed from the Pasadena Freeway behind it.

7. Abbey San Encino, 1909-25
Clyde Browne
6211 Arroyo Glen Street

A miniaturized stone abbey which reads as a child's medieval castle. Browne was a printer who, like his hero William Morris, collected the literati of the area in his living room. The house begins with Mission Revival and ends with Spanish Colonial.

8. Bungalow Court, ca. 1915
337 Avenue 61

Big, independent units along the court with a two-story duplex at the end. A Craftsman ensemble with Oriental flourishes.

9. House, 1890
5905 El Mio Drive at Avenue 59

A Queen Anne mansion with a great view in every direction.

10. Yoakum House, ca. 1900
140-45 Avenue 59

Rather rare Tudor Revival.

11. House, ca. 1905
5903 Echo Street at northwest corner of Avenue 59

Colonial Revival.

12. House, ca. 1910
5915 Echo Street

Colonial Revival again but this time made Californian with Islamic arches!

13. Duplex, ca. 1900
5960-62 Hayes Avenue

Mission Revival with holly leaves in leaded glass.

14. House, ca. 1895
6028 Hayes Avenue

A one-story Queen Anne reminiscent of some of the simpler southern plantation houses.

15. Ebell Club, 1912
Sumner Hunt and Silas Burns
127 Avenue 57

Ever since this building was constructed it has been the civic, educational, and social center of Highand Park. The style is Mission Revival with Italianate brackets, but the broad overhanging eaves suggest the Midwestern Prairie style.

16. Hall of Letters, 1904-1905
Old Campus, Occidental College
Northwest corner of Figueroa Street and Avenue 50

In this red brick, now non-descript (but once vaguely French Renaissance) building, Robinson Jeffers once studied English literature.

17. Three Duplexes, ca. 1900
Echo Street at southeast corner of Avenue 50

Exactly alike, the adjoining buildings

resemble Neo-Classical city houses of 1870s London.

17. *Three Duplexes*

18. Craftsman Row, 1904-1911
4967-4985 Figueroa Street

Five shingled houses in the manner Gustav Stickley would have approved. It appears that all were put up by the same builder.

19. Hiner House and Sousa Nook, 1922
4757 Figueroa Street at Pasadena Avenue Terrace

This was the house of Edwin M. Hiner, the director of the most popular brass band in the Los Angeles area. He founded the music department at the old Los Angeles Normal School, now UCLA. The Tudor house done in boulders is unusual. The nook is more conventional Craftsman bungalow style, but John Philip Sousa slept here!

20. Bent House, ca. 1909
Hunt, Eager, and Burns
End of Avenue 49 next to Pasadena Freeway

Another (but very different) flat-roofed Craftsman/Tudor house whose picturesque oak and boulder strewn garden once wandered down into the Arroyo Seco.

21. "Casa de Adobe," 1917
Theodore Eisen
4603 N. Figueroa Street

An interesting effort (because it is early) to re-create an authentic hacienda of the Spanish-Mexican period. It is, in spite of a few modernisms, completely successful. It houses a museum of materials from the late Mexican and early Anglo periods in Los Angeles history, and is administered by the Southwest Museum on the hill above it.

22. Mount Washington Cable Car Station, 1909
200 West Avenue 43

A small Mission Revival building that housed a waiting room for people riding the funicular railway to their homes on Mount Washington. The operation was closed down in 1919, apparently a victim of the automobile.

23. ▪Lummis House ("El Alisal"), 1898-1910
Charles F. Lummis
200 East Avenue 43

Lummis, a graduate of Harvard who had taken courses from Charles Eliot Norton, an authority on the Greek culture, a friend of Ruskin and first president of the Boston Society of Arts and Crafts, built this house of boulders from the Arroyo and named it for the huge sycamore in the patio. Little of the original furniture exists, but there is a great deal about the place that evokes the presence of this amazing man whom his friend Charles Keeler called "William Morris gone Indian." Lummis was the founder of the Southwest Museum, one of the important repositories of Native American art in the United States. You can see Lummis's admiration of the Indian culture in the magnificent pottery that was left after the 1971 earthquake dashed most of his personal collection to pieces, and also in the lantern slides fixed in one window showing Indian dances. The doors and some built-in furniture were designed by Maynard Dixon, as was the magnificent hardware on the main door on the garden side. And there is even an Art Nouveau fireplace designed by Gutzon Borglum long before he sculptured the stone faces on Mount Rushmore. Be sure to notice the Mission style gable on the dining room wing with a bell given to Lummis by the King of Spain. This reminds us that among his many other contributions to the culture of Southern California Lummis founded (1895) the California Landmarks Club that, in its efforts to save the California missions, was one of the first preservation organizations in the United States.

24. Heritage Square
End of Homer Street, south off Avenue 43 (Pasadena Freeway off-ramp)

Whatever you may think of such projects, it is quite clear that none of the buildings moved here in the last two decades would exist if some enterprising people had not decided to do something about retaining these disjointed shards of the Victorian culture. Ruskinian purists in preservation do not like to see buildings moved from sites to which they were meant to relate (in some cases). But what do you do when buildings of the obvious quality of these are being vandalized and would otherwise be demolished? The obvious solution: move them. And it may be significant for the image of Los Angeles that two of these buildings had been moved before—one of them twice! The site has been described as "a freeway-isolated arroyo littoral" (Nathan Weinberg, *Preservation in American Towns and Cities,* p. 63). It is not ideal but with landscaping, the problems of the site are being diminished. And then it has the advantage that you can take it all in as you travel on the Pasadena Freeway.

Listed from north to south:

24. Heritage Square

a. Palms Railroad Station, ca. 1886

An Eastlake building brought from Palms near Century City.

b. Perry House ("Mount Pleasant"), 1876
Ezra F. Kysor

An Italian villa being restored by the Colonial Dames. Probably it was the finest house in Los Angeles when it was built by William Hayes Perry in Boyle Heights.

c. ▪Hale ("C. M.") House, ca. 1885
Attributed to Joseph Cather Newsom

Queen Anne proportions with Eastlake and Queen Anne details. Restoration is almost complete inside and outside. Named for the Hale family that was its longest resident though high in the front gable are the letters "C. M." carved in a shield, the initials of Charles Morgan, the original owner.

d. Shaw ("Valley Knudson Memorial") House, ca. 1877

A French Second Empire (mansard) cottage built originally for Richard E. Shaw in East Los Angeles. The restoration has been liberally endowed by the Bel Air Garden Club of which Mrs. Knudsen was a founder and president.

e. Ford ("Beaudry Street") House, ca. 1885

Queen Anne, Eastlake, and Italianate mixed. But the style is not so important as the elaborate decoration on such a small house. The first owner, John J. Ford, was a wood carver of extraordinary imagination and talent. The house was moved from Beaudry Street where a computer center now stands.

f. Lincoln Avenue Methodist Church, 1898-1899
George W. Kramer; W. A. Benshoff, supervising architect

Moved from Pasadena to make way for a new and strikingly hideous post office, this is a good Eastlake Gothic building that will make a good meeting place at the Square. The door, with its pilasters and pediment, is at the corner suggesting that the interior is laid out on the famous Methodist "Akron Plan"— the pulpit at the opposite corner with the pews in arcs around it.

25. Southwest Museum, 1912 and later
Sumner Hunt and Silas R. Burns
Northwest corner of Museum Drive and
Marmion Way

A monument of the Mission Revival with definite references to the siting and exterior of the Alhambra and its site. This building houses a fine collection of Native American art. Its specialty is, of course, Southwestern, but there are some fine Californian, Plains, and Alaskan things. Enter through the Mayan portal at the base of the hill and through a long corridor that leads to what must be the slowest elevator in the world, finally letting you out at the museum.

25. Southwest Museum

26. Aldama Apartments, 1961
A. E. Morris
5030-5038 Aldama Avenue near Avenue 50

These stepped stucco boxes clinging to the hill evoke the spirit of Schindler's apartment houses of the twenties and thirties but are more openly mannered than their ancestors.

Mount Washington

Artists' nests abound in this area above Highland Park and the real world. When you get to the top of San Rafael Avenue, you realize that Mount Washington was invaded in the early twentieth century and people have been building ever since. It is said that Mount Washington is above the smog. Not true. But it does, in spite of winding streets, give a sense of neighorhood as few places in Southern California do. Incidentally, we are sorry that Jack Smith's house cannot be viewed properly, and we have thus been forced to leave out this fabled structure. Perhaps it is best left to legend.

1. Birtcher-Share House, 1942
Harwell H. Harris
4234 Seaview Lane (between Seaview Drive and Seaview Avenue)

Influenced by Wright's Usonian houses, Harris nevertheless seems to straighten the Master out. This large, one-story wood house is one of his masterpieces. Another small view of it can be obtained from Seaview Avenue unless the bushes have grown too high by the time this book comes out.

2. Hinds House, 1947
Richard J. Neutra
3941 San Rafael Avenue

Yes, you can see the house if you get out of your car. The number is on the lower part of the small cliff. It is one of Neutra's few wood-sheathed houses.

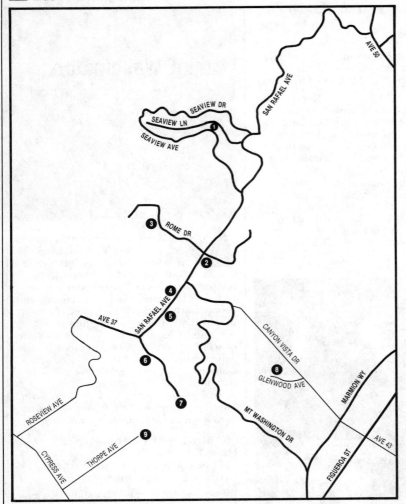

3. Mauer House, 1949
John Lautner
932 Rome Drive

Subdued for this architect, the derivation from Frank Lloyd Wright's Usonian houses of the 1930s is clear.

4. House, ca. 1910
3855 San Rafael Avenue

A great Mission Revival structure with massive columns. While here you will want to look at the large house across the street now owned by the Vedanta Society. Although big it is not distinguished architecture.

5. House, ca. 1925
3820 San Rafael Avenue

An adobe structure with adobe wall and gate. In spite of its late date it is much more convincing than most of the nineteenth-century adobes. Across the street is a good Craftsman **house** often attributed to the Greenes but apparently mistakenly.

6. Byler House, 1937
Gregory Ain
914 Avenue 37

Vertical boards stained brown and looking very Craftsman. It is amazing how many Ain houses have weathered the years and come out looking as if they were brand new. The architect must have satisfied the owners.

7. House, 1941
Raphael S. Soriano
End of Avenue 37

This is a big, unfinished house which is impressive here but even more impressive from the Golden State Freeway far below.

7. House

8. Williams House, 1948
Smith and Williams
4211 Glenwood Avenue

From the street this house is a simple box with huge protruding eaves.

9. Jeffries House, ca. 1905
End of Thorpe Avenue east of Cypress Avenue

It is significant that Jim Jeffries, the famous pugilist, would build a refined Classical Revival house as his ideal in life. Ah, that someone would see his intelligence and restore it!

Eagle Rock

When Occidental College moved from Highland Park to Eagle Rock in 1914, the town was a crossroads whose only other real ornament was a huge rock with a naturally-formed image of a spread-winged eagle on its face. The rock and the area around it had been a significant Indian site at the beginning of the nineteenth century and earlier. Later it was a favorite picnic site for city folk who rode the old trolley line out Figueroa Street.

In the twenties the town grew, as is evidenced by the thousands of bungalows that cover the land between Glendale and Pasadena. Few of these small dwellings have claims to aesthetic significance, but as a whole they signify a pleasant and respectable way of life in the American tradition of single-family housing. More expensive houses were erected on the hills, but again the architectural talent displayed is not outstanding. Two Schindler houses, the Lowe House #1 (1923), and the Lowe House #2 (1937), were domolished when the Ventura Freeway was constructed. The old buildings that stood at the corners of Colorado and Eagle Rock boulevards, and that once gave a kind of Midwestern charm to the place, have been demolished or remodelled beyond recognition. Eagle Rock Boulevard has somehow managed to become even more hideous than it was when our first architectural guide came out.

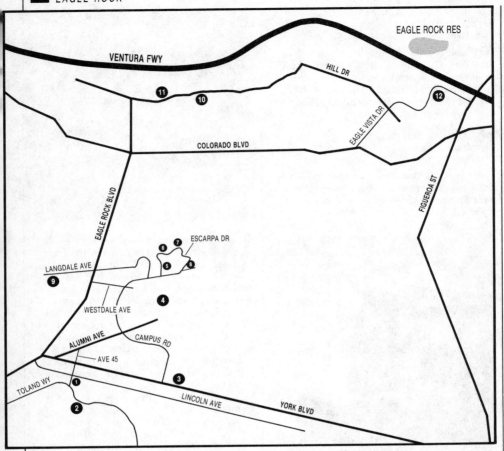

1. Sparkletts Drinking Water Corporation, 1925-29
Attributed to a "Mr. King"
4500 Lincoln Avenue

A mosque of the first water. Unfortunately the 1971 earthquake so shook its minarets that they had to be removed.

2. Kapin House, 1935
George Kapin
4512 Toland Way

Situated above the Sparkletts plant, this house seems to be related to it.

3. Motels R Us, 1983
4855 York Boulevard

This building defies all canons of taste and must be mentioned for its sheer horror, impossible to experience in black and white.

4. Occidental College, 1911-13
Myron Hunt; Beatrix Farrand, landscape architect
1600 Campus Road

The architecture of the college contrasts sharply with that of the community. It seems, in spite of its many tile-roofed buildings, to have been transplanted from New England, so orderly and understated is its campus style, a kind of regionalized Palladianism. Jarring intrusions, such as the chapel, are all the more irritating because of the overall unity throughout the campus that was achieved by hiring Myron Hunt and H. C. Chambers to design almost all the buildings right up to the mid-thirties.

We have listed only the most interesting buildings:

4. Occidental College

a. Swan, Johnson, and Fowler halls, 1914
Myron Hunt

These buildings, dedicated by the great educator Booker T. Washington, *were* the college until a modest flurry of building in the twenties transformed the campus. Indeed, they set the tone for future building. Hunt originally designed a columned hall to connect Johnson and Fowler, but this part of his plan was never carried out. In 1968 the **Coons Administrative Center,** designed by William Pereira Associates, was placed where Hunt envisioned a colonnade. Most of the building is invisible but not quite underground. The second level is almost entirely sheathed in glass so that it has, perhaps unkindly, been dubbed "the Chrysler Showroom."

b. Clapp Library, 1924
Myron Hunt and H. C. Chambers

Extensions at each side of the original tiny Mediterranean style building doubled its size in 1954. Then in 1969 an addition in "State College Modern" was made by Neptune and Thomas, again doubling the size of the building. Except for the fact that the old book stacks are separated from the new ones, the entire building functions well.

c. Herrick Chapel, 1964
Ladd and Kelsey

Distinguished by its slip-form concrete construction — marvelous to view when construction was underway but unremarkable when finished — and its magnificent stained glass windows by Perli Pelzig.

d. Freeman Union, 1928
Myron Hunt and H. C. Chambers

The charming, double-arcaded entrance patio is good for dancing. In 1956 Chambers and Hubbard added a large extension to the old building. The extension is efficient but not charming.

e. Thorne Hall (Auditorium), 1938
Myron Hunt and H. C. Chambers

The last of Hunt's major designs for Occidental. The incidents surrounding its construction figure prominently in Aldous Huxley's *After Many a Summer Dies the Swan,* in which Occidental is "Tarzana College."

f. Booth Music-Speech Center, 1929
Myron Hunt and H. C. Chambers

The old building is comprised of studios and a small recital hall around an arcaded court. A large classroom, office, and theatre addition was made by Charles Luckman Associates in 1960.

g. Orr Hall, 1925
Myron Hunt and H. C. Chambers

The loveliest dormitory on the campus, it seemed doomed because it was built before strict earthquake codes were in force. But there are plans afoot to reinforce it and use it as an art center.

h. Erdman Hall, 1927
Myron Hunt and H. C. Chambers

Another example of civilized student housing.

i. Faculty Club (originally President's House), 1922
Myron Hunt and H. C. Chambers

Eastern Colonial Revival at its best.

j. Dean of Students' (now Vice President's) House, 1951
Smith and Williams

Unassuming rationality with a hint of Orientalism.

k. Dean of the Faculty's House, 1932
Myron Hunt and H. C. Chambers

Monterey style. Well planned for entertaining.

l. President's House, 1932
Myron Hunt and H. C. Chambers

Monterey Revival again, bigger than the Dean's House but not so well planned—or seen.

m. Bird Hillside Theatre, 1925
Myron Hunt and H. C. Chambers

Very Greek, this amphitheatre is used for commencement exercises, recreation, and excellent summer drama. A beautiful place to watch the sun set through eucalyptus trees.

n. Norris Residence Hall, 1966
Pereira and Associates

Bay Area style plastered on Harvard-inspired clustered apartments around stairs. The scale is too small for active students.

5. Chambers House, 1923
2068 Escarpa Drive

The Chambers were enthusiasts for American Indian designs and thus had their house built in the style of the Pueblo Revival. The Hopi symbol for happiness— ▬ᴸ —is used again and again in details as well as floor plan.

6. Martin House, 1966
Donald Martin
2039 Escarpa Drive

Designed by the architect for his parents, this house shows the influence of Richard J. Neutra.

7. Four Houses, 1962-68
Oakley Norton
1955 (remodeled), 2003, 2009, and 2026 Escarpa Drive

These neo-Craftsman houses cling to the hill for a view of Mount Verdugo and, though they didn't ask for it, the Ventura Freeway.

8. Paxson House, 1971
Buff and Hensman (Conrad Buff)
1911 Campus Road

The Craftsman tradition revived.

9. Mason House, 1916
2434 Langdale Avenue

This house has often been attributed to Irving J. Gill though few of the details suggest his work.

10. House, ca. 1925
2403 Hill Drive

Hill Drive has some very good Spanish Colonial Revival houses. This is one of the best.

11. Bryce House, 1923
Egasse and Brauch
2327 Hill Drive

The general impression is Tudor until you see the drooping swags of stucco at the point of the front gable. Hansel and Gretel appear. It is likely that this house was once painted more colorfully.

12. Eagle Rock Playground Clubhouse, 1953
Richard J. Neutra and Associates (Dion Neutra)
1100 Eagle Vista Drive

A Neutra house enlarged, an unexpected International Style Modern building in this area.

12. Eagle Rock Playground Clubhouse

Lincoln Heights

Northeast Los Angeles is now bisected by the east/west San Bernardino Freeway and the north/south Golden State Freeway. The section west of the Golden State Freeway is industrial/railroad, with some modest residential sections to the north. There is a smattering of modest late nineteenth-century Queen Anne cottages and houses still standing in and around Workman and Griffin streets. Equally nineteenth century in feeling is Lincoln Park with its small lake. The major visible monument in the Mission Road area is the Los Angeles County Hospital, but the real architectural gem is Ernest Coxhead's Epiphany Chapel of 1888-89.

1. Los Angeles County/USC Medical Center, 1928-33 and later Allied Architects of Los Angeles: Edwin Bergstom, Myron Hunt, Pierpont Davis, Sumner P. Hunt and William Richards
1200 N. State Street

The twenty-story central concrete and steel unit of the hospital has remained as *the* landmark in northeastern Los Angeles. Its basic form is PWA monumental

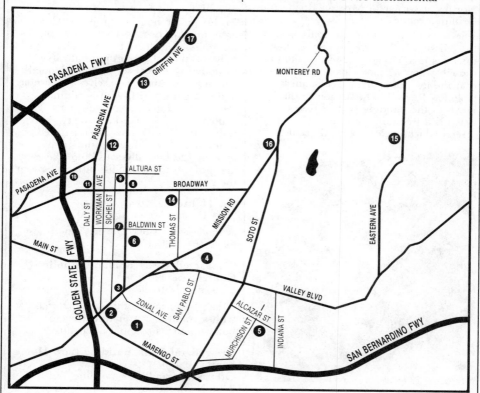

Moderne—with more than a slight hint of the influence of Bertram G. Goodhue. Its design of sculptural volumes and heavy arches slightly suggests early Romanesque. High relief sculpture on a grand scale adorns the major entrance from the west. This entrance, which is still partially preserved, has an axial walkway and garden leading up to the building. Not much can be said of the many later additions to the building except that they look as if they were put up quickly and cheaply (which they probably were not).

2. Administration Building, Los Angeles County Hospital, ca. 1912
1100 N. Mission Road

An Austrian/German Secessionist design in the classical manner. The center of the building exhibits a low dome.

3. University of Southern California School of Medicine, Administration Building, ca. 1920
Northwest corner of Mission Road and Griffith Avenue

The rows of arches, stucco walls, and the Mission bells leave no one in doubt that this is a Mission Revival Building, though when we look closer we will find that the low tower is in fact Spanish Colonial Revival. The arcade to the north of the building (with Mission bells) is a freestanding wall—really a screen which encloses a small garden.

3. *University of Southern California School of Medicine, Administration Building*

4. Lincoln Park (formerly **East Lake Park**), 1874
East corner of Mission Road and Valley Boulevard

This forty-five-acre park contains a picturesque lake (man-made, of course) and until recently a wonderful carousel (which burned). The park's first carousel now resides in Golden Gate Park in San Francisco. In the late nineteenth century and through the early years of the twentieth century the park was widely know for its exotic planting, its ostrich farm, and its alligator farm. Alas, it is all quite tame nowadays.

5. Ramona Gardens Public Housing, 1940-41
George G. Adams, Walter S. Davis, Ralph C. Flewelling, Eugene Weston, Jr., Lewis Eugene Weston, and Lloyd Wright; Katherine Bashford and Fred Barlow, Jr., landscape architects
Between Alcazar, Murchison, and Indiana streets

In this public housing project, 102 concrete units of two stories provide 610 living units on a thirty-two-acre site. The hilly location of the project with its meandering streets seems well planned. The housing units themselves are simple and straightforward, with a minimal sense of "architecture" about them. The contemporary (of the last twenty years) wall murals which have been painted on a number of the housing units may perhaps be ideologically satisfying, but they add little to the home-like atmosphere of the project.

6. House, ca. 1890
2054 Griffin Avenue

A modest two-story Queen Anne (most likely spec) dwelling.

7. Sacred Heart Roman Catholic Church, ca. 1900
2210 Sichel Street

A late Victorian Gothic brick church, with a traditional square corner tower but without its original high spire.

8. Federal Bank Building (now **Home Savings**), 1910
Otto Neher and C. F. Skilling
2201 N. Broadway

A V-shaped building with a semi-circular pavilion where the angled streets come together. The public banking room is covered by a delightful, quite small glass dome.

8. Federal Bank Building (now Home Savings)

9. Epiphany Chapel, 1888-89
Ernest Coxhead
Southeast corner of Sichel and Altura streets

A really fine, small Coxhead design. Low stone walls support a slightly projecting single gable with an over-scaled round window. As usual, Coxhead maneuvers the shingles across the surface in a highly original fashion. The building has most fortunately been recently restored.

10. Engine Company No. 1 Fire Station, 1940
2230 Pasadena Avenue

10. Engine Company No. 1 Fire Station

A Streamline Moderne design, its rear more Modern than Moderne. The street elevation of this two-story building comes close to being pure two-dimensional design, with the windows and entrance door as an L-shaped form articulated in the lower section with horizontal fins, the lettering treated as a horizontal line, and then the two firetruck entrances as two deep rectangles.

11. Department of Water and Power Building, ca. 1937
S. Charles Lee
2417 Daly Street

Regency Moderne. The slightly convex facade of glass suggests the product (at least one of them) which this public department sells. The marquee with its projecting lettering can be seen best at night when the glass behind is lighted.

12. Cottage, ca. 1889
2652 Workman Avenue

A well-preserved Queen Anne cottage. The gable end over the front bay is decorated with sawed relief work. The entrance porch still contains its sawed and turned work decoration.

13. House

13. House, ca. 1890
Attributed to Joseph Cather Newsom
3537 Griffin Avenue

A two-story Queen Anne dwelling with a number of sharp angular Eastlake details in wood. Especially unusual is the double-gabled dormer on the third floor.

14. Sturgis House, 1889-90
Ernest Coxhead
2345 Thomas Street

One suspects that this design is supposed to evoke the feeling of the Colonial Revival. As with a good number of Coxhead's designs of the 1890s, the Sturgis House seems to be a composition of architectural fragments, each of which strongly stands on its own. The street elevation of the entrance porch sits as a screen with its paired columns and independent entablature. Above, the arched opening of the small second floor porch contrasts with the pair of high, vertical, transomed windows to the side.

15. Farmdale School Building, 1889
2839 N. Eastern Avenue (at the rear of the school grounds)

A more-than-usually elaborate Queen Anne Revival style schoolhouse with a large, open, square bell tower.

16. Lunch Pail Restaurant Building, ca. 1930
4067 Mission Road

A small fast-food restaurant which suggests a pail with perhaps a milk bottle on top.

17. Group of Spec Bungalows, ca. 1910
4000 block of Griffin Avenue

This group of spec Craftsman bungalows provides an excellent glimpse of what many of the residential streets of Los Angeles looked like by the mid-teens.

Alhambra

One of the oldest suburbs of Los Angeles, this town was set out (1873) in five- to ten-acre lots by Benjamin D. Wilson (who later became mayor of Los Angeles) between the Arroyo San Pasqual and the Old Mill Wash. He called it Alhambra because his wife was rather belatedly reading Washington Irving's *Tales* at the time. The shrewd land speculator had found a theme and named the streets after incidents and characters in the romance. The present Main Street was, for instance, called Boabdil for the last king of Granada, who wept as he surveyed his beloved city seized from him by Ferdinand and Isabella in 1492. The name was soon changed because the residents found it impossible to pronounce. Unfortunately, almost every evidence of the world of "Don Benito" has been erased, some fairly recently. As usual, most of the old buildings were situated in the town center where urban renewal, early and late, got them.

The main commercial street dates from the fifties with a little twenties decoration interspersed. The local urban conservationists have wisely decided to restore each building to its original state, even if it has the fifties blahs. A strong element in the design of the entrances to these buildings is often a terrazo floor, sometimes elaborately designed in pastels. Alhambra has other good things, some on the outskirts:

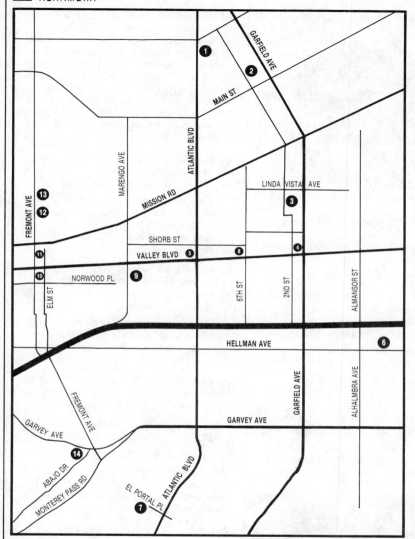

1. Descanso Court, ca. 1915
509 Atlantic Boulevard

Eight Oriental bungalow units.

2. Alhambra Women's Club, ca. 1910
204 S. Second Street

A good Craftsman building with interiors intact.

3. House, ca. 1937
Southeast corner of Second Street and Linda Vista Avenue

A Streamline Moderne structure — a ship's bridge sailing into Second Street.

4. Service Station, ca. 1938
Northwest corner of Valley Boulevard and Garfield Avenue

This is bigger than the last entry, but the inspiration is the same Streamline Moderne.

2. Alhambra Women's Club

5. "Crawford's Corner" Shopping Center, ca. 1965
Northwest corner of Valley and Atlantic boulevards

Victoriana again raises its head.

6. Mark Keppel High School, 1939
Marston and Maybury
501 E. Hellman Avenue

A huge Streamline Moderne structure. The brick base is vaguely pre-Columbian while still being Moderne.

7. Cascades Park, ca. 1928
Ralph D. Cornell, Cook, Hill, and Cornell, landscape architects
Atlantic Boulevard and El Portal Place, Monterey Park (South of Alhambra)

Here is a real estate developer's dream if there ever was one! At the west end of El Portal Place a small hill rises on

7. Cascades Park

which has been constructed an elaborate tile fountain with cascade. At the other end is a Spanish Colonial Revival building with the original "El Encanto" sign in place, apparently once a restaurant and offices. It faces El Mercado, a commercial district that never developed. Across the street from El Encanto is an adobe bungalow court which looks early. The whole area was finally built up in the fifties.

8. Fire Station and City Administration Building, ca. 1938
Sixth Street north of Valley Boulevard

The complex is extremely picturesque, but the most attention has been given to the fire station. The buildings are sheathed in pink brick, painted white and allowed to weather.

9. Church of Saints Simon and Jude (Episcopal Home for the Aged), 1926
Reginald D. Johnson
1428 Marengo Avenue

Spanish Colonial Revival on an almost doll-house scale by the son of the (then) Episcopal Bishop of Los Angeles and dedicated to an earlier one.

10. Fire Station No. 4, ca. 1938
Northwest corner of Norwood Place and Elm Street near Fremont Avenue

A Spanish Gothic surprise.

11. Cajal House, 1907
Attributed to A. J. Cajal
1350 S. Fremont Avenue

The wooden lions on the capitals of the porch are very unusual, as is the whole Chinese-influenced house.

12. C. F. Braun and Company, ca. 1929-37
Marston and Maybury
1000 S. Fremont Avenue

We mean no sneer when we say that these buildings are comparable to the best work of Albert Speer in the Germany of the thirties. Austere red brick with almost peep-hole fenestration, they owe nothing to the International Style Modern.

11. Cajal House

13. Sears Complex, 1971
Albert C. Martin and Associates
900 S. Fremont Avenue

This group of buildings set within a landscaped site is dominated by a great mirrored glass box.

14. Saint Steven's Serbian Orthodox Cathedral, 1949-52
North side of Garvey Avenue west of intersection with Abajo Drive

Serbian Romanesque with two glistening tile domes, the church is done in California's favorite ecclesiastical material — concrete with the impression of the forms still showing.

Montebello, Pico Rivera

This Italian name was once applied to a large section of the Repetto Ranch which the Anglo pioneer Harrison Newmark purchased in 1887. When he subdivided a portion of the ranch and established a town, he, of course, called it "Newmark." In 1920 the town's name was changed to Montebello. Notwithstanding its poetic name, Montebello and the regions to the south and west are now basically industrial, originally spawned by the discovery of oil shortly after 1900. As a commercial retail strip Whittier Boulevard is well worth a cruise (though do note that it is often closed at night to automobiles because of drag racing and other social problems). The facades of many of the one-story (and a few two-story) commercial buildings along Whittier Boulevard exhibit a number of variations on the late 1930s Streamline Moderne, plus a sprinkling of other exotic images.

Montebello Park, south of Whittier Boulevard between Gerhart and Vail avenues, was laid out in 1925 by the planning and landscape architectural firm of Cook and Hill. On paper the plan looks fine, but in actuality there is little of great inspiration to be found in either the landscaping or the modest houses which line the streets.

Montebello marks the beginning of what is a great industrial park (the City of Industry sprawls nearby). Huge complexes of factories and warehouses are erected in an anonymous architecture

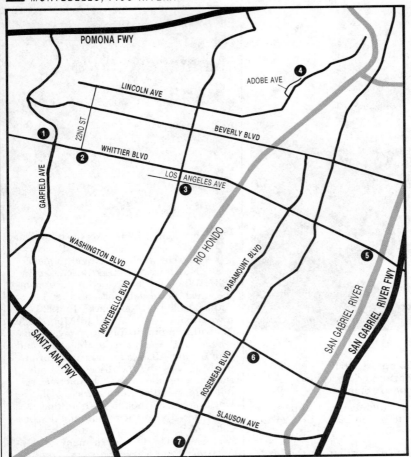

that might best be called "Computer Moderne," a style that is even more salient in the Irvine area.

Pico Rivera, which lies to the east of Montebello between the Rio Hondo and San Gabriel rivers, is a recent creation (1958), when the towns of Pico and Rivera were combined. Like Montebello, it is an industrial city whose principal architectural glory is the commercial strip of Whittier Boulevard.

1. The Tamale, 1928
6420 Whittier Boulevard, East Los Angeles

An often-illustrated example of California's programmatic architecture, we have here a small roadside restaurant in the form of one of its products—a tamale. The poor little structure is now pressed in by buildings on both sides, and it is no longer painted or signed as it was when built, but we should be happy that it is still with us.

2. Marcel and Jeanne French Cafe, ca. 1930
Southeast corner of Whittier Boulevard and 22nd Street, Montebello

A doll-house-scaled French Norman cottage right out of a children's storybook. Do not miss the final mark of France—a small version of the Eiffel Tower as the restaurant's sign.

2. Marcel and Jeanne French Cafe

3. House, ca. 1915
Southeast corner of Montebello Boulevard and Los Angeles Avenue, Montebello

A clapboard dwelling, of modest size, which almost succeeds in being Moorish.

4. Juan Matias Sanchez Adobe, 1845, mid-1850s, and later
945 N. Adobe Avenue (off Lincoln Boulevard), Montebello

Here on the west bank of the Rio Hondo River is an impressive story-and-a-half adobe. The oldest section of the adobe is that part which runs parallel to the river, while the mid-1880s wing was extended at a right angle to the original house. The wide, hipped roof with dormer windows and much of the woodwork are twentieth century. Nonetheless, the adobe and its site do an excellent job of conveying what Southern California was like in the 1840s and 1850s. It is now used as a museum by the City of Montebello and is open to the public on Wednesdays, Saturdays, and Sundays, 1-4 P.M.

5. Mount Baldy Inn, 1927
9608 Whittier Boulevard, Pico Rivera

A good-sized programmatic roadside restaurant in the form of the snow-capped peak of Mount Baldy. At this writing the restaurant is no longer in use, so see it quickly while it is still around.

5. Mount Baldy Inn

6. Santa Fe Passenger Station (now Pico Rivera Chamber of Commerce), ca. 1880
9122 E. Washington Boulevard, Pico Rivera

This early, Eastlake style railroad station has been moved, restored, and converted into offices for the Chamber of Commerce.

7. United Auto Workers Union Building, 1961
Neutra and Alexander (Dion Neutra) 8503 S. Rosemead Boulevard, Pico Rivera

A Neutra Modern machine image exercise indoor and out with courtyards, pools, plantings, and covered walkways. When you walk in and out and through a building of this quality, you sense how unfortunate most commercial design of the sixties was.

Whittier

A Quaker organization, the Pickering Land and Water Company, founded the community of Whittier in 1887. A college was formed in 1887 but succumbed in the bust of 1888 and was reorganized as the Whittier Academy in 1891. Though the extensive orange, lemon, avocado, and walnut orchards are now gone, the city does retain a pleasant, small-town atmosphere, quite separate from the rest of the valley to the south and west.

1. Whittier Theatre, 1928
David S. Bushnell
11608 Whittier Boulevard

A Spanish lighthouse tower looks down on the theatre and its connected retail shopping center. The patio to the north of the theatre provides a semi-enclosed public space upon which the small retail stores open. This building type (a theatre combined with a forecourt of retail stores) came into being in California in the mid-1920s.

2. Whittier Union High School, 1939-40
William H. Harrison
Northeast corner of Philadelphia Street and Whittier Avenue

PWA Moderne structures, the best of which is the auditorium with its lettering high on each corner and its undulat-

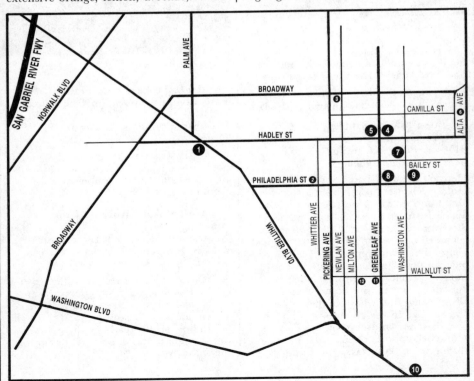

ing facade which comes close to the then-popular Hollywood Regency.

3. Lincoln School, ca. 1935
Attributed to William H. Harrison
Southwest corner of Broadway and Newlin Avenue

PWA Moderne, more classically monumental than the nearby High School building. One wall of the kindergarten classroom wing folds aside to combine garden with classroom.

3. Lincoln School

4. Harvey Apartment Building, 1913
Northeast corner of Greenleaf Avenue and Hadley Street

California's own Neo-Florentine, expressed in a two-story stucco box. Huge brackets support the broadly cantilevered roof. The name of the apartment is on a stucco scroll, the design of which comes

4. Harvey Apartment Building

close to the European Art Nouveau. This is one of the almost identical "Four Bricks" that were built on each of the corners of Hadley Street and Greenleaf Avenue by C. W. Harvey, a local promoter. The year 1888 was, of course, a bad one economically and the buildings stood idle even after the recovery. Finally in 1913 Harvey decided to convert this one to apartments and added the fancy Florentine brackets and miscellaneous decoration. The other three "bricks" were demolished long ago.

5. First Christian Church, 1923
Northwest corner of Greenleaf Avenue and Hadley Street

A nice minor effort in Beaux Arts Neo-Classicism.

6. Lou Henry Hoover School, 1938
William H. Harrison
East end of Camilla Street at Alta Avenue

The severity of this Regency Moderne building is lightened by the concave central bay with a Wedgewood-like relief panel depicting the *Pageant of Education* by Bartolo Mako.

7. Whittier Post Office, 1935
Louis A. Simon
Northwest corner of Washington Avenue and Bailey Street

A single-story, rather mild PWA Moderne building which fits well into the streetscape of downtown Whittier.

8. National Trust and Savings Building, ca. 1935
William H. Harrison
Northeast corner of Philadelphia Street and Greenleaf Avenue

Monumental Moderne. Bunched fluted shafts at each side of the entrance terminate in four stylized (NRA!) eagles.

9. Charles House, 1893
6537 S. Washington Avenue

A simple, well-maintained, two-story Queen Anne.

10. Krause House, 1950-52
Raphael S. Soriano
8513 La Sierra Avenue (Whittier Boule-

vard to Catalina Avenue, left on Mar Vista Street, right to Sierra Vista Avenue, then right)

A large, single-story steel modular post-and-beam house, most of the walls being infilled with glass, masonry, and corrugated fiberglass. The front wall facing the auto court has a narrow band of windows carried just below the roof. The precise geometry of the house contrasts with the luxurious planting of the grounds.

11. Service Station, ca. 1934
Southwest corner of Greenleaf Avenue and Walnut Street

A prefabricated Streamline Moderne service station. Except for its signage and pumps, all seems original.

12. Cottage, ca. 1900
7602 Milton Avenue

A late Queen Anne cottage composed of parts which somehow remain separate from one another. Two low gable wings press in on a central, hipped-roof pavil-

ion. It all adds up to a delightful architectural oddity.

13. Governor Pio Pico Adobe, 1842, 1882; restored 1913, 1946
Pioneer and Whittier boulevards just west of San Gabriel River Freeway (Whittier Boulevard off-ramp)

According to some accounts, this adobe was once two stories in height and contained thirty-three rooms. Hard to believe, but Pio Pico, the last of the Mexican governors of California, was a very successful manager of real estate until financial problems in the 1880s forced him into bankruptcy. The house was flooded in 1867 and rebuilt on a more modest scale and then restored three more times! Nevertheless it remains one of the most credible of the adobes because the present curators have kept the early Victorian furnishings good but sparse as they probably were in Pico's day. It is a State Historic Park and is open to the public, Wednesday-Sunday, 10 to 5.

6. *Lou Henry Hoover School*

Santa Fe Springs

This community was founded in 1873 when J. E. Fulton established the Fulton Sulpher Springs and Health Resport. The town was renamed Santa Fe Springs in 1886 and, as was true of much of this area of Los Angeles County, it remained agricultural until oil wells were brought in during the early 1920s. The city was incorporated in 1957 and the basic impression one has is that it is all quite new. While there are a number of recent office and commercial buildings located around Telegraph Road, the real point of architectural interest is the handsome, small-scaled **Santa Fe Springs Town Center.** Within a beautifully landscaped park are located a group of one-story concrete block public buildings. While none of these buildings is architecturally assertive, they do seem to work well with one another, and within the context of the park. These buildings are:

1. Fire Station, 1959
Marson and Varner

This red brick building was the first in the civic center, and it does reflect a somewhat different architectural image than the others. But because of its scale and the planting around it, it seems compatible with the other structures.

2. City Hall, 1967
William L. Pereira and Associates

In a traditional California fashion, the covered walkway around the building is in fact the corridor for the interior spaces.

3. Library, 1976
Anthony and Langford

A very pleasant building within. Do stop and see the ceramic mural at the entrance. By Raul Esparza, it depicts events in the history of the community.

4. Town Center Hall, 1971
William L. Pereira and Associates

5. Santa Fe Springs Post Office Building, 1969
William L. Pereira and Associates

The Santa Fe Springs Town Center is located on the south side of Telegraph Road between Alburtis Street and Pioneer Boulevard.

Downey

Norwalk

Though the city was subdivided as early as 1865 by Governor John G. Downey, it, like the neighboring communities, is essentially a product of the post-World War II years. At the southwest corner of Lakewood Boulevard and Florence Avenue is a monument of roadside architecture, America's first **McDonald's** drive-in hamburger restaurant (1953). This was the first restaurant established before the chain itself developed. It preceeded by one year the McDonald's at 563 E. Foothill Boulevard in Azusa, and it was also earlier than the one often mentioned in the Midwest. The design consists of two neon-lighted elliptical arches which plunge through the typical fifties shed-roofed restaurant building. Architecturally, this design, in contrast to the later classic McDonald's Restaurant buildings, poses somewhat mid-way between popular and serious architecture. Also do take note (as if you could avoid it) of the impressive, well-lighted sign at the corner. Like the restaurant building, it is part and parcel of the entire composition of sign, parking lot, and building.

Norwalk was founded in 1877, and two years later a post office was established. The early commercial center of the community was laid out around Front Street, which parallels the Southern Pacific tracks. A few of the older commercial buildings, including a turn-of-the-century Beaux Arts **bank building,** still remain on Front Street, although most of these have been remodelled over the years. At the northwest corner of Pioneer Boulevard and Rosecrans Avenue is one of Southern California's greatest freestanding signs, which announces the **Norwalk Square Shopping Center.** The very high sign is composed of an inverted open metal triangle topped by an open metal rectangle (upon which the letters are placed), and finally a series of four upward-reaching loops — it is all similar in feeling to the central spaceship restaurant at the Los Angeles International Airport. This extravaganza was designed between 1951 and 1954 by Stiles Clements for the Pacific Mutual Life Insurance Company, which sponsored (as an investment) the shopping center. Further to the north on the northeast corner of San Antonio Drive and Sproul Street is an excellent Art Deco Moderne former **auto show room** (now used for the sale of auto parts). The building is designed around a low, squat, square tower, and it is ornamented (in cast concrete) with horizontal bands of connected chevrons. It dates from about 1930. In **Norwalk**

Park (at Sproul Street and Norwalk Avenue) you will find an Eastlake cottage (ca. 1889), the **Gilbert Sproul House.** It is now maintained as a house museum by the city and is open Wednesday, Thursday, and Friday, 10 to 2; and Saturday and Sunday, 1 to 5.

Artesia

Norwalk Square Shopping Center Sign

This town, located south of Norwalk, was set out in the 1870s by the Artesian Water Company, though as is so often the case nothing really remains from these early years. The character of the community is primarily post-World War II, both in its commercial buildings and in its housing. Like Bellflower·to the northeast, the town in located on the Southern Pacific Railroad tracks and it is adjacent to the San Gabriel River. The architectural gem of Artesia is the former **First National Bank Building** (1925), on the northwest corner of Pioneer Boulevard and 187th Street, designed by the Los Angeles architect Henry Withey. This Mediterranean building is a simple rectangular box with an elegant, three-arched loggia resplendent with doubled twisted Saracenic columns. The community has also done much better than most with its new **Post Office Building** (1970-71; Donald M. Forker), located at the northeast corner of 183rd Street and Alburtus Avenue. The Post Office is a low adobe-appearing (it is of slumpstone) building with deeply-splayed recessed windows, a low-pitched tiled roof, and a wide and cool portale.

Bellflower

This community is situated on the west bank of the lower San Gabriel River. It was founded in 1906, but most of its growth has occurred in the 1960s and 1970s. Its older commercial core is located in and around Bellflower Boulevard just north of the San Gabriel Freeway (Highway 91). The commercial center is dominated close up and from afar by the now-unused marquee and the expansive sign of the **Holiday Theatre** (located on the west side of Bellflower Boulevard north of Flower Avenue). This theatre building was built at the end of the 1920s, though the wonderous curved and open theatre sign dates from the post-World War II years (ca. 1950). South of the Theatre on Bellflower Boulevard, at the northeast corner of Arkansas Avenue, is a programmatic fast food establishment, the **Taco Hour.** This is composed of a hugh doughnut on the rooftop with the hands of a clock contained within the doughnut (ca. 1960). At the southeast corner of Woodruff Avenue and South Street is the **Dutch Village Shopping Center** (ca. 1960 and later). A shingled Dutch Windmill proclaims the principal entrance to the complex, and north across South Street, another smaller windmill marks the Dutch Mill Bowling building.

East of Bellflower and Artesia, not far from the Los Angeles/Orange County line, are two new "wonders" of the Southern California architectural scene. One of these is a pure programmatic building, the **Bear Tree** (1982-83; Bea de Armond with Jason and Michelle Walker), and the other is the **Doll and Toy Museum** (1979; "created by" Jay and Bea de Armond). The Bear Tree is in the form of a huge tree stump, with you and me as the little people who inhabit it. The Doll and Toy Museum is, according to the building's legend, a half-scale replica of the White House in Washington, D. C. Both of these structures form a part of **Hobby City,** which is located at 1238 South Beach Boulevard.

The Bear Tree

San Fernando Valley

Charles Lummis wrote that the Franciscans "unerringly chose from the California wilderness the garden spots, and a hundred years of experiment have failed to find anything better than their first judgment." Early pictures show the San Fernando Mission in pastureland, dependent on the winter rains for life. But the Franciscans dammed the springs near the mission (the dam is its oldest fragment) and then the Los Angeles River in the rainy season. The fertile land bloomed.

Heavy settlement waited for the Yankees, who carved up the former Mexican holdings. In the early 1870s a Bavarian immigrant, Isaac Lankershim, and his friend, I. N. Van Nuys, both large landholders in northern California, set out the southern part of the valley to sheep ranches and to wheat that was dry farmed. Charles Maclay, a Methodist minister turned land speculator, bought the northern valley a few years later thanks to a loan of $60,000 from Leland Stanford, who seems to have trusted Methodists.

Stanford sustained his interest. He made San Fernando the northern terminus of his Southern Pacific Railroad and shipped some railroad equipment there to make the designation look realistic. In fact, Maclay's deal determined the route of the line that in 1876 broke through the mountains and linked San Francisco and Los Angeles, leaving San Fernando a way station between two great cities.

The railroad brought more people to the Valley. They settled in old towns such as Calabasas and Chatsworth, both of which had been stagecoach stations, and, of course, San Fernando. But there were new settlements at Zelzah (now Northridge), Reseda, Pacoima, Roscoe (now Stonehurst), Sunland, Lankershim, Burbank, and Glendale. These towns, like the railroad, serviced a magnificent agricultural area, made more magnificent by the completion in 1913 of Mulholland's aqueduct bringing what at that time seemed unlimited water from the High Sierra 250 miles to the north.

Then, gradually at first, began the transformation of the landscape from wheat and citrus to what has been called "L.A.'s bedroom." Hollywood spread across the Santa Monica Mountains to form North Hollywood. Glendale oozed northwest. Though the scent of orange blossoms filled the air until World War II and even after, the rural idyll was then approaching the transformation into miles of dull tract housing, streets of apartment buildings, shopping centers, and commercial strips that mark it today. Ventura Boulevard was the great commercial strip to the south and the beginning of the main inland route to Ventura and Santa Barbara until the Ventura Freeway took its place in the mid-sixties. The immediate effect of the freeway was to further disintegrate the community, but, as in so many cases, the long-term effect has been to renew it, especially at Sherman Oaks and Encino, where mediocre high-rise is beginning to obscure the mountains.

Yes, the Valley is becoming super-respectable in places. In fact, it has been denounced too often. The stately rows of trees on east-west streets such as Sherman Way and the dry winds that sweep through them near sunset are as much of the present as they are of the past.

Glendale

Long inhabited by Mexican rancheros, the huge Rancho San Rafael was, before the Yankees came, mainly grazing land interspersed with a few farms which raised wheat, corn, beans, and hay. After the Gringo conquest the land was subdivided, the southern half comprising what is now Glendale, as well as Eagle Rock and part of Pasadena.

With the extension of the Southern Pacific Railroad north in 1873, the town (originally called Riverdale), was planned. Then in 1876, when the railroad was completed to San Francisco and with Los Angeles County thus open to transcontinental emigration, the community now called Glendale began to grow. It was supposed to grow wildly in the land boom of the 1880s. The obligatory extravagant hotel designed by Joseph Cather Newsom was built, but when the boom collapsed in 1888, the hotel stood finished but empty. After serving as a girls school and then a tuberculosis sanitarium, it was demolished in the twenties.

Significantly, it is very difficult to find anything left of Glendale's Victorian past. Its real history begins with the

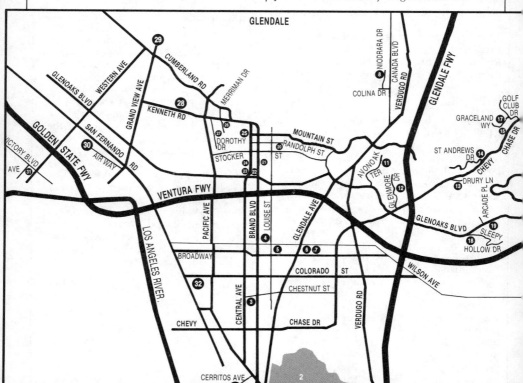

early twentieth century when the Pacific Electric Railroad (Interurban) extended (1904) its tracks from Central Los Angeles to Glendale. The city is thus well-bungalowed and in its upper reaches and along its main street (Brand Boulevard) well-stocked with the architecture of the twenties, which is either being spruced up or demolished and in some cases replaced with architecture that looks as if it came from the twenties or wished it had. Most of the newest buildings are clichés derived from old issues of *Progressive Architecture* — banal reformatory hives in concrete, or glass aviaries punctured with angular extrusions *a la* James Stirling. These, along with pretentious street lights at corners and brick pedestrian walkways across streets, make Glendale super-Mod. Oh yes, it has a Galleria (shopping mall) that is so successful that it appears that it eventually will consume the entire business district.

1. Southern Pacific Railroad Station,
ca. 1922
MacDonald and Couchot
Southwest end of Cerritos Avenue at Railroad Avenue

If there ever was a stage set, this is it! The Spanish Colonial Revival appears here at its most cloying. But it still works.

2. Forest Lawn Memorial Park,
1917 — present
Frederick A. Hansen, landscape architect

Entrance just north of the intersection of San Fernando Road and Glendale Boulevard. Map of grounds available at Information Booth near entrance and "Art Guide" at Administration Building near Information Booth.

The man behind this famed Southern California inspiration was Dr. Hubert L. Eaton, who planned it as "a great park, devoid of misshapen monuments. . . a place where lovers new and old shall love to stroll." In other words Forest Lawn was calculated to be something more than an architectural experience.

But architecture resides here. Behind the Tudor **Administration Building**

(1918 and later), designed by Charles Kyson and given ornamental enrichment by Austin Whittlesey (who also designed the Kerckhoff Monument), is the **Church of the Flowers** adapted (1918) by A. Patterson Ross from the church at Stoke Poges about whose cemetery Thomas Gray composed his "Elegy." It is the best piece of architecture at Forest Lawn and is often missed. F. A. Hansen's inexact copy of the **Wee Kirk of the Heather** is here, as is Anson Boyd's **Church of the Recessional,** which is supposed to be an exact copy of Rudyard Kipling's home church at Rottingdean. It isn't.

The main program here is, of course, sculptural, with more copies of Michelangelo's work than exist anywhere else on earth. Also an awful lot of modern Italian stuff, the most arresting being E. Gazzeri's *The Mystery of Life* in the Court of Memory. Just as interesting for other reasons is *The Dream of Peace* by Gutzon Borglum in his Art Nouveau phase.

We could go on, but will only add that in spite of all the generally execrable art, Forest Lawn does preserve an awful lot of open space.

2. *Church of the Flowers, Forest Lawn*

3. Glendale Chamber of Commerce Building (now Sons of the American Revolution Genealogical Library and Patio Gallery), ca. 1925
600 Central Avenue, at southeast corner of Chestnut Street

A one-story Spanish Colonial Revival building whose walls preserve their original burnt umber coloring.

4. Alex Theatre, 1924-25
Arthur G. Lindley and Charles R.
Selkirk; front added 1939.
268 N. Brand Boulevard

An Art Deco Moderne piece that puts
the more recent architecture on Brand
Boulevard to shame. The central pylon
erupting out of curved forms gives dramatic emphasis to the fact that the silver
screen is inside. Probably the most salient feature of the building is its lobby,
which combines Greek Doric columns
with chandeliers that resemble giant
heliotrope blossoms.

5. Glendale Post Office, 1933-34
George M. Lindsay; J. A. Wetmore
313 E. Broadway

Italian Renaissance with a good interior.

5. Glendale Post Office

6. Glendale City Hall, 1940-42
Albert E. Hansen
Northwest corner of Broadway and
Howard Street

Crisp Classical Moderne with a clock
tower.

7. Glendale Municipal Services Building, 1965
Albert C. Martin and Associates
(Merrill W. Baird)
Northwest corner of Broadway and
Glendale

Toned-down concrete Brutalism hovering
on stilts over a plaza with fountain.

8. Rodriguez House, 1941
R. M. Schindler
1845 Niodrara Drive

The angled roof with its wooden projections protects the rectangular de Stijl
composition below. Unfortunately, the
extraordinary structural gymnastics of
the house are largely screened from public view by fences and planting.

9. Paietta House, 1928
Southeast corner of Verdugo Road and
Sparr Boulevard

A hillside Spanish Colonial Revival extravaganza thrown together by a builder
with a lot of money and even more
spirit.

10. Leavitt House, 1948
A. Quincy Jones and Frederick E.
Emmons
1919 Bayberry Drive

A woodsy, late Craftsman bungalow all
on one floor. Variations on the same
theme are to be seen at 3068 Chevy
Chase Drive and at 1709 Golf Club
Drive (see entry number 16 below).

11. House, 1980
950 Avonoak Terrace, north of Glenoaks
Boulevard

It is encouraging to see that fantasy is
still with us. A small castle.

12. House, ca. 1920
680 Glenmore Drive, off Chevy Chase
Drive

The stone facade of the house and the
garden layout are similar to those at
Tujunga, which is one of Southern
California's meccas of boulder architecture.

13. House, 1929
2322 Drury Lane, at Chevy Chase
Drive

Unsophisticated but very romantic
Spanish Colonial Revival, almost Hansel
and Gretel. Quantities of such houses
abound in Glendale, especially in the
area above the Ventura Freeway.

14. Derby House, 1926
Lloyd Wright
2535 Chevy Chase Drive, at Saint Andrew's Drive

Built mainly in what Wright's father,
Frank Lloyd Wright, called his "textile
block" construction, Lloyd claimed it as

his own invention. The design of the concrete blocks was inspired by pre-Columbian ornament, but the general effect of the house is Islamic. Since the road has been widened practically to the front door, there is no problem in seeing the house.

14. Derby House

15. Calori House, 1926
Lloyd Wright
3021 Chevy Chase Drive

An abstract arrangement of shed and gable roofs hovers incongruously over the volumes below, while two massive brackets, supporting a small enclosed balcony, create a cave-like entrance to the house. A very free interpretation of the Spanish Colonial Revival.

15. Calori House

16. Fuller House, 1948-49
A. Quincy Jones and Frederick E. Emmons
3068 Chevy Chase Drive

As noted in entry number 10, this house was a variation on a theme established by the architects for several houses. Nearby at 1709 Golf Club Drive the **Kett House** (1948-49) preserves its woodsy, Craftsman exterior.

17. Lewis House, 1926
Lloyd Wright
2948 Graceland Way

This stucco structure has been modified, but the south elevation is similar to the strong vertical components of the Millard House by Wright's father. (Lloyd was just finishing the studio for Mrs. Millard at this time.)

18. House, ca. 1927
2414 E. Glenoaks Boulevard, at Sleepy Hollow Terrace

A rare use of the Zigzag Moderne in domestic architecture.

19. Bauer House, 1938
Harwell H. Harris
2528 E. Glenoaks Boulevard, at Arcade Place

A fence screens this house from the street, but what can be seen is good late Craftsman in style.

20. House, ca. 1905
Southwest corner of Randolph and Louise streets

A Mission Revival house which once was a famous Mexican restaurant, Casa Verdugo, at the end of the Pacific Electric Line.

21. Saint Mark's Episcopal Church, 1948
Carleton M. Winslow
1020 N. Brand Boulevard

Poured concrete construction with the wooden forms indented in the exterior surface, this large Gothic image building shows the strength of the Episcopalians in Glendale.

21. Saint Mark's Episcopal Church

22. Church of the Incarnation Roman Catholic Church, 1951
Northwest corner of Brand and Glenoaks boulevards

Both inside and out, this is a superb period piece of late Classical Moderne. This building and its adjacent school, along with the Methodist church down the block and the Mormon church nearby (next two entries), form a shrine for the Moderne enthusiast.

23. North Glendale Methodist Church, 1941
Harry W. Peirce
Northwest corner of Glenoaks Boulevard and Central Avenue

Gothic Moderne. One of the parishioners said she liked it because it wasn't "this far-out stuff."

24. Glendale Second Ward, Church of Jesus Christ of Latter-day Saints (Mormon), 1939
Georgius Y. Cannon
Northwest corner of Dryden Street and Central Avenue

Rather academic but very good Streamline Moderne.

25. House, ca. 1927
Southwest corner of Central Avenue and Spencer Street

A fairytale castle with a lovely tile band wrapped around the tower.

26. House, ca. 1905
Southeast corner of Merriman Drive and Kenneth Road

22. Church of the Incarnation Roman Catholic Church

A two-story tribute to the eastern Colonial tradition.

27. Adobe San Rafael, 1865 (restored 1932)
1330 Dorothy Drive

A one-story, beautifully maintained structure with Monterey style porch. It is notable that such buildings evoke New England as much as they do the West. The house and gardens are open to the public Sunday and Wednesday afternoons, 1-4.

28. Senator Madison Jones House, 1902
727 Kenneth Drive

A two-story Ionic portico with Adamesque front door is the pride of this house. Tradition has it that Senator Jones's brother was the architect.

29. Brand House ("El Miradero"), 1902-4
Nathaniel Dryden
1601 W. Mountain Street, at north end of Grandview Avenue

Certainly worth a trip to Glendale. This Islamic folly is supposed to have been inspired by the East Indian Pavilion at the World's Columbian Exposition in Chicago in 1893. It was the home of Leslie C. Brand, the Glendale booster who brought the Pacific Electric to Glendale in 1904. He gave his estate to the city on the condition that it be a public library and park, and so it is. The house and its harmonious addition (1969) by Jones and Walton is now an art library and cultural center. The grounds are beautiful. Since the publication of our last *Guide* the Queen Anne **Doctor's House** (ca. 1887), formerly at Wilson Avenue and Belmont Street, has been moved into the park and is being restored.

30. Grand Central Air Terminal, 1928
Henry L. Gogerty
1310 Air Way

A surviving Spanish Colonial Revival curiosity, since the airport has disappeared and has been replaced by factories and warehouses.

29. Brand House ("El Miradero")

31. Two Bungalows, 1935
246 and 248 Jesse Avenue, at Victory Boulevard

Tiny treasures of the Streamline Moderne with glass brick and portholes.

32. Joy Company, 1972-73
Craig Ellwood Associates
4565 Colorado Street

One Miesian box cantilevered over another, this fine example of Ellwood's taste can be best viewed from the Golden State Freeway across the Los Angeles River channel (paved, of course). Travelling north on the freeway in this area you will also get a good view of public art of a sort: huge cat faces that have been painted around drainage ducts emptying into the river.

Burbank

Contrary to popular assumption, this city was not named for Luther Burbank, the horticulturist, but for a typical Angelino, Dr. David Burbank, a dentist who was one of the happy subdividers in 1887. Too much fun has been made of "beautiful downtown Burbank." It has a shopping mall that seems to work, i.e., where you see people. It is amusing that almost everything worth seeing is on or just off Olive Avenue, a street that cuts diagonally southwest through the conventional grid which lines up on the Los Angeles River, of all things.

We begin, however, in the northwest, near the very busy Burbank Airport:

1. Memorial Rotunda, 1927
Kenneth MacDonald, Jr.
End of Valhalla Drive just off Hollywood Way, south of the main runway of the airport.

One of L. A.'s extravagant gems; an open-domed temple richly embellished with cast concrete ornament almost worthy of San Francisco's Bernard Maybeck. This was to have been the entrance to a sumptuous memorial park.

2. House, ca. 1955
7630 Glenoaks Boulevard, near Cabrini Drive (just outside the Burbank boundary)

The house seems to be a takeoff on the brittle Neo-Classicism of Sir John Soane. But the real sight is the front garden, alive with old street lights. A local wag has dubbed it, therefore, the "Villa Luminaria."

1. Memorial Rotunda

3. Adolph's Office Building, 1951-53
Raphael S. Soriano
1800 Magnolia Boulevard, at Parish Place

The post and lintel modular system taken to the point where it almost becomes an anonymous building.

4. Bungalow, ca. 1920
Southwest corner of Olive Avenue and Ninth Street

One of the handsomest and most characteristic "airplane" bungalows in the region.

5. Two bungalows, ca. 1920
Northeast corner of Olive Avenue and Ninth Street

Indigenous boulder architecture.

6. Saint Robert Bellarmine Complex
Northwest and southwest corners of Olive Avenue and Fifth Street

Monsignor Martin Cody Keating, the priest who envisioned this, deserves some kind of medal. Next to God, his hero was Thomas Jefferson. The **Jefferson-Bellarmine Elementary School,** a rebuilding in the thirties of the old Holy Trinity Church, is thus partly Neo-Classical, supposedly based on Jefferson's stables at Monticello, and partly Moderne. It was designed by Paul Kingsford. The nearby **Saint Robert**

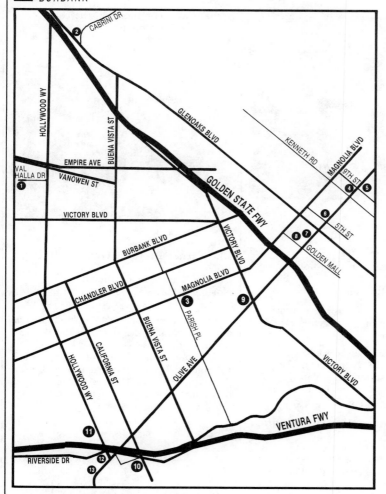

Bellarmine Church (1939; George Adams), at the southeast corner of 5th Street and Orange Grove, is similarly Neo-Classical with its portico modelled on the south front of Monticello. Then back on Olive Avenue is the **Jefferson-Bellarmine High School** (1945; Barker and Ott) a facsimile of Independence Hall with a splendid facsimile of the Liberty Bell in the entrance hall under the tower. All this is followed by a Classical Roman **auditorium** (1952; Barker and Ott), inspired by Jefferson's Library at the University of Virginia. Three cheers for the architect(s) and the priest who conceived of (and for the church who endorsed) this Fourth of July celebration.

7. Burbank City Hall, 1941
William Allen and George Lutzi
Southwest corner of Olive Avenue and Third Street

A classic of the PWA Moderne with matching fountain decorated with WPA bas-relief (by Bartolo Mako) on the Third Street side, the whole carried out with great delicacy. The lobby has retained all of its original pizazz.

7. Burbank City Hall

8. The Golden Mall, 1967
Simon Eisener and Lyle Stewart

A tree-lined pedestrian way along a section of San Fernando Road from San Jose Avenue to Tujunga Avenue.

9. Grist Mill Restaurant, ca. 1950
Southwest corner of Olive Avenue and Victory Boulevard

A skirted windmill whose slats, edged with lights, actually twirl and make you nostalgic for those old blue Van de Kamp's bake shops of the twenties and thirties.

10. Warner Brothers Records Building, 1975
A. Quincy Jones Associates
South side of Riverside Drive at junction of Warner Boulevard and California Street

Natural wood framed in metal softens the International Style Modern building.

11. Bungalows, ca. 1930
300 Block of Hollywood Way

A block-long row of tiny, terribly quaint, Hansel and Gretel cottages with some "intrusions."

12. Warner/Elektra/Atlantic Corporation Building, 1981
Gibbs and Gibbs
Northwest corner of Olive Avenue and Hollywood Way

The building appears to be a vast assemblage of huge Tinker Toy beam

perhaps as a comment on the early Craftsman movement.

12. Warner/Elektra/Atlantic Corporation Building

13. Warner Brothers Office Building, 1979
Charles Luckman Partnership
Northeast corner of Olive Avenue and Maple Street

A Post-Modern and very conscious revival of the Streamline Moderne of the thirties by the firm whose head once ironically participated in the design of New York's International Style Modern Lever House that pioneered the Miesian aesthetic in post-World War II America. In every way the new building is monumental!

13. Warner Brothers Office Building

Toluca Lake

This lovely residential section, roughly bordered by the Ventura Freeway, the Los Angeles River, Cahuenga Boulevard, and the border with Burbank, is a real surprise in the Valley. The drawing card for the well-heeled gentry coming in the thirties and later was the lake and the country club. The winding, tree-lined streets are up to Pasadena standards. Yet, as in so many parts of beautifully landscaped Los Angeles County, very little noteworthy architecture exists in the shade of the trees.

The mildly International Style Modern **MacFadden House** (1948) at 1052 Toluca Lake Avenue near the intersection with Tolofa Avenue was designed by J. R. Davidson as, one would like to think, a foil for its "traditional" neighbors. The **Elliott House** (1951) at 10443 Woodbridge Street, near Strohm Avenue, is one of Harwell H. Harris's late Craftsman masterpieces. Rather unexpectedly at 4217 Navajo Street near the corner of Valley Spring Lane you will find a large **Streamline Moderne house** whose roof is adorned with a huge antenna obviously tuned to "Buck Rogers in the Twenty-fifth Century." The house was designed by Kenneth Worthen, Sr. in 1935. The latest addition to Toluca Lake's small trove of outstanding architecture is Frank O. Gehry and Associates' **World Savings Building** (1982) at 10064 Riverside Drive (intersection with Mariota Avenue). It is definitely Post-Modern with its false back, including fenestration.

World Savings Building

Universal City

Tucked in below Toluca Lake and the Los Angeles River to the north and the Hollywood Freeway to the south at the intersection of Cahuenga and Lankershim boulevards is the old lot of Universal Studios, now turned into an amusement park with a fringe on Lankershim Boulevard of elegant **office buildings** by Skidmore, Owings, and Merrill (1970-present). It all began with a black glass tower and three lower volumes, also black glass boxes. Then, as if the architects had changed their minds, huge horizontal, brown, travertine marble slabs began appearing as if the fragments of a long-lost Schindler design had developed elephantiasis. The latest is a new tower, the headquarters (1984) of the Getty Oil Company (Skidmore, Owings, and Merrill). What next?

Oh yes, we should mention the restaurants. **The Victoria Station** (1980; Swinerton and Walberg Company) and **Fung Lum's** (1981; Tracey Price) are architecturally the most sensational.

North Hollywood

The sister of the Hollywood over the hill, North Hollywood owes its existence to the film industry that found the Valley photogenic and less hazy than the L.A. Basin. Not the faintest trace of Isaac Lankershim's wheat barony remains except for his name attached to a street that has the gall to cut diagonally across a grid firmly based on north-south, east-west axes. North Hollywood had an unusual number of parks and other spaces, but the freeway engineers have taken advantage of almost all of them in order to easily put through their great works. So much for parks.

Not much really exotic or monumental architecture exists in the acre upon acre of tract housing, apartments, and condominiums. But North Hollywood is far from a total loss:

1. Saint Charles Boromeo Roman Catholic Church, 1959
J. Earl Trudeau

Parish Hall, 1938
Laurence Viole
Southwest corner of Moorpark Street and Lankershim Boulevard

Impressive when viewed from the Ventura Freeway, this Spanish Colonial Revival edifice is not as bold when closely inspected. The ascetic Mission Revival **Parish Hall** adjoining it is more impressive architecturally.

1. Saint Charles Boromeo Roman Catholic Church

2. La Caña Restaurant Building, ca. 1935
Near northeast corner of Lankershim Boulevard and Vineland Avenue

An enlarged root beer barrel, a programmatic that enlivens an otherwise dreadful area.

3. DWP Building, 1939
Attributed to S. Charles Lee
5108 Lankershim Boulevard

A tasteful exposition of the fragile Streamline Moderne.

4. Methodist Church, 1949
Northeast corner of Riverside Drive and Tujunga Avenue

A Spanish Colonial Revival building with a sort of Mudejar tower ending in two stages that might have been designed by Asher Benjamin.

5. Masonic Temple, 1951
Robert Stacy-Judd
5122 Tujunga Avenue

Egypto-Mayan, by California's most passionate pre-Columbian exponent. This structure maintains the tradition of off-beat architecture established by the Freemasons in early California.

5. Masonic Temple

6. Los Angeles County Regional Branch Library, ca. 1929
Weston and Weston
Near northwest corner of Magnolia Boulevard and Tujunga Avenue

Spanish Colonial Revival with strange, non-functional porch.

4. Methodist Church

Studio City

I t is difficult to distinguish Studio City from North Hollywood except that its heart (the word seems inappropriate) is south of the Los Angeles River and along Ventura Boulevard which begins here. In fact, this section of Ventura marks one of the earliest (1930s) commercial strips in the Valley. Its remains can still be seen.

Also, Studio City is blessed with a considerable amount of good to excellent architecture, much of it by R. M. Schindler.

1. Ward House, 1939
Richard J. Neutra
3156 Lake Hollywood Drive

Low, sleek, private, its inner complexities are masked by an International Style Modern facade.

2. ▪Hay House, 1939
Gregory Ain
3432 Oakcrest Drive

This modular box, done mainly in wood, looks as if it had just been finished. The International Style Modern at its most beautiful.

3. Showboat Restaurant, 1968
Cahuenga Boulevard near Bennett Drive at Hollywood Freeway ramp.

Well, *part* of a Mississippi showboat with its pair of metal smokestacks, appropriately situated near the Los Angeles River.

4. Centrum Office Building, 1982
Johannes Van Tilburg and Partners
3575 Cahunga Boulevard, near Multiview Drive

Described as "futuristic," this vast hulk seems somewhat old-fashioned—brutal at the bottom moving into Sterling-like

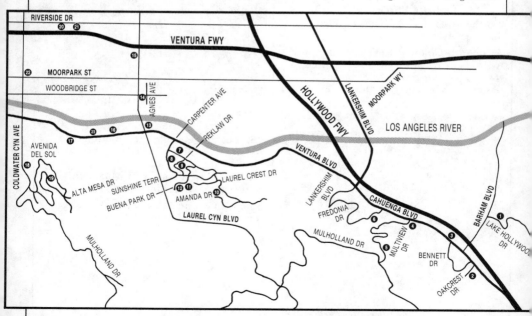

tipped glass panels at the top. Nevertheless, it acts as a nice foil for the "less-is-more" of Universal City directly across the freeway.

3. Showboat Restaurant

5. Kallis House, 1947
R. M. Schindler
3580 Multiview Drive

This angular cliff-hanger, now sequestered in foliage, is one of Schindler's most dramatic houses.

5. Kallis House

6. Fredonia Apartment Building, 1964
Raymond L. Kappe
3625 Fredonia Drive, off Ventura Boulevard

An ellipse of glass and stucco set into the hill, this small but luxurious building commands a magnificent view of the Valley.

7. Laurelwood Apartment Building, 1948
R. M. Schindler
11833-37 Laurelwood Drive

Two rows of simple, stucco box, de Stijl designs step up the small rise of land. At the time of this writing they are somewhat the worse for the wear, but we should rejoice in the fact that at least they are still here.

8. Goodwin House, 1940
R. M. Schindler
3807 Reklaw Drive

Not much can be seen of this small-scaled de Stijl composition from the street.

9. Gold House, 1945
R. M. Schindler
3758 Reklaw Drive

From the gate you will get a good view of Schindler's imaginative maneuvering, both vertically and horizontally, of light stucco volumes.

10. Lechner House, 1948
R. M. Schindler
11606 Amanda Drive

Actually, the best view is from Laurelvale Drive below. Schindler gives conventional builders' forms the stamp of his genius in this tent-like structure.

10. Lechner House

11. Waxman House, 1964
J. Barry Moffat
3644 Buena Park Drive

A theatrical essay in vertical and horizontal thrusts.

12. Roth House, 1945
R. M. Schindler
3624 Buena Park Drive

Another "builder's house" whose flaring porch at the curve of the road is a major exterior feature.

13. Home Savings and Loan Building, 1968
Millard Sheets
Northeast corner of Ventura and Laurel Canyon boulevards

Sheets's huge mosaic over the door adds zest to an area that needs it.

14. Presburger House, 1945
R. M. Schindler
4255 Agnes Avenue

Not much can be seen, but this house with its high clerestory window running full length was imitated many times by contractors in the L.A. area.

15. Campbell Hall School, 1951
Jones and Emmons
4533 Laurel Canyon Boulevard

Modest International Style Modern on a small, shaded campus.

16. Medical Arts Building, 1945
R. M. Schindler
12307 Ventura Boulevard

Very chaste, this structure remains almost exactly as Schindler designed it, which is more than we can say for the next entry.

17. Lingenbrink Shops, 1939-42
R. M. Schindler
12632-68 Ventura Boulevard

A complex of ten small offices and shops compromised by modernization. But there are recognizable fragments, as well as the wonderful jagged roofline, mauled to be sure by signage.
To the east at 12601 Ventura Boulevard, note the two Southern Pacific Railroad cars that have been turned into **Carney's Express Restaurant** (ca. 1978).

16. Medical Arts Building

18. Saint Savior's Chapel, Harvard School, 1914
Reginald D. Johnson
3700 Coldwater Canyon Avenue

In 1937 this building was moved from the old campus at Venice Boulevard and Western Avenue in Central Los Angeles. It is mildly Gothic inside — supposedly based on a chapel at Rugby. The exterior is based upon rural Spanish models.

19. Stevens House, 1941
Rodney Walker
3642 Altamesa Drive

All you can see are some Mexican pots hanging from a pergola, but this view is suggestive of Walker's romanticism.

20. Dorman/Winthrop Clothiers Building, 1966
Pulliam, Zimmerman, and Matthews (Bernard Zimmerman)
12640 Riverside Drive

A glistening International Style Modern glass box pushed up against the Ventura Freeway; its street front is almost a classical temple.

21. Riverside Law Building, 1972
Goldman/Brandt (Ron Goldman)
12650 Riverside Drive

Brownstone and wood, this two-story office building is designed around a small court. It looks fine and the lawyers say that it works.

22. Office Building, 1983
Ebbe Videriksen
4400 Coldwater Canyon Avenue

Twenty-eight thousand square feet of English Queen Anne.

23. Kinsey Office Building, 1978
Pulliam, Matthews, and Associates
12345 Ventura Boulevard

A beautifully articulated, brick cut-into box with the front covered with plates of glass set behind metal columns.

Pacoima

This section of the Valley is not rich in architecture, but until recently it had two houses designed by Joseph Cather Newsom. One has been moved to Mission Hills and the other (1887) at 13204 Judd Street has had its fine Queen Anne lines covered with stucco. A good **stone house** of the twenties is at 13333 Filmore Street.

18. Saint Savior's Chapel, Havard School

Sherman Oaks

A residential development of the thirties with a commercial strip along Ventura Boulevard, Sherman Oaks was changed by the intersection here of the Ventura and San Diego freeways in the early sixties. Sherman Oaks is now exposed to medium high-rise, all of it boring. The process has continued to the present with the same results. Nowhere is the aphorism "change and decay" more apt. In the last few years Smith and Williams's Goldman Medical Building (1948) has been demolished and an awful thing put in its place. The "dazzling scraffito work" on the Fiore d'Italia Restaurant has been painted over, though the exciting facade remains. The best here is elderly.

1. Notre Dame High School Building, ca. 1938
Northeast corner of Woodman Avenue and Riverside Drive

Mission style of the thirties for the buildings facing Woodman Avenue and Riverside Drive. It is difficult to say what was the model for the Depression-period, Churrigueresque-styled gymnasium that makes a diagonal behind the corner.

1. Notre Dame High School Building

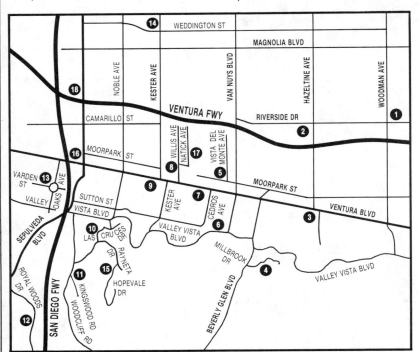

2. Sunkist Headquarters Building, 1969
Albert C. Martin and Associates
14130 Riverside Drive

A huge, four-square wine crate on stilts, all in concrete; it works well from the freeway.

2. Sunkist Headquarters Building

3. Bungalow Court, ca. 1930
South side of Ventura Boulevard just west of Hazeltine Avenue

A conversion of this Craftsman staple of the Southern California diet to a restaurant and shops. Well done.

4. Schwenck House, 1940
Harwell H. Harris
14239 Millbrook Drive

A barely-visible "Brown and Brown" clinging to the hillside.

5. Bungalow, ca. 1935
Northwest corner of Moorpark Street and Vista del Monte Avenue

A tiny stucco cottage exhibiting a complete checklist of all elements of Streamline Moderne.

6. Mesner House, 1951 and later
Gregory Ain (Ain, Johnson, and Day)
14571 Valley Vista Boulevard

Everything but the jutting roof is swamped in foliage.

7. La Reina Theatre, 1938
S. Charles Lee
Southwest corner of Ventura Boulevard and Cedros Avenue

A small Moderne structure with multi-sided marquee supporting a crown. A little of the etched glass is left in the otherwise disappointing interior.

8. Esplanade Apartment Building, 1967
Kamnitzer, Marks, and Vreeland
4617 Willis Avenue

International style Modern with a bit of color.

9. Fiore d'Italia Restaurant Building, ca. 1965
14928 Ventura Boulevard

Formerly, the general tone of this area was Wild West, to which this once marvelously decorated building served as a foil. Now the scraffito work is gone and even the restaurant has become Wild West. Ironically, the Disneyland neighbors have almost disappeared in new building.

10. ■Foster House, 1950
John Lautner
4235 Las Cruces Road

Anyone who remembers the fine Julius Shulman photograph of this house in our 1965 *Guide* will now have difficulty in seeing what was intended before nature took over.

11. Elterman house, 1961
Gregory Ain
15301 Kingswood Lane

Spartan sophistication. Again, little can be seen.

12. Handman House, 1963
Raymond E. Kappe
3872 Woodcliff Drive

A late Constructivist-Craftsman piece lost in foliage.

18. *Castle Miniature Golf Course*

13. Smith House, 1948
Rodney Walker
15435 Varden Street

Designed in International Style Modern simplicity before the architect developed his strong tendency toward romanticism.

14. Kester Avenue Elementary School Building, 1951
Richard J. Neutra; addition 1957; Dion Neutra
Northwest corner of Kester Avenue and Weddington Street

A refinement of the open-air school, for which Neutra is famous.

15. Willheim House, 1978-79
Charles Moore (Urban Innovations Group); with Elias Torres and John Rubel
3944 Hopevale Drive

A plaster and wood castle clinging to a hillside.

16. Sherman Oaks Galleria, 1980
Albert C. Martin and Associates; Interior mall, Charles Kober Associates
Southeast corner of Sepulveda Boulevard and Camarillo Street

A vast assemblage of white, late International Style forms stretching for a long city block.

17. Zimbalist Apartment Building, 1973
B. H. Bosworth
4520 Natick Avenue

This L.A. Post-Modern endeavor consists of a large ellipse of classical columns and pediments.

18. Castle Miniature Golf Course
5000 Block, Sepulveda Boulevard

Begun in the late sixties, this elaborate development of Hansel and Gretel forms and fantasy fountains is a nice stage set for the off-ramp from the Ventura to the San Diego freeway.

Encino

The Portola expedition (1769) referred to what we now call the San Fernando Valley as "Santa Catalina de Bononia de los Encinos" for the many great oaks found in the area. The development of Encino, beginning with the introduction of an alternate route of the Southern Pacific Railroad in 1890, did not banish the oaks, many of which still exist. For example, the low, Ranch style **Plaza de Oro Shopping Center** (1971-72), at the northeast corner of Ventura Boulevard and Louise Avenue, was designed by Ebbe Videriksen in order to preserve the trees for which the city was named. Significantly one of the oldest (1000 years) oaks in the state is just southwest of the shopping center on Louise Avenue just below Ventura Boulevard.

If you continue on Louise Avenue and then turn west on Rancho Street, you will have a pleasant drive back to Ventura Boulevard where at 16661 you will see the **Travelers Insurance Building** (1966) designed by Howard Lane in a Neo-Streamline Moderne mode. Not far away and just off Ventura Boulevard (turn north on Petit Avenue) at 16756 Moorpark Street is the two-story masonry Greek Revival house (1849) of the **Rancho de los Encinos,** a State monument of California open 1-4, Wednesday through Sunday. Back on Ventura Boulevard at the northwest corner of Genesta Avenue is an intriguing row of **Tudor shops** that seems to hail from the twenties.

When you experience either the Ventura Freeway west of its interchange with the San Diego Freeway or the San Diego Freeway north of the Ventura Freeway you will see off to the northwest the spillway of the **Sepulveda Flood Control Dam.** This rock-faced dam was built between the years 1939 and 1941 as a flood control point on the Los Angeles River. The central concrete flood gates and tower are one of the most impressive examples of the PWA Moderne to be found in the Los Angeles Basin. As with so many of the dams and similar utilitarian constructions of the 1930s, the spillway section of the dam was designed through the eyes of the Streamline Moderne — beautiful, curved surfaces for the water channels, and even round porthole windows for the concrete control tower. In order to reach the dam you must park at its north end, just off Burbank Boulevard, north of Sepulveda Boulevard, and then walk to the spillway and tower. The spillway and tower are off-limits, but you can wander around in the basin and below the basin obtain a close view of its design.

Tudor Shops

Tarzana, Woodland Hills

Griffith Ranch House

T here is really no distinguishing these bedroom communities along the Ventura strip. Tarzana has the more colorful name, given it by express permission of Edgar Rice Burroughs, whose ranch covered much of the area. Its chief point of architectural interest is the **Barclays Bank Building** (1971) by Honnold, Reibsamen, and Rex at 18321 Ventura Boulevard. See also the **Medical Center of Tarzana** (1973) just north of it (via Etiwanda Avenue and Clark Street) by Rochlin and Baran and Associates.

In Woodland Hills, R. M. Schindler's **Van Dekker House** (1940) may be viewed from a distance at 5230 Penfield Avenue. It is sited on the slope of a small hill. A dramatic shed roof corners the living room and is intersected by layers of low horizontal roofs; the walls are made of wood, stucco, and stone.

A new addition (1984) to the Woodland Hills landscape is the **Struckus House** (1982-84) just northwest of the corner of Saltillo Street and Canoga Avenue. It resembles an eighteenth-century birdcage strung between four oak trees. It was designed by Bruce Goff (his only house in Southern California) just before his death in 1983.

The **Griffith Ranch House** (1936) by Lloyd Wright is almost invisible at 4900 Dunman Avenue. In this dwelling, Wright took the theme of the late thirties California Ranch house and imposed a Prairie cruciform plan upon it.

To the east on the hillside at the northwest corner of Ventura Boulevard and Del Moreno Drive is a new three-story Spanish Colonial Revival **Office Building** (1983). From the Ventura Freeway its large round tower, tile roofs, and white walls look romantic; but unfortunately it is not as impressive close up. Further to the west on the Ventura Freeway you see what appears to be a half-timber **Medieval building.** This structure, located behind 20631 Ventura Boulevard is an addition to what was a small, two-story restaurant building (ca. 1970). The restaurant is now an accounting office, and the new building to the rear (ca. 1980) contains a ground-level garage and two floors of additional offices. Next door to the east is one of the **Victoria Station** Restaurants—in the usual form of a railroad car.

Medieval Building

Calabasas

Leonis Adobe

One of the oldest settlements in the Valley, Calabasas was a stagecoach stop on the Camino Real route from Santa Barbara to Los Angeles. Only a few simple brick buildings remain from the late nineteenth-century commercial district and these have been Disneyized in order to create an image of the Wild West that will amuse if not edify. A touch of reality at 23400 Calabasas Road is the beautifully restored two-story **Leonis Adobe** (ca. 1850) with its wooden Queen Anne gingerbread added by Miguel Leonis when he moved there in the 1870s. The back lawn, shaded by one of California's greatest oaks, helps to create a nineteenth-century atmosphere even with the freeway only a hundred yards away. Thanks to the late Catharine S. Beachey and her family this may be one of the best endowed house museums in the country. Open to the public Wednesday, Saturday, and Sunday, 1-4, no admission charge.

About a mile southwest of Calabasas (via Calabasas Road and Park Granada Boulevard) is a new subdivision called **Calabasas Park.** The landscape of the lake area was designed in 1972 by Julian George. The Country Club (1972) was laid out by Robert Trent Jones. The surrounding condominiums and townhouses (1974-later) were designed by Dorman/Munselle Associates who chose the Spanish Colonial Revival image. Along with the provision of a multitude of trees, the whole enterprise fits well into the landscape.

Almost directly south of Calabasas (Mulholland Drive, then Val Mar Road to Bluebird Drive) are the remnants of the **Park Moderne,** conceived by L.A.'s early patron of the Moderne and Modern, William Lingenbrink, in 1929 (*see* **Lingenbrink Shops,** Studio City) for "Lovers of Modernistic Art," meaning both the de Stijl and Art Deco phases of that passion. He employed European-educated R. M. Schindler and Jock Peters to design houses "along Modern lines." Due to the Depression, few of these houses were built. We don't want to encourage you to make a desperate effort to see what is left but thought it our duty to record the facts:

5. House

1. House, 1931
Jock Peters
Northeast corner of Bluebird Drive and Meadowlark Drive

Art Deco (Zigzag) Moderne transformed by later hands into an English Cottage.

2. Community Building (now a private residence), 1931
Jock Peters
23031 Bluebird Drive

Close to European Modern of the twenties with a strong contrast between the horizontal corner windows and the vertical fins and piers.

3. Fountain, 1930
Jock Peters
South side of Blackbird Way, south of Meadowlark Drive

Art Deco (Zigzag) Moderne in concrete.

4. House, ca. 1931
South side of Blackbird Way, south of Meadowlark Drive

Remodelled Art Deco (Zigzag) Moderne.

5. House, 1929
R. M. Schindler
3978 Blackbird Way

Of the three houses Schindler designed for Lingenbrink at Park Moderne one remained a project, a second was built and subsequently demolished. Only this one remains. In scale it is a single-floor cabin, dominated by strong horizontals — projecting flat roofs and narrow bands of clerestory windows.

6. Well-house, 1931
Attributed to Jock Peters
Opposite 22959 Hummingbird Way

Angular Art Deco (Zigzag) Moderne in cast concrete.

7. House, (ca. 1931)
22912 Bluebird Way

The best preserved house of this early period, and Pueblo Revival to boot. Except for the Southern California vegetation, it seems to be in Santa Fe.

Canoga Park

The early seat of the Orcutts and the Workmans, this area is really Valley—meaning that it is given over to tract housing that was the subject of cartoons in the fifties. If you wish to view this phenomenon, it is best to take the north-south streets off the main boulevards—Roscoe, Saticoy, Sherman Way (magnificent lines of Imperial palms) and Vanowen. You should also see these same areas from the air for, the glint of the sun off the unused swimming pools is quite charming. Some good things on the ground:

1. Canoga Mission Gallery Building,
1934-36
Francis Lederer
23130 Sherman Way,

Lederer, the famous cinema idol of yesteryear, designed this building as stables in the simple, very late Mission mode. But when the city decided to cut through his estate in order to extend Sherman Way, the road led right past the stables. Mrs. Lederer, sensing an opportunity, remodelled the stables to serve as a gift shop selling Mexican and Californian crafts. In fact, it also serves

1. Canoga Mission Gallery Building

as a kind of social hall for this part of the Valley.

2. W. W. Orcutt House ("Rancho Sombra del Roble"), ca. 1930
23555 Justice Street

Orcutt was an early oil baron who bought this property that had years before provided the timber used in firing the kilns producing bricks for the San Fernando Mission. His Spanish Colonial Revival house is rarely open to the public and is barely visible from the street.

3. Workman House ("Shadow Ranch"), 1869-72; remodelling ca. 1935
Lawrence Test; Charles Gibbs Adams, landscape architect
22633 Vanowen Street

Both visible and accessible, this house was remodelled to look more "Colonial" than the original. It is really lovely, set in a public park with some of the oldest eucalyptus groves in the state.

4. Great Western Savings Building, 1966
Kurt Meyer and Associates
6601 Topanga Canyon Boulevard

A huge, Neo-Brutalist temple in exposed concrete and glass. The projecting roof is supported on both sides of the entrance by two sets of double columns.

5. Bullock's Woodland Hills, 1972-73
Welton Becket and Associates
Promenade Shopping Center, 6000 block, Topanga Canyon Boulevard (actually in Canoga Park)

The sparingly-fenestrated, white slumpstone facade evokes the image of the walls of a Mexican village—on a very large scale, to be sure.

6. Canoga Park Post Office, 1938
Louis A. Simon, supervising architect
Northwest corner of Sherman Way and Jordan Avenue

The building is simple Spanish Colonial Revival with Moderne tendencies. Inside is a fine Federal Arts Project (WFA) mural, *Palomino Ponies,* painted by Maynard Dixon in 1942.

7. Crippled Children Society ("Rancho del Valle"), Main Building, 1979
John Lautner
6530 Winnetka Avenue

A wing of this radially-planned, one-story building has been erected. It has all the drama that we have come to expect of Lautner designs.

8. ▪Platt Office Building, 1981
T. W. Layman
19725 Sherman Way (just west of Corbin Avenue)

Parts of buildings, formerly on Bunker Hill, have been assembled here to give us something more than a new Victorian (Queen Anne) commercial building. This is a bona fide and very welcome folly.

8. Platt Office Building

Chatsworth

Northridge

This old town has, in spite of growth, managed to avoid being submerged. It began its Anglo Yankee life as a small settlement at the southeast end of the Santa Susana Pass, where it was a stop on the inland stagecoach route opened in 1861 between San Francisco and provincial Los Angeles. The trail down the pass (parts are still visible) was so steep that the wheels of the coaches were locked and timbers hauled behind in order to control the descent. Harried travelers were relieved when the stagecoach line was relocated (1874) along the Camino Real (*see* Calabasas), but the trail was used by travelers to and from the Simi Valley until the railroad tunnels were built in 1904. Now a freeway to the north of the town communicates with Simi.

The great outcrop of rock known as **Stony Point** has often been used as scenery in Wild West movies. Earlier it marked the site of Indian settlements. The very active Chatsworth Historical Society is an excellent source of information on Indian lore. It is also the agency chiefly responsible for moving the picturesque Eastlake-Gothic **Methodist Church** (1904) to the **Oakland Cemetery** (10000 block of Valley Circle Boulevard) when the church was threatened by progress.

First named Zelzah (in 1908), the settlement's current respectable name was suggested in 1935 by Carl S. Dentzel, a founding member of the Los Angeles Cultural Board who lived in the area. Immediately after World War II this part of the valley was sparsely settled, as agricultural land planted in orange groves and truck crops. In the fifties a little **Modern tract housing** (Smith and Williams, 1954) was tried near Reseda Boulevard. The block bounded by Chase Street, Darby Avenue, and Rathburn Avenue contains the highest proportion of original, relatively un-remodelled examples. Obviously builders' tract housing took off from there.

Also, in the early sixties Northridge became the seat of **San Fernando Valley State College** ("Valley State") which in a few years raised itself to a university (California State University, Northridge) that is roughly bounded by Reseda Boulevard, Lassen Street, Zelzah Avenue, and Nordhoff Street (where there is a little visitor parking). The architect chosen for this institution was Richard J. Neutra (with Robert E. Alexander) whose nearby Streamline landship, the Von Sternberg House (1935), now destroyed, may have suggested him to the trustees. Unfortunately, only the **Fine Arts Building** (1959) was designed by Neutra. The architects of several other buildings have tried to imitate his design featuring elongated sunshades, but they

Brown's Burger Bar

have succeeded only in reproducing State College Modern dullness.

In places, Reseda Boulevard retains memories of its strip development in the thirties. In fact, just off Reseda Boulevard at 18448 Saticoy Street is a Streamline Moderne diner, **Brown's Burger Bar** (ca. 1940). North of Saticoy Street are several of the now-plentiful stucco box **apartments.** The variety of images possible in this medium is suggested by 7923 Reseda Boulevard, which is Polynesian (ca. 1958), and the one at the northwest corner of Reseda Boulevard and Strathern Street, where a large corner mosaic of a winged bull proclaims its Assyrian heritage (ca. 1960).

Teledyne Systems Company

Farther west, on and off Tampa Avenue, are some equally interesting developments. **Bullock's Northridge** (1972), designed by Welton Becket and Associates, is in the Northridge Plaza near the southwest corner of Plummer Street and Tampa Avenue. It is all roof with its two ends resembling sawed-off pyramids. Southwest of it at 190601 Nordhoff Street (northeast corner of Corbin Avenue) is the black, sophisticated **Teledyne Systems Company** (1968) that Cesar Pelli designed for Daniel, Mann, Johnson, and Mendenhall before Post-Modern tendencies struck him. At the Corbin Avenue corner is a tiny grove of orange trees and across the street a large wood lot with green fields behind it. South on Tampa Avenue at the west end of Cantara Street there is actually a large barn. But this arcadian bliss is passing, as the large **Northridge Hospital** (1968—later) by Rochlin and Baran and Associates attests. This complex, just east of the intersection of Roscoe Boulevard and Reseda Boulevard, is superficially a spin-off from Louis Kahn's Richards Medical Center in Philadelphia.

Bullock's Northridge

Granada Hills, Mission Hills

Van Nuys, Panorama City, Sepulveda

This area of the northern San Fernando Valley began its residential development in the late fifties, and the newer tracts reach right up to the Santa Susana Mountains. Its green space has been enhanced by golf courses and parks in a manner very uncharacteristic of the normal tendencies in Southern California. To be sure, some of these spaces are cemeteries.

Most of the housing is conventional middle-middle-class stuff, a better-than-average tract being reached by driving north on Balboa Boulevard to Westbury Drive and then west to Jimeno Avenue. Jimeno Avenue, Lisette Street, Nanette Street, and Darla Avenue were developed by Joseph Eichler. The housing was designed by Jones and Emmons (1963-64) around courtyards.

Mission Hills has as its great claim to fame a **Victorian Queen Anne house** (1887) moved there from Pacoima. It was designed by Joseph Cather Newsom as one of a group of spec houses. The house, moved to 17410 Meyerling Street (between Shoshone and Andasol Avenues), has a two-story, side-hall plan and exhibits the usual array of Newsom's ornament in sawed and turned wood.

The name *Van Nuys* is the only thing that memorializes the great wheat rancher. The area has not seen wheat for years. It is dignified by having a branch of the Los Angeles City Hall, around which some urban renewal is going on. Otherwise, there is not much to distinguish it from its neighbors, Panorama City and Sepulveda, to the north. Thus, if you get off the freeway here, you might as well see them all.

1. Post Office, ca. 1926
14540 Sylvan Street

Modest Spanish Colonial Revival, but worth protecting against urban renewal. Next door at 14550 is one of those charming Moderne **gas stations** (Richfield) of the thirties and next to it is a small, dumpy Classical Revival **office building**. An imaginative urban designer could give great interest to this group.

2. Valley Municipal Building, 1932
Peter K. Schabarum
14410 Sylvan Street

An eight-story Art Deco/(zigzag) Moderne office building which certainly stands out in this area of the Valley. According to rumor, it may not be with us much longer.

3. U.S. General Services Administration, 1974
Lyman Kipp

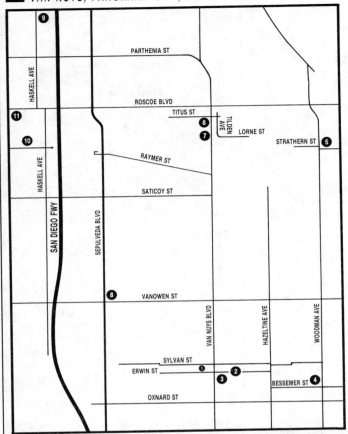

Southeast corner of Van Nuys Boulevard and Erwin Street

This long, sleek, four-story example of modern classicism in white brick and concrete is ultra-sophisticated for the Valley. In case there is a misunderstanding of the relationship between architecture and art, the building's cornerstone bears the following: "Federal Art in Architecture Program."

4. House, 1935
Just behind apartments at northwest corner of Woodman Avenue and Bessemer Street

At least the extremely picturesque Spanish Colonial Revival house was preserved when the front yard was taken over by progress. Incidentally, George Brent once lived here—before progress.

3. U.S. General Services Administration

5. The Taos West Apartments, 1972
7924 Woodman Avenue

Pueblo Revival that no resident of Taos would recognize as home, but which gets some points for its outrageous parody of folk architecture.

6. Great Western Savings Bank, ca. 1970
Northwest corner of Van Nuys Boulevard and Titus Street, Panorama City

We admire bankers who have the nerve to go so deeply into the architecture of fantasy. This is not great architecture, but it certainly pokes convention in the nose.

7. Carnation Research Building, 1952-3
8015 Van Nuys Boulevard at Lorne Street

An understated, post-World War II Streamline Moderne building, if such is possible.

8. Valley Presbyterian Hospital, 1983-84
Thomas, Bobrow, and Associates
Northeast corner of Sepulveda Boulevard and Vanowen Street

The non-descript fifties buildings have been included in a new site plan of Bobrow and Thomas. The first phase of their plan has provided a new entrance at the center of the complex which joins two of the older buildings together. Also, new parking facilities have been added. The entrance and the other new additions express a reserved, sophisticated version of the late Modern mode, realized in exposed concrete and glass.

9. Greer House, 1940
Lloyd Wright
9200 Haskell Avenue

Some touches of Streamline Moderne (portholes) adorn this building, now easily accessible since it has been incorporated with the church next door.

10. Ninety-fourth Aero Squadron Headquarters Restaurant, 1973
Lynne, Paxton, Paxton, and Cole
16320 Raymer Street

French Provincial with a vengeance, this large farmhouse at the Van Nuys Airport even has bales of hay apparently ready to be pulled into the loft. The only thing that is missing is the pile of manure that would give this marvelous creation the sense of complete authenticity.

10. Ninety-fourth Aero Squadron Headquarters Restaurant

11. The Torrington Manufacturing Company, 1953
Marcel Breuer (Craig Ellwood, supervising architect)
16300 Roscoe Boulevard

Incredibly close (a few blocks) to the previous entry, this long, two-story monument to Bauhaus modularism stands (perhaps as it should considering its attack on history) in a visual wasteland. In spite of its age, it looks just fine — one of the things that should slow you up on your way to Bakersfield.

Mission San Fernando Rey De España

Convento, 1810-22

Iglesia, 1974 (based on church of 1804-06)
15151 San Fernando Mission Boulevard, just east of Sepulveda Boulevard and the Golden State Freeway. (A map of the Mission complex is given to you when you buy your ticket to the grounds.)

The Mission was founded by Padre Fermin Lasuen in 1797. Nothing architectural remains from this period except the ruins of the dam that provided a water supply for the acres of wheat and corn. The church looks and is new. The earthquake of 1971 shook the old building so badly that it had to be demolished. The 1974 building, while in concrete, is faithful to the former one, but it must be noted that the previous church was in its turn a rather imaginative reconstruction (1935) by M. R. Harrington of the original. With few hints as to the details of the first building, Harrington set out to investigate the decoration of other missions and imitated what he found in order to give romantic appeal to the new church, an appeal which the good fathers have attempted to render in the 1974 building.

The **Convento,** the first thing that you see when you approach the entrance, is old. It used to *look* old until the 1974 restoration which spread from the church to the outbuildings. Stucco was swished over everthing (especially exposed adobe bricks), and painted so that the Mission complex *in toto* looks brand new. The interior, whose simplicity was earlier broken only by the Baroque headings of its windows, has now been enhanced by several gilt triumphal arches (source?) donated by some well-intentioned but misguided friend.

The **cemetery,** containing the graves of Indian converts and early white settlers, is just north of the church. Across the street from the Convento is a lovely park which, with its fountain, gardens, and statue of Junípero Serra, almost makes you forget the follies of contemporary restoration projects.

By jogging south on Columbus just west of the mission, you will encounter, amidst a trailer court and other skulch, the **Andres Pico Adobe.** Its address is 10940 Sepulveda, well marked. The house was the home of the Mexican who in 1845 leased the entire San Fernando Valley and began its development. In 1873, after the American occupation, Pico decided to remodel the adobe (begun in 1834) in American style, adding Yankee sash, a second story, and other fashionable details. The house has been remodelled and enlarged many times, particularly by Dr. M. R. Harrington in the 1930s when the Spanish Colonial porch was added. It is, in the mess of the Valley, an oasis of civilization.

Andres Pico Adobe

San Fernando

Some attempts to invent a Spanish Colonial past have been made in the new buildings by the use of stucco walls and tile roofs, but the effect is not as successful as the similar effort at Santa Barbara. An exception is **Saint Ferdinand's Roman Catholic Church** (1949) just across Maclay Avenue from the Lopez Adobe. The church takes its sculptural forms from the simple mission churches, even going so far away as Taos, New Mexico, for its inspiration.

This town is the oldest in the Valley. It was settled northeast of the Mission which is, by a fluke of politicking, in Los Angeles and not in separately incorporated San Fernando. Its short boom began in 1874 when the Southern Pacific Railroad, coming up from the south, reached it. The one remaining shred of this Victorian period is the **Gerónimo López Adobe** (1878) at the northwest corner of Pico Street and Maclay Avenue. It is two-story Monterey style with some pretty Queen Anne sawed gingerbread across the gallery. Otherwise all signs of the old town have disappeared, except for the railroad.

Saint Ferdinand's Roman Catholic Church

Gerónimo López Adobe

A typical **stone house** of the twenties, so evocative of the picturesque image of the Valley, appears on the northeast side of Laurel Canyon Boulevard near Brand Boulevard. The **Municipal Light, Water, and Power Building** (ca. 1937)

Stone House

at 313 S. Brand Boulevard near the corner of Pico Street is a semi-precious gem of the Streamline Moderne. But don't go out of your way to see the oldest town in the Valley.

Municipal Light, Water, and Power Building

Newhall, Saugus, Valencia

In your eagerness either to enter or to leave Los Angeles you may forget that a good deal of history, mainly transportation and engineering, took place in this area. Beside you on the Golden State Freeway is **The Cascade** that in 1913 marked the termination of William Mulholland's Los Angeles Aqueduct that brought water from the Owens River Valley so that Los Angelenos would never be thirsty—or so it seemed at the time. Near this place is an off-ramp marked *The Old Road* meaning the famous *Ridge Route* that was opened in 1915 and in spite of its curves cut off many miles between Los Angeles and San Francisco. Much of the concrete is still there, but the roadhouses and gas stations are all gone.

By turning northeast on the Antelope Valley Freeway you will soon come to the **Placerita Canyon State Park and Nature Study Center.** Here you can see the "Oak of the Golden Dream" under which Francisco Lopez discovered in 1842 the first gold to be found in California in commercial quantities. Architecturally the award-winning **Nature Center** (1973), a collection of low, hipped-roof buildings designed by Richard L. Dorman and Associates, is more rewarding.

Turn back (west) on the Sierra Highway, then north on San Fernando Road. In a few hundred yards you will see a State Landmark sign directing you to the first commercial **oil refinery** (1876) in California, a plausibly restored group

William S. Hart Ranch House

of buildings in a strangely picturesque setting. Continue north on San Fernando Road to the **William S. Hart Park,** once the estate of the famous cowboy movie star. The original ranch house (ca. 1910) is a log cabin, but by climbing the hill you will come upon the mansion (Arthur Kelley, 1925), which will delight followers of the Spanish Colonial Revival.

Back to San Fernando Road and north again at Drayton Street you will come to the bracketed **Southern Pacific Railroad Station** (ca. 1900) which should remind you that in 1876 about ten miles east of this place the last section of track was completed on the railroad link between Los Angeles and San Francisco, thus joining with the transcontinental railroad to bring thousands of people to Southern California, eventually transforming Los Angeles from a sleepy village into questionable urbanity.

Heading north again on San Fernando Road, you will almost immediately see Magic Mountain Parkway. Turn left on it and then left again on Valencia Boulevard and then again on Newhall Avenue, which becomes McBean Parkway. To the south of this road is the community of **Valencia** which you may wish to visit because it was planned (1966) by Thomas L. Sutton, Jr. and Victor Gruen Associates as a New Town (like Westlake Village and Irvine). It will be, according to the descriptive literature, "a semi-contained urban element" with its own industry as well as retail centers and housing. The promoters expect a town of 150,000 people by the year 2020. The housing (designed by Barry Berkus, Maxwell Starkman and Associates, Edward C. Malon, and others) ranges from garden apartments to single-family dwellings and, in spite of its essential dullness, works out better than most project housing because of excellent planning and landscaping. Parks, greenbelts, and bike paths were provided.

Near the intersection of the McBean Parkway with the Golden State Freeway, you will see the entrance to the **California Institute of the Arts** whose main buildings were designed by Ladd and Kelsey (1969-70) in brown slumpstone and concrete. One would expect better architecture considering the competence of the architects and the wherewithal of the Walt Disney estate that is behind it financially, but the architecture is only a cut above that of the tract housing nearby.

After looking around Valencia, cross under the Golden State Freeway (Highway 5) to Magic Mountain Parkway. Go to the end (west) and you will arrive at the **Magic Mountain Amusement Park** (now **Six Flags Magic Mountain**) designed in 1970 by Thomas L. Sutton for the Newhall Land and Farming Company, the developer of Valencia. After establishing clearly where you have parked you car in relation to the "auto gate," go on to the ticket counter and entrance. Until 1982 you entered through the gates of a French chateau and moved ahead into a formal garden with a fountain and geometrical planting. Visually this arrangement helped to bring a sense of order before you plunged into the exuberance of the park. Unfortunately this has all been changed. A new entrance designed in serious High Modern-High Tech provides no joy or tone of fantasy.

The same seriousness pervades the High Tech image of the **Texas Instruments Computer Discovery Center** (1982). Notwithstanding these recent movements away from the original lightheartedness of Magic Mountain, its glory remains its landscaping designed by Emmet Wemple and Associates who also designed the old French forecourt. The architecture runs the full range from the Oriental (perhaps it is Japanese, but who can be sure?) to German, Swiss, and English Medieval to American Colonial and Victorian. And California's own tradition of the Mission Revival can be seen in the forecourt of the "Revolution." The Monterey style is featured in the Holiday Bazaar. Magic Mountain is far more informal and easygoing than the highly organized environment of Disneyland, its chief rival to the south.

Palmdale, Lancaster

This country is hardly an architectural oasis. Lancaster's **Western Hotel** (1874), a plain, two-story building with columned porch at 557 W. Lancaster Boulevard, is a remnant of pioneer days. Beyond Palmdale, about fifteen miles along Avenue O, you will come to Avenue 170 East. Go north on it and then west on Avenue M. Almost immediately you will come upon the **Antelope Valley Indian Musuem** (1928), a simple wooden building intended by its creator, H. Arden Edwards, to embody elements of Indian design, but tending to look more like a Swiss chalet than any example we know of Native American architecture. The collection of Indian artifacts, particularly Southwestern rugs, is excellent. The Kachina Hall will attract the Craftsman enthusiast. Open only on weekends and Monday holidays.

La Crescenta Valley

I f you have visited Newhall, Valencia, and Magic Mountain and wish to return to Los Angeles by a different route, exit from the Golden State Freeway onto the Foothill Freeway (Pasadena signs!). You thus skirt the eastern side of San Fernando and eventually, after some beautiful, lonely, and almost desert landscape, enter Sunland, from which you can make an amusing diversion south on Sunland Boulevard to Sun Valley.

Actually, Sun Valley is closer to the Golden State Freeway so you can make your choice between the Golden State Freeway and the Foothill Freeway. If you choose the former, exit at Sunland Boulevard and go north to the city of Sunland. Thereafter, you should probably stay on Foothill Boulevard visiting the towns as we have listed them. You will come out at Pasadena, as you will if you take the Foothill Freeway.

A general map of the area will make all this clear and also, we believe, make you sympathize with our problems of establishing a rational plan for visiting the Los Angeles area.

If you want to get the feel of working class Southern California in the 1920s and 1930s, you cannot get it anymore in Hollywood. The epicenter of "Old Wide-open Southern California" is in the Sunland-Tujunga area. It is hot, dusty, occasionally smog-ridden, but with exceptions which you must learn to cancel out (especially along Foothill Boulevard) here are almost the last of the freewheeling communities with close ties to nature, golden hills, and monuments to dreams. For instance, the **Villa Rotunda** (ca. 1955) at 8618 La Tuna Canyon Road. What is it? Why is it round?

The delight of the area is the quantity of its boulder ("cobblestone" out here) architecture. The **house** (ca. 1922) at 8642 Sunland Boulevard near Olinda Street is a good introduction. But the mecca for boulder enthusiasts is the old town of Roscoe (now Stonehurst). Here forty or so stone bungalows were built, according to the story, for $100 apiece, some say by Indian labor. You can see that we are hedging on facts. There is disagreement about them as there is about the English colony that is supposed to have lived here and the movie stars that are supposed to have vacationed in Roscoe with the idea of "roughing it." Stick to what you see along Stonehurst Avenue and Sheldon, Thelma, Allegheny, and Wicks streets.

Going east along Sunland and Foothill boulevards you will encounter more delights, though, we are sorry to say, a great many have disappeared in recent years. But venture into the side streets. Try going north on Orovista Avenue to Hillrose Circle. The whole area is delightful, but it is simply preparing you for Tujunga.

Tujunga

Parts of the Tejunga and La Cañada ranchos were subdivided in the boom of the 1880s, and it was thought that the picturesque acreage which now comprises Sunland and Tujunga (new spelling) would take off economically. Soon, however, most of the town plots were "sold for taxes." Another try at building came in 1907 when M. V. Hartranft, whose family had speculated in land in other parts of Los Angeles County, attracted a little group of Socialists with his slogan, "A Little Land and a Lot of Living," thus settling "La Ciudad de los Terrenitos" or the "Little Landers." Their boulder **Clubhouse,** whose cornerstone was laid on April 12, 1913, is still at 10116 Commerce Avenue and has recently been restored. The **boulder houses,** which until the 1971 earthquake made the town very picturesque, dated from the twenties. Some remain, along with their wonderful boulder retaining walls. Several of them are spectacular. We have tried to list the best, but we have undoubtedly missed some. The town is best seen by walking along Commerce, Samoa, Pinewood, and Fairgrove avenues. It is easily as funky as Venice West. But see it soon. Slummy apartment houses are rapidly taking the place of stone follies. The end of camp ambience is near.

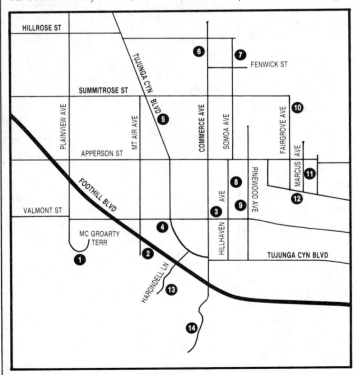

3. *Bolton Hall (now Tujunga City Hall)*

1. McGroarty House, 1923
Arthur B. Benton
7570 McGroarty Terrace, south of Foothill Boulevard at end of Plainview Avenue

The architecture is not much, even with the leaded art glass windows given to John Steven McGroarty, once Poet Laureate of California, by Frank Miller, the host of the Mission Inn at Riverside where McGroarty wrote his once famous *Mission Play* (the inspiration, incidentally, for the building of the Mission Playhouse in San Gabriel). This house took the place of an earlier house which burned. The original furniture that survived is as delightfully bombastic as the play.

2. Harris House, ca. 1910
George Harris
7320 Foothill Boulevard, east of Mount Air Avenue

Perched just below street level, this bungalow is remarkable for still existing on a street which has gone honky-tonk commercial. Harris came west as a representative of an eastern publishing house. He doffed his Prince Albert, donned corduroy vest and knickers and began making curious garden furniture in what must be called the "Rustic Baroque" style. A suggestion of this is the concrete railing along the walk (bridge) to his house. His most important piece of architecture is the next entry.

3. Bolton Hall (now known as Tujunga City Hall), 1913
George Harris
10116 Commerce Avenue

If you think that the exterior of this boulder, Mission style-influenced building is extraordinary, you should see the wood beamed interior! It was originally the clubhouse for the "Little Landers" and was called Bolton Hall for the New York Socialist of the same name.

4. "Blarney Castle", ca. 1925
10217 Tujunga Canyon Road, at southwest corner of Valmont Street

A stucco two-story house with a round tower that now guards the parking lot of a large shopping center.

5. House, ca. 1925
10428 Tujunga Canyon Boulevard, south off Summitrose Street

A long, low, boulder house enhanced by new boulder walls in the front.

6. Weatherwolde Castle, 1928
Dumas
10633 Commerce Avenue, near southwest corner of Hillrose Street

A stucco suggestion of Normandy.

7. Reavis House, 1923
10620 Samoa Avenue, north off Fenwick Street

A boulder gem built for a blind man who was attracted to Tujunga by McGroarty's *Mission Play.*

8. House, ca. 1925
10142 Samoa Avenue

A fine boulder house in the Craftsman tradition.

9. Tujunga American Legion Hall, ca. 1928
10039 Pinewood Avenue

Egyptoid and Art Deco Moderne combined. A real surprise in bungalowland.

10. House, ca. 1925
10420 Fairgrove Avenue

A very tidy Craftsman-boulder structure.

11. House, ca. 1925
10226 Marcus Avenue

This towered boulder house with its matching garage is really delightful; apparently it was originally a schoolhouse.

12. House, ca. 1915
6915 Day Street

Not one of the best boulders (upper clapboard story added) but interesting because it is supposed to have been a Wells Fargo station. Hard to believe, but it's part of local lore.

13. Rock of Ages House, ca. 1925
9920 Hirondelle Lane

Self-explanatory; very nicely designed.

14. Bungalow, ca. 1920
9725 Hillhaven Avenue

A good Craftsman house beautifully sited on a hillside.

La Crescenta

This community, settled in the 1880s, is still unincorporated. It continues the commercial strip along Foothill Boulevard with fine residential areas on each side. Try **Briggs Avenue** and the streets east of it. **Orange Cove Avenue** with its shingle and boulder Craftsman architecture (numbers 2301, 2321, and 2346) is good.

La Crescenta also has an extremely picturesque boulder church—**Saint Luke's of the Mountains** (1924; S. Seymour Thomas)—at the northeast corner of Foothill Boulevard and Rosemont Avenue.

Saint Luke's of the Mountains

La Cañada-Flintridge

1. House, ca. 1927
2143 Montrose Avenue at Rincon Avenue

The Craftsman house is all right but the tile is better.

2. Egyptian Gardens, ca. 1935
2254 Foothill Boulevard near Ocean View Boulevard

Two sphinxes guard the gate.

3. Wallace House ("El Nido"), 1911
Arthur B. Benton
End of Castle Knoll Road

A vaguely Medieval Venetian folly built as a summer home for a lieutenant governor. It is known locally as the "Pink Castle."

4. Lewin House, 1962
Gregory Ain
15310 Jessen Drive

Very simple International Style Modern, barely visible from the street.

F lintridge and La Cañada, both subdivided in 1920, have recently joined and become incorporated as a hyphenate. Both parts are very upper-middle-class. Montrose to the south is a step lower on the social ladder.

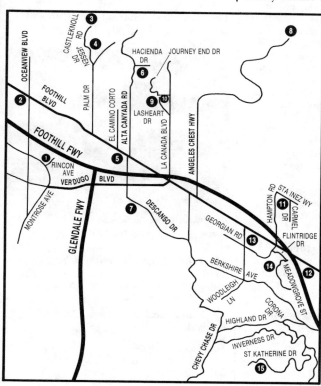

5. Lutheran Church in the Foothills, ca. 1965
Foothill Boulevard on southeast corner of El Camino Corto

It is the campanile rather than the church that is visually striking. The bland shaft is topped by a huge sculpture of Christ preaching.

6. House, ca. 1927
Southeast corner of Alta Canyada Boulevard and Hacienda Drive

This splendid Spanish Colonial Revival house has the quality of a John Byers design, though it is not by him. There is a splendid Byers house, the **Robbins House,** at 717 Hillcrest Avenue (1931), but it is very difficult to see from the road. Note the fine garden. In fact, almost all of Alta Canyada is beautifully landscaped.

7. Descanso Gardens, 1937, 1941-later
1418 Descanso Drive

In 1937, E. Manchester Boddy, editor of the old *Los Angeles Daily News,* bought the 165 acres on which the gardens are now situated and began setting out camelias in a forest of live oaks. When in 1941 Japanese-American nurserymen and their families were sent to relocation camps, Boddy was able to acquire thousands of camelias and azaleas. The County bought the gardens in 1953, and they are now a branch of the County Arboretum. In 1966 the Descanso Guild commissioned Whitney Smith and Wayne Williams to design a Japanese-inspired teahouse. Here you may sip tea while you take in the natural beauty and listen to the mockingbirds sing their hearts out. Open year round during daylight hours.

8. Mount Wilson Observatory, 1913
Daniel H. Burnham and Company
Mount Wilson Road off Angeles Crest Highway

One of the last buildings designed by Burnham, completed after his death.

9. House, 1945-48
J. R. Davidson
4756 Lasheart Drive

The Moderne lamps on the gate posts are about all that you can see.

10. Gainsburg House, 1946
Lloyd Wright
1210 Journeys' End Drive

A variation on the Usonian houses, but more theatrical than his father's work.

11. Cottage, ca. 1925
Southwest corner of Santa Inez Way and Carmel Road

A rustic hunting lodge gone bungalow. Notice the magnificent planting. In fact, the streets in this area seem to have been planted with a variety of trees, all of which have flourished. The houses, mostly small, have a great deal of charm.

12. Flintridge Country Club (now **Saint Francis High School**), 1921
Myron Hunt and H. C. Chambers
Just east of off-ramp of Foothill Freeway at intersection with Daleridge Road

The hacienda section of the Club still exists with its long portal.

12. *Flintridge Country Club (now Saint Francis High School)*

13. La Cañada Thursday Club, ca. 1930
Henry Newton and Robert Murray
4440 Woodleigh Lane

Beautifully scaled Spanish Colonial Revival.

14. House, 1928
Myron Hunt and H. C. Chambers
535 Meadow Grove Street

Georgian Revival and livelier than most of Hunt's work. Important houses by Hunt, Paul Williams, Wallace Neff, and the rest of the Pasadena crowd are in this section of town but, as in Bel Air, they have been landscaped out of sight.

13. La Cañada Thursday Club

15. The Flintridge Biltmore (now **Flintridge Sacred Heart High School**), 1927
Myron Hunt and H. C. Chambers
Saint Katherine Drive (take Corona Drive off Highland Drive and follow signs)

More impressive from the valley of the Arroyo Seco than up close, this is an ample but dry building in Hunt's usual Spanish Colonial manner. The Biltmore saw a few good years. Then the Great Crash and the building's remoteness from anything did it in, but not before the management had commissioned two huge pictures (1929) for the lobby by George Fisher and Desmund Rushton. One is rather strange (considering the context): a group of Plains Indians on horseback. The other depicts a highly diverse procession of people in their national costumes moving toward the then-new Los Angeles City Hall.

15. Flintridge Biltmore (now Flintridge Sacred Heart High School)

A Note on Route 66

The Main Street of America" of old still plies its way east along Colorado, Boulevard through Pasadena and Arcadia connecting with Huntington Drive, which becomes Route 66 until Huntington suddenly becomes Foothill Boulevard just west of Azusa, when it then joins Alosta Avenue. When Alosta runs into the City of San Dimas, it becomes Foothill Boulevard again and with that name continues to Claremont and on through Cucamonga, beyond the L.A. County line. For many years the "camp" ambience of roadhouses, gas stations, and motels seemed to have passed, but the nearby Foothill Freeway that should have been the final blow to America's Main Street has ironically brought Route 66 back, not as a highway but as an access road. Almost every single building dating from as far back as the twenties has been spruced up and in some cases recycled. In fact it is fun to try to pick out the old places from the cheap, modern horror that surrounds them.

Significantly, it is where the Foothill Freeway now stops at San Dimas that you easily begin to pick up the forlorn monuments to the early days of transcontinental driving. If the freeway is completed as proposed it will veer north and leave the old roadside civilization along Foothill decaying as it is at present.

Pasadena

It is said that Pasadena means "Crown of the Valley" in the language of the Chippewas, an Indian tribe that never set foot in the area. The land on which the city was built was first occupied by Gabrielino Indians and then by the Spanish and the Mexicans who built several adobes. (One, **Adobe Flores,** still exists in South Pasadena.) The history of Yankee settlement really began in 1874 when the San Gabriel Orange Grove Association acquired most of the land of the old Rancho San Pasqual east of the Arroyo Seco to the present Fair Oaks Avenue and sold it to prospective citrus growers from Indiana.

The Indiana Colony, as it was called, flourished in the gently rolling land dotted with clumps of oaks and sycamores and later orange and olive groves. But the surge of growth came in the eighties and nineties when the Southern Pacific and Santa Fe railroads entered the town, and, with the aid of local boosters, the farming community turned into a fashionable winter resort with large hotels on the scale of those at Atlantic City, Miami, and the White Mountains of New Hampshire. The grandest hotel was the Raymond, on a small hill just inside the South Pasadena boundary. But the Green Hotel near the Santa Fe station, whose location was not as picturesque, was so popular that it had to be enlarged three times, the second time to a site on the other side of the street

and connected to the older building by a picturesque "Bridge of Sighs." The Maryland, the Wentworth (now Huntington), and the Vista del Arroyo were other hotels patronized into the twenties and beyond. (The Huntington is still a very popular Pasadena institution.)

The resort atmosphere was of great significance for Pasadena's architectural history. It drew conservative and often very rich emigrants, some of whom eventually decided to become permanent residents of a city that could provide plenty of sun and a cog-railroad up past the Echo Mountain House to Mount Lowe. A local legend has it that in 1900 there were fifteen millionaires on Orange Grove Avenue (now Boulevard). Naturally these people desired mansions in the latest eastern styles and especially those that easterners thought most suitable for the West. Architects such as Harry Ridgeway, A. B. Parkes, and Frederick L. Roehrig made sure that supply kept up with demand. Lawrence Test, an architect who grew up in this environment of building, answered when he was asked how he happened to go into architecture: "Why, there was never any other thought in my mind about my profession. With so much building going on, how could I think of anything else but architecture?" And he added slyly, "I wonder what would have become of me if I had been raised in Glendale or Monrovia!"

From the beginning Pasadenans were partisans of cultural uplift. The Orange Grove crowd was drawn to the Valley Hunt Club, from which they set out to catch more coyotes than foxes. They founded that excessively famous Pasadena institution, the Tournament of Roses, whose parade once ended with a chariot race *a la Ben Hur* rather than the present football game. Another group, highly educated and usually residents of the area around the picturesque Arroyo Seco, created the Coleman Chamber Music Association (1904) and the Pasadena Playhouse Association (1917), two pillars of Pasadena culture — the former still alive and well, the latter struggling to be reborn.

The abundance of money meant that Pasadenans would have expensive homes. What is just as interesting is that on Orange Grove these people would engage in an elaborate Victorian Baroque street planning with traffic circles at major intersections and a parkway in the center in the shape of two giant lozenges linked together. Apparently part of this 1874 plan was carried out. The pattern east of Orange Grove was the usual grid with the business center at Fair Oaks Avenue and Colorado Boulevard. By the nineties the commercial district was already moving east along Colorado with an array of business blocks designed in Victorian styles whose boldness should shame the fainthearted efforts of modern architects. In the twenties Colorado Boulevard was widened and all of these buildings lost their fanciful facades. Most were then refaced with Art Deco and Spanish fronts, so that Colorado as far as Euclid Avenue, in spite of recent encroachments, still has a twenties air out front and Victorian red brick in the alleys to the rear.

In the old residential districts many Queen Anne cottages remain. The grand Victorians on Orange Grove have been completely eliminated and replaced by garden apartments, now mainly condominiums. Elsewhere a few pretentious gingerbreads have stood up against change. But, in spite of the fact that Barney Williams' **"Hillmont"** has one of the finest ensembles of nineteenth-century interiors in America, Pasadena is not strong in Victoriana. Its great treasury of building (and great it is!) comes from the period 1900 to 1940, the first years dominated by the woodsy Arts and Crafts aesthetic, so much appreciated by Gustav Stickley in his *Craftsman* magazine (1901-1916), and the later years devoted to the period revivals. The Arts and Crafts or Craftsman style, a kind of amalgam of Swiss Chalet, Tudor, and Oriental forms, can best be savored on the eastern side of the Arroyo Seco. There, just north of the Ventura Freeway, the greatest concentration of work by the now-famous architects Charles and Henry Greene still stands. South of the freeway important houses by less familiar names such as Louis B. Easton, Arthur and Alfred Heineman, G. Lawrence Stimson, and

Jeffrey, Van Trees, and Millar, provide the finest collection of Craftsman architecture outside Berkeley.

Pasadena's architectural heritage of the twenties and thirties, on the other hand, parallels the accomplishments of Santa Barbara. In fact, the two cities often used the same architects. Besides Bertram G. Goodhue and George Washington Smith, and J. Wilmer Hersey (who worked in both places), Pasadena residents employed Roland E. Coate, Reginald D. Johnson, Garrett Van Pelt, Gordon B. Kaufmann, and Wallace Neff—the last coming closest to Smith in originality and assurance within the forms of the Spanish Colonial Revival. Their work is most magnificent on the western edge of the Arroyo Seco and best viewed from Arroyo Boulevard on the eastern side. Smaller but still ambitious Period Revival architecture is more easily seen in the Oak Knoll district. Lombardy Road is particularly rich.

As in most of Los Angeles County, the greatest amount of fine architecture is domestic, but Pasadena is ahead of most of her neighbors in public architecture. The **Civic Center** is one of the few successes of the "City Beautiful" movement. The 1923 general plan was designed by the Chicago firm of Bennett, Parsons, Frost, and Thomas. The same year a competition was announced for the design of the main buildings. The winners were Myron Hunt for the Library, Edwin Bergstrom of the firm of Bennett and Haskell for the Auditorium, and Bakewell and Brown (San Francisco) for the City Hall whose proposed facade was an incredible enlargement of the *campanario* of the San Gabriel Mission. This design was eventually discarded in favor of the present, more respectable triumphal arch and dome. The imagery of all three of these buildings was Classical Mediterranean.

The result of this planning is magnificent. The major axis running along Holly Street toward City Hall begins with the **YMCA** designed by the important Pasadena firm of Marston and Maybury and the **YWCA** by Julia Morgan. Neither is among these architects' best buildings, but both illustrate Pasadena's historic mission to wed ethics and aesthetics. Bakewell and Brown's **City Hall** is a wonderful stage set, or better, a wedding cake, less elaborate than the same firm's San Francisco City Hall, but much more entertaining. In front of it runs Garfield Street, the minor axis of the Beaux Arts plan. At its north end is Hunt and Chamber's **Public Library.** The south end of the axis was once closed by Bergstrom's **Civic Auditorium** on Green Street. Now up front on Colorado is the stupid arch designed by Kober Associates as a supposed link between the two extremities of the **Plaza Pasadena.** Other horrors have intruded, such as the vertically striped court building near the library, but the grand plan is still evident and effective especially since it stands aside from Colorado Boulevard, the main commercial artery, and thus does not interfere with traffic and business. It is in every sense a triumph of California's own version of Beaux Arts ideas.

The skyline of the city should be viewed from the steps of the **Norton Simon Museum** or even better from the campus of **Ambassador College** to the south. Besides the dome of City Hall, church spires appear at just the right places. Unfortunately, the cityscape is marred by the tasteless, out-of-scale **Parsons Tower** and outbuildings which cannot be landscaped out of sight. It is sad to say that even greater blemishes are being planned.

Like most California cities, Pasadena has not invested in many parks. Its high moral tone has never interfered with real estate values. Partial compensation for the paucity of open spaces is the very large park in the valley of the Arroyo Seco that runs in a southerly direction through the western part of the city. When visiting the site in 1911 Teddy Roosevelt is supposed to have said, "The Arroyo would make one of the greatest parks in the world." It is not quite that, but it is Pasadena's greatest natural treasure besides its view of the mountains, often clouded with smog. The northern part of the Arroyo is broad and includes a golf course and an exhibition area as well as the famous **Rose Bowl,** which is used more often for flea markets than for athletic endeavors. At a narrowing of the gorge is a new freeway bridge modelled as closely as possible on the lines of the old **Colorado Street Bridge** (1912-13) alongside it. The huge concrete arches of both bridges are spectacular, especially when seen from Arroyo Boulevard which cuts through them. Unfortunately the stream bed has been paved with a concrete channel, but the palisades on both sides are covered with trees and are very picturesque.

Nature and architects were, until the fifties, very good to Pasadena. Modern architecture has not fared so well. Certainly the city continues the tradition of rearing and attracting excellent architects, but their work tends to be elsewhere. The business district is full of new buildings, mostly mediocre and designed by outsiders. Single-family dwellings of distinction are now rarely built and, needless to say, the quality of most apartment houses and condominiums is undistinguished. Naturally there are exceptions to these observations, and we have tried to include them.

Upper Arroyo Seco

This area north of the Ventura Freeway is one of the richest architectural districts in the West. The Linda Vista Avenue (western) side is hilly, exclusive, and well guarded. Some beautiful architecture is there, but it can best be viewed in the pages of the sumptuous *Architectural Digest* of the twenties and thirties. The east side is even richer in art if not in banknotes. It contains two monuments of American architecture—the **Millard House ("La Miniatura")** by Frank Lloyd Wright, and the **Gamble House** by the Pasadena architects Charles and Henry Greene. In fact, one whole street, Arroyo Terrace, was designed by the Greenes and another, Grand Avenue, has works by them, by Myron Hunt, and by other architects of equal talent.

The entire Arroyo Seco should be declared a national monument. The architecture is as important as that of Charleston, South Carolina, and the scenery is much better.

1. Matthews House, 1966
Mortimer Matthews (Pulliam, Matthews, and Associates)
1435 Lindaridge Road

The arresting roofline of this house can best be seen from the curve below it.

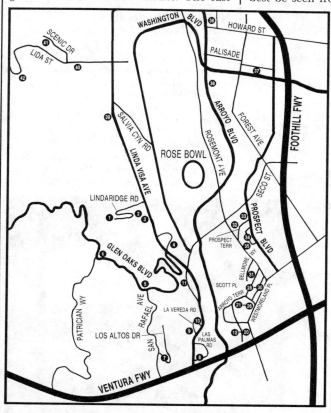

2. Ralphs House, 1950
Ain, Johnson, and Day
1350 Lindaridge Road

One of Ain's largest houses, it has been well maintained over the years.

3. Schonbach House, 1946
Leland Evison
701 Linda Vista Avenue

A modular post and beam system in which the frames are made of asbestos; concrete panels exposed.

4. House, 1946
Henry Eggers
1043 Pine Oak Lane

A brick house of extreme simplicity.

5. Ladd Studio, 1950
Thornton Ladd
1085 Glen Oaks Boulevard

You catch a glimpse of this International Style Modern building from the street below. Sliding panels make it possible to close off the interior spaces within the rectangular grid.

6. Ladd House, 1956
Thornton Ladd
1280 Glen Oaks Boulevard, at Patrician Way

Perched just below the crest of a hill, this low-lying, modular structure is as handsome as when it was built.

7. Wilbur House, 1928
Gordon B. Kaufmann
25 Los Altos Drive

This Mediterranean style house peers through trees at the Annandale Golf Club. It is on a private road but can be seen from San Rafael Avenue.

8. Fowler House, 1927
Edward W. Fowler
825 Las Palmas Road

Apparently Fowler got his ideas from magazine illustrations. This Andalusian house, the **Basque house** around the corner on El Circulo Drive and the **Majorcan house** at 95 El Circulo were all designed by him and certainly seem to have come out of a picture book, all the more incredible since now the enormous arches of the freeway bridge tower over this quaint assemblage.

9. Smith House, 1929
David A. Ogilvie
181 La Vereda Road

A Tudor villa on a pleasant street.

10. Kubly House, 1964
Craig Ellwood and Associates
215 La Vereda Road

Ellwood in his Miesian phase. This is one of his most elegantly detailed houses, gaining strength of character from its exposed timber framing.

11. Two Houses, ca. 1924
Train and Williams
373 and 405 Mira Vista Terrace

Both are Bavarian hunting lodges, especially significant because they were designed by the only architectural firm

5. Ladd Studio

to be directly affiliated with the Arroyo Guild of Fellow Craftsmen.

12. Halsted House, 1905
Charles and Henry Greene
90 N. Grand Avenue

The Greenes were just finding their way here, but this is a fine Craftsman house in spite of frequent alterations during the teens and twenties.

13. Park House, 1904
130 N. Grand Avenue

An awkward but fascinating example of turn-of-the-century Colonial Federal Revival.

14. Newcomb House, 1910, 1922
141 N. Grand Avenue

A Tudor mansion complete with necessary gatehouse and servants' quarters. Just around the corner on an extension of Arroyo Terrace is "200-236," a group of condominiums designed (1980) by Buff and Hensman. We mention them because they are good examples of the currently fashionable Neo-Craftsman mode.

15. Myron Hunt House, 1905
Myron Hunt
200 N. Grand Avenue

Simplified Doric columns mark the entrance of this otherwise Craftsman house.

16. House, ca. 1887
203 N. Grand Avenue

A Queen Anne pearl that was moved from the site (across the street) of the present Culbertson House. This must have been one of the first houses in this area. Notice the original carriage house in the rear.

17. Van Rossem House, 1904
Charles and Henry Greene
210 N. Grand Avenue

Josephine Van Rossem, a real estate speculator, built this brown, barn-like Craftsman house just after having built another Greene and Greene around the corner on Arroyo Terrace.

18. Speirs House, 1904
Attributed to Hunt and Grey
230 N. Grand Avenue

A good, early example of the Dutch Colonial Revival.

19. Duncan-Irwin House, 1900, 1906
Charles and Henry Greene
240 N. Grand Avenue

One of the largest and finest houses by Greene and Greene, this house began its history as a single-story bungalow which was incorporated in the Irwins' 1906 extension that we see today. The composition of the facade is more beautiful than the much more elegant Gamble House.

19. Duncan-Irwin House

20. James A. Culbertson House, 1902, 1914
Charles and Henry Greene
235 N. Grand Avenue

Little of the original, very important house is left. Only the bay window, the front door with its Tiffany glass, and the magnificent pergola and wall along Grand were designed by the Greenes. They would also have been demolished except for the protests of the architects Smith and Williams who remodelled the house in 1953.

21. Charles Sumner Greene House, 1901, 1906, 1912, 1914
Charles and Henry Greene
368 Arroyo Terrace

Charles was naturally mainly responsible for the design of this house and its additions. It is not as richly appointed as the nearby Gamble House, but its Craftsman details are just as fine.

22. White Sisters House, 1903
Charles and Henry Greene
370 Arroyo Terrace

Charles Greene's sisters-in-law lived in this once completely shingled house. Notice the crescendo of the retaining wall made of clinker brick and Arroyo Seco boulders.

23. Van Rossem-Neill House, 1903, 1906
Charles and Henry Greene
400 Arroyo Terrace

Carefully restored, this shingled house looks very much as it did when it was pictured in *The Craftsman* magazine in 1915.

23. Van Rossem-Neil House

24. Hawks House, 1906
Charles and Henry Greene
408 Arroyo Terrace

Almost identical to the contemporaneous **Bentz House** on Prospect Boulevard.

25. Willett House, 1905
Charles and Henry Greene
424 Arroyo Terrace

A Craftsman house completely remodelled on the exterior by another architect who chose the Spanish Colonial Revival mode.

26. Ranney House, 1907
Charles and Henry Greene
440 Arroyo Terrace

Another Oriental Craftsman, two-story house; recently beautifully restored. This completes the row of Greene and Greene houses but, of course, there are many more nearby.

27. Fenyes House, 1906
Robert Farquhar
170 N. Orange Grove Boulevard

Neo-Classical, expensive, but not Farquhar at his best (see **Clark Library** on West Adams and the **California Club** in Central Los Angeles). This design nevertheless suggests the high style of living that once characterized Orange Grove Avenue. It can be visited Tuesday and Thursday afternoons courtesy of the Pasadena Historical Society whose headquarters are here.

28. Neighborhood Church, 1972
Whitney R. Smith
1 Westmoreland Place

Modern Shingle style evoking memories of the old Neighborhood Church on California Street. The pines and other trees are beginning to give the area the park-like atmosphere that the architect had in mind.

29. Cole House, 1906
Charles and Henry Greene
2 Westmoreland Place

The Greenes hit their stride here. The interior has been remodelled for use as church parlors, but the exterior is almost precisely as the Greenes designed it. Notice the monumental boulder chimney to the south, which emerges from the ground like a tree trunk.

30. ■Gamble House, 1908
Charles and Henry Greene
4 Westmoreland Place

Certainly this is the masterpiece of these master architects, not because of its facade or its plan (which is conservative even by late Victorian standards) but for the rich interiors, unmatched for loving attention to detail. Like most architects, the Greenes were happiest when they had a rich client who gave them an open purse. But what is remarkable is that the intricate teak interiors that they designed could be carried out with such incredible craftsmanship, forget the price. Containing almost all of the original Greene-designed furniture, this is probably one of the five finest house museums in America. Thanks to the Gamble family, and to the City of Pasadena and the University of Southern California who jointly administer it, this house is open to the public. For tour hours and admission fees, call the Gamble House (818-793-3334 or 213-681-6427).

Note the **stone gateposts and wrought iron gates** (1913) at the Rosemont Avenue entrance to Westmoreland Place. They are also by the Greenes.

31. Dickinson House, 1941
Lawrence Test (Woodbridge Dickinson, associate)
429 Belmore Way

An understated, dark wood house in the Craftsman tradition. This is the best house on a street of good houses built during and just after World War II.

32. McMurran House, 1911
Frederick L. Roehrig
499 Prospect Terrace

Roehrig could and did design in every style. This house shows him expansive in the Mission style.

32. McMurran House

33. Hindry House, 1909
Arthur S. Heineman (Alfred Heineman, associate)
781 Prospect Boulevard

A huge Mission style mansion overlooking the Arroyo Seco. Arthur Heineman

saw the clients and worked out the floor plans. His brother Alfred, who had just joined the firm, elaborated the details as he continued to do until the firm broke up in the thirties. The leaded glass in the dining room was carried out to Alfred's designs by the Judson Studios in Garvanza. The fireplace in the hall may have been designed by Charles Greene.

34. Bentz House, 1906
Charles and Henry Greene
657 Prospect Boulevard

The architects at their most restrained. The house is perfectly maintained.

Prospect Boulevard deserves special praise. The houses on it are comfortable and some are of high quality. But the real attraction is the camphor trees that line it — one of the loveliest sights in Pasadena. The final touch is to know that the **gates** (1906) at Orange Grove Boulevard were designed by Greene and Greene.

35. Millard House ("La Miniatura"), 1923
Frank Lloyd Wright
645 Prospect Crescent

The first of Wright's "textile block" constructions, La Miniatura has the feeling of a Mayan ruin set in a jungle ravine. The famous view of it is from a gate on Rosemont. The studio at the west side of the pond is by Lloyd Wright (1926).

35. Millard House ("La Miniatura")

36. Franks House, 1932
Palmer Sabin
1260 N. Arroyo Boulevard

A well-turned Monterey Revival house overlooking the Arroyo.

37. Grover Cleveland Elementary School, 1934
Robert H. Ainsworth
524 Palisade Street

PWA Moderne with a direct message bas-relief of a child reading.

38. Byles and Weston House, 1950
H. Douglas Byles and Eugene Weston III
1611 Kenneth Way

An understated vertical batten house.

39. Wadsworth House, 1925
1145 Linda Vista Avenue

The supreme Craftsman statement—a two-story log cabin.

40. House, ca. 1887
1360 Lida Street

This Queen Anne cottage is a relic of the tiny hamlet of Linda Vista.

41. Hernly House, 1949
Lawrence Test
1475 Scenic Drive

The siding is three-quarter-inch plywood with the inside face exposed in rooms. The skilled workmanship is an echo of the Craftsman era. The use of unusual materials is representative of the experimental work that was done just before and after World War II.

42. Art Center College of Design, 1977
Craig Ellwood and Associates
1700 Lida Street

Every follower of Mies must have wanted to design a bridge that was also a building. Here Ellwood had his opportunity. This is a very striking building and yet notice how it is sited so as to avoid spoiling the natural landscape. The mess of equipment on the roof was not designed by the architect.

Lower Arroyo Seco, North

O n a map the lower Arroyo seems to be cut off from the upper by the freeway, but in reality Arroyo Boulevard connects the two areas as it always has. It is a lovely drive, and is favored by bicyclists, joggers, and people who like to stroll. In fact, it is one of the few residential sections in Southern California where you see people walking because there is something to experience—lovely scenery and interesting-to-distinguished architecture set in well-kept gardens.

In the nineteenth century, the edges of the Arroyo were not considered desirable places to build. Too many vapors! The Arroyo itself was used as a wood lot by the millionaires on Orange Grove Boulevard and also for picnics and the collecting of wild flowers. The western bank pitched abruptly into the stream bed but the eastern side was moderated by two natural terraces before it too dropped into the valley. This land provided the locale for elaborate gardens, the most extensive being that of Adolphus Busch, the beer tycoon. The Busch Gardens, in fact, ran into the Arroyo. They were open to the public until subdivided in the late thirties.

As the gardens disappeared, so did most of the Orange Grove mansions that were eventually replaced by pleasant but unremarkable garden apartments. But the lower slopes had, beginning around 1900, become attractive to people of moderate means and often of intellectual and artistic pretention. Many of them

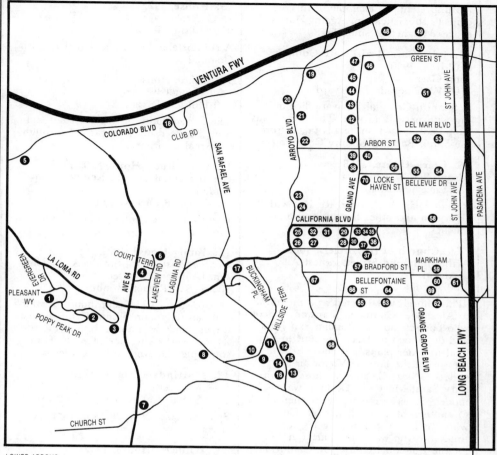

LOWER ARROYO

built bungalows and larger houses in the "ostentatious simplicity" of the Arts and Crafts (Craftsman) movement. Almost all of these brown, woodsy houses remain, many in almost pristine condition. There are even a few new ones. It is for this reason that we have included so many entries for this section.

1. Laing House, 1935
Harwell H. Harris
1642 Pleasant Way

Simplified Wright, but Harris understood the Orient much better than the Master.

2. Kempton House, 1961
Lyman Ennis
1685 Poppy Peak Drive

Austere stucco with even more austere slit windows. A late rendering of the Pueblo Revival.

3. ■Perkins House, 1955
Richard J. Neutra
1540 Poppy Peak Drive

Neutra's ability to make a small space seem large by turning it into the outdoors is seen here at its best.

4. Harris House, 1939
Harwell H. Harris
410 N. Avenue 64

An unpretentious example of this architect's sophistication. Again, Harris evokes Wright but simplifies.

5. John Carr Real Estate Company Building, 1950
John Carr
1400 W. Colorado Boulevard

A Spanish Colonial Revival office building with pergola in rear. The design was supposedly based on details taken from the Santa Barbara County Courthouse.

6. Clark House, 1968
Alson Clark
430 Lakeview Road

Recent Spanish Colonial Revival with Georgian and other highly innovataive touches.

7. ■Church of the Angels, 1889
Arthur Edmund Street; Ernest A. Coxhead
1100 Avenue 64

This church was erected as a memorial to Alexander Campbell-Johnston, a Scot who bought most of Rancho San Rafael and developed it. His wife went to England to order plans and chose Street, the son of the famous Victorian architect George E. Street, whose Holmbury Saint Mary's in Dorking was the model. Street's drawings were then given to another Britisher, Ernest A. Coxhead, who was living in Los Angeles at the time and who was semi-official architect for the Episcopal Church in California. Coxhead took great liberties with the design, the result being one of his several masterpieces. The interior is almost precisely the way it was in the nineteenth century. So is the exterior, except that the 1971 earthquake knocked off the belfry with its Saxon columns. Luckily, the earthquake spared the Gothic and Romanesque blend of the main fabric.

8. Puelicher House, 1960
Boyd Georgi
901 Laguna Road

An International Style Modern box with an unusual amount of color in its bank of louvers.

9. House, 1927
L. C. Brockway
976 Hillside Terrace

A comfortable looking shingled English Colonial.

10. Tabor House, 1950
Paul Haynes
969 Hillside Terrace

The horizontality of this International Style Modern house is carried through with real assurance.

11. Case Study House #10, 1947
Kemper Nomland and Kemper Nomland, Jr.
711 S. San Rafael Avenue

Beautifully sited International Style Modern.

12. Young House, 1927
George Washington Smith; A. E. Hanson, landscape architect
808 S. San Rafael Avenue

A two-story Andalusian house of which you can only gain glimpses. But notice the entrance wall and gate and the south facade overlooking one of A. E. Hanson's splendid Andalusian gardens.

13. Martindale House, 1924
Joseph Kucera
1000 S. San Rafael Avenue

Spanish Colonial walled off from the street.

14. ■Crowell House, 1952
Smith and Williams
949 S. San Rafael Avenue

The architects working in a Japanese mood; one of Pasadena's best fifties houses.

15. House, 1913
Eager and Eager
910 S. San Rafael Avenue

A sort of Danish country home in dressed stone.

16. Gallion House, 1956
Arthur B. Gallion
1055 S. San Rafael Avenue

Japanese-style Modern by a city planner and former Dean of the USC School of Architecture.

17. Cunningham House, 1980
Pulliam, Matthews, and Associates
969 Buckingham Place

A large cut-into box house with vertical wood sheathing.

Something must be said about the array of houses on **San Rafael Avenue** north of the intersection with La Loma Road. They are large, private behind their security systems, and some are fine works of art by Marston and Maybury, Morgan, Walls, and Clements, Paul R. Williams, Reginald D. Johnson, Gordon B. Kaufmann, and other distinguished architects. Almost none can be even vaguely glimpsed from San Rafael Avenue, though there is a tantalizing view of them from Arroyo Boulevard across the Arroyo Seco. All we can say is that we hope that you will watch for house tours, particularly those put on by Pasadena Heritage. Often the San Rafael mansions are the backdrops for movie and television shows and commercials. Naturally the credits never indicate the location.

18. Messler House, ca. 1950
Paul Haynes
136 Club Road

A clapboarded house in the Harwell H. Harris tradition.

19. Colorado Street Bridge, 1912-13
John Drake Mercereau, designer and engineer

19. Colorado Street Bridge

This long, high concrete bridge spanning the Arroyo was curved so that it would get solid footing. The aesthetic result has been compared to that achieved by the aqueduct in Segovia, Spain.

20. La Casita del Arroyo, 1934
Myron Hunt
177 S. Arroyo Boulevard

Very uncharacteristic Hunt, this small meetinghouse was inspired by the Pasadena Garden Club's interest in spurring employment during the Depression. The main funds came from the PWA. Hunt donated his services and designed this structure using boulders and sand from the Arroyo, fallen trees from higher up the canyon, and even parts of the bicycle track abandoned after its use in the 1932 Olympics.

21. Barber House, 1925
Roland E. Coate
270 S. Arroyo Boulevard

An attractive Cape Cod Colonial in brick. The landscape architect was Katherine Bashford.

22. House, 1983
Buff and Hensman
Northeast corner of South Arroyo Boulevard and Arbor Street

An elaborate Craftsman bungalow.

23. Cheesewright House #2, 1912
Jeffrey, Van Trees, and Millar
490 S. Arroyo Boulevard

A beautifully sited Craftsman house.

24. Mannheim House, 1909
Jean Mannheim
500 S. Arroyo Boulevard

Mannheim, a distinguished regional painter, had earlier been associated with Frank Brangwyn, one of the few painters in the English Arts and Crafts movement.

25. Batchelder House, 1909, 1913
Ernest A. Batchelder
626 S. Arroyo Boulevard

A shingled Craftsman house with a brick terrace entrance and a large, second-floor sleeping porch. Batchelder was, by the twenties, one of the country's most successful producers of decorative tile. It all began in the backyard of this house, where his kiln house still stands. He was also a frequent contributor of articles on design and aspects of the Arts and Crafts movement for *The Craftsman* magazine. His wife, a professional pianist, founded the Coleman Chamber Music Association, the oldest such organization in the United States.

26. Clark House, ca. 1910
George A. Clark
648 S. Arroyo Boulevard

Another Swiss chalet, well publicized in the periodicals of the time and featured in H. von Holst's *Modern American Homes* (1915). Incidentally, Clark was a haberdasher!

27. Wright House, ca. 1909
Timothy Walsh
691 La Loma Avenue

Craftsman with classical touches, illustrated and discussed in *The Craftsman* of January 1910. Walsh was a Boston architect who came out to Los Angeles to do the new Roman Catholic Cathedral. The church never got off the drawing boards, but Walsh was quickly converted to the Pasadena style.

28. Austin House, 1909
Grable and Austin, designers
629 S. Grand Avenue

The architectural historian Clay Lancaster believes that this true (i.e. one-story) bungalow was based on an ancient Lycian house illustrated in the *American Architect and Building News* in 1908. If he is correct, Grable and Austin followed through quickly since this house was published in the *Western Architect* in 1909. An almost identical twin is at 990 Vermont in Oakland.

28. Austin House

29. House, ca. 1910
Timothy Walsh
619 S. Grand Avenue

A Craftsman chalet; or better, a Bavarian hunting lodge.

30. Volney-Craig House, 1908
Louis B. Easton
620 S. Grand Avenue

A simple Rocky Mountain cabin on the outside, this house exhibits all the Craftsman paraphernalia on the interior—redwood framing and panelling, inglenook, and even a burnt-wood sideboard.

31. Williams House, 1911
Grable and Austin, designers
638 W. California Street

A fine bungalow in mint condition.

In spite of our heavy coverage of this area, we are mentioning only what we consider to be the best examples of the Craftsman architecture here. You should plan to walk Grand Avenue, California Street, Arroyo Boulevard, La Loma Avenue, and Bradford Street.

32. Cheesewright House #1, 1910
Jeffrey, Van Trees, and Millar
686 W. California Street

E. J. Cheesewright, an Englishman, was one of the leading interior designers in Southern California. Perhaps he suggested the feeling of a thatched-roof Cotswold cottage for this otherwise Craftsman house.

33. House, ca. 1910
550 W. California Street

Possibly by Easton, this excellent Craftsman house was moved around the corner from La Loma Avenue.

34. De Forest House, 1906
Charles and Henry Greene
530 W. California Street

A fine, large bungalow; one of the best-preserved specimens of the Greenes' early work.

35. Norton House, 1905
Alfred Heineman
520 W. California Street

Heineman designed this house before joining his brother Arthur's firm. It is worthy of comparison with the Greene and Greene next door.

36. Noble House, ca. 1910
475 La Loma Avenue

The Tudor Craftsman mode.

37. Clapp House, 1874
549 La Loma Avenue

A simple but refined Italianate dwelling. One of the oldest buildings in Pasadena, it housed the city's first school. It was moved before the turn of the century from the southwest corner of Orange Grove Boulevard and California Street.

38. Francis House, 1929
Reginald D. Johnson
415 S. Grand Avenue

One of Johnson's best Georgian efforts.

39. Boult House, 1893
Seymour Locke and Jasper Newton Preston
395 S. Grand Avenue

A large cobblestone and shingle house. Another strongly Richardsonian **house** (1895) by the same firm is at 325 S. Grand Avenue.

40. House, 1910
G. Lawrence Stimson
390 S. Grand Avenue

Dressed-up Craftsman, this house is similar in style to **Myron Hunt's house** at 200 N. Grand Avenue.

41. House, 1926
Marston and Van Pelt
293 S. Grand Avenue

A French Provincial mansion.

42. Tod Ford House, 1919
Reginald D. Johnson
257 S. Grand Avenue

A grand Mediterranean style mansion with beautifully landscaped forecourt and impressive gardens terraced into the valley of the Arroyo Seco.

43. Freeman Ford House, 1907
Charles and Henry Greene
215 S. Grand Avenue

This house cannot be seen from the street, but it is one of the Greene's major works and must be mentioned. The gardens were set out by Robert Gordon Fraser, the landscape architect for the Busch Gardens.

44. Robinson House, 1905
Charles and Henry Greene
195 S. Grand Avenue

The gates have Oriental lanterns but the house, with its suggestion of half-timbering, seems Tudor.

45. Shakespeare Club, ca. 1925
Marston, Van Pelt, and Maybury
(Sylvanus Marston)
171 S. Grand Avenue

A severe Florentine villa.

46. Vista Grande Townhouses, 1981
Buff and Hensman
72-108 S. Grand Avenue

This linked-together stucco and wood style has become very popular in this area thanks in large part to this firm. See also the similar and impressive **condominiums** by Harrison, Beckhart, and Mill just around the corner at 1 S. Orange Grove Boulevard.

47. Vista del Arroyo Hotel, 1920
Marston and Van Pelt
Tower, 1930; George Wiemeyer
125 S. Grand Avenue

This hotel began its life as Mrs. Bang's Boarding House. Needless to say it prospered, only to suffer a loss of patronage in the thirties. It was taken over by the Federal Government during World War II. Today it is being converted for use as an appelate court building. The so-called bungalows in the extensive gardens are mostly by Marston and also Myron Hunt.

48. Memorial Flagpole, 1927
Bertram G. Goodhue
Northeast corner of Orange Grove Boulevard and Colorado Boulevard Boulevard

The sculpture is by Lee Laurie, who worked with Goodhue on many buildings, including the Nebraska State Capitol and the Los Angeles Public Library.

49. Pasadena Museum of Art (now **Norton Simon Museum**), 1969
Ladd and Kelsey
411 W. Colorado Boulevard

To a degree, this building, with its curved forms, draws upon the Streamline Moderne of the thirties. The collection it houses is superb. The hours are Thursday-Sunday, 12-6 P.M.

50. Elks Club Building, 1924
Myron Hunt and H. C. Chambers
400 W. Colorado Boulevard

A pleasing variation on Mount Vernon.

50. Elks Club Building

51. Ambassador College Campus
Between Green Street, West Colorado Boulevard, Del Mar Boulevard, and Saint John Avenue

The administration of Ambassador College deserves special praise for its efforts to preserve and use the old houses which remained on the land it purchased in the fifties. More than that, the college has demolished fences in order to develop old backyards into a magnificent park with views of the city through palms and oaks. The new buildings are flamboyant Modern, some deserving attention. A tour, including some interiors, may be arranged at the Information and Administrative Center on Green Street. The buildings that follow are some highlights:

a. Scofield House, 1909
Frederick L. Roehrig
280 S. Orange Grove Boulevard

A merging of the styles of Harvey Ellis as illustrated in *The Craftsman* and of Will Bradley (who, incidently, lived for a time in South Pasadena). There is more than a little of Frank Lloyd Wright, too, especially in the entrance hall.

51a. Scofield House

b. Sprague House, 1903
A. A. Sprague
Behind Scofield House

A vast, half-timbered Tudor pile.

c. Merritt House, 1905-06
W. F. Thompson

An Italian Renaissance palace set between two large waffles near the corner of Green Street and Orange Grove Boulevard.

d. Information and Administrative Center, 1969

Peter Holstock (for O. K. Earl Corporation)

Influenced by early Yamasaki.

e. Student Center, 1966
Gerd Ernst (for Daniel, Mann, Johnson, and Mendenhall)

A pleasing pavilion.

f. Auditorium, 1974
Daniel, Mann, Johnson, and Mendenhall

This building is already famous for its opulence and good acoustics.

52. Mead House, 1910
Louis B. Easton
380 W. Del Mar Boulevard

A monument of the Craftsman movement by a brother-in-law of Elbert Hubbard. Recently restored. The porte cochere is not a part of the original design.

53. Bolton House, 1906
Charles and Henry Greene
370 W. Del Mar Boulevard

The shingle exterior shows only a few signs of the Orientalism which was to emerge full-blown in the Greene's work two years later. The staircase bulge was added by Garrett Van Pelt in 1918. The house has gone through many interior changes but is now restored and somewhat modernized.

54. Rhodes House, 1906
W. J. Saunders
365 W. Bellevue Drive

Worthy of Maybeck, this huge Bavarian hunting lodge deserves study.

54. Rhodes House

55. Condominium, 1982
Batey-Mack
371-379 Bellevue Drive

Clear stucco abstraction worthy of Irving J. Gill.

55. Condominium

56. Wrigley House, 1911
G. Lawrence Stimson
391 S. Orange Grove Boulevard

Mission Revival with delusions of Beaux Arts grandeur, this mansion, though itself of no great quality, is set in ample gardens that give an idea of the high style once common on Orange Grove Boulevard. It is now the headquarters of the Tournament of Roses Association.

56. Wrigley House

57. Fitzpatrick House, 1980
Leland Hershberger
549 Bradford Street

Craftsman Revival in an area that is worthy of it. Certainly special credit goes to Rodger Whipple, the master carpenter, along with the architect and the imaginative owner.

58. Apartment Building, 1926
Robert H. Ainsworth
339-353 W. California Boulevard

Andalusian Spanish Colonial Revival giving variety of design within the uniformity of the U-shaped plan.

59. Wilmans House, 1900
337 Markham Place

A Georgian Revival dwelling.

60. Blankenhorn-Lamphear House, 1893
346 Markham Place

A beautiful and typical example of the Queen Anne style.

61. McCarthy House, 1937
Donald McMurray
762 Saint John Avenue

If the Long Beach Freeway is completed, this fine Monterey Revival house will be demolished.

62. Hollister House, 1899
Charles and Henry Greene
310 Bellefontaine Street

Early Greene. They tried out the English Colonial Revival and showed their allegiance to the vogues of the eastern seaboard, particularly the work of McKim, Mead, and White.

63. Ware House, 1913
Charles and Henry Greene
460 Bellefontaine Street

Here the Greenes seem to be moving away from their Swiss and Oriental influences. The house looks more like their early work, e.g. the Hollister House.

64. Phillips House, 1906
Charles and Henry Greene
459 Bellefontaine Street

A large, very characteristic, brown chalet. The only Greene and Greene style that you do not experience in these Bellefontaine houses is, strangely enough, the Japanese.

65. Thomas House, 1911
Sylvanus Marston
574 Bellefontaine Street

Tudor Craftsman.

66. Marshall-Eagle House (now **Mayfield School**), 1917
Frederick L. Roehrig
500 Bellefontaine Street

A huge Beaux Arts mansion whose grounds have been well maintained.

67. House, 1927
Donald McMurray
850 S. Arroyo Boulevard

One of the finest Monterey Revival houses in Pasadena.

67. House

68. Pergola House, ca. 1910
Attributed to Robert Gordon Fraser
1025 S. Arroyo Boulevard

This remains among only a few relics of the Busch Gardens begun in 1903 under

Fraser's direction. He had trained at the great Horticultural Gardens in his native Edinburgh. So far as is known, he had no architectural background, but the idea of a platform from which to view Camel's Hump must have been his. Now the circular building has been incorporated in a relatively modern house.

69. Buckingham House, 1918-19
Sylvanus Marston
325 Bellefontaine Street

A handsome example of the late Queen Anne Style that Vincent Scully has called the Shingle style. Two more examples are nearby at 707 and 721 Saint John Avenue. The fomer dates from 1890 and the latter from 1897 (Frederick L. Roehrig). Both will be demolished if the Long Beach Freeway is completed.

69. Buckingham House

70. Three Houses
Southeast corner of South Grand Avenue and Lockhaven Street

These houses have been moved to the property once occupied by the La Solana Inn. The one on Lockehaven is a marvelous Queen Anne extravaganza (1887; Merithew and Ferris) that was originally at 626 W. 30th Street near the USC campus. The dwelling at 440 S. Grand is a high-strung, Shingle style, two-story house made more nervous by the paint job. Just south of it an early twentieth century Colonial Revival is being reconstructed.

Lower Arroyo Seco, South

When the city of South Pasadena was laid out in 1886, there was a movement to incorporate it with Pasadena. But the good people of this area held out against "the diabolical traffic" in liquor tolerated by the Presbyterians to the north. South Pasadena was, in the words of the historian Hiram Reid, "compelled by sheer necessity for self-protection to incur the expense and trouble of forming a city corporation." The town fought alcohol well into this century. Perhaps that is the reason that it is not so rich in architecture as its northern neighbor.

But the tradition of otherwise-mindedness also has its rewards. More recently South Pasadena has taken a gallant stand against the Long Beach Freeway that would cut down Meridian Avenue, the old main street of South Pasadena, demolishing old commercial buildings and a fine residential district which includes important Victorian houses, two houses by Greene and Greene, and one by R. M. Schindler.

We do not mean to create ironies, but the simple fact is that freeways, while often destroying major and minor monuments, do not, when properly constructed, divide cities as they seem to do on maps. If elevated, or especially if depressed and bridged, they may actually reduce the traffic flow on surface streets and preserve neighborhoods. The Pasadena Freeway, in spite of its dangerous on and off ramps, is almost invisible as it bends out of the Arroyo and

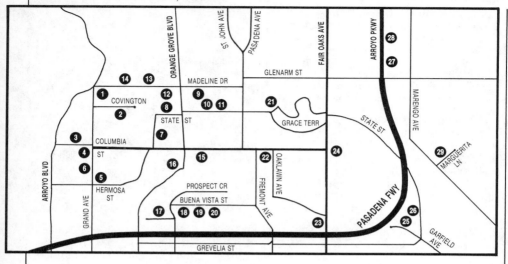

through the northern part of South Pasadena. Thus, at the risk of inflaming the passions of people in both Pasadena and South Pasadena, we have included a part of South Pasadena in the following section and then in a later section rather courageously gone on to move east through the main part of South Pasadena. We do this not to confuse but to help the knowledgeable admirer of architecture who cares nothing for political boundaries, particularly since they were drawn on the principles of the Anti-Saloon League.

1. House, 1938
Donald McMurray
Southeast corner of Grand Avenue and Madeline Drive, Pasadena

A Spanish urban house of great quality. Its model was a seventeenth-century house in Antigua, Guatemala.

1. House

2. House, 1950
Leland Evison
520 Covington Place

Good conservative Modern with oiled redwood exterior.

3. Jeffries House, 1922
Bertram G. Goodhue
695 Columbia Street

Unfortunately, when this once-huge house was divided a few years ago, the wonderful Churrigueresque entrance was removed. But we are told that it is stored somewhere on the grounds. It is still possible to see some of the architect's intentions from a gate on Columbia Street.

4. Tanner-Behr House, 1917
Reginald D. Johnson
Southwest corner of Columbia Street and Grand Avenue, South Pasadena

A rather formidable essay in the Mediterranean style, now best viewed from the gate on Grand Avenue. The two Roman busts at the tops of the gate posts always have wreaths around them at Christmastime. Notice also the lovely antique pink wall.

5. House, ca. 1925
H. Roy Kelley
Northeast corner of Hermosa Street and Grand Avenue, South Pasadena

A compact Tudor villa in brick.

5. House

6. House, ca. 1925
Donald McMurray
309 N. Grand Avenue, South Pasadena

With its scalloped wall and beautiful maintenance, this Spanish Colonial Revival house is almost too good to be true.

7. ■Davis House, 1936-37
Roland E. Coate
1230 Hillside Road

Federal Revival in painted brick. Note the arcaded office on the one-story wing to the south.

8. Perrin House, 1926
Garvin Hodson
415 W. State Street

Monterey Revival with mannered touches strongly suggesting the influence of George Washington Smith.

9. Westridge School, 1906-1980
324 Madeline Drive, South Pasadena

The campus, most of whose buildings can easily be seen from the street, is a veritable museum of the works of Pasadena's architectural worthies. Remember that the school is private property. Buildings are listed in clockwise fashion.

a. Administration Building, 1923
Marston, Van Pelt, and Maybury

A modest Tudor Revival structure by a firm that was more at home with the congeries of Mediterranean.

b. Performing Arts Building, 1909
Frederick L. Roehrig
North wing added 1932; Bennett and Haskell
Stage designed 1958; Henry Dreyfuss

Most of the Roehrig design has been covered up or remodelled. The later wing harmonizes with the Tudor Administration Building. The stage is, of course, the product of one of the world's greatest industrial designers, who incidentally lived a few blocks away.

c. Hoffman Gymnasium-Auditorium, 1980
Whitney R. Smith

A shingled box reminiscent of Smith's Neighborhood Church.

d. Pitcairn House (now Fine Arts Building), 1906
Charles and Henry Greene
Interior remodelled 1973
Roland E. Coate, Jr. (Timothy Andersen, associate)

The Greenes in beautiful form. This building is now a good example of recycling. The interior retains many of the old features; the exterior, with its wonderful stepped windows reflecting the interior staircase, remains exactly as built.

e. Laurie and Susan Frank Art Studio, 1978
Whitney R. Smith

Seeley G. Mudd Science Building, 1978
Whitney R. Smith

How do you design new buildings next to a major work by the Greenes? Smith chose shingles but wisely understated the design, though the Art Studio may have been modelled on the Gamble House garage—a good model.
The landscaping of the south half of the campus is by Yosh Kuromiya.

f. Ranney House Classrooms, 1962
Henry Eggers and Walter W. Wilkman

Gladys Peterson Building, 1962
Henry Eggers and Walter W. Wilkman

Library (south wing of Administration Building), 1962
Henry Eggers and Walter W. Wilkman

The most "modern" looking buildings on the campus.

g. Gertrude Hall Building and Classrooms, 1955
George Vernon Russell

Barely visible from the street (Madeline Drive), these buildings are compromises between Modern architecture and the Tudor Revival Administration Building nearby.

10. Mervin House, 1904
Charles and Henry Greene
267 W. State Street

A columned porch identifies this otherwise Craftsman house.

11. Rolland House, 1903
Charles and Henry Greene
225 W. State Street

A Craftsman bungalow (now painted white) with a recessed window in the middle of the roof. Incidentally, Henry Greene's own house (demolished) once was across the street.

12. Cravens House, ca. 1929
Lewis P. Hobart
430 Madeline Drive

In spite of its present address, this French chateau by a San Francisco architect is the best remaining example of the Orange Grove style of life. It is now Pasadena's Red Cross Headquarters and can be visited from 8:30 A.M. to 5 P.M. on weekdays. The gardens, designed by the Olmsted Brothers, have been subdivided and lost.

13. Old Mill of Banbury Cross, ca. 1907; additions later, especially in the twenties
Attributed to Robert Gordon Fraser
485 Madeline Drive

The Hansel and Gretel mill was the teahouse in the old Busch Gardens. It cannot be seen from the street but the lychgate entrance is a fine piece of street furniture.

14. Dunham House, 1956
Carl L. Maston
495 Madeline Drive

The best view of this International Style Modern structure is from Stoneridge Drive.

15. House, ca. 1885
919 Columbia Street, South Pasadena

Professor Thaddeus Lowe lived in this expansive Queen Anne villa while his own great house, now demolished, was being built on Orange Grove Boulevard.

16. Porter House, 1875
215 N. Orange Grove Boulevard, South Pasadena

A Queen Anne cottage built by one of the founders of the San Gabriel Orange Grove Association that sold the first eighty-four lots to the Hoosier settlers of Pasadena.

17. Prospect Houses, 1948
Van E. Bailey and William Gray Purcell
543 and 545 Prospect Lane (alley just north of Pasadena Freeway and off Prospect Circle), South Pasadena

Rare examples of Purcell's late work. Simple slip form concrete structures with wide, overhanging eaves; somewhat reminiscent of Wright's Usonian houses.

18. House, ca. 1895
929 Buena Visa Street, South Pasadena

Huge turn-of-the-century Tudor with lots of shingles. Note also the fine, **shingled mansion** next door at number 917.

19. Garfield House, 1904
Charles and Henry Greene
1001 Buena Visa Street, South Pasadena

The Greenes designed this modest but respectable house for the widow of President James A. Garfield. It is a Craftsman Swiss chalet without the Oriental touches that they were beginning to display in other commissions.

20. Longley House, 1897, 1910
Charles and Henry Greene
1005 Buena Vista Street, South Pasadena

This is a strange but significant work. Here the Greenes were trying their wings in architecture—and they seem to have tried almost everything. It includes Mission style, Moorish, Richardsonian Romanesque, Oriental, and even Georgian Revival elements.

These Buena Vista houses are all in the path of the proposed extension of the Long Beach Freeway and may be demolished in spite of the fact that the Greene and Greene houses are on the National Register.

21. House, ca. 1900
135-137 Grace Terrace, South Pasadena

A shingled, Mission Revival edifice.

Oaklawn Avenue, dating from the early 1900s, has many handsome Craftsman houses. See especially numbers 216, 217, 304, 309, 317, and 325.

22. Oaklawn Gates, 1905
Charles and Henry Greene
On Columbia Street at Oaklawn Avenue

A Craftsman redwood fence ends in boulder pillars supporting beautiful tile roofs.

22. Oaklawn Gates

23. Oaklawn Bridge and Waiting Station, 1906
Charles and Henry Greene
Oaklawn Avenue at Fair Oaks Avenue, South Pasadena

The bridge across the tracks of the Southern Pacific and Santa Fe railroads was an unsuccessful but amusing sally of the Greenes into engineering. The waiting station is an amazing concoction of redwood beams with tile roof.

24. Waiting Station and Cobblestone Wall, ca. 1902
Attributed to T. W. Parkes
Southeast corner of Fair Oaks Avenue and Raymond Hill Road, South Pasadena

A fine Craftsman shelter where guests of the Raymond Hotel, once on the hill above, used to wait for the "Big Red Cars" on the Pacific Electric line—a branch of what was once one of the greatest rapid transit systems in the country.

25. "Adobe Flores," Casa de Jose Pérez, 1839; 1849-50
1804 Foothill Street, South Pasadena

A single-floor, L-shaped adobe, now covered with a tile roof. The Mexican Army headquarters during the Mexican-American War, this adobe was restored and "enhanced" in 1919 by the well-known exponent of the Spanish Colonial Revival, Carleton M. Winslow, Sr. In the twenties it was a teahouse with a high cultural tone. It is now a private residence.

26. Group of Adobes, 1925-27
Carleton M. Winslow, Sr.
West side of Garfield Avenue north of Foothill Street, South Pasadena

In spite of their late date, these are much more "convincing" structures than the previous entry.

27. Royal Building, 1968
Nyberg and Bissner
East side of Arroyo Parkway north of Glenarm Street

A stilted pavilion related to Edward D. Stone's projects but without his Moorish screens.

28. Grieger Building, 1972
Daniel, Mann, Johnson, and Mendenhall
900 S. Arroyo Parkway

A strong Streamline Moderne building of almost monumental proportions.

29. Spanish Colonial Revival Village, ca. 1928
Marguerita Lane (on curve of Marengo Avenue below Glenarm Street)

A group of very pretty cottages— actually a bungalow court.

Oak Knoll

B esides Pasadena proper there were other real estate ventures aimed at appeasing the voracious appetites of Midwesterners for Paradise. The Oak Knoll area, now a part of Pasadena but in the 1880s a separate

subdivision, was bought by a Mr. Rosenbaum, a New York speculator, and was laid out by the R. R. Staats Realty Company. Land contours (some determined by earthquake faults!) and native oaks were preserved by curving streets. Oak Knoll was from the beginning an area of fine houses on estates originally almost as extensive as those on Orange Grove Boulevard. All of these were broken up in the twenties so that houses in the Craftsman idiom are cheek-to-jowl with period revivals.

1. Experimental Dome House, 1946
Wallace Neff
1097 S. Los Robles Avenue

A thin-shell concrete dome by this famous exponent of the Spanish Colonial Revival. Neff was looking for a practical, low-cost structure that would replace the balloon frame.

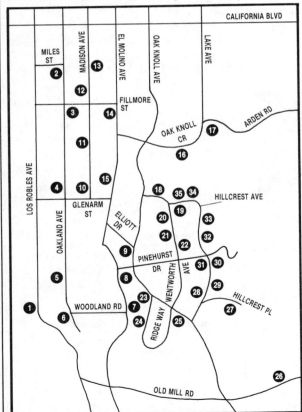

2. House, ca. 1887
Southwest corner of Oakland Avenue
and Miles Street

A colorful Queen Anne two-story with
picket fence.

3. Flintoft House, ca. 1910
G. S. Bliss, contractor
800 S. Oakland Avenue

A two-story Craftsman house. Fine
Craftsman houses, some bungalows, pop
up elsewhere on this street. See espe-
cially numbers 755, 903, 911, and 1315.
Bliss constructed many bungalows in
Pasadena.

4. Toleston House, 1913
E. P. Zimmerman
965 S. Oakland Avenue

American Georgian with Dutch and
Federal elements.

5. House, 1915
Rossiter-Banfield Company
1205 S. Oakland Avenue

A Pueblo Revival house, unusual in this
area.

6. Rochester House, ca. 1910
T. Beverly Keim
1365 S. Oakland Avenue

The Rochesters chose a Los Angeles architect to design this magnificent Beaux
Arts mansion for them.

7. Grey House, 1911
Elmer Grey
1372 S. El Molino Avenue

Although touches of Italian influence appear in the architect's own house, the
broad circular front porch is very
Californian, the composition of the
rough stucco walls reminds you of Voysey or even Mackintosh. The house is
beautifully sited on the hillside.

7. Grey House

8. Van Pelt House, 1926
Garrett Van Pelt
1212 S. El Molino Avenue

This important architect chose a variation on a French Provincial theme for
his own house.

9. Ross House, 1911
Arthur S. Heineman (Alfred Heineman,
associate)
674 Elliott Drive

The Craftsman aesthetic in its later
stage, this house is often mistaken for a
work by the Greenes.

10. House, 1910
Sylvanus Marston
1011 S. Madison Avenue

West Coast Prairie style.

11. Ioannes House, 1911
Louis B. Easton
885 S. Madison Avenue

A rather well-turned effort in Mission
style stucco by an architect who usually
used wood.

12. E. J. Blacker House, 1912
Charles and Henry Greene
675 S. Madison Avenue

Obviously this house does not bear comparison with the one that the Greenes
had built earlier for another Blacker (see
entry **#19**). It is nevertheless a good
Craftsman design as is the one (1907) at
805 S. Madison Avenue by Frederick L.
Roehrig.

13. Blood House, 1911
654 S. Madison Avenue

An excellent U-plan Craftsman bungalow painted yellow in the latter day.

14. House, ca. 1911
Arthur S. Heineman (Alfred Heineman,
associate)
885 S. El Molino Avenue

Although painted, this two-story house
still shows its Craftsman origins.

15. Crow-Crocker House, 1909
Charles and Henry Greene
979 S. El Molino Avenue

Actually, this Craftsman masterpiece was
designed entirely by Henry Greene.

16. McDonald House, ca. 1927
W. F. Staunton
800 Oak Knoll Circle

A good Monterey Revival two-story.

17. "Tara West," 1978
Thornton and Fagan Associates
Southeast corner of Lake Avenue and
Arden Road

A folly if there ever was one! It is sup-
posed to be modelled on Scarlet
O'Hara's mansion in the late-thirties film
Gone with the Wind.

18. Garford House, 1919
Marston and Van Pelt
1126 Hillcrest Avenue

A rather dry but dignified version of the
Spanish Colonial Revival. Just north of
it and running along Oak Knoll Avenue
is an Orientalized gunnite wall designed
by the Greenes.

19. R. R. Blacker House, 1907
Charles and Henry Greene
177 Hillcrest Avenue

Like the Gamble House across town,
this is one of the very finest of the
Greenes' Craftsman-Japanese designs. Its
magnificent gardens have been subdivided and built upon. The chauffeur's
and gardener's houses, now separate
dwellings on Wentworth Avenue, give an
idea of the grandeur of the ensemble.

19. R. R. Blacker House

20. Lunkenheimer House, 1906
Joseph Blick
1215 Wentworth Avenue

Mission Revival, very similar to the
work of Lester S. Moore.

21. House, ca. 1913
Arthur S. Heineman (Alfred Heineman,
associate)
1233 Wentworth Avenue

The Craftsman aesthetic moving directly
into a version of Cotswold Hansel and
Gretel.

21. House

22. Campbell House, 1924
Roland E. Coate
1244 Wentworth Avenue

One of this architect's best Spanish
Colonial Revival houses.

23. ■O'Brien House, ca. 1912
Arthur S. Heineman (Alfred Heineman,
associate)
1327 S. Oak Knoll Avenue (corner of
Ridge Way)

A beautifully-crafted house in the
Heinemans' special fusion of Oriental
details with the feeling of a Cotswold
cottage.

24. Ledyard House ("Idyllwild"), 1909
1361 Ridge Way

An extraordinary Craftsman house
framed in logs.

25. Wentworth Hotel (now
Huntington-Sheraton), 1906, 1913
Charles Whittlesey; Hunt and Grey
1401 S. Oak Knoll Avenue

Whittlesey, well known for his Mission
Revival railroad stations and hotels in
the Southwest, continued the tradition
here in this great hotel catering to
Easterners and Midwesterners trying to

escape the cold months back home. Hunt and Grey greatly increased the size of Whittlesey's intentions. Unfortunately a series of remodellings has left very little of the original interior decor. But the exterior, now vine-covered, is still impressive and the gardens are excellent. See also the **rustic bridge** with murals (ca. 1933) by Frank M. Moore.

26. ■El Molino Viejo, 1816
1120 Old Mill Road, San Marino

Built under the direction of Father Zalvidéa on the outer limits of the San Gabriel Mission property, it served as a flour mill until the "new" and presumably more efficient mill put it out of service. It mouldered until the twenties, when it was refurbished and used as a house with painted decoration added to interior walls. Both Myron Hunt and Carleton M. Winslow, Sr. were involved in the restoration. Certainly it is one of the most picturesque of the old adobe structures remaining in Los Angeles County.

27. Hamish House, 1951
Henry Eggers and Walter W. Wilkman
940 Hillcrest Place (watch the bumps in the road)

Actually, all you can see is one wall of the house, but it is a beautiful wall.

28. Landreth House, ca. 1918
Reginald D. Johnson
1385 Hillcrest Avenue

A grand American Classical Revival mansion.

29. Spinks House, 1909
Charles and Henry Greene
1344 Hillcrest Avenue

A blend of barn and Swiss Chalet.

30. Freeman House, 1913
Arthur S. Heineman (Alfred Heineman, associate)
1330 Hillcrest Avenue

The once-rolled eaves have now been clipped, but this is still a great Craftsman house. Notice the extensive use of Batchelder tile. There is more inside.

31. Prindle House, 1926, 1928
George Washington Smith
1311 Hillcrest Avenue

Bold Spanish Colonial Revival forms mark this house; its tour de force is the loggia garden to the rear.

31. Prindle House

32. Elliott House, 1925
Wallace Neff
1290 Hillcrest Avenue

Extremely dignified Spanish Colonial Revival.

33. Griffith House, 1924
Johnson, Kaufman, and Coate
1275 Hillcrest Avenue

Spanish Colonial Revival. See also the house in the same style next door.

34. Hurshler House, 1950
Ain, Johnson, and Day
1200 Hillcrest Avenue

A low, single-story International Style Modern house beautifully sited.

35. Cordelia Culbertson House, 1911
Charles and Henry Greene
1188 Hillcrest Place

This gunnite-sheathed house with green
tile roof seems more Chinese than Japanese. It is roughly L-shaped with a
Moorish fountain in the central court.
The back of the house, which once
looked down on extensive terraced
gardens, is almost pure Segovia. Only a
suggestion of the gardens remains.

35. Cordelia Culbertson House

Pasadena, Central Business District

The commercial heart of nineteenth century Pasadena was at Fair Oaks Avenue and Colorado Boulevard, mostly on Fair Oaks. Indeed, a small and precious fragment remains. But, contrary to early expecta-tions, the main business developed along Colorado Boulevard and the result was a congeries of taste that we have already described. Spanish and Art Deco Moderne facades hooked to Victorian structures line the street from Delacey to El Molino avenues with an interruption on the south side between Arroyo Park-way and Los Robles Avenue where the new **Plaza Pasadena,** a commercial suc-cess but an architectural disaster, ap-pears like a yellow brick fortress. It has been suggested that the intersection at Garfield Avenue be renamed the Place d' la Bastille.

As in most California communities, Colorado Boulevard (Pasadena's main street) was, until the fifties, pretty much a commercial strip with single-family residential areas spreading behind al-most within the same block both north and south. Recently this pattern has changed with the building of hotels, banks, and condominiums to the south of Colorado and the development of the Parsons Engineering firm to the north-west. This new growth has wiped out many neighborhoods and several land-marks, but it has been accompanied by a growing awareness of the importance of old buildings, an awareness that is visible in the restoration of storefronts,

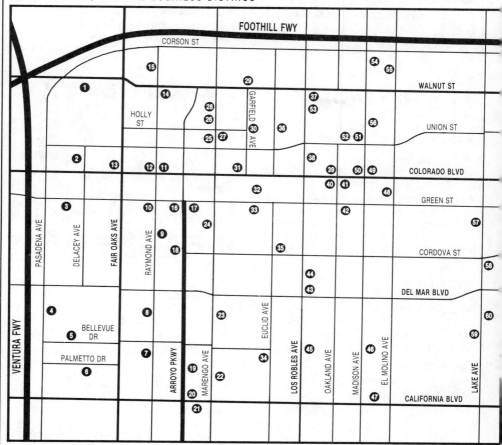

the cleaning of the brick backs and alleys, and restrictions on signage. Other indications of responsibility are an extremely active urban conservation program emanating from City Hall and a resourceful private support organization, Pasadena Heritage.

1. Ralph M. Parsons Company, Office Tower, 1974
William Pereira Associates
100 W. Walnut Street

Two almost identical **office buildings**, 1979 and 1981; Skidmore, Owings, and Merrill

Sorry to begin this section on a negative note, but the tower in particular is something that should stand as a monument to what should be avoided. Architecturally dull, its bulk is an insult to the fine scale of the older buildings on the skyline. The other two major buildings, designed in Skidmore, Owings, and Merrill's latest wrap-around style, are not much better, though there is a rather striking view of the older one from the picturesque alley to the south of it.

2. Pennsylvania Oil and Tire Warehouse, 1930
Bennett and Haskell
33 Delacey Avenue

The lower portion of the structure has been remodelled but the tower remains pretty much as it was envisioned by the architects—Art Deco (Zigzag) Moderne

with a programmatic frieze of automobile wheels.

3. Friend Paper Company, 1965
Smith and Williams
100 W. Green Street

A surprising place for this sophisticated,
typically regionalized (softened), International Style Modern design to have
been erected. The deep bays were landscaped by Eckbo, Dean, and Associates.

4. Stahlhuth House, 1907
Charles and Henry Greene
380 S. Pasadena Avenue

Originally, you would be unable to distinguish this bungalow from the
hundreds of others that once surrounded
it. It now has a fine view of the uncom-
pleted Long Beach Freeway.

5. House, 1893
Wood Taylor
101 Bellevue Drive

A charming two-story Queen Anne
dwelling with characteristic ornament in
the gable. You have to imagine it in its
orange grove.

6. Palmetto Court, 1915
A. C. Parlee, builder
100 Palmetto Drive

Fourteen tiny Craftsman bungalows.

7. Royal Laundry Building, 1927 (ad-
dition ca. 1935)
Gordon B. Kaufmann
443 S. Raymond Avenue

Restrained Spanish Colonial Revival enhanced by a fine tile doorway almost Art
Deco Moderne in design. The later addition is in Streamline Moderne. All this
is on the site of the once-sensational
Moorish Revival Lowe's Opera House.

8. Pasadena Humane Society Build-
ing, 1932
Robert Ainsworth
361 S. Raymond Avenue

A fine Mediterranean style building.

9. Santa Fe (AMTRAK) Railroad
Passenger Station, 1935
H. L. Gilman
222 S. Raymond Avenue

The Chief (demoted from Superchief)
still stops at this colorful Spanish
Colonial Revival depot. Note the
magnificent Batchelder tiles in the waiting room.

9. Santa Fe (AMTRAK) Railroad Passenger Station

10. Hotel Green (now Castle Green Apartments and Hotel Green Apartments), 1898, 1903
Frederick L. Roehrig
50 E. Green Street, at southwest corner
of Raymond Avenue

The Hotel Green, once one of the great
resort hotels, has now been converted
into apartments and condominiums.
Both are very private but quite often the
owners of the Castle Green play host to
Pasadena Heritage, and it is possible to
see the public rooms, almost completely
intact with even some of the Moorish
furniture in place. These buildings are
late additions to an older hotel that was
on the other side of Raymond Avenue.

10. Hotel Green

Thus the "Bridge of Sighs" is now cut off at the sidewalk. The Staats Company is partly housed in what is left of the old hotel which was designed by Strange and Carnicle (southeast corner of Raymond and Green). Note the original curved entrance at the corner.

11. United California Bank (now **Bank Theatre Building**), 1929
Bennett and Haskell
Northeast corner of Raymond Avenue and Colorado Boulevard

A crisp brick essay in Art Deco (Zigzag) Moderne.

12. Kinney-Kendall Building, 1897; remodelled 1925
Charles and Henry Greene; remodelled by Bennett and Haskell
65 E. Colorado Boulevard, at northwest corner of Raymond Avenue

As a result of the 1920s set-back and the stripping away of almost all ornament, this rare example of the Greenes' commercial work bears little resemblance to their original ideas. While it was never a great building the Greene and Greene cult should take it in hand and restore it.

13. Old Pasadena
Fair Oaks Avenue and Raymond Avenue, two blocks north and south of Colorado Boulevard

Here is the commercial heart of old Pasadena. It has been pretty badly handled by time, neglect, and remodelling, but the **White Block** (1887), at one time the City Hall, at the southwest corner of Union Street and Fair Oaks Avenue, the **Slavin Block** next door on Fair Oaks, the **Venetian Revival Building** (1887; Harry Ridgeway), and further down the street at number 9-17, are presently being restored and recycled. A good example of what can be accomplished is the **Renaissance Revival Block** (1894; Frank Hudson) at 32 S. Raymond Avenue, and there are other good refurbishings all around. Best of all are the brick alleys that are gradually being drawn upon for their highly picturesque quality.

14. Entrance to Old Pasadena Public Library, 1887
C. W. Buchanan
Southeast corner of Walnut Street and Raymond Avenue

This relic of the Richardsonian Romanesque library remains as a garden ruin at the corner of a small park. Across the street at 145 N. Raymond Avenue is the stunning PWA Moderne **California State Armory,** now the Pasadena Badminton Club. It was designed by Bennett and Haskell and built in 1932. Notice also the rare group of clapboard **row houses** (1901) at the opposite corner.

14. Entrance to Old Pasadena Public Library

15. Saint Andrew's Roman Catholic Church, 1927
Ross Montgomery
311 N. Raymond Avenue

Early Christian fabric with Romanesque campanile right out of old Ravenna. The rich interior is as marvelous as the contribution of the outlines of the church to the cityspace. Best seen from the Foothill Freeway going east at sunset.

16. Pasadena Datsun Building, 1946
Bennett and Bennett
Southwest corner of Green Street and Arroyo Parkway

Chiefly distinguished by its two flamboyant Streamline Moderne signs.

17. Bankamericard Center Building, 1975
Edward D. Stone
Southeast corner of Green Street and Arroyo Parkway

Late Stone, a huge pink marble block without windows (presumably because computers do not need light). One wag has suggested that it looks like the box that the **Conference Center** (across Marengo Avenue) came packaged in.

18. U.S. Post Office, Arroyo Annex, 1940
Cyril Bennett
Arroyo Parkway at west end of Cordova Street

Originally a skating rink, this Streamline Moderne mass evokes nostalgia for the FDR era.

19. Bryan's Cleaners, 1938
Eliot Construction Company
544 Arroyo Parkway

A well-turned essay in the Streamline Moderne.

20. Hunt Offices and Display Rooms, 1925
George Hunt
Northeast corner of Arroyo Parkway and California Boulevard

Hunt was the foremost furniture maker to the rich in the twenties. This Monterey Style structure was good advertising.

20. Hunt Offices and Display Rooms

21. Architects' Offices, 1929
Wallace Neff and Ernest Torrance
186 E. California Boulevard

Very picturesque, rural Andalusian Spanish Colonial Revival, still so in spite of its setting behind a new gas station.

22. Two Houses, 1905
Louis B. Easton
530 and 540 S. Marengo Avenue

Easton, Elbert Hubbard's brother-in-law, built number 540 improvising upon a plan he found in a book. But according to a legend, which should be true even if it isn't, in designing number 530 he cast away precedent and relied on his own best judgment. It is the better of the two, in the Swiss Chalet version of Craftsman architecture. It has recently been restored by Pasadena Heritage and is now a bed and breakfast hotel.

23. Don Carlos Court, 1927
Burrell and Company, builders
374-384 S. Marengo Avenue

A pleasant bungalow court in the Spanish Colonial Revival mode. South Marengo still has many bungalow courts. Some are being recycled as this street becomes commercial. Others are in limbo.

24. House, ca. 1887
255 S. Marengo Avenue

A lovely Queen Anne holding on for dear life against the tides of change.

25. First Baptist Church, 1926
Carleton M. Winslow, Sr. and Frederick Kennedy
75 N. Marengo Avenue

Italian Romanesque in exposed concrete with a beautiful tower that adds to the cityscape.

26. Turner and Stevens Mortuary, 1922
Marston and Van Pelt
95 N. Marengo Avenue

A long, low, brick structure in the English Gothic mode.

27. YWCA Building, 1920-22
Julia Morgan

Southeast corner of Marengo Avenue
and Holly Street

A disappointing, very bland Mediterranean style work by a major architect.
The addition is, of course, not to be
blamed on her.

28. American Legion Post, 1925
Marston and Van Pelt
131 N. Marengo Avenue

Spanish Renaissance. As the ranks of
this once-active American institution
dwindle, the future of such fine buildings as this and the even greater one in
Hollywood is insecure.

29. Pasadena Public Library, 1927
Myron Hunt and H. C. Chambers
285 E. Walnut Street

Spanish Renaissance. The rich
Plateresque entrance beyond the screen
on the street is unusual for Hunt, whose
works are often on the dry side. See Occidental College.

29. Public Library

30. ▪Pasadena City Hall, 1925-27
John Bakewell, Jr. and Arthur Brown, Jr.
100 N. Garfield Avenue

One of several exceptions to the rule
that Pasadena's best buildings were
designed by Pasadena architects, this
giant wedding cake is by the San Francisco firm that is responsible for that
city's marvelous headquarters. Pasadena
was less generous so the interiors are not
as opulent as the earlier San Francisco

City Hall, but its central patio with
fountain and beautiful garden makes up
for the absence of all that marble. The
Spanish Baroque dome and western facade are stunning in the late afternoon
sun.

Notice also the handsome **Gas Company
Building** (1929) at the northwest corner
of Garfield Avenue and Ramona Street
and across Garfield on the northeast corner, the old **Court Buildings** (1952;
Breo Freeman), the latter distinguished
by being well executed Spanish at so late
a date and the former for its rare
scraffito-work in the second story.

31. Old Pasadena Post Office, 1913
Oscar Wenderoth. Addition 1938; Marston and Maybury
Northwest corner of Garfield Avenue
and Colorado Boulevard

This Italian Renaissance palace is notable not only for its facade with light relief decoration but also for its interior
space enclosed in colorful marble walls
paid for by the people of Pasadena,
mind you, and not the federal government. The electric blue walls in the rear
are recent and lamentable. The building
is now a branch of the downright hideous new Central Post Office at Lincoln
Avenue and Orange Grove Boulevard.

32. Plaza Pasadena, 1980
Kober Associates
South side of Colorado Boulevard, between Marengo and Los Robles avenues

We have already paid our respects to
this monstrous cliché that photographs
well if the photographer gets the right
angle (see *Progressive Architecture,* July
1981, page 94-97, that gave it an award).
Come, experience it, and you will go
home shouting the praises of Frank O.
Gehry's **Santa Monica Place** (1980).

33. Pasadena Civic Auditorium, 1932
Edwin Bergstrom (J. E. Stanton, decorator); Bennett and Haskell
300 E. Green Street

A low-silhouette, Italian Renaissance
palace that was once the "City Beautiful"
southern anchor of the minor Garfield
Avenue axis dominated by City Hall
and anchored at the north by the Public
Library.

34. Pasadena Conference Center, 1975
John Carl Warnecke

At both sides of the auditorium are what one little old Pasadena lady has called "The Pig Sties," low structures with most of their interior spaces underground. The intention of the architect was to avoid competing with the Auditorium. Very commendable except that he was in a Brutalist phase and the roofs do intrude, but thankfully not so much as the lines of the heavy-handed Plaza Pasadena across the street.

35. ■Condominiums, 1981
Eric Moss and John Stafford
475 S. Euclid Avenue

Really, in Pasadena? A Post-Modern extravaganza in stucco with window panels in stepped glass brick. A large ear appears on the roof of this object, so much in contrast with its Craftsman and Spanish Colonial neighbors.

36. Masonic Temple, 1926
Bennett and Haskell
200 S. Euclid Avenue

A Beaux Arts Renaissance structure of great dignity.

37. All Saints Episcopal Church, 1925
Johnson, Kaufman, and Coate, (Roland E. Coate)

Parish House and Rectory, 1930
Bennett and Haskell

Interior of Parish House totally remodelled after fire, 1979
Warren Callister
132 N. Euclid Avenue

English country Gothic without and within, including Tiffany windows from an earlier church. The Episcopalians seem to have unfailing good taste. This observation applies to the new interiors of the Parish House. *Joyful* is the best word to describe them.

38. First Congregational Church, 1904, 1916
Buchanan and Brockway
Southeast corner of Walnut Street and Los Robles Avenue

A large English Gothic church that dignifies a rather forlorn commercial area.

39. Grace Nicholson Building, (now Pacific-Asia Museum), 1924
Marston, Van Pelt, and Maybury
46 N. Los Robles Avenue

A real surprise—a Chinese palace. A dealer in Oriental art and books on the Orient, Ms. Nicholson built it as a shop and home. Later it became the Pasadena Museum of Art, until that institution moved to new quarters. Now it is the Pacific-Asia Museum, which has done very well by it by giving unusually good exhibitions and building a lovely Chinese garden in the central court (1979; Erikson, Peters, Thomas, and Associates).

40. Warner Building (A. Schmidt and Sons Company), 1927
Marston and Maybury (Jess Stanton, designer)
481 E. Colorado Boulevard

One suspects that under the paint on the marvelous Art Deco seashell and flower ornament lies black and gold. It could easily be restored.

40. Warner Building

41. First United Methodist Church, 1926
Thomas P. Barber
Southwest corner of Oakland Avenue and Colorado Boulevard

On the outside, this English Gothic church is notable for the pleasant entrance court and the lovely tracery of the large east window, best viewed in the morning. The interior has the usual Methodist central plan with curved pews and curved balcony surrounding the pulpit. But it is the fan vaulting of the ceiling that is remarkable. If you look closely you will see that the intricate plasterwork ingeniously encloses the ventilating system.

42. Singer Building, 1926
Everett Phipps Babcock
520 E. Colorado Boulevard

A good, as-yet-unspoiled example of Spanish Colonial Revival commercial work.

43. First Church of Christ, Scientist, 1909
F. P. Burnham
Southeast corner of Oakland Avenue and Green Street

Like most churches of this denomination, this is a variation on the Neo-Classical "Mother Church" in Boston. It is one of the first large exposed concrete structures in the area.

44a. ■Throop Memorial Unitarian-Universalist Church, 1923
Frederick Kennedy
Northeast corner of Los Robles Avenue and Del Mar Boulevard

An exposed concrete (now plastered over) Gothic design that gives sophistication to this area.

44b. E. W. Smith House, 1910
Charles and Henry Greene
272 S. Los Robles Avenue (next door to Throop Church)

A large, two-story Craftsman house that shows very little evidence of the Greene's affair with the Orient. Converted to commercial use without damaging the integrity of the architecture, this building is a model of adaptive re-use.

45. Pages Victorian Court, 1981
Thornton and Fagan Associates
430 S. Los Robles Avenue

Talk about a protest against the Modern movement, this is it — a humorous, not-too-authentic-but-still-recognizable Eastlake Revival extravaganza.

46. Pasadena Town Club, 1931
Roland E. Coate
378 S. Madison Avenue

This chaste, one-story Monterey style building, with a good Greek Revival door, exudes respectability.

47. Casa Torre Garden Court, 1927
Everett Phipps Babcock
611-27 E. California Boulevard

A two-story, L-shaped Spanish Colonial Revival apartment building that looks as if it is about to be gobbled up by modernism.

48. Pasadena Playhouse, 1924-25
Elmer Grey
Interiors, Dwight Gibbs
37 S. El Molino Avenue

Once the very heart of Pasadena culture, this theatre and school came upon hard times in the fifties and collapsed in the mid-sixties. The wonder is that it is still with us. At present it is being refurbished and hopefully will resume its old spirit and ambience. The official State Theatre.

48. Pasadena Playhouse

49. First Trust Building (now Lloyds Bank), 1928
Bennett and Haskell
595 E. Colorado Boulevard at Madison Avenue

This dignified Renaissance Revival building is most impressive inside. The banking room was decorated by Giovanni Smeraldi and is hung with four large paintings by Alson Clark.

56. Scottish Rite Cathedral

Also, this happens to be the first building in Pasadena built to resist earthquakes. In 1971 it met the test.

50. Pasadena Presbyterian Church, 1976
Gougeon-Woodman
Northwest corner of Colorado Boulevard and Madison Avenue

Architectural expressionism at its very height, this church replaces a Collegiate Gothic structure (1904) by F. L. Roehrig that was badly damaged in the 1971 earthquake.

51. Blaisdell Medical Building, 1952
Smith and Williams (Whitney R. Smith)
547 E. Union Street

A small reinforced concrete building with central patio. Smith was obviously influenced by Wrightean ideas. He did not design the recent wooden fence.

52. Earl Apartment House, 1912
Charles and Henry Greene
527 E. Union Street

The Greenes working in the Mission style though they could not resist occasional Oriental touches.

53. Blinn House (now Women's City Club), 1906
George W. Maher
Oakland Avenue at Ford Place

So far as is known this is the only house in the West designed by the well-known Chicago architect, friend of Sullivan and Wright. (Incidentally, Maher's only other western building is, of all things, a combined public library and water tower in Fresno.) Stylistically the Blinn House is distantly related to the Mission Revival, though it is hard to place the corner windows on the second floor. The interior, somewhat remodelled, is nevertheless still exciting, particularly the staircase and glazed tile fireplace.

54. Bungalow Court, 1910
Attributed to Hunt and Grey
270 N. Madison Avenue

A handsome Tudor court.

55. Lukens House, 1887
267 N. El Molino Avenue

This beautifully restored house in its garden is one of the few vestiges of Victorianism left in this part of town. It is Queen Anne with dripping lathwork similar to that on Lucky Baldwin's Guest House in Arcadia.

56. Scottish Rite Cathedral, 1924
Joseph Blick
150 N. Madison Avenue

Pre-PWA Classical Moderne with guardian sphinxes.

57. First City Bank, 1961
Ladd and Kelsey
123 S. Lake Avenue

A beautifully articulated Miesian box.

58. Retail Shops (Abacus, Konditori), 1961
Pulliam, Matthews, and Associates
230 S. Lake Avenue

Very civilized International Style Modern, including an outdoor cafe.

59. Bullock's Pasadena, 1947
Wurdeman and Becket
401 S. Lake Avenue

The building extends the Streamline Moderne idiom into the post-war era. The elegance of the interior craftsmanship, now beginning to show wear, evokes the Arts and Crafts tradition in Pasadena. There are rumors of imminent remodelling. We hope not.

See also **Robinson's Pasadena** nearby at 777 E. Colorado Boulevard, designed in 1950 by Pereira and Luckman.

60. The Burlington Arcade, 1982
Symonds/Deenihan
380 S. Lake Avenue

A galleria of two, two-story tiers of shops facing each other, reminiscent of the building of the same name. These architects also designed **The Commons** (1982), a courtyard shopping center up the street at S. Lake Avenue. This time they chose the Mansard mode.

East Pasadena

The section of the city east of Lake Avenue and south of the Foothill Freeway is fairly recent Pasadena with products of the twenties and thirties appearing in the western portion. Then about Hill Avenue at Pasadena City College shards of the fifties begin to pop up, at first on commercial Colorado Boulevard and then south of it in the residential districts. It is easy to brush this stuff off as kitsch culture, but who knows what forthcoming Ph.D. candidate will pronounce it not just significant but profound!

1. Trinity Lutheran Church, 1927
Frederick Kennedy, Jr.
997 E. Walnut Street at Catalina Avenue

Vaguely English Gothic in revealed concrete. Kennedy was a strong advocate of concrete construction in the Los Angeles area and his work deserves a careful study.

2. Sanborn House, 1903
Charles and Henry Greene
65 N. Catalina Avenue

This is a large, angular Craftsman structure, never very good and made worse by a nasty paint job. But it is by Greene and Greene and significant, for in 1903 they were on the brink of their great creative period.

3. Thatcher Medical Center and other buildings, 1948-49
L. G. Scherer
960 E. Green Street at Mentor Avenue

A collection of offices, shops, and apartments in the New Orleans Mansard style, rather strange to encounter in Pasadena.

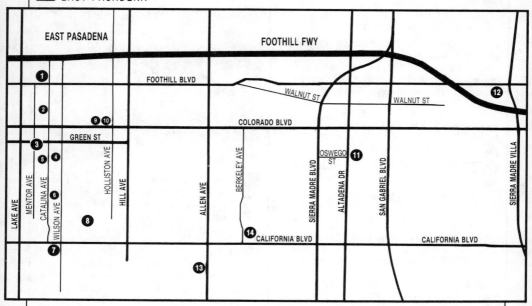

4. Apartment Building, 1963
Pulliam, Matthews, and Associates
241 S. Wilson Avenue

Elegant International Style Modern simplicity on a tree-lined street notable for apartments designed with less sophistication, to put it mildly.

5. Charlotte Perkins Gilman House, ca. 1900
239 S. Catalina Avenue

A Colonial Revival cottage of no great architectural distinction, but it was the last home of Charlotte Perkins Gilman, the great American feminist who resigned from the Women's Suffrage Movement because it did not go far enough in its advocacy of women's rights. Gilman died here.

6. House, ca. 1915
Arthur S. Heineman (Alfred Heineman, associate)
516 S. Catalina Avenue

The rolled-eave treatment of this house is almost a trademark of Heineman work in the teens.

7. Polytechnic School, 1907
Hunt and Grey
1030 E. California Street at Wilson Avenue

This is probably the first fully realized bungalow school. Not only does it manage to get all the classrooms on one floor, but it also opens these rooms with ranks of doors to the outside, pioneering the idea of the indoor-outdoor school that has won wide popularity in California and elsewhere. The old building has been remodelled but the idea is still clear.

8. California Institute of Technology, 1908-present
California Boulevard between Wilson and Hill avenues

The first campus plan and buildings for Cal Tech were designed by the firm of

Myron Hunt and Elmer Grey. Their scheme provided a Beaux Arts axial mall, open at one end and surrounded by two-story Mission Revival structures on the enclosed sides. Their principal building, which terminated the major axis, was **Throop Hall (Pasadena Hall)** of 1910. Hunt and Grey continued their work on the campus over a period of eight years, from 1908 through 1915. In 1915 they were replaced by Bertram G. Goodhue. Goodhue enlarged and elaborated on the original axial plan, making the landscape more Moorish and the buildings more Spanish Churrigueresque. After Goodhue's death in 1924 his firm, Goodhue Associates, continued to design buildings for the campus through the late 1930s. As with most American academic institutions after World War II, the Modern Movement entered the scene. The results have added little of merit, and they have done much to destroy the strong character of the original campus plan and its architecture.

The most interesting buildings that remain are:

a. Gates Chemistry Laboratory (now **Administration Building**), 1917
Bertram G. Goodhue and Elmer Grey

Its exterior is dominated by a fine Churrigueresque door. The interior has been recycled (1983) by Bobrow and Thomas; Peter de Bretteville and Stefanos Polyzoides. The **Gates Annex** (1927) is by the Goodhue Associates and is Spanish mixed with Art Deco Moderne.

b. Bridge Physics Laboratory, 1922
Bertram G. Goodhue

Again, rather severe Spanish with relief given by a Churrigueresque entrance.

c. West Court Buildings, 1928-30
Goodhue Associates

The main (Wilson Avenue) entrance to Cal Tech consists of two long, arcaded buildings somewhat reminiscent of the Campo Santo at Pisa. The rows of Italian cypresses in front of them were recently cut down.

d. Athenaeum (Faculty Club), 1930
Gordon B. Kaufmann

A marvelous, Mediterranean (Italian) style building without and within.

8c. California Institute of Technology, West Court Buildings

e. Dormitories, 1931
Gordon B. Kaufmann

Designed around three courtyards, these vaguely Spanish/Italian Romanesque buildings, with capitals in the cloisters featuring the heads of aviators and scientists, are real treasures.

f. Beckman Auditorium, 1963
Edward D. Stone

A fanciful Islamic image in Stone's World's Fair phase.

California Boulevard east of Cal Tech

This street, extending into San Marino and San Pasqual, has fine houses in the period revivals of the twenties and thirties. It is a good place to walk. Even better is **Lombardy Road,** one block below California, but, since most of Lombardy is in San Marino, we have included it in our San Marino section.

9. Howard Austin Company Building, ca. 1927
1285 E. Colorado Boulevard

Huge, gaping jaws full of plate glass are framed by cast stone Plateresque ornament.

10. Holliston Avenue United Methodist Church, 1899
John C. Austin
Northwest corner of Holliston Avenue and Colorado Boulevard

This large Gothic structure (which looks Richardsonian) was moved stone-by-stone from its original site at Marengo Avenue and Colorado Boulevard where it had been First Methodist. It lost its tower in the 1971 earthquake, but it otherwise speaks of the late Victorian age. The interior is based on the Akron Plan with its semicircular seating oriented to the northwest corner pulpit area.

9. Howard Austin Company Building

11. Pasadena Public Library, Lamanda Park Branch, 1966
Pulliam, Matthews, and Associates
140 S. Altadena Drive at Oswego Street

Though one-story, the massive concrete post-and-lintel frame makes this building seem monumental. The interior is well planned for use and beauty.

12. ■Stuart Pharmaceutical Company, 1958
Edward D. Stone; Thomas D. Church, landscape architect
3300 block of East Foothill Boulevard near Sierra Madre Villa Avenue

This building and the American Embassy in New Delhi are Stone's best designs in the post-World War II era. Like the embassy, the Stuart Building poses as a delicate Islamic box set in an Oriental pond. Church's design for the garden fully acknowledges the mood that Stone was trying to convey.

13. Longfellow-Hastings (Octagon) House, 1893
85 S. Allen Avenue

This building was once in the midst of orange groves. It was moved to its present location many years ago and lost its wrap-around veranda in the process. This octagon house is one of the few tributes to Orson Squire Fowler's ideas remaining in California.

14. Ten Spec Houses, ca. 1927
Wallace Neff
500 Block, of South Berkeley Avenue, San Marino

A delightful group of modest-sized Spanish Colonial revival houses by an architect who usually designed much larger ones.

11. Pasadena Library, Lamanda Park Branch

14. Spec House

North Pasadena

T his area, bounded on the west and south by the Foothill Freeway, on the east by Michillinda Avenue, and on the north by the boundary with Altadena is listed from west to east, generally alternating streets south-north and north-south.

1. Savage House, 1924
Henry Greene
1299-1301 N. Marengo Avenue

A Spanish Colonial Revival duplex distinguished only by the name of its architect. It was done after his partnership with his brother Charles was dissolved.

2. House, 1895
1249 N. Garfield Avenue

The American Colonial Revival at its best, this beautifully detailed house awaits restoration.

3. Lewis House ("Mansion Adena"), 1886
Northeast corner of Garfield Avenue and Adena Street

This otherwise Queen Anne house sports a mansard tower.

4. Rust-Smiley House, 1887
730 N. Garfield Avenue

Another good Queen Anne well set back from the street.

3. Lewis House ("Mansion Adena")

5. Bowen Court, 1913
Arthur S. Heineman (Alfred Heineman, associate)
539 Villa Street

This is one of the first bungalow courts. It is set in tall trees and extends in an arc around to North Oakland Avenue. Note the rustic "playhouse" (now glassed in) which is toward the center of the court. **Two other bungalow courts** of the same period—one Mission style, the other Craftsman—are at 567 and 572-574 N. Oakland Avenue respectively. The former is quite simple but retains marvelous Mission style lanterns in the center of the court.

6. House, 1914
Southwest corner of Orange Grove Boulevard and El Molino Avenue

A huge airplane bungalow on a boulder base.

7. Westminster Presbyterian Church, 1928
Marston, Van Pelt, and Maybury
1757 N. Lake Avenue

Certainly a landmark as Lake Avenue rises toward the mountains, this church seems vaguely modelled on Saint Maclou at Rouen.

8. Saint Elizabeth's Roman Catholic Church, 1924
Wallace Neff
1849 N. Lake Avenue, Altadena (north of Westminster Presbyterian Church)

The monumental but simple facade of this Spanish Colonial Revival church is marred only by a bad sculpture of the saint over the door.

8. Saint Elizabeth's Roman Catholic Church

9. House, ca. 1910
Southwest corner of Michigan Avenue and Washington Boulevard

Mission style with red trim.

10. Houses, ca. 1912
800 N. Michigan Avenue

A number of Craftsman bungalows, not by the Greenes, are to be found in almost mint condition in this area. See also from about the same period number 885 and 1399 N. Michigan Avenue, 835 and 897 N. Holliston Avenue, and 1261 N. Mar Vista Avenue.

11. Williams House ("Hillmont"), 1887
Harry Ridgeway
Northwest corner of Hill Avenue and Mountain Street

This Queen Anne house of extraordinary quality is set in beautiful grounds. Ridgeway was Pasadena's first professional architect. Hiram Reid in his *History of Pasadena* (ca. 1895) wrote that Ridgeway "never wanted any man to be able to point out any structure and say 'that's one of Ridgeway's designs—it shows the earmarks of his style.' He sought and achieved that ideal freedom from style called the artlessness of art."

Just west of the house at 1507 Mountain Street is the utterly nondescript **Thum House** (1925) by Henry Greene.

11. Williams House ("Hillmont")

Altadena

12. Gartz Duplex, 1921
Irving J. Gill
950 N. Oakland Avenue

Very simple stucco walls and an arch —
very characteristic of Gill in a highly
puritanical mood.

13. Craig Adobe ("The Hermitage"),
ca. 1880
2121 Monte Vista Street, just west of
Craig Avenue

Except for its walls, this is a Queen
Anne cottage with fish-scale shingles in
the gable.

14. Pasadena Jewish Temple and Center, 1957
1434 N. Altadena Drive, just above
Washington Boulevard

Classical Moderne.

15. Saint Luke's Hospital, 1934
Gene Verge, Sr.
2632 E. Washington Boulevard near Altadena Drive

Classical Moderne with strong Spanish
Colonial Revival elements.

16. Hale House, ca. 1910
835 N. Holliston Avenue

A sturdy example of the Craftsman aesthetic in a predominantly Swiss Chalet
version.

Altadena is unincorporated, but,
as its name implies, it is culturally an extension of Pasadena.
Here large estates existed by the
late nineteenth century. Although by
now almost all of them have been subdivided several times, the relaxed style
of living can still be imagined — citrus
groves and chicken farms!

In our citation of buildings we generally move from west to east.

1. House, ca. 1906
Louis B. Easton
403 W. Ventura Street, near Lincoln
Avenue

By a miracle this Craftsman house, perhaps a bunkhouse, was not torn down
when the C. C. Curtis ranch house was
demolished. It is, along with the Volney-
Craig House in Pasadena, one of
Easton's finest designs, which is to say
that it is one of the best examples of the
Craftsman aesthetic anywhere.

The house across the street is also
probably by Easton. In 1925 additions
were made to it by Henry Greene.

2. ■McNally House, 1888
Frederick L. Roehrig
Just east of southeast corner of
Mariposa Street and Santa Rosa Avenue

A towered, simplified Queen Anne
(Shingle style) building now almost obscured by later building. A. N. McNally
(of Rand-McNally) was a commissioner
of the World's Columbian Exposition in
Chicago in 1893. According to the story,

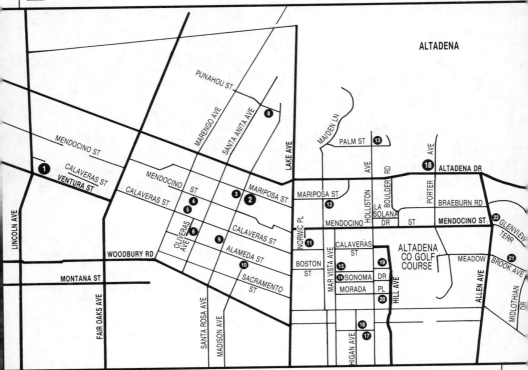

ALTADENA

he liked the interior of the Turkish display so much that when it was dismantled he had parts of it crated and sent to Altadena where, presumably with the aid of Roehrig, they were added to the main house as a "smoking room." In fact, remembering Roehrig's Islamic pretentions, we rather imagine that he was the instigator of this delightful enterprise.

3. Altadena Public Library, 1967
Boyd Georgi
600 E. Mariposa Street, southwest corner of Santa Rosa Avenue

The International Style Modern box softened by Orientalism.

4. House, 1917
Myron Hunt

396 E. Mendocino Street, east of Marengo Avenue

A stucco Anglo-Colonial Revival dwelling. Very gracious.

5. House, 1923
369 E. Calaveras Street

Egyptian Revival. This town has everything!

6. House, 1938
Whitney R. Smith
2320 N. Oliveras Avenue

A very simple Modern structure.

7. Bowen House, 1905
Charles and Henry Greene
443 E. Calaveras Street, at northwest corner of Santa Anita Avenue

One of the Greenes' best early bungalows, enlarged and almost totally changed at a later date.

8. Lowe House, 1933-34
Harwell H. Harris (Carl Anderson, associate)
596 E. Punahou Street, between Santa Anita and Santa Rosa avenues

An impressive classic of the thirties. The garage to the street and the L-shaped house enclose the entrance court. Small, wood-walled enclosures extend from each bedroom so that it is possible to sleep out-of-doors in privacy. The feeling is Japanese but also very personally Harris.

9. Case Study House #20, 1958
Buff, Straub, and Hensman
2275 N. Santa Rosa Avenue

An elegant, small house set in bosky ("Christmas Tree Lane") surroundings.

10. Woodbury House, ca. 1885
2606 N. Madison Avenue, on cul-de-sac just north of Sacramento Street

An old ranch house in the Italianate manner.

10. Woodbury House

11. "Little Normandy," 1925
J. Wilmer Hershey
Norwic Place just east of Lake Avenue and off Mendocino Street

A group of quaint dollhouse dwellings intended to be reminiscent of rural France. Unfortunately, there were some intrusions in the early fifties.

11. "Little Normandy"

12. Serrurier House, 1905
Charles and Henry Greene
1086 Mariposa Street, at southeast corner of Maiden Lane

A tiny Craftsman bungalow.

13. Gateposts, ca. 1910
Northeast corner of Holliston Avenue and Palm Street

An impressive boulder entrance to an old ranch.

13. Gateposts

14. Williams House

14. Williams House, 1915
Charles and Henry Greene
1145 Sonoma Drive at northeast corner
of Mar Vista Avenue

The stuccoed house, with its green tile
roof, seems almost Spanish until you no·
tice the Oriental touches. It is interesting to compare it with the Earl Apartments (1912) and the Cordelia
Culbertson House (1911) by the same
architects.

15. House, ca. 1915
Northeast corner of Boston Street and
Mar Vista Avenue

A Pueblo Revival bungalow with matching pergolas jutting from the central
"upper room."

16. House, ca. 1915
Northeast corner of Woodbury Road
and Michigan Avenue

A late example of the Mission style with
corner gate.

17. House, ca. 1915
1290 E. Woodbury Road

Mission style simplicity placed on an almost monumental rustic cobblestone
base. Very strange.

18. ■Parsons Bungalow, 1909
Arthur S. Heineman (Alfred Heineman,
associate)
1605 E. Altadena Drive at Porter
Avenue

This is simply one of the finest, most
characteristic California bungalows to be
found anywhere. And its siting at a diagonal to the nearby mountain is spectacular. In our 1977 *A Guide to Architecture in Los Angeles and Southern California* it
was still at the corner of Los Robles
Avenue and California Street in
Pasadena. But times change. Incidentally, it proved impossible to move the
original cobblestone foundations and pillars but they were rebuilt by modern
craftsmen.

There are some fascinating neighborhoods in this area. You will not believe **Boulder Road** just west of the previous entry and nearby **La Solana**, a street devoted to the Spanish Colonial Revival. Farther south, **Mar Vista Avenue** above and below New York Drive is a very characteristic pre-World War I street.

19. Keyes Bungalow, 1911
1337 E. Boston Street, west of Altadena Country Club

A first-rate example of the "airplane bungalow," called that for its wingspread. It is obvious that it once was surrounded with much more open space.

20. Dorland House, 1949
Lloyd Wright
1370 Morada Place, west of Altadena Country Club

A large glass prow accents the street facade.

21. Beard House, 1935
Richard J. Neutra
1981 Meadowbrook Drive, between Allen Avenue and Midlothian Drive

A small but elegant machine image house with walls and roof of H. H. Robertson ribbed steel panels.

22. House, ca. 1925
1960 Mendocino Lane, facing Allen Avenue

This is a striking sight—it is almost as if the street were designed to show off this rather unusual and large Mediterranean style house here at the east end of Mendocino.

22. House

South Pasadena, Central Section

We have already introduced South Pasadena under the Lower Arroyo, South section. The following listing cover the business district of South Pasadena and its immediate surroundings.

1. House, ca. 1910
499 Monterey Road, at southwest corner of Indiana Court

A large Tudor-Craftsman chalet with Mission touches.

2. Bungalow, ca. 1900
1102 Indiana Avenue, north of Monterey Road, near the Santa Fe Railroad tracks

A marvelous misinterpretation of Vitruvius on a very small scale.

2. Bungalow

3. Bilike House, ca. 1905
Entrance at 699 Monterey Road

An uphill drive takes you to this Mission Revival house that is now an educational center and church office for the nearby United Methodist Church. Also, the view of Pasadena and the mountains can be magnificent.

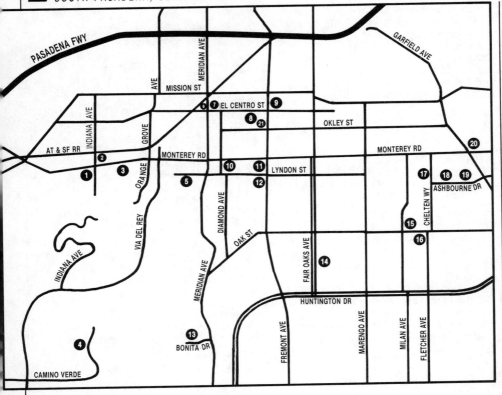

4. Chiat House, 1967
Carl Maston
612 Camino Verde

In an area of pleasant but unremarkable houses, this vertically planked Miesian box stands out as one of the best pieces of architecture in South Pasadena.

5. Graham House ("Wynyate"), 1887
W. R. Norton
851 Lyndon Street

This triumph of the Queen Anne style was a meetingplace for such worthies as John Muir, Mary Austin, and Charles F. Lummis. Imagine it with its porte cochere and tall chimney restored!

6. Meridian Iron Works, ca. 1890
913 Meridian Avenue

An example of the Pioneer False Front style, rare in this area.

7. Watering Trough and Wayside Station, 1905
Norman F. Marsh
On Meridian Avenue, just aross the street from the Iron Works.

This large boulder cairn was a rest stop for horses and their riders on their way between Los Angeles and Pasadena.

8. South Pasadena Public Library, 1930
Marsh, Smith, and Powell; new addition, Howard H. Morgridge and Associates, 1982
1115 El Centro Street

Only the Renaissance Revival facade of the 1930 building has been retained in the new construction. All traces of the older (1907) Carnegie Library (with dome, of course) have been destroyed. But the new building is harmonious with the old as it now stands.

9. South Pasadena Presbyterian Church (now **Grace United Brethren Church**), 1906
Northeast corner of Fremont Avenue and El Centro Street

Mission style monumentality screening the apse of the much earlier (1886) Pasadena Presbyterian Church, that was moved from the site at Colorado and Madison when the 1906 church by Frederick L. Roehrig was built.

10. Cottage, ca. 1890
1103 Monterey Road, southeast corner of Diamond Avenue

A Queen Anne relic.

11. Saint James Episcopal Church, 1907
Cram, Goodhue, and Ferguson (Carleton M. Winslow, Sr., associate)
Southwest corner of Monterey Road and Fremont Avenue

Some points of similarity to the West Point Chapel (by the same firm) on the outside — heavy Gothic mixed with Romanesque — but the interior is airy and elegant.

12. South Pasadena High School Auditorium, 1937
Marsh, Smith, and Powell; murals by Millard Sheets; sculptured panels by Merrill Gage
Southwest corner of Fremont Avenue and Lyndon Street

PWA Classical Moderne rather delicately worked. South of the high school there are some good streets of bungalows; Ramona Street has some sophisticated designs; Diamond Avenue is another interesting street. East of Fair Oaks Avenue are more bungalows and other Craftsman houses; also, try Milan Avenue. It may be of interest that Henry Saylor, whose publication *Bungalows* (1911) is one of the classics in the literature of that genre, lived in South Pasadena — in a bungalow, of course.

13. Grokowsky House, 1928
R. M. Schindler
816 Bonita Dive off Meridian Avenue

Schindler in a modest example of his early de Stijl phase.

13. Grokowsky House

14. 1414 Fair Oaks Building, 1959
Smith and Williams; Eckbo, Dean, and Associates, landscape architects
1414 Fair Oaks Avenue

A building as a sun screen with gardens and enclosed spaces underneath. Some grievous alterations have been made by the new tenants.

15. Bungalow, ca. 1910
Northeast corner of Oak Street and Milan Avenue

Pictured in Sweet's *Bungalows* (ca. 1911), the design may be by the Heinemans.

16. House, ca. 1905
Southwest corner of Oak Street and Fletcher Avenue

Mission style with Oriental touches.

17. Miltimore House, 1911
Irving J. Gill
1301 Chelten Way

This house is one of Gill's best; puritanical, based on Mission style. Note the extensive pergolas that provide the transition between house and garden. Also compare the houses nearby—very different in imagery but only a little earlier. This section around the intersection of Chelten Way and Ashbourne Drive was once called Ellerslie Park, full of ancient oaks. It was privately developed with many of the live oaks being saved by curving the streets around them, a perverse twist dear to the hearts of ecologists, old and young.

18. House, 1926
David A. Ogilvie
2000 Ashbourne Drive

The yellow brick walls of this Tudor villa give it a Cotswold feeling.

19. Baer House, 1930
Roland E. Coate
2040 Ashbourne Drive

Spanish Colonial Revival somewhat corrected by reference to the eastern Colonial. It is swamped in foliage.

20. House, 1923
Roland E. Coate
1148 S. Garfield Avenue, at northeast corner of Monterey Road

This house is one of the first uses of the Monterey Revival style. It was often illustrated and mentioned in discussions of that style in the twenties and thirties.

21. Rialto Theatre, 1925
L. A. Smith
Northwest corner of Fair Oaks Avenue and Okley Street

The exterior, once mildly Plateresque with Baroque touches, is defaced. But the mainly Spanish interior is still intact. Note an Egyptian influence here and there.

San Marino

It should be obvious from its architecture that this town, settled on the Henry H. Huntington estate of the same name, is largely inhabited by members of the monied class. Its "high tone" was set by Huntington, who put his house and then his library on a fine prominence with a distant view of the Pacific (still seen occasionally). In the twenties and thirties the would-be barons gathered within his regal estate. Even the subdividing of properties in recent years and the consequent building of houses closer and closer together has not really interfered with the picture of opulence. This is the way all people should be able to live even if they do not wish to do so. Try **Saint Albans Road** north of Huntington Drive to get a feeling for "the way of life."

A rule never boldly stated in this book but sometimes implied is that good architecture and a great deal of money are constant companions. In San Marino this "rule" often breaks down. It is not that there isn't a lot of beautiful building; it is just that the expenditure should have produced more, particularly since nearby Pasadena has always had excellent architects ready to cross the border. As a matter of fact, most of the best work is significantly near Pasadena.

1. House, 1970
B. R. Offenhauser
1045 Oak Grove Place

An unusual and very knowing play on the Mediterranean style.

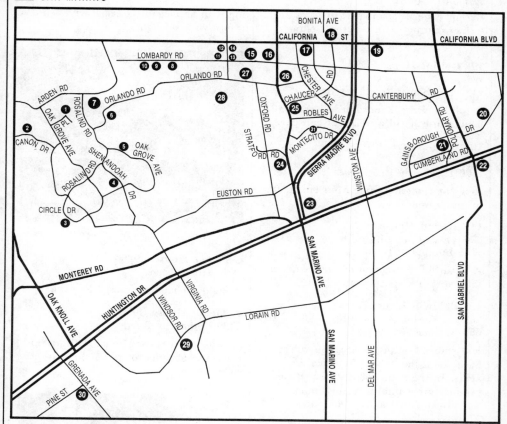

2. House, 1960
Lynn V. Maudlin
931 Canon Drive

A return to the Oriental Craftsman tradition. The setting is lovely.

3. House, 1932
Roland E. Coate
1435 Circle Drive

A turn at the Georgian Revival.

4. House, 1929
John Atchinson
1215 Shenandoah Road

Tudor finery.

5. Romboz House, 1927
Weston and Weston
1762 Oak Grove Avenue

Spanish Colonial Revival Mudejar with a gorgeous entrance.

6. House and Outbuildings, ca. 1915
870 Orlando Road

A Mission Revival complex of great interest. It is rare to be able to see all the main buildings from the street. This is a picturesque ensemble with Orientalized chimney and green tile roofs.

7. Mays House, 1927
Roland E. Coate
945 Orlando Road

New Orleans, Georgian, and Tudor styles mixed very nicely.

8. Marlow House, 1981
B. R. Offenhauser
1556 Lombardy Road, Pasadena

Recent eastern Colonial Revival in the former cutting garden of the Collins House next door.

9. Collins House, 1927
Wallace Neff
1550 Lombardy Road, Pasadena

A solid-looking, handsome, Mediterranean house set in a well-kept garden.

10. Fong House, 1976
Miller Fong
1500 Lombardy Road, Pasadena

Airy International Style Modern. It "fits in" quite well.

11. ■Ostoff House, 1924
George Washington Smith
1778 Lombardy Road

A beautiful abstraction of rural Andalusia transferred to opulent suburbia.

12. Baldwin House, 1925
George Washington Smith
665 S. Allen Avenue

Rid yourself of any reservation you may have about the uses of historical imagery. In the hands of an artist, it can produce great things, as this romantic Spanish dwelling and garden attest.

13. House, ca. 1927
Wallace Neff
Northeast corner of Lombardy Road and Allen Avenue

Another Spanish Colonial Revival masterpiece with a marvelous staircase in front.

14a. Milligan House, 1928
Roland E. Coate
1850 Lombardy Road

Monterey Revival with a trace of Regency.

Other nearby examples of Roland Coate's work are:

b. Le Fens House, 1933.
691 Holladay Road

A painted stone Monterey Revival dwelling with an elegant Greek Revival entrance with sidelights.

14c. Pitner House

c. Pitner House, 1928.
1138 Arden Road

A highly refined Monterey Revival.

d. Heath House, 1930
2080 Lombardy Road

A two-story Regency house with an unusual use of fluted piers for the two-story porch.

14d. Heath House

15. House, 1948
R. H. Ainsworth
1910 Lombardy Road

A Classical Revival giant portico on a delicate Federal (Adamesque) Revival fabric. See 1945 Lombardy Road for an almost identical twin (1941) by the same architect.

16. Bourne House, 1927
Wallace Neff
2035 Lombardy Road

One of the finest of Neff's Spanish Colonial Revival houses. Here he enlarged the theme of the white, stuccoed, Andalusian farmhouse to a stately villa.

16. Bourne House

17. House, ca. 1940
Whitney R. Smith
705 Canterbury Road

Monterey style—and good—by an architect best known for his early Modern work.

18. House, ca. 1910
580 Bonita Avenue at northeast corner of California Street

A fine Craftsman house in an otherwise Mediterranean style area.

19. Fitzgerald House, 1919
Roland E. Coate
708 Winston Avenue

Coate was, of course, always at home with the Monterey style.

20. Packard House, 1924
R. M. Schindler
931 N. Gainsborough Road

Maybeckian spaces and the tidy line of the early International Style Modern;

Schindler was a master of both. The original rolled composition roof has been shingled over. Three wings project out of the central core kitchen.

21. Day House, 1932
H. Roy Kelley
2871 Cumberland Road

Compact Monterey style.

22. Carver Elementary School, 1947
Marsh, Smith, and Powell
1300 San Gabriel Boulevard at Huntington Drive

It is interesting to compare this brick, International Style Modern school (with its continuation of the indoor-outdoor classroom tradition) with Hunt's and Grey's much earlier (1907) **Polytechnic School** in Pasadena.

23. Sobieski House, 1946
Harwell H. Harris
1420 Sierra Madre Boulevard, just north of Huntington Drive

The beautifully crafted, two-story shingle and wood garage is about all that can be seen from the street.

24. House, 1948
Wallace Neff
1173 San Marino Avenue

The architect in one of his French Norman moods.

25. House, 1933
Rainer and Adams
2170 Chaucer Road (but visible only from San Marino Avenue gatehouse)

This fine Tudor Revival house with its extensive black-and-white work encourages great expectations for the almost invisible mansion behind it. Records are confused, but it would appear that the gatehouse came first and that the mansion was designed (1937) by Girard R. Colcord.

26. House, ca. 1928
Wallace Neff
2115 Orlando Road

A characteristic Neff Tuscan villa with an inset second-floor loggia placed above the front entrance.

27. Wallace Neff House, 1929
Wallace Neff
1883 Orlando Road

A larger version of entry number 26, this Tuscan house was even more impressive before the entrance court was changed and the fence added.

27. Wallace Neff House

28. Henry E. Huntington Art Gallery, Library and Gardens

Gallery (originally the house), 1910
Myron Hunt and Elmer Grey

Library, 1925
Myron Hunt and H. C. Chambers
Entrance is at end of Allen Avenue at Orlando Road

Public areas are open, free of charge (donation suggested!) 1-4:30 every afternoon except Monday. Reservations required on Sunday. Closed in October and on all major holidays.

You will enter through a mildly Beaux Arts gate and orientation building designed by Whitney Smith (1981). The main **Gallery** is reserved, academic, Beaux Arts Neo-Classicism. Architecturally, the salient points are the Palladian-like porch and the interior grand staircase. The treasure is the collection, assembled for the railroad magnate by Lord Joseph Duveen. English eighteenth-century painting may not turn you on, but the main gallery, with Lawrence's *Pinkie* on the side and Gainsborough's *Blue Boy* on the other and Reynold's *Mrs. Siddons as the Tragic Muse* at the end, is something to behold.

The later separate **Library** building is also Beaux Arts with a decidedly French feeling. The main collections can be used only if you have a Ph.D. or similar credentials. But there is a large, recently renovated exhibition hall where you can gaze at such things as a Guttenberg Bible, Thoreau's manuscript of *Walden,* or an architectural drawing by Thomas Jefferson.

The **gardens** — French, Shakespearean, Japanese, Cactus, etc. — begun in

Henry E. Huntington Library

1904 by William Hertrich and extended by Wilbur David Cook, are among the most beautiful in the world. The Japanese garden (begun 1911) is especially fine with a teahouse (1906), much changed since it was taken from the Japanese Tea Garden that once stood at the northeast corner of California Boulevard and Fair Oaks Avenue in Pasadena. More recently, a Zen garden designed by Robert Watson has been added.

Do not miss the impressive **Huntington Mausoleum** (1933) designed by America's prominent Beaux Arts architect John Russell Pope, the designer of the National Gallery in Washington, D.C. Here Pope explores the theme of the circular and domed Classical Temple, a theme he returned to again and again.

Nearby and just completed (1983-4) is the ▪**Virginia Steele Gallery of American Art** designed by Paul Gray (Warner and Gray). It is a sensitive and lively continuation of the Classical tradition of Pope with its principal space organized around an open dome.

29. Sheppard House, 1934
Jock Peters
1390 Lorain Road

A rare executed example in Streamline Moderne of the gifted architect who was the principal interior designer of Bullocks Wilshire in Los Angeles.

30. House, ca. 1925
Southwest corner of Pine Street and Granada Avenue, Alhambra

The strange Hansel and Gretel feeling of this building suggests that it was designed by the Heineman firm in Pasadena.

31. "The Mosque", 1980
2250 Montecito Drive

This is the name that neighbors have aptly given this house — a little out of place in San Marino.

San Gabriel Valley

The San Gabriel Valley is roughly bounded by the San Gabriel Mountains to the north, the desert on the east, the Whittier Hills to the south, and the Arroyo Seco to the west. Not all of it is covered here because the Los Angeles County line cuts down the middle of it. It is an area of many towns, a large number founded by land speculators attached to the Southern Pacific and Santa Fe railroads. Some towns still show their nineteenth century origins in their display of Victorian architecture, but instead of the citrus groves and vineyards that once surrounded them, you see acres and acres of tract housing, most of it tedious. It has come to resemble the San Fernando Valley except that you see few trees outside the boundaries of the old towns. Also, sadly, the San Gabriel Valley, particularly the eastern side, often gets the worst smog in the county.

San Gabriel

I t all began with the founding of the San Gabriel Mission in 1771, near the present site of Montebello. When the Mission was relocated in 1776, the town also moved. What is left of this later settlement dates from 1791 to 1850 and there is precious little of it. Early photographs show, however, that in the 1890s West Mission Road was a charming country town street with adobes extending their pitched roofs over the sidewalks. But in 1913 the residents voted for incorporation and progress. Their decision meant the wholesale destruction of the visible past, a process which has continued until fairly recently, leaving few shards besides the Mission (itself in bad shape even today). The Mission, in spite of its woebegone appearance (and its gift shop, unmatched for its bad taste), is still considerably more convincing than the next in the chain—San Fernando—which has been restored beyond credibility.

1. Rose House, 1862
7020 La Presa Drive, off Huntington Drive

Said to be the oldest frame house in the San Gabriel Valley, it looks the part. It is a simple house without style but it is nevertheless picturesque in its beautiful garden.

2. Miller Water Garden, 1925-later
Bill Miller
6221 N. San Gabriel Boulevard

Driving by, you might think that this was just another nursery, but take time to muse. The garden furniture takes you back to early California. This is distributed among concrete grottoes, rustic concrete bridges, and rare aquatic plants and fish. There is even a concrete log cabin.

3. San Gabriel Union Church and School, 1936
Northwest corner of Las Tunas Drive and Pine Street

Basically, this building is Classical PWA Moderne with an update of Streamline touches, such as a porch with chrome trim intact.

4. "The Alamo", ca. 1929
522 E. Broadway

Yes, this residence has an entrance that vaguely resembles that of The Alamo in San Antonio.

5. San Gabriel Village, ca. 1938
Percy Bitton Limited, developer
Fairview Avenue west of Del Mar Avenue

This settlement was to have 840 units selling for around $4000 each. The houses are not much, but efforts at low-cost housing in the thirties deserve mention.

6. Ortega-Vigare Adobe, 1792-1805
616 S. Ramona Street

Only half of this one-story adobe remains, but it is old in spite of its restored appearance. Originally, the roof was flat and the corridor was completely open.

7. Mission San Gabriel Archangel, 1791-1806 and later
Mission and Junipero Serra drives

The Mission was established in 1771 and was moved to its present site in 1776. The stone church, begun in 1791, replaced an earlier small adobe church. When first built, the long nave of the church was covered with a barrel vault, but because of earthquake damage this was replaced by a timber roof in 1804. The building was designed to receive the stone vaulting thus explaining the rows of buttresses, which create the fortress-like quality of the church. The square

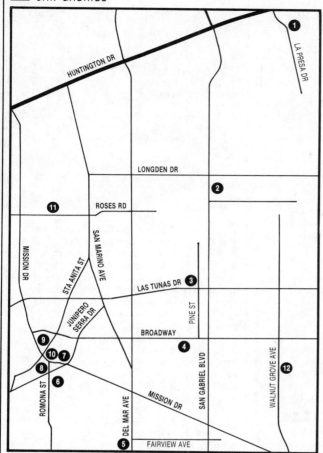

tower which stood to the right of the entrance and much of the fabric of the church was severely damaged in the earthquake of 1812. The church was then rebuilt, although the present campanario was not added until 1828.

8. San Gabriel City Hall and Municipal Buildings, 1923
Walker and Eisen
Southwest corner of Mission Drive and Ramona Street

Spanish Colonial Revival without zest.

9. San Gabriel Civic Auditorium ("Mission Playhouse"), 1923-27
Arthur B. Benton
Northwest corner of Mission Drive and Santa Anita Street

This huge Mission style building (the prototype was the Mission of San Antonio de Padua near the present town of Jolon) was designed specifically for the production of John Steven McGroarty's *Mission Play* that between 1912 and 1933 presented 3200 performances. The emblems of Spanish provinces that adorn the interior were given by the King of Spain. The building also houses a fine theatre organ.

10. Lopez de Lowther Adobe, 1792-1806
330 S. Santa Anita Street

This single-room-wide, gabled-roof adobe was probably one of the Mission outbuildings. It has escaped the wrecker by being on a side street. It is open to the public on Sunday afternoons, 1-4.

11. Church of our Savior (Episcopal), 1872-later
535 W. Roses Road, near Rosemont Boulevard

Only the portion of this rural English Gothic church behind the entrance is old, but it retains some good Tiffany windows.

12. Sorg House, 1926
R. M. Schindler
5204 N. Walnut Grove Avenue

A tight de Stijl composition, with pergola sunroof and garage. The rows of two-by-six supports suggest the wood stud wall construction behind the stucco-covered walls.

12. Sorg House

Sierra Madre

Named by its developer, Nathaniel C. Carter, in 1881, Sierra Madre was intended to be a boom town, but it never quite made it. It still evokes the image of a Midwestern crossroads village of the turn of the century. Its big industry was tuberculosis sanitariums, almost all of which have now disappeared. But it attracted more than its share of distinguished architects—Ernest A. Coxhead, Joseph Cather Newsom, Charles and Henry Greene, Timothy Walsh, Irving J. Gill, Wallace Neff, Harwell H. Harris, and John Gougeon.

1. ▪Mulrihill House, 1949
Harwell H. Harris
580 N. Hermosa Avenue

Although this house has been remodelled, it still bears comparison with the same architect's Johnson House in Bel Air of exactly the same year.

2. Lewis Courts, 1910
Irving J. Gill
Northeast corner of Mountain Trail and Alegria Avenue

In this project Gill provided an individual terrace and an enclosed porch or loggia for each of the small stucco-walled, two-bedroom bungalows. The open courtyard in the center contained a pergola and a croquet court. The complex is now changed almost beyond recognition and is threatened with demolition, but it is so famous that we felt that we had to include it.

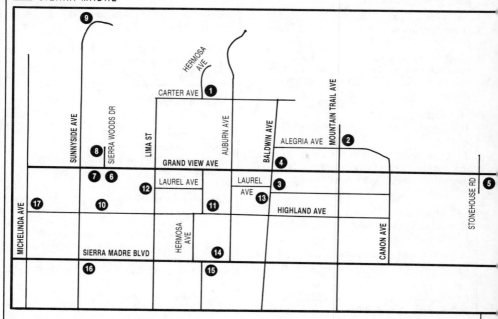

2. Lewis Courts

Modern Expressionist with a slight Spanish flavor. Gougeon's later Pasadena Presbyterian Church goes even further.

3. Church of the Ascension

3. Church of the Ascension, 1888
Ernest A. Coxhead
Northeast corner of Baldwin and Laurel avenues

One of Coxhead's storybook churches. Some remodelling has been done by Carleton M. Winslow, Jr. who also designed the parsonage.

4. Saint Rita's Church, 1969
John Gougeon
Northeast corner of Baldwin and Grand View avenues

4. Saint Rita's Church

5. House, ca. 1890
Near southeast corner of Grand View Avenue and Stonehouse Road, Arcadia

A stone structure, originally built as a maintenance building for the northern section of "Lucky" Baldwin's extensive ranch.

6. Cabin, ca. 1900
468 Grand View Avenue, east of Sierra Woods Drive

Tiny, vertical board and batten building that suggests the back-to-nature atmosphere that Sierra Madre once boasted.

7. House, ca. 1905
506 Grand View Avenue, west of Sierra Woods Drive

A good Craftsman house, stucco on the first floor and shingle on the second.

8. Edgar Camp House, 1904
Charles and Henry Greene
327 Sierra Woods Drive

One of the Greenes' most picturesque bungalows with later additons. It is almost visible from the street.

9. Passionist Fathers Monastery and Retreat House, 1928-31
Timothy Walsh
North end of Sunnyside Avenue

Two huge Spanish Colonial Revival piles with very little ornament; large but on the dry side in the manner of so much of the work of Myron Hunt. Walsh had come west to design a new Roman Catholic Cathedral of Our Lady of Guadalupe in Los Angeles. The design was not dry but richly Churrigueresque, somewhat in the manner of the great cathedral at Santiago de Campostella. It should have been built, but financial problems struck even before the Depression. This monastery must be seen in the light of the Great Crash. As far as we know, Walsh's only other buildings are two Craftsman houses in Pasadena (*see* Lower Arroyo Seco).

10. House, ca. 1910
481 Highland Avenue

A long, two-story, shingled Craftsman house with horizontality worthy of the Prairie School.

11. Sierra Madre School, ca. 1930
Marsh, Smith, and Powell
North side of Highland Avenue between Hermosa and Auburn avenues

Spanish Colonial Revival in poured concrete.

12. Pinney House, 1886
Joseph Cather Newsom
225 Lima Street, west end of Laurel Avenue

Originally, this building was a large but rather plain hotel on the order of the other Newsom hotel still standing in San Dimas. Then in the thirties a movie company added the outsized spindle work on the porch and the equally mannerist swans neck pediment, both from a house being demolished on Wilshire Boulevard in Los Angeles. The result is overwhelming.

12. Pinney House

13. House, 1911
171 N. Baldwin Avenue

A beautifully maintained shingled Craftsman house.

14. Church of the Nazarene, 1890
191 W. Sierra Madre Boulevard

A Victorian Gothic structure in wood, somewhat botched around the entrance and, unfortunately, painted white.

14. Church of the Nazarene

15. Congregational Church, 1928
Marsh, Smith, and Powell
170 W. Sierra Madre Boulevard

Some parts of this church are said to date from 1886, but they do not show under the Romanesque exterior.

16. Essick House, ca. 1905
550 W. Sierra Madre Boulevard

A large, true bungalow (one story) with flat roof above a thin, horizontal, latticed attic for ventilation.

17. Barlow House (now **Alverno School**), 1923-24
Wallace Neff
Northeast corner of Michillinda and Highland avenues

This villa was built by Dr. James Barlow for his wife, who had visited the Villa Collazzi (sometimes attributed to Michelangelo) outside Florence and who wanted a house just like it. Neff gave them what they desired and included a superb southern *cortile* from which they had magnificent views of the San Gabriel Valley below them through Italian cypresses, palms, and formal gardens.

Arcadia

Arcadia is best known for the **Santa Anita Racetrack,** where Los Angelenos go to sin, and the **Santa Anita Mall,** where they go to spend. Neither has architectural merit, though the latter tries. (The former was once by Gordon B. Kaufmann, but none of his architecture remains.) The best thing in town—in fact one of the high points in Los Angeles County—is the County **Arboretum,** on what was once the old Rancho Santa Anita, the estate of E. J. Baldwin, one of the most eccentric millionaires that California has ever produced.

The Santa Anita Ranch was granted during the Mexican period to Hugo Reid in 1841. Either just before that date or shortly thereafter, he built an adobe on the ranch. From evidence now available, we know this adobe was a single-floor dwelling with a corridor running along one side, and it was covered by a flat roof. This adobe was later incorporated into a large house. Between 1948 and 1960, the **Hugo Reid Adobe** was rebuilt; this rebuilding has been recently updated by the California Conservations Corporation. A new garden of herbs and flowers characteristic of the Mexican period has been planted by the adobe.

In 1875, E. J. "Lucky" Baldwin purchased the Rancho, and over the years he extensively planted the area and dredged the picturesque lake. Baldwin was interested in horses, gold mines, real estate, and horticulture. In fact, he was interested in everything and almost everything he touched turned into gold. Thus, his nickname "Lucky." Having literally struck pay dirt in Northern California, he bought the rancho east of Los Angeles, possibly with the idea of "roughing it," for he moved (1875) into the Hugo Reid Adobe and started raising horses—and money! He also planted a wide variety of trees, the nucleus of the Arboretum, though now it is much more lush than Lucky would have imagined possible. Incidentally, the early growth was the site of the filming of the first *Tarzan* movies.

Baldwin was also interested in architecture. Like many other Americans, he was excited by the Queen Anne buildings that the British erected for their pavilions at the Philadelphia Centennial Exhibition in 1876. When he returned to California he hired A. A. Bennett, one of the architects of the Capitol Building at Sacramento, to design a **Queen Anne Cottage** (1881) as a guest house for the ranch. Although not closely related to the British pavilions and not really Queen Anne, it was and is pretentious both inside and out. The

exterior has ornament extracted from Eastlake and is painted to suggest what Vincent Scully has called the "Stick style." There are also Islamic touches. The original features inside are Victorian Baroque with marble fireplaces and art glass windows that would have been the pride of San Francisco, where they were probably made.

Perhaps more fascinating are the ample **stables and dog house** in the same style as the exterior of the guest house. Oh, yes—a Queen Anne **railroad station** (1890) that Baldwin built on the Santa Fe right-of-way has now been moved to the grounds.

The California Arboretum Foundation took over the operation of the Arboretum in 1948, and it was opened to the public in 1955. The Arboretum may be visited every day except Christmas, from 8:30 A.M. to 4:30 P.M. for a small admission charge.

As if grateful for this architectural success, Baldwin married the architect's daughter. The marriage was not so fortunate and the couple soon separated. A previous marriage (there were four) had produced a beloved daughter, Anita, to

Queen Anne Cottage

whom he gave a large section of his ranch to the north. In 1910 she built a large but nondescript house, **Anoakia,** which she proceeded to furnish with large numbers of Tiffany chandliers and some rather astonishing murals by Maynard Dixon. There is also a small Palladian temple in the gardens! All this Californiana at the northwest corner of Baldwin Avenue and Foothill Boulevard is the well-maintained headquarters of a developer. It is occasionally open, but is private property.

Anita Baldwin's estate has, of course, been subdivided and is now called Santa Anita Oaks. It is a pleasant piece of suburbia that exhibits acre after acre of the California Ranch houses of the thirties and forties, as well as some impressive historic-image designs by H. Roy Kelley and others. One of the best of these is at **1225 Rodeo Road** just north of Foothill Boulevard above Sycamore Avenue. It was designed by Wallace Neff, (ca. 1936) one of the greatest of the purveyors of the Mediterranean style, who here sheaths his familiar architectural forms in grey shingles. The rest of the area is genially soporific, but lushly so.

Another architectural attraction of Arcadia is an excellent Art Deco Moderne **retail store building** (ca. 1932) at 53 Huntington Drive. The relief sculpture on the building is by J. J. Mora. Another, more recent landmark is the **Great Scott Restaurant,** (ca. 1967) at the northeast corner of Santa Anita Avenue and Wheeler Street. Its image is that of an English pub, not from England or Scotland, but from a Hollywood stage set.

Great Scott Restaurant

Monrovia

All of the towns in the shadow of the San Gabriel Mountains owe their existence to the Santa Fe Railroad, which came through the valley in the 1880s. This town is named for a construction engineer, William N. Monroe, who saw the opportunities of this beautiful spot and platted the town in 1886. Though now thoroughly built over, Monrovia still demonstrates its nineteenth-century origins better than most of the San Gabriel Valley communities. Its Victorian houses are sprinkled around town, usually at street corners—evidence of a land speculator's dream that did not materialize until the twentieth century. Old photographs show Queen Anne and Eastlake houses amid orange groves and vineyards. Monrovia must have been lovely.

Like its neighbor, Sierra Madre, Monrovia was a health resort with tuberculosis sanitaria distributed through the upper reaches of the city—a deep irony, for now it gets some of the worst smog in the county, both from friendly Los Angeles and from the industry miserably sprawled to the southwest. The Foothill Freeway which runs through the southern section does nothing to improve the atmosphere. But stop by, if only to see the **Aztec Hotel** (in the Mayan style!), one of the most exotic things that you will ever encounter.

1. Monrovia High School, 1928
John C. Austin and Frederic M. Ashley (Austin Whittlesey)
Northeast corner of Madison Avenue and Colorado Boulevard

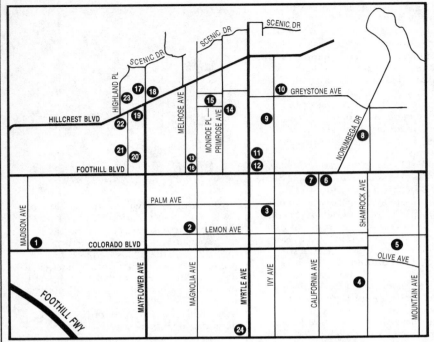

A Palladian facade on an otherwise Spanish Colonial Revival building. Whittlesey, the designer, was well known for his books on Spanish architecture.

4. Cottage

2. House, ca. 1915
423 S. Magnolia Avenue

This remodelled house has all the marks of a Irving J. Gill design.

3. United Methodist Church, 1911
(addition 1923)
Southwest corner of Ivy and Palm avenues

An imposing piece of early-twentieth-century Beaux Arts Neo-Classicism.

4. Cottage, ca. 1887
823 S. Shamrock Avenue

It is conceivable that this one-and-a-half-story Queen Anne building was designed by one or both of the Newsoms.

5. Park, 1923
Cook and Hill, landscape architects
Between Shamrock and Mountain avenues; Olive and Lemon avenues

This is Monrovia's only park of any size—but, of course, there are the mountains!

6. Saint Luke's Episcopal Church, 1926
Carleton M. Winslow
Southeast corner of California Avenue and Foothill Boulevard

A very severe handling of Spanish Romanesque and Gothic in poured concrete. The interior is even more severe.

6. Saint Luke's Episcopal Church

7. Four Bungalows, ca. 1910
Tifal Brothers, builders
Southwest corner of California Avenue and Foothill Boulevard

A row of bungalows in mint condition. Actually, there are more, apparently by the same builders, on Wild Rose Avenue on the south side of the same block.

8. Dumond House, ca. 1925
270 Norumbega Drive

Pure Hansel and Gretel, the house-studio of an artist.

9. Watt Bungalow, ca. 1910
231 N. Ivy Avenue

A flat-roofed, single-story house—right out of a "bungalow book."

10. Butts House, 1894
Arthur B. Benton
Northeast corner of Ivy and Greystone avenues

An angular example of the Shingle style with a boulder first story and mannerist touches above.

11. Burr House, 1893
150 N. Myrtle Avenue

A two-story Queen Anne with a suggestion of the Colonial Revival.

12. United Presbyterian Church, ca. 1926
Harry L. Pierce

Northeast corner of Myrtle Avenue and Foothill Boulevard

A Mission Revival tower, but otherwise rather academic Spanish Colonial Revival. The interior has hints of the Rococo.

13. Stewart House, ca. 1887
117 N. Magnolia Avenue

A two-story Queen Anne dwelling.

14. House, ca. 1887
Solon I. Haas
250 N. Primrose Avenue

Another Queen Anne, but this time with a tall, narrow, mansard tower, still crowned with iron railing and pinnacles.

15. Monroe House, 1887
225 Monroe Place

This is the Queen Anne house of William N. Monroe, who founded the town and for whom it was named.

16. Aztec Hotel, 1925
Robert Stacy-Judd
Northwest corner of Magnolia Avenue and Foothill Boulevard

Words fail. By the mid-twenties, Stacy-Judd had emerged as one of America's most flamboyant apologists for the pre-Columbian Revival, which he thought, since it was "native American," should form the basis for a true American style in the future. Here he presents it in cast concrete and stucco.

16. Aztec Hotel

17. Mills House ("Mills View"), 1887
329 N. Melrose Avenue

It is possible that this house was designed by Joseph Cather Newsom. It has the mark of his outrageous aesthetics in its Queen Anne mass with mansard tower at the southwest corner.

18. Case House, 1887
Northeast corner of Hillcrest Boulevard and Mayflower Avenue

A Queen Anne/Colonial Shingle style dwelling.

19. Pile House ("Idlewild"), 1887-88
Joseph Cather Newsom
255 N. Mayflower Avenue near corner of Hillcrest Boulevard

A two-story Queen Anne with a strange bracket at the corner; the wonderful interiors are well preserved.

20. Mellenthin House, ca. 1912
Frank O. Eager
168 Highland Place

A fine, shingled Craftsman house in the Swiss Chalet vein.

21. Everest House, ca. 1912
Arthur Kelly
173 Highland Place

Another Craftsman two-story, almost worthy of Charles and Henry Greene. The **Daniels House** across the street (number 174) was *once* by Arthur Kelly.

22. Badger House, ca. 1912
Attributed to Arthur Kelly
225 Highland Place

Craftsman shingles again.

23. Wood House, ca. 1925
Herbert J. Gerhardt
338 Highland Place

Another evidence of the search for Native America, here realized through the Pueblo Revival.

24. Santa Fe Railroad Passenger Station, ca. 1925
William H. Mohr
Just above Duarte Road on west side of Myrtle Avenue

A small Hispanic building.

Duarte

This community, founded in 1886 southeast of Monrovia, was once covered with rural estates dating mainly from the teens and twenties. After World Ward II these succumbed to the growth syndrome and were subdivided. A few good houses remain behind gates and high hedges, but your experience of the "better day" will be only the magnificent trees. Duarte does have a beautiful Mission Revival **school** (1908) by F. S. Allen at 1247 Buena Vista Street. Its paired towers and pedimented gables are easily visible from the nearby Foothill Freeway, so you won't really even need to slow down.

Bradbury

Very exclusive, mostly behind locked gates. Everything is post-World War II. It does have the honor of having an excellent hilltop house by Frank Lloyd Wright—the **Pearce House** (1950)—behind locked gates at 5 Bradbury Hills Road.

Azusa

Any reader over fifty will remember this town, along with Cucamonga and Anaheim, as one of Jack Benny's stops on his imaginary railroad journeys around Southern California. It was founded in 1887. One of its sons, the eminent historian Robert Glass Cleland, wrote that Azusa had in the late nineteenth century "more saloons than Protestants." And he continued, "So, also, certain priceless gifts—freedom and space, simplicity and leisure, blue skies overhead, and unfailing kindness and friendship in the hearts of our neighbors."

The Civic Center buildings are good examples of the "City Beautiful" movement. The **City Hall** (1909) looks newer than the wings (1925) that flank it. The little grey stone **Iglesia Presbiteriana** (ca. 1900) nearby at the northwest corner of Alameda Avenue and Foothill Boulevard is picturesque. And the **Wells Fargo Bank** at the northeast corner of Azusa Avenue and Foothill Boulevard designed (1918) by Robert H. Orr in a mixture of Romanesque, Classical, and Moderne forms, adds interest to an otherwise uninspiring business district.

Glendora

Where Azusa was Presbyterian in its early religious orientation, Glendora, also on the Santa Fe Railroad, was firmly Methodist, a saving grace of nearby Monrovia. Glendora had a strong Dixie element. As late as 1935 the local chapter of the United Daughters of the Confederacy would announce in the *Glendora Press* an essay contest in which "ten points will be deducted in judging any manuscript that uses the term 'Civil War' when speaking of the War Between the States." Today the sleepy southern crossroads town comes to mind particularly on Glendora Avenue. The northern part of Glendora has simply been taken over by developers for tract housing to the point that the town's original reason for being, its citrus industry, is gone. Surely Citrus College at the west end of town, will change its name.

In the foothills behind Glendora there is still some evidence of truck farming. Beautifully tended nurseries cling to the slopes of the hills, as do some Victorian houses, none of great architectural quality. The best work is early-twentieth-century Craftsman. In town the **Tudor two-stories** (ca. 1920) at the northwest corner of Minnesota Avenue and Foothill Boulevard and at the northwest corner of Bennett and Vermont avenues, and the **bungalows** (ca. 1915) at the northwest corner of Foothill Boulevard and Wabash Avenue and at the southeast corner of Bennett and Vermont avenues (beautiful bevelled glass door) are cases in point. The modern work at **Citrus Junior College** by Neptune and Thomas is bland.

San Dimas

Another town inspired by the Santa Fe Railroad and the boom of the 1880s, San Dimas is almost exactly midway between Los Angeles and San Bernardino, to which the railroad had completed its tracks in 1885. As in other boom cities, the first building of consequence was a **hotel** (1885-87) designed by Joseph Cather Newsom in the Queen Anne style. Again paralleling the history of many such enterprises, the hotel was finished just as the boom collapsed and never functioned as a hotel. In 1889 J. W. Walker bought this thirty-room structure and used it as his home. Such has been its use until recently when it has been transformed into an excellent restaurant. Address: 121 N. San Dimas Avenue.

Recently San Dimas's business street has been remodelled into someone's version of a Wild West town but the residential streets, with their modest, late-nineteenth-century cottages and later bungalows, are pleasant.

Hotel, San Dimas

La Verne

Originally named Lordsburg for I. W. Lord, who laid it out in 1888, La Verne was another of the Santa Fe Railroad enterprises based on health and citrus. It is the seat of **La Verne University** (formerly College) which never made it to Claremont as Pomona did. The college looks like the one in Sinclair Lewis's *Elmer Gantry,* which you couldn't distinguish from the County Poorhouse except for the sign out front. The grand exception is the absolutely outlandish (and successful) **Student Center and Drama Laboratory** (1973), designed by the

Student Center and Drama Laboratory, La Verne University

Shaver Partnership to resemble tents. In fact, the five large episodes *are* tents coated with Teflon! Otherwise the best building in town is the **Church of the Brethren** (1930) at the southwest corner of 5th and E streets. It is flamboyant Gothic with suggestions of the Moderne roughed out in reinforced concrete and was designed by Orr, Strange, and Inslee.

On the west side of town below Foothill Boulevard at the intersection of Moreno Avenue and Gladstone Street is the **Water Filtration and Softening Plant** (1940) designed by Daniel A. Elliot with monumental Spanish forms in reinforced concrete. It is one of the substations on the 392-mile aqueduct that brings water to Los Angeles from the Colorado River.

La Verne may not have much to offer architecturally, but it has some of the most beautiful trees of any town in the state.

Temple City, El Monte

Mostly depressing, but the **Security Savings Bank** (1976) by Pulliam, Matthews, and Associates slipped in at Las Tunas Drive and Cloverly Avenue in Temple City. To the south in El Monte the **High School** (1938-39) designed by Marsh, Smith, and Powell through PWA funding at Tyler Avenue and Badger Street is a good Moderne work whose best effect is the bas-relief sculpture by Bartolo Mako on the Administration Building. It depicts *The End of the Santa Fe Trail* beginning with a covered wagon and ending with a coed with tennis racket. While in El Monte you may want to take a look at the **Busway Terminal** (1973) designed by Daniel, Mann, Johnson, and Mendenhall (at the west end of Romano Boulevard near Santa Anita Avenue) to encourage people in the area to give up their cars at the parking lot and ride the buses into L.A. The attempt by architects to achieve absolutely anonymous architecture seems to have reached its complete fulfillment here.

Covina, West Covina

Covina, a product of land speculation in the late 1880s, has real presence in spite of the calculated designs of its political and commercial leaders to destroy it. The area around the intersection of Citrus Avenue with Badillo Street can be brought back in the mind's eye to a better day before modernization took over. How wonderful the broad-eaved Arcade Apartments must have been before their face-lifting! How majestic the Ionic beauty of the First National Bank before its new owners decided to block out its rich architrave with a concrete slab! Thank God for sparing Arthur B. Benton's Holy Trinity Episcopal Episcopal Church (1910), a shard of a better day. A few Queen Anne cottages even remain around the town.

1. Church of the Holy Trinity, 1910-11
Arthur B. Benton
Northeast corner of Badillo Street and 3rd Avenue

Benton has put aside his Mission style (Mission Inn, Riverside) for the Episcopalian's preferred Eastlake-Gothic. The strong tower and fabric of the church was made of stones dragged from the San Gabriel River. The interior is well-wooded and has good stained glass windows.

2. First National Bank, ca. 1918
Train and Williams
Northeast corner of Citrus Avenue and College Street

A well-proportioned Ionic pile, now somewhat altered.

3. Masonic Hall, ca. 1900
Southwest corner of 2nd Avenue and School Street

A huge, Classical Revival, rather awkward building made of wood. The Masons have as many architectural pretensions as the Episcopalians, and we are glad of that.

4. Saint Martha's Episcopal Church, 1956-62
Carleton M. Winslow, Jr.
Northeast corner of Lark Ellen Avenue and Service Street, West Covina

Very exotic, the facade is enriched by metal stars suspended a couple of feet in front of the walls and held in place by wires.

1. Church of the Holy Trinity

Industry, La Puente

3. Workman Adobe

ndustry is what it says it is — an industrial park, though the word *park*
hardly seems appropriate. Much of it
is faceless, computerized building,
eminently forgettable. La Puente seems
to be inhabited but has very little else to
offer. Here is what we turned up:

1. Puente Hills Mall, 1974
Victor Gruen Associates
Southeast corner of Pomona Freeway
exit and Azusa Avenue

Nothing really holds this ninety-four-
acre shopping center together except the
parking lot. A few buildings, especially
the **Sears** store, are noteworthy.

2. Francisco Grazide Adobe, ca. 1875
South of Puente Hills Mall (turn east on
Colima Road, then south on Batson
Avenue)

A single-floor adobe picturesquely situated on a tiny lake.

**3. Workman Adobe ("Rancho La
Puente"),** 1842, greatly altered 1872
Ezra Kysor

Temple Hall, 1919-23
Walker and Eisen
15415 E. Don Julian Road (Hacienda
Boulevard exit from Pomona Freeway,
then north to Don Julian Road, then
west to Rancho entrance)

William Workman ("Don Julian" to his
contemporaries) led the first wagon train
of Yankees into the Los Angeles area in
1841. Because he had a Mexican wife
and thus had a right to claim land, he
and his friend John Rowland received

the enormous Rancho La Puente which
they shared in common for awhile. Finally the ranch was divided, Workman
taking the western half. As his business
ventures prospered in Los Angeles, he
decided to remodel his ranch-house to
resemble what he remembered an English country house to look like. The result was to Gothicize it and remove almost all traces of the simple adobe, at
least on the exterior.

Ironically, it was his grandson, Walter
P. Temple, who revived the Spanish tra-
dition by building Temple Hall ("La
Casa Nueva") next door in the vigorous
Spanish Colonial Revival style — with a
Manueline (Portuguese) front door!
Temple Hall has been immaculately re-
stored by Raymond Gervigian and is a
veritable house museum of the taste of
the twenties.

The grounds also contain the oldest private cemetery in Los Angeles County. In it among the graves of other pioneers are those of Pio Pico and his wife, Maria Ygnacia. The houses and grounds are open (free) to the public Tuesday through Friday, 1-4 and Saturday and Sunday 10 A.M. to 4 P.M. Groups by reservation.

4. The Donut Hole, 1968
John Tindall, Ed McCreany, and Jesse Hood
Southeast corner of Elliott Avenue and Amar Road, La Puente (near Hacienda Boulevard, north of "Rancho La Puente")

The first of the Donut Hole establishments was built in 1963 in Covina; by the end of the 1960s there were five examples in Southern California. In these programmatic buildings you drive through the hole in the giant doughnut, pick up your sack of doughnuts, and then exit through a large doughnut at the other end. The whole experience is consummated without your having to get out of your car.

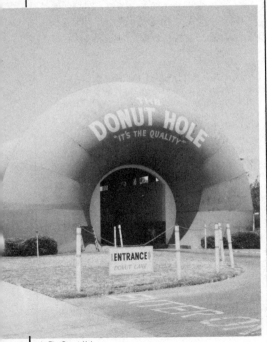

4. The Donut Hole

Pomona

Named for the Roman goddess of fruit trees, Pomona has exchanged the scent of orange blossoms for the stink of smog. It was founded in the 1880s, another railroad town—this time the Southern Pacific. It was the commercial center of a very large agricultural region in the east San Gabriel Valley until very recently when changing population and economic patterns turned the area toward housing and industry. Also, the smog, the worst in Southern California, quite literally has wiped out citrus groves and vineyards that would otherwise still be producing. Incidentally, much of this smog is not really the crepitation of Los Angeles but of local industry. The economy being what it is, people are afraid to enforce rules that might drive industry elsewhere.

In truth, the business district, in spite of some good tries, looks terrible. In 1960 Gruen and Associates, with the best intentions, put in a pedestrian mall along 2nd Street between Gordon and Palomares streets. It didn't work. Business moved elsewhere. Several banks were built in the late sixties and a new **city hall, public library,** and **post office** were constructed in the same period. While in some cases moderately good architecture, they nevertheless demonstrate all the problems of the "City Beautiful" movement that Jane Jacobs has so eloquently deplored in her *Death and Life of Great American Cities.*

Generally, Pomona is an unfortunate area, especially when compared to neighboring Claremont, which remained residential and collegiate. Nevertheless, there are some fascinating things in Pomona, especially from the turn of the century.

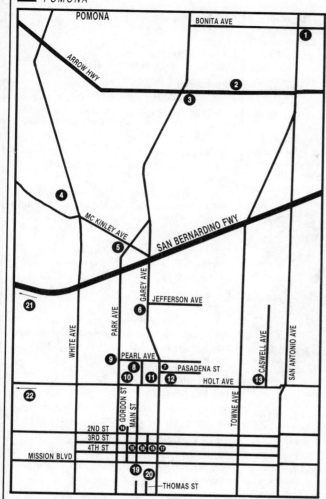

1. Xerox Corporation Manufacturing Facility, 1967
Craig Ellwood
800 E. Bonita Avenue, at southwest corner of Towne Avenue (just above Arrow Highway)

Miesian, large, but spartan, this building just misses the look of having been turned out by a computer.

2. Palomares Adobe, ca. 1850-54
491 E. Arrow Highway in Palomares Park

A single-story, **L**-shaped adobe with a shingle hipped roof. A corridor runs around the **L**, and originally a second corridor faced the patio. The adobe was substantially restored in 1939.

3. Bungalow, ca. 1920
178 E. Arrow Highway

An example of the Boulder style much more plentiful in the communities to the north.

4. Los Angeles County Fairgrounds
Northwest corner of McKinley and White avenues

Most of the buildings date from the mid-1930s and thus have Moderne pretensions. Note particularly the sculpture (1939) near Gate 3—man's tribute to his equine friend done by Lawrence Tenney Stevens in the heroic style often associated with Nazi art. Remember that this style was not the product of dictatorship (though Mussolini and Hitler went for it) but a more general movement in the history of taste not yet completely analyzed. Everybody will love the **Santa Fe Railroad Station** (ca. 1885) brought from Arcadia. It is a tight mixture of Queen Anne and Stick style forms, almost dollhouse in scale. Why would Arcadia let this go?

4. *Railroad Station, Los Angeles County Fairgrounds*

5. La Casa Primera Adobe (Ygnácio Palomares Adobe), ca. 1837-later
Southwest corner of McKinley and North Park Avenues

A single-floor, five-rooms-in-a-line adobe with a corridor along the front and on one side. It is the headquarters of the Pomona Valley Historical Society.

6. House, ca. 1887
Southwest corner of Garey and Jefferson avenues

A big, angular, Queen Anne house with intricate ornament.

7. Pilgrim Congregational Church, 1911
Robert H. Orr
East side of Garey Avenue between Pasadena and Pearl streets

A large Gothic complex, including cloister, offices, parish house, etc., all in red brick.

8. House, ca. 1900
Southwest corner of Pearl and Main streets
Classical Revival with a double-columned, two-story portico.

9. Park Place, ca. 1920
Park Avenue at Pearl Street

A highly unusual compound. Four rows of two-story apartment units all sheathed in boulders.

10. House, ca. 1887
Northeast corner of Holt and Park avenues

Such Queen Anne houses make you realize how marvelous Victorian Pomona must have been. A hideous little building has been dumped in the front yard.

11. First Baptist Church, ca. 1900
Norman F. Marsh
Garey and Holt avenues

Education Building, 1963
Everett L. Tozier

A lot of Classical elements have been strung across and around the facade of this structure. The effect is challenging, not to say unnerving.

12. House, ca. 1910
143 Holt Avenue

A two-story Classical Revival house set at a respectable distance from the street.

13. Ebell Club, ca. 1910
Ferdinand Davis
Northwest corner of Holt and Caswell avenues

This two-story, L-shaped building is a monument to the women's club movement of the turn of the century and to the sober, shingled Craftsman style.

14. Great Western Savings and Loan Association, 1965
Kurt Meyer and Associates
300 Pomona Mall West (2nd Street)

A big temple with concrete roof slab and concrete columns.

15. Seventh-Day Adventist Church, ca. 1895
Ferdinand Davis
Southeast corner of 3rd and Gordon streets

A mad concoction of Queen Anne, Gothic, and Italianate forms mercifully preserved in the midst of progress.

15. *Seventh-Day Adventist Church*

16. Fox Theatre, 1931
Balch and Stanberry
Southwest corner of Garey Avenue and 3rd Street

A late example of Art Deco Moderne. The fate of this theatre hangs in the balance.

17. Wells Fargo Bank, 1972
Northeast corner of Garey Avenue and 4th Street

Classical Moderne Revival.

18. Masonic Hall, ca. 1900
Ferdinand Davis
Northwest corner of 4th and Thomas streets

A fancy building with mansard roof. Davis's work needs more study.

18. *Masonic Hall*

19. Pomona City Hall and Council Chambers, 1969
Welton Becket and Associates (B. H. Anderson)
South side of Mission Boulevard west of Garey Avenue

The City Hall is square; the Council Chambers building is round. Both are dull. They are included because they are testaments to the big try.

20. Pomona Central Library, 1965
Welton Becket and Associates (Everett L. Tozier)
Northwest corner of Garey Avenue and 6th Street

This fussy interpretation of the International style is not outstanding architecture, but it seems to work.

21. California State Polytechnic University, Pomona
Valley Boulevard turnoff from San Bernardino Freeway

An agricultural college turned technical in the sixties, Cal Poly has several interesting modern buildings.

The **School of Environmental Design** (1971) by Carl Maston is an asymmetrical massing of cubic forms. The **Student Health Center** (1976) designed by Mosher, Drew, Watson Associates of La Jolla is also well done. Probably the best building on the campus is the **Student Union** (1976) whose architects were Pulliam, Matthews, and Associates, proponents of the Cut-into Box style.

22. Phillips House, 1875
2640 W. Pomona Boulevard, off Corona Freeway below Holt Avenue

An elegant French Second Empire house that seems dreadfully alone in this part of the world.

Claremont

Claremont was named for its view and for Claremont, New Hampshire, the hometown of one of the directors of the Pacific Land and Improvement Company that settled the property along the Santa Fe Railroad. It was plotted in 1887 and by the next year a large hotel was rising to accommodate the visitors who, it was assumed, would soon be thronging the area. Then the "Boom of the Eighties" busted. At first it appeared that the town would also expire.

But every economic cloud has a silver lining. A college had been founded by the Congregationalists at Pomona in 1887. Then suddenly, no money! But there was that empty new hotel in nearby Claremont. Pomona College moved into the hotel during Christmas vacation in 1888-89 and named it Sumner Hall in honor of the wife of a Congregational minister. At first it was thought that with good times the college would move back to Pomona, but Claremont proved to be its permanent home. It became the nucleus of a group of "Associated Colleges"—Claremont Graduate School (1925), Scripps College (1926), Claremont Men's (now Claremont-McKenna) College (1946), Harvey Mudd (1955) and Pitzer (1963). The Southern California School of Theology, originally connected with the University of Southern California in Los Angeles, is also here, though not formally associated. All these schools share faculty and libraries.

This is to indicate that even though founded by the Santa Fe Railroad, Claremont has always been a college town—and looks the part except for the area south of the tracks. In fact everything about the town is small and pleasant. The east side is devoted to the colleges and the west side (roughly west of Harvard Avenue) to housing on beautiful tree-lined streets. Claremont is a lively and attractive place on a smog-free day. Like its neighbors, Upland and Ontario, it looks and is civilized.

A note on **Base Line Road:** this road, which begins in Azusa, gives up in Glendora and then picks up again in San Dimas, stretches in an almost straight east-west line out into the desert. It is a fascinating route to explore. In L.A. County it runs through land that was once devoted to citrus and grapes, but now the pitiful orange groves and vineyards are interrupted repeatedly by intervals of tract housing. But it is still possible in places to conjure up an older California—1900-1930. Many Craftsman bungalows and Spanish Colonial Revival houses remain, as do a few Victorian efforts mainly of the vertical board-and-batten shack variety. The most interesting features of the man-made landscape are the boulder (cobblestone) pumphouses and reservoirs and barns that remind us that this area was once green. Note especially the stone structures at Benson and Padua Avenue in the Claremont area.

1. Webb School, 1922-later
1175 W. Baseline Road

This boy's preparatory school was founded in 1922 by Thompson Webb, a native of Tennessee, and his California-born wife, Vivian. The aim was that the boys should live with nature in a gentlemanly manner. Except for Webb's late Craftsman house, the Spanish Colonial Revival was chosen as the style of the early buildings. Apparently Webb and the contractor worked together on these. The **gymnasium** is extraordinarily picturesque both inside and out. Recent buildings are mainly by Allen Siple. The **Jones Dormitory** and the house next to it are by Roland E. Coate, Jr. the **Museum** was designed (1965) by Millard

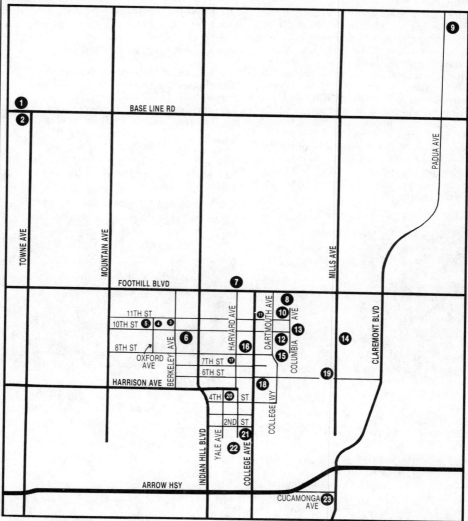

Sheets with one of his Neo-WPA murals over the door. The loveliest building on the campus is the **Vivian Webb Chapel** (1944) that Webb designed as a memorial to his wife. It is a tiny Mission church. Webb, the faculty, the student body, and friends in Claremont literally built it with their own hands. Even the adobe brick was made from the earth of the campus.

Back of the Webb School near the junction of Live Oak Canyon Road and Summit Road is a small collection of

houses (1960s) designed by Foster Rhodes Jackson, a student of Frank Lloyd Wright. The few that can be seen from the road are impressive.

2. Pitzer House, 1913
Robert H. Orr
Southwest corner of Towne Avenue and Base Line Road

This house is tragically near the proposed extension of the Foothill Freeway. Pitzer hired Orr to design a bungalow that would reflect the rustic environment which can still be sensed to the north. Orr chose to sheath it in boulders. The plan is essentially a box almost split by an interior patio whose walls are encased in boulders and whose ceiling is the sky. Although seemingly carefully calculated in floor plan, the effect of the arrangement seems very informal when it is experienced. As usual in a house of this kind, the most important rooms, besides the patio, are the living and dining rooms, the former having a boulder fireplace framed with art glass windows depicting a Dutch boy and girl. The house and gardens are currently being carefully restored.

1. Vivian Webb Chapel, Webb School

3. House, ca. 1927
Southwest corner of Berkeley Avenue and 11th Street

Probably designed by Helen Wren, a local architect of talent who usually worked in the Anglo-Colonial Revival of which this Monterey Revival is an intended off-shoot. The street planting is even better than the house. Praise water and the absence of Dutch elm disease!

4. House, ca. 1965
Vincent Savoy
East side of Oxford Avenue between 10th and 11th streets

A sophisticated International style essay in brick and glass.

5. Criley-Patterson House, ca. 1965
Attributed to Vincent Savoy
782 W. 11th Street

Similar to the previous entry.

6. Lincoln House, ca. 1927
Helen Wren
472 W. 10th Street

Monterey Revival in miniature.

7. Southern California School of Theology, 1960-61
Pereira and Luckman
Entrance is near the intersection of Harvard Avenue and Foothill Boulevard

This is not one of the firm's greatest works. What a shame at such a site! The only salient feature is the **Kresge Memorial Chapel** (1961), and it is by Edward D. Stone!

7. Southern California School of Theology

8. Harvey Mudd College, 1957-later
Edward D. Stone; Heitschmidt and Thompson, supervising architects
Between Columbia and Mills avenues

Stripped Neo-Classical in concrete blocks.

8. Harvey Mudd College

9. Padua Hills

At the northeastern boundary of Claremont is the entrance to Padua Avenue. About three miles north is a tiny community that grew up around the Padua Hills Theatre and Dining Room, an institution in Claremont's culture since the twenties. Here the stage version of Helen Hunt Jackson's *Ramona* was played. The cluster of houses on Via Padova includes the **Hansch House** (1955) by Richard J. Neutra at number 4218 and a **house**(ca. 1965) by Foster Rhodes Jackson at number 4161.

10. Four College Science Center, 1970
Caudill, Rowlett, and Scott
Near northwest corner of 11th Street and Columbia Avenue

Cleaned up Brutalism, especially effective set off against the dullness of Harvey Mudd College nearby.

11. Daggs House, ca. 1910
1102 N. College Avenue

A beautifully-sited Craftsman house with vertical board and batten siding.

12. Garrison Theatre, 1963, addition 1970
Millard Sheets Associates and S. David Underwood
Northeast corner of Dartmouth Avenue and 10th Street

Sheets, once a member of the faculty of the Claremont Colleges, knows modern architecture. He believes that the International style is too severe. Obvious solution: soften it by giving a Saarinen-inspired classicism some hoopla in the form of mosaics and sculpture. The result is this drama center, strongly related to the Home Savings and Loan Association buildings that he designed or remodelled all over the county in the fifties and sixties. There is one of these, in fact, in downtown Claremont.

13. Scripps College, 1927-later
Gordon B. Kaufmann; Edward Huntsman-Trout, landscape architect
Access at Columbia Avenue and 10th Street

Scripps has to be one of the prettiest colleges in the country. It has a small and select student body and looks that way largely thanks to Kaufmann, who designed most of the buildings. His **Denison Library** (1930) is especially well done in the Spanish Colonial Revival style of most of the campus. The **Balch Administration Building** (1929) was designed by Sumner Hunt and Silas R. Burns and fits in beautifully. Note the Shakespearean bas-reliefs by John Gregory that were the casts for ones ornamenting the Folger Library in Washington, D.C. Other, more recent, buildings on the campus were designed by Smith and Williams, Criley and McDowell, and Warnecke and Associates.

13. *Balch Administration Building, Scripps College*

14. Pitzer College, 1964-and later
Criley and McDowell
Entrance at 9th Street off Mills Avenue

Not very distinguished in general except for the **McConnell Center** (1967) which was designed by Killingsworth, Brady, and Associates. Its projecting "rafters" suggest an attempt to break with the International style. See also the **Zetterberg House** (1906), a handsome, Orientalized Craftsman house that was moved (1977) to the Pitzer campus from 721 Harrison Avenue and restored by faculty and students.

15. Honnold Library, 1952
Kaufmann and Stanton. Addition 1956; Stanton and Stockwell
College Way at intersection of Dartmouth and Columbia avenues

The facade is stripped Moderne so crisp that it has a Regency look. This is the main library of the Associated Colleges.

16. Darling House, 1903
Charles and Henry Greene
Northwest corner of College Avenue and 8th Street

A significant house in the Greenes' *ouvre* for it is one of the first of their houses in the true Craftsman—in this case Swiss Chalet, with Oriental touches—mode.

17. Sugg House, ca. 1930
Helen Wren
Northwest corner of 7th Street and Harvard Avenue

This large house is Anglo-Colonial, Wren's favorite style.

18. Pomona College, 1887-and later
Ralph Cornell, landscape architect
Both sides of College Avenue between 2nd and 6th streets

This is the oldest and largest of the colleges with a congeries of styles and architects. The **gates** (1914) at Sixth Street and College Avenue are by Myron Hunt, as is the **Bridges Hall of Music** (1915). The latter, based on a Mannerist triumphal arch, is one of Hunt's best buildings. Just east of it is the **Harwood Garden** (1921) laid out by Ralph Cornell and remaining close to his original ideas. Beyond it is **Sumner Hall**, the hotel that was Pomona's first building, but it has been so heavily remodelled that it is worth only a glance. Dating from 1908 and looking older is the **Carnegie Building** designed by Franklin P. Burnham. The **Bridges Auditorium** (1931) by San Diego architect William Templeton Johnson is vaguely Romanesque enlivened with a little Art Deco (Zigzag) Moderne. The interior, with its frescoed ceiling, is a period piece. Also notable is **Frary Hall** (1929), not for its architecture by Webber and Spaulding but for its murals. Just inside the entrance porch is a striking one by Rico Lebrun called *Genesis* (1960). In the dining hall you will find one of California's most famous murals, *Prometheus* (1930), by Jose Clemente Orozco.

18. Bridges Hall of Music, Pomona College

22. Santa Fe Railroad Passenger Station

19. Claremont-McKenna (formerly Mens) College, 1948 and later
Allison and Rible
Mills Avenue and 6th Street

Not inspired architecture, but the two residential towers, **Fawcett Hall and Claremont Hall** (both 1966) designed by Ladd and Kelsey are worth mentioning because high-rise, even medium high-rise, seems odd in Claremont. Also the scoops taken out of the corners of the buildings seem an obvious, planned dig at the International style.

20. Bungalow, ca. 1910
Southeast corner of Yale and Harrison avenues

Brown in color, of course, with vertical board-and-batten siding. Just behind this house at 428 N. Yale Avenue is another well maintained Craftsman house.

21. Sumner House, 1887
105 N. College Avenue

A two-story Queen Anne mansion built just before the bust.

22. Santa Fe Railroad Passenger Station, ca. 1925
William H. Mohr

1st Street and railroad tracks, just west of the end of Harvard Avenue

At the moment, things look bad for this Churrigueresque extravaganza. It is in the middle of a great deal of construction. But it is still there—boarded up, vandalized, but still not ruined.

23. Russian Village, 1928-later
South Mills Avenue (approached from the north by Claremont Avenue) just below Arrow Highway

Thirteen picturesque houses built of cast-off materials such as concrete pavement torn up from Holt Avenue when it was being repaved. Its creator was Steve Stys, a Czech, who began with 290 S. Mills Avenue, rather conservatively fashioned by Stys from fieldstone and other materials that he had accumulated. He figured that it cost him $35 to build it. Later he went on to use broken concrete, boulders, and, after the Long Beach earthquake of 1933, marble and other parts of the ruins. He did not build all of the thirteen houses, but his imagination obviously dominated the project.

Mission San Gabriel Archangel, 1791-1806 and later. San Gabriel. (p. 392, #7)

La Iglesia de Nuestra Señora la Reina de Los Angeles, 1818-22; 1861-62; 1875; 1912; 1923. Los Angeles. (p. 240, #1)

El Molino Viejo, 1816. San Marino. (p. 363, #26)

Antonio José Rocha (Gilmore) Adobe, 1828-30; ca. 1925. Restored by John Byers. Wilshire District, Los Angeles. (p. 194, #2)

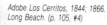

*Adobe Los Cerritos, 1844; 1866.
Long Beach. (p. 105, #4)*

Ranco de los Encinos, 1849. Encino. (p. 315)

(From right to left:) Masonic Temple, 1858; Merced Theatre, 1870, attributed to Ezra F. Kysor; Pico House, 1869-70, Ezra F. Kysor. Downtown Los Angeles, the Plaza. (p. 241, #4,5,6)

House, ca. 1885. San Pedro (p. 86, #8)

Hale House, Heritage Square, ca. 1887, attributed to Joseph Cather Newson. Highland Park, Los Angeles. (p. 272, 24c)

Sessions House, 1888. Joseph Cather Newsom. Angelino Heights, Los Angeles. (p. 190, #2g)

*Church of the Angels, 1889.
Ernest A. Coxhead. Lower Arroyo
Seco. Pasadena (p. 348, #7)*

*McNally House, 1888. Frederick
L. Roehrig. Altadena. (p. 379, #2)*

House, ca. 1895. MacArthur Park-East, Los Angeles. (p. 215 #13d)

Stimson House, 1891. Carroll H. Brown. Exposition Park-East, Los Angeles. (p. 253, #1)

Bradbury Building, 1893. George H. Wyman. Downtown, Los Angeles. (p. 229, #49)

"El Alisal," Lummis House, 1898-1910. Charles F. Lummis. Highland Park, Los Angeles. (p. 271, #23)

Fitzgerald House, 1903. Joseph Cather Newsom. Exposition Park-East, Los Angeles. (p. 252, #6)

*Brady (Hibernian) Building, 1903.
John Parkinson. Downtown, Los
Angeles. (p. 232, #71)*

*Museum and Exposition Building,
Exposition Park, 1910-13. Hudson
and Munsell. Exposition Park-
East, Los Angeles. (p. 257, #25)*

St. Thomas the Apostle Roman Catholic Church, 1905. McGinnis, Walsh and Sullivan. MacArthur Park-West, Los Angeles. (p. 203, #11)

Gamble House, 1908. Charles and Henry Greene. Upper Arroyo Seco, Pasadena. (p. 344, #30)

Parsons Bungalow, 1909. Arthur S. Heineman (Alfred Heineman, Associate). Altadena. (p. 382, #18)

Los Angeles Examiner Building, 1912. Julia Morgan. Downtown-South. Los Angeles. (p. 243, #1)

O'Brien House, ca. 1912. Arthur S. Heineman (Alfred Heineman, Associate). Oak Knoll District, Pasadena. (p. 362, #23)

Bernheimer Bungalow (now Yamashiro Restaurant), 1913. Franklin M. Small. Central Hollywood, Los Angeles. (p. 164, #17)

Krotona Court (now Goldwater Villa Apartments), 1914. Mead and Requa. Central Hollywood, Los Angeles. (p. 168, #46)

Barnsdall (Hollyhock) House, Olive Hill, 1917-20. Frank Lloyd Wright. East Hollywood, Los Angeles. (p. 178, #22a)

Horatio West Court, 1919-21. Irving J. Gill. Santa Monica South. (p. 60, #4)

St. Vincent de Paul Roman Catholic Church, 1923-25. Albert C. Martin. Exposition Park-East, Los Angeles. (p. 253, #2)

Ennis House, 1924. Frank Lloyd Wright. Los Feliz District, Los Angeles. (p. 117, #16)

Ostoff House, 1924. George Washington Smith. San Marino. (p. 388, #11)

W. P. Fuller Paint Company Building, 1924. Morgan, Walls and Clements. Downtown, Plaza and Northeast, Los Angeles. (p. 242, #13)

Los Angeles Public Library, 1922-26. Bertram G. Goodhue and Carleton M. Winslow. Downtown, Los Angeles. (p. 223, #14)

Pasadena City Hall, 1925-27. Bakewell and Brown. Central Business District, Pasadena. (p. 369, #30)

Sowden House, 1926. Lloyd Wright. Los Feliz District, Los Angeles. (p. 176, #11)

"Mausoleum of the Golden West," Calvary Cemetery, 1927. Ross Montgomery. Boyle Heights, Los Angeles. (p. 249, #25)

Samson Tyre and Rubber Company Building, 1928-29. Morgan, Walls, and Clements. Boyle Heights, Los Angeles. (p. 250, #29)

The Flintridge Biltmore Hotel Building, 1927. Myron Hunt and H. C. Chambers. Flintridge. (p. 337, #15)

Lovell House, 1929. Richard J. Neutra. Los Feliz District, Los Angeles. (p. 179, #25)

Bullocks-Wilshire Department Store Building, 1928. John and Donald Parkinson; Feil and Paradince; Jock Peters. MacArthur Park-West, Los Angeles. (p. 207, #40)

The Eastern Columbia Building (now 849 Building), 1929. Claude Beelman. Downtown, Los Angeles. (p. 231, #66)

Sunset Towers, 1929. LeLand A. Bryant. West Hollywood. (p. 153, #9)

Hamilton House, 1931. John Byers (with Edla Muir). Brentwood. (p. 121, #37)

*Los Angeles Times Building,
1931-35. Gordon B. Kaufmann.
Downtown, Los Angeles.
(p. 232, #69)*

*Beverly Hills Post Office, 1933.
Ralph Flewelling. Beverly Hills.
(p. 146, #16)*

Sunset Plaza, 1934-36. Charles Selkirk; Honnold and Russell. West Hollywood. (p. 151, #1)

Sten-Frenke House, 1934. Richard J. Neutra. Santa Monica Canyon, Pacific Palisades. (p. 43, #2)

Union Passenger Terminal, 1934-39. John and Donald Parkinson; J.H. Christie, H. L. Gilman, R. J. Wirth. Downtown, Plaza and Northeast. (p. 242, #10)

Pan Pacific Auditorium, 1935-38. Wurdeman and Becket. Wilshire District, Los Angeles. (p. 194, #4)

Temple House, 1935-36. John Byers (with Edla Muir). Brentwood. (p. 119, #25)

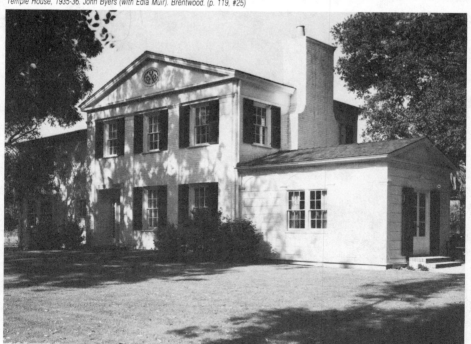

Davis House, 1935. Roland E. Coate. Lower Arroyo, South, Pasadena. (p. 357, #7)

Lane Wells (now Winnie and Sutch) Building, 1938-39. William E. Meyer. Huntington Park. (p. 266, #6)

Coca-Cola Bottling Plant, 1936-37. Robert V. Derrah. Downtown- South, Los Angeles. (p. 244, #5)

Bubeshko Apartment Building, 1938; 1941. R. M. Schindler. Silver Lake. (p. 184, #4)

Academy Theatre, 1939. S. Charles Lee. Inglewood. (p. 108, #8)

Federal Building and Post Office (now U. S. Federal Courthouse), 1938-40. Louis A. Simons; Gilbert Stanley Underwood. Downtown Civic Center, Los Angeles. (p. 238, #6)

Music Corporation of America Building (now Litton Industries), 1940. Paul R. Williams. Beverly Hills. (p. 146, #18)

Hay House, 1939. Gregory Ain. Studio City. (p. 308, #2)

Sturges House, 1939, Frank Lloyd Wright. Brentwood. (p. 119, #13)

Mulrihill House, 1949. Harwell H. Harris. Sierra Madre. (p. 94 #1)

Wayfarer's Chapel, 1949 and later. Lloyd Wright. Palos Verdes. (p. 80, #3)

Millron's (now Broadway) Department Store Building, 1949. Gruen and Krummeck. Westchester. (p. 70, #4)

Tischler House, 1949. R. M. Schindler. Westwood, West. (p. 129, #16)

Foster House, 1950. John Lautner. Sherman Oaks. (p. 313, #10)

Crowell House, 1952. Smith and Williams. Lower Arroyo Seco, Pasadena. (p. 348, #14)

Shulman House, 1950. Raphael S. Soriano. Hollywood Hills. (p. 174, #10)

Perkins House, 1955. Richard J. Neutra. Lower Arroyo Seco, Pasadena. (p. 347, #3)

Reynolds House, 1958. John Woolf. Wilshire District, Los Angeles. (p. 199, #40)

Restaurant, 1959-62. William Pereira and Associates. Los Angeles Airport Area. Los Angeles. (p. 70, #1)

*Apartment Building, ca. 1960.
Northridge. (p. 322)*

*Rosen House, 1962. Craig
Ellwood Associates. Brentwood.
(p. 120, #28)*

Perpetual Savings Bank Building, 1962. Edward D. Stone. Beverly Hills. (p. 145, #4)

Kappe House, 1968. Raymond Kappe. Pacific Palisades. (p. 46, #20)

One Park Plaza, 1971-72. Daniel, Mann, Johnson, and Mendenhall (Anthony J. Lumsden.) MacArthur Park-West. (p. 207, #39)

Los Angeles Bonaventure Hotel, 1974-76. John Portman and Associates. Downtown, Los Angeles. (p. 222, #4)

Pacific Design Center, 1975. Gruen Associate. (Cesar Pelli). West Hollywood. (p. 156, #30)

O'Neill House, 1978-83. Don Ramos. Beverly Hills. (p. 141, #9)

Rodes House, 1978-79. Moore, Ruble, Yudell. Brentwood. (p. 119, #20)

Wells Fargo Building, 1979. Albert C. Martin and Associates. Downtown, Los Angeles. (p. 223, #13)

St. Matthew's Episcopal Church, 1982-83. Moore, Ruble, Yudell; Campbell and Campbell, landscape architects. Pacific Palisades. (p. 41,#11)

Sun Tech Townhouses, 1981. Urban Forms (Steve Andre and David Van Hoy). Santa Monica-South. (p. 62, #18)

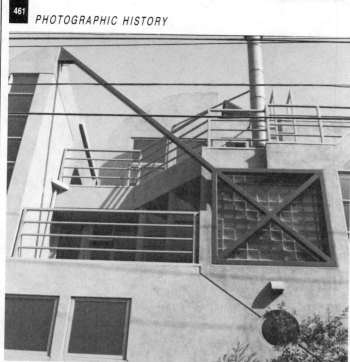

Condominium townhouses, 1981-82. Stafford-Bender. Santa Monica, South. (p. 60, #3)

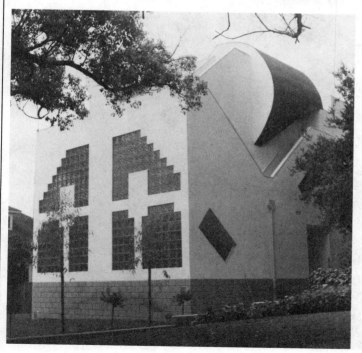

Condominiums, 1981. Eric Owen Moss and John Stafford. Central Business District, Pasadena. (p. 370, #35)

Platt Building, 1981. T. W.
Layman. Canoga Park.
(p. 320, #8)

Villa de Malaga Townhouses,
1982-83. Santa Monica.
(p. 54, #32)

"Petal House," 1982. Eric Owen Moss. Baldwin Hills. (p. 111, #1)

Santa Monica Transportation Center, 1982-83. Kappe, Lotery and Boccato. Santa Monica. (p. 57, #47)

Aerospace Museum, Exposition Park, 1982-84. Frank O. Gehry and Associates. Exposition Park-East. (p. 257, #25)

Virginia Steele Gallery of American Art, 1983-84. Warner and Gray (Paul Gray). San Marino. (p. 390, #28)

Style Glossary

One of the joys and banes of architecture is the question of style (image)—not only for the architecture historian, but also for the architect and for those who simply enjoy and experience buildings. During the 1920s and 1930s, the exponents of "modern" architecture sought to eliminate the study of history, so that architects and society would be able to create buildings which were not concerned with style. But it quickly became apparent that the "modern" architects themselves ended up creating the new and very impressive International Style. Styles (images) are the vocabulary and ultimately the language of architecture, and can only be eliminated by eliminating architecture itself.

Each period during the past 200 years has thought of its current mode as modern or contemporary—with the implication that it is obviously better and an improvement on the immediate past. Each period as well has responded differently to the past—both in the way that the past has been used and also in how it has been viewed and defined. While there is a degree of unanimity in regard to pre-1800 architectural styles, confusion and continual disagreement seem to abound regarding most of those styles which came about from the late nineteenth century through much of the twentieth.

Catalogs of architectural styles generally fall into two groups: those that split and split, making finer and finer distinctions; and those that tend to lump the numerous episodes into a few pigeon holes. In the following style glossary we have tended to fall into the latter group, but in the notes on individual buildings we have continually pointed out how in many instances two or even three styles may be present. We are still uneasy with certain style categories which have been coined in more recent times—such as Vincent Scully's Stick style and his Shingle style. We have also made clear our reservation about the single term Art Deco to describe the Moderne of the 1920s and the very different Moderne of the 1930s.

The past itself was rather loose, and delightfully so when it came to definitions of style. This is beautifully expressed in an 1886 volume on architecture, which noted that "the majority of buildings now being erected . . . are designed in the Free or Knickerbocker, Picturesque, Eastlake, Queen Anne, Colonial and Renaissance styles; with Moorish embellishments." We may all have a general idea of what the Eastlake, Queen Anne, Colonial, and Renaissance imply, but most people would probably have some trouble in determining the other styles.

Since the late 1950s we have been living in a period of instant history, when new movements such as the *New Brutalism* or *Post-Modernism* have been coined even before the movements have really gotten underway. At the rate that instant history is going, we may, by the end of the decade, be coining our style terms based on abstract concepts before the movements actually commence.

If you wish to consult an excellent bird/flower guide to American architecture then pick up a copy of Marcus Whiffen's enjoyable *American Architecture Since 1780* (Cambridge, 1969). He provides us with forty pigeon holes with which to play. Two newer guides to style in American architecture are: John Poppeliers, S. Allen Chambers, and Nancy B. Schwartz's *What Style Is It?* (Washington, 1977), and John J. G. Blumenson's *Identifying American Architecture* (Nashville, 1977). Another new volume devoted to domestic architecture is Virginia and

Lee McAlester's *A Field Guide to American Houses* (New York, 1984).

For architecture of the past fifteen years or so, one cannot avoid the writings of Charles Jencks, though his view of styles is often more conceptual than visual. See his *Modern Movements in Architecture* (New York); *The Language of Post-Modern Architecture* (New York, 1980). 1978); and *Late-Modern Architecture* (New York, 1980).

The Hispanic Tradition (ca. 1770s-1850s)

The mission churches built in Southern California were provincial adaptations of late Churrigueresque and Neo-Classic designs, primarily of Mexico. Since these church buildings were designed by untrained priests, they often mixed the elements of the Neo-Classic with earlier Plateresque and Churrigueresque features or with other remembrances which the early fathers brought with them. As in any remote provincial area, the design of these church complexes was tightly conditioned by available resources — generally limited to nonexistent skilled labor, available materials, and the desire to create a new church building as rapidly as possible. In the more sophisticated examples, domes, vaulting, and carved stonework occurred. Bell towers, usually of the tiered variety, were built singly or in pairs. One of the most common elements was the long, low arcade with just a slight suggestion of piers supporting the spring of the arches.

Mission San Gabriel Archangel, San Gabriel

The adobe style is, in a sense, not a style at all. It was simply the direct, logical manner of constructing secular buildings. These were normally one room wide, with the rooms arranged in a row, side by side. The width of a room was determined by the available length of timbers. Roofs were flat, shed, or gabled. They were covered first with asphalt and later with tile or wood shingles. Exterior and interior walls were washed with white lime cement as soon as it was available and could be afforded. Floors at first were of packed adobe, later of tile, and finally of wood joists and flooring. The more elaborate of these Hispanic houses were L or U plans; very few were large enough to form a complete square enclosing a patio. Window and door openings were at the beginning kept at a minimum. Only with the coming of the Yankee and sawmills were glass windows (usually double-hung) and panelled wood doors made available. Yankees brought other changes. Most exterior porches found on adobe houses are later additions (generally after 1820). Other "innovations," introduced from the 1830s on were clap-board sheathing, wood shingles, and fireplaces. The Yankee additions often transformed the Hispanic adobe buildings into something which was vaguely Greek Revival or, as it is often labeled, Monterey (for the Monterey style see *Greek Revival*).

Greek Revival (Monterey) style (ca. 1840s-1860s)

The arrival of the Yankee in California in the 1820s and later came at the moment the Greek Revival was enjoying great popularity throughout the country. As a fashionable form it ceased to be important in the larger urban areas of the East after 1850, though it continued as a provincial style in the rural East and Midwest well on into the 1860s. Many examples which we loosely label in California as Greek Revival are, in fact, a late carryover of the ca. 1800 Federal style. The Greek Revival as manifest in California normally conjures up examples of the Monterey style—two-story buildings, generally with walls of adobe, cantilevered second-floor balconies (or two-story porches supported by simple, thin square posts), double-hung windows, and perhaps an entrance with sidelights and a transom light. These houses represent the additions of provincial Yankee Greek and Federal wood details to the earlier Hispanic adobe. There are examples as well of single-story Monterey adobes, and there are (or were) a number of examples of modern churches and other buildings which are essentially Greek in imagery. The Monterey style occurs throughout California, and is in no way restricted to the Monterey area. Nor is it even specifically Californian, for similar nineteenth century examples are found throughout the American Southwest in Texas, Arizona, and New Mexico.

Adobe Los Cerritos, Long Beach (p. 105, #4)

Characteristics:

- rectilinear, gabled-roof volumes, one or two stories, horizontal in character, roof at low pitch
- symmetrical, balanced plan and disposition of windows and doors (the side-hall plan is simply one-half of a symmetrical unit)
- wide entablatures, occasionally with dentils
- gable ends form classical triangular pediment with horizontal roof eave/cornice carried across gable end
- frequent occurrence of engaged piers at corner
- flat or pedimented windows and doors
- use of Doric (occasionally Ionic) columns
- entrances with side and transom lights
- use of narrow wood porches and second-floor balconies
- roofs often covered with wood shingles

Italianate style (ca. 1860s-1870s)

The nineteenth-century Italianate style represented the best of two worlds — classical order and control, and the picturesque. It began in the United States in the mid-1830s and continued in popularity in the larger urban centers of the East through the early 1860s. As a style, its sources can be found in late eighteenth-century paintings depicting the northern Italian landscape. Other more direct sources came from England via the popularity of the work of John Nash and others, and English pattern books. The Italianate can be divided into two phases: the Italianate Villa and the High Victorian Italianate. The first mode is fundamentally a rural or suburban form, usually characterized by an irregular mass — its hallmark being a campanile-like tower placed within the L of two major wings. The High Victorian Italianate tended to employ a single volumetric form, richly articulated by sharp, angular details.

Perry House, Los Angeles (p. 272, #24b)

Characteristics:
- emphasis on the vertical in volumes and details
- broadly projected roofs supported by elaborate, three-dimensional patterns of brackets
- round, segmented, or straight-sided rectangular arched windows; groups of double-arched windows
- frequent use of angular bays
- heavy articulation of headers over windows and doors
- quoined corners
- use of thin (almost Gothic), arched colonnettes
- classic spindled ballustrades
- tower with low-pitched, hip roof

Gothic Revival (ca. 1850s-1900s)

The Gothic provided one of the most intense of the picturesque styles which developed in the United States. Nineteenth-century Gothic can be divided into three phases: Literary Picturesque, Victorian Gothic, and the "correct" Gothic which developed toward the end of the century. The few early examples of Gothic found in Southern California are all relatively simple, relying on only a few elements to suggest the style. The earliest Gothic Revival churches and houses were often classical Greek Revival buildings (horizontal emphasis) with Gothic details attached. Later in the Victorian Gothic phase (ca. 1870s-1880s) the volumes and details accentuated the vertical. Gothic was occasionally used throughout California for story-and-a-half wood frame houses.

Characteristics:
- volumes covered by high-pitched roofs
- use of barge boards on gable cornice
- lancet, pointed windows
- open Tudor arches, especially in porches
- split pilasters (posts) for porches
- occasional crenelated parapets
- projecting pinnacles
- board and batten walls often employed in early examples
- multi-colored bands (especially in brick examples) characterize surfaces of the Victorian Gothic
- in final phase, elements of English Perpendicular and French High Gothic predominate

Sacred Heart Roman Catholic Church, Los Angeles (p. 280, #7)

Late Carpenter's Gothic Revival
(1860s-early 1900s)

Most of Southern California's late-nineteenth-century churches represent late Carpenter's Gothic. The designs for these churches generally came from (or seem to have been inspired by) one or another of the numerous pattern books which were published throughout the century. Sometimes the carpenter (with the local parson and building committee) would recreate a familiar design from the East. Often he would work out a free adaptation of the pattern book or previously known design. During the 1870s and 1880s these pattern-book churches were almost always simple, rectangular, gabled-roof structures with a central entrance tower attached to the front gable-end of the buildings. Later variations introduced the double tower, side towers, and the like. Detailing in wood and glass was frequently derived from other contemporary popular styles, especially the Eastlake and the Queen Anne. At the end of the century, elements of both the Colonial Revival and the Arts and Crafts mode were incorporated into these buildings.

Characteristics:
- rectangular, gable-roof volumes; at first, of the entrance tower type; later, with paired towers and corner towers
- windows of the lancet (pointed) type
- main entrance usually of segmented or lancet arch form
- tower normally broken into superimposed levels; belfry openings usually of lancet type; tower roofs of pointed spire type

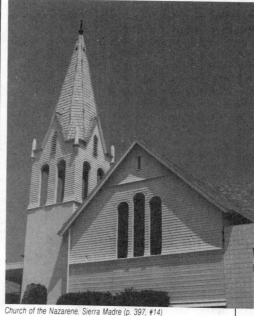

Church of the Nazarene, Sierra Madre (p. 397, #14)

Eastlake (ca. 1870s-1880s)

The supposed origins of this style came from the writings and drawings for interiors and furniture of the English architect Charles Eastlake, though he strongly and continually denied he had anything to do with the style to which his name was attached. (Eastlake's *Hints on Household Taste* was first published in London in 1868, and then in New York in 1872.) The pure Eastlake style was not widely popular in California, and there are only a few examples of it still around. In most instances, the elements of this mode were mixed with other styles, especially with the Queen Anne. The 1850s-60s stylistic features which historian Vincent Scully has combined under the heading "Stick style" share a number of similarities with the early Eastlake.

Arcadia Railroad Station, Pomona (p. 410)

Characteristics:

- thin, tenuous vertical volumes, surfaces, details; all of a fragile nature
- exposure (in myth or fact) of structural members — posts, dentils, corner bracing, angled struts, etc.
- surface divided into panels, each area defined by flat board molding, inner surface covered with lap siding, tongue-and-groove siding, diagonal siding, vertical siding, and occasionally shingles
- profusion of jigsaw and lath work in wood
- ornament often rendered by the outline of cut-out patterns, drilled holes, and thin, layered wood (with all edges very sharp)
- ornamentation often confined to gable ends and to porch posts and entablatures
- frequent use of projecting turned knobs as single or repeated decoration

Queen Anne Revival (ca. 1885-1900)

The Queen Anne Revival started in England in the late 1860s and was closely associated with the architectural designs of Richard Norman Shaw. The first American architect to fully take up the mode was Henry Hobson Richardson in the mid-1870s. The American Queen Anne was *the* picturesque style in late-nineteenth-century America. The form of these buildings was highly irregular, and special emphasis was given to the varied silhouette of the roofs — different gables, dormers, high chimneys, towers, turrets, and pinnacles. Corner towers (often bay towers), round or hexagonal with conical pointed roofs, were essential to the style. So, too, were extensive entrance-living porches which often wrapped themselves around the house. In plan, the best of these houses were of the living-hall type with wide openings being provided between the hall and all of the other family living spaces. Most of the detailing tended to be directly and indirectly classical. By the early 1880s certain architects began to simplify the picturesque form, surfaces, and detailing of the Queen Anne. Out of this developed the Colonial Revival (a phase of which is the Shingle style of Vincent Scully).

Wright-Mooers House, Los Angeles (p. 215, #15a)

Characteristics:

- irregular plan, elevations, roof silhouettes
- vertical emphasis at first, later increasingly horizontal
- surfaces covered with a variety of tactile patterns — clapboard, patterned shingles (especially of fish-scale pattern)
- extensive wrap-around porches on first floor
- balconied porches cut into second floor and third floor attic
- corner (sometimes bay) towers, roofed with a variety of different shapes: conical, segmented concave, bulbous
- classical detailing: columns, dentils, scrolls, engaged columns, and piers
- tall, recessed, panelled chimneys
- leaded, stained glass windows; especially the stair landing window

French Second Empire (ca. 1870s-1880s)

The origin of this style was the public and private domestic architecture developed in France during the reign of Napoleon III (1850s-1870s). As a style, it came to be used extensively in the East and Midwest for public buildings, commercial blocks, and for large- and small-scaled houses. The style took hold in the U.S. after the Civil War and continued through the early 1880s. It often became mixed with the Italianate, and in many instances a building could just as easily be thrust in the Italianate pigeon hole as in the Second Empire. The style was never extensively employed in Southern California. When used it was often combined with the Italianate.

Cottage, ca. 1885, Los Angeles

Characteristics:
- emphasis on elongation and the vertical
- use of tower pavilions, central pavilion, corner pavilions
- high mansard roof sometimes gently convex or concave in form, usually flat on top, with its summit surrounded by a cast iron railing
- use of a wide variety of domes and other dome-like forms
- dormers often break through walls and roofs; form of dormers varied from pediment types to round arch forms to circular with surrounding cartouches *(oeil-de-boeuf)*
- surfaces of the building were, in the more elaborate examples, rich in three-dimensional classical detailing: superimposed orders with entablatures and cornices; projecting pedimented and semi-circular headed windows with bold side framing and sills; rusticated lower floor or basement
- heavily projecting roof cornices with brackets
- entablature filled with a variety of classical details
- porch balustrades of thick, turned spindles

Richardsonian Romanesque Revival (ca. 1870s-1890s)

This highly personal version of the Romanesque first came into existence in Henry Hobson Richardson's design for Trinity Church in Boston (1872). By the early 1880s the Romanesque was *the* style of great prestige. It came to be used for churches, government buildings, business blocks, large-scale private residences, and multiple housing. Only a few buildings in this style were constructed in Southern California, and of these only a handful now remain. It should be pointed out, though, that features of this style were incorporated into numerous Queen Anne and Mission Revival buildings.

Pasadena Public Library (old entrance), Pasadena (p. 367, #14)

Characteristics:

- weight and mass are the essential ingredients
- form of building conjures the medieval and picturesque; these qualities are realized by a minimal number of elements
- rough masonry walls, with detailing, arches, and dentils of a different color, smoother, more polished stone
- predominance of the arch, either singly or as an arcade; repeated use of the early Christian arch from Syria, which often seems to spring from the ground
- rectangular window openings divided into a rectangular patterns by stone mullions and transoms
- in larger buildings, windows grouped between tall, narrow, clustered piers and arches
- windows sometimes grouped horizontally (with either arched or flat headers) as a band directly under projecting roof soffit
- gable ends carried up as a parapet
- round towers with pyramid or convex roofs
- use of bands of engaged colonnettes

Chateauesque Revival (ca. 1890s-1910)

This style was derived from the hunting lodges and castles built principally in France during the reign of Francis I (1515-47) and was popularized in the eastern U.S. by Richard Morris Hunt after the Civil War. As a style it was infrequently used in the West, though features of it were occasionally mixed with other concurrent styles. The few examples built in Southern California were designed around the turn of the century. Since the original French style was a combination of the late Medieval and the early French Renaissance, the American version could be both controlled and picturesque at the same time.

House. ca. 1895. Los Angeles (p.215, #13d)

Characteristics:
- irregular, non-symmetrical plans and silhouettes, with an open play between the horizontal and vertical
- roofs with high-pitched surfaces; wall and roof dormers with pedimented parapets; tall chimneys and high pinnacles
- smooth-cut stone surfaces for walls
- projecting round corner turrets with thin conical roofs
- windows, either round-arched or flat-lintel, both accompanied by classical detailing
- some doors and windows of Gothic segmented arch pattern
- detailing (in stone) both Classical and late Gothic

Colonial Revival (ca. 1890-1915)

Very early, the American Queen Anne architects began to substitute eighteenth-century American Georgian and Federal style elements for the purely Queen Anne classical elements used by the English designers. The Shingle style was the first major execution of a nostalgic return to the simplicity and puritanism of America's earlier years. By the 1890s the Colonial Revival was fully on its way. At first this simply meant that the picturesque Queen Anne designs were simplified and classical Georgian and Federal detail substituted for the loose classical features which had been used. By 1900 the Georgian and Federal Revival had fully arrived in form, plan, and detail. From 1900-1915, these Colonial Revival buildings became increasingly "correct," i.e., architects and their clients became more knowledgeable as to the original prototypes, and they also became more sensitive to the original scale, plans, and details. Southern California abounds with examples of the Colonial Revival. The only aspect of this Revival which was in short demand was the Shingle style, which surprisingly never caught hold (especially surprising when compared to its popularity in Northern California). The remaining major monuments of the Shingle version of the Colonial Revival in Southern California are the churches of Ernest Coxhead.

Apartment Building, Los Angeles (p. 225, #22)

Characteristics:
- simple rectangular volumes, covered by gabled or hip roofs
- symmetrical, balanced dispensing of windows and doors
- surfacing of clapboard or brick (shingles earlier)
- classical, colonial detailing: columns, engaged piers, cornices and entablatures, shuttered windows
- double-hung, small-paned windows

Beaux Arts, City Beautiful Classicism (ca. 1890-1930)

Beaux Arts Classicism embraces a variety of historic classical modes which came to be used in the U.S. from the early 1890s through the 1920s. The great buildings associated with the style are a mixture of late-nineteenth-century Parisian Neo-Baroque, a renewed grandiose fascination with Roman Imperial architecture, and a continued interest in Italian Renaissance architecture. The American Beaux Arts also embraces the late-nineteenth-century Renaissance Revival and what loosely could be called the Neo-Classical Revival. As a style it usurped all others to become close to the only packaging for a public building, ranging from the smallest of Carnegie Public Libraries to the design of state capitols. It also became an almost universal form for railroad stations, skyscrapers, and above all for banks. Examples of this style began to appear in Southern California in the late 1890s, and it continued to be popular for banks, skyscrapers, office blocks, and public buildings through the 1920s.

Second Church of Christ, Scientist, Long Beach (p. 98, #12)

Characteristics:
- formally, ponderously scaled; purposely non-reference to point-of-scale reference
- symmetrical and balanced facade
- use of columned drums and domes (with resulting interior rotundas)
- interior spaces place major emphasis on sequences of spaces—halls, corridors, staircases, public meeting chambers—rather than on utilitarian office and other spaces
- monumental flights of stairs
- often used central projecting pavilion
- fondness for classical porticos, usually Ionic or Corinthian orders
- later Beaux Arts examples (Neo-Classical) became increasingly correct and relied on broad or decorated surfaces

Gothic style (ca. 1895-1940)

These Late Gothic buildings are architecturally more accurate (though on occasion dryer and more pretentious) in form and detail than the picturesque Gothic of the nineteenth century. Sources of the style for church and public buildings were the late English Perpendicular Gothic and the late northern French Gothic. In domestic architecture borrowing was from the Tudor and French Norman traditions. The religious aspect of this Late Gothic movement was closely associated with the Boston architect Ralph Adams Cram. In Southern California the style was employed for schools and churchs (and even for a few skyscrapers), but on the whole it was never as popular as the Romanesque or the Byzantine.

Throop Memorial Unitarian—Universalist Church, Pasadena (p. 371, #44a)

Characteristics:

- simple, smooth surfaces of stone (often inside as well as out)
- employment of terra-cotta for details
- elaborate stained, leaded glass windows
- stucco and half-timbering, brick and stone for houses and smaller institutional buildings like libraries and clubs
- round, conical roof tower placed within L of two major wings of building
- designed low to ground; molded to irregularities of site

Craftsman (Arts and Crafts)
(1895-1920)

The Craftsman style was almost exclusively a domestic style closely associated with suburbia and the middle class. Though its ultimate source was the English Arts and Crafts movement and the architecture of M. H. Baillie Scott and Charles F. A. Voysey, the architectural forms developed in the U.S. were generally quite distinct from their English prototypes. The style was most aptly expressed in the designs published in the pages of *The Craftsman* magazine (1901-16) and in the emergence of the California bungalow. In a broad sense all of the "innovative" designs ca. 1900-1910 are examples of the craftsman aesthetic (including the Midwestern Prairie School). The specific design sources for the style were complex, ranging from the English (Medieval) cottage forms of Voysey and Scott to the earlier Queen Anne Shingle tradition and the Japanese. Southern California, and particularly Pasadena, can rightly be considered the home of the architectural aspects of the movement. No architects ever equaled the high art Craftsman dwellings of the brothers Charles and Henry Greene, and nowhere else in the U.S. did the low-cost builder's bungalow reach such a high point.

House, Pasadena (p. 368, #22)

Characteristics:

- direct, simple, box-like shapes; low-pitched roofs
- informal plans and non-symmetrical elevations
- even in large houses, scale suggests the intimate and informal
- stucco a favored sheathing, although clapboard, shingles, or board and batten also used
- brick occasionally employed (especially clinker bricks) for foundations, parapet walls of porches and terraces, chimneys
- river boulder sheathing of lower portion of walls also encountered
- exposure of some structural members, especially roof rafters, struts to support roof, projecting end beams, etc.
- screened sun and sleeping porches, terraces, pergolas

- in best examples, the Craftsman house was low to the ground and mirrored the irregularity of the site

Mission Revival (ca. 1890-1912)

The Mission Revival began in California in the early 1890s and by 1900 examples were being built across the country. Its high point of popularity was in the fifteen-year period 1900-1915. As a style it was used successfully for a wide variety of building types, ranging from railroad stations and resort hotels to schools, service stations, apartments, and single-family dwellings. As a style it easily lent itself to available methods of construction, from stucco and wood stud to hollow tile and reinforced concrete. Since it relied on only a limited number of stylistic elements, it could readily be organized to satisfy new functional needs.

First Presbyterian Church (Now Grace Brethren Church), South Pasadena (p. 385, #9)

Characteristics:
- white, plain stucco walls
- arched openings — usually with the pier, arch, and surface of buildings treated as a single plane
- tile roofs of low pitch
- scalloped, parapeted gable ends
- paired bell towers, often covered with tile, hip roofs
- quatrefoil windows (especially in gable ends and accompanied by surrounding cartouches)
- occasional use of domes
- ornament when present cast in terracotta or concrete; patterns often Islamic and Sullivanesque

Prairie style (1905-1920)

The Midwestern Prairie style came into existence around 1900 in the Chicago work of Frank Lloyd Wright. By 1910 it had become a set style and was being employed by architects and builders across the country. The form most often used was the low, horizontal, square box dwelling which Wright first published in 1906 in the pages of the *Ladies Home Journal*. But each of the major Prairie architects developed his own personal and recognizable version of the style. These styles ranged from the classical, monumental designs of George W. Maher to the loose, highly varied designs of William G. Purcell and George G. Elmslie. Though we tend to think of the Prairie style as a domestic style, it also evolved a recognizable commercial and institutional counterpart (occasionally referred to as *Sullivanesque*), used in small-scaled banks, libraries, schools, churches, and public buildings. Los Angeles's adoption of the Prairie style was marginal compared to the great acceptance it gained in the Bay Area of Northern California.

House, Los Angeles (p. 153, #16)

Characteristics, domestic:
- usually stucco boxes with horizontal emphasis
- openings arranged in horizontal patterns; bands or windows placed directly under roof soffit
- facades (especially street facade) symmetrical and balanced
- usually one or more open or closed single-floor porches symmetrically projecting off house; second-floor sleeping porches often present
- pattern of boards, especially horizontal boards (usually stained) used to connect windows, doors, and other elements
- casement windows favored in more elaborate examples

Characteristics, non-domestic:
- preference for single brick-sheathed box
- facades almost always balanced and symmetrical
- free-standing engaged piers (not supporting any entablature) used to orchestrate facades
- Richardsonian Syrian arch used
- use of Sullivanesque patterned ornament in colored terra-cotta
- geometric patterned stained, leaded glass windows and skylights

English Tudor (1900-present)

The English Medieval mode was spoken of at times as English Half-timber or English Elizabethan. In Southern California this image was used almost exclusively for single-family residential architecture. It also occurred in some multiple housing, especially in bungalow courts in the teens and twenties. And in the 1970s and 1980s it has been employed throughout the Los Angeles area for condominium townhouses. Most of the examples in Southern California have as their source the rural or small village cottages and houses of England, especially those of the Cotswold district. The English Tudor image was a picturesque one, and in some of the best examples the forms evoke the mood of a cottage which might be encountered in a child's fairytale. These buildings tend towards the informal, and details such as windows, doors, half-timbering, and high-pitched gables are meant to hug the building to the ground. Tall chimneys are treated as major design elements, the windows are casement with small lights. The landscaping around the dwelling is usually informal, and ideally meant to partially enshroud the house.

Barnett House, Pacific Palisades (p. 41, #11)

French Norman (1900-present)

The difference between the Medievalism of the French Norman image and that of the English Tudor often narrowed down to whether or not a round, conical-roofed tower was provided. The specific sources for the style were the farm houses and small manor houses of France, especially those of Normandy and Brittany. Knowledge of this image developed in the teens, as an outcome of the First World War, and on into the 1920s through the publication of numerous illustrative books and articles. The most typical form for the houses was that of an L with a tower placed within the junction of the two volumes. In the more correct examples the roofs were hipped and quite steep, and wall dormers with narrow windows were used. Walls were stuccoed, occasionally of brick, and half-timbering was generally employed only on the upper sections of the walls.

Bungalow Court, Los Angeles (p. 187, #31)

Mediterranean (Spanish and Italian) Revival (1900-present)

California architects and their clients have never been particularly precise as to what made a dwelling Mediterranean rather than Spanish, though there indeed was a difference. That which was labeled *Mediterranean* during the teens and twenties should perhaps have been called *Italian,* or even more pointedly the *Tuscan Rural style.* The source in this instance came from one or another of the numerous books published between 1900 and 1930 that illustrated Italian rural villas and their gardens. Generally, the twentieth-century revivalist looked to Italian villas of the sixteenth rather than the fifteenth century, for these tended to be more classical and formal. In California the Mediterranean villa appealed to those who wished to continue the classical tradition, and at the same time wished to suggest a form which was picturesque and regional. The California examples generally employed a symmetrical composition for the street elevation (or at least a portion of the facade was symmetrical), and the basic form of the building was that of a single rectangular volume. The walls were of smooth stucco, shutters were often used, the roof had a pronounced overhang, and the form of the roof was low pitched and hipped. Details (generally in cast stone) were restrained in their classical references. Gardens were axial and were directly related to the symmetry of the building, its plan, and interior spaces.

House, San Marino *(p. 390, #27)*

Spanish Colonial Revival (1915-present)

The Spanish Colonial Revival was a direct outgrowth of the earlier Mission style, and examples were built as early as the 1890s in Southern California. The symbolic beginning of the revival was the San Diego Exposition of 1915 and the buildings designed for the fair by Bertram G. Goodhue and Carleton M. Winslow. By the 1920s it became *the* style for Southern California. Hispanic or, as they were often called, Mediterranean designs were employed for the full range of building types. Many Southern California communities adopted the style as the only image allowed.

The term *Spanish Colonial Revival* entails a number of related historic styles — including the provincial Italian of northern Italy, the Plateresque, the Churrigueresque and the Neo-Classic of Spain and her colonies, and the Islamic from Southern Spain and North Africa. Its most formal exercises generally looked to the Italian while the Andalusian was employed for informal designs. The acknowledged master of the style was the Montecito architect George Washington Smith. The style's greatest period of popularity was 1920-1930.

From the mid-1920s on the Spanish Colonial Revival traditon provided a source for the Monterey Revival and for the California Ranch house. In more recent years, in the 1970s and 1980s, variations on the Spanish Colonial Revival theme have frequently been used for the images of shopping centers, office buildings, for condominium townhouses, and for single-family houses.

Adamson House, Malibu (p. 37, #12)

Characteristics:

- stucco surfaces which predominate over the openings
- low-pitched tile roofs
- limited number of openings (best if deeply cut into the wall surfaces)
- closely related to outdoors through use of French doors, terraces, pergolas
- gardens designed in a formal, axial manner
- use of decorative ironwork for windows, doors, balconies, and roof supports
- glazed and unglazed tile used for walls and floors
- commercial buildings generally organized their facades in deep-set vertical bands (with windows and spandrels recessed)
- Plateresque and especially rich Churrigueresque ornament of cast concrete or terra-cotta occurred in many commercial buildings and occasionally in domestic designs

Pueblo Revival (1900-1930)

The Pueblo Revival was based upon forms developed in the late eighteenth and early nineteenth centuries in the Southwest, and especially in the Rio Grande Valley of New Mexico. Surprisingly it was never a widely used style in Southern California, though features of the style like projecting vigas and parapeted roofs were employed as elements on what otherwise was Spanish Colonial Revival design. As a style it remained exotic for the Southland. Examples are primarily residential.

Atwater Bungalows, Los Angeles (p. 192, #14)

Characteristics:
- general profile low, earth-hugging
- thick adobe-appearing walls, sometimes fake, sometimes real
- adobe walls extend vertically as horizontal parapet, usually with edge of parapet curved to suggest the handmade feeling of adobe architecture
- roofs flat and invisible behind parapets
- rows of projecting vigas
- tree trunks for porch columns
- brick used for terraces, porch, and interior floors
- small windows, usually of casement type
- oven-type corner fireplaces

Monterey Revival (1928-1941)

The Monterey Revival provided a fusion of Spanish and the American Colonial, and even in some instances with the Regency. The first of the Monterey Revival houses were built in the mid-1920s and its popularity supplanted that of the Spanish Colonial Revival of the 1930s. The style tended to be limited to domestic architecture, though occasionally it was used for small shops, offices, and motels. Its first examples were more Spanish, the later examples more Colonial or Regency. Two of its gifted proponents in the Southland were Roland E. Coate and H. Roy Kelley.

Kerr House, Brentwood (p. 121, #40)

Characteristics:

- single, two-story rectilinear volume; occasionally with wings
- stuccoed surfaces; in some examples board and batten used, especially to sheath second floor
- low-pitched gable roof covered in most instances with wood shingles
- projecting second-floor balcony with simple wood supports and wood railing
- "Colonial" entrances with panelled doors, sidelights, fanlights, panelled recesses
- double-hung wood windows with mullions; occasional Greek Revival detailing of wood frame
- "Colonial" interior detailing— fireplaces, built-in cupboards, wood panelled walls, etc.

Moderne (Art Deco and Streamline Moderne) (1920-1941)

The popular Moderne divides itself into two different phases: the Zigzag Moderne of the 1920s and the Streamline Moderne of the 1930s. The Art Deco Zigzag Modern developed from classical-inspired designs of the teens and early twenties by Bertram B. Goodhue, from the vertical Gothic schemes of Eliel Saarinen; from the work of the Viennese Seccessionists, from the forms and ornamentations of the Paris Exposition des Arts Décoratif of 1925, as well as the teens and twenties designs of Frank Lloyd Wright. The Streamline Moderne was an outgrowth of the machine aesthetic, the curved aerodynamic form of the airplane, and of the newly-developing International Style Modern. Though the term *Art Deco* has recently been employed to describe the Moderne, it is not satisfactory, since it does not take into account the diversity of sources, nor does it mirror the major differences between the Moderne of the twenties and the Moderne of the thirties. It would be best to limit the term to the first phase which took place in the 1920s.

Fox-Wilshire Theatre Building, Los Angeles (p. 159, #53)

Characteristics, Zigzag or Art Deco Moderne:
- smooth-surfaced volumes, windows arranged in sunken vertical panels; elimination of any classical or medieval termination at the top of the building
- symmetry and balance for each elevation
- frequent use of central tower, whose summit recedes in a stepped pattern
- flat roof, usually headed by parapets
- tendency for buildings to be monumental, formal, and heavy
- ornamentation of zigzags, chevrons, sunbursts, spirals, and stylized plant motifs; stylized animals such as deer and gazelle employed

Characteriestic, Streamline Moderne:
- stucco boxes, often with rounded corners, and even rounded parapets
- emphasis on the horizontal through banded surfaces, windows, etc.
- curved projecting wings
- glass brick

Federal Reserve Bank, Los Angeles (p.227, #36)

- round windows (as ship portholes)
- steel (ship) railing
- brightly colored vitrelite.

PWA Moderne (1930-1941)

During the last years of the presidency of Herbert Hoover and throughout the Depression years of the thirties, architects merged the Beaux Arts Classical (its Neo-Classical phase) with the Art Deco and Streamline Moderne. The style is most closely associated with Federal governmental architecture, but it was also used for private commercial buildings as well. These buildings were fundamentally classical and formal, but just enough Moderne details were injected to convey a contemporary Moderne feeling as well as the traditional authority of the classical. Southern California, along with the rest of the country, acquired a wealth of these buildings during the thirties. The largest number of these were public school buildings.

Characteristics:

- emphasis on mass rather than volume
- basic classical balanced and symmetrical form; classical horizontal proportions
- piers used rather than columns; piers occasionally fluted, but generally had no capitals or bases
- windows arranged as vertical, recessed panels
- surfaces smooth and flat; terra-cotta used for ornament
- most examples sheathed in smooth stone; polished marble, granite, and terrazzo used both within and without
- use of relief sculpture and interior murals

Los Angeles Branch, Federal Reserve Bank of San Francisco (p.227, #36)

International Style (Modern)
(1935-present)

The International style developed in Europe in the 1920s in the hands of Le Corbusier, Walter Gropius, and Mies Van der Rohe. A highly personal version of the new style was introduced in the Los Angeles area by R. M. Schindler, and later by Richard J. Neutra, J. R. Davidson, Kem Weber, and Jock Peters. Probably the purest examples of the style were the late 1930s houses of Raphael S. Soriano. From 1935-1941 Los Angeles was the center of the International Style Modern in the U.S., though the Southern California examples of the style were far different from those in Europe or even in the Eastern U.S.

After World War II the preferred form was the Miesian post and beam, metal-and-glass-sheathed box, often called the *Corporate International Style.* Variations of this mode have continued right down to the present day.

Lukens House, Los Angeles (p. 252, #9)

Characteristics:
- light, horizontal volumes often cantilevered out over the landscape
- horizontality strongly emphasized
- walls and glass surfaces kept in same plane
- stucco walls conveying lightness
- flat roofs, usually without parapets
- extensive use of glass
- machine, hospital-like image cultivated

California Ranch house (1935-present)

The California Ranch house developed out of the turn-of-the-century Craftsman bungalow and the period style bungalows of the twenties. The ranch house is a single-floor dwelling, low in profile and closely related to terraces and gardens. Its specific historic images were both the nineteenth-century California adobe house and the nineteenth-century California single-wall, board-and-batten rural farm buildings. The characteristic ranch house did and still does employ a variety of historic images, but the classic design mingles modern imagery with the Colonial. Los Angeles designer Cliff May can be considered the author of this informal style of suburban residential design. Versions of the California Ranch house were designed as early as the 1920s. But its "hey day" was in the post-World War II years.

Cliff May Ranchhouse

Characteristics:

- single-floor dwelling, composed of informal arrangement of volumes
- low-pitched hip or gable roof with wide overhangs
- sheathed in stucco, board and batten, shingles, clapboard, or a combination of one or more of these
- windows often treated as horizontal bands
- glass sliding doors lead to covered porches, terraces, or pergolas
- interior spaces open, and of low horizontal scale

Corporate International Style (Modern) (1945-present)

In the U.S. the Lever House in New York of 1951-52 (designed by Skidmore, Owings, and Merrill) can be said to be the first full realization of this style. The concept of clothing a building in a moduled, thin metal and glass skin independent of the structural skeleton, derived from the 1920s designs of Ludwig Mies Van der Rohe. In the early examples, the repeated pattern of sheathing was simple and rectilinear; by the end of the 1950s innumerable variations had been worked out on the theme. Corporate International style buildings seek to convey the precision image of the machine and of anonymity. Los Angeles and Southern California in general have acquired a full range of these buildings, and in fact, the style is still being used in the 1980s.

Carson Roberts Building, Los Angeles (p. 158, #47)

Characteristics:
- vertical box, with a suggestion of being set above the ground on stilts
- skin of machine-produced elements; windows and vertical surfaces all on same plane and all as weightless as possible
- buildings appear fragile
- the horizontal layering of floors, and the repetitious cell-like character of interior space can be read in the exterior fenestration

Brutalism (1960-present)

Brutalism (actually *New Brutalism*) was originally coined to describe the 1950s work of certain British architects who created an aesthetic based on the blunt exposure of all of a building's guts—its frame (concrete or steel); its sheathing (often brick), and all of the innards, pipes, ducts, etc. But very quickly the term began to be applied to the monumental rough concrete buildings of Le Corbusier and others. The Brutalist aesthetic represents a revolt against the Corporate International style. The Brutalist building is heavy, monumental, and emphatically permanent. Concrete is dealt with in an openly crude fashion, and all the innards of the building are laid before us. The end result is that the building has once again become a monumental piece of sculpture—one, which in many examples, is purposefully not beautiful, at least in a traditional architectural sense. The Southland began to acquire its first examples of this style in the early 1960s.

Liberty Building, Los Angeles (p. 112,#8)

Characteristics:

- building frequently composed of picturesque variety of forms; volumes project horizontally and vertically; contradicting shapes, shed roofs, cylinders introduced
- walls and structure of concrete are one again
- where wall and structure are separate, brick or other materials used as a separate infill which does not hide structure; and structure, not infill, predominates
- openings introduced as holes; occasionally as random holes
- concrete surfaces left exposed within and without; tactile quality interjected through leaving the pattern of wooden form work
- pipes, vents, ducts, etc., left exposed

New Formalism (ca. 1960-present)

The New Formalism (or *Neo-Palladianism*) represents yet another twentieth century effort to enjoy the advantages of the past and also the full advantages of the present. In this compromise the Miesian aesthetic of the Corporate International style returns to the Classical. Symmetry, classical proportions, arches, and traditional rich materials such as marble and granite are now used. The form of the building often tends to be a symmetrical pavilion set on a podium. The style came about in the hands of Edward D. Stone, Philip C. Johnson, and Minoru Yamasaki. Since the New Formalism shares many points of similarity with the earlier Regency Formalism, it is difficult to indicate a specific date for the early examples in Southern California. By the early 1960s, with the work of Stone himself in Southern California, the style was well on its way.

Perpetual Savings, Westwood (p. 131, #14)

Characteristics:
- single volume preferred
- buildings separated from nature and usually set on podium
- often an exotic Near Eastern/Indian flavor
- suggestion of classical columns (piers) and entablatures
- arches, elliptical and others
- wall surfaces smooth, often elegantly sheathed in stone
- delicacy of all details — no heavy, monumental qualities
- grilles of polished metal, concrete, and stone
- formal landscape: pools and fountains; frequent use of monumental High Art sculpture

Cut-into Box (1965-present)

The Cut-into Box style emerged out of the New Brutalism, the classic element of the New Formalism, and specifically from the 1960s designs of Louis I. Kahn. In most cases the horizontal imagery of the International style is maintained; but now the building is transformed into something monumental and permanent, and the traditional separateness of interior and exterior space is again cultivated. Design elements, such as Kahn's vertical service stacks or his diagonal splitting of a volume, and Charles Moore's use of unifying cores, are now employed as style devices, devoid in most instances of their original conceptual origin. As a style in Southern California, it has been mostly used for offices and other commercial usages.

Characteristics:
- rectangular volumes; usually several rather than one
- volume articulated horizontally
- surface sheathed in brick; skin hides structure
- windows and other openings deeply cut into surface; usually with slanted apron sills
- exteriors tend to be monotone both in color and in use of single surface material

Century Bank Building, Los Angeles (p. 159, #52)

Post-Modern (1970-present)

Post-Modern is a loose stylistic designation (coined by Charles Jencks in the mid-1970s) which refers to a self-conscious use of traditional architectural elements, usually added as "decoration" to what is essentially a late Modern building. The close-to-exclusive historic imagery used is that of the Classical tradition, derived from Italian examples from the High Renaissance, Mannerism, and Baroque; from French, German, and English "Rationalist" architects just before and after 1800; and early twentieth century classicists such as Sir Edwin Lutyens and Josef Hoffmann. The column, arch, and entablature are the components most often employed, but these features are seldom integral to the total design. Other traditional elements in the way of proportions, symmetry, and axial orientation are rarely used, and when they are they are generally seen as points of contradiction within the total design. In Southern California some Mediterranean/Spanish design elements have been employed by the Post-Modernists, but in most instances these regional design elements have been utilized in period revival image buildings of the 1970s and 1980s, rather than in Post-Modernist designs. In Los Angeles the favorite Post-Modern imagery is that of the early high art Modern of the 1920s conveying the High Tech image of the machine.

Burlington Archade, Pasadena (p. 373, #60)

Characteristics:

- image of the machine via the visual language of the early Modern of the 1920s — nautical portholes, railings, metal stairs, banded windows, stucco walls
- use of Classical columns (usually a version of the Tuscan Order)
- columns or piers coupled with arches; arches often boldly defined by voussoirs and keystone
- use of circular and lunette windows; roof and wall dormers
- entrance played up with pilasters and entablature
- use of pronounced entablatures and projecting cornices
- occasional use of closed Classical pediments
- building itself (its enclosed space) seems to sit behind a screen or partial screen of historic elements
- pergolas employed to counter or deny extension of interior spaces

High Tech style (1970-present)

The High Tech style represents one of the many aspects of Post-Modern. The image of the machine, as an ideal, has been a dominant theme for all aspects of Modern architecture in this century. The image of the machine revealed through high art painting and sculpture and through the transportation machine (especially the ocean liner) served as the bases for the early International Style Modern in the 1920s and 1930s. The recent references to the idea of the machine have been equally, if not more indirect, than those of the twenties and thirties. All of the contemporary instances of High Tech buildings in Southern California see the machine through the eyes of the early Modernists of the 1920s, together with a serious glance at the high art world of minimal sculpture of the 1960s and early 1970s. The contemporary High Tech style has developed two approaches: the first depicts the building as if it were composed of a series of separate, independent machine parts akin to the design of an automobile of the 1920s; the second approach seems to have simply taken the forms of minimal sculpture and enlarged them into a building. The language used for the later is that of elemental shapes — cylinders, angular volumes—which are articulated by fragile skins of glass, often colored or reflective. The first of the High Tech modes has a fondness for revealing the buildings innards (symbolically, not in fact) via exposed piping and metal chimneys. These are coupled with everyday machine products such as corregated metal sheathing. Finally historical references are made to the vocabulary of the early International Style Modern — glass bricks, metal stairs and pipe railings, etc. Like the automobiles of the twenties bright colors are often employed to bring added emphasis to each of the separate parts.

Condominium Townhouses, Santa Monica (p. 63, #20)

Bibliography

One can gain some idea of the mountains of literature of Los Angeles by thumbing through Doyce B. Nunis, Jr.'s *Los Angeles and Its Environs in the Twentieth Century,* (now over ten years old) with its 9,895 entries contained within 501 pages. And this bibliography is only for the twentieth century from 1900 through 1973. While every state and every American city had its array of PR sales literature in the nineteenth century, no region or city comes close to equaling the output of literature on Southern California and Los Angeles. And the last ten years has seen no letdown in the interest in publishing articles and books about Los Angeles (in part due to the celebration of the city's bicentennial in 1981).

The accompanying bibliography lists those writings which we have found most useful in forming our understanding of the built environment of Los Angeles. Though of real value in research we have on the whole left out those ponderous "histories," mostly written in the early twentieth century. Periodicals that concern themselves at least in part with architecture in the Southland are *Sunset, Westways,* and the *Home* section of the *Los Angeles Times.* Those specifically devoted to architecture which we continually consult are *Architectural Digest, L.A. Architect,* and *Arts and Architecture* (formerly *Pacific Coast Architect, California Arts and Architecture,* and *Arts and Architecture,* an important periodical which has recently been revived under the editorship of Barbara Goldstein). Other magazines no longer published but of great value to us have been: *Architect and Engineer, California Home Owner, Bungalow Magazine, Land of Sunshine* (later *Outwest*), and the all-too-brief *West* magazine of the Sunday *Los Angeles Times.* The real estate section of the Sunday *Los Angeles Times* has always provided a revealing clue as to what was and is occurring in Los Angeles architecture (especially commercial and popular spec architecture). Then there are those very valuable articles written by the architectural critics of the *Los Angeles Times:* John Pastier, John Dreyfus, Art Seidenbaum, and Sam Hall Kaplan: those written by Joseph Giovannini for the *Los Angeles Examiner.* Los Angeles and the Southern California scene in general was well presented in many of the national magazines, such as *House and Home,* which are no longer published. Also no longer published but very revealing of Los Angeles and its environs was the environmental planning magazine *Cry California.*

Institutions notable for their collections on Los Angeles architecture are the Huntington Library, the History Department of the Los Angeles Public Library, the History Division of the Los Angeles County Museum of Natural History, the Los Angeles Cultural Heritage Board, the Pasadena Urban Conservation Program, the UCLA Special Collection, Research Library, Art and Architectural Library, the Art and Architecture Library, the University of Southern California, and the Special Collections, Library at the University of California, Santa Barbara.

Original architectural drawings and archives are of great value in the study of architecture in Los Angeles and the Southland. The largest single collection is contained in the Architectural Drawing Collection, University Art Museum, University of California Santa Barbara. Other collections of drawings are to be found at the Huntington Library, at the Gamble House of the University of Southern California in Pasadena, and at the library, UCLA.

As one would expect there was a real spate of literature published at the time of Los Angeles's bicentennial in 1981, and by far the most useful of these was Paul Gleye's *The Architecture of Los Angeles*. Earlier works which have continually influenced us are Esther McCoy's *Five California Architects* (first published in 1960; republished in 1975), and Reyner Banham's *Los Angeles: The Architecture of Four Ecologies* (1974). More generally Robert Venturi and Denise Scott Brown (Venturi) and Charles Moore have informed and inspired us. Their pioneering publications on Los Angeles and vernacular architecture have been continued by John Margolies, Jim Heiman, Rip George, John Chase, and John Beach. Los Angeles will never be the same.

Anonymous. 1912. "California's Contribution to a National Architecture." *The Craftsman* 22 (Aug.): 352-547.

_____. 1912. *Southern California: The Land of Heart's Desire: Its People, Homes, and Pleasures: Art and Architecture*. Los Angeles: *Los Angeles Morning Herald*.

_____. 1914. *Handbook of Southern California, Los Angeles and San Diego Standard Guide*. New York.

_____. 1923. "The Los Angeles Civic Center." *Architect and Engineer* 73 (June): 65-67.

_____. 1941. "Work of Some Contemporary Los Angeles Architects." *Pencil Points* 60 (May): 306-33.

_____. 1943. "The Housing Authority of the City of Los Angeles Presents a Solution." *California Arts and Architecture* 60 (May): 47-66.

_____. 1973. "Street Art Exploration in Los Angeles." *Sunset* 150 (April): 110-13.

_____. 1976. "The Los Angeles 12." *Architectural Record* 160 (Aug.): 81-90.

Abeloe, William N., et. al. 1966. *Historic Spots in California*. Stanford.

Allison, David C. 1918. "The Work of Myron Hunt." *Architect and Engineer* 53 (April): 38-68.

Amos, Patrick. 1983. *At Home with Architecture*. La Jolla.

Andersen, Timothy J., Eudorah M. Moore, Robert Winter. 1974. *California Design 1910*. Pasadena. Reprint 1980, Salt Lake City.

Andre, Herb. 1971. *John Byers. Domestic Architecture in Southern California 1919-1960*. Unpublished M.A. Thesis, University of California, Santa Barbara.

Architectural Design. 1973. "Architectural Design Goes West." *Architectural Design* 43, no. 8.

Austin, John C. 1905. *Architecture in Southern California*. Los Angeles.

Austin, Mary. 1903. *Land of Little Rain*. Boston.

_____. 1914. *California: Land of the Sun*. London.

Baer, Kurt. 1963. *Architecture of the California Missions*. Berkeley.

Bangs, Jean Murray. 1948. "Greene and Greene." *Architectural Forum* 89 (Oct.): 80-82.

_____. 1961. "Los Angeles. . .Know Thyself." *Home, Los Angeles Times* (Oct. 14): 4-11

Banham, Reyner. 1971. "L.A.: The Structure Behind the Scene." *Architectural Design* 41 (April): 227-30.

_____. 1974. *Los Angeles: The Architecture of Four Ecologies*. London.

_____. 1974. "A London-L.A. Love Affair." *West, Los Angeles Times* (June 6): 9-14.

Basten, Fred. 1974. *Santa Monica by the Bay: Its First 100 Years*. Los Angeles.

Baum, Dwight James. 1928. "Ecclesiastical Architecture of California." *American Architecture* 34 (July): 71-78.

Baum, George C. 1919. "The Spanish Mission Type." *Architectural Styles for Country Houses* by Henry H. Taylor. New York.

Baylis, Douglas and Joan Parry. 1956. *California Houses of Gordon Drake*. New York.

Beach, John. 1983. "Lloyd Wright's Sowden House." *Fine Homebuilding* (April/May): 66-73.

Benton, Arthur B. 1896. "Architecture for the Southwest." *Outwest (Land of Sunshine)* 4 (Feb.): 126-30.

_____. 1911. "The California Mission and Its Influence on Pacific Coast Architecture." *Architect and Engineer* 24 (Feb.): 35-45.

_____. 1914. "The Work of the Landmark Club of Southern California." *AIA Journal* 2 (Sept.): 469-81.

Beronius, George. 1976. "Those

Astonishing Murals of East Los Angeles." *Home, Los Angeles Times* (April 11): 12-17, 22-23.

_____. 1976. "Paradise for Porkers." *Home, Los Angeles Times* (April 18): 19-21.

Billiteu, Bill. 1979. "Simon Rodia's Incredible Towers." *Art News* 78 (April): 92-96.

Bledsoe, Jane. 1983. "Added-on Ornament," *Home Sweet Home, American Domestic Vernacular Architecture.* Edited by Charles W. Moore, etc., 30-34. New York.

Bowman, Lynn. *L.A.: Epic of a City.* Los Angeles.

Boyarsky, Nancy and Bill. 1971. "The Highway Game." *West, Los Angeles Times* (Feb. 28): 7-15.

Bradley, Bill. 1979. *The Last of the Great Stations.* Glendale.

_____, (compiler). 1981. *Commercial Los Angeles, 1925-1947: Photographs from the "Dick" Wellington Studio.* Glendale.

Brady, Francis. 1962. "The Spanish Colonial Revival in California Architecture." Unpublished M.A.. thesis, California State University, Long Beach.

Brantner, Cherri and Gregory Cloud, eds. 1978. "The Essential Pico Blvd." *SCAN* 1 (Nov.): 2-7.

Braupton, Ernest. 1946. *The Garden Beautiful in California.* Los Angeles.

Bricker, David. 1983. *Cliff May and the California Ranch House after 1945.* Unpublished M.A. thesis, University of California, Santa Barbara.

Bricker, Lauren Weiss. 1982. *The Residential Architecture of Roland E. Coate.* Unpublished M.A. thesis, University of California, Santa Barbara.

Brino, Giovanni. 1978. *La Citta Capitalista: Los Angeles.* Florence.

Brodsly, David. 1981. *L.A. Freeway: An Appreciative Essay.* Berkeley.

Brook, Harry Ellington. 1915. *Los Angeles, California: The City and County.* Los Angeles.

Brown, Robert G. 1964. "The California Bungalow in Los Angeles: A Study in Origins and Classifications." Unpublished M.A. thesis, University of California, Los Angeles.

Browne, F. E. 1896. *Comfortable Los Angeles Homes and What People Say Who Live in Them.* Los Angeles.

Bryant, Lynn. 1983. "Edward Huntsman-Trout, Landscape Architect," *Review,* Southern California Chapter, Society of Architectural Historians, II, no. 1 (Winter): 1-6.

Buergen, Anne Luise, Robert Alexander, Calvin Hamilton, Albert Martin. 1979. "Downtown L.A." *L.A. Architect* 5 (Feb.): 3-6.

Burdette, Robert J. 1906. *Greater Los Angeles and Southern California.* Chicago.

California Institute of Technology (Baxter Art Gallery). 1983. *Caltech, 1910-1950.* Exhibition catalog with essays by Alice Stone and Judith Goodstein, Richard Oliver, Joseph Giovannini, Alson Clark, Helen Searing, Stefanos Polyzoides, and Peter de Bretteville. Pasadena.

Cameron, Robert. 1976. *Above Los Angeles.* Los Angeles.

Campbell, Regula. 1981. "Notes on Landscape Design in Southern California." *L.A. Architect* 7 (Oct.): 4-5.

Caughey, John W. and La Ree. 1976. *Los Angeles: Biography of a City.* Berkeley.

Chalk, Warren. 1968. "Up the Downramp." *Architectural Design* 38 (Sept.): 404-07.

Chapman, John L. 1967. *Incredible Los Angeles.* New York.

Chase, John. 1981. "Map Guide to Recent Architecture in L.A." *L.A. Architect* 7 (Oct.): 2, 7.

_____. 1982. *Exterior Decoration: Hollywood's Inside-out Houses.* Los Angeles.

_____. 1982. "Typecasting Style: New Condominiums in Santa Monica, California." *Arts and Architecture* 1: 51-58.

_____. 1983. "The Garret, the Boardroom, and the Amusement Park." *Journal, Los Angeles Institute of Contemporary Art* 4: 21-27.

Chase, John and John Beach. 1983. "The Stucco Box," *Home Sweet Home, American Domestic Vernacular Architecture,* pp. 118-129. New York.

Case, Walter. 1927; 1974. *History of Long Beach and Vicinity.* New York.

Clark, Alson. 1982. "The California Architecture of Gordon Kaufmann," *Review*, Southern California Chapter, Society of Architectural Historians I, no. 3 (Summer): 1-7.

_____. 1983. "The Architecture of Los Angeles: An Introduction," *Review*, Southern California Chapter, Society of Architectural Historians II, no. 1 (Winter): 6-7.

Clark, David. 1972. *L.A. on Foot*. Los Angeles and San Francisco.

_____. 1981. *Los Angeles: A City Apart*. Woodland Hills.

Clark, Robert Judson and Thomas S. Hines. 1983. *Los Angeles Transfer: Architecture in Southern California 1880-1980*. William Andrews Clark Memorial Library, Los Angeles.

Cohen, Gloria. 1982. "Allyn E. Morris, Architect." *L.A. Architect* 8 (May): 2-3.

Coombs, Robert. 1983. "The New Victorians," *Westways* 75 (May): 31-33, 69.

Crocker, Donald W. 1968. *Within the Vale of Annandale*. Pasadena.

Crofutt, George A. 1878-79. *Crofutt's New Overland Tourist and Pacific Coast Guide*. Chicago.

Croly, Herbert D. 1906. "The California Country House." *Architect and Engineer* 7 (Dec.): 24-39.

Crump, Spencer. 1962. *Ride the Big Red Cars*. Los Angeles.

Current, William R. and Karen. 1974. *Greene and Greene, Architects in the Residential Style*. Fort Worth.

Cutts, Anson B., Jr. 1933. "The Hillside Home of Ramon Navarro, A unique setting created by Lloyd Wright." *California Arts and Architecture*, 44 (July): 11-13, 31.

Dash, Norman. 1976. *Yesterday's Los Angeles*. Miami.

David, Arthur C. 1906. "An Architect of Bungalows in California." *Architectural Record* 20 (Oct.): 306-15.

Del Zoppo, Annette and Jeffrey Stanton. 1978. *Venice, California, 1904-1930*. Venice.

Dickinson, R. B. 1896. *Los Angeles Today—Architecturally*. Los Angeles.

Dietz, Lawrence. 1969. "There Was Once a Woman Who Lived in a Shoe." *West, Los Angeles Times* (Nov. 30): 12-15.

_____. 1969. "Raymond Chandler's L.A." *Western Architect* 32 (Aug.): 87-90.

Dirección General De Arquitectura y Vivienda. MOPU 1984. *R. M. Schindler Arquitectura*, with articles by Esther McCoy, Hans Hollein, Stofanos Polyzoides, and David Gebhard. Madrid.

Duell, Prentice. 1923. "The New Era of California Architecture." *Western Architect* 32 (Aug.): 87-90.

Dumke, Glen S. 1970. *The Boom of the Eighties in Southern California*. San Marino.

Faulstick, Paul. 1977. *A Guide to Claremont Architecture*. Claremont.

Feldman, Eddy S. 1972. *The Art of Street Lighting in Los Angeles*. Los Angeles.

Fink, Augusta. 1966. *Time and the Terraced Land*. Berkeley.

Flanagan, Barbara. 1980. "Terminal Oasis: The Uncanny Survival of Union Station." *L.A. Architect*, 6 (Feb.): 2-3.

Flood, Francis B. 1941. "A Study of the Architecture of the Period 1868-1900 Existing in Los Angeles in 1940." Unpublished M.A. thesis, University of Southern California, Los Angeles.

Fogelson, Robert M. 1967. *The Fragmented Metropolis: Los Angeles, 1850-1930*. Cambridge.

Gallion, Arthur B. 1956. "Architecture of the Los Angeles Region." *Architectural Record* 119 (May): 159-66.

Gaut, Helen Lukens. A frequent contributor to *The Craftsman* (1901-1916) and other journals, she was a Pasadenan who had strong ties to the Arts and Crafts movement.

Gebhard, David. 1964. "Architecture in Los Angeles." *Artforum* 2 (Summer): 10-11.

_____. 1964. *George Washington Smith*. Santa Barbara.

_____. 1967. "The Spanish Colonial Revival in Southern California." *Journal of the Society of Architectural Historians* 26 (May): 131-47.

_____. 1970. "L.A., The Stucco Box." *Art in America* 58 (May-June): 130-33.

_____. 1972. *Schindler*. London and New York. Reprint 1980. Salt Lake City.

_____. 1974. "Getty's Museum." *Architecture Plus* 2 (Sept.-Oct.): 56-61.

_____. 1978. "Charles Moore and the West Coast." *Architecture and Urbanism* 5: 45-48.

_____. 1980. "Los Angeles: An Architectural Tour." *Portfolio* 2 (Sept.-Oct.): 106-109.

_____. 1980. "Architectural Imagery: The Missions and California." *Harvard Architectural Review* 1 (Spring): 136-45.

_____. 1982. "The Monterey Tradition: History Re-ordered." *New Mexico Studies in the Fine Arts* 7: 14-19.

_____. 1983. "Tile, Stucco Walls, and Arches; The Spanish Tradition in the Popular American House." *Home Sweet Home, American Domestic Vernacular Architecture.* Edited by Charles W. Moore. Pp. 104-11. New York.

Gebhard, David and Susan King. 1976. *A View of California Architecture 1960-1976.* San Francisco.

Gebhard, David and Harriètte Von Breton. 1968. *1868-1968: Architecture in California.* Santa Barbara.

_____. 1969. *Kem Weber. The Moderne in Southern California, 1920-1941.* Santa Barbara.

_____. 1971. *Lloyd Wright, Architect.* Santa Barbara.

_____. 1975. *L.A. in the Thirties.* Salt Lake City.

_____. 1983. "Preserving the Common Place." *Journal L.A.I.C.A.* 4 (Spring): 50-57.

Gebhard, David, Harriette Von Breton Lauren Weiss. 1980. *The Architecture of Gregory Ain: The Play between the Rational and High Art.* Santa Barbara.

Gebhard, David, Harriette Von Breton Robert Winter. 1979. *Samuel and Joseph Cather Newson: Victorian Architectural Imagery in California, 1878-1908.* Los Angeles.

Gebhard, David, Lauren Weiss Bricker, David Bricker. 1982. *Fort MacArthur, San Pedro—A Public Report.* Washington, D.C.

Gebhard, David and Robert Winter. 1965. *A Guide to Architecture in Southern California.* Los Angeles.

_____. 1977. *A Guide to Architecture in Los Angeles and Southern California.* Salt Lake City.

Gill, Brendan. 1982. *The Dream Come True: The Great Houses of Los Angeles.* New York.

Gill, Irving J. 1916. "The Home of the Future: The New Architecture of the West." *The Craftsman* 30 (May): 140-41, 220.

Giovannini, Joseph. As architectural critic for the *Los Angeles Herald Examiner* from 1978 to 1983, Giovannini contributed greatly to our understanding of the local architectural and planning scene.

_____. 1981. "The Environment of Movement." *California History* 60 (Spring): 82-83.

_____. 1984. "A Chronicler of California Architecture (Esther McCoy)." *The New York Times* (June 21): 21.

Gleen, Constance W. 1977. *Egypt in L.A.* Long Beach.

Gleye, Paul. 1981. *The Architecture of Los Angeles.* San Diego.

Goodhue, Bertram G. and Carleton M. Winslow. 1916. *The Architecture and Gardens of the San Diego Exposition.* San Francisco.

Greene, Charles S. 1908. "Bungalows." *The Western Architect* 12 (July): 3.

_____. 1915. "Impressions of Some Bungalows and Gardens." *The Architect* 10 (Dec.): 251-52, 278.

Grenier, Judson A., Doyce B. Nunis, Jr. Jean Bruce Poole. 1978. *A Guide to Historic Places in Los Angeles County.* Dulrique.

Grey, Elmer. 1905. "Architecture in Southern California." *Architectural Record* 17 (Jan.): 1-17.

_____. 1922. "Some Country House Architecture in the Far West." *Architectural Record* 51 (Jan.): 308-15.

Griffin, Helen S. 1938. "Some Two-Story Adobe Houses of Old California." *Historical Society of Southern California Quarterly* 20 (March): 5-21.

Gudde, Erwin G. 1968. *California Place Names: Origin and Etymology of Current Geographical Names.* Berkeley.

Guinn, J. M. 1897. "Los Angeles in the Adobe Age." *Historical Society of Southern California Quarterly* 4: 49-55.

Haley, A. L. Ca. 1910. *Modern Apartments.* Los Angeles.

Halprin, John. 1979. *Los Angeles: Improbable City.* New York.

Hamlin, Talbot F. 1939. "What Makes it American: Architecture in the Southwest and West." *Pencil Points* 20 (Dec.): 762-76.

_____. 1941. "California Whys and Wherefores." *Pencil Points* 22 (May): 339-44.

Hancock, Ralph. 1949. *Fabulous Boulevard* (Wilshire). New York.

_____. 1955. *The Forest Lawn Story.* Los Angeles.

Hannaford, Donald R. 1931. *Spanish Colonial or Adobe Architecture in California, 1800-1850.* New York.

Hanson, A. E. 1978. *Rolling Hills: The Early Times.* Rolling Hills.

_____. 1984. *An Aradian Landscape, The California Gardens of A. E. Hanson, 1920-1931.* Edited and introduced by David Gebhard. Los Angeles.

Hanson, Earl and Paul Beckett. 1944. *Los Angeles: Its People and Its Homes.* Los Angeles.

Harrel, Mary Ann Beach. 1983. "The Vernacular Castle." *Home Sweet Home, American Domestic Vernacular Architecture.* Edited by Charles W. Moore. Pp. 72-75. New York.

Harris, Allen. 1922. "Southern California Architects: Walker and Eisen." *Building Review* 22 (Oct.): 43-52.

Harris, Frank and Weston Bonenberger. 1951. *A Guide to Contemporary Architecture in Southern California.* Los Angeles.

Harris, Harwell Hamilton. 1965. *Harwell Hamilton Harris—A Collection of his Writings.* Raleigh, N.C.

Hastings, Miles. 1914. "The Continuous House." *Sunset* 32 (Jan.): 110-16.

Hatheway, Roger. 1981. "El Pueblo: Myth and Realities," *Review,* Southern California Chapter, Society of Architectural Historians I, no. 1 (Fall): 1-5.

Hays, William C. 1917. "One Story and Open-Air Schoolhouses in California." *Architectural Forum* 27 (Sept.): 57-65.

Heiman, Jim and Rip George. Introduction by David Gebhard. 1980. *California Crazy.* San Francisco.

Heisley, George D. 1909. "Seeing America: Los Angeles." *Outwest* 30 (March): 193-224.

_____. 1909. "Seeing America: Some More About Los Angeles." *Outwest* 30 (May): 509-18.

Henstell, Bruce. 1980. *Los Angeles: An Illustrated History.* Los Angeles.

Hess, Alan. 1983. "Golden Architecture." *Journal, Los Angeles Institute of Contemporary Art* 4 (Spring): 28-30.

_____. 1983. "California Coffee Shops," *Arts and Architecture* 2, no. 2: 42-50.

Hill, Laurence L. 1929. *La Reina: Los Angeles in Three Centuries.* Los Angeles.

Hines, Thomas S. 1982. "Housing, Baseball, and Creeping Socialism: The Battle of Chavez Ravine, Los Angeles, 1949-1959." *Journal of Urban History* 8 (Feb.): 123-45.

_____. 1982. *Richard Neutra and the Search for Modern Architecture.* New York.

Hitchcock, Henry-Russell. 1940. "An Eastern Critic Looks at Western Architecture." *California Arts and Architecture* 57 (Dec.): 21-23, 40.

Holder, Charles. 1888. *Southern California—A Guide Book.* Los Angeles.

Honnold, Douglas. 1956. *Southern California Architecture: 1769-1956.* New York.

Hopkins, Una Nixon. 1908. "The Development of Domestic Architecture on the West Coast." *The Craftsman* 13 (Jan.): 450-57. Hopkins, a resident of Pasadena, was a frequent contributor to *The Craftsman,* writing about the Southern California scene.

Hume, H. (compiler). 1902. *Los Angeles Architecturally.* Los Angeles.

Hunt, Myron. 1912. "The Work of Messrs. Allison and Allison." *Architect and Engineer,* 42: 39-75.

Hunter, Paul and Walter L. Reichardt, eds. 1939. *Residential Architecture in Southern California.* Los Angeles.

Hylen, Arnold. 1976. *Bunker Hill: A Los Angeles Landmark.* Los Angeles.

_____. 1981. *Los Angeles Before the Freeways.* Los Angeles.

Inaya, Beata. 1974. *The Three Worlds of Los Angeles.* Text by Beata Inaya, David Gebhard, Reyner Banham, Dan McMasters, Hans Hollein, and Yona Freidman. Los Angeles.

Jackson, Helen Hunt. 1904. *Glimpses of California and the Missions.* Boston.

James, George Wharton. 1914. *California, Romantic and Beautiful.* Boston.

_____. 1927. *In and Out of the Old Missions.* Boston.

Jencks, Charles. 1976. "The Los Angeles Silvers." *Urbanism* (Oct.): 13-14.

————. 1978. *Daydream Houses of Los Angeles.* New York.

————. 1982. *Architecture Today.* London and New York.

Jenney, William L. E. 1906. "The Old California Missions and Their Influence on Design." *Architect and Engineer* 6 (Sept.): 25-33.

Johnson, Paul (ed.). 1968. *Los Angeles: Portrait of an Extraordinary City.* Menlo Park.

Johnson, Reginald D. 1926. "Development of Architectural Styles in California." *Architect and Engineer* 87 (Oct.): 108-9.

Jones, A. Quincy and Frederick E. Emmons. 1957. *Builder's Homes for Better Living.* New York.

Jordy, William H. 1972. *Progressive and Academic Ideals at the Turn of the Century.* New York.

Kamerling, Bruce. 1979. *Irving Gill: The Artist as Architect.* San Diego.

Kapp, Glenn and Geoff Miller. 1961. "Our Backyard Riviera." *Los Angeles* 2 (April): 18-21.

Kirker, Harold. 1960. *California's Architectural Frontier.* San Marino. Reprint 1973. Salt Lake City.

————. 1972. "California's Architecture and its Relations to Contemporary Trends in Europe and America." *California Historical Quarterly* 51 (Winter): 289-305.

Knight, Arthur and Eliot Elisofon. 1969. *The Hollywood Style.* New York.

Kuehn, Gernot. 1978. *Views of Los Angeles.* Los Angeles.

Lancaster, Clay. 1958. "The American Bungalow." *Art Bulletin* 15 (Sept.): 239-53.

————. 1963. *The Japanese Influence in America.* New York.

Laporte, Paul. 1962. *Simon Rodia's Towers in Watts.* Los Angeles.

Lautner, John. 1971. "You've Got to Fight for Great Design." *Home, Los Angeles Times* (Feb. 14): 16-18,21.

Lazlo, Paul. 1947. *Paul Lazlo — Designed in the U.S.A. 1937-1947.* Beverly Hills.

Le Barthon, J. L. 1904, *Our Architecture: Morgan and Walls, John Parkinson, Hunt and Eager.* Los Angeles.

Lewin, Susan Grant and Stanley Tigerman. 1982. *The California Condition: A Pregnant Architecture.* La Jolla.

Lewis, Oscar. 1957. *Here Lived the Californians.* New York.

Lindley, Walter, and J. P. Widney. 1896. *California of the South.* New York.

Lingenbrink, William. Ca. 1933. *Modernistic Architecture.* Los Angeles.

Littlejohn, David. 1984. *Architecture: The Life and Work of Charles W. Moore.* New York.

Litter, Charles. 1939. "A Dream Come True." *California AIA* (June): 28-29.

Long Beach Museum of Art. 1957. *Arts in California. I: Architecture.* Introduction by Jerome Allen Donson. Long Beach.

Los Angeles Architectural Club. 1910, 1912, and 1913. *Yearbook.* Los Angeles.

Los Angeles Chamber of Commerce. 1904. *Los Angeles and Vicinity.* Los Angeles.

Los Angeles Conservancy (The Conservancy has printed a number of tours of Los Angeles. Among them (undated) are:
Alvarado Terrace House Tour.
Buildings Reborn in Los Angeles.
Cruisin' L.A.
Old Monrovia House Tour.
Would You Believe Hollywood Boulevard?
Would You Believe Los Angeles?
The Los Angeles Conservancy's *News,* also contains helpful information about architecture and planning in Los Angeles.

Los Angeles Regional Planning Commission. 1940, 1941, and 1942. *Annual Reports.* Los Angeles.

————. 1941. *A Comprehensive Report on the Master Plan of Highways for Los Angeles County.* Los Angeles.

————. 1941. *Master Plan for Land Use — Inventory and Classification.* Los Angeles.

Los Angeles Department of Planning. 1964. *City Planning in Los Angeles: A History.* Los Angeles.

Luitjens, Helen. 1968. *The Elegant Era.* Palm Desert.

Luitjens, Helen and Katherine La Hue. 1975. *A Sketch Book of Pacific Palisades, California.* Santa Monica.

Lummis, Charles F. 1909. "The Making of Los Angeles." *Outwest* 30 (April): 227-57. See also his many other articles for this journal and its predecessor, *The Land of Sunshine.*

Mackey, Margaret G. 1938. *Los Angeles Proper and Improper*. Los Angeles.

Makinson, Randell L. 1960. "Greene and Greene," in *Five California Architects* by Esther McCoy. New York.

_____. 1974. *A Guide to the Work of Greene and Greene*. Salt Lake City.

_____. 1977. *Greene and Greene: Architecture as a Fine Art*. Salt Lake City.

_____. 1979. *Greene and Greene: Furniture and Related Designs*. Salt Lake City.

Margolies, John. 1973. "Roadside Mecca." *Progressive Architecture* 54 (Nov.): 123-28.

_____. 1980. *The End of the Road*. New York.

Marsh, Norman F. 1906. "Venice of America." *Architect and Engineer* 3 (Jan.): 19-25.

Marquez, Ernest. 1976. *Port of Los Angeles*. San Marino.

May, Cliff. 1952. *Sunset Western Ranch House*. Menlo Park.

Mays, Morrow. 1933. *Los Angeles*. New York.

McClurg, Verner B. 1945. *A Catalogue of Small Homes of California*. Hollywood.

McCoy, Esther. 1956. *Roots of California Contemporary Architecture*. Los Angeles.

_____. 1958. *Irving Gill, 1870-1936*. Los Angeles.

_____. 1960, 1975. *Five California Architects*. New York.

_____. 1960. *Richard Neutra*. New York.

_____. 1961. "Wilshire Boulevard," *Western Architect and Engineer* 222, no. 3 (Sept.): 25-51.

_____. 1962. *Modern California Houses: Case Study Houses, 1945-1962*. New York. (Reprinted as *Case Study Houses*.)

_____. 1968. "R. M. Schindler," *Lotus* 5: 92-105.

_____. 1968. *Craig Ellwood, Architect*. New York.

_____. 1979. *Vienna to Los Angeles: Two Journeys*. Santa Monica.

_____. 1982. "The Greenhouse: Energy Efficient Home in Venice, California." *Arts and Architecture* 1, no. 3: 45-59.

_____. 1982. "Charles Greene's Presence," *Review*, Southern California Chapter, Society of Architectural Historians 1, no 2 (Spring): 1-2.

_____. 1984. *The Second Generation*. Salt Lake City.

(The above listing of writings by Esther McCoy relating to Los Angeles and Southern California represents only a small proportion of her numerous articles and studies.)

McCoy, Esther and Evelyn Hitchcock. 1983. "The Ranch House," *Home Sweet Home, American Domestic Vernacular Architecture*. Edited by Charles W. Moore. Pp. 84-89. New York.

McGroarty, John Steven. 1921. *Los Angeles from the Mountains to the Sea* (3 vols.). Chicago.

McMillian, Elizabeth. 1979. *1929-1979 A Legend Still: Bullocks Wilshire*. Los Angeles.

_____. 1983. "Five Basic Classifications of Building Production." *Journal, Los Angeles Institute of Contemporary Art* 4 (Spring): 43-49.

McMillian, Elizabeth and Leslie Heumann. 1981. "Old Venice-New Venice." *Newsletter, Southern California Chapter, Society of Architectural Historians* 5 (April): 1-6.

McPherson, William. 1873. *Homes of Los Angeles City and County*. Los Angeles.

McWilliams, Carey. 1946. *Southern California: An Island on the Land*. Reprinted 1973 with new introduction. Salt Lake City.

Melnick, Robert and Mimi. 1974. *Manhole Covers of Los Angeles*. Los Angeles.

Millon, Wendy et. al. 1980. *The Best of Los Angeles: A Discriminating Guide*. Los Angeles.

Moore, Charles W. 1966. "You Have to Pay for the Public Life." *Perspecta* 9/10: 57-97.

_____. 1967. "Plug It in Rameses and See if It Lights Up." *Perspecta* 11: 33-43.

Moore, Charles W. and Gerald Allen. 1976. *Dimensions: Face, Shapes, and Scale in Architecture*. New York.

Moore, Charles W., Peter Becker, and Regula Campbell. 1984. *Los Angeles: The City Observed — A Guide to its Architecture and Landscapes*. New York.

Moore, Charles W., Kathryn Smith, and Peter Becker, eds. 1983. *Home Sweet Home, American Domestic Vernacular Architecture* New York.

Moran, Thomas. 1976. "L.A. Pop Architecture." *Los Angeles Free Press* 13 (April 7-8): 6-7.

Moran, Thomas and Tom Sewell. *Fantasy by the Sea: A Visual History of the American Venice.* Venice.

Morrow, Irving F. 1938. "Recent Architecture of Allison and Allison," *Architect and Engineer* 133: 2-34.

Murmann, Eugene O. 1915. *California Gardens.* Los Angeles.

Nadeau, Remi. 1960. *Los Angeles, from Misión to Modern City.* New York.

_____. 1965. *City Makers: The Story of Southern California's First Boom.* Los Angeles.

Nairn, Janet. 1976. "Frank Gehry: The Search for 'No Rules' Architecture." *Architectural Record* 159 (June): 95-102.

Neff, Wallace. 1964. *Architecture in Southern California.* Chicago. A survey of his own designs, no others!

Neuerburg, Norman. 1975. *Herculaneum to Malibu.* Malibu.

Neutra, Richard J. 1929. "Architecture Conditioned by Engineering and Industry." *Architectural Record* 66 (Sept.): 272-74.

_____. 1962. *Life and Shape.* New York.

Newcomb, Rexford. 1927. *The Spanish House for America.* Philadelphia.

_____. 1928. *Mediterranean Domestic Architecture in the United States.* Cleveland.

_____. 1925. *The Old Mission and Historic Houses of California.* Philadelphia.

_____. 1937. *Spanish Colonial Architecture in the United States.* New York.

Newsom, Joseph Cather. 1888. *Artistic Buildings and Homes of Los Angeles.* San Francisco. (Reprinted 1981 with an introduction by Jenne C. Bennett, and a foreword by R. L. Samsell, Los Angeles.)

_____. 1890. *Picturesque and Artistic Homes and Buildings of California.* San Francisco.

_____. Ca. 1893. *Modern Homes of California.* San Francisco.

Newsom, Samuel and Joseph Cather Newsom. 1884. *Picturesque California Homes* (No. 1); *Picturesque California Homes* (No. 2). San Francisco. (Reprinted in 1978 with an introduc-

tion by David Gebhard, Los Angeles.)

Nordhoff, Charles. 1878. *California for Pleasure and Residence.* New York.

Nunis, Doyce B. (ed.) 1973. *Los Angeles and its Environs in the Twentieth Century: A Bibliography of a Metropolis.* Los Angeles.

Nystrom, Richard Kent. 1968. *UCLA, An Interpretation Considering Architecture and Site.* Los Angeles.

Oberhind, Robert. 1977. *The Chili Bowls of Los Angeles.* Los Angeles.

O'Conner, Ben H. 1941. "Planning the Supermarket." *Architect and Engineer* 146 (Sept.): 14-19.

O'Flaherty, Joseph. 1977. *An End and a Beginning: The South Coast and Los Angeles, 1850-1887.* Hicksville, N.Y.

_____. 1978. *Those Powerful Years: The South Coast and Los Angeles, 1887-1917.* Hicksville, N.Y.

Ostroff, Roberta. 1971. "Up Against the Wall." *West, Los Angeles Times* (Jan. 31): 22-27.

Owen, J. Thomas. 1960. "The Church by the Plaza: A History of the Pueblo Church of Los Angeles." *Historical Society of Southern California Quarterly* 42 (June): 186-204.

Padilla, Victoria. 1961. *Southern California Gardens.* Berkeley.

Papademitriou, Peter. 1976. "Images from a Silver Screen." *Progressive Architecture* 57 (Oct.): 70-73.

Pastier, John. During the years 1969-1975 Pastier wrote weekly columns for the *Los Angeles Times* on the city's architecture and planning problems. At first these were published in the real estate section of the Sunday edition, later in the *View* section on Mondays. There is not space here to list these perceptive and important articles, but anyone who has tried to understand the local architectural scene in those years has thanked Pastier for his insights.

_____. 1974. "Evaluation; Utility and Fantasy in Los Angeles's 'Blue Whale'." *AIA Journal* 67 (May): 38-45.

_____. 1981. "Downtown Los Angeles: Guide Map." *Arts and Architecture* 1 (Fall): 49-53.

_____. 1983. "MOCA Builds." *Arts and Architecture* 2: 31-35.

Peand, Frank F. (publisher) 1911. *Land of Heart's Desire — Southern California: Her People, Homes and Pleasures, Art and Architecture.* Los Angeles.

Pelli, Cesar. 1974. "Tour Days in May." *Architecture and Urbanism* 45 (Sept.): 19.

Peterson, Kirk. 1983. "Eclectic Stucco," *Home Sweet Home, American Domestic Vernacular Architecture.* Edited by Charles M. Moore. Pp. 112-121. New York.

Peders, William Fredrick. 1980. *Lockwood de Forest, Landscape Architect: Santa Barbara, California, 1896-1949.* Unpublished M.A. thesis, University of California, Berkeley.

Phillips and Co. (publisher) 1889. *Phillips California Guide.* Los Angeles.

Pildas, Ave. 1979. *Art Deco Los Angeles.* New York.

Pinney, Joyce. 1978. *A Pasadena Chronology, 1769-1977: Remembering — When. . .Where.* Pasadena.

Plagens, Peter. 1972. "Los Angeles: The Ecology of Evil." *Artforum* 11 (Dec.): 67-76.

—————. 1973. "The L.A. Connection.: *Architectural Design* 43 (Aug.): 571-74.

Polyzoides, Stefanos, Roger Sherwood, and James Tice, with photographs by Julius Shulman. 1982. *Courtyard Housing in Los Angeles.* Berkeley.

Powell, Lawrence Clark. 1952. *Land of Fiction.* Los Angeles.

Price, C. Matlock. 1915. "Panama-California Exposition: Bertram G. Goodhue and the Renaissance of Spanish Colonial Architecture." *Architectural Record* 37 (March): 229-51.

Rand, Christopher. 1967. *Los Angeles, the Ultimate City.* New York.

Rand-McNally Guide to Los Angeles and Environs. Ca. 1925. New York.

Regan, Michael. 1965. *Mansions of Los Angeles.* Los Angeles.

—————. 1966. *Mansions of Beverly Hills.* Los Angeles.

Rey, Felix. 1924. "A Tribute to the Mission Style." *Architect and Engineer* 76 (Oct): 77-78.

Richey, Elinor. 1973. *Remain to Be Seen: Historic Houses Open to the Public.* Berkeley.

Rickard, J. A. 1923. "Los Angeles — The Wonder City of America." *Engineering News Record* 91 (Oct. 4): 554-58.

Rider, Freemont. 1925. *Rider's California: A Guide Book for Travelers.* New York.

Robbins, George W. and Deming L. Tilton, eds. 1941. *Los Angeles: Preface to a Master Plan.* Los Angeles.

Robinson, Charles Mulford. 1906. "Los Angeles Parks," *House and Garden* 10, no. 3 (Sept.): 114-15.

—————. 1910. "Los Angeles California, The City Beautiful," *Architectural Record* 26: 303-4.

Robinson, Paul and Walter Reichardt. 1939. *Residential Architecture in Southern California.* Los Angeles.

Robinson, W. W. 1942. *What They Say About Los Angeles.* Pasadena.

—————. 1953. *Panorama: A Picture-History of Southern California.* Los Angeles.

—————. 1968. *Los Angeles: A Profile.* Norman, Okla.

Rolle, Andrew F. 1963. *California, A History.* New York.

Rubin, Barbara. 1977. "A Chronology of Architecture in Los Angeles," *Annals of the Association of American Geographers* 67, no. 4: 521-37.

Rubin, Barbara, Robert Carlton, and Arnold Rubin. 1979. *L.A. In Installments. Forest Lawn.* Santa Monica.

Ruscha, Edward. 1965. *Some Los Angeles Apartments.* Los Angeles.

—————. 1966. *Every Building on the Sunset Strip.* Los Angeles.

—————. 1967. *Thirty-four Parking Lots.* Los Angeles.

Sanford, Trent E. 1950. *The Architecture of the Southwest.* New York.

Saylor, Henry H. 1917. *Bungalows.* New York.

Schindler, Pauline, ed. 1935. "Special Issue Devoted to Modern Architecture in Southern California." *California Arts and Architecture* 47 (Jan.).

Schmidt-Brummer, Horst. 1973. *Venice, California: An Urban Fantasy.* New York.

Schuyler, Montgomery. 1908. "Round About Los Angeles." *Architectural Record* 24 (Dec.): 430-40.

Scott, Mel. 1942. *Cities are for People.* Los Angeles.

—————. 1949. *Metropolitan Los Angeles: One Community.* Los Angeles.

Sears, Urmy. 1930. "A Community Approaches Its Ideal." *California Arts and Architecture* 38 (June): 19-21, 70, 72.

Seidenbaum, Art. 1972. "Los Angeles: The New Neighborhood." *Home, Los Angeles Times* (Dec. 31): 6-12.

————. 1975. *This Is California: Please Keep Out.* New York.

Seidenbaum, Art and John Malmin. Foreword by Will Durant. 1980. *Los Angeles 200: A Bicentennial Celebration.* New York.

Sewell, Elaine K., Ken Tantanaka, and Katherine W. Rinne. 1983. "A. Quincy Jones: The Oneness of Architecture," *Process: Architecture* 41.

Sexton, Randolph W. 1927. *Spanish Influence on American Architecture and Decoration.* New York.

————. 1930. "A New Yorker's Impression of California Architecture." *California Arts and Architecture* 39 (Oct.): 23-25, 64.

Shinn, Charles. 1878. *Pacific Coast Rural Handbook.* San Francisco.

Shulman, Julius. 1962. "The Architect's Perspective." *Architectural Digest* (May-June): 72-79.

————. 1968. *Cultural-Historic Monuments.* Los Angeles.

————. 1977. "A Photographer's Perspective on Neutra." *AIA Journal* 66 (March).

Sillo, Terry and John Manson. 1976. *Around Pasadena: An Architectural Study of San Marino, Sierra Madre, and Arcadia.* Pasadena.

Smith, Jack. 1976. *The Big Orange.* Los Angeles.

————. 1980. *Jack Smith's L.A.* New York.

Smith, Kathryn. 1979. "Frank Lloyd Wright, Hollyhock House and Olive Hill, 1914-1924." *Journal of the Society of Architectural Historians* 38 (March): 15-33.

Smith, Richard Austin. 1965. "Los Angeles: Prototype of Super City." *Fortune* (March).

Smith, Sarah Bixby. 1925, revised 1974. *Adobe Days.* Fresno.

Spalding, William A., compiler. 1931. *History and Reminiscences: Los Angeles, City and County, California* (3 vols.). Los Angeles.

Stacy-Judd, Robert B. 1934. "Some Local Examples of Mayan Adaptions." *Architect and Engineer* 116 (Feb.): 21-30.

Starr, Kevin. 1973. *Americans and the California Dream.* New York. Reprint 1980, Salt Lake City.

Stephens, James C. 1937. *The Development of County Planning in California.* Unpublished M.A. thesis, University of California. Los Angeles.

Strand, Janann. 1974. *A Greene and Greene Guide.* Pasadena.

Streatfield, David. 1976. "The Evolution of the Southern California Landscape: 1. Settling into Arcadia," *Landscape Architecture* 66 (Jan.): 39-78.

————. 1976. "The Evolution of the California Landscape: 2. Arcadia Compromised," *Landscape Architecture* 66 (March): 117-27.

————. 1977. "The Evolution of the California Landscape: 3. The Great Promotions," *Landscape Architecture* (May): 229-39.

————. 1977. "The Evolution of the California Landscape: 4. Suburbia at the Zenith," *Landscape Architecture* 67 (Sept.): 417-24.

Thompson and West, publisher. 1880. *History of Los Angeles County.* Reprint, 1959, Berkeley.

Tomlinson, Russell P. 1968. "Mobile Home Parks as a Settlement Type in Los Angeles, Orange, and Riverside Counties." Unpublished M.A. thesis, California State University at Los Angeles.

Torrance, Bruce. 1979. *Hollywood: The First 100 Years.* Hollywood.

Tracy, Robert Howard. 1982. *John Parkinson and the Beaux-Arts City Beautiful Movement in Downtown Los Angeles 1894-1935.* Unpublished Ph.D. thesis, University of California, Los Angeles.

Trillin, Calvin. 1974. "Simon Rodia: Watts Towers," in *Naives and Visionaries.* Walker Art Center, Minneapolis.

Truman, Ben. C. 1874. *Semi-Tropical California.* San Francisco.

————. 1885. *Homes and Happiness in the Golden State of California.* San Francisco.

Van Dyke, Theodore S. 1886. *Southern California.* New York.

Van Petten, O. W. 1969. "Westwood: The Case of the Bartered Bride,"

West, Los Angeles Times (Oct. 26): 23-33.

Walker, Derek, ed. 1981. *Los Angeles: Architectural Design Profile — AD/USC Look at L.A.* London.

Warner, Charles Dudley. 1891. *Our Italy.* New York.

Weaver, John D. 1973. *El Pueblo Grande.* Los Angeles.

Weber, Msgr. Francis J. 1976. *Saint Vibiana's Cathedral.* Los Angeles.

Weitze, Karen. 1983. *California's Mission Revival.* Los Angeles.

Welch, Ileana. 1980. *Historic-Cultural Monuments as Designated by the Cultural Heritage Board, Los Angeles.* Los Angeles.

West, Nathaneal. 1950. *The Day of the Locust.* New York.

Whitnall, Gordon. 1930. "Tracing the Development of Planning in Los Angeles." *Annual Report of the Los Angeles Planning Commission.* Los Angeles.

Whittlesey, Charles F. 1905. "Concrete Construction." *Architect and Engineer* (Dec.): 43-47.

————. 1908. "Reinforced Concrete Construction—Why I Believe in It." *Architect and Engineer* 12 (March): 35-57.

Wiley, Stephen. 1976. "Los Angeles: 200 Years, 200 Buildings." Compiled by Regula Campbell, John Chase, Elizabeth McMillian, and John Pastier. *L.A. Architect* 6 (Sept.).

Williams, Paul R. 1945. *The Small Home of Tomorrow.* Hollywood.

————. 1946. *New Homes for Today.* Hollywood.

Wilson, William. 1970. "The Colossus of the Roads (The Billboard as Pop Art)." *West, Los Angeles Times* (Dec. 31): 14-21.

————. 1970. "Where Has All the Neon Gone?" *West, Los Angeles Times* (April 19): 8-11.

————. 1973. "The L.A. Fine Arts Squad: Venice in the Snow and Other Visions." *Art News* 72 (Summer): 28-29.

Winter, Robert W. 1974. "The Arroyo Culture." *California Design 1910,* by Timothy J. Andersen, Eudorah M. Moore, and Robert Winter. Pasadena. Reprint 1980, Salt Lake City.

————. 1980. *The California Bungalow.* Los Angeles.

————. 1981. "The Architecture of the City Eclectic." *California History* 60 (Spring): 72-75.

————. 1983. "The Common American Bungalow." *Home Sweet Home, American Domestic Vernacular Architecture.* Edited by Charles W. Moore. Pp. 98-101. New York.

Withey, Henry F. and Elsie R. 1956. *Biographical Dictionary of American Architects.* Reprint 1970, Los Angeles.

Wolfe, Tom. 1968. "I Drove Around Los Angeles and It's Crazy: The World is Upside Down." *West, Los Angeles Times* (Dec. 1): 18-22, 24, 27.

Wood, Ruth K. 1915. *The Tourist's California.* Los Angeles.

Woollett, William L. 1966. "Los Angeles Landmarks." *Historic Preservation* 18 (July-Aug.): 160-63.

Works Progress Administration (WPA) 1939. *California: A Guide to the Golden State.* New York.

————. 1941. *A Guide to the City of Los Angeles.* New York.

Wurman, Richard Saul. 1982. *L.A./Access.* Los Angeles.

Yost, Lloyd Morgan. 1950. "Greene and Greene of Pasadena." *AIA Journal* (Sept.): 115-25.

Young, Betty Lou and Thomas Young. 1975. *Rustic Canyon and the Story of the Uplifters.* Santa Monica.

————. 1983. *Pacific Palisades.*

Young, Robert B. 1905. *Architecture of Robert B. Young.* Los Angeles.

Zarakov, Barry Neil. 1977. *California Planned Communities of the 1920s.* Unpublished M.A. thesis, University of California, Santa Barbara.

Zierer, Clifford M., ed. 1934. "San Fernando, A Type of Southern California Town." *Annals of the Association of American Geographers* 24: 1-28.

Index